D0235421

Latin American Urbanization:

A Guide to the Literature, Organizations and Personnel

by

Martin H. Sable

Associate Professor

University of Wisconsin-Milwaukee

The Scarecrow Press, Inc.

Metuchen, N.J. 1971

ISBN 0-8108-0354-2
Library of Congress Catalog Card Number: 74-145643

THIS BOOK IS DEDICATED

TO

MY DEAR WIFE,

MINNA

Foreword

The present work is a continuation of the interdisciplinary approach inherent in A Guide to Latin American Studies, a source (also compiled by Dr. Martin H. Sable) which has as its scope the entire gamut of activities and fields of knowledge as these relate to the study of Latin America.

Treated in the present reference book are problems of urbanization and of allied fields, including urban education, public health, transportation and communications, industrialization, social change, housing, crime and juvenile delinquency, cost of living, employment, public welfare, municipal government and finance, and the urban matrix for literature and the arts among the thirty-odd areas covered. A considerable body of literature is available on these topics, and various types of materials have been brought together for use of students and faculty, municipal researchers and other specialists, who will be concerned with research on one or more of these aspects of Latin American civilization.

For the 1967-68 Seminar offered by the Latin American Center at UCLA, the topic of Urbanization in Latin America (entering upon and being influenced by disciplines in the social, natural and applied sciences, as well as the arts and humanities) was chosen. Latin America is destined to be an urban continent. It was therefore logical to assume that those problems currently plaguing urban centers in Latin America will be with us for a considerable time. Granted the assumption that population control methods were to be universally adopted in Latin America, housing, public health, urban education and transportation, urban crime, social security and "the quality of life in the urban matrix" would, among other topics, continue to present themselves as prime areas of concern awaiting solutions.

Primary to solutions, however, are the twin prior stages of exposition of the problems and alternatives to be followed. It is in response to these needs, preparatory to suggesting solutions, that Dr. Martin H. Sable has compiled the detailed bibliographies and the specialized directories of "working" and research organizations, and the list of urbanization specialists. It is hoped that this reference source will facilitate research and intercommunication by scholars working in the areas concerned.

Johannes Wilbert
Director, Latin American Center
University of California,
Los Angeles.

Prólogo

El presente trabajo es una continuación del método interdisciplinario en la obra, A Guide to Latin American Studies (recopilada también por el Dr. Martin H. Sable), que tiene como campo toda la gama de actividades y aspectos conocidos relacionados con el estudio de Latinoamérica. En el presente libro de referencia se tratan problemas de urbanización y campos afines, incluyendo educación urbana, salud pública, transporte y comunicaciones, industrialización y cambio social, vivienda, crimen y delincuencia juvenil, costo de vida, empleo, bienestar público, gobierno y finanzas municipales, y la ciudad como centro de fomento para la literatura y las artes, entre las 30 particulares áreas cubiertas. Un apreciable volumen de literatura sobre estos temas está disponible y varias clases de material han sido recopiladas para ser usadas por estudiantes y profesores, por los investigadores municipales y otros especialistas interesados en la investigación de uno o más de estos aspectos de la urbanización latinoamericana.

Para el Seminario del Centro Latinoamericano de la UCLA de 1967-68 el tema "Urbanización en Latinoamérica" (interconectado con las disciplinas de ciencias sociales, naturales, y con las ciencias aplicadas, así como también con las artes y las humanidades) fué escogido. Latinoamérica está destinada a ser un continente urbano. Por eso es lógico asumir que los problemas que actualmente afectan los centros urbanos en Latinoamérica permaneciesen por largo tiempo. Aún si los métodos del control del crecimiento de la población fueran adoptados totalmente en Latinoamérica, la vivienda, salud pública, educación urbana, transporte, criminalidad urbana, seguridad social y el "estilo de vida en los centros urbanos" se presentarían, entre otros tópicos, como problemas urgentes en espera de soluciones urgentes.

Previamente a la adopción de soluciones, es necesaria la descripción de los problemas, análisis científico de los mismos, y formulación de alternativas. En respuesta a las necesidades anteriormente expuestas, Dr. Martin H. Sable ha recopilado las bibliografías detalladas y los directorios especializados de instituciones de investigación científica y organizaciones de acción social, así como la lista de expertos en urbanización. Se espera que esta obra de consulta facilitará la investigación y la intercomunicación entre los estudiosos de la urbanización en la América Latina.

Johannes Wilbert
Director, Latin American Center
University of California,
Los Angeles

Author's Preface*

According to the 1965 Encyclopaedia Britannica (Volume 22, page 894-A), urbanization may be defined as "a process of population concentration such that the ratio of urban people to the total population in a territory increases."

In our own day we perforce tend to take it for granted that this process of urbanization is an irresistible phenomenon. The fact of the matter is that throughout the nineteenth century urban populations in the United States were continually expanding by a greater percentage than rural ones. Obviously rural-urban migrations and large-scale settlement of European immigrants in U. S. metropolitan areas were key factors here, and despite the fact that U. S. rural birth rates still exceed those in urban areas, urbanization in the United States grows apace.

The first manifestation of the "urban revolution" in recorded history, as Professor V. Gordon Childe terms it, occurred about 3,000 B. C., when a great percentage of the inhabitants of Egypt, Mesopotamia and the Indus Valley in Northwest India quit their primitive agricultural activity to become traders and artisans. Instead of dwelling in isolated farming areas, they became incorporated into self-sufficient and independent towns (Encyclopedia Americana, international edition, 1965, Volume 7, page 24). The 1966 edition of Encyclopaedia Britannica (Volume 15, page 406) states that during the Late Formative Period in Middle America (800-100 B. C.), urbanization appeared as a significant characteristic. One urban zone has been identified in the Valley of

*(The author was instrumental in the development of the Documentation and Publications Section, Latin American Center at UCLA, which published four of his reference books on Latin America. He is currently Associate Professor in the School of Library and Information Science, University of Wisconsin-Milwaukee, where he also is active in the work of the Latin American Center).

Mexico, and another in the Guatemalan Basin, at Kaminaljuyu. The urban element prevailed through the Classic Period (100 B. C. -900 A. D.) and became even more prominent between 900 and 1250 A. D. in the Post-Classic Period.

In this connection it is interesting to take note of the recent establishment of the Center of Ekistics at the Athens Technological Institute, Athens, Greece, with collaborating researchers located at universities around the world. Ekistics, the new science of human settlement, bids fair to add to our store of knowledge concerning not only the history of urban manifestations, but also with respect to many of the current problems attendant upon the urbanization phenomenon. In February of 1965 the World Society for Ekistics was established in London. Although the presidency is currently held by Lord Llewellyn Davies, Professor of Architecture at University College in London, the Society's headquarters remain in Athens. It is anticipated that Latin America will figure in the research program of the World Society for Ekistics.

Urban studies may be defined "as a field of research . . . interdisciplinary, somewhat problem-oriented endeavor (like all academic fields, as distinguished from disciplines) focused on the structure and function of communities that are relatively urban in character, on the causes, conditions and consequences of urbanizing processes as they become manifest within communities, and on the physical and societal-cultural environments in which such communities and processes are imbedded" (In Urban Studies Center: the first five years, 1961-1966. New Brunswick, Rutgers, the State University, 1966, p. 16).

The beginnings of urbanization as an interdisciplinary field of study in the United States date from the 1920's, when University of Chicago Sociology Professor Ernest W. Burgess wrote his Introduction to the science of sociology, and edited the 1925 Proceedings of the American Sociological Society, published as The urban community (Chicago, University of Chicago Press, 1926, 268 pp.). He contributed (with Robert E. Park and R. D. McKenzie) to another early work entitled The city (Chicago, University of Chicago Press, 1925, 239 p.). In 1929 the Holt Publishing Company of New York City issued Principles of rural-urban sociology, by Pitirim Sorokin and Carle C. Zimmerman. Arthur Schlesinger, Sr., among interested historians, contributed a volume entitled The rise of the city (New York, Macmillan, 1933, 494 pp.) to the History of American Life series.

During the 1930's and 1940's, Howard Mumford Jones of Harvard treated urban life and urban physical surroundings in his voluminous works. In 1964 Dr. Burgess joined University of Chicago Sociology Professor Donald J. Bogue in editing Contributions to urban sociology for the University of Chicago Press.

Maturation of Urban Studies on the U. S. academic scene, and the delineation of those disciplines most directly concerned, have been succinctly described by Dr. David Popenoe, Director of Research at the Urban Studies Center of Rutgers, the State University of New Jersey:

> The field first developed in its modern academic form as the outcome of the research interests of city planners, sociologists, geographers, economists, political scientists, public administrators, architects and others who felt the need for an interdisciplinary approach to phenomena which each of the disciplines had previously been studying in a piecemeal fashion. City planners, who most consciously felt the need for better organized and integrated knowledge of urban areas arising from the demands of their work activities, played perhaps a major role in bringing the disciplines together around a common focus.
>
> At the same time many universities have discovered that they are increasingly being called upon to be of direct service to the communities in which they are located. Urban studies... has become a term used to denote emerging forms of active involvement of university intellectual resources directed toward the solution of pressing urban problems of our time; problems which range from race relations to transportation. Thus, the field consists of both an interdisciplinary research and educational focus on the phenomena of urbanization and urbanism and the direct involvement of university personnel in social action and social change. [1]

With respect to the university assistance mentioned above, the University Program of Community Action of the Institute of Regional and Urban Planning, a division of the Universidad Nacional del Litoral (Santa Fé, Argentina) has the following aims: to make known the advantages of planning (since it is the means which makes possible the integral development of the individual in a physically and spiritually appropriate atmosphere), and to foster popular participation in activities contributing to the advancement of planning, inasmuch as each city must obviously contribute to its own future welfare. This Program should serve as a model for universities located in metropolitan areas worldwide, for in addition to assisting in planning development, it involves the public in the planning process through direct communication.

Currently two of the foremost urbanization experts are Philip M. Hauser (Professor of Sociology at the University of Chicago and Director of its Population Research and Training Center) who has had extensive experience in housing, and Leo F. Schnore (Professor of Sociology at the University of Wisconsin). In 1965 they edited The study of urbanization for the New York City publishing firm of John Wiley. This work, containing chapters (including one on Latin America) by outstanding specialists, appears to be the definitive work on the field, as of January, 1969. Solid contributions to the literature have been made, over a period of years, by Dr. Francis Violich, Professor of City Planning, University of California at Berkeley, who ranks among the world's foremost Latin Americanists in his own specialty. Dr. Violich has been working on Latin American city planning and urbanization topics for approximately twenty-five years.

Closely allied to city planning is urban geography, a profession destined to expand greatly as the urbanization process accelerates throughout the world. On page 10 of the pamphlet entitled A career in geography (authored by the Joint Committee on Careers of the Association of American Geographers together with the National Council for Geographic Education, and published in 1965 by the Chicago-based Geographical Research Institute of the Denoyer-Geppert Company), the duties of and job opportunities for urban geographers are discussed:

> The problems of urban geography are many and vital, for cities have their difficulties. Some have grown too fast, some have grown outward leaving dead or dying areas near the center; others haven't grown as fast as their citizens wanted them to. It is with such important problems as these that the urban geographer can make helpful suggestions after sufficient study. There is much work to be done, and urban geography is a relatively new subject. For that very reason it is one with growing opportunities and a field that may very well be worth watching

as time goes on and preparing for, if one is so inclined.

What does an urban geographer do? He studies cities, of course. But since cities are many and their problems are varied he is likely to specialize on certain aspects of cities or upon a particular city or group of cities. A few geographers are working at the difficult problems of describing and defining the parts of a city accurately. Everyone knows that a city has a central business district, but just how large is it in any particular city, and what businesses does it contain? Others would like to know how to find which industries and businesses actually support the city and which ones are there merely because the people are there. Some study the inter-relations of the city and its supporting region, or hinterland. Finding the answers to these problems is intriguing, but difficult.

Not all urban geographers are interested in as sweeping problems as these. Some are attacking definite, immediate problems. Where are parking areas most needed? Where should new schools or new shopping areas be located? How should through arterials be rerouted to give the greatest relief to congested traffic? Many of these problems an urban geographer cannot solve by himself, but he can help others to find the best solution as problems in urban planning are studied.

As you may have surmised, urban geographers find their jobs quite largely in city planning offices, though a few teach in universities and make urban geography their special research and teaching field.

What does an urban geographer need to know? In addition to his regular geographic training, he needs to know all he can about cities--their physical, demographic, and political structure, their engineering problems, their economic problems, and their social problems. Economics, sociology, and political science are all good additional training...

As the new science of urbanization came into its own in the 1960's, the United States Government converted its once-minuscule housing agencies into a full-fledged cabinet post, the

Department of Housing and Urban Development. Pressure is currently being exerted to treat problems of mass transportation on a similar level. A Center for Urban Education has recently been established in New York City. Urban crime rates in the United States multiply geometrically, while attendance at concerts and museums, and the use of large metropolitan-area public libraries continue to break pre-existing records. There is a trend to form groups country-wide with the aim of improving the appearance of their respective cities, and all this while the impersonality of city life, and the "one continual city" from Boston to Washington, D. C. remain topics of the day.

What may surprise U. S. urban planners is the fact that the identical theme is being discussed in Mexico. To quote Jim Budd (The News, Mexico City, August 21, 1967, p. 30): "According to one urbanologist, by the year 2000 Mexico will have a megalopolis of its very own. From Puebla on to the capital, then to Toluca, Querétaro and León, cities will grow out, one merging with the next. Hopefully, the scene will be no more hideous than the scar running diagonally through New Jersey." It should here be noted that Mexico City[2] is at present building a huge subway system to transport its nearly 7, 000, 000 inhabitants and workers, who despite an intricately-woven, frequent low-cost bus service, and the 22, 000 taxicabs serving the city, are hard-pressed to navigate in what has become the world's sixth most populated metropolis. (Note: Caracas, Venezuela will construct its subway system (1968-73) at an approximate cost of $300 million). The growth of Mexico City as a cosmopolitan center of culture and entertainment is in direct contrast to Brasilia, from which wholesale weekend evacuations of government executives takes place, due to the lack of diversion to which they are accustomed in Rio de Janeiro.

Not usually considered within the framework of urbanizing areas are resort towns, usually on the ocean or adjacent to inland lakes, where people find repose and escape from the hustle and bustle of metropolitan cities. A few examples would include San Carlos de Bariloche, Argentina, Viña del Mar, Chile, and Chapala, Mexico. The quantity (and quality) of their influential residents renders them ever more urban in character. In 1967 the town of Chapala, situated on beautiful Lake Chapala in the State of Jalisco, erected street lights on paths marked out in fields adjacent to the Lake and already zoned for residential and commercial areas. The population of the town, which includes many U. S. citizens and currently totals approximately

10,000 people, has grown five-fold in thirty years. It supports a modern supermarket and bids fair to double itself by 1985. Guadalajara,[2] capital of Jalisco State, now boasts over 1,000,000 people (including 10,000 U.S. citizens), a wide variety of expanding industries, operetta companies from Spain, and an international airport with direct flights to the United States and Europe. It was practically rebuilt in the 1960's (including a completely new water supply and drainage system), and is now the second largest city in the Mexican Republic.

Formerly in second place was Monterrey,[2] commonly termed the "Pittsburgh of Mexico." Long known for its excellent Institute of Technology (which boasts a computer center), as of Friday, August 18, 1967, when the first Borgward cars were completed, Monterrey has the distinction of being the site of the first and only all-Mexican automobile factory. This is also a "first" for Latin America. A Mexican syndicate purchased *in toto* the German Borgward auto firm. Monterrey is headquarters for complete production and world wide export of Borgward cars and auto accessories.

While Monterrey has enjoyed a long-term reputation as an industrial center, by means of a Mexican government industrial program U.S. manufacturers have (since 1966) been establishing industrial plants in several cities along the U.S.-Mexican border. Low-cost but qualified supplies of labor, exemptions (for imports into Mexico of machinery and production materials) from Mexican customs duties, and the proximity to U.S. sales outlets has led these U.S. firms to set up factories in Matamoros, Tijuana, Ciudad Juarez, and several other Mexican border cities. What has begun, therefore, as an industrial-commercial advantage for manufacturers in the United States bids fair, if continued, to industrialize cities and towns which otherwise might have continued to eke out their existences from the disbursements of U.S. tourists who have "been to Mexico."

The transcendent significance of urbanization, and the problems attendant upon it, have attracted the attention of the Adlai E. Stevenson Institute for International Affairs, which was established at Robie House, near the University of Chicago, on February 6, 1967, in memory of the late U.S. ambassador to the United Nations. The Institute undertakes research on domestic problems as well as in international affairs, with emphasis on those problems currently faced by a host of the family of nations. It is worthwhile pointing out that high on the list of priorities for research will be a study of urbanization on a world-wide basis.

In its news release dated November 30, 1967, the Ford Foundation stated that it had allocated $10, 800, 000 to Columbia and Harvard Universities, the University of Chicago, and to the Massachusetts Institute of Technology, for the purpose of endowing new professorships in the urban aspects of the following fields: economics, engineering, education, law, management, political science, sociology, systems analysis, and urban planning. In announcing that graduate fellowships would be offered in the various programs, the Foundation pointed out that although university interest in urban problems has been one of long standing, until recently organized efforts in terms of financial commitment and standing within the traditional academic hierarchy for Urban Studies as an interdisciplinary field have been scattered. In view of the dire need, the Ford Foundation through its action, planned to attract more first-rate scholars and scientists to the study of urban problems. Although the program concentrates wholly on U. S. cities, because of the Foundation's traditional keen interest in and awareness of Latin American problems, it is hoped that subsequently attention might be directed to that area's urban difficulties.

In general the problems of living in large metropolitan areas everywhere in the world are becoming more complex. To quote Dr. Roger Revelle, Director of the Center for Population Studies, Harvard University: "In the megalopolis of the future, the problems of water, air, and food supply, of removal of waste and avoidance of pollution, of transport and communications, above all of maintaining human life on a human scale, will all be of a magnitude never faced before in the history of cities."[3]

Why does the average Latin American rural citizen leave the familiar surroundings in which his forebears have dwelt for centuries to face unknown ways of life in the city? The lure of "bright lights" and the chance to gain wealth have been traditional replies. And yet one wonders whether other reasons (better health and educational facilities, the ever-worsening living grubbed from overworked land and a burgeoning rural population unable to feed itself, or simply, on the other hand, leaving for the city because "it's the thing to do" currently) might in some nations be prime considerations. One can cite additional highly appropriate reasons for rural-urban migration varying with the individual:

women migrate to marry; many people seek the wider variety of jobs available; youth seeks education and escape from boredom; criminals marvel at the wide variety of opportunities and the masses, which give more security from detection. It is of importance to observe that the Instituto Mexicano de Estudios Sociales, A. C., a non-profit research organization based in Mexico City which seeks to apply the results of research to the solution of problems of socio-economic development, has been studying the backgrounds, motivations (impelling them to migrate), attitudes and ways of life of rural migrants to slum areas around Mexico City. The information thus obtained will serve as the basis for a pilot project which will take the form of a Rural-Urban Migration Studies Center.

Rural-urban migration, often considered the essence of the urbanization problem, is a significant contributor, but not the "end and all" of the matter. Research has demonstrated that urban migrants come to large cities in considerable number from cities and towns of secondary and tertiary importance. In most nations the tendency is to proceed from the countryside to larger towns; true, some rural migrants use these larger towns as temporary "stopovers" on their way to the city; in many instances their children, born in such towns, will complete the transition. A considerable number, however, remain in these larger towns permanently. Concern over problems of rural-urban migration in Mexico is apparent in the United States, where the National Science Foundation in 1967 granted over $41,000 to Dr. John M. Ball of the Department of Geography of the University of Georgia, for the purpose of studying the relationship between migration and trends in growth of the Mexican population on the one hand, and socio-economic conditions, on the other.

One solution to the problem of heavy rural-urban migration was suggested by the author in a previous publication, specifically with respect to the Argentine situation:

> ...established contacts (between rural and urban populations) must be broadened and new ones introduced in order to make rural life sufficiently attractive (in addition to economically worthwhile, by means of government financial and technical assistance to agriculture), so that those now crowded into Buenos Aires might seek their livelihoods 'on the land.'... Clearly, assistance... is indicated in the forms of (1) water supply development; (2) school and library improvement;

(3) extended electric power development; (4) highway improvement and railroad renewal; (5) housing; (6) increased newspaper and magazine distribution; (7) increased radio and television program transmission; (8) improvement of art and natural history museums; (9) programs of musical and dramatic performances by road companies; (10) youth and "senior citizen" centers; (11) rural hospital development.

(See Argentine Agriculture: Proposal for Progress, by Martin H. Sable, in his A Guide to Latin American Studies, v. 1. Los Angeles, Latin American Center, University of California, 1967, p. 33).

In this connection it is significant to consider the recommendations concerning world urban development contained in the Report on Activities of the International Cooperation Year, submitted in June of 1966 by the Committee on Foreign Affairs, U. S. House of Representatives, 89th Congress, Second Session (Washington, U. S. Government Printing Office, 1966, p. 47):

> Urbanization, once a manageable, gradual, and slow-moving force in man's history, has accelerated and has made such impact on the last 50 years that it must be accounted one of the truly great revolutionary forces of the 20th century. Urbanization has made this the century of the city. And in terms of man's welfare and well-being the conclusion must be drawn that this is all to the good. Urbanization poses many perplexing and anxious problems, but it is indeed a net advantage to mankind and an integral and essential element of progress. The task men face is to minimize the problems and to maximize the benefits of urbanization. The International Cooperation Year provides a framework for achieving some of these ends, and it is in this spirit that the Urban Development Committee makes the proposals which follow:
>
> 1. The United States should give higher priority and more recognition to urban development programs in its bilateral assistance and should move to secure comparable priority and recognition for urban development programs within the United Nations assistance programs. In particular, the United States should vigorously seek to secure

adequate budget and personnel for the newly established United Nations Center for Housing, Building, and Planning.

2. The United States should take the initiative within the United Nations to inaugurate a concerted international program, supported by voluntary contributions of member nations, to attack the specific problem of slums and squatter settlements in developing countries.

3. Additional attention and consideration should be focused on the problem of financial resources for carrying out urban development programs. The heartening successes of such undertakings as savings and loan and credit union institutions recently organized in Latin America are an augury of what might be done by even more zealous promotion of these institutions or the introduction of other imaginative and practical instruments or policies.

4. The United States should establish a World Urban Development Research Laboratory and Institute. This Laboratory and Institute would be sponsored by the United States, be financed principally by the United States, and be headquartered in the United States. It would function, however, as a world organization, with full international participation, possibly with branches in other regions of the world, and its products would be for all nations.

5. The United States should sponsor a United Nations World Conference on Urban Development to emphasize the importance of urban development and to gain understanding and support from decision-makers in the countries concerned.

With regard to international assistance to Latin American municipal governments, the Inter-American Development Bank allocates approximately 40% of its Social Progress Trust Fund to Latin American cities. Why such a large percentage to cities? The proliferation around major and secondary metropoli in Latin America of bidonvilles, barrios bajos, tugurios, favelas, cantegriles, ranchos, villas miserias, callampas, barriadas, or just plain slums, if you will, with the resulting low ebb of human existence and concomitant threats to public health, education, morals, economic and political security are sufficient response. It is a fact that by the year 2000 Latin America is destined to be an urban continent. In view of this fact, as well as the statement that "the trek to the city" has been gaining in importance as a Latin American sociological manifestation since 1920,[4] it behooves us to consider seriously not only those factors motivating the phenomenon, but in addition the impacts reverberating upon all aspects of life in the city.

That the same realization is shared by universities far and wide is corroborated by Cornell University's AID-financed five-year research program on "Urban Housing Policy in Latin America: Its Demographic, Economic, Health, Political and Social Implications." New York University's Graduate School of Arts and Sciences and Columbia University both offer courses on urbanization in Latin America, as does the University of Buenos Aires. The Haitian Social Science Research Center in Port-au-Prince researches the topic. Furthermore, faculty members from the University of Florida are conducting research under a Ford Foundation contract on problems (including industrialization and social change, education, health, transportation and municipal government) facing the city of Cali, Colombia. Their base of operation will be the Universidad del Valle, in Cali, at which institution they will also lecture. Under a five-year Ford Foundation grant focusing on "Basic Problems of Education in Latin America," Harvard University's Center for Studies in Education and Development has begun researching on the school's role in the urbanization and industrialization of the Guayana section of Venezuela. This topic, involving urbanization, is the initial and prime element in a five-pronged investigation into the nature and characteristics of this newly and rapidly urbanizing area of Venezuela. In 1967, M. I. T. established a "Special Program for Urban and Regional Studies of Developing Areas."

The fact that problems incidental to the metropoli of Latin America are of world-wide concern is borne out by the convening of a special Colloquium on the Capitols of Latin America, held under auspices of the French Government's National Council of Scientific Research, in Toulouse, France, at the Institute of Spanish, Latin American and Luso-Brazilian Studies of the University of Toulouse, on February 24-27, 1964.[5]

As of 1967, the Documentation Center of the Institute for Advanced Studies of Latin America at the University of Paris became headquarters for the French Government's

National Scientific Research Council, Cooperative Research Project on the Regional Role of Cities in Latin America. Under the direction of Dr. Olivier Dollfus, noted geographer, the Center will gather materials on the regional economics, geography and planning of Latin America. In the same year (June 9 and 10, 1967) the University of Texas held a Conference on Problems of Urbanization in Latin America, at its El Paso campus. The Conference was a success, and plans were made to meet again in June 1968.

The Sécrétariat des Missions d'Urbanisme et d'Habitat, 11, rue Chardin, Paris 16, France, conducts research in the fields of documentation methodology and terminology with respect to planning and housing. It is a prime information source, especially for the world's underdeveloped nations. The fact that such an organization exists stresses the need for data organized in logical sequence, as stated above.

The seriousness with which Latin American intellectuals and government officials view urbanization problems is pointed up by the convening of a Seminar on Urban Development in Latin America, at Rosario, Santa Fé Province, Argentina, from October 15 to 17, 1965. Broad areas covered at the Seminar included: (a). Social Aspects of Urbanization (effects of rural-urban migration and its influence on urban development, standard of living, etc.); (b). The Urban Economy (Centralization vs. decentralization, municipal finance problems, public services, etc.); (c). The Urban Structure (Urban planning; the influence of the means of transportation on the city's physical profile); (d). Administrative and legal matters. What is significant is that the major thrust of the Seminar aimed at the identification and evaluation of available information in each of these areas, with a view to setting priorities for future research. Here, then, is an additional example of the importance of definitive and carefully categorized information assigned by scholars to urbanization research.

Latin American literary men traditionally deal with city life. One may cite the work of the contemporary Argentine poet, Jorge Luis Borges, with respect to his treatment of the streets of Buenos Aires. Society in 18th century Lima, Peru is the topic of the series entitled Tradiciones peruanas, by Ricardo Palma (1833-1919). In Chile Joaquín Edwards Bello (1888-1968) wrote about underworld life in Santiago. Eduardo Barrios (1884-1963) and Augusto G. Thomson known as Augusto D'Halmar (1880-1950) also treated social problems in the city. The most recent work in this vein treats the problem of juvenile delinquency in Santiago. Titled simply Manuel (and written by Christopher Jackson, a Chilean university professor), it tells of the seamy side of life in Santiago and its psychological effects on an adolescent who finally murders an influential businessman. The work has been published in English (New York, Knopf, 1964, 251 p.).

Interest in the quality of city life has been a continuing phenomenon among writers in Latin American nations (and in Spain, for that matter). But the extension of this interest into a newer branch of language, the science of Linguistics, is a more recent innovation. From October 24-29, 1966, there was held, in Madrid, the First Meeting of Representatives of the International Office of Information and Observation of the Spanish Language, and of the Commission of Latin American Linguistics and Dialectology of the Inter-American Program for Linguistics and Language Teaching. The Meeting had as its purpose to pinpoint the basic aspects of its upcoming project in studying URBAN SPEECH in Latin American capital cities and in Spain. An invitation was accorded to scholars in Rio de Janeiro and in Lisbon (as well as in San Juan, Puerto Rico) to join their colleagues in undertaking speech research in their respective cities. Scholars from universities and research institutes in each of the following cities will participate in studies on normal speech patterns, which will include speech of families and the speech of the upper classes, in Barcelona, Bogotá, Buenos Aires, Havana, Lima, Madrid, Mexico City, Montevideo, and Santiago. Tape recordings will be made for studying the phonology, morpho-syntax, lexicon and colloquial speech structures in each city. The Office of Information and Observation of the Spanish Language in Madrid has set a target date of late 1969 for publication of results.

Within the past few years, urbanization research on Latin America has greatly increased.

For the benefit of those interested in specific research topics, the author would like to suggest the following as being worthwhile (he believes several to be unique with respect to Latin America):

1. The city and its religious elements

2. Natural areas for recreation in large cities, and

clearance of "eyesores" for aesthetic purposes

3. The study of university cities (such as those in Bogotá, Quito, Mexico City, San José, etc.) in relation to the city of which they are parts

4. Legal, political and financial bases in the development of Brasilia

5. Factors in consideration of the locating of shopping centers

6. Health, recreation, aesthetic and lebensraum factors with respect to the location of industrial plants in São Paulo

7. Citizen participation in the "carrying-out" aspect of urbanization, and problems of interpersonal relations and communication

8. Municipal research bureaus in Latin American city governments

9. Problems resulting from urban renewal of central trading areas in large cities (relocation of masses, or firms): legal and economic aspects, as well as social change experienced

10. Elements of urbanization (characteristics common in social change in large cities, including economic changes) which also occur in rural areas which have undergone economic development, even partly

11. Possibilities for the decentralization of Buenos Aires

12. Climatic and economic-geographic factors in the choice of Latin American capital cities' location

13. Comparative study of Bogotá-Santiago-Caracas; São-Paulo-Rio de Janeiro; Tegucigalpa-Managua; Valparaíso-Cali; Buenos Aires-Paris

14. Comparative legal-municipal government studies: Brazil-Argentina; Colombia-Venezuela-Chile; Mexico-Guatemala

15. Urban research centers and the teaching of urban studies in Latin American universities

Because of the wide variety of causes resulting in the transformation of most of Latin America to an urban region by the end of the twentieth century, research in the field has only begun to scratch the surface.

The bibliography section of the present reference source treats all aspects of life in urban areas of Latin America, no matter whether such areas of activity fall into the natural and applied sciences (e. g., air pollution, water supply, health, housing, public utilities, etc.), the social sciences (education, urban history, municipal government and finance, poverty, employment and cost of living, transportation and communications, urban crime and juvenile delinquency, industrialization and social change, public welfare and social security, etc.), or in the arts and humanities (the quality of religious life in the city, the urban matrix for literature and the arts, and urban planning and recreation). For specific sub-topics of these broad fields please refer to the Table of Contents and to the Geographic-Subject Index. In addition, there are sections devoted to urban research, wherein topics, approaches and research methodology in general are treated. The category entitled Bibliography actually renders the entire work a bibliography of bibliographies; the section of books on Urban Research contains statistical sources covering most fields listed above. Because community development techniques may be applied to solving of problems of large cities, a section covering this topic has been included. Urbanization (general) treats the general topic (in both book and periodical-article sections) in order to present items of a general nature as an introduction and background to the material with special reference to Latin America to be found in the subsequent section, Urbanization--Latin America. The entire bibliography is divided under each subject field, into two sections: (1) text and reference books, pamphlets, government documents, periodicals, conference proceedings, and theses; and (2) periodical articles.

Although the bulk of the materials included is in Spanish and English, a very good representation in Portuguese, covering all aspects of urbanization in Brazil, forms a vital section of this work. Coverage has also been extended to Western European publications in French and German, as well as to items published in French in Haiti.

The bibliography is arranged (1) in five broad activity

areas; (2) in 30 subject fields, subdivided by physical form, as defined above. The term "books", as used in the example below, includes government documents, conference proceedings, pamphlets, theses, text and reference books; (3) by subheading, with a general section listing basic works in each field; (4) geographically by nation in alphabetical order, Latin America preceding Argentina, Bolivia, Brazil, etc.; (5) alphabetically by author within each nation-grouping. The following example will portray this procedure:

IV. Sociological (broad activity area)

PUBLIC HEALTH (subject field)

Air Pollution (subheading)

Books: (physical form)

General

Johnson, James. Pollution problems. Chicago, Jones Publishing Co., 1960, 199 p.

Latin America (geographically)

Arnold, John. Air pollution in the Americas. Washington, Grapevine Press, 1966, 200 p.

Baker, Roy. Latin America and Pollution of the air. Boston, Vacuum Cleaner Press, 1960, 1243 p.

Argentina, etc.

Periodical Articles: (physical form)

General

Latin America, etc.

In instances in which periodical-article entries contain no place of publication, it is understood that such serials and periodicals are issued in the United States of America. "Santiago" refers to Santiago, Chile, in every instance unless stipulated otherwise in the given book or article entry.

Due to the fact that there are many articles, conference proceedings, and monographs without authors appearing in bibliographic citations, and inasmuch as the titles of these works cover a multitude of topics in thirty varying fields, users of this sourcebook are strongly urged to utilize the Geographic-Subject Index so as to ascertain that they have made fullest use of the materials contained herein.

Each bibliographic item has been numbered consecutively throughout, and it is important to note that the subject headings in the Geographic-Subject Index have names of places following them, either cities or nations. Thus, for example, "Air Pollution, São Paulo, Brazil", followed by the number, let us say "750", would inform the user interested in this topic of the availability of such a study on São Paulo, Brazil. To obtain the reference, he would quickly locate number 750 in the body of the work. It should be understood that where no geographic designation is given, the item in question is general in nature. Efforts have been expended to provide representation for all Latin American nations and European dependencies.

While the bibliography section was compiled primarily for the use of scholars within the various disciplines and applied fields concerned with Latin American urbanization, it is important for specialists, scholars and researchers not primarily concerned with the urbanization process to realize that the bibliographies in the individual fields may be utilized in and of themselves, with only incidental reference to urbanization. For example, a linguistic scientist might very profitably consult the listing of books, pamphlets and periodical articles on the urban speech of the Latin American nation or nations in which he is primarily interested. Likewise, specialists in Religion, Social Security, Transportation, Communications, Urban History, Social Change, Industrialization, or any one of many additional fields may utilize the bibliography in their respective areas of professional activity.

Furthermore, within various fields there are main and sub-topics impossible or extremely difficult to locate bibliographically elsewhere. Examples under Public Health include Air Pollution, Mental Hygiene, Sanitary Engineering, Hospital and Medical Care, Water Supply. The same holds true for additional topics such as Unemployment (under Poverty), Films, Newspapers, Radio and Television (under Communications), Crime and Juvenile Delinquency, Public Utilities, Municipal Finance, Rural-Urban Migration, Music and Painting (under the heading Urban Matrix for Literature and the Arts), Employment and Recreation Facilities. In connection with these topics, it is suggested that bibliographic lacunae have been filled to a significant degree.

Of necessity many items included refer to an entire nation. Inasmuch as hospital and school facilities, labor unions, social security payments, city planning and industrialization are characteristic of urban areas, materials on these and most of the other topics covering an entire nation apply to the larger cities in the given nation. In certain instances a given book or periodical article may contain material on both urban and rural areas, and in one specific field, that of Community Development, the emphasis is almost wholly on development of communities in rural areas. Community Development has been included because of the recently-established theory that community development techniques might successfully be applied in larger Latin American cities*, especially those in which there are hosts of new arrivals from rural areas.

The Directory, containing names and addresses of entities world-wide in scope, is divided into three sections: (1) research centers, institutes and organizations, mainly attached to universities, but also including private and government bureaus; (2) "Working" organizations, such as professional associations and departments of governments on various levels; units of activity cover those engaged in the urbanization process generally as well as those concerned with specific fields; (3) specialists in various fields of activity involved in the urbanization process, located in the United States, Latin America, and in Western Europe.

It is in the nature of such a compilation that errors are an inevitable, albeit unintentional result. While the attempt has been made to gather reliable data, such data as presented herein are offered without warranty as to their accuracy, timeliness or completeness.

It is anticipated that this sourcebook will be updated periodically. Suggestions for improvement of this work, in

*The Peace Corps trains some of its volunteers for urban community development work in Latin America. AID finances projects in low-income neighborhoods in Latin America.

terms of bibliographic entries, and organizations in the fields represented, will be gratefully received by the compiler.

It is the hope of the undersigned that researchers, students, government officials, international agencies, foundations and specialists concerned with various aspects of Latin American urbanization will utilize materials in this sourcebook for the ultimate improvement for living conditions--physical, economic, and governmental--and of the quality and tone of life in the metropolitan areas of Latin American nations. If, as a by-product of his efforts, inter-American relations should be improved, then he shall indeed be compensated.

I wish to thank Miss Elizabeth Ann Davies, a major in Social Welfare at the University of Wisconsin-Milwaukee, for her assistance in proofreading this manuscript.

Finally, I wish to dedicate this work to my dear wife, Minna. In order to pay sufficient tribute, I have no recourse but to resort to the words of the poet who wrote:

> This woman, whom thou mad'st to be my help
> And gav'st me as thy perfect gift, so good,
> So fit, so acceptable, so divine.

Martin H. Sable

Notes

1. Annual report: The Center of Community and Metropolitan Studies. St. Louis, University of Missouri at St. Louis, July 1967, pp. 1-2.

2. Guillermo Luna, in "Megalopolis Trends in Mexico" (Athens, Ekistics, volume 24: # 140, July 1967, pp. 19-20), states that by the year 2000 Mexico City, Guadalajara and Monterrey will be megalopolitan areas with populations of 14 million, 6-1/2 million and 5 million, respectively).

3. Roger Revelle, Science and Social Change (In Proceedings of the Special National Conference called by the U. S. National Commission for Unesco, New Orleans, La., 18-20 September, 1966. Washington, U. S. National Commission for Unesco, 1966, p. 31).

4. According to the 1965 Encyclopaedia Britannica (Volume 13, p. 768), the urban population of Latin America

grew from 33% in 1925 to 45% in 1960. Although Argentina led in the percentage of its inhabitants residing in cities (60%, according to 1960 figures), the other Latin American nations were rapidly urbanizing, with the major metropoli expanding more rapidly in population than smaller cities. Between 1950 and 1960, Caracas, Venezuela's population grew more than twice in size, while that of Sao Paulo, Brazil, multiplied from 2, 017, 025 in 1950 to over 3, 600, 000 in 1960. In the decade following the Second World War the urban populations of Colombia, Venezuela, Panama, and Mexico expanded by 58%, 57%, 54% and 50%, respectively.

These _Encyclopaedia Britannica_ statistics are more than confirmed by the computations of Professor Montague Yudelman of the Center for Research on Economic Development, University of Michigan, who asserts that Latin American urban centers are growing in population (as of 1966) by 5% annually.

5. That this topic is of continuing interest is borne out by the fact that a group of concerned faculty members of the University of Toulouse is preparing a study entitled, _The Cities of Latin America_, currently scheduled for publication during 1969, in a special issue of _Caravelle_, the journal of the Institute. Volume 3 (1964) included papers delivered by specialists at the February 1964 Colloquium.

Prefacio

De acuerdo con la Enciclopedia Británica (volumen 22, página 894-A) urbanización puede ser definida como "un proceso de concentración de la población, tal como la proporción de la población de las ciudades crece en comparación con el total de la población."

En nuestros días, por la fuerza debemos admitir que este proceso de urbanización es un fenómeno irresistible. El hecho es que a través del siglo XIX la población urbana en los Estados Unidos se ha expandido en un mayor porcentaje que la rural.

Ciertamente la migración rural-urbana y el gran número de inmigrantes europeos hacia las áreas metropolitanas fué el factor clave en los EE. UU. Aunque todavía la tasa de nacimientos en las zonas rurales es mayor que la de las urbanas, la urbanización en los EE. UU. aún crece rapidamente.

Según el Profesor V. Gordon Childe, la primera manifestación de la revolución urbana ocurrió 3,000 años A. C. cuando un gran porcentaje de habitantes de Egipto, Mesopotamia y el Valle Indus al Noroeste de la India dejaron sus trabajos de agricultura por el de comerciantes y artesanos. En lugar de localizarse en áreas aisladas, se incorporaron en poblaciones independientes y capaces de abastecerse por si mismas. (Enciclopedia Americana, edición internacional, 1965, volumen 7, página 24).

La edición de la Enciclopedia Británica (año 1966, tomo 15, página 406) manifiesta que durante el Período Formativo Ultimo en Centro-América (años 800-100 antes del Cristo), se observó la urbanización como calidad significativa. Se identificaron dos zonas urbanas, la primera en el Valle de México, y la segunda en Kaminaljuyu, en la Cuenca Guatemalteca. El elemento urbano prevaleció durante el Período Clásico (entre el año 100 antes de Cristo hasta 900 D. C.) y se hizo aún más importante entre los años 900-1250 D. C., en el Período Post-Clásico.

En este respecto es interesante tomar nota de lo establecido recientemente en el Centro de Ekistics en el Instituto Tecnológico de Atenas, en Atenas, Grecia, con la colaboración de investigadores de universidades de todo el mundo. Ekistics, la nueva ciencia de sedenterización humana, es muy capaz de agregar a nuestros conocimientos no solamente lo concerniente a la historia de manifestaciones urbanas, sino también con respecto a los actuales problemas sobre el fenómeno de urbanización. En febrero de 1965 la Asociación Mundial de Ekistics fué establecida en Londres. Aunque la presidencia es actualmente (1967) ejercida por Lord Llewellyn Davies, profesor de Arquitectura en la University College en Londres, la oficina principal de la Sociedad continua en Atenas. Queremos anticipar que Latinoamérica figurará en el programa de investigación, de la Sociedad Mundial de Ekistics.

Se puede definir Los Estudios Urbanos como: "Campo de investigaciones... interdisciplinario, una tentativa para orientar los problemas (tal como la mayor parte de los ramos académicos, en comparación con las disciplinas puras) concentrado en la estructura y función de las comunidades relativemente urbanas, en las causas, condiciones y resultados de los procesos de urbanización tal como se manifiestan dentro de las mismas comunidades, y en sus ambientes físicos y socio-culturales" (En Urban Studies Center: the first five years, 1961-1966. New Brunswick, Rutgers, The State University, 1966, p. 16).

El comienzo de la urbanización como un campo interdisciplinario de estudio en los Estados Unidos viene desde los años veinte, cuando el Profesor de Sociología Ernest W. Burgess, de la Universidad de Chicago, escribió su Introducción a la ciencia de la sociología, y redactó en 1925 las actas de la American Sociological Society, publicadas como The urban community (Chicago, University of Chicago Press, 1926, 268 p.). El contribuyó con Robert E. Park y R. D. McKenzie a otra obra pionera titulada The city (Chicago, University of Chicago Press, 1925, 239 p.). En 1929 la Holt Publishing Company de Nueva York publicó Principles of rural urban sociology, por Pitirim Sorokin y Carle C. Zimmerman. Arthur Schlesinger, entre otros historiadores interesados, contribuyó con un volumen titulado The rise of the city (Nueva York, MacMillan, 1933, 494 p.) a la serie de "History of American Life."

En los años 30 y 40, Howard Mumford Jones de Harvard trató de la vida urbana y las circunstancias físicas urbanas, en sus voluminosos trabajos. En 1964 Dr. Burgess se asoció con Donald J. Bogue, Profesor de Sociología en la Universidad de Chicago, en la edición de Contributions to urban sociology para la Editorial de la Universidad de Chicago.

El Doctor David Popenoe, Director de Investigaciones del Centro de Estudios Urbanos de Rutgers, la Universidad del Estado de New Jersey, ha escrito lo siguente sobre la historia del desarrollo de los Estudios Urbanos en los EE. UU. de Norte-América, y la participación de los campos relacionados:

> El campo surgió en forma moderna como resultado de los intereses investigativos de planificadores de ciudades; sociólogos, geógrafos, economistas, profesores de la ciencia política y de administración pública, arquitectos y otros quienes buscaban acercamiento inter-disciplinario al fenómeno que anteriormente estudiaba cada uno aisladamente. Puesto que los planificadores de ciudades necesitaban constantemente un cuerpo de información mejor organizado e integrado, ellos hicieron el papel más importante en reunir las varias materias alrededor de su orientación común. Simultaneamente las ciudades de los Estados Unidos pedían ayuda en la resolución de sus problemas, a las universidades localizadas dentro de sus límites. Se utiliza el término Estudios Urbanos para designar las formas modernas de envolvimiento activo de los recursos intelectuales universitarios disponibles para la resolución de los problemas urbanos urgentes y actuales, problemas de todo tipo, desde el tópico de las relaciones entre razas y hasta el transporte. Así que el campo de Estudios Urbanos se compone, por un lado, de la investigación inter-disciplinaria y enfoque educativo sobre el fenómeno de la urbanización y urbanismo, y por otro, el envolvimiento directo del personal universitario en la acción y el cambio sociales.[1]

Con respecto a la ayuda universitaria arriba-mencionada, el Programa de Acción Comunal Universitaria del Instituto de Planeamiento Regional y Urbano de la Universidad Nacional del Litoral tiene los siguientes objetivos: difusión de las ventajas de la planificación (por que es el camino correcto que posibilita el desarrollo integral del hombre en un ambiente física y espiritualmente propicio), y promoción de la participación popular en iniciativas que contribuyan al mejor cumplimiento de las premisas de la planificación, porque es la misma ciudad la que tiene que construir su futuro. Este Programa debe servir como modelo para esas universidades localizadas en metrópolis (en todas partes del mundo), puesto que además de ser el instrumento necesario para llevar a cabo la planificación, comunica a la población toda información respectiva.

Actualmente, dos de los expertos más destacados en urbanización son: Philip M. Hauser (Profesor de Sociología de la Universidad de Chicago y Director de Population Research and Training Center), quien ha tenido una vasta experiencia en vivienda, y Leo F. Schnore, Profesor de Sociología en la Universidad de Wisconsin. En 1965 ellos editaron por la editorial de John Wiley en la ciudad de Neuva York, The study of urbanization. Este trabajo contiene capítulos (incluyendo uno sobre Latinoamérica) por distinguidos especialistas. Este parece ser el más importante trabajo en el campo, hasta enero de 1967. Sólidas contribuciones a la literatura han sido hechas durante varios años por el Dr. Francis Violich, Profesor de Planificación de Ciudades en la Universidad de California en Berkeley, a quién se considera mundialmente entre los más avanzados latinoamericanistas en su propia especialidad. El Dr. Violich ha estado trabajando en planificación de ciudades latinoamericanas y otros temas de urbanismo por aproximadamente 25 años.

Estrechamente aliado con urbanismo se halla el campo de Geografía Urbana, profesión destinada a tomar mucha importancia a medida que se acelere el proceso de urbanización en todas partes del mundo. En la página 10 del folleto, A career in geography (recopilaod por el Comité Central de la Asociación de Geógrafos Americanos, con la ayuda del Consejo Nacional para Educación Geográfica, y editado en 1965 por el Instituto de Investigaciones Geográficas de la Denoyer-Geppert Company, de Chicago), hay una discusión de las funciones y oportunidades de empleo para Geógrafos Urbanos:

> Son muchos y vitales los problemas de Geografía Urbana, en vista de las dificultades de las ciudades. Algunas crecieron demasiado rapidamente, otras se expandieron, dejando zonas muertas (o en vías de) cerca de los centros; otras no crecieron bastante rapidamente, de

acuerdo con los deseos de sus cuidadanos. Para tales problemas y otros semejantes, el Geógrafo Urbano puede ofrecer sugerencias de soluciones, basadas en suficientes investigaciones. Hay mucho que hacer, y es la Geografía Urbana un campo relativamente nuevo. Por esa misma razón ofrece oportunidades crecientes, y muy posiblemente vale la pena formarse en este campo, si existe la vocación personal.

Qué hace el Geógrafo Urbano? Estudia ciudades, naturalmente. Pero, puesto que hay muchas cuidades y debido al hecho de la heterogeneidad de los problemas, en general se especializa en ciertos aspectos de la ciudad o bien sobre una ciudad determinada o grupo de ciudades. Unos cuantos Geógrafos están trabajando sobre los problemas difíciles relacionados con la descripción y definición precisa de los sectores de una ciudad.

Todo el mundo sabe que en una ciudad hay una zona central comercial, pero ¿Qué tamaño tiene en tal o cual ciudad, y qué tipos de actividad económica abarca? Otros desean saber como averiguar, cuales plantas industriales y firmas comerciales realmente sostienen economicamente la ciudad, y cuales existen solamente porque hay gente en la ciudad. Algunos estudian las relaciones entre la ciudad y la región, o provincia que la sostiene. La búsqueda de las respuestas a estos problemas es atrayente y a la vez difícil.

Ne se interesa todo Geógrafo Urbano por problemas tan comprehensivos como los anteriores. Algunos atacan problemas específicos e inmediatos: Cuales zonas necesitan áreas de estacionamiento mas urgentemente? En donde se debe localizar neuvas escuelas y áreas de compras? Cómo se deberían atrazar las arterías públicas de modo que se obtenga alivio del tránsito congestionado? El Geógrafo Urbano no puede resolver muchos de estos problemas por si mismo, pero puede ayudar a otros para hallar le mejor solución.

Tal como se supone, los Geógrafos Urbanos consiguen sus puestos, generalmente, en oficinas municipales de planificación, aunque unos cuantos enseñan en la universidad y hacen Geografía

Urbana como su campo de investigación y enseñanza.

Qué debe saber el Geógrafo Urbano? Adicionalmente a su formación ordinaria de Geógrafo necesita saber todo lo posible con respecto a ciudades: su enstructura física, demográfica y política, sus problemas de ingeniería, sus problemas económicos, y sus problemas sociales. Vale la pena, como formación adicional: Economía, Sociología y Ciencia Política...

Como la nueva ciencia de urbanización se formó en la década de los 60, el Gobierno de los Estados Unidos convirtió lo que eran sus minúsculas agencias caseras en una agencia con rango presidencial: El Ministerio de Vivienda y Desarrollo Urbano.

Es corriente que se ejerza presión para tratar los problemas del transporte de masas, en forma similar. Un Centro de Educación Urbana ha sido establecido recientemente en Nueva York. La tasa de criminalidad urbana en los Estados Unidos se multiplica geometricamente en tanto que la asistencia a conciertos, museos y el uso de las bibliotecas públicas en las grandes áreas urbanas continua quebrando los records anteriores. A solicitud de la Señora Johnson, esposa del Presidente de los EE, UU., se forman organizaciones a todo lo largo del país con el ánimo de mejorar la apariencia de sus respectivas ciudades. Todo esto sucede mientras la impersonalidad de la vida en la ciudad y la idea de "Ciudad Continua" desde Boston hasta Washington, D. C. permanece como tema del día.

Lo que puede sorprender a los planeadores urbanos de los Estados Unidos es el hecho que el tema idéntico está por discutirse en México. Cotizando a Jim Budd (The News, Ciudad de México, 21 de Agosto de 1967, página 30): "de acuerdo con un especialista en la urbanización, por el año 2000 México tendrá su propia metrópolis. Desde Puebla hasta la Capital luego a Toluca, Querétaro y León, ciudades crecerán, la una mezclándose a la siguiente. Es de esperar que el panorama no sea más feo que la cicatriz que corre diagonalmente a través de New Jersey."

Deberá notarse que la Ciudad de México[2] actualmente construye un sistema subterráneo (la Ciudad Caracas, Venezuela, entre 1968 y 1973, hará lo mismo, al costo de US $300 millones, aproximadamente) muy grande para transportar cerca de 7, 000, 000 de sus habitantes y trabajadores, quienes a pesar de un servicio de autobuses eficiente, barato y frecuente, y no obstante los 22, 000 taxis sirviendo la Ciudad, viajan con mucha dificultad en lo que se ha hecho la sexta metrópolis más poblada del mundo. El crecimiento de la Ciudad de México como centro cosmopolitano de cultura y placer es en contraste directo a Brasilia, del cual durante los fines de semana occurren salidas al por mayor de funcionarios, debido a la falta de diversiones, a las cuales están acostumbrados en Rio de Janeiro.

Los pueblos de temporada localizados cerca del océano o contiguos a lagos interiores, en donde la gente encuentra descanso y comodidad por el ruido molesto de las cuidades metropolitanas, regularmente no se consideran dentro del sistema de áreas urbanizadas. He aquí unos pocos ejemplos: San Carlos de Bariloche, Argentina, Viña del Mar, Chile, Chapala, México. La cantidad (y calidad) de sus residentes influyentes rinden sus características aún más urbanas. En 1967 el pueblo de Chapala, situado cerca del hermoso Lago de Chapala en el Estado de Jalisco, construyó faroles sobre las beredas marcadas en campos contiguos al Lago, ya en zonas destinadas para áreas residenciales y comerciales. La población del pueblo, la que incluye muchos ciudadanos estadounidenses y que actualmente suma aproximademente hasta 10, 000 personas, se ha multiplicado cinco veces durante los últimos treinta años. Sostiene supermercado moderno y tiene posibilidades de duplicarse por el año 1985. Guadalajara, [2] Jalisco tiene una población actual de más de 1, 000, 000 de personas (inclyuendo 37, 000 de ciudadanos estadounidenses), diversas industrias en proceso de desarrollo rápido, conjuntos de zarzuelas de España y un aeropuerto internacional con vuelos directos a Los Estados Unidos y a Europa. Durante la década de los 1960 practicamente ha sido reconstruida (incluyendo un sistema de abastecimiento de agua y drenaje), y es actualmente la segunda ciudad de la República Mexicana.

Anteriormente era en segundo lugar Monterrey, [2] popularmente denominado "El Pittsburgh de México." Es conocido desde hace muchos años por la eficiencia de su Instituto Tecnológico (que tiene un centro de computadores). Desde Viernes, 18 de Agosto, 1967, cuando el primer automóvil de la marca Borgward salió de la línea, tiene la distinción de ser la sede de la primera y única fábrica de automóviles completamente fabricados en México, o en Latino America. Una sociedad anómima mexicana compró en total la firma alemana de automóviles Borgward.

Monterrey será la matríz para la fabricación completa y exportación mundial de automóviles y de refacciones Borgward.

Aunque Monterrey goza de una fama prolongada de centro industrial, por medio de un programa del Gobierno Mexicano, fabricantes estadounidenses (desde 1966) establecen plantas en algunas ciudades a lo largo de la frontera México-Estados Unidos. Debido a la disponibilidad de trabajadores calificados y a una escala barata de pago, franquicias aduanales para maquinaria y materiales de producción (ofrecidas por parte del Gobierno Mexicano), así como la proximidad a los mercados en los Estados Unidos, estas firmas norteamericanas instituyeron fábricas en Matamoros, Tijuana, Ciudad Juarez y en otras ciudades fronterizas mexicanas. De modo que lo que empezó como ventaja industrial-comercial para fabricantes estadounidenses, si continua, podría resultar en la industrialización de ciudades y pueblos que hasta la fecha ganan sus vidas de los desembolsos de turistas norteamericanos quienes quieren "ver México."

La importancia transcendental de urbanización, así como los problemas afines, han llamado la atención del Instituto de Asuntos Internacionales Adlai E. Stevenson, establecido en la Casa Robie, muy cerca a la Universidad de Chicago, el día 6 de Febrero de 1967, <u>in memoriam</u> al difunto embajador estadounidense a las Naciones Unidas. El Instituto desempeñará investigaciones sobre problemas nacionales (de los EE. UU.), así como en cuanto a asuntos internacionales, con énfasis en los problemas que actualmente enfrentan una multitud de naciones. Vale la pena señalar el hecho que un estudio de la urbanización, a base mundial, ocupa lugar de primer categoría en la lista de proyectos para investigación.

La acción del Instituto Stevenson pronosticó el interés de otras entidades por problemas de la urbanización. El día 30 de Noviembre de 1967, la Fundación Ford manifestó que había otorgado US $10.800.000 a las Universidades de Chicago, Columbia, Harvard y al Instituto Tecnológico de Massachusetts, para fines de establecer cátedras en los campos siguientes pero relacionados al estudio de problemas de la urbanización: economía, ingeniería, educación, leyes, administración pública, ciencia política, sociología y análisis de sistemas, así como en planificación urbana. La Fundación anunció la disponibilidad de becas, subrayando el hecho que aún ha habido interés universitario de larga duración por los problemas urbanos, recientemente se han hecho esfuerzos para respaldar los Estudios Urbanos dentro de la jerarquía académica tradicional como campo interdisciplinario, y financiarlos. En vista de la urgente necesidad, la Fundación Ford, como resultado de su acción, abrigó la esperanza para atraer más estudiosos y científicos de primera clase al estudio de los problemas urbanos. Aunque se enfoca el programa enteramente sobre las ciudades de los EE. UU., debido al interés tradicional de la Fundación por los problemas de Latinoamérica, se espera que posteriormente se ponga atención a las dificultades de esa región.

En general el problema de vivir en grandes áreas metropolitanas en cualquier parte del mundo se está volviendo más complejo. Citando las palabras del Dr. Roger Revelle, Director del Centro de Estudios sobre Población de la Universidad de Harvard:

> En la megalópolis del futuro los problemas de agua, aire, suministro de comida, recolección de vasuras, control de la contaminación, el transporte y las comunicaciones, y sobre todo de la conservación de la vida humana en un nivel humano estará más allá de cualquier magnitud nunca antes presentada en la historia de las ciudades. [3]

Porqué el promedio del ciudadano latinoamericano rural deja el terruño familiar donde sus antepasados han habitado por muchos años para irse a una vida desconocida entre las luces de la ciudad? La atracción de las "brillantes luces" y la oportunidad de obtener beneficios, han sido las respuestas tradicionales. Y todavía uno se plantea otras razones (más facilidades educacionales y sanitarias, el eterno empeoramiento de la subsistencia por la tierra sobretrabajada y el incremento violento de la población rural incapaz de alimentarse por si misma o simplemente por otra parte, irse para la ciudad porque "está de moda" de ordinario). Estas pueden ser en muchas naciones consideraciones primordiales.

Es posible enumerar motivos bastante apropiados resultando en la migración rural-urbana de varias clases de personas: las mujeres se migran para casarse; mucha gente prefiere el surtido muy amplio de empleo; los jóvenes buscan la educación y quieren evitar el fastidio; les gustan a los reos la gran variedad de ocasiones, y la seguridad (en contra el descubrimiento) ofrecida por parte de las masas. Es importante observar que existe en la Ciudad de México una organización investigativa que trata con los problemas de desarrollo socio-económico. Esta organización estudia a fondo las vidas enteras de las migrantes rurales (motivos resultando en las migraciones, actitudes y modos de vivir) en los barrios bajos de la Ciudad de México. Se utilizarán las informaciones obtenidas para fines de un proyecto piloto en la forma de un Centro de Estudios sobre las Migraciones Rural-Urbanas.

Aunque se considera la migración rural-urbana la causa principal de los problemas tipo urbanización, no es el único factor: vienen los migrantes a la metrópoli de ciudades de segunda y tercera clase en muchos países. En casi todos los países latinoamericanos es la tendencia proceder de la campaña a las ciudades más grandes, y son muchos los migrantes quienes permanecen ratito en estas ciudades, en su rumbo a la metrópoli. Muchas veces son los niños de los migrantes originales quienes terminan la migración de sus padres.

En los Estados Unidos de América hay bastante interés por la migración rural-urbana mexicana. En 1967 otorgó la National Science Foundation US $41, 000 al Doctor John M. Ball, Catedrático en el Departamento de Geografía de la Universidad de Georgia, para fines de investigar la conexión entre las migraciones y el crecimiento de la población mexicana, por un lado, y las condiciones socio-económicas, por otro.

Una solución al problema de las migraciones rural-urbanas fué publicada en una obra previa del autor, especificamente con respecto a la situación argentina:

> ... los contactos establecidos (entre poblaciones rurales y urbanas) deben ser aumentados e introducidos otros neuvos con el fin de hacer suficiente atrayente la vida rural (además de ser valiosa económicamente, con la ayuda del gobierno y por medios tecnológicos y financieros a la agricultura) de modo que aquellos que están ahora apiñados en Buenos Aires podrían buscar ganarse la vida "en la tierra"... Claramente, la ayuda... se necesita para (1) el desarrollo de abastecimiento de agua; (2) el mejoramiento de las escuelas y las bibliotecas; (3) la extensión del desarrollo de la potencia eléctrica; (4) mejoramiento de carreteras y renovación de ferrocarriles; (5) vivienda; (6) aumento de la distribución de periódicos y revistas;

(7) incremento de la transmisión de programas de radio y televisión; (8) mejoramiento de museos de arte e historia natural; (9) programas de música y actuaciones dramáticas por compañías viajeras; (10) centros para la juventud y "ciudadanos mayores"; (11) desarrollo de hospitales rurales.

(Véase Argentine Agriculture: Proposal for Progress, por Martin H. Sable, en su libro, A Guide to Latin American Studies, tomo I. Los Angeles, Latin American Center, University of California, 1967, p. 85).

En este aspecto es importante considerar las recomendaciones referentes al desarrollo urbano universal contenido en el Reporte de Actividades del Año de la Cooperación Internacional presentado en junio de 1966 por la Junta de Asuntos Extranjeros de la Camara de Diputados de los EE. UU., 89º Congreso, segunda sesión (Washington, EE. UU. Imprenta Oficial, 1966, p. 47).

La urbanización, una vez en la historia del hombre una fuerza gradual, lenta y manejable, se ha acelerado y ha hecho tal impacto en los últimos 50 años, que debe ser considerada como una de las grandes fuerzas revolucionarias del siglo XX. La urbanización ha hecho de este siglo el "Siglo de la Ciudad." En cuanto al bienestar del hombre y sus posibilidades, debe de concluirse como completamente beneficiosa. La urbanización presenta muchos confusos y urgentes problemas, pero es indudable algo de beneficio para la especie humana y un elemento esencial e integral de progreso. La misión del hombre es minimizar los problemas y obtener los máximos beneficios de la urbanización. El Año de la Cooperación Internaciónal brinda la oportunidad para activar la consecución de algunos de estos fines, y en este sentido La Junta de Desarrollo Urbano propone:

1. Los Estados Unidos deben dar destacada prioridad y mayor reconocimiento a los programas de desarrollo urbano en su asistencia bilateral, y debe gestionar para obtener similar prioridad y reconocimiento para programas de desarrollo urbano en los programas de asistencia de las Naciones Unidas. En particular los Estados Unidos deben hacer esfuerzos para conseguir adecuado presupuesto y el personal necesario para el

recientemente establecido Centro de Vivienda y Planifacación.

2. Los Estados Unidos deben tomar la iniciativa entre las Naciones Unidas para establecer un programa internacional organizado, sostenido por contribuciones voluntarias de las naciones miembros para atacar los problemas específicos de los tugurios y la localización de nuevos pobladores en las ciudades de los países en desarrollo.

3. Adicional atención y consideración debe concentrarse en los problemas de recursos financieros para sostener los programas de desarrollo urbano. El éxito entusiasta de las entidades ahorro y préstamo recientemente organizadas en Latinoamérica son un augurio de los que puede hacerse por medio de la entusiasta promoción de estas instituciones o por medio de la introducción de otros imaginables y prácticos instrumentos o políticas.

4. Los Estados Unidos deberían establecer un Instituto Laboratorio de Investigación del Desarrollo Mundial de la Urbanización. Este Instituto y Laboratorio serían patrocinados y financiados principalmente por los Estados Unidos, y su sede estaría allí. Debería funcionar, sin embargo, como una organización mundial con plena participación internacional y posiblemente con sucursales en otras regiones del mundo y sus beneficios serían para todas las naciones.

5. Los Estados Unidos deberían promover una Conferencia Mundial sobre Desarrollo Urbano para enfatizar la importancia del desarrollo urbano y para conseguir comprensión y ayuda de los gobernantes en los países interesados.

Con referencia a la asistencia internacional a los gobiernos municipales en Latinoamérica, el Banco Interamericano de Desarrollo distribuye aproximadamante un 40% de su Fondo Especial del Progreso Social para las ciudades Latinoamericanas. Por qué este gran porcentaje para las ciudades? La proliferación en las afueras de las metrópolis primarias y secundarias en todas las naciones latinoamericanas, de barrios bajos , tugurios, ranchos, favelas, barriadas, cantegriles, villas miserias, callampas y bidonvilles, con la resultante decadencia de la existencia humana, y la concomitante amenaza a la salud pública, educación, moral, seguridad económica y política son respuesta suficiente. Es un hecho que en el año dos mil Latinoamérica está destinada a ser un continente urbano. En vista de este punto, también como la declaración que "el viaje a la ciudad" ha estado ganando en importancia en Latinoamérica como una manifestación sociológica desde 1920,[4] nos incumbe considerar seriamente no sólo los factores que han motivado este fenómeno, sino también los impactos que han repercutido sobre los aspectos de la vida en la ciudad.

Es un hecho que esta actitud es compartida por varias universidades, adicionales a UCLA, tal como Cornell University, donde la Agencia Internacional de Desarrollo de los EE. UU. financia un programa de cinco años de investigaciones sobre "La Política de Vivienda Urbana en Latinoamérica, sus Implicaciones Demográficas, Económicas, de Salud, Políticas y Sociales." El Graduate School of Arts and Sciences de la Universidad de Nueva York, así como Columbia University ofrecen cursos en Urbanización en la América Latina. El Instituto de Tecnología de Massachusetts en 1967 organizó un "Programa Especial para Estudios Urbanos y Regionales para Areas en Desarrollo." La Universidad de Buenos Aires ofrece cursos, y el Centro Haitiano de Investigaciones Sociales en Puerto de Príncipe trata el asunto.

Además, profesores de la Universidad de Florida realizarán investigaciones en la ciudad de Cali, Colombia, sobre educación, salud, transporte, gobierno municipal, desarrollo industrial y desarrollo social, en colaboración con la Fundación Ford. Su base de operaciones será la Universidad del Valle, en Cali, donde además se dictarán conferencias sobre el tema.

Bajo un programa de cinco años patrocinado por La Fundación Ford, el Centro de Estudios en Educación y Desarrollo de la Universidad de Harvard ha comenzado una investigación sobre el rol de la escuela en la urbanización e industrialización de la Guayana de Venezuela. Este tópico sobre la urbanización es la iniciación y primer elemento en el programa de cinco aspectos de investigación sobre la naturaleza y características de esta área en Venezuela, en vías de una urbanización acelerada. El hecho de que los problemas referentes a las metrópolis Latinoamericanas conciernen al mundo entero, se confirma por la convocatoria a una Reunión especial sobre las Capitales de Latinoamérica auspiciada por el Consejo Nacional de Investigación Científica del Gobierno Francés, en el Instituto de Estudios Españoles, Latinoamericanos y Luso-Brasileños de la Universidad de Toulouse, Francia, en Febrero de 1964.[5] Desde 1967, el Centro de Documentación del Instituto de Estudios Superiores de la América Latina de la Universidad de París ha sido la oficina principal para el Proyecto de Investigación Cooperativa en la Parte Regional de Ciudades en Latinoamérica, de la misma entidad (Consejo Nacional de Investigación Científica del Gobierno Francés). Bajo la dirección del Dr. Olivier Dollfus, famoso geógrafo, el Centro reunirá materiales sobre la economía, geografía y planeación regional de Latinoamérica. En el mismo año (los días 9 y 10 de Junio de 1967), la Universidad de Texas organizó una Conferencia sobre Problemas de la Urbanización en Latinoamérica, en El Paso, Texas.

Esta obra fué recopilada por otra razón: la necesidad de tener a mano, sistematizada y lista para su uso... "la documentación necesaria, sobre todo en materia estadística... si en el futuro no se prepara esta documentación más precisamente y cuidadosamente, será imposible preveer de manera inteligente y sensata la metamórfosis de una realidad en estado de cambio constante." Aunque se incluyen fuentes estadísticas en la mayoría de los campos de la obra, las secciones de Urban Research y Demography contienen cantidades de referencias bibliográficas, específicas, de las naciones latinoamericanas. De esta manera llenan la laguna para tales datos requeridos por parte de las Naciones Unidas, la Organización de Estados Americanos y la Oficina de Trabajo Internacional, en su publicación.[6]

Le Secrétariat des Missions d'Urbanisme et d'Habitat (El Secretariado de Asuntos de Urbanismo v Vivienda), 11, rue Chardin, Paris 16, Francia, desempeña investigaciones en los campos de metodología documental y terminología, con respecto a planificación y vivienda; es fuente de información de primer orden, especialmente para los países subdesarrollados del mundo. El hecho de la existencia de esta organización confirma la necesidad de datos sistematizados en una secuencia lógica, como ya lo hemos manifestado.

La seriedad con que los intelectuales y funcionarios latinoamericanos consideran los problemas de urbanización se subraya por la convocación de un Seminario sobre Desarrollo Urbano en Latinoamérica, en Rosario, Argentina, del 15 al 17 de Octubre de 1965. En este Seminario trataron los asuntos siguientes: (a). Aspectos Sociales de la Urbanización (efectos de la migración rural-urbana, y su influencia sobre desarrollo urbano, nivel de vida, etc.); (b). La Economía Urbana (centralización vs. descentralización, problemas de finanzas municipales, servicios públicos, etc.); (c). La Estructura Urbana (planificación urbana; la influencia del transporte municipal sobre el perfil físico de la ciudad); (d). Asuntos Administrativos y Legales. Lo significativo aquí se Señala en el hecho que el empuje del Seminario se dirigió hacia la identificación y evaluación de la información disponible en cada una de estas áreas, con mira hacia el establecimiento de prioridades para investigaciones futuras. Tenemos, pues, un ejemplo adicional de la importancia, concedida por los expertos, a la documentación y clasificación precisa de la información, con respecto a los problemas de urbanización.

Escritores latinoamericanos han tratado el tema de la ciudad. Se pueden mencionar las obras del poeta argentino contemporáneo, Jorge Luis Borges, con respecto a sus descripciones íntimas de las calles de Buenos Aires. La sociedad de Lima, Perú, se estudia profundamente en la serie, Tradiciones peruanas de Ricardo Palma (1833-1919). En Chile, Joaquín Edwards Bello (1888-1968) escribió sobre el mundo del hampa de Santiago. Eduardo Barrios (1884-1963) y Augusto G. Thomson (mejor conocido bajo el seudónimo de Augusto d'Halmar 1880-1950) trataron el asunto de los problemas sociales de la ciudad en Chile. Una obra reciente que ganó fama internacional estudia la delincuencia juvenil en la ciudad de Santiago. Llevando el título Manuel (y escrito por parte de Christopher Jackson, profesor universitario chileno), describe el lado peor de la vida santiagüena, y sus efectos psicológicos en un adolescente quien acaba por matar a un comerciante influyente. La obra fué traducida al inglés (Nueva York, Knopf, 1964, 251p.).

El interés por el estilo de la vida urbana ha sido y continua siendo tema de primer orden entre los escritores latinoamericanos (y españoles). Pero unicamente en años recientes se extendió este interés en el nuevo ramo del estudio de las lenguas, la ciencia de la lingüística. Entre el 24 y 29 de Octubre de 1966, tuvo lugar en Madrid la Primera Reunión de Representantes de la Oficina Internacional de Información y Observación de la Lengua Española, y de la Comisión de Lingüística Latinoamericana y Dialectología del Programa Interamericano para le Enseñanza de Lingüística y Lenguas. La Reunión tuvo como propósito especificar los aspectos básicos de su próximo proyecto: el estudio del estilo y forma del lenguaje urbano en las capitales latinoamericanas y en España. Fueron invitados a colaborar en las investigaciones de lingüística urbana (en sus metrópolis respectivas) especialistas en lingüística en universidades e institutos de Barcelona, Bogotá, Buenos Aires, Havana, Lima, Madrid, Ciudad de México, Montevideo, Rio de Janeiro, San Juan de Puerto Rico, y Santiago de Chile. Grabaciones en cintas magnéticas se efectuarán para investigar la fonología, la morfo-sintáxis, el léxico y las estructuras familiares de cada ciudad. La Escuela de Investigaciones Lingüísticas de la Oficina de Información y Observación de la Lengua Española en Madrid ha fijado una fecha límite (fines de 1969) para la conclusión del proyecto y la publicación de los resultados.

El autor se permite sugerir a los interesados en la investigación los siguientes tópicos como de primera importancia e interés para América Latina:

1. La ciudad y sus elementos religiosos.

2. Areas naturales para recreación en ciudades grandes y embellecimiento de las ciudades.

3. Estudio de las ciudades universitarias (como las que existen en Caracas, Bogotá, Quito, Ciudad de México, San José, etc.) en relación con las ciudades en las que están localizadas.

4. Bases legales, políticas y financieras en el desarrollo de Brasilia.

5. Factores a considerar en el establecimiento de centros comerciales.

6. Salud, recreación, embellecimiento y espacio vital como factores para la localización de las plantas industriales en São Paulo.

7. Participación ciudadana en la implementación de todos los aspectos implícitos en el proceso de la urbanización, y problemas de relación y comunicación interpersonal.

8. Oficinas de investigación municipal en las ciudades latinoamericanas.

9. Problemas resultantes de la remodelación urbana en las áreas comerciales en el centro de las grandes ciudades (reubicación de los grupos y de las actividades comerciales: aspectos legales y económicos, y el cambio

social involucrado.

10. Elementos de la urbanización (características comunes del cambio social en las grandes ciudades, incluyendo el cambio económico) los cuales también se presentan en las áreas rurales que experimentan un pequeño proceso de desarrollo económico.

11. Posibilidades para la descentralización de Buenos Aires.

12. Factores climáticos y geo-económicos en la escogencia de la localización para las capitales latinoamericanas.

13. Estudios comparativos de Bogotá, Santiago, Caracas; São Paulo, Rio de Janeiro; Tegucigalpa, Managua; Valparaíso, Cali; Buenos Aires, París.

14. Estudios comparativos de las leyes municipales en: Brasil, Argentina, Colombia, Venezuela, Chile; México, Guatemala.

15. Centros de investigación urbana y la enseñanza de los estudios sobre la urbanización en las universidades latinoamericanas.

La sección de bibliografía en la presente fuente de referencia trata todos los aspectos de la vida en las áreas urbanas de Latinoamérica, representados en Las Ciencias Naturales y Aplicadas (contaminación del aire, abastecimientos de agua, salud, vivienda, servicios públicos, etc.) o Ciencias Sociales (educación, historia urbana, gobierno municipal y finanzas, pobreza, empleo y costo de vida, transporte y comunicación, crimen urbano, delincuencia juvenil, industrialización y cambio social, bienestar y seguridad de la comunidad, etc.) o en Artes y Humanidades (el nivel de vida religiosa en la ciudad y patrón urbano de la literatura y las artes, el planeamiento urbano y la recreación). Para los sub-tópicos específicos en este campo, referirse a la Tabla de Contenido y al Indice Geográfico de Temas. Además, hay secciones dedicadas a la investigación urbana, incluyendo estudios específicos, estudios de aproximación y metodología. La sección de libros en Investigación Urbana contiene fuentes estadísticas que cubren la mayoría de los temas enumerados anteriormente. Puesto que las técnicas de desarrollo de la comunidad pueden ser aplicadas para solucionar los problemas de las grandes ciudades, una sección que abarca estos tópicos ha sido incluida. El tema "Urbanización (General)" trata el tópico (en las dos secciones de libros y artículos de revista) con la presencia de fichas bibliográficas de naturaleza general como una introducción y base al material que se refiere especialmente a Latinoamérica. Cada tema tratado en la bibliografía está dividido en dos secciones: 1). Textos y libros de referencia, folletos, documentos oficiales, revistas, actas de conferencias, y tésis; 2). Artículos de revista.

Aún cuando la mayoría del material incluido está en Español y en Inglés, una buena representación en Portugués que cubre todos los aspectos de la urbanización en Brasil, constituye una de las principales secciones de este trabajo. También está representado un buen grupo de publicaciones francesas y alemanas así como unas publicaciones en francés para Haití.

La bibliografía está organizada: 1). En cinco extensas áreas de actividad. 2). En treinta temas subdivididos físicamente, como se definió anteriormente. El término Libros como se usa en el ejemplo siguiente incluye documentos oficiales, actas de conferencias, folletos, textos y libros de referencia. 3). En subtópicos, con una sección general que contiene los trabajos básicos de cada campo. 4). Geograficamente por naciones en órden alfabético, empezando con la sección general sobre Latinoamérica y después Argentina, Bolivia, Brasil, etc. 5). Alfabeticamente por autor para cada nación. El siguiente ejemplo ilustrará el procedimiento:

IV. SOCIOLOGIA (Campo de actividad)

SALUD PUBLICA (Tema)

Contaminación del Aire (Subtema)

Libros: (Categoría física)

General

Johnson, James. Pollution Problems. Chicago, Jones Publishing Co., 1960, 100p.

Latinoamérica (Categoría geográfica)

Arnold, John. Air pollution in the Americas. Washington, Grapevine Press, 1966, 200p.

Baker, Roy. Latin America and pollution of the air. Boston, Vacuum Cleaner Press, 1960, 1243p. (Alfabeticamente por autor)

Argentina, etc.

Artículos de Revista (Categoría física)

General

Latinoamérica, etc.

En el caso de cuando las fichas bibliográficas de artículos de revista no manifiestan lugar de publicación, se entiende que tales revistas se editan periodicamente en los Estados Unidos de América. En todo caso "Santiago" significa Santiago de Chile, a menos de que se especifique de otra manera, para libros y revistas. Por el hecho de haber muchos artículos, actas de conferencias y monografías sin autores en las citas bibliográficas y a causa de la gran cantidad de fichas en treinta campos de la urbanización, los que utilicen este trabajo se verán urgidos a utilizar el Indice Geográfico de Temas para asegurarse de un mejor uso de los datos. Cada ficha bibliográfica ha sido numerada consecutivamente; es importante observar que los temas de encabezamiento en el Indice Geográfico de Temas tienen a continuación nombres de lugares, ciudades o naciones. Así por ejemplo "Contaminación del Aire, Sao Paulo, Brasil," seguido por el número, digamos "750," informa al investigador interesado en este tópico de la disponibilidad de tal estudio sobre Sao Paulo, Brasil. Para obtener la referencia, él podría localizar rapidamente el número 750 en el contenido de la obra. Es sobre entendido que cuando la designación geográfica no es dada, el tema en cuestión es de naturaleza general. Muchos esfuerzos han sido invertidos por representar todas las naciones Latinoamericanas y dependencias europeas.

Puesto que la bibliografía fué recopilada en primer lugar para el uso de investigadores en disciplinas y campos afines al fenómeno de la urbanización latinoamericana, es importante que los especialistas, estudiosos e investigadores no-interesados directamente por problemas de la urbanización se percaten de que pueden utilizar las bibliografías de las varias secciones para sus específicos campos. Por ejemplo, un científico lingüista puede muy provechosamente consultar las fichas bibliográficas, en la sección de Lengua Urbana, para las naciones de sus interéses. De la misma manera expertos en Religión, Seguridad Social, Transporte, Comunicaciones, Historia Urbana, Cambio Social, Bienestar Público, Gobierno Municipal, Vivienda, Industrialización, Nivel de Vida, o cualquier de los campos individuales adicionales pueden utilizar la bibliografía de su propio campo de interés, o actividad professional.

Además, bajo varios campos hay grupos de subtópicos muy difíciles de localizar. He aquí unos cuantos ejemplos: bajo Salud Pública: Contaminación del Aire, Higiene Mental, Ingeniería Sanitaria, Atención Hospitalaria y Médica, Abastecimiento de Agua y Nutrición; fichas bibliográficas sobre grupos religiosos en Latinoamérica (bajo Religión); Literatura, Música y Pintura (bajo Urban Matrix for Literature and the Arts); Desempleo (bajo Poverty); Cine, Periódicos, Radio y Televisión (bajo Communications); todo nivel de educación, con énfase en universidades (bajo Education); Crimen y Delincuencia Juvenil, Servicios Públicos, Finanzas Municipales, Migración Rural-Urbana, Pobreza, Empleo, y Facilidades de Recreación. Para la mayoría de los tópicos arriba-mencionados no existe, para ciudades latinoamericanas, ninguna bibliografía completa en cualquier lengua: esta bibliografía abarca cinco lenguas. Por eso apreciamos que algunas lagunas bibliográficas han sido llenadas en un grado significativo.

Necesariamente, muchos de los temas incluidos son referentes a naciones enteras. Como las facilidades de escuelas y hospitales, sindicatos, sistemas del seguro social, planeamiento e industrialización son características de las áreas urbanas, estos tópicos cubren una nación entera, y por su naturaleza altañen directamente a las grandes ciudades de cada nación. En ciertos casos libros y artículos de revista contienen material sobre las áreas rurales y urbanas y, en un específico aspecto del Desarrollo de la Comunidad, el énfasis es totalmente en el desarrollo de las comunidades rurales. Desarrollo de la Comunidad ha sido incluido por la teoría recientemente establecida de que las técnicas del desarrollo de la comunidad podrían ser aplicadas con todo éxito en ciudades latinoamericanas, * especialmente en

*El Cuerpo de Paz adiestra algunos de sus voluntarios para trabajo en desarrollo de las comunidades urbanas en Latinoamérica. La Agencia para Desarrollo Internacional (AID) de los EE. UU. financia proyectos en barrios bajos de ciudades latinoamericanas.

aquellas donde hay gente recien llegada de las áreas rurales. En el caso de las comunidades marginales que rodean las metrópolis, poblaciones rurales enteras convergen en dos o tres centros numerosamente poblados, de aquí, que logicamente las técnicas del desarrollo de las communidades pueden aplicarse a ciertos problemas de la urbanización.

El directorio que contiene nombres y direcciones de entidades del mundo entero, está dividido en tres secciones: (1) Centros de investigación, institutos y organizaciones principalmente conectadas con universidades; también se incluyen instituciones privadas y del gobierno. (2) Organizaciones de acción social, asociaciones profesionales y departamentos gubernamentales en varios niveles; las entidades de acción social se ven necesariamente incluidas en el proceso de urbanización y generalmente también en lo que se refiere a los campos específicos. (3) Especialistas en varios campos de actividad envueltos en el proceso de urbanización, localizados en los Estados Unidos, Latinoamérica y Europa Occidental.

En un trabajo de esta naturaleza es inevitable que se produzcan algunos errores, aunque estos sean obviamente accidentales. Se ha hecho un esfuerzo para recopilar información que sea confiable. Dicha información aquí se ofrece sin garantía en cuanto a su precisión, su ubicación en el tiempo y su integridad.

Se espera publicar nuevas ediciones de esta obra de consulta periodicamente. El autor está dispuesto a recibir indicaciones motivando el mejoramiento del libro: items bibliográficos, organizaciones, centros de investigaciones, etc.

El autor espera que investigadores, estudiantes, funcionarios gubernamentales, agencias internacionales, fundaciones y especialistas interesados en los varios aspectos de la urbanización latinoamericana utilicen el material que se ofrece en este libro, para el eventual mejoramiento de las condiciones de vida: físicas, económicas y gubernamentales, y el estilo y nivel de vida en las áreas metropolitanas de Latinoamérica. Si, como residuo de este esfuerzo las relaciones interamericanas se mejoran, el autor indudablemente se sentirá compensado.

Finalmente, considero justo dedicar este trabajo a mi querida esposa, Minna. Para rendirle suficiente tributo, no tengo otro recurso que identificarme con el poeta que escribió:

Esta mujer que habeis hecho para que sea mi ayuda
Y me habeis dado como vuestro regalo perfecto, tan
bueno,
Tan idóneo, tan acceptable, tan divino.

Martin H. Sable

Notes

1. Annual report: The Center of Community and Metropolitan Studies. St. Louis, University of Missouri at St. Louis, July 1967, pp. 1-2.

2. Guillermo Luna en "Megalopolis Trends in Mexico" [Atenas, Ekistics, Tomo 24: # 140, Julio 1967, pp. 19-20], manifiesta que por el año 2000 la Ciudad de México, Guadalajara y Monterrey serán áreas metropolitanas con poblaciones de 14 millones, 6-1/2 millones y 5 millones respectivamente).

3. Roger Revelle, Science and social change. (En Actas de la Conferencia Nacional Especial Convocada por la Comisión Nacional de los Estados Unidos para Unesco, New Orleans, La., 18-20 Septiembre 1966. Washington, Comisión Nacional de los EE. UU. para Unesco, 1966, pág. 31).

4. De acuerdo con la Enciclopedia Británica (1965, Volúmen 13, pág. 768), la población urbana en América Latina creció de un 33% en 1925 a un 45% en 1960. Aunque Argentina fué el primer país en porcentaje de población urbana (60%, de acuerdo con las cifras de 1960), las otras naciones latinoamericanas también se urbanizaban rapidamente con un crecimiento superior en las metrópolis que en las ciudades pequeñas. Entre 1950 y 1960 la población de Caracas, Venezuela se sobreduplicó en tamaño mientras que la de Sao Paulo, Brasil, cambiaba de 2. 017. 025 en 1950, a aproximadamente 3. 600. 000 en 1960. En la década siguiente a la Segunda Guerra Mundial la población urbana de Colombia, Venezuela, Panamá, y México crecieron hasta un 58%, 57%, 54%, y 50%, respectivamente.

   Estas estadísticas de la Enciclopedia Británica son

confirmadas por las estimaciones del Profesor Montague Yudelman del Centro de Investigación del Desarrollo Económico de la Universidad de Michigan, quien afirma que la población de los centros urbanos de Latinoamérica crecía en un 5% anual para 1966.

5. El hecho de que este asunto es de continuo interés se comprueba, por ejemplo, con la existencia de un grupo de profesores de la Universidad de Toulouse, quienes preparan un estudio bajo el título de Las Ciudades de Latinoamérica, el cual será publicado en 1969 en un número especial de Caravelle (revista del Instituto). Volumen 3 (1964) abarcó ponencias por especialistas en el Coloquio de Febrero del 1964.

6. Seminar on Urbanization Problems in Latin America, Santiago de Chile, 1959. Urbanization in Latin America; Proceedings. Paris, Unesco, 1961, p. 26.

"Seek the welfare of the city whither I have caused you to migrate,
And pray to the Lord for it." Jeremiah 29:7.

* * * *

"Busque el bienestar de la ciudad a la cual le causé migrarse,
Y rece a Dios por ella." Jeremias 29:7.

Introduction to the Table of Contents

Latin American urbanization: a guide to the literature, organizations and personnel contains material in its bibliography section on practically every topic concerned with Latin American cities. These run the entire gamut from urban history, religion and culture to materials on air pollution and garbage collection. Prospective tourists may utilize the section on "Description and Travel" to obtain books and articles on travel to Latin American cities of primary, secondary, and even tertiary importance. There follows here a description of the areas and sub-areas included within the topical divisions of the bibliography.

"The City in Latin American Literature" is an area which begins with "Literature, General," a "catch-all" term covering correspondence and reminiscences, sketches and general descriptions of life in Latin American cities at various periods of their existences. Those concerned with the topic are advised to check items listed under Urban History. There follow, in order, subdivisions for Drama, Novel, Poetry and Short Story. Combinations of these are also to be found under "Literature, General."

"Description and Travel," a field containing books and periodical articles on travel to Latin American cities, was an afterthought which completes a bibliography covering perhaps every aspect of the lives and descriptions of Latin American cities. Included here are materials on cities such as Payssandú (Uruguay), Oruro (Bolivia), San Pedro Sula (Honduras), Barquisimeto (Venezuela), Bahia (Brazil), Camaguey (Cuba), Medellín, (Colombia), and hosts of additional Latin American cities not of cardinal significance.

"Planning" is here considered to include the architectural laying out of streets and thoroughfares, placement of buildings, and the planning of the physical profile of the city, making allowances for "green" areas.

"Recreation," a relatively recent entrant into the "community of scholarship, covers in this bibliography parks, and other recreational facilities, the recreational use of "open spaces," and sports activities. It should be noted that although baseball is a great favorite in many nations of Latin America, soccer's popularity is growing by leaps and bounds, to the extent that it is rapidly advancing in number of players and devotees in the United States of America. Despite the uniqueness of the field for Latin America, the reader is directed to item 975 for a study of the use of recreation in Caracas, Venezuela.

"Religion" concerns not only church histories, but also studies on social change with relation to religion currently manifested. Entries on the Protestant, Afro-American and Jewish religions are also included, in addition to items on Catholicism.

In the field of "Urban History" are to be found not only histories of the founding and development of Latin American cities, but also material on social customs of their inhabitants and vignettes on the "life of the times" in various periods.

"The Urban Matrix for Literature and the Arts" is a broad area which points up those intellectual components of a metropolis which foster the growth and development of culture: learned institutions (libraries and museums, etc.), painting and sculpture, music, theatre and the dance, and literature. For an incisive treatment of the situations of The Writer (by Dr. Fred P. Ellison) and The Artist (by Dr. Gilbert Chase), see pages 79 and 101, respectively, in Continuity and Change in Latin America, edited by Professor John J. Johnson (Stanford, Stanford University Press, 1964, 282p.).

"Urban Speech" covers all aspects of linguistics as related to major Latin American cities. In addition to scholarly studies and research reports, there are included dictionaries of words and phrases as used in the cities of each country. There is an ample section for the Creole French of Haiti, and much attention is devoted to the linguistic atlas for Colombia, compiled by specialists of the Instituto Caro y Cuervo, of Bogotá.

"Cost and Standard of Living" is well-represented by an abundance of periodical literature on the topic. A highly valuable feature of this literature is its time-spread: articles range in publication dates from 1929 to mid-1967. The "General" sections in both book and periodical divisions contain indexes of cost of living in various countries, including those outside Latin America, a highly valuable tool for international comparative purposes.

"Industrialization" has grown apace in many Latin American cities. Many sections of São Paulo, Brazil, suffer from over-industrialization with a resulting "swallowing up" of recreation areas and friction between industrialists and residents of industrializing zones. Under "Industrialization" are to be found many entries in the field of economic development.

"Poverty" covers not only unemployment, but also life in slum areas of large Latin American cities. Social problems attendant upon, and resulting from poverty are treated under corresponding categories.

"Transportation" covers railroads, motor cars, buses and trucks. Here is another field which requires more in-depth research, and the resulting reports of same. Studies on motor car, bus and truck transportation are in especial need of attention. To the compiler's knowledge, only one such study now exists in English; it covers all of Latin America, and was published by the U. S. Department of Commerce. One of the few U. S. specialists on transportation is Dr. David Snyder of Yale University, who made studies of the transportation problems in Montevideo, Uruguay, among other metropoli.

With respect to problems of "Urban Employment," see The Urban Worker (by Professor Frank Bonilla of M. I. T., and former correspondent in Latin America for the American Universities Field Staff), in Dr. John J. Johnson's Continuity and Change in Latin America (Stanford, Stanford University Press, 1967, pp. 186-205). Trade unions are also included in our bibliographical coverage. For the topic of unemployment, see "Poverty."

Under the topic of "Municipal Finance," bibliographic items on legal aspects of the funding of municipal activities and services are located. Relationships between cities, and state and federal governments are likewise included.

Constitutional and legal bases fundamental to the organization and administration of cities are listed under "Municipal Government and Legal Matters." It is advisable to consult data under "Urban History," especially with respect to Spanish colonial administration prior to Independence.

Within the scope of "Public Utilities," typically telephone, electric and gas companies (both publicly and privately operated), there are entries concerning legal aspects. Allied topics to be consulted are Transportation, and Sanitary Engineering and Water Supply (the latter two under "Public Health").

The field of "Communications" covers the sub-topics of newspapers, radio and television, publishing and the motion picture industry. The field of communications has given birth to a considerable body of literature, mainly the result of field research carried out by the Programa Interamericano de Información Popular, with headquarters in San José, Costa Rica, and a branch in Lima, Peru. Operating under Rockefeller funds, this research organization has been studying the transmission of information among farmers; it has recently turned some of its attention to the problems of city-dwellers.

The problem of establishing contact among city slum-dwellers, for purposes of arousing identification and a sense of community, just as has been done in rural areas in the process of developing small towns, is one to which the field of communications can indeed render valued and needed service.

"Community Development," an area of activity traditionally relegated to rural locales, is currently being applied to Latin American metropoli, around which "shanty-towns" spring up, peopled by migrants from the country and from smaller towns. The desperate living conditions of the "shanty-towns", similar (and often inferior) to those which the migrants knew in their former surroundings, demand constructive measures bound up in community development programs, fostered by public, private, religious and social-service organizations and associations, both domestic and foreign.

"Crime and Juvenile Delinquency" are areas which have received considerable attention in most of the Latin American nations. Professor Manuel Zamorano Hernández of the Institute of Sociology, University of Chile, an expert on the topic, in 1967 published a work entitled Çrimen y literatura, which analyzes Chilean novels, written between 1875 and 1962, setting forth bibliographic data, plots, critiques, and criminological material. The work is unique and of great value to students of sociology as well as Chilean literature.

"Demography" here refers not so much to urban growth (a topic covered under "Urbanization" and "Rural-Urban Migration"), but mainly to the makeup of urban populations in Latin America. Although a few studies on social classes are included here, those concerned with that subject are directed to the field of "Social Change." "Demography" concerns itself with the "races of mankind" in Latin American cities, as well as problems impinging upon their cultural backgrounds. Those concerned with population statistics are referred to the sources given under "Urban Research."

Developments in the study and teaching of Demography bid fair to equal the growth rate of the world's population. In 1967 a Department of Demography was established by the University of California at Berkeley in its College of Letters and Science. It is the only such academic department in the United States, and is the result of an interdepartmental graduate program, the Group in Demography, which also offered the first doctoral curriculum of its type in the United States; it awards both the M.A. and Ph.D. degrees. Under an agreement between the General Secretariat of the Organization of American States and the French Government, a three-month special training program on population and development in Latin America was offered under auspices of the National Institute of Demographic Studies, Paris, France, from October, 1967 through January, 1968. Participants comprised Latin American government officials and professionals whose work is concerned with these matters.

"Education" is an area covering all levels from primary school through the university, as well as teacher-training and administration. Some works are general in nature, covering an entire nation; however, because of the propensity for education to be available in larger cities rather than in rural areas, the items *per se* have to do with education in cities.

With respect to "Housing," "in 1960 the United Nations Organization surveyed 29,905 homes, where 5.1 persons were housed *per unit*; it concluded that 48% of such dwellings were *undesirable*, from a social standpoint. To overcome this deficiency, urban centers should be built to serve as community settlements, to aid the social life of the neighborhoods in cities. But urban growth has been largely unplanned; homes, schools, buses are over crowded now..." (from *Review of the economic situation of Mexico*

[XLIII: 500] July, 1967, p. 6). It should be noted, therefore, that the need for replacement housing is a problem, in addition to slum dwellings in shanty-towns which surround Latin American cities.

"Public Health" includes the following sub-areas: Air Pollution, Hospital and Medical Care, Mental Hygiene, Nutrition, Sanitary Engineering, and Water Supply. Air pollution problems grow apace as industrialization of metropoli increases. Cities such as São Paulo, Brazil, Santiago, Chile, Mexico City, and San José, Costa Rica, have experienced smog disturbances. The pollution in San José, Costa Rica, occurred as a result of the activation of the Irazú Volcano nearby (during 1964) rather than from industrial causes.

Many items are included on the history of hospitals and insane asylums, under Hospital and Medical Care, and Mental Hygiene, respectively, in addition to works on each of these fields *per se*. There is an abundance of nutrition studies for various Latin American cities, including many on children. The need exists for fuller in-depth research reports on Sanitary Engineering and Water Supply; the latter topic here includes studies concerning water pollution.

According to the November 20, 1967 issue of the Alliance for Progress *Weekly Newsletter*, 82% of the total urban population in Latin America has the advantages of running water either in the home, or has it available nearby. This figure surpasses the 70% one written into the Alliance for Progress Charter at Punta del Este in 1961, which was at that time expected to be reached by the year 1971. Furthermore, Brazil, during 1967, announced that 36,000,000 of its citizens (mainly urban residents) enjoy the benefits of pure water and sewage disposal, adding that it has set up a National Council for Sanitation.

Social service and social work play an important role in bibliographic coverage of the field of "Public Welfare." Those concerned with this topic are advised to seek out allied items under "Social Security," and under "Public Health," as well as "Community Development." Entries in the specialty of industrial social service are also included.

Within the field of "Social Change" may be found entries on social mobility, and on social classes, as well as studies of changes in the social structure occasioned by industrialization and other facets of urbanization. One such study, published in 1968 by the Latin American Center at

UCLA, focus on migration of Venezuelan Indians to the city of Maracaibo, and is entitled Guajiro Personality and Social Change. The author is Dr. Lawrence J. Watson, Assistant Professor of Anthropology at San Diego State College.

The concept of "Social Security" in Latin America differs markedly from that of the average U.S. citizen. Complete "medicare" service, covering every aspect of physical and mental health, is usually the rule in Latin America; vocational training and recreational activities are also provided, these being in addition to the unemployment compensation, accident-insurance payments, and old-age pensions typically associated with "social security" in the United States of America.

Within the vast literature of social security, a segment of which is presented herewith, there is a considerable bibliographic coverage of legal aspects. Social security in Latin America has received the attention of the U.S. Government's Social Security Administration as well as that of Ibero-American Social Security Organization, in Madrid.

"Urbanization" has pervaded the very vitals of Latin American cities. According to the U.N. Economic Commission for Latin America, during the decade 1950-60 fourteen million persons migrated to cities. During this period, urban growth was 56% while rural growth amounted to only 17%. One of every three Argentine citizens resides in Buenos Aires, just as one of every three Chileans lives in Santiago; one out of every two Uruguayans makes his home in Montevideo. In addition, it should be noted that 75% of the citizens of Argentina and Uruguay reside in cities, while 67% of Chileans and Venezuelans do likewise. In Brazil, Colombia and Mexico, the proportion is 1:1. Only Central American nations thus far have not concentrated their populations into cities to the extent that other Latin American nations have. (Note: figures are recorded in Review of the economic situation of Mexico [XLIII:500] July, 1967, p. 5).

Within "Urbanization Research" are to be found statistical materials and sources, as well as research techniques and methodology studies from a wide variety of approaches. This is a field in which a goodly supply of studies should be forthcoming as more attention is directed to Latin America. One source should be the Center for Economic and Demographic Studies of the Colegio de México, where research on the nature of the urbanization process in Mexico is being conducted.

As a topic for research in U. S. universities, Latin American urbanization is just now coming of age. As of Autumn 1967, Dr. David Denslow, Jr. of the Economics Department, Yale University, was working on the economic causes of Latin American urbanization in the nineteenth century, while Miss Rebecca Baird (of Bolívar House, Stanford University) was researching the topic, "Urban Interest Group Responses to the Negro in Rio de Janeiro, 1888-1908." It is expected that in future years all phases of the urbanization process in Latin America will be represented.

The compiler expresses the wish that the preceding "directional signals" of this vehicle which traverses the cities of Latin America will point the way as efficiently as those of the most expensive 1971 models.

M. H. S.

Introducción a la Tabla Del Contenido

Latin American Urbanization: a Guide to the Literature, Organizations and Personnel contiene en su sección bibliográfica material sobre casi cada asunto relacionado con las ciudades latino-americanas. Estos representan la escala entera de tópicos relacionados con la urbanización, desde historia, religión y cultura urbanas hasta materiales sobre la contaminación del aire y la recolección de basura. Turistas futuros pueden utilizar la sección de "Description and Travel" para conseguir libros y artículos de revista en cuanto a viajes a las ciudades latino-americanas de importancia primaria, secundaria y tercera. Sigue más adelante una descripción de asuntos y sus correspondientes divisiones incluidas dentro de las varias secciones de la bibliografía.

"The City in Latin America Literature" es una área que empieza con "Literatura, General," un término general abarcando correspondencia y memorias, reseñas y descripciones generales de la vida en las ciudades latino-americanas en varios períodos de sus existencias. (Estas personas interesadas por el asunto deberían verificar las fichas bajo Historia Urbana). En orden consecutivo siguen subdivisiones para Drama, Novela, Poesía y Cuento. Las combinaciones de éstas también se hallan bajo "Literatura general."

"Description and Travel," una sección que abarca libros y artículos de revistas sobre viajes a las ciudades latino-americanas, fué el resultado de una idea tardía, lo que termina una bibliografía sobre casi todo aspecto de las vidas y descripción de las ciudades de Hispano América. Se incluyen fichas bibliográficas sobre ciudades tales como: Payssandú (Uruguay), Oruro (Bolivia), San Pedro Sula (Honduras), Barquisimeto (Venezuela), Bahía (Brasil), Camaguey (Cuba), Medellín (Colombia) y una multitud de ciudades latino-americanas adicionales no de suma importancia.

"Planning" se considera aquí incluir el diseño arquitectónico de calles y vías, la localización de edificios y la planeación del perfil físico de la ciudad, teniendo en cuenta las "áreas verdes".

"Recreation," campo principiante en la comunidad de disciplinas eruditas, cubre en esta bibliografía parques y otras facilidades recreativas, el uso recreativo de "lugares abiertos," y actividades deportivas. Debería notarse que aunque el beisbol es el deporte favorito en muchos países latino-americanos, la popularidad del soccer aumenta rapidamente, hasta que actualmente atrae muchos aficionados aún en los Estados Unidos de Norte América. A pesar del carácter reciente de la Recreación en Latino América, el lector se dirige a la ficha bibliográfica # 975 para un estudio del uso de la recreación en Caracas, Venezuela.

"Religión," concierne no solamente historias de iglesias, sino también estudios sobre cambios sociales manifestados actualmente, con respecto a la religión. Se incluyen también fichas sobre las religiones protestante, afro-americanas y judía, además de ésas sobre catolicismo.

En el campo de "Urban History" hay historias no solamente en cuanto a la fundación y desarrollo de ciudades latino-americanas, sino también sobre costumbres de sus habitantes y viñetas en la vida durante varios períodos.

"The Urban Matrix for Literature and the Arts" es una área extensa que da importancia a estos rasgos intelectuales de una metrópolis los cuales fomentan el crecimiento y desarrollo de la vida intelectual: Instituciones culturales (bibliotecas y museos, etc.), pintura, escultura, música, teatro, baile y letras. Para una discusión a fondo de las situaciones de The Writer (por el Dr. Fred P. Ellison) y The Artist (por el Dr. Gilbert Chase), ver páginas 79 y 101, respectivamente en Continuity and Change in Latin America, editado por el profesor John J. Johnson (Stanford, Stanford University Press, 1967, 282p).

"Urban Speech" cubre todo aspecto de la lingüística relacionado a las principales ciudades de Hispano-América. En adición a los estudios eruditos e informes de investigaciones, se incluyen diccionarios de palabras, frases y refranes como se usan en las ciudades de cada país. Hay una sección amplia para el francés criollo de Haití, y se pone mucha atención al Atlas Lingüístico para Colombia, recopilado por expertos del Instituto Caro y Cuervo de Bogotá.

"Cost and Standard of Living" se representa por una abundancia de artículos de revista. Rasgo muy valioso de estos artículos es la época extensa: hay algunos del año 1929 hasta la primavera de 1967. Las secciones llamadas "General" en ambas divisiones de libros y artículos de revista contienen índices del costo de la vida en varios países del mundo, herramienta bastante útil para fines de comparación internacional.

"Industrialization" ha crecido mucho en diversas ciudades latino-americanas. En varias secciones de Sao Paulo, Brasil, hay demasiada industria; resultan la absorción de "áreas verdes" y fricción entre industriales y residentes. Bajo "Industrialization" se hallan muchas fichas bibliográficas del campo de desarrollo económico.

"Poverty" abarca no solamente desempleo, sino también la vida en los tugurios de las grandes ciudades latino-americanas; los problemas sociales que resultan de la pobreza se clasifican bajo categorías correspondientes y afines.

"Transportation" cubre ferrocarriles, automóviles, autobuses y camiones. He aquí otro campo que requiere más investigaciones e informes. Hay gran escasez de estudios sobre transporte por automóviles, autobuses y camiones. Hasta que sepa el autor, existe en inglés un solo estudio, publicado por parte del Departamento de Comercio de los Estados Unidos, que cubre toda Latino-América. Uno de los pocos especialistas estadounidenses sobre el campo del transporte de Latino-América es el Dr. David Snyder de la Universidad de Yale, quién realizó estudios sobre los problemas de transporte de Montevideo, Uruguay, entre otras metrópolis.

Con respecto a los problemas de "Trabajos Urbanos" ver The Urban Worker, (por el Profesor Frank Bonilla del Instituto Tecnológico de Massachusetts, ex-corresponsal en Latino-América para American Universities Field Staff), en la obra del Dr. John J. Johnson titulada Continuity and Change in Latin America (Stanford, Stanford University Press, 1967, pp. 186-205). Los sindicatos laborales también se incluyen en esta bibliografía. Ver "Poverty" para el asunto de desempleo.

Dentro de "Municipal Finance" hay fichas bibliográficas sobre los aspectos legales en cuanto a los fondos para actividades y servicios municipales. También se incluyen materiales sobre las relaciones entre municipalidades, entidades federales y estaduales.

"Municipal Government and Legal Matters" abarca las bases constitucionales y legales fundamentales a la organización y administración de municipalidades. Es conveniente consultar materiales bajo "Urban History, " sobre todo con respecto a la administración colonial española antes de la Independencia.

Dentro de "Public Utilities" (servicios de teléfonos, electricidad y gas, organizados por la municipalidad o particularmente), hay fichas sobre los aspectos legales. Se notifica a los interesados ver las secciones sobre Transporte, Ingeniería Sanitaria y Abastecimiento de Agua (las últimas 2 secciones bajo "Public Health").

El campo de "Communications" cubre las subdivisiones de periódicos, publicación, radio y televisión y la industria de cine. Del ramo de las comunicaciones surgió un cuerpo considerable de publicaciones, por mayor parte el resultado de investigaciones desempeñadas por parte del Programa Interamericano de Información Popular, con sede en San José de Costa Rica, y sucursal en Lima, Perú, bajo auspicios de los Rockefeller. Esta organización ha sido estudiando la transmisión de información entre agricultores; recientemente pone alguna atención a los problemas de poblaciones urbanas.

El problema de establecer contacto entre residentes urbanos de tugurios, con el propósito de despertar un sentido de identificación y de comunidad, tal como se ha hecho en regiones rurales como parte del desarrollo de pueblos, es una de las dificultades a la cual puede ofrecer el campo de comunicaciones servicio valioso y necesitado.

"Community Development, " una área de actividad destinada tradicionalmente a las zonas rurales, actualmente se aplica a las metrópolis latino-americanas, alrededor de las cuales surgen barrios bajos poblados por migrantes del campo y de los pueblos. Las condiciones de vida desesperadas, similares (y muchas veces inferiores) a las que existen en el campo, exigen resoluciones constructivas relacionadas con programas de desarrollo de comunidades, y fomentados por organizaciones y asociaciones públicas, particulares, religiosas y de servicio social, nacionales y extranjeras.

"Crime and Juvenile Delinquency" han llamado mucha atención en la mayoría de las naciones latino-americanas. El profesor Manuel Zamorano Hernández del Instituto de Sociología de la Universidad de Chile, un especialista del ramo, en 1967 publicó una obra titulada Crimen y Literatura, la cual analiza las novelas chilenas escritas entre 1875 y 1962. Presenta datos bibliográficos, resúmenes, críticas, y mucho material de tipo criminológico. El libro es único en su género y de valor inestimable para estudiantes de sociología así como de letras chilenas.

"Demography" se refiere al crecimiento urbano (asunto tratado bajo "Urbanization" y "Rural-Urban Migration"), pero atribuye principalmente al estudio de las características de las poblaciones urbanas en Latino-América. Aunque se incluyen aquí pocas investigaciones sobre clases sociales, los interesados en este tópico se dirigen al campo de Cambio Social. "Demography" se concierne con "las razas de la humanidad" en las ciudades latino-americanas, así como con los problemas tropezando sobre sus medios culturales respectivos. Los interesados en estadísticas de población se dirigen a las fuentes dadas bajo "Investigaciones Urbanas."

El avance en el campo de Demografía iguala el crecimiento rápido de la población mundial. En 1967 fué establecido en la Universidad de California en Berkeley el primer Departamento de Demografía en los EE. UU. Es el único en las universidades de los EE. UU., y ofrece los títulos de Maestro en Artes, y Doctor de Filosofía, en Demografía. Desde octubre de 1967 y por un espacio de tres meses, se desarrolló en París, Francia un programa especial de capacitación sobre población y desarrollo en América Latina. Esta iniciativa se concretó mediante un acuerdo entre la Secretaría de la Organización de Estados Americanos y el Gobierno Francés. El programa estuvo a cargo del Instituto Nacional de Estudios Demográficos, organismo autónomo del Ministerio de Asuntos Sociales del Gobierno Francés. Participaron funcionarios gubernamentales y profesionales de varios países latinoamericanos, cuyas labores están relacionadas con los problemas de la población y el desarrollo en sus respectivos países.

"Education" es una área que cubre todo nivel de la escuela primaria hasta la universidad, así como formación de maestros y administración. Algunos libros son de tipo general y tratan una nación entera; sin embargo, debido a la mayor disponibilidad de escuelas en grandes ciudades y no en regiones rurales, las fichas bibliográficas obviamente tienen que ver con educación en las ciudades.

Con respecto a "Housing," "en 1960 la Organización de las Naciones Unidas, reconoció 29,905 casas en las cuales residían 5.1 personas por unidad; concluyó que 48% de tales viviendas fueron nocivas desde un punto de vista social. Para superar esta deficiencia se deberían construir centros urbanos para servir como establecimientos comunitarios, en forma de auxilio a la vida social en los barrios urbanos. Pero el crecimiento urbano no ha sido planeado, en general; viviendas, escuelas, autobuses están actualmente atestados..." (de Review of the Economic Situation of Mexico [XLIII:500] Julio, 1967, p. 6), Se debería notar obviamente, que hay necesidad para reemplazar viviendas antigüas, en adición al problema de las casuchas en los tugurios alrededor de las ciudades latino-americanas.

"Public Health" abarca las siguientes subdivisiones: Contaminación del Aire, Cuidados Médicos y Hospitalarios, Higiene Mental, Nutrición, Ingeniería Sanitaria, y Abastecimiento de Agua. La contaminación del aire se aumenta a medida que avanza la industria en las metrópolis. Las ciudades tales como: São Paulo, Brasil, Santiago de Chile, La Ciudad de México y San José de Costa Rica han experimentado disturbios del smog. La contaminación en San José de Costa Rica ocurrió como resultado de la erupción del cercano volcán Irazú (durante el año de 1964) y no de causas industriales.

Hay fichas bibliográficas sobre la historia de hospitales y manicomios bajo Cuidados Hospitales y Médicos, e Higiene Mental, respectivamente, en adición a escritos acerca de cado uno de estos campos per se. Hay una abundancia de estudios sobre nutrición en varias ciudades de Latino-América, incluso muchos en niños. Existe la necesidad para más informes completos de investigaciones a fondo sobre Ingeniería Sanitaria y Abastecimiento de Agua; en esta bibliografía hay estudios sobre la contaminación del agua bajo el rubro de Abastecimiento de Agua.

De acuerdo con el número 47 (volúmen V, de fecha 20 de noviembre de 1967), de Weekly Newsletter de la Alianza Para el Progreso, 82% de la población total de Latinoamérica goza de las ventajas de agua corriente en casa, o la tiene disponible muy de cerca. Esta cifra de 82% sobrepasa la de 70%, planificada (de acuerdo con la

Carta de la Alianza Para el Progreso) para realizarse en el año 1971. Es más: durante el año 1967, el Gobierno del Brasil anunció que 36.000.000 de sus ciudadanos (la mayoría residentes urbanos) están servidos por sistemas de agua potable y drenaje, y que se estableció un Consejo Nacional de Sanitación.

Servicio social y trabajo social juegan un papel importante en la bibliografía de "Public Welfare." Los interesados en este asunto se les avisa buscar fichas similares bajo Seguridad Social, Salud Pública y Desarrollo de la Comunidad. También se incluyen bajo "Public Welfare" estudios sobre servicio social industrial.

Dentro del campo de "Social Change" hay fichas bibliográficas sobre movilidad social, clases sociales así como sobre los cambios en la estructura social ocasionados por la industrialización y otros aspectos de la urbanización. Uno de estos estudios publicado en 1968 por el Centro Latino Americano de la Universidad de California en Los Angeles, se enfoca en la migración de indígenas venezolanos a la Ciudad de Maracaibo, y se intitula Guajiro personality and social change. El autor es el Dr. Lawrence J. Watson, Profesor Ayudante de Antropología en San Diego State College.

El concepto de "Social Security" en Latino-América y en los Estados Unidos de Norte América varía mucho. Servicio hospitalario y médico completo, abarcando cada aspecto de salud física y mental, es regularmente la guía en Latino-América; formación vocacional y actividades recreativas también se abastecen, éstes siendo adicionales al seguro contra cesantía, pagos de seguro contra accidente, y vejez pensionada, los últimos tres tipos de seguros comunmente asociados con seguridad social en Los Estados Unidos de Norte América.

Dentro de la literatura de la seguridad social una parte de la cual se presenta aquí, hay muchas fichas bibliográficas sobre los aspectos legales. La seguridad social en Latino-América ha recibido la atención de la Administración de Seguridad Social de los Estados Unidos así como la de la Organización Iberoamericana de Seguridad Social de Madrid.

"Urbanization" ha penetrado a fondo las ciudades latino-americanas de acuerdo con la Comisión Económica de las Naciones Unidas para la América Latina; durante la década 1950-1960 migraron a las ciudades 14 millones de personas. En este mismo período el crecimiento urbano fué 56%, mientras que el crecimiento rural sumó unicamente 17%. Uno de cada tres ciudadanos argentinos reside en Buenos Aires, lo mismo que uno de cada tres chilenos tiene su domicilio en Santiago; uno de cada dos uruguayos reside en Montevideo. Es más, debería notarse que 75% de los ciudadanos de la Argentina y de Uruguay habitan en las ciudades mientras que 67% de chilenos y venezolanos hacen lo mismo. En Brasil, Colombia y México, la proporción es 1:1. Unicamente las naciones centro-americanas hasta la fecha no han concentrado sus poblaciones en ciudades al mismo grado alcanzado por los demás países latino-americanos. (Nota: las cifras arriba-amencionadas se registran en Review of the Economic Situation of Mexico [XLIII:500] Julio, 1967, p. 5).

Dentro de "Urbanization Research" se hallan materiales y fuentes estadísticas así como técnicas y métodos de investigaciones de varios puntos de vista. Esto es un campo en la cual debería haber buen número de estudios, a medida que se ponga más atención a Latino-América. El Centro de Estudios Económicos y Demográficos del Colegio de México desempeña investigaciones sobre el proceso de la urbanización en México. De este Centro se espera recibir publicaciones de categoría en cuanto al asunto.

La urbanización como tópico para investigaciones en las universidades estadounidenses acaba de manifestarse. Durante el otoño de 1967, el Dr. David Denslow, Jr., del Departamento de Economía de la Universidad Yale trató las causas económicas de la urbanización latino-americana en el siglo XIX, mientras que la Señorita Rebecca Baird (de la Casa Bolívar, Universidad de Stanford) investigó el asunto de "Las Reacciones de un Grupo Urbano al Negro en Rio de Janeiro, 1888-1908." Se espera que se investigue todo aspecto del proceso de la urbanizacion en Latino-América en el futuro.

El autor expresa el deseo de que las "señales de sentido" anteriores de este vehículo, el cual viaja por las ciudades de Latino-América, señalarán el camino tan eficiente como las de los modelos de 1971 más caros.

M.H.S.

Table of Contents

Bibliography Section

Directory Section

Indices

Tabla Del Contenido

Seccion Bibliográfica

Sección Directoria

Indices

BIBLIOGRAPHY SECTION

Part I

AESTHETICS AND HUMANITIES

THE CITY IN LATIN AMERICAN LITERATURE

(Note: Main classifications used are literature: general, drama, novel, poetry, and short story. Where only a nation, as opposed to a specific city is mentioned, it is understood that the larger cities of that nation represent the scene of the given work. "Literature, General" consists of general works, such as correspondence, reminiscences, descriptive works, etc., and works which combine drama, novels, poetry or short stories).

Literature, General

Books

Argentina

1 Gobello, José
Historias con ladrones. Buenos Aires, Eds. Bastion, 1957, 117p. (Buenos Aires)

2 González Arrili, Bernardo
Calle Corrientes entre Esmeralda y Suipacha. Buenos Aires, Kraft, 1952, 199p. (Buenos Aires)

3 Martínez Cuitiño, Vicente
El Café de Los Inmortales. Buenos Aires, Kraft, 1950, 393p. (Buenos Aires)

4 Soboleosky, Marcos
Después de la nada. Buenos Aires, Eds. La Reja, 1958, 171p. (Buenos Aires)

Bolivia

5 Noel, Eugenio
Tríptico de Potosí, una breve antología de escritos de Eugenio Noel y Ernesto Giménez Caballero, y poema de Alberto Saávedra Nogales. Potosí, Ed. "Potosí," 1956, 68p. (Potosí)

Brazil

6 Amado, Gilberto
Minha formação no Recife. Rio de Janeiro, Olympio, 1955, 373p. (Recife)

7 Americano, Jorge
São Paulo atual, 1935-1962. São Paulo, Eds. Melhoramentos, 1963, 373p. (São Paulo)

8 Bandeira, Manuel, & Carlos Drummond de Andrade, eds.
Rio de Janeiro em prosa e verso. Rio de Janeiro, Olympio, 1965, 581p. (Rio de Janeiro)

9 Braga, Roberto
Gente do Rio. Rio de Janeiro, Pongetti, 1956, 204p. (Rio de Janeiro)

10 Bruno, Ernani Silva, & Diaulas Riedel, eds.
Histórias e paisagens do Brasil. 10v. São Paulo, Cultrix, 1958-1960.

11 Cavalcanti, Emilio di
Reminiscencias líricas de um perfeito carioca. Rio de Janeiro, Ed. Civilização Brasileira, 1964, 97p. (Rio de Janeiro)

12 Freyre, Gilberto
Assombrações do Recife velho. Rio de Janeiro, Eds. Condé, 1955, 124p. (Recife)

13 Ivo, Ledo
A cidade e os dias: crônicas e históricas. Rio de Janeiro, Eds. O Cruzeiro, 1957, 234p. (Rio de Janeiro)

14 Latif, Miran Monteiro de Barrios
A comédia carioca, na ribalta da rua. Rio de Janeiro, Eds. do Autor, 1962, 188p. (Rio de Janeiro)

15 Lemoine, Carmen Nícias de
Tradições da cidade do Rio de Janeiro do século 16 ao 19. Rio de Janeiro, Irmãos Pongetti Eds., 1965, 255p. (Rio de Janeiro)

16 Mattos, Waldemar
A Bahia de Castro Alves. 2d ed. São Paulo, Instituto Progresso Ed., 1948, 174p.

17 Molles, Osvaldo
Piquenique classe C. Crônicas e flagrantes de São Paulo. São Paulo, Boa Leitura Ed., 1962, 346p. (São Paulo)

18 Pacheco, Jacy
Noël Rosa e sua época. Rio de Janeiro, Penna, 1955, 186p. (Rio de Janeiro)

19 Pinheiro, Péricles da Silva
Manifestações literárias em São Paulo na época colonial. São Paulo, Comissão de Literatura, Conselho Estadual de Cultura, 1961, 139p. (São Paulo)

20 Rebêlo, Marques (pseud.)
O trapicheiro. São Paulo, Martins, 1959, 471p. (Rio de Janeiro)

21 Requião, Hermano
Itapagipe: minha infância na Bahia. Rio de Janeiro, Olympio, 1949? 128p.

22 Thiollier, René
Episódios de minha vida. São Paulo, Ed. Anhembi, 1956, 210p. (São Paulo)

23 Vianna, Antônio
Casos e coisas da Bahia. Bahia, Secretaria da Educação e Saúde, 1950, 165p.

Chile

24 Edwards Bello, Joaquín
Valparaíso; fantasmas. Santiago, Nascimento, 1955, 413p. (Valparaíso)

25 Zamorano Hernandez, Manuel
Crimen y literatura: ensayo de una antología criminológico-literaria de Chile. Santiago, Facultad de Filosofía y Educación, Universidad de Chile, 1967, 468p.

Colombia

26 Acosta de Samper, Soledad
Los piratas en Cartagena. Bogotá, Ministerio de Educación, 1946, 230p. (Cartagena)

27 García Valencia, Abel
Medellín en el mundo, en la poesía y en la historia. Medellín, Pubs. de la Revista "Universidad de Antioquia," 19- , 14p. (Medellín)

El Salvador

28 Mechin, T.P. (pseud.)
La muerte de la tórtola, o Malandanzas de un corresponsal. 2d ed. San Salvador, Ministerio de Cultura, 1958, 249p. (San Salvador)

Haiti

29 Lescouflair, Georges
Mon vieux carnet. Montreal, Librairie Beauchemin, 1958, 178p. (Port-au-Prince)

30 Trouillot, Hénock
Les origines sociales de la littérature haïtienne. Port-au-Prince, Impr. Théodore, 1962, 376p.

Mexico

31 Dromundo, Baltasar
Mi barrio de San Miguel. México, Robredo, 1951, 136p. (Mexico City)

Panama

32 Beleño C., Joaquín
Luna verde; diario dialogado. Panamá, Ed. Panamá América, 1951, 249p.

Peru

33 Bermejo, Vladimiro, comp.
Historiadores y prosistas. Arequipa, 1958, 165p. (Arequipa)

Venezuela

34 Insausti, Rafael A.
El valle, la ciudad y el monte. Caracas, Sursam, 1959, unpaged. (Caracas)

35 Jiménez Arráiz, Francisco
La ciudad de los crepúsculos. Edición conmemorativa del IV centenario de la ciudad de Barquisimeto. Caracas, Avila Gráfica, 1952, 133p. (Barquisimeto)

36 Picón Salas, Mariano
Las nieves de antaño; pequena añoranza de Mérida. Maracaibo, Eds. de la Universidad de Zulia, 1958, 140p. (Mérida)

Periodical Articles

Argentina

37 Castellanos, C. de
"Aproximación a la Obra de Ernesto Sábato." Madrid, Cuadernos hispanoamericanos LXI, 1965, p. 486-503.

38 García, G.
"Argentina: Capítulo para una Biografía Novelada." Santa Fé, Universidad 54, October-December 1962, p. 87-108.

39 Gibbs, Beverly J.
"El Túnel: Portrayal of Isolation." Hispania XLVIII, 1965, p. 429-436.

Brazil

40 Batchelor, C.M.
"Arthur Azevedo e a 'Comédia Carioca!'" México, Revista ibero-americana (22:43), January-June 1957, p. 61-69. (Rio de Janeiro)

41 Simões, R.
"A Metrópole Paulistana e seus Ficcionistas." São Paulo, Revista brasiliense 47, May-June 1963, p. 107-114. (São Paulo)

Mexico

42 Mead, Robert G.
"Aspects of Mexican Literature Today." Books abroad 34, 1960, p. 5-8.

Drama

Books

Latin America

43 Jones, Willis K.
Behind Spanish American footlights. Austin, University of Texas Press, 1966, 609p.

44 Carballido, Emilio
Un pequeño día de ira. Havana, Casa de las Américas, 1962, 69p.

Argentina

45 Carlo, Omar del
Proserpina y el extranjero. El jardín de ceniza. Buenos Aires, Ed. Nova, 1956, 157p.

46 Dragun, Osvaldo
Heroica de Buenos Aires. Havana, Casa de las Americas, 1966, 185p.

47 Gorostiza, Carlos
El puente. Buenos Aires, Eds. de Losange, 1954, 124p.

48 Karnis, M.V.
Social issues in Argentine drama since 1900. Ann Arbor, University Microfilms, 1954, 259p.

49 Marial, José
El teatro independiente. Buenos Aires, Alpe, 1955, 260p. (Buenos Aires)

50 Meyrialle, Horacio S.
Todo el año es navidad. Buenos Aires, Eds. Mariel, 1960, 142p. (Buenos Aires)

51 Ordaz, Luis, ed.
El sainete porteño. (In his Breve historia del teatro argentino. Buenos Aires, Ed. Universitaria, 1964, 198p.). (Buenos Aires)

52 Solly, pseud.
El crack. Buenos Aires, Nueva América, 1960, 61p. (Buenos Aires)

53 Villegas Vidal, Juan C.
El llamado; obra en 45 escenas. La Plata, Municipalidad de La Plata, 1962, 169p.

Brazil

54 Callado, Antônio
A cidade assassinada. Rio de Janeiro, Olympio, 1954, 109p. (São Paulo)

55 Souza, Affonso Ruy de
História do teatro na Bahia: séculos XVI-XX. Salvador, Universidade da Bahia, 1959, 129p.

Colombia

56 Mejía de Gaviria, Regina
Calle Tal, Número Tal. Medellín, Eds. La Tertulia, 1963, 147p.

Haiti

57 Fouchard, Jean
Le théâtre à St.-Domingue. Port-au-Prince, Impr. de l'Etat, 1955, 353p.

Mexico

58 Basurto, Luis G.
Los reyes del mundo. México, Col. Teatro Mexicano, 1959, 83p. (Mexico City)

59 Cantón, Wilberto L.
Malditos; obra en dos actos. México, Colección Teatro Mexicano, 1959, 102p. (Mexico City)

60 Carballido, Emilio
D.F. (14 obras en un acto). Xalapa, Universidad Veracruzana, 1962, 197p.

61 Magaña, Sergio
Los signos del zodíaco. México, Colección Teatro Mexicano, 1953, 171p.

62 Montoya, María T.
El teatro en mi vida. México, Eds. Botas, 1956, 365p.

Uruguay

63 Deugenio, Rubén
Quiniela. El ascenso. Montevideo, Ed. El Siglo Ilustrado, 1962, 96p. (Montevideo)

Periodical Articles

Latin America

64 Berruti, A.E.
"Historietas de Don Alejandro. Adaptación de Rubén Pesce." Buenos Aires, Talia (6:25), Supplement, 1964, p. 1-26.

Colombia

65 Jaramillo Arango, R.
"Cita a las Cuatro. Feria de Vanidades en Tres Actos." Bogotá, Revista de las Indias (33:105), September-October 1950, supplement No. 10, 31p. (Bogotá)

Venezuela

66 Rojas, A.
"Orígenes del Teatro en Caracas." Caracas, Crónica Caracas, año 4 (4:19), August-December 1954, p. 575-587. (Caracas)

Novel

Books

Latin America

67 Dessein, Eduardo M.
Los comienzos. Buenos Aires, Eds. Botella al Mar, 1954, 119p.

Argentina

68 Barletta, Leónidas
Primer cielo de Buenos Aires. Buenos Aires, Ed. Goyante, 1960, 209p. (Buenos Aires)

69 Canto, Estela
El hombre del crepúsculo. Buenos Aires, Ed. Sudamericana, 1953, 141p.

70 Canto, Estela
La noche y el barro. Buenos Aires, Ed. Platina, 1961, 164p.

71 Capdevila, Arturo
Crónicas dolientes de Córdoba. Buenos Aires, Emecé, 1963, 240p. (Córdoba)

72 Cerretani, Arturo
La violencia. Buenos Aires, Eds. Doble P, 1956, 220p. (Buenos Aires)

73 Cortázar, Julio
Rayuela. Buenos Aires, Ed. Sudamericana, 1963, 635p. (Buenos Aires)

74 Denevi, Marco
Rosaura a las diez. Buenos Aires, Kraft, 1955, 258p.

75 Dickman, Max
Los habitantes de la noche. Buenos Aires, Santiago Rueda, 1952, 360p. (Buenos Aires)

76 Fernando, Valentín
Desde esta carne. Buenos Aires, Ed. Sudamericana, 1952, 283p. (Buenos Aires)

77 Gambaro, Griselda
Madrigal en ciudad. Buenos Aires, Ed. Goyanarte, 1963, 106p. (Buenos Aires)

78 Gómez Bas, Joaquín
Barrio gris. Buenos Aires, Emecé Eds., 1952, 209p. (Buenos Aires)

79 Goyanarte, Juan
Fin de semana. Buenos Aires, Ed. Goyanarte, 1955, 239p. (Buenos Aires)

80 Goyanarte, Juan
Tres mujeres. Buenos Aires, Ed. Goyanarte, 1956, 140p. (Buenos Aires)

81 Guido, Beatriz
La caída. Buenos Aires, Ed. Losada, 1956, 140p. (Buenos Aires)

82 Guido, Beatriz
Fin de fiesta. Buenos Aires, Ed. Losada, 1958, 260p.

83 Hosne, Roberto
Gente sencilla; novela. Buenos Aires, Ed. Stilcograf, 1957, 109p.

84 Lozzia, Luis M.
Domingo sin fútbol. Buenos Aires, Ed. Sudamericana, 1956, 202p. (Buenos Aires)

85 Mallea, Eduardo
Los enemigos del alma. Buenos Aires, Ed. Sudamericana, 1950, 363p. (Bahia Blanca)

86 Manauta, Juan J.
Los aventados. Buenos Aires, Ed. Hemisferio, 1952, 158p. (Buenos Aires)

87 Martel, Julián, pseud.
La bolsa. Buenos Aires, Ed. Estrada, 1946, 298p. (Buenos Aires)

88 Moog, Juan J.
Plaza de Mayo, 16 de junio, 1955; cita del destino. Buenos Aires, Ed. Periplo, 1955? 112p. (Buenos Aires)

89 Mujica Láinez, Manuel
Misteriosa Buenos Aires. Buenos Aires, Ed. Sudamericana, 1951, 317p. (Buenos Aires)

90 Novión de los Ríos
Los culpables. Buenos Aires, Schapire, 1955, 334p. (Buenos Aires)

91 Onetti, Juan C.
El astillero: novela. Buenos Aires, Cía. General Fabril Ed., 1961, 218p.

92 Pelayo, Félix M.
El financista. Buenos Aires, Guiferma, 1947, 425p. (Buenos Aires)

93 Peyrou, Manuel
Acto y ceniza. Buenos Aires, Emecé Eds., 1963, 384p. (Buenos Aires)

94 Plá, Roger
Los Robinsones. Rosario, Ed. Rosario, 1946, 464p. (Buenos Aires)

95 Sábato, Ernesto R.
El túnel. 4th ed. Buenos Aires, Emecé, 1952, 158p. (Buenos Aires)

96 Silberstein, Enrique
El asalto. Buenos Aires, La Reja, 1956, 145p. (Buenos Aires)

97 Soboleosky, Marcos
Las aguas de Mara. Buenos Aires, Ed. Goyanarte, 1960, 167p. (Buenos Aires)

98 Sol, Alvaro
Los trece en la feria. Buenos Aires, Instituto Amigos del Libro Argentino, 1964, 189p. (Buenos Aires)

99 Speroni, Miguel A.
La puerta grande: aventura y desventura de Buenos Aires. Buenos Aires, Claridad, 1947, 388p. (Buenos Aires)

100 Vera, Humberto B.
Aroma de tilos; estudiantina. Buenos Aires, Signo, 1953, 163p. (La Plata)

Brazil

101 Albuquerque, Matheus de
A juventude de Anselmo Tôrres. 3d ed. Rio de Janeiro, Organização Simões, 1956, 241p. (Recife)

102 Alencar, José Martiniano de
Romance urbano. (In his Obra completa. Rio de Janeiro, Ed. J. Aguilar, 1959, 201p.) (Rio de Janeiro)

103 Araújo, Benito
Futuros congelados. Recife, Ed. Capibaribe, 1955, 125p. (Recife)

104 Barreto, Affonso Henríques de Lima
Clara dos Anjos. Rio de Janeiro, Mérito, 1948, 303p. (Rio de Janeiro)

105 Barreto, Affonso Henríques de Lima
Vida urbana. (In His Obras. v. 11. São Paulo, Ed. Brasiliense, 1956, 306p.)

106 Benedetti, Lúcia
Nocturno sem leito. Rio de Janeiro, Olympio, 1948, 263p. (Rio de Janeiro)

107 Carneiro, Jorge
A visão do quatro séculos. São Paulo, Martins, 1954, 330p. (São Paulo)

108 Carrazedo, Renato O.
Os despojados. Rio de Janeiro, Irmãos Pongetti Eds., 1964, 122p. (Rio de Janeiro)

109 Condé, José
Um ramo para Luísa. Rio de Janeiro, Civilização Brasileira, 1959, 145p.

110 Coutinho, Galeão
Confidências de Dona Marcolina. São Paulo, Saraiva, 1950, 229p. (São Paulo)

111 Cox, Dilermando Duarte
Os párias da cidade Maravilhosa. Rio de Janeiro, Olympio, 1950, 232p. (Rio de Janeiro)

112 Donato, Mário
Domingo com Christina. São Paulo, Livraria Martins, 1963, 223p. (São Paulo)

113 Ferreira, Ondina
Vento de esperança. 2d ed. São Paulo, Boa Leitura Ed., 1962, 253p. (São Paulo)

114 Fontana, Maria E.
Biografia de uma rua. Rio de Janeiro, O Cruzeiro, 1954, 223p. (Curitiba)

115 Holanda, Gastão de
O burro de ouro. Recife, Ed. Igarassu, 1960, 303p. (Recife)

116 Issa, Otávio
Os inquietos. São Paulo, Cia. Ed. Nacional, 1957, 230p. (São Paulo)

117 Machado, Aníbal M.
João Ternura. Rio de Janeiro, Olympio, 1965, 230p.

118 Machado, Dionélio
Passos perdidos. São Paulo, Livraria Martins, 1946, 296p. (São Paulo)

119 Mársico, Gladstone Osório
Gatos à paisana. Pôrto Alegre, Livraria Salina, 1962, 174p.

120 Martins, Ibiapaba
Sangue na pedra. São Paulo, Martins, 1955, 296p. (São Paulo)

121 Miranda, Maio
Memórias de um casaco verde. São Paulo, Ed. Art, 1963, 234p. (São Paulo)

122 Mulholland, Lúcia Izaguirre
A morte de Osvaldo. Rio de Janeiro, Konfino, 1959, 235p. (Rio de Janeiro)

123 Nascimento, Esdras do
Solidão em família. Rio de Janeiro, Ed. Civilização Brasileira, 1963, 233p. (Rio de Janeiro)

124 Paezzo, Sylvan
Diário de um transviado. Rio de Janeiro, Ed. Civilização Brasileira, 1963, 163p. (Rio de Janeiro)

125 Pardini, Armando
Maria das bonecas. Bêlo Horizonte, Ed. Itatiaia, 1962, 239p. (São Paulo)

126 Pereira, Lúcia M.
Cabra-cega. Rio de Janeiro, Olympio, 1954, 202p. (Rio de Janeiro)

127 Pimentel, Matos
Lodo contro o céu. Rio de Janeiro, Pongetti, 1947, 370p. (Rio de Janeiro)

128 Pires, J. Herculano
Um deus vigia o planalto. São Paulo, Livraria Francisco Alves, 1964, 117p. (São Paulo)

129 Pontes, Eloy
Favela. Rio de Janeiro, Olympio, 1946, 419p. (Rio de Janeiro)

130 Queiroz, Amadeu de
A rajada. São Paulo, Ed. Saraiva, 1954, 167p. (São Paulo)

131 Raimundo, Angelo
Brasilia, Paralelo 15'. Rio de Janeiro, Livraria São José, 1960, 229p. (Brasilia)

132 Rocha, Luiz Marcondes
Café e polenta: romance histórico. São Paulo, Livraria Martins, 1964, 246p. (São Paulo)

133 Rodrigues, Francisco Pereira
Memórias dum vereador. Pôrto Alegre, Livraria Sulina, 1955, 182p.

134 Rodrigues, Paulo
Se a cidade contasse . . . Rio de Janeiro, Livraria São José, 1964, 115p. (Rio de Janeiro)

135 Sabino, Fernando Tavares
O encontro marcado. Rio de Janeiro, Civilização Brasileira, 1956, 281p. Bêlo Horizonte & Rio de Janeiro)

136 Santos, Geraldo
Loucos, poetas, amantes. Rio de Janeiro, Livraria São José, 1957, 73p. (São Paulo)

137 Verissimo, Erico
Noite. Pôrto Alegre, Ed. Glôbo, 1954, 210p. (Rio de Janeiro)

138 Vieira, José
Um reformador na cidade do vício. Rio de Janeiro, Olympio, 1948, 218p. (Rio de Janeiro)

Chile

139 Alegría, Fernando
Mañana los guerreros. Santiago, Ed. Zig-Zag, 1964, 273p. (Santiago)

140 Atías, Guillermo
El tiempo banal. Santiago, Nascimento, 1955, 309p.

141 Blest Gana, Alberto
La aritmética del amor. Santiago, Ed. Zig-Zag, 1950, 508p. (Santiago)

142 Cassigoli, Armando
Angeles bajo la lluvia. Santiago, Eds. "Alfa," 1960, 157p.

143 Donoso, José
Coronación. 2d ed. Santiago, Zig-Zag, 1962, 240p.

144 Droguett, Carlos
100 gotas de sangre y 200 de sudor. Santiago, Zig-Zag, 1961, 198p.

145 Edwards, Jorge
Gente de la ciudad. Santiago, Ed. Universitaria, 1961, 124p. (Santiago)

146 Edwards Bello, Joaquín
La chica del crillón. 5th ed. Santiago, Ed. Ercilla, 1943, 236p. (Santiago)

147 Edwards Bello, Joaquín
En el viejo almendral. Santiago, Ed. Orbe, 1943, 635p.

148 Gertner, María E.
Islas en la ciudad. Santiago, Ed. del Nuevo Extremo, 1958, 190p. (Santiago)

149 González Vera, José S.
Vidas mínimas. Santiago, Ercilla, 1950, 111p. (Santiago & Valparaíso)

150 Guzmán, Nicómedes
La sangre y la esperanza. Santiago, Ed. Orbe, 1943, 412p. (Santiago)

151 Hidalgo, Ramón
El barón de Valparaíso. Santiago, Arancibia Hnos., 1961, 155p. (Valparaíso)

152 Laso, Jaime
El cepo. Santiago, Ed. Zig-Zag, 1958, 131p.

153 Palazuelos, Juan A.
Muy temprano para Santiago. Santiago, Zig-Zag, 1965, 239p. (Santiago)

154 Reyes, Salvador
Valparaíso, puerto de nostalgia. Santiago, Ed. Zig-Zag, 1955, 205p. (Valparaíso)

155 Rojas, Manuel
Punta de rieles. Santiago, Zig-Zag, 1960, 255p. (Santiago)

156 Teitelboim, Volodia
La semilla en la arena. Santiago, Empresa Ed. Austral, 1957, 564p.

157 Urzúa Alvarez, Waldo
Esas niñas Ugarte. Santiago, Ed. del Pacifico, 1954, 208p. (Santiago)

158 Vergara, José M.
Don Jorge y el dragón. Santiago, Ed. del Pacífico, 1962, 156p.

Colombia

159 Airó, Clemente
La ciudad y el viento. Bogotá, 1961, 349p. (Bogotá)

160 Beltrán, Germán
El diablo sube al telón. Bogotá, Espiral, 1955, 213p. (Bogotá)

161 Castrillón Arboleda, Diego
Sol en Tambalimbu. Bogotá, Kelly, 1950, 314p. (Bogotá)

162 Delgado Nieto, Carlos
El hombre puede salvarse. Bogotá, Espiral, 1951, 136p. (Bogotá)

163 Sanín Echeverri, Jaime
Una mujer de cuatro en conducta. 2d ed. Bogotá, Iqueima, 1950, 212p. (Medellín)

Costa Rica

164 Dobles, Fabián
Los leños vivientes. San José, 1962, 136p.

165 Gutiérrez, Joaquín
Puerto Limón. Santiago, Nascimento, 1950, 380p. (Puerto Limón)

Cuba

166 Juárez Fernández, Bel
En las lomas de El Purial. Havana, Eds. Revolución, 1962, 114p.

Dominican Republic

167 Sanz-Lejara, J.M.
Caonex. Buenos Aires, Americalee, 1950, 348p. (Ciudad Trujillo)

Ecuador

168 Icaza, Jorge
El chulla Romero y Flores. 2d ed. Quito, Ruminahui, 1959, 280p.

169 Icaza, Jorge
En las calles. 3d ed. Quito, Casa de la Cultura Ecuatoriana, 1959, 359p. (Quito)

170 Mata, Gonzalo H.
Sal. Cuenca, Casa de la Cultura Ecuatoriana, Núcleo del Azuay, 1963, 275p. (Cuenca)

171 Mujica, Elisa
Los dos tiempos. Bogotá, Iqueima, 1950, 244p. (Bogotá & Quito)

172 Vera, Pedro J.
Los animales puros. Buenos Aires, Ed. Futuro, 1947, 238p. (Guayaquil)

Haiti

173 Brierre, Jean F.
Les horizons sans ciel; province. Port-au-Prince, Henri Deschamps, 1951, 234p. (Port-au-Prince)

174 Cinéas, J.B.
Le choc en retour. Port-au-Prince, Eds. Deschamps, 1948, 292p. (Port-au-Prince)

175 Saint-Aude, Magloire
Parias. Port-au-Prince, Impr. de l'Etat, 1950, 100p. (Port-au-Prince)

Mexico

176 Aguirre, Manuel J.
Guadalaxara, la ciudad errante; novela histórica. México, 1951, 201p. (Guadalajara)

177 Azuela, Mariano
La mujer domada. México, Ed. del Colegio Nacional, 1946, 197p. (Mexico City)

178 Banda Farfán, Raquél
Cuesta abajo. México, Eds. de Andrea, 1958, 210p. (Mexico City)

179 Bernal, Rafael
Un muerto en la tumba; novela policíaca. México, Ed. Jus, 1946, 159p. (Oaxaca)

180 Bobes Ortega, Evelina
La ciudad y la música. México, Eds. Botas, 1951, 265p. (Mexico City)

181 Castro, Dolores
La ciudad y el viento. Xalapa, Universidad Veracruzana, 1962, 111p. (Mexico City)

182 Corona Rojas, Benigno
La barriada. México, Omega, 1948, 246p. (Mexico City)

183 Crabbe de Rubín, Madeleine
La ciudad de México en la novela mexicana del siglo XIX. México, 1951, 120p. (Mexico City)

184 Fuentes, Carlos
Los días enmascarados. México, Los Presentes, 1954, 97p.

185 Fuentes, Carlos
La región más transparente. México, Fondo de Cultura Económica, 1958, 460p.

186 Galindo, Sergio
La comparsa. México, Ed. Joaquín Mortiz, 1964, 142p. (Jalapa)

187 Leñero, Vicente
Los albañiles. Barcelona, Ed. Seix Barral, 1964, 250p.

188 Ochoa Campos, Humberto
El tigre emplumado: historia de tres generaciones. México, México-Lee Eds., 1962, 227p.

189 Sarquis, Francisco
Mezclilla. México, 1933, 240p. (Jalapa & Veracruz)

190 Spota, Luis
Casi el paraíso. México, Fondo de Cultura Económica, 1956, 453p. (México City)

191 Spota, Luis
La pequena edad. México, Fondo de Cultura Económica, 1964, 525p.

192 Velásquez, Rolando
Entre la selva de neón: novela de la ciudad. San Salvador, Ministerio de Cultura, Depto. Editorial, 1956, 265p. (Mexico City)

Panama

193 Beleno C., Joaquín
Luna verde: diario dialogado. Panamá, Ed. Panamá América, 1951, 249p. (Panama City)

194 Jurado, Ramón H.
San Cristóbal. 2d ed. Panamá, Depto. de Bellas Artes y Pubs., Ministerio de Educación, 1963, 180p.

Peru

195 Castro Arenas, Mario
El líder. Lima, Eds. Tawantinsuyu, 1960, 129p.

196 Congrains Martín, Enrique
Lima, hora cero. Lima? Círculo de Novelistas Peruanos, 1954, 167p. (Lima)

197 Congrains Martín, Enrique
No una, sino muchas muertes. Buenos Aires, Embajada Cultural Peruana, 1957, 201p.

198 Ribeyro, Julio R.
Los gallinazos sin plumas. Lima, Círculo de Novelistas Peruanos, 1955, 135p. (Lima)

199 Wagner de Reyna, Alberto
La fuga. Santiago, Ed. Zig-Zag, 1955, 252p. (Lima)

Uruguay

200 Benedetti, Mario
La tregua. Montevideo, Ed. Alfa, 1960, 183p.

201 Más de Ayala, Isidro
Montevideo y su cerro. Buenos Aires, Rueda, 1956, 220p. (Montevideo)

202 Méndez, Ariel
La ciudad contra los muros. Montevideo, Ed. Alfa, 1961, 153p. (Montevideo)

203 Méndez, Ariel
La encrucijada. Montevideo, Ed. Rosgal, 1950, 259p. (Montevideo)

204 Silva, Clara
El alma y los perros. Montevideo, Ed. Alfa, 1962, 182p.

205 Trobo, Claudio
Sin horizonte. Montevideo, Eds. de Marcha, 1963, 112p.

Venezuela

206 Corda, José
Doce horas por las calles de Caracas; cuadros novelados. Caracas, Ed. Avila Gráfica, 1948, 163 p. (Caracas)

207 Munoz Rueda, Enrique
Beatriz Palma. Caracas, Edime, 1956, 207p. (Caracas)

208 Rial, José A.
Venezuela, imán. Caracas, Eds. Edime, 1955, 507p. (Caracas)

209 Vallenilla Lanz, Laureano
Allá en Caracas. Caracas, Eds. Garrido, 1954, 367p. (Caracas)

Periodical Articles

Argentina

210 Lewald, H.E.
"Society and 'La Bolsa' in the Argentine Novel." Hispania XLIII, 1960, p. 198-200.

Colombia

211 Hernández de Mendoza, C.
"Humorismo Bogotáno en Germán Arciniegas."
Bogotá, Noticias culturales--Instituto Caro y Cuervo 76, May 1, 1967, p. 9-12.

Mexico

212 González, M. P.
"Luis Spota, Gran Novelista en Potenciá."
Revista hispánica moderna 26, 1960, p. 102-106.

Poetry

Books

Latin America

213 Solana, Rafael
Alas: viñetas de Roberto Montenegro. México, Estaciones, 1958, 139p.

Argentina

214 Biagioni, Amelia
La llave. Buenos Aires, Emecé Eds., 1957, 105p.

215 Borges, Jorge L.
Poemas, 1922-1943. Buenos Aires, Ed. Losada, 1943, 181p. (Buenos Aires)

216 Capdevila, Arturo
Otoño en el flor. Córdoba Assandri, 1952, 128p. (Córdoba)

217 Capitaine Funes, Carlos
Barrio nativo, General Paz de la ciudad de Córdoba. Prosa y verso. Santa Fé, Castellví, 1959, 77p. (Córdoba)

218 Casagrande, Adolfo
Ciudad del corazón. Buenos Aires, Ed. Huemul, 1961, 76p.

219 Castelpoggi, Atilio J.
Destino de Buenos Aires. Buenos Aires, Ed. Pleamar, 1961, 27p. (Buenos Aires)

220 Cousté, Alberto
The difficult new time. (In Pan American Union. General Secretariat. Young poetry of the Americas . . . v. 1. Washington, 1967? p. 3-5.)

221 Etchenique, Nira
Horario corrido y sábado inglés. Buenos Aires, Colección Ventana de Buenos Aires, 1957, 52p. (Buenos Aires)

222 González Tuñon, Raúl
A la sombra de los barrios amados. Buenos Aires, Ed. Lautaro, 1957, 152p. (Buenos Aires)

223 Gorbea, Guillermo J.
Reportaje a Buenos Aires. Buenos Aires, 1954, 61p. (Buenos Aires)

224 Guibert, Fernando
Poeta al pie de Buenos Aires. Buenos Aires, Santiago, Rueda, 1953, 206p. (Buenos Aires)

225 Huasi, Julio
Sonata popular en Buenos Aires. Buenos Aires, Cuadernos de la Cultura, 1959, 61p. (Buenos Aires)

226 Martelli, Juan C.
Ciudad de Buenos Aires. Buenos Aires, 1955, 12p. (Buenos Aires)

227 Negro, Héctor
Bandoneón de papel. Buenos Aires, Gleizer, 1957, 77p. (Buenos Aires)

228 Nicotra, Alejandro A.
Cuadernos de Córdoba. Santa Fé, Castellví, 1957, 88p. (Córdoba)

229 Pedrido, Federíco G.
Poesías de la sonrisa áspera. Buenos Aires, 1950, 108p. (Buenos Aires)

230 Pedro, Valentín de, ed.
Nuevo parnaso argentino. Barcelona, Maucci, 1927?, 304p.

231 Riccio, Gustavo
Un poeta en la ciudad. Gringo puraghei. Buenos Aires, Instituto Amigos del Libro Argentino, 1955, 140p. (Buenos Aires)

232 Rivera, Héctor M.
Edad de Buenos Aires. La Plata, Municipalidad de La Plata, 1959, 44p. (Buenos Aires)

233 Seminara, Roberto O.
Poema a la soledad de la calle, y otros poemas. La Plata, Municipalidad de La Plata, 1959, 29p. (Buenos Aires)

234 Varela, Juan de la Cruz
Poesías. Buenos Aires, Talleres Gráficos Argentinos, L.J. Rosso, 19- ?, 314p.

235 Vasquez, Abelardo
Buenos Aires en las malas; poemas. Mendoza, Eds. Pampano, 1963, 27p. (Buenos Aires)

Bolivia

236 Guerra, José E.
José Eduardo Guerra; cuadernos quincenales de poesía. 2. La Paz, Ed. Letras, Dirección General de Cultura, Municipalidad de La Paz, 1957, 49p. (La Paz)

237 Jaimes Freyre, Raúl
El instante que pasa. La Paz, Ed. Charcas, 1945, 79p. (Sucre)

Brazil

238 Andrade, Mário de
Lira paulistana . . . Sao Paulo, Martins, 1946? 90p. (Sao Paulo)

239 Bandecchi, Brasil
Romancero paulista. 3d ed. São Paulo, Ed. Obelisco, 1962, 113p. (São Paulo)

240 Castro, Luis Paiva de
Guia poético da cidade do Rio de Janeiro. Rio de Janeiro, Ed. Civilização Brasileira, 1965, 114p. (Rio de Janeiro)

241 Castro, Luis Paiva de
O ofício das coisas. Rio de Janeiro, José Alvaro Ed., 1965, 93p. (Rio de Janeiro)

242 Dantas, Donatilla
Candango; poesia. Capad e Benjamin. Rio de Janeiro, Minerva, 1959, 61p. (Brasilia)

243 Entrambasagues y Pena, Joaquín de
Poemas cariocas. Valencia, 1955, 45p. (Rio de Janeiro)

244 Feijo, Luiz C.
Morro que morre; poemas. Rio de Janeiro, Ed. do Professor, 1964, 73p. (Rio de Janeiro)

245 Goes, Jayme de Faria
Festas tradicionais da Bahia. Salvador, Progresso, 1961, 106p.

246 Goes, Jayme de Faria
Trovas que a Bahia inspirou. Rio de Janeiro, Freitas, Bastos, 1962, 64p.

247 Griz, Jayme
Rio Una. Recife, Diário da Manha, 1951, 211p. (Recife)

248 Guimaraes Filho, Alphonsus de
A cidade do sul. Bêlo Horizonte, Panorama, 1948, 109p. (Belo Horizonte)

249 Leonardos, Stella
Romanceiro de Estácio. Rio de Janeiro, Secretaría General de Educação e Cultura, Estado da Guanabara [n. d.] 99p. (Rio de Janeiro)

250 Lima, Stella Leonardos da Silva
Rio cancionero. Rio de Janeiro, Libraria São José, 1960, 90p. (Rio de Janeiro)

251 Mora, Octavio
Ausência viva. Rio de Janeiro, Livraria São José, 1956, 84p. (Belo Horizonte)

252 Orico, Osvaldo
Feitiço do Rio. Rio de Janeiro, Serviço Gráfico, Instituto Brasileiro de Geografia e Estatística, 1958, 77p. (Rio de Janeiro)

253 Pena Filho, Carlos
Livro geral. Rio de Janeiro, São José, 1959, 123p. (Recife)

254 Rangel, Otávio
Reportagens cariocas em verso, de ontem e de hoje. Rio de Janeiro, Gráfica Ed. Aurora, 1959, 165p. (Rio de Janeiro)

255 Ribeiro, Pacífico
Urtigas e malaguetas; motivos da Bahia. Salvador, Progresso, 1962, 140p.

256 Silva, Domingos Carvalho da, et al, eds.
Antologia da poesia paulista. São Paulo, Comissão de Literatura, Conselho Estadual de Cultura, 1960, 171p. (São Paulo)

257 Sousa, Afonso F. de
Album do Rio: poemas. Rio de Janeiro, Livros de Portugal, 1965, 79p. (Rio de Janeiro)

258 Tamayo Vargas, Augusto
Estación y éxtasis: poemas en Rio de Janeiro. Lima, Mejía Baca, 1957, 79p. (Rio de Janeiro)

Central America

259 Menéndez Alberdi, Adolfo
Poemas del pueblo. Havana, Impr. Marón, 1959, 60p.

Chile

260 Liscano, Juan, et al
Fuego de hermanos: a Pablo Neruda. Caracas, Ed. Arte, 1960, 34p. (Santiago)

Colombia

261 Bustamante, José I.
La poesía en Popayán, 1536-1954. 2d ed. Popayán, Ed. Universidad del Cauca, 1954, 495p. (Popayán)

262 Cote Lamus, Eduardo
La vida cotidiana. Bogota? Eds. Mito de Poesía, 1959, 70p.

Costa Rica

263 Aguilar, Marco
Nocturn to the light. (In Pan American Union. General Secretariat. Young poetry of the Americas . . . v. 1. Washington, 1967? p. 47.)

264 Doblez Yzaguirre, Julieta
Unfinished prayer. (In Pan American Union. General Secretariat. Young poetry of the Americas . . . v. 1. Washington, 1967? p. 45-46.)

Cuba

265 Casal, Julián del
Poesías completas. Havana, Dirección de Cultura, Ministerio de Educación, 1945, 349p.

266 Riverón Hernández, Francisco
Caimán sonoro. Havana, 1959, 173p.

267 Sánchez de Fuentes y Sell, Luis
Estampas de la Habana . . . y Tríptico de los fundadores. Havana, 1958, 128p. (Havana)

Dominican Republic

268 Morel, Tomás E.
La calle de mi casa. Santiago, D.R., Ed. Yagüe 1951, 55p. (Santiago, D.R.)

Ecuador

269 Cordero y León, Rigoberto
Acuarelas cuencanas. Cuenca, Casa de la Cultura Ecuatoriana, Núcleo del Azuay, 1951, 28p. (Cuenca)

270 Falconi Villagómez, José A.
Los precursores del modernismo en el Ecuador: César Borja y Fálquez Ampuero. Quito, Ed. Casa de la Cultura Ecuatoriana, 1959, 89p. (Guayaquil)

271 Romero y Cordero, Remigio
Ambato y sus romances . . . Ambato, 1951, 214p. (Ambato)

272 Urarte Alvarez de Eulate, José
Azucena de Quito; ramillete de poesías. Quito, Ed. "La Prensa Católica," 1958, 212p. (Quito)

273 Vela, Pablo H.
Ante las ruinas de Ambato. Quito, Tall. Gráf. Nacionales, 1951, 47p. (Ambato)

Guatemala

274 Ovalle López, Werner
El canto vivo; poesía suburbana. Guatemala, Impr. Iberia, 1952, unpaged.

Haiti

275 Brierre, Jean F.
Belle. Port-au-Prince, Impr. de l'Etat, 1948, 26p. (Belladère)

276 Lubin, Maurice A.
Poésies haïtiennes. Rio de Janeiro, Casa do Estudante do Brasil, 1956, 147p. (Port-au-Prince)

Mexico

277 Durán, Manuel
Ciudad asediada. México, Tezontle, 1954, 95p.

278 Gibson, Percy
Yo soy; Cuernavaca, México, 1949. [n. p., 1950?] 26p. (Cuernavaca)

279 González, Juan N.
Elegías de Tenochtitlán. México, Ed. Guaranía, 1953, 80p. (Mexico City)

280 López Bermúdez, José
Canto a Cuauhtemoc. México, Universidad Nacional Autonoma de México, unpaged. (Mexico City)

281 Moreno Machuca, Ernesto
Paisaje espiritual de mi barriada; poesía en el ámbito de Puebla. Puebla, 1959, 161p. (Puebla)

282 Pellicer, Carlos
Teotihuacán y 13 de agosto: ruina de Tenochtitlán. México, Revista de Poesía Universal, 1966, 21p. (Mexico City)

Nicaragua

283 Doña, William H.
El espíritu de Managua, managuadas. México, Ed. Ibero-Mexicana, 1956, 245p. (Managua)

Peru

284 Nieto, Luis C.
Romancero de pueblo en armas. Cuzco, Eds. Sol y Piedra, 1957, unpaged. (Arequipa)

285 Velarde, Hernán
Lima de antaño, cuadros costumbristas. 1st ed. Lima, Mar del Sur, 1952, 133p. (Lima)

Uruguay

286 Acuña de Figueroa, Francisco E.
Obras completas. 12v. Montevideo, Vazquez Cores, 1890.

Venezuela

287 Castillo Vásquez, Andrés
Y te espero en Valencia. Caracas, 1961, 50p. (Valencia)

288 Gerbasi, Vicente
Tirano de sombra y fuego. Poema basado en la leyenda del tirano Aguirre. Caracas, La Nación, 1955, 80p. (Valencia)

289 Montesinos, Roberto
La lámpara enigmática y otros poemas. Ed. conmemorativa del IV centenario de la ciudad de Barquisimeto. Caracas, Ed. Avila Gráfica, 1951, 194p. (Barquisimeto)

290 Paredes, Pedro P.
Patria del sueño, San Cristóbal. San Cristóbal, Sociedad "Salón de Lectura," 1961, 7p. (San Cristóbal)

West Indies and the Caribbean

291 Morand, Florette
Mon coeur est un oiseau des iles, poèmes. Paris, Ed. de la Maison des Intellectuels, 1954, 47p.

Periodical Articles

Argentina

292 Borges, Jorge L.
"Buenos Aires." Buenos Aires, Davar, revista literaria 111, October-November-December, 1966, p. 3.

293 Gómez Bedate, P.
"Sobre Borges." Madrid, Cuadernos hispanoamericanos LV, 1963, p. 268-276. (Buenos Aires)

294 Lagmanovich, D.J.
"Poesía Buenos Aires, 1950-1960: una Revista Argentina de Vanguardia." México, Revista iberoamericana XXIX, 1963, p. 283-298. (Buenos Aires)

295 Morello-Frosch, M.E.
"Elementos Populares en la Poesía de Jorge Luis Borges." San Juan, Asomante (18:3), July-September 1962, p. 26-35. (Buenos Aires)

296 Uset, R. D.
"Poesía de Buenos Aires." Buenos Aires, Estudios 550, December 1963, p. 769-770. (Buenos Aires)

Colombia

297 García Valencia, Abel
"Medellín en el Mundo, en la Poesía y en la Historia." Medellín, Universidad de Antioquia (26:104), September-November 1951, p. 625-638. (Medellín)

298 Zalamea, L.
"Jorge Rojas: Poeta, Agricultor y Urbanista." Américas 15, December 1963, p. 35-39.

Guatemala

299 Landívar, R.
"A la Ciudad de Guatemala." San José, Educación (8:30-31), March-June 1962, p. 138. (Guatemala City)

Honduras

300 Muñoz Cota, J.
"Comayagüela." Tegucigalpa, Honduras rotaria (año XXIII, no. 232), October-November 1966, p. 14. (Comayagüela)

Panama

301 "Cantores de la Patria." Panamá, Lotería (7:84), November 1962, p. 10-26.

Peru

302 Velarde, H.
"Lima Colonial: Relato de mi Abuela." México, Arquitectura México (18:76), December 1961, p. 242-243. (Lima)

Uruguay

303 Gamba, C. T.
"Las Ciudades que Amé. I-IV." Montevideo, Revista nacional (58:174), June 1953, p. 321-337. (Montevideo)

Venezuela

304 Armas Chitty, J.A. de
"Canto a la Ciudad que Regresa." Caracas, El farol (24:201), July-August 1962, p. 15-16.

Short Story

Books

Argentina

305 Onetti, Juan C.
La cara de la desgracia: novela. Montevideo, Ed. Alfa, 1960, 49p.

306 Onetti, Juan C.
El infierno tan temido. Montevideo, Ed. Asir, 1962, 71p.

307 Plá, Roger
Paño verde. Buenos Aires, Cía. Fabril Ed., 1962, 155p.

308 Rozenmacher, Germán N.
Cabecita negra y otros cuentos. Buenos Aires, Ed. Anuario, 1962, 159p.

309 Tapia, Atols
Tres cruces. Buenos Aires, Seijas y Goyanarte Eds., 1963, 97p.

310 Victoria, Marcos
Un verde paraíso, precedido de La Rosarito, Un genio, El tema. Buenos Aires, Losada, 1960, 149p. (Buenos Aires)

Bolivia

311 Llanos Aparicio, Luis
Cuentos para oficinistas y otros del ambiente paceño. La Paz, Empresa Ed. "Universo," 1960, 118p. (La Paz)

Brazil

312 Andrade, Mário de
Contos novos. São Paulo, Martins, 1947, 152p. (São Paulo)

313 Antônio, João
Malagueta, Perus e Bacanaço. Rio de Janeiro, Ed. Civilização Brasileira, 1963, 159p. (São Paulo)

314 Carvalho, Ruy, ed.
A cidade e as ruas. Novelas cariocas. Rio de Janeiro, Ed. Lidador [n. d.] 273p. (Rio de Janeiro)

315 Lessa, Orígenes
Zona sul. 2d ed. Rio de Janeiro, José Alvaro, 1963, 101p. (Rio de Janeiro)

316 Medeiros, José Cruz
Bicho-carpintero. Rio de Janeiro, A Estante, 1959, 151p. (Rio de Janeiro)

317 Tozzi, César (pseud.)
Jovens contos. Rio de Janeiro, Organização Simões, 1959, 143p. (Rio de Janeiro)

Chile

318 Acuña, Luis A.
Contrabando. Santiago, Arancibia Hermanos Eds., 1962, 115p.

319 Alonso, Carmen de
La cita. Santiago, Arancibia Hermanos Eds., 1962, 107p.

320 Cornejo Gamboa, Luis
Barrio Bravo. 2d ed. corr. Santiago, Aranciba Hermanos Eds., 1964, 85p.

321 Délano, Poli
Gente solitaria, y otros cuentos. Santiago, Eds. Mazorca, 1960, 58p. (Santiago)

322 Morand, Carlos
Una larga espera. Santiago, Eds. Alerce, 1961, 53p. (Santiago)

Costa Rica

323 Durán Ayanegui, Fernando
Dos reales, y otros cuentos. San José, Asociación Nacional de Fomento Económico, 1961, 60p. (San José)

Dominican Republic

324 Lafourcade, Acab
La fiesta del rey Acab. Santiago, Ed. del Pacífico, 1959, 244p.

Ecuador

325 Gangarotena y Jijón, Cristóbal de
Al margen de la historia: leyendas de pícaros, frailes y caballeros. 2d ed. Quito, Casa de la Cultura Ecuatoriana, 1960, 193p. (Quito)

El Salvador

326 Salarrué (pseud.)
La espada y otras narraciones. San Salvador, Ministerio de Cultura, Depto. Editorial, 1960, 290p. (San Salvador)

Mexico

327 Cruz, Salvador de la
Balada de la ciudad. Jalapa, El Caracol Marino, 1962, 18p. (Mexico City)

328 Dávila, Amparo
Música concreta. México, Fondo de Cultura Económica, 1964, 148p.

329 Guerrero, Jesús R.
Reflejos de la luz humana. México, Eds. Botas, 1948, 208p. (Mexico City)

330 Lenero, Vicente
La polvareda y otros cuentos. México, Ed. Jus, 1959, 188p.

Nicaragua

331 Calera Orozco, Adolfo
Cuentos nicaragüenses. Managua, Academia Nicaragüense de la Lengua, 1957, 176p.

Panama

332 Valdés Alvarez, Ignacio de J.
Cuentos de Carnaval. Panamá, Ed. Panamá América, 1949, 27p. (Panama City)

333 Valdés Alvarez, Ignacio de J.
Cuentos panameños de la ciudad y del campo. 2d ed. corr. and enl. Panamá, Impr. Nacional, 1955, 172p. (Panama City)

Paraguay

334 Bazán, Juan F.
Polen al viento: cuentos de ambiente paraguayo. Asuncion, Ed. de Agencia de Librerías de Salvador Nizza, 1954, 171p. (Asunción)

Peru

335 Cuadros Escobedo, Manuel E.
Cinco cuentos cuzqueños. Cuzco? Ed. Garcilaso, 1960, 32p. (Cuzco)

336 Fajardo, Jesús V.
Cofre serrano. Lima, Crédito Ed. Victory, 1951, 164p. (Ayacucho & Huamanga)

337 Ribeyro, Julio R.
Cuentos de circunstancias. Lima, Ed. Nuevos Rumbos, 1958, 96p.

338 Torre, Alfonso la
En la noche: cuentos. Lima, 1958, 175p. (Lima)

Uruguay

339 Banchero, Anderssen
Mientras amanece. Montevideo, Eds. de la Banda Oriental, 1963, 78p. (Montevideo)

340 Benedetti, Mario
Esta mañana. Montevideo, 1949, 151p. (Montevideo)

341 Benedetti, Mario
Montevideanos; cuentos. Montevideo, Ed. Alfa, 1959, 124p. (Montevideo)

342 Benedetti, Mario
El último viaje, y otros cuentos. Montevideo, Número, 1951, 70p. (Montevideo)

343 Castro, Manuel de
Humo en la isla: cuentos y relatos. Montevideo, Eds. de la Banda Oriental, 1962, 81p.

344 Gómez Cruz, Ramón
Temas salteños. Salto, 1955, 101p. (Salto)

Venezuela

345 Díaz, Manuel G.
La virgen caraqueña; Bolívar, dios y diablo; otros cuentos frívolos, por Blas Millán, pseud. Caracas, Ed. Avila Gráfica, 1950, 340p. (Caracas)

346 Trejo, Oswaldo
Cuentos de la primera esquina. Caracas, Impr. Cruz del Sur, 1952, 68p. (Caracas)

Periodical Articles

Honduras

347 Durón, R.E.
"El Cuento Hondureño: La Campa del Reloj." Tegucigalpa, Honduras rotaria (año XXIII, no. 233) December 1966-January 1967, p. 21-23.

DESCRIPTION AND TRAVEL
(including guidebooks)

Books

Latin America

348 American Automobile Association. International Travel Dept. Touring Central and South America. New York, 1953, 173p.

349 Aspinall, Algernon E.
The pocket guide to the West Indies and British Guiana, British Honduras, Bermuda and the Spanish Main, Surinam, the Panama Canal. 10th ed. rev. by Sidney Dash. London, Methuen, 1960, 474p.

350 Butler, George P., & Erica Butler
South America. Princeton, Van Nostrand, 1960, 300p.

351 Carr, Archie F.
High jungles and low. Gainesville, University of Florida Press, 1953, 226p.

352 De Sherbinin, Betty
River Plate Republics: Argentina, Uruguay, Paraguay. New York, Coward-McCann, 1949, 276p.

353 Hanson, Earl P., ed., et al
The new world guides to the Latin American republics. 3v. New York, Duell, Sloan & Pearce, 1943-45.

354 Howell, Mark
Journey through a forgotten empire. New York, Collins, 1964, 200p.

355 Kane, Robert S.
South America, A to Z . . . Garden City, Doubleday, 1962, 370p.

356 Morris, James
Cities. New York, Harcourt, Brace, 1963, 375p.

357 Pan American-Grace Airways
How to get the most out of your trip to South America. New York, 1961, 128p.

358 Russell, William R.
The Bolivar countries: Colombia, Ecuador, Venezuela. 1949, 308p.

359 The South American handbook, 1924-. London, South American Pubs., 1924- Annual.

360 Swan, Michael
The marches of El Dorado; British Guiana, Brazil, Venezuela. Chester Springs, Dufour, 1964, 304p.

361 Williams, Elizabeth A.
High heels in the Andes. New York, Crowell, 1959, 194p.

Argentina

362 Alcolea, Santiago
Côrdoba. Barcelona, Ed. Artes, 1951, 208p.

363 Daufresne, Julio, & A. Isola
Usos y costumbres de Buenos Aires. Buenos Aires, Librería l'Amateur, 1960, 15p.

364 Dĩaz Ulloque, Fernando J.
Nunca olvidaré a Córdoba. Buenos Aires, Nuevo Cabildo, 1962, 110p.

365 Genesoni Rossi, Julio
Mirador mendocino, semblanzas y evocaciones. Mendoza, D'Accurzio, 1947, 145p.

366 Gómez de la Serna, Ramón
Explicación de Buenos Aires. Madrid, 1948, 303p.

367 Guía anual de turismo, Mendoza, Argentina, Chile. Mendoza, 1949- .

368 Guzzo, Emeterio G.
El tropero inmortal; el apellido Sosa al servicio de la independencia. 1st ed. Mendoza, 1952, 110p.

369 Makarius, Sameer
Buenos Aires y su gente: ensayo fotográfico. Buenos Aires, Cía. General Fabril, 1960, 22p.

370 Meyer, Gordon
The river and the people. London, Methuen, 1965, 223p.

371 Molina, Ricardo
Córdoba. Barcelona, Ed. Noguer, 1953, 37 plus 40p.

372 Moores, Guillermo H.
Estampas y vistas de la ciudad de Buenos Aires, 1599-1895. 2d ed. Buenos Aires, 1960, 197p.

373 Nicasio, Alberto
Iglesias de Córdoba; estampas xilográficas. Córdoba, Oficina del Album del VI Congreso Eucarístico Nacional, 1959, 10p. plus 12 plates.

374 Pérez Olivares, Rogelio
La Mezquita de Córdoba. Madrid, 1948, 327p.

375 Pessano, Carlos A.
Ciudad de Buenos Aires. Buenos Aires, Kraft, 1955, 120p.

376 Pinasco, Eduardo H.
El puerto de Buenos Aires en los relatos de 20 viajeros. Buenos Aires, 1947, 182p.

377 Rodríguez-Trío, David F.
Gran guía "Trío" de la ciudad de Buenos Aires. Buenos Aires, Trío, 1952? 80 plus 144p.

378 Schauman, Francisco I.
La Mendoza de mis años mozos. Buenos Aires, Colombo, 1959, 152p.

379 Schumacher, Werner
Buenos Aires y bellezas de la Argentina. Buenos Aires, 1955, 96p.

380 Streeter, Stephen
This is Buenos Aires. New York, McBride, 1954, 223p.

381 Ziechmann, Ernesto
Rincones evocativos del viejo Buenos Aires, dibujos. Buenos Aires, Kraft, 1948, 16p.

Bolivia

382 Asturias, Miguel A.
Bolivia: an undiscovered land. Tr. by Frances Hogarth-Gante. Chester Springs, Dufour, 1962, 116p.

383 Díaz Arguedas, Julio
Síntesis biográfica, histórica y geográfica de los nombres de las calles, avenidas, plazas y parques de la ciudad de La Paz. La Paz, 1951, 111p.

384 Guía comercial y turística de Cochabamba. Cochabamba, 1947- .

385 Guía general de Cochabamba. Cochabamba, Ed. Canelas, 1961- .

386 Guía práctica de La Paz. La Paz, Banco Popular del Perú, 1951- .

387 Hanke, Lewis
The imperial city of Potosí; an unwritten chapter in the history of Spanish America. The Hague, Nijhoff, 1956, 60p.

388 Marín, Rufino
La Paz, alma de Bolivia. Buenos Aires, Rego, 1947, 158p.

389 Molins, W.J.
La ciudad única, Potosí. 2d ed. Buenos Aires, 1927, 159p.

390 Pan American Union
La Paz. Washington, 1946, 23p.

391 Paredes, Manuel R.
La Paz y la Provincia El Cercado. La Paz, Ed. Centenario, 1955, 148p.

392 Urquidi, Guillermo
Monografía del Departamento de Cochabamba. Cochabamba, 1954, 366p.

Brazil

393 Coaracy, Vivaldo
Memorias da cidade do Rio de Janeiro. 2d ed. rev. + enl. Rio de Janeiro, Olympio, 1965, 557p.

394 Cruls, Castão
Aparência do Rio de Janeiro; notícia histórica e descritiva da cidade. 2v. Rio de Janeiro, Olympio, 1949.

395 Dos Passos, John R.
Brazil on the move. New York, Doubleday, 1963, 205p.

396 Eckschmidt, Jan
São Paulo no limiar do seu quinto século. São Paulo, Gráfica Ed. Michalany, 1955, unpaged.

397 Eichner, Erich
A cidade maravilhosa, Rio de Janeiro, e seus arrededores. The marvellous city . . . Rio de Janeiro, Kosmos, 194- ? 184p.

398 Gerson, Brasil
História das ruas do Rio de Janeiro. Rio de Janeiro, Souza, 1954, 350p.

399 Guia pitoresco e turístico de São Paulo . . . São Paulo, Livraria Martins, 1949?--.

400 Guia turístico da cidade de São Paulo e de seus arrededores. São Paulo, Eds. Melhoramentos, 1954, 199p.

401 Karfeld, Kurt P.
Rio de Janeiro . . . São Paulo, Eds. Melhoramentos, 1955, 24p.

402 Karfeld, Kurt P.
São Paulo, album com fotografias em cores. São Paulo, Eds. Melhoramentos, 195- ? 27 plus 36p.

403 Knox, John, & France Knox
Rio de Janeiro. New York, Doubleday, 1965, 59p.

404 Magalhaes, Aloisio, & Eugene Feldman
Doorway to Brasilia. Philadelphia, Falcon Press; dist. by G. Wittenborn, New York, 1959- .

405 Maurois, André
Rio de Janeiro. Images de Jean Manzon. Paris, F. Nathan, 1951, 185p.

406 May, Stella
Brazil. Grand Rapids, Fideler Co., 1963, 128p.

407 Milano, Miguel
Os fantasmas da São Paulo antiga; estudo histórico-literário da cidade de São Paulo. São Paulo, Ed. Saraiva, 1949, 111p.

408 Orico, Osvaldo
Brasil, capital Brasília. Rio de Janeiro, Serviço Gráfico do IBGE, 1958, 257p.

409 Prado, Caio
Evolução política do Brasil, e outros estudos. 3d ed. São Paulo, Ed. Brasiliense, 1961, 264p.

410 Rio de Janeiro et ses environs. Paris, Hachette, 1955, 128p.

411 Sarthou, Carlos
Relíquias da cidade do Rio de Janeiro. Rio de Janeiro, Gráfica Olímpica, 1961, 149p.

412 Stendardo, Alfredo
Visões do Rio de Janeiro. Rio de Janeiro, Irmãos Pongetti, 1961, 68 + 68p.

413 Tavares de Sá, Hernâne
A guide to Rio de Janeiro. New York, Farnam Associates, 1950, 31p.

414 Touring Club do Brasil
Rio de Janeiro. Rio de Janeiro, Cartografía Turística Ed., 1948? 35p.

415 Varzea, Alfonso
Geografia do Distrito Federal. 2d ed. Rio de Janeiro, Prefeitura do Distrito Federal, Secretaria Geral de Educação e Cultura, 1957?-.

British Honduras

416 Anderson, A. H.
Brief sketch of British Honduras. 5th ed. rev. Belize? Government Printer, 1948, 86p.

Central America

417 Cordan, Wolfgang
Secret of the forest; on the track of Maya temples. Tr. by Basil Creighton. New York, Doubleday, 1964, 225p.

418 Clark, Sydney A.
All the best in Central America. New York, Dodd, Mead, 1964, 292p.

419 Long, Edward J.
Central America. Garden City, Doubleday, 1964, 64p.

420 Ordish, George
Man, crops, and pests in Central America. Oxford, Pergamon Press, 1964, 119p.

421 The world and its peoples; the Caribbean region and Central America. New York, Greystone Press, 1965, 216p.

Chile

422 Beals, Carleton
Long land: Chile. New York, Coward-McCann, 1949, 244p.

423 Bianchi, Lois
Chile in pictures. London, Oak Tree Press, 1965, 64p.

424 Butland, Gilbert J.
Human geography of southern Chile. London, George Phillips & Son, 1958, 132p.

425 Chile. Instituto Geográfico Militar
Guía y planos de Santiago. Santiago, 1958, 186p.

426 Freeling, Nicholas
Valparaiso. New York, Harper & Row, 1965, 216p.

427 Guia de Santiago. Santiago, Kegan, 1950- .

428 Ossandón Guzmán, Carlos
Guia de Santiago . . . Santiago, Ed. Zig-Zag, 1962, 169p.

Colombia

429 Acevedo Latorre, Eduardo
Guia de turista . . . Bogotá, Librería Nueva, 1933, 132p.

430 Blomberg, Rolf
Buried gold and anacondas. Tr. by F.H. Lyon. Toronto, Nelson, Foster & Scott, 1959, 144p.

431 Bogotá, d. e. Bogota, Cámara de Comercio de Bogotá [n. d.] unpaged.

432 Esta es, this is Barranquilla; la puerta de oro de Colombia. Tr. by Alfred C. Clarke. Barranquilla, Ed. Colombo-Americana, 1954, unpaged.

433 Gers, José (pseud.) & Raúl Echevarría Barrientos
Cali en coloramor. Cali, 1960, 78p.

434 Geonaga, Miguel
Lecturas locales; crónicas de la vieja Barranquilla . . . Barranquilla, 1953, 452p.

435 Gómez Pérez, Fernando, ed.
Guía de Medellín. Medellín, Asesores Pubs., 1956, 120p.

436 Hernández de Alba, Guillermo
Guía de Bogotá, arte y tradición. Bogota, Librería Voluntad, 1948, 235p.

437 Katich D., Dragan, ed.
Bogotá y alrededores. Bogotá, 1960, variously paged.

438 Medellín: algunos artículos y un reportaje gráfico. Bogotá, Librería Colombiana-Camacho Roldán, 1962, unpaged.

439 Moser, Brian, & Donald Tayler
The cocaine eaters. Don Mills, Longmans Canada Ltd., 1965, 204p.

440 Ortega Ricaurte, Daniel
Album del sesquicentenario. Bogotá, Aedita Eds., 1960? 173p.

441 West, Robert C.
Pacific lowlands of Colombia; a negroid area of the American tropics. Baton Rouge, Louisiana State University Press, 1957, 278p.

Costa Rica

442 Costa Rica. Instituto Geográfico Nacional
Carreterras del área metropolitana, San José, Costa Rica. San José, 1958, 71p.

443 Lundberg, Donald E.
Adventure in Costa Rica. London, Bailey Bros. & Swinfen Ltd., 1960, 238p.

444 Pan American Union. Travel Division
Visit Costa Rica. Washington, 1954, 32p.

445 Quirós Amador, Tulia
Geografía de Costa Rica. San José, 1954, 192p.

Cuba

446 Clark, Sydney A.
All the best in Cuba. 2d ed. rev. New York, Dodd, Mead, 1956, 235p.

447 Franco, Victor
The morning after; a French journalist's impressions of Cuba under Castro. Tr. by Ivan Kats & Philip Pendered. New York, Praeger, 1964, 248p.

448 Guía de la Habana, Marianao, y sector de Miami. Graphic tourist guide of the city of Havana, Marianao and sector of Miami. Havana, 1955?-.

449 Iglesias, Ramiro E.
Guía de información y plano de la Habana; calles, rutas de omnibus, numeración, clínicas, hospitales, etc . . . Information guide and map to Havana; streets, bus routes, house numbers, Havana, Impr. Solana, 1947, 36p.

450 Roberts, Walter A.
Havana, the portrait of a city. New York, Coward-McCann, 1953, 282p.

Dominican Republic

451 Harding, Bertita L.
Land Columbus loved: the Dominican Republic. New York, Coward-McCann, 1949, 246p.

452 Incháustegui Cabral, Joaquín M.
Geografía descriptiva de la República Dominicana. 7th ed. rev. & corr. Ciudad Trujillo, Librería Dominicana, 1950, 110p.

453 Pan American Union. Dept. of Public Information
Dominican Republic. Washington, 1964, 47p.

454 This is the Dominican Republic. New York, Consulate General of the Dominican Republic, 1954? 44p.

Ecuador

455 Bemelmans, Ludwig
The donkey inside. New York, Dutton, 1964, 224p.

456 Blanchard, Dean H.
Ecuador, crown jewel of the Andes. New York, Vantage Press, 1963, 228p.

457 Bravo Aráuz, Bolívar
Quito monumental y pintoresco. Quito, Ed. Universitaria, 1961, 307p.

458 Dolinger, Jane
The forbidden world of the jaguar princess. London, Robert Hale, Ltd., 1964, 191p.

459 Enríquez Bermeo, Eliecer, ed.
Guía espiritual de Quito . . . Quito, Ed. "Los Andes"; dist. Librería Universitaria, 1953, 244p.

460 El libro de la ciudad de San Francisco de Quito hasta 1950-51. Quito, Eds. Cegan, 1951, variously paged.

461 La Orden Miracle, Ernesto
Elogio de Quito. Bilbao, Eds. Cultura Hispánica, 1950, 122p.

462 Quito al día; guía. Quito, 1947- .

463 Quito: guía. Quito, 1961, variously paged.

464 Von Hagen, Victor W.
A guide to Guayaquil. New York, Farnam Associates, 1950, 32p.

El Salvador

465 Mertens, Robert
El Salvador. Biologische reise im lande der vulkane. Frankfurt am Main, Kramer, 1952, 116p.

466 Osborne, Lilly de Jongh
Four keys to El Salvador. New York, Funk & Wagnalls, 1956, 221p.

467 Pan American Union. Travel Division
Visit El Salvador. Washington, 1958, 24p.

468 Salvador. Junta Nacional de Turismo
Conozca El Salvador. San Salvador, 195- , 28p.

469 Salvador, Secretaría de Información
El Salvador, país en marcha ascendente. San Salvador, Impr. Nacional, 1953, 119p.

French Guiana

470 Mazière, Francis
Expedition Tumuc-Humac. Tr. by Fernand G. Renier & Anne Cliff. New York, Doubleday, 1955, 249p.

Guatemala

471 Directoria; aspectos gráficos de Guatemala, Quezaltenango y Retalhuleu. Guatemala, Unión Tipográfica, 1955- .

472 Lloyd, Joan
Guatemala, land of the Mayas. London, Robert Hale, Ltd., 1963, 175p.

473 Nach, James
Guatemala in pictures. London, Oak Tree Press, 1966, 64p.

474 Woodman, James M.
Discovering Yucatan; a complete guide to the Yucatan Peninsula of Mexico, cradle of Mayan civilization, including Cozumel and neighboring Guatemala. New York, Doubleday, 1966, 84p.

Guyana

475 Carr, David, & John Thorpe
From the cam to the cays; the story of the Cambridge expedition to British Honduras, 1959-60. Chester Springs, Dufour, 1964, 190p.

476 Cummings, Leslie P.
Geography of Guyana. New York, Collins, 1965, 64p.

477 Great Britain. Central Office of Information. Reference Division
British Guiana. New York, British Information Services, 1959, 30p.

478 Jeeves, Stanley
Journey to the lost world. London, University of London Press, 1965, 95p.

479 Norwood, Victor G.
Jungle life in Guiana. London, Robert Hale, Ltd., 1965, 158p.

480 Roth, Vincent
Where is it? A gazetteer of British Guiana. Rev. ed. Georgetown, Daily Chronicle, 194-? 137p.

481 Smith, Raymond T.
British Guiana. New York, Oxford University Press, 1962, 218p.

Haiti

482 Catalogne, Gérard de
A guide to Cap Haïtien and the citadel of King Christophe. Cap Haïtien, King Christophe Travel Organization, 1956, 56p.

483 Cave, Hugh B.
Haiti, high road to adventure. New York, Holt, Rinehart and Winston, 1952, 306p.

484 Métraux, Alfred
Haiti: black peasants and voodoo. Tr. by Peter Lengyel. New York, Universe Books, 1960, 109p.

485 Rodman, Selden
Haiti; the black republic; the complete story and guide. New rev. ed. New York, Devin-Adair, 1961, 168p.

486 Roy, Adrien L.
Projet d'aménagement des grands travaux de la Grand Rue . . . Port-au-Prince, Impr. de l'Etat, 1958, 157p.

487 Wilson, Ruth (Danenhower)
Here is Haiti. New York, Philosophical Library, 1957, 204p.

Honduras

488 Aguilar Pinel, Carlos
Geografía de Honduras. 3d ed. Tegucigalpa, 1955, 248p.

489 Bonilla, Marcelina
Diccionario histórico-geográfico de las poblaciones de Honduras. 2d ed. Tegucigalpa, Impr. Calderón, 1952, 310p.

490 Houlson, Jane H.
Blue blaze; danger and delight in strange islands of Honduras. New York, Bobbs-Merrill Co., 1934, 305p.

491 Keenagh, Peter
Mosquito coast. Boston, Houghton, Mifflin, 1938, 286p.

492 Pan American Union. Travel Division
Visit Honduras. Washington, 1958, 22p.

Jamaica

493 Bent, Rupert M., & E. L. Bent-Golding
A complete geography of Jamaica. New York, Collins, 1966, 128p.

494 Cargill, Morris, ed.
Ian Fleming introduces Jamaica. New York, Hawthorne Books, 1966, 240p.

495 Cave, Hugh B.
Four paths to paradise; a book about Jamaica. Toronto, Doubleday, 1961, 308p.

496 Great Britain. Directorate of Overseas Surveys
Jamaica 1: 10,000: Kingston. 1st ed. Tolworth, Surrey, 1962- .

497 Jamaica. Survey Dept.
Kingston (Parish) 1: 2,500 series: Kingston and vicinity. Kingston, 1958- .

498 Jones, Wilfrid L.
From steps to steeple; poetical selections, sketches and careers of prominent citizens. In honor of Kingston's 150th anniversary. Kingston [n. d.] 1953? 48p.

499 Roberts, Walter A., ed.
The capitals of Jamaica: Spanish Town, Kingston, Port Royal. Kingston, Pioneer Press, 1955, 112p.

500 William's street guide and service index of Greater Kingston, including a street guide of Mandiville, Montego Bay, and Spanish Town. Kingston, Sangster's Book Store [n. d.] 309p.

Mexico

501 Cantón, Wilberto L.
La ciudad de México, águila y sol de su vida. México, Secretaría de Educación Pública, 1946, 74p.

502 Cohen, John M.
Mexico City, Mexico. London, Spring Books, 1966, 159p.

503 Covarrubías, Ricardo
Las calles de Monterrey. Monterrey, Tip. Garza y Jiménez, 1947- .

504 Crespo de la Serna, J. J.
Cinco intérpretes de la ciudad de México. México, Ed. Guarania, 1952, 123p.

505 Dörner, Gerd
Mexico. Tr. by Gladys Wheelhouse. New York, Doubleday, 1964, 61p.

506 Ford, Norman D.
Fabulous Mexico; where everything costs less. Greenlawn, Harian Publications, 1965, 143p.

507 Howe, Alice
Guadalajara, the majestic capital of Jalisco, Mexico. 1st ed. Guadalajara? 1955, 188p.

508 Icaza, Alfonso de
Así era aquello . . . 60 años de vida metropolitana. México, Eds. Botas, 1957, 318p.

509 León, Nicolás
El Santo Desierto de Guajimalpa, o Desierto de los Leones. México, 1922, 24p.

510 México y sus alrededores. Ed. centenaria. México, 1961, 11p.

511 Nash, Joe
El Paseo de la Reforma: a guide. México, Esquivel, 1959, 127p.

512 Páez Brotchie, Luis
Guadalajara capitalina y su cuarto centenario. Ed. del H. Ayuntamiento Constitucional. Guadalajara, 1961, 224p.

513 Poniatowska, Elena
Todo empezó el domingo. México, Fondo de Cultura Económica, 1963, 260p.

514 Romero, José
My Mexico City and yours. Garden City, Doubleday, 1962, 237p.

515 Schalkwijk, B.
Mexico City, Mexico. London, Spring Books, 1966, 160p.

516 Simon, Kate
Mexico: places and pleasures. New York, Doubleday, 1965, 461p.

517 Stoppelman, Joseph W.
People of Mexico. London, Phoenix House Pub., 1964, 178p.

518 Timmons, W. L.
Should you drive in Mexico? El Paso, Tourists' Protective Association, 1966, 107p.

519 Wilhelm, John
Guide to Mexico City. Mexico, Eds. Tolteca, 1960- .

520 Baus, Ruth, & Emily Harvin
Who's running this expedition! New York, Coward-McCann, 1959, 256p.

521 Palmer, Mervyn G.
Through unknown Nicaragua. London, Jarrolds Publishers, 1946, 150p.

522 Pan American Union. Travel Division
Visit Nicaragua. Washington, 1957, 24p.

523 Tweedy, Maureen
This is Nicaragua. Ipswich, East Anglian Magazine, 1953, 116p.

Panama

524 Henry, Marguerite
Panama in story and pictures. Chicago, Albert Whitman & Co., 1942, 32p.

525 Pan American Union. Travel Division
Visit Panama. Rev. ed. Washington, 1958, 32p.

526 Pellaton, May, & Henry Larsen
The forests of Panama. Tr. by Irene Salem. London, Harrap, 1964, 136p.

527 Rodman, Selden
The road to Panama. New York, Hawthorne Books, 1966, 224p.

528 Rubio y Muñoz-Bocanegra, Angel
La ciudad de Panamá: biografía, funciones, diagnosis, paisaje. Panamá, Banco de Urbanización y Rehabilitación, 1950, 217p.

529 Rubio y Muñoz-Bocanegra, Angel
Pequeño atlas geográfico de Panamá. 5th ed. rev. Panamá, Eds. Oasis, 1959, 63p.

530 U.S. Army. Caribbean Command
City plan, Panama City, Republic of Panama. Corozal, C.Z., 7465AU Engineer, 1954, 19p.

Paraguay

531 Ferreira Gubetich, Hugo
Geográfia de Paraguay. 4th ed. Asunción, 1960, 252p.

532 Gibson, Christopher
Enchanted trails. London, Museum Press, Ltd., 1948, 272p.

533 Land of lace and legend. An informal guide to Paraguay. 2d ed. Compiled by Las Amigas Norteamericanas del Paraguay. Asunción, La Colmena S.A., 1960? 162p.

534 Meyer, Gordon
The river and the people. New York, International Publications Service, 1965, 223p.

535 Pan American Union. Travel Division
Visit Paraguay. Washington, 1955, 32p.

536 Paraguay. Dirección General de Turismo
Guía de turismo. Asunción, 1958, 231p.

537 Smith, W.H., & V.G. Smith
Paraguayan interlude; observations and impressions. Scottdale, Mennonite Publishing House, 1950, 184p.

Peru

538 Alayza Paz Soldán, Luis
La Ciudad de los Reyes y los trovadores galos. Lima, Ed. Médica Peruana, 1958, 128p.

539 "Aurora"; guía de bolsillo. #1- , 1949- .

540 Caparo, A., José D.
Guía auxiliar manual de la ciudad de Arequipa. 5th ed. corr. & enl. Arequipa, 1960, 196p.

541 Cornejo Bouroncle, Jorge
Arequipa, homenaje y recuerdo. Cuzco, Ed. Rozas, 1952, 35p.

542 Dolinger, Jane
Gypsies of the Pampa. New York, Fleet Pub., 1958, 179p.

543 Lima. Museo del Arte
Presencia de la arquitectura virreinal de Lima. Lima, 1962, 64p.

544 McBride, Barrie St. C.
Amazon journey; 7,000 miles through Peru and Brazil. London, Robert Hale, Ltd., 1965, 200p.

545 Malinovsky, Constantino
Así es Lima; manual de turismo, industria y comercio. Lima, Sparrow, 1947, 448p.

546 Perú. Oficina Nacional de Planeamiento y Urbanismo
Guía de ciudades del Perú . . . Lima, 1955, unpaged.

547 Pino González, Juan J. de
Guía de turismo y de vialidad de la ciudad de Ayacucho. Cuzco, 1953, 95p.

548 Polar, Jorge
Arequipa; descripción y estudio social. 3d ed. Arequipa, 1958, 239p.

549 Slesser, Malcolm
The Andes are prickly. New York, Doubleday, 1966, 254p.

550 Travada, Ventura
El suelo de Arequipa convertido en cielo; historia general de Arequipa, año de 1752. Arequipa, 1958, 121p.

551 Von Hagen, Victor W.
Huancayo and Ayacucho. New York, Farnam Associates, 1950, 32p.

552 Woodcock, George
Incas and other men; travels in the Andes. London, Faber and Faber, 1965, 268p.

Uruguay

553 Barrios Pintos, Aníbal
Salto, voz de la tierra y del hombre. Montevideo, Ed. Minas, 1962, unpaged.

554 Guía de las calles, plazas, plazuelas, parques, pueblos, barrios, villas, etc., del departamento de Montevideo. Montevideo, Guías Araújo, 1951- .

555 Instituto Histórico y Geográfico del Uruguay
Iconografía de Montevideo. Montevideo, 1955, 250p.

556 Montevideo, Intendencia Municipal
Aspectos de Montevideo. Montevideo, 1953, unpaged.

557 Palhoriès, Lucien
Atlantique austral; escales en Amérique du Sud. Paris, Puyfourcat, 1959, 215p.

Venezuela

558 Bangor, Edward H. H. W.
New El Dorado; Venezuela. London, Robert Hale, Ltd., 1957, 189p.

559 Boehm, Lincoln A.
Venezuela in pictures. London, Oak Tree Press, 1966, 64p.

560 Clemente Travieso, Carmen
Las esquinas de Caracas . . . Caracas, Ed. "Ancora," 1956, 285p.

561 Felice Cardot, Carlos
Tierra y hombres; discursos. Madrid, 1953, 158p.

562 Garavini di Turno, Sadio
Diamond River. Tr. by Peter Green. New York, Harcourt, Brace & World, 1963, 186p.

563 Gasparini, Graziano
Promesa de Venezuela . . . Caracas, Presidencia de la República, 1964, 236p.

564 General Drafting Company, Inc.
Mapa del norte de los Estados Unidos de Venezuela. 5th ed. Caracas, Creole Petroleum Corp., 1952- .

565 González Guinán, Francisco
Tradiciones de mi pueblo, Valencia, Venezuela. Caracas, Ed. "Ragón," 1954, 217p.

566 Gran guía de turismo Caracas. Caracas, Ed. Rex, 1955, 285p.

567 Jiménez Arráiz, Francisco
La ciudad de los crepúsculos . . . Barquisimeto, Ed. Avila Gráfica, 1952, 133p.

568 Matiz, Leo
Algo de Caracas. Caracas? 195- , unpaged.

569 El Mes Financiero y Económico de Venezuela (periodical)
Así es Caracas. Caracas, 1951, unpaged.

570 Mudarra, Miguel A.
Barquisimeto. Caracas, Empresa "El Cojo," 1952, 72p.

571 Núñez, Enrique B.
Figuras y estampas de la antigua Caracas, primera serie. Caracas, Pubs. del Consejo Municipal del Distrito Federal, 1962, 107p.

572 La pequeña Venecia del Estado Zulia; anécdotas, problemas, costumbres. Importancia de la región lacustre de Maracaibo. Maracaibo, 1949, 72p.

573 Reyes, Vitelio
Dos interpretaciones históricas: la Ciudad de Barquisimeto y El lago de Maracaibo . . . Caracas, Impr. Nacional, 1952, 132p.

574 Tariffi, Terzo, & Natalia Rosi de Tariffi
Caracas; guía histórico-artística e indicador general. Caracas, Ed. "Nueva Venezuela," 195- , 366p.

575 Venezuela. Dirección de Turismo
Guía fomento de Caracas. Caracas, 1957, 98p.

576 Vilá Camposado, Marco A.
Monografía geográfica del Valle de Caracas. Caracas, Pubs. del Grupo de Caracas de la Sociedad Interamericana de Antropología y Geografía, 1947, 122p.

577 Villaneuva, Carlos R.
La Caracas de ayer y de hoy, su arquitectura colonial y la reurbanización de "El Silencio" . . . Paris, 1950, 87p.

West Indies and the Caribbean

578 Clark, Sydney A.
All the best in the Caribbean, including the Bahamas and Bermuda. New York, Dodd, Mead, 1959, 470p.

579 Graves, Charles P.R.
Fourteen Islands in the sun. London, Leslie Frewin, Ltd., 1965, 220p.

580 Jonckheer, C.L.H., comp.
The Netherlands Antilles; guide for Curaçao. Willemstad, Government Information Service, 1958, 64p.

581 Macpherson, John
Caribbean lands; a geography of the West Indies. New York, International Publications Service, 1965, 180p.

582 Redgrave, William J.
Islands in the wind; what to see and how to cut costs in the West Indies, the Bahamas, and Bermuda. Greenlawn, N.Y., Harian Pubs.; trade distributor: Greenberg, 1958, 227p.

Periodical Articles

Latin America

583 Bourjaily, V.
"Memo from an Excited Traveler: South America's Infinite Variety," Esquire 55, January 1961, p. 75-87.

584 Garcia, L.J.
"Circling South America." Travel 101, February 1954, p. 7-10.

585 Knight, P.
"The Traveler's Guide to South America." Sports Illustrated 17, November 12, 1962, p. 60-62.

Argentina

586 Arrue Gowland, A.
"El Puerto de Rosario." Rosario, Revista de la Bolsa de Comercio de Rosario (41:1,000), September 15, 1953, p. 3-12.

587 Bostick, P.
"Around Buenos Aires." Travel 108, November 1957, p. 50-52.

588 Everill, K.
The City of Buenos Aires." London, Latin American World, September 1930, p. 12-14.

589 Joseph, R.
"Buenos Aires Report . . ." Holiday, November 1946, p. 20-25.

590 Klappenback, H.R.
"Sidewalks of Buenos Aires." Américas 5, April 1953, p. 33-34.

591 Pahlen, K.
"Sinfonía de una Gran Ciudad." Buenos Aires, Revista geográfica americana (218-219), November-December 1953, p. 193-204.

592 Reynolds, L.
"Mendoza: South America's Biggest Little City." Buenos Aires, Comments on Argentine trade, November 1945, p. 54-62.

Barbados

593 McCarthy, J.
"Barbados Without Tours." Holiday 33, February 1963, p. 96.

594 Mankowitz, W.
"Flying Fish and Sugar Cane." Holiday 35, February 1964, p. 72-78.

Bolivia

595 Beltrán Heredia, B. A.
"Contenido Mitológico, Histórico y Religioso del Carnaval Orureño." La Paz, Khana (1:15-16), March 1956, p. 133-140.

596 Nazoa, Aquilés
"Viaje a la Capital de Cholitas." Caracas, Revista shell (7: 27), June 1958, p. 48-53.

597 Ocampo Moscoso, E.
"Potosí Colonial y Republicano." Cochabamba, Revista jurídica (13: 52), June 1950, p. 187-217.

598 Pritchett, V. S.
"La Paz: Madness at 12,000 Feet." Holiday 23, June 1958, p. 52.

599 Samper, Armando
"Portrait of La Paz." Américas (7:11), November 1955, p. 8-13.

Brazil

600 Azevedo, Aroldo de
"São Paulo, Metrópole Moderna." São Paulo, Boletim paulista de geografia 5, July 1950, p. 53-61.

601 Frontini, R.M.
"Sao Paulo Landmarks." Américas (9:4), April 1957, p. 22-25.

602 Guimaraes, J.
"Marvelous City: Rio's 400th Anniversary." Américas 17, March 1965, p. 1-10.

603 Joseph, R.
"Why They're Still Flying Down to Rio." Esquire 60, December 1963, p. 214-217.

604 Krauss, W.A.
"Rio." Holiday 14, December 1953, p. 106-111.

605 Llewellyn, R.
"Sao Paulo, City of Promise." Holiday 33, February 1963, p. 68-77.

606 Moore, W.R.
"Rio Panorama." National geographic magazine, September 1939, p. 283-324.

607 Morse, Richard M.
"Sao Paulo Since Independence: a Cultural Interpretation." Hispanic American historical review (34:4), November 1954, p. 419-444.

608 Pires, F.D. de A.
"Floating Community of Amazonas." Natural history 74, October 1965, p. 12-17.

609 "Rio: Portrait of a Startling City." Life 37, November 1, 1954, p. 83-90.

610 Taunay, Affonso de Escragnolle
"Iconografia Carioca." Rio de Janeiro, Revista do Instituto Histórico e Geográfico Brasileiro 203, April-June 1949, p. 3-94.

611 Tavares de Sá, Hernane
"Metropolis Made to Order: Brasilia." National geographic magazine (117:5), May 1960, p. 704-724.

612 Tavares de Sá, Hernane
"Spectacular Rio de Janeiro." National geographic magazine (107:3), March 1955, p. 289-328.

British Honduras

613 Killgrove, J.
"Little-Known British Honduras." Travel 102, September 1954, p. 24-26.

614 Lewis, N.
"Letter from Belize." New Yorker 31, October 15, 1955, p. 136.

Central America

615 "Central America." Look 18, January 12, 1954, p. 54-57.

Chile

616 Bellani Nazeri, R.
"Santiago de Chile, la Ciudad Monumental de los Andes." Buenos Aires, Revista geográfica americana, August 1946, p. 65-76.

617 Cid, D. Martí de
"Valparaíso." Havana, Carteles (33:28), July 13, 1952, p. 16-17, 80.

618 Durand, L.
"Concepción: El Aguila Negra en Campo de Oro." Concepción, Atenea (99:304), October 1950, p. 5-15.

619 Llewelyn, R.
"Santiago, Bright Star of Chile." Holiday 34, November 1963, p. 76-81.

620 Maples Arce, M.
"Recordando a Santiago." Concepción, Atenea (109:333), March 1953, p. 307-333.

621 Tait, B.
"City of the Southern Sun." Grace log (27:3), May-June 1952, p. 15-20.

Colombia

622 "Bogotá y sus Gentes." Buenos Aires, Continente 53, August 1951, p. 32-35.

623 Coester, Alfred L. "Lessons Learned at Bogotá." Hispania, February 1939, p. 68-72.

624 Davis, M.M. "Down and up in Bogotá." Travel 122, July 1964, p. 50-53.

625 Forero, Manuel J. "Ciudades de Colombia: Bucaramanga." Bogotá, Vida 40, October-November 1950, p. 41-43.

626 Holguin, B. de "Rare Pair." Travel 108, August 1957, p. 24-27.

627 Martínez Cabana, Carlos "Instantáneas de Medellín." Bogotá, Cromos, April 6, 1946, p. 3-5, 56-57.

628 Meek, G.D. "Medellín." Américas (12:5), May 1960, p. 27-30.

629 Ogletree, J. "Breathless in Bogotá." The Panamerican, December 1944, p. 6-10.

Costa Rica

630 Samper, Armando "Through the Streets of San José." Américas (11:8), August 1959, p. 8-12.

Cuba

631 Andrews, P. "Havana, Queen City of the Caribbean." Mademoiselle 46, January 1958, p. 96-97.

632 Basso, H. "Havana." Holiday (12:6), December 1952, p. 64–70, 138-144.

633 Hemingway, M.
"Havana." Saturday review 48, January 2, 1965, p. 40-41.

634 Maribona, A.
"Havana; or, The Art of Living." UN world 5, February 1951, p. 49-51.

635 Planas, Juan M.
"La Habana Dentro de 50 años." Havana, Ingeniería civil (10:4), April 1959, p. 223-236.

636 Ruiz, G.G.
"Desdicha y Esperanza de Holguin." Havana, Carteles, May 28, 1950, p. 26-29.

637 Sutton, H.
"Chez Papa." Saturday review 37, March 13, 1954, p. 41-46.

638 Viamontes Enríquez, L.M.
"Nuestro Legendario Camagüey." Havana, El federado escolar (11:121-122), March-April 1953, p. 43-46.

Dominican Republic

639 Fiori, A.
"Oldest City in the New World." UN world 5, February 1951, p. 62-63.

640 Hull, M.H.
"Castle of Columbus: Dominican Home of the Discover's Son." Américas 10, September 1958, p. 22-25.

641 Klemfuss, H.C.
"Ciudad Trujillo." Exporters' digest (27:4), April 1953, p. 1-4.

642 Welles, Sumner
"Santo Domingo: an Ideal Winter Resort for the American Tourist." Pan American Union bulletin 64, January 1930, p. 16-30.

Ecuador

643 Beard, A.H.
"The River Port that Became a Seaport: Puerto Marítimo." Américas 15, May 1963, p. 17-19.

644 Cross, W.
"Sounds of Sites." Travel 119, March 1963, p. 32-33.

645 Estrada, E.
"Guayaquil." Madrid, Mundo hispánico 93, supplement, 1955, p. 26-27.

646 Forero, Manuel J.
"Ciudades del Ecuador." Bogotá, Vida 51, May-June 1952, p. 43-45.

647 Kilmer, E.B.
"This is Quito." Américas (12:1), January 1960, p. 10-13.

648 Linke, Lilo
"What's Happening to Guayaquil?" Américas 9, June 1957, p. 3-8.

649 Moscoso Cárdenas, A.
"Between the Earth and the Sky: Quito, Capital of Ecuador." Américas 10, May 1958, p. 14-19.

650 Ortega, M. de
"Portrait of San Francisco de Quito." Américas 13, June 1961, p. 10-13.

651 "Quito." Madrid, Mundo hispanico 93, supplement, 1955, p. 20-25.

El Salvador

652 Holguin, B. de
"Enchanting El Salvador." Travel 110, October 1958, p. 36-40.

653 Killgrove, J.
"El Salvador." Travel 99, March 1953, p. 36-39.

654 Lainez, J.J.
"San Salvador de los Ojos Cerrados." San Salvador, Sintesis (1:6), September 1954, p. 5-8.

655 Morse Delgado, O.
"Crónica de Viaje: Sal Salvador." Havana, Arquitectura (23:266), September 1955, p. 414-418.

French Guiana

656 Smith, N.
"Color Glows in the Guianas, French and Dutch." National geographic magazine 83, April 1943, p. 459-480.

Haiti

657 Bervin, A.
"Port-au-Prince." Havana, El heraldo de Haiti (4:41), May 1956, p. 28-30.

658 "Caribbean Carnival." Life 28, March 13, 1950, p. 98-105.

659 Fligelman, B.
"Letter from Haiti." The nation 170, June 24, 1950, p. 633-635.

660 Gold, H.
"Americans in the Port of Princes." Yale Review (44:1), September 1954, p. 85-98.

661 "Haiti Holiday." Américas 1, December 1949, p. 2-5.

662 Johnson, M.E.
"Throbbing Voodoo Drums, Villa Hotels Heighten Haiti's Spell-Binding Allure." Travel 109, May 1958, p. 37-40.

663 Krauss, W.A.
"Haiti." Holiday 7, March 1950, p. 98-110.

664 Otis, D.
"Going Places and Finding Things in Haiti." House & garden 120, December 1961, p. 160-167.

665 Thompson, L.E.
"Port-au-Prince." *American foreign service journal*, November 1934, p. 588-591.

Honduras

666 Kilmer, E.B.
"Tegucigalpa." *Américas* (12:4), April 1960, p. 25-28.

667 Lamb, E.S.
"A Gringo Looks at Tegucigalpa." *Pan American Union bulletin 82*, May 1948, p. 262-267.

668 Reina Valenzuela, J.
"San Pedro Sula: su Pasado, su Presente, su Porvenir." Tegucigalpa, *La pajarita de papel* (3:19-21), October-December 1951, p. 89-104.

Jamaica

669 Davis, M.M.
"Editor's Report: Jamaica." *Travel 100*, December 1953, p. 13-16.

670 Moore, W.R.
"Jamaica: Hub of the Caribbean." *National geographic magazine 105*, March 1954, p. 333-362.

Mexico

671 Aguilar Olmos, R.
"Guadalajara." México, *El mundo gráfico*, November 1933, p. 363-387.

672 Alba, O.L.
"Monterrey, las Canas de la Joven Ciudad." México, *Hoy*, July 6, 1946, p. 68-69.

673 Birmingham, S.
"Life in the Vibrant Capital." *Holiday 32*, October 1962, p. 106-111.

674 García, R.
"Señuelos de Monterrey." México, *Todo 834*, September 1, 1949, p. 36-37, 43.

675 Lemert, B. F.
"Mexico: Urban Life." Journal of Geography, January 1936, p. 1-7.

676 Lemert, B. F.
"Guadalajara, Mexico." Journal of Geography, May 1941, p. 173-180.

677 "Mexico City." Sunset 131, August 1963, p. 42-57.

678 "San Luis Potosí, City of 'Extraordinary Riches.'" México, Mexican-American review (23:12), December 1955, p. 30-31, 44-51.

679 "Sinking City." México, Mexican-American review, April-May 1948, p. 12-15.

680 Sutherland, M.
"Mexico's Booming Capital." National geographic magazine (100:6) December 1951, p. 785-825.

681 Sutton, H.
"Second City." Saturday review 47, March 7, 1964, p. 27-28.

Nicaragua

682 Curtis, William E.
"Managua, la Capital de Nicaragua." Guatemala, Anales de la Sociedad de Geografía e Historia de Guatemala (26:3-4), September-December 1952, p. 414-429.

683 Darío, R.
"No Hay Patria Pequeña." México, Centroamericana (1:2), April-June 1954, p. 57-58.

684 Quintana González, O.
"León de Nicaragua." León, Mercurio, July-December 1946, p. 26-27.

685 Solórzano Díaz, A.
"Managua Revisited." Américas (10:12), December 1958, p. 29-32.

Panama

686 Artel, J.
"Rambles in Panama City." Américas (12:1), January 1960, p. 36-39.

687 Bermúdez, R.J.
"Panama City Then and Now." Américas (8:7), July 1956, p. 18-22.

688 Winchester, J.H.
"Surprise Stopover: Panama." Travel 119, June 1963, p. 34-37.

Paraguay

689 Carter, D.S.
"Snapshots of Asunción." Américas 10, October 1958, p. 34-35.

690 McAdams, J.
"Guaraní Spoken Here." Américas 2, July 1950, p. 9-11.

691 Velasco, G. Granda Vásquez de
"Assunçao, a Capital do Paraguai." Sao Paulo, Engenharia municipal (2:4), December 1956, p. 41-43.

Peru

692 Bermejo, Vladimiro
"Arequipa: Historia, Geografía y Arquitectura." Lima, Boletín de la Sociedad Geográfica de Lima 70, 1st-2d quarter 1953, p. 6-23.

693 Bissell, R.
"Lima, I Love You, Oddly Enough." Holiday 35, June 1964, p. 46-55.

694 Cornejo Bouroncle, Jorge
"Arequipa." Cuzco, Revista universitaria (41:102), 1st quarter 1952, p. 57-81.

695 "Cusco." Lima, Hora del hombre (1:3), May-June 1950, p. 1-28.

696 Eddy, A.
"Cuzco, Machu Picchu and Urubamba." Lima, Peruvian times (17:841), February 1, 1957, p. 11-14.

697 Fernández del Castillo, Antonio
"Lima." México, Memoria de la Academia Nacional de Historia y Geografía (14:6), 1958, p. 33-35.

698 Gutiérrez Ferreira, Pedro P.
"Lima, Ciudad de los Reyes." Madrid, Cuadernos hispanoamericanos (41:121), January 1960, p. 83-95.

699 McCoun, G.K.
"Ayacucho, an old Peruvian City of the Andes." Lima, Peruvian times (16:831), November 23, 1956, p. 7.

700 Perl, S.
"Lima Today." Opera news 30, December 25, 1965, p. 13-15.

701 Romero, E.
"Quito y Cuzco, Ciudades Paralelas." Lima, Mar del sur (3:7), September-October 1949, p. 1-5.

702 Sánchez, Luis A.
"Retrato de Lima." La nueva democracia (39:3), July 1959, p. 76-80.

703 Tejada, C.
"Echoes of Lima." Américas 2, February 1950, p. 15-19.

704 Valle, E. del
"Cuatro Estampas del Callao." Lima, Pensamiento peruano, January 1948, p. 36-42.

705 Weaver, K.F.
"Five Worlds of Peru." National geographic magazine 125, February 1964, p. 212-266.

Surinam

706 Clark, Sydney A.
"Surprising Surinam." Travel 112, September 1959, p. 22-26.

707 McDowell, B., & M. McDowell
"Surprise-Laden Surinam." Travel 102, December 1954, p. 23-26.

Trinidad

708 Messinesi, D.
"Trinidad Pleasure." Vogue 145, January 15, 1965, p. 121.

709 Morris, J. A.
"They Go Carnival Crazy in Trinidad." Saturday evening post 225, June 6, 1953, p. 28-29.

Uruguay

710 Bracker, M.
"Gayest Spot South of the Border." Saturday evening post 223, November 11, 1950, p. 30-31.

711 Callorda, P. E.
"Montevideo." Bogotá, Revista de América (5:15), March 1946, p. 369-376.

712 Capurro, R.
"Paysandú Heróica y Cordial, Marcha Hacia el Futuro." Montevideo, Mundo uruguayo, July 31, 1947, p. 6-7.

713 Carrío, E.
"Paysandú: una Ciudad que Despierta." Buenos Aires, La chacra, September 1947, p. 58-59.

714 Potenze, J.
"Sentimental Journey Through Montevideo." Américas (11:9), September 1959, p. 30-34.

Venezuela

715 Alvarado, A. L.
"Barquisimeto, la Ciudad Panorámica." Caracas, Revista Shell (6:23), June 1957, p. 45-47.

716 Arraiz, A.
"Red Roofs and Skyscrapers." *UN world* (5:7), July 1951, p. 46-48.

717 "Asi es Caracas." Caracas, *El mes financiero y económico de Venezuela 1*, February 1950, p. 33-59.

718 "Barquisimeto." Caracas, *El agricultor venezolano*, August-September 1952, p. 11-45.

719 Corporación Venezolana de Fomento
"Maracaibo." Caracas, *Cuadernos de información económica* (6:2), March-April 1954, p. 11-27.

720 Corporación Venezolana de Fomento
"Valencia." Caracas, *Cuadernos de información económica* (6:1), January-February 1954, p. 19-34.

721 Díaz Sánchez, R.
"Sinfonía de Caracas." Caracas, *El farol* (15:150), February 1954, p. 18-27.

722 "Valencia, IV Centenario." Caracas, *Producción 104*, March 1955, p. 5-25.

West Indies and the Caribbean

723 "Caribbean, Ho!" *Life 42*, February 11, 1957, p. 24-33.

724 Folliard, E.T.
"Martinique, Caribbean Question Mark." *National geographic magazine*, January 1941, p. 47-55.

725 "Lands in the News." *UN world 7*, July 1953, p. 30-33.

726 Logan, Rayford W.
"A Caribbean Anomaly: Curaçao and Aruba." *Pan American* (11:6), November-December 1950, p. 21-24.

727 Thruelsen, W.
"Overlooked Islands." Saturday evening post 232, February 20, 1960, p. 26-29.

728 "West Indies Escape: Southern Islands of the Lesser Antilles." Life 36, January 11, 1954, p. 76-89.

PLANNING

(Planning here refers to all activities concerning architectural design and the physical profile and structure of the city. For items on economic planning, see Industrialization).

Books

General

729 Alomar Esteve, Gabriel
Comunidad planeada, principios de sociología aplicada al urbanismo y al planeamiento rural. Madrid, Instituto de Estudios de Administración Local, 1955, 229p.

730 Alomar Esteve, Gabriel
Teoría de la ciudad; ideas fundamentales para un urbanismo humanista. Madrid, Instituto de Estudios de Administración Local, 1947, 240p.

731 American Public Health Association. Committee on the Hygiene of Housing
Planning the neighborhood. Chicago, Public Administration Service, 1960, 94p.

732 Branch, Melville C.
Planning: aspects and applications. New York, Wiley, 1965, 269p.

733 Breese, Gerald W., & Dorothy E. Whiteman, eds.
An approach to urban planning. Princeton, Princeton University Press, 1953, 147p.

734 Caplow, Theodore, ed., et al
City planning; a selection of readings in its theory and practice. Minneapolis, Burgess, 1950, 226p.

735 Conference (2nd) on Urban Planning Information Systems & Programs, University of Pittsburgh, September 24-26, 1964. Urban information and policy decisions: selected papers. Pittsburgh, Institute of Local Government, University of Pittsburgh, 1965, 268p.

736 Davies, J.C.
Neighborhood groups and urban renewal. New York, Columbia University Press, 1966, 235p.

737 Gallion, A.B., & S. Eisner
The urban pattern. 2d ed. London, Van Nostrand, 1963, 433p.

738 García Ramos, Domingo
Iniciación al urbanismo. 1st ed. México, Escuela Nacional de Agricultura, Universidad Nacional Autónoma de Mexico, 1961, 304p.

739 Harth-Terré, Emilio
Filosofía en el urbanismo. Lima, Ed. Tierra y Arte, 1961, 142p.

740 Iglesias, Santiago
Planificando alrededor del mundo . . . Hato Rey, Impr. Real Hnos., 1960, 192p.

741 International Federation for Housing & Planning
International glossary of technical terms used in housing and town planning. 2d rev. & enl. ed. . . Amsterdam, 1951, 144p.

742 International Federation for Housing & Planning
News sheet # 57. The Hague, December, 1960- .

743 Joint Center for Urban Studies
The effectiveness of urban planning. Washington, G.P.O., 1964, 209p.

744 Johnson-Marshall, Percy E.A.
Rebuilding cities. Chicago, Aldine Press, 1966, 374p.

745 Journal of the Town Planning Institute. Newcastle, University of Newcastle (52:2-5), February-May, 1966- .

746 Klaasen, L.H.
Area economic and social redevelopment. London, H.M.S.O., 1965, 113p.

747 Labovitch, Peter C.
Strategies for shaping model cities. Cambridge, A.D. Little, Inc., 1967, 60p.

748 Lavedan, Pierre
Géographie des villes. Paris, Gallimard, 1959, 341p.

749 Lopez Otero, M., et al
Estudios de urbanismo. Zaragoza, Institución "Fernando el Católico," 1960, 288p.

750 Melvin, Ernest E.
Community self assistance; monograph # 7. Athens, Institute of Community & Area Development, University of Georgia, 1963, 5p.

751 Mumford, Lewis
From the ground up; observations on contemporary architecture, housing, highway building, and civic design. New York, Harcourt, Brace, 1956, 243p.

752 Pastor, José M. F.
Urbanismo con planeamiento; principios de una nueva técnica social. Buenos Aires, Ed. Arte y Técnica, 1947, 419p.

753 Paulsson, Gregor
The study of cities; notes about the hermeneutics of urban space. Copenhagen, Munksgaard, 1959, 92p.

754 Plan. Toronto (VI:2), December 1965- .

755 Problems and prospects of community planning in the urban age . . . Ed. by Kenneth Kraemer. Los Angeles, Center for Training & Career Development, University of Southern California, 1967, 164p.

756 Ragon, M.
Les cités de l'avenir. Paris, Eds. Planète, 1966, 250p.

757 Tommasi López, Leopoldo
La ciudad de ayer, de hoy y de mañana. México, Ed. Cultura, 1951, 338p.

758 United Nations
Report of the United Nations Symposium on the Planning and Development of New Towns, Moscow, USSR, 24 August-7 September 1964. New York, 1966, 48p.

759 U.S. Housing & Home Finance Agency. Office of International Housing
Bibliography on housing, building and planning: for use of overseas missions of the U.S. Agency for International Development. Washington, 1964, 52p.

760 Uribe Uribe, Leonardo
Historia del urbanismo y técnicas de planificación. Medellín, Universidad Pontificia Bolivariana, 1962, 223p.

761 Webber, M.M., et al
Explorations into urban structure. Philadelphia, University of Pennsylvania Press, 1964, 264p.

762 Webster, D.H.
Urban planning and municipal policy. New York, Harper & Row, 1958, 572p.

763 Whiffen, Marcus, ed.
The architect and the city; papers from the A.I.A.-A.C.S.A. Teacher Seminar, Cranbrook Academy of Art, June 11-22, 1962. Cambridge, M.I.T. Press, 1965, 301p.

764 Wilson, James Q.
Urban renewal: the record and the controversy. Cambridge, M.I.T. Press, 1966, 197p.

Latin America

765 Boltshauser, João
Noções de evolução urbana nas Américas. 3v. Belo Horizonte, Eds. Escola de Arquitetura, 1959-61.

766 Instituto de Estudios de Administración Local. Seminario de Urbanismo
Planos de ciudades iberoamericanas y filipinas existentes en el Archivo de Indias . . . Madrid, 1951- .

767 Mantilla Bazo, Víctor
Vivienda y planeamiento en América Latina; bibliografía preliminar. Washington, División de Vivienda y Planeamiento, Depto. de Asuntos Económicos y Sociales, Unión Panamericana, 1952, 112p.

768 Mora, Santiago E. de la
Planeamiento vs. arquitectura. Bogotá, Ed. Iqueima, 1952, 140p.

769 Morse, Richard M.
Latin American cities, aspects of function and structure. (In Friedmann, John, & William Alonso, eds. Regional development and planning. Cambridge, 1964, p. 361-381.)

770 Pan American Union. Division of Labor & Social Affairs.
Informe final, seminarios regionales de asuntos sociales: vivienda y urbanismo . . . Washington, 1952, 140p.

771 Schneider, Wolf
De Babilonia a Brasilia; las ciudades y sus hombres. Tr. by Juan Godó Costa. Barcelona, Ed. Noguer, 1961, 526p.

772 Seminario de Técnicos y Funcionarios en Planeamiento Urbano, Bogotá, 1958
Tema III; El plan general urbano como instrumento básico para guiar el desarrollo urbano. Bogotá, CINVA, 1958, 34p.

773 Sociedad Interamericana de Planificación
Revista. # 1- , Cali, 1967- .

774 Violich, Francis, & Carlos Bernal Salinas
Bibliography on landscape architecture in relation to urban planning in Latin America. Eugene, Council of Planning Librarians, 1964, 18p.

775 Violich, Francis, & Juan B. Astica
Community development and the urban planning process in Latin America. Los Angeles, Latin American Center, University of California, 1966, 115p.

776 Violich, Francis
Problems and techniques of land use control in Latin American cities. 2v. in 1. Berkeley, University of California, 1958?

777 Wilhelmy, Herbert
Südamerika im spiegel seiner städte. Hamburg, Kommissions-Verlag Cram, DeGruyter, 1952, 450p.

Argentina

778 Calcaprina, Gino
Planificación regional; enfoque de un plan para la vida del noreste argentino. Tucumán, Instituto de Arquitectura y Urbanismo, Universidad Nacional de Tucumán, 1950, 89p.

779 Calcaprina, Gino, & Enrique Tedeschi
Urbanismo con legislación; el problema legislativo de la planificación urbana y rural. Tucumán, Instituto de Arquitectura y Urbanismo, Universidad Nacional de Tucumán, 1950, 91p.

780 Greca, Alcides
Problemas del urbanismo en la República Argentina. Santa Fé, Impr. de la Universidad Nacional del Litoral, 1939, 213p.

781 Klein, A.
Urbanismo; código nacional y legislación provincial para la promoción del planeamiento regulador de los poblados argentinos. Buenos Aires, 1956, 73p.

782 Pastor, José M.F., & José Bonilla
Estudio sobre uso de la tierra. Buenos Aires, Instituto de Planeamiento Regional y Urbano, 1958, 273p.

783 Universidad Nacional del Nordeste. Instituto de Vivienda y Planeamiento
Instituto de Vivienda y Planeamiento, Universidad Nacional del Nordeste; medio social, enseñanza, investigación. Resistencia, 1957, 29p.

Bolivia

784 Avis S., Julio A. d'
Propiedad, expropriación y plusvalia. Cochabamba, Impr. Universitaria, 1952, 50p.

Brazil

785 Almeida, Theodoro Figueira de
Brasília, a cidade histórica da América. Rio de Janeiro, Depto. de Impr. Nacional, 1960, 72p.

786 Azevedo, Aroldo de, et al
A cidade de São Paulo, estudos de geografía urbana. 4v. São Paulo, Cía. Ed. Nacional, 1958.

787 Baltar, Antonio Bezerra
Diretrizes de um plano regional para o Recife. Tese de concurso para o provimento da cadeira de urbanismo e arquitetura paisagística na Escola de Belas Artes da Universidade do Recife. Recife, 1951, 156p.

788 Brasilia: história, urbanismo, arquitetura, construção/ History, city planning, architecture, building. 2d ed. São Paulo, Acropole, 1960, 132p.

789 Caldas, Ney Ulrich
A conjuntura nacional e os problemas do Rio Grande do Sul; necesidade do planejamento regional. Pôrto Alegre, Dist. exclusiva: Livraria Sulina, 1963, 118p.

790 Carmin, Robert L.
Anápolis, Brazil: regional capital of an agricultural frontier; research paper # 35. Chicago, Dept. of Geography, University of Chicago, 1953, 172p.

791 Magalhães, Aloisio, & Eugene Feldman
Doorway to Brasilia. Philadelphia, Falcon Press; distributed by G. Wittenborn, New York, 1959, variously paged.

792 Robock, Stefan H.
Brazil's developing northeast; a study of regional planning and foreign aid. Washington, Brookings Institution, 1963, 213p.

793 Santos, Milton
O centro da cidade do Salvador; estudo de geografia urbana. Salvador, Universidade da Bahia, 1959, 196p.

794 Santos, Milton
A cidade como centro de regiao; definiçoes e métodos de avaliaçao da centralidade. Bahia, Laboratorio de Geomorfologia e Estudos Regionais, Universidade da Bahia, 1959, 28p.

795 Sao Paulo, Brazil (City) Depto. de Urbanismo
O Dia do Urbanismo, 8 de Novembro de 1950. Ademar de Barros, et al. Sao Paulo, 1950, 69p.

796 Staubli, Willy
Brasilia. New York, Universe Brooks, 1966, 199p.

797 Szilard, Adalbert, & José de Oliveira Reis
Urbanismo no Rio de Janeiro. Rio de Janeiro, Ed. "O Constructor," 1950, 157p.

Chile

798 Valdés Valdés, I.
La transformación de Santiago. Santiago, Lit. Barcelona, 1917, 68p.

Colombia

799 Inter-American Housing & Planning Center
Estudios para la rehabilitación del barrio inglés, en la ciudad de Bogotá. Bogotá, 1952, 76p.

800 Medellín, Colombia. Oficina del Plan Regulador
Informe. Medellín, 1958, 58p.

801 Reunión Nacional de Oficinas de Planes Reguladores
Informe final. Bogotá, 1958- .

Ecuador

802 Paz y Miño, Luis T.
Apuntaciones para una geografía urbana de Quito. México, Instituto Panamericano de Geografía e Historia, 1960, 73p.

El Salvador

803 Sumner, Harold A.
Urbanismo, funciones, organización; estudio. San Salvador, Publicaciones del Ministerio de Obras Públicas, 1953, 43p.

Guatemala

804 Rodríguez O., José
Ciudad y zonificación. Guatemala, 1950, 39p.

Jamaica

805 Clarke, Colin G.
Problemas de planeación urbana en Kingston Jamaica. (In International Geographical Union. Proceedings of the First Latin American Regional Conference, Mexico City, August 2-8, 1966. v. 1. Mexico, 1966, p. 411-431.)

Mexico

806 Espacios (periodical)
Reorganización funcional física; la construcción del gran Centro Urbanístico de la Secretaría de Comunicaciones. México, 1955, unpaged.

807 Gándara Mendieta, Manuel
De la administración municipal. Urbanismo. México, 1953, 172p.

808 Instituto de Estudios Sociales de Monterrey, A. C.
Apuntes para el plan regulador de la ciudad de Monterrey. Monterrey, 1950, 34p.

809 Instituto Nacional de la Vivienda
Tacubaya, problemas y soluciones. México, 1958, 23p.

810 Mexico (City) Universidad Nacional. Escuela Nacional de Arquitectura
Arquitectura y urbanismo en México. México, Dirección General de Publicaciones, Universidad Nacional Autónoma de México, 1961, 87p.

811 México. Dirección General de Pensiones Civiles de Retiro
Centro Urbano Presidente Aleman. México, 1949, 133p.

812 Stanislawski, Dan
The anatomy of eleven towns in Mexico. Austin, University of Texas Press, 1950, 77p.

813 Tata, Robert
El uso de los análises sobre el potencial de espacio localizado para el establecimiento de la industrialización mexicana. (In International Geographical Union. Proceedings of the First Latin American Regional Conference, Mexico City, August 2-8, 1966. v. 2. Mexico, 1966, p. 625-646.)

Nicaragua

814 Nicaragua. Oficina Nacional de Urbanismo
Planificación urbana; apuntes gráficos del proceso. Managua, Ed. Los Angeles, 1959, 109p.

Panama

815 Rubio y Muñoz-Bocanegra, Angel
Geografía y planificación regional; conferencia dictada en la Universidad de Panamá el día 19 de diciembre de 1952 en el programa de extensión cultural "Viernes Universitarios." Panamá, 1953, 51p.

Peru

816 Harth-Terré, Emilio
Apuntaciones a un plan orgánico para la ciudad de Lima. Contribución al VI Congreso Panamericano de Arquitectos. Lima, 1947, 20p.

817 Perú. Oficinal Nacional de Planeamiento y Urbanismo
Lima metropolitana. Algunos aspectos de su expediente urbano y soluciones parciales varias. Lima, 1954, 35p.

818 Perú. Oficina Nacional de Planeamiento y Urbanismo
Memoria. Lima, 1959- .

Surinam

819 Surinam-American Technical Cooperative Service
Final report. Paramaribo, 1965? 43, 14p.

Uruguay

820 Abella Trías, Julio C.
Montevideo; la ciudad en que vivimos; su desarrollo, su evolución y sus planes. Montevideo, Ed. Alfa, 1960, 334p.

821 Arroyo Mendoza, José P.
La ciudad del mañana . . . Montevideo, 1964, 62p.

Venezuela

822 Aragón, Victor
Lo mejor del urbanismo y de la moderna arquitectura en Caracas. The best in city planning and modern architecture in Caracas . . . Caracas? Mendoza & Mendoza, 1957, unpaged.

823 Friedmann, John R.
Regional development policy: a case study of Venezuela. Cambridge, M.I.T. Press, 1966, 279p.

824 General Drafting Company, Inc.
Mapa de la República de Venezuela, con planos de Barcelona, Barquisimeto, Ciudad Bolívar, Maracaibo, Maracay, Puerto Cabello, Puerto La Cruz, San Cristobal, Valencia. Caracas, Creole Petroleum Corp., 1956, 1p.

825 Rodwin, Lloyd
Ciudad Guayana, a new city. (In Scientific American, periodical. Cities. Ed. by Dennis Flanagan. New York, Knopf, 1965, p. 88-104.)

826 Venezuela. Ministerio de Obras Públicas. Comité de Remodelación de Barrios
Programa preliminar para la remodelación de barrios, área metropolitana de Caracas. Caracas, 1963, 39p.

827 Villanueva, Carlos R.
La Caracas de ayer y de hoy, su arquitectura colonial y la reurbanización de "El Silencio . . ." Paris, 1950, 87p.

West Indies and the Caribbean

828 Caribbean Commission. Central Secretariat
Town and country development planning in the Caribbean: selected from the documentation and report of the Conference on Town and Country Development Planning in the Caribbean, Trinidad, November 14-23, 1956. Hato Rey, Puerto Rico, 1958, 217p.

Periodical Articles

General

829 Aleshire, R. A.
"The Metropolitan Desk; a New Technique in Program Teamwork." Public administration review (26:2), June 1966, p. 87-95.

830 Anhaia Mello, Luis de
"A Cidade Cellular." Sao Paulo, Boletím do Instito de Engenharia, September 1933, p. 131-142.

831 Bardet, Gaston
"Los Grandes Problemas del Urbanismo." Havana, Arquitectura, July 1946, p. 215-220.

832 Branch, Melville C.
"Simulation, Mathematical Models, and Comprehensive City Planning." Urban affairs quarterly (I:3), March 1966, p. 15-38.

833 Burotto, M. C., & G. Geisse G.
"Dos Juicios sobre la Planificación Urbana y Regional en Estados Unidos de Norteamérica." Santiago, Planificación 2, December 1965, p. 25-36.

834 Carrasco, Lorenzo
"Los Métodos y las Técnicas de la Planificación." México, Revista de economía (25:9), September 1962, p. 327-338.

835 Dyckman, J.W.
"The Scientific World of City Planners." American behavioral scientist (VI:6), February 1963, p. 40-45.

836 Fagin, Henry
"Planning for Future Urban Growth." Law & contemporary problems 30, Winter 1965, p. 9-25.

837 Harth-Terré, Emilio
"Filosofía en el Urbanismo." Lima, El arquitecto peruano 279-299, April-June 1962, p. 7-11.

838 Hufschmidt, M.
"Environmental Planning." American behavioral scientist (10:1), September 1966, p. 6-8.

839 Kallen, H.M.
"City Planning and the Idea of the City: Considerations Especially About New York." Social Research (23:2), Summer 1956, p. 186-198.

840 Lorca F., F.
"La Planificación del Desarrollo y el Problema Metropolitano." Santiago, Economía (20:75-76), 2nd-3rd quarter 1962, p. 45-54.

841 McKinley, H.
"Metropolitan Planning for the Small City." Public management 40, June 1958, p. 130-133.

842 Meyerson, Martin
"El Futuro de la Planificación." Buenos Aires, Nuestra arquitectura 386, January 1962, p. 45-46.

843 Pomeroy, H.R.
"Trends and Forecasts Affecting Cities in Planning." Public management 33, October 1951, p. 223-226.

844 Rebora, L.A.
"La Ciudad en el Planeamiento Regional." Córdoba, Revista de la Universidad Nacional de Córdoba (4:3-4), July-October 1963, p. 605-627.

845 Rose, A.
"Coordination in Physical and Social Planning in a Metropolitan Area." Social service review 32, December 1958, p. 374-386.

846 Trebbi del Trevigiano, R.
"Urbs y Civitas, Estética Urbana vs. Planificación." Santiago, Planificación 3, June 1966, p. 63-70.

847 Vigier, F.C.
"An Experimental Approach to Urban Design." Journal of the American Institute of Planners 31, February 1965, p. 21-31.

848 Violich, Francis
"El Planeamiento Urbano en Relación a las Tendencias del Crecimiento Urbano." Havana, Arquitectura, (25:283), January 1957, p. 46-48.

849 Violich, Francis
"El Proceso de la Planificación." Caracas, Hombre y expresión 3, January 1957, p. 49-55.

850 Winsborough, H.H.
"Social Consequences of High Population Density." Law & contemporary problems 30, Winter 1965, p. 120-126.

Latin America

851 Bens Arrarte, José M.
"Inicio de Urbanismo Colonial en Hispanoamérica: Comentarios a las Leyes de Indias en lo Referente a la Fundación de Ciudades." San Juan, Boletin # 3, Union Interamericana del Caribe, 1942, p. 79-102.

852 Carlson, E.
"La Renovación Urbana y los Servicios Públicos en América Latina. Los Casos de Cali, Bogotá y Maracaibo." New York, Servicios públicos (7:1), January/February 1960, p. 38-44.

853 Gaines, Frank S.
"La Planificación Urbana en las Américas." Havana, Arquitectura, March 1946, p. 93-98.

854 García Ramos, Domingo
"Urbanismo." México, Arquitectura México (20:83), September 1963, p. 279-282.

855 Journaux, A.
"Problèmes du Site et l'Extension à Caracas, Bogota, Quito." Paris, Information géographique (24:2), March-April 1960, p. 47-55.

856 Maia, A. Prestes
"Bibliografia de Planejamento . . ." Rio de Janeiro, Revista de administração municipal (9:52), May-June 1962, p. 257-268.

857 Solow, Anatole A.
"Urban Development in Latin America." New York, American city, July 1948, p. 78-79.

858 Stanislawski, Dan
"Early Spanish Town Planning in the New World." Geographical review 1947, p. 95-105.

859 Torre Revello, J.
"Tratados de Arquitectura Utilizados en Hispanoamérica: Siglos XVI a XVIII." Revista interamericana de bibliografía (6:1), January-March 1956, p. 3-23.

860 Violich, Francis
"Control del Uso de Tierras en Ciudades de América Latina: Problemas y Técnicas." Buenos Aires, Nuestra arquitectura (8:358), September 1959, p. 41-44.

861 Violich, Francis
"A Cuatrocientos Años de la Planificación Urbana de los Incas." Buenos Aires, Ingeniería, February 1944, p. 84-91.

862 Violich, Francis
"Visitando Nuevamente las Ciudades de la América Latina." Lima, El arquitecto peruano (20:243-244), October/November 1957, p. 33-34.

Argentina

863 Ahumada, José M.
"Plan Regional de la Ciudad de Buenos Aires." Buenos Aires, Boletín Honorable Consejo Deliberante, January-May 1942, p. 7-28.

864 Frías, P. J.
"Algo por Hacer: la Ciudad Argentina." Buenos Aires, Criterio 35, April 26, 1962, p. 286-287.

865 Palacio, Eudosio de J.
"Cuarto Centenario de Santiago del Estero, 1550-1950." Córdoba, Revista de la Universidad Nacional de Córdoba (37:5), November/December 1950, p. 1287-1351.

866 Pastor, José M. F.
"Ejecución de Planes Reguladores en Argentina." Córdoba, Revista de la Universidad Nacional de Córdoba (4:3-4), July-October 1963, p. 629-660.

867 Sarrailh, E. J.
"Esquema de Organización Intermunicipal entre la Comuna de Buenos Aires y Sus Municipios Limítrofes, para Crear una Misma Area de Planeamiento." Havana, Revista Municipal Interamericana (9:3/4), January/June 1959, p. 12-16.

868 Torre Revello, J.
"Un Proyecto del Gobernador Bucareli para Embellecer a Buenos Aires." Buenos Aires, Boletín del Instituto de Investigaciones Históricas, July-December 1931, p. 40-75.

869 Villanueva, Guillermo A.
"Plan Financiero para la Reedificación de San Juan." Buenos Aires, Ingeniería, April 1944, p. 228-234.

Bolivia

870 Anaya A., Franklin
"Estudio de la Planificación Territorial y Urbana de Bolivia." La Paz, Khana (3:11/12), October 1955, p. 147-165.

871 Hawthorn, H. B., & A. E. Hawthorn
"The Shape of a City: Some Observations on Sucre, Bolivia." Sociology & social research 33, 1948, p. 87-91.

Brazil

872 Almeida, Paulo de Camargo
"Projeto de Remembramento do Centro do Distrito Federal, em Relação ao Novo Traçado dos Terrenos Conquistados com o Futuro Desmonte do Morro de Santo Antônio." Rio de Janeiro, Revista municipal do engenharia, March 1939, p. 141-152.

873 Azevedo, Washington
"A Organisação Technica dos Municipios. Parecer quanto à Organização da Divisão dos Negocios Municipaes." São Paulo, Boletim do Instituto de engenharia, July 1934, p. 13-38.

874 Baltar, A. Bezerra
"Planos Diretores para as Cidades Pequenas e Médias do Brasil." Rio de Janeiro, Revista de administração municipal (13:46), February-March 1963, p. 32-47.

875 "Brasilia, Síntese Histórica." Rio de Janeiro, Revista brasileira dos municipios (10:39-40), July-December 1957, p. 205-210.

876 "Brazil Builds a New City: Cidade dos Motores." Progressive architecture, September 1946, p. 52-73.

877 Carvalho, A.
"Salvador e a Organização do seu Espaço Imediato." Salvador, Boletim baiano de geografia 5-6, 1961, p. 37-46.

878 Correia Lima, V. Ferrer, & T. de Vilanova Monteiro Lopes
"A Companhia Urbanizadora da Nova Capital do Brasil; Recursos, Organização e Funcionamento." Rio de Janeiro, Revista do serviço público (83:2), May 1959, p. 136-140.

879 Correia Lima, V. Ferrer, & T. de Vilanova Monteiro Lopes
"Fundamentos Históricos, Sociais e Econômicos da Construção de Brasilia." Rio de Janeiro, Revista do serviço público (82:1-3), January-March 1959, p. 6-10.

880 Costa, V. Ribeiro da
"Brasilia, Marco para Conquista do Oeste." Rio de Janeiro, Revista do serviço público (80:3), September 1958, p. 201-209.

881 Ferreira, João da Costa
"A Cidade do Rio de Janeiro e Seu Termo; Ensaio Urbanológico." Rio de Janeiro, Revista do Instituto Histórico e Geográfico Brasileiro (164:2), 1933, p. 7-354.

882 Freyre, Gilberto
"A Brazilian's Critique of Brasília." Rio de Janeiro, Brazilian business (40:4), April 1960, p. 64-66.

883 Garcia, Heitor J. Eiras
"Urbanização de São José do Rio Preto." São Paulo, Engenharia municipal (2:4), December 1956, p. 16-21.

884 Kelley, Wilfrid D.
"Settlement of the Middle Rio Grande Valley." The journal of geography (54:8), November 1955, p. 387-399.

885 Kelly, Prado
"Integração da Cidade e do Estado do Rio de Janeiro." Rio de Janeiro, Síntese política, economica, social (1:4), October/December 1959, p. 11-26.

886 Lacerda, Carlos
"City-Planning of Rio de Janeiro." Rio de Janeiro, Brazilian-American survey (10:20), 1963, p. 22-25.

887 Lima, Lauro de Oliveira
"Plano Urbanístico de Fortaleza." Rio de Janeiro, Revista de Administração municipal (10:56), January-February 1963, p. 3-6.

888 Mendes, H. Nobrê
"Plano de Expansão da Cidade do Rio de Janeiro, a sua Ligação à Niterói e a Criação de uma Cidade Satélite." Rio de Janeiro, Revista do Clube de Engenharia (22:161), January 1950, p. 11-17.

889 Niemeyer, Oscar
"Minha Experiencia de Brasilia." Rio de Janeiro, Módulo (2:12), February 1959, p. 17-19.

890 Passos, Edison
"Plano de Melhoramentos da Cidade do Rio de Janeiro." Rio de Janeiro, Revista municipal de engenharia, July 1941, p. 212-223.

891 Peçanha, Celso
"Uma Experiência Fluminense de Administração Planificada; Recuperação e Desenvolvimento do Municipio de Río Bonito." Rio de Janeiro, Revista do serviço público (87:1-2), April-May 1960, p. 61-91.

892 Queiroz, M. Vinhas de
"Arquitetura e Desenvolvimento." Brasilia, Revista do Instituto de Ciencias Sociais da Universidade do Brasil (1:1), January-June 1962, p. 71-198.

893 Reis, José de Oliveira
"Métodos para Integrar nos Planos Regionais as Necesidades Urbanas." Rio de Janeiro, Revista brasileira dos municipios (15:57), January-June 1962, p. 16-23.

894 Ribeiro, J.O. Saboja
"Urbanização da Esplanada de Santo Domingo." Rio de Janeiro, Revista municipal de engenharia, 1944, p. 9-16.

895 Ribeiro, P. Leite
"An inconsistent City Planning: New State of Guanabara's Major Problem." Rio de Janeiro, Brazilian-American survey (8:15), 1961, p. 30-32.

896 Saia, L.
"Notas para a Teorizaçao de Sao Paulo." Paris, Acrópole XXV, June 1963, p. 209-221.

897 Snyder, David E.
"Alternate Perspectives on Brasilia." Economic geography 40, January 1964, p. 34-45.

898 Torres, Matio H.G.
"Planning Progress in Brazil." Journal of the American Institute of Planners, Summer-Fall 1947, p. 14-18.

899 Vannier, Stephane
"Urbanismo no Estado de Rio." Rio de Janeiro, Revista do Clube de Engenharia, August 1945, p. 46-50.

900 Wiener, Paul L.
"Cidade dos Motores, Brasil." Buenos Aires, Revista de arquitectura, October 1946, p. 38-409.

Chile

901 Alzamora K., P.
"Pueden los Gobiernos Municipales Planificar el Desarrollo de Sus Comunas?" Santiago, Planificación 3, June 1966, p. 93-106.

902 Antolin López, M.
"Comentarios sobre Aspectos Metodológicos de la Planificación Regional." Santiago, Planificación 1, December 1965, p. 37-48.

903 Guarda Gewitz, Fernando
"El Urbanismo Imperial y las Primitivas Ciudades de Chile." Santiago, Finis terrae (4:15), 3rd quarter, 1957, p. 48-64.

904 Mardones, Francisco
"Plano Regulador de Santiago." Santiago, Boletín municipal, October 1934, p. 25-39.

905 Martínez, R., & J. de Fierro
"Santiago: un Análisis Visual." Santiago, Planificación 3, June 1966, p. 35-50.

906 Muñoz Maluchka, Luis
"Manual de Urbanismo. Para Uso de los Alcaldes y Directores de Obras Municipales." Santiago, Boletín Municipal de la República, July 1933, p. 21-25.

907 "Primer Congreso Chileno de Urbanismo." Pan American Union bulletin 72, September 1938, p. 536-545.

908 Urbina V., R.
"Hacia una Superior Enseñanza de la Planificación Urbana y Regional en Chile." Santiago, Planificación 1, October 1964, p. 71-94.

909 Violich, Francis
"Crecimiento y Planeamiento Urbanos en Chile." New York, Servicios públicos (5:5), September/October 1959, p. 52-62.

Colombia

910 Martínez, Carlos
"Las Mejores Urbanizaciones Están en el Centro de Bogotá." Bogotá, El mes financiero y económico, August 1945, p. 143-146.

911 Moreno Clavijo, Jorge
"Bogotá Se Va a Transformar el Plan Soto-Bateman." Bogotá, Cromos, August 1944, p. 8-9, 60-62.

912 "Reconstrucción de Bogotá. Primera Etapa: Remodelación del Sector Central, Plano Piloto, Reparcelaciones." Bogotá, Proa, June 1946, p. 11-17.

913 Ruiz, J.M.
"'Ciudades Nuevas' También para Colombia." Medellín, Ciencias económicas (6:18), November 1962, p. 470-474.

914 Violich, Francis
"Organización para el Planeamiento Regional y Fomento Urbano en Colombia." New York, Servicios públicos (7:3), May/June 1960, p. 56-57.

Cuba

915 Dyer, D. R.
"Urbanism in Cuba." Geographical review (47:2), 1957, p. 224-233.

916 Harth-Terré, Emilio
"Nuestra Ciudad de Ayer y de Mañana." Havana, Arquitectura, July 1946, p. 211-214

Dominican Republic

917 Dominican Republic. Laws, statutes, etc.
"By an Executive Decree, a Commission for the Development and Embellishment of the City of Santo Domingo Has Been Created." Pan American Union bulletin 63, January 1929, p. 86.

918 Dominican Republic. Laws, statutes, etc.
"Ley No. 1558 que Amplia el Artículo 34 de la Ley sobre Urbanización, Ornato Público y Construcciones. [October 30, 1947]". Ciudad Trujillo, Gaceta oficial, November 5, 1947, p. 7-9.

919 Dominican Republic. Laws, statutes, etc.
"Ley No. 1874, que Amplia el Artículo 38 de la Ley sobre Urbanización, Ornato Público y Construcciones. [December 14, 1948]". Ciudad Trujillo, Gaceta oficial (70:6881), January 8, 1949, p. 7-8.

920 Dominican Republic. Laws, statutes, etc.
"Ley No. 4045, que Modifica el Párrafo III Agregado por la Ley No. 3027 al Artículo 16 de la Ley sobre Urbanización, Ornato Público y Construcciones. [February 3, 1955]". Ciudad Trujillo, Gaceta oficial, February 12, 1955, p. 10-11.

El Salvador

921 El Salvador. Laws, statutes, etc.
"Declárase de Utilidad Pública y Necesidad Urgente la Fundación de una Ciudad Comprendida entre las Siguientes Coordenadas Geodésicas Basadas en el Datum Centroamericano de Ocotepeque . . ." San Salvador, Diario oficial, June 6, 1951, p. 3462-3463.

922 "Un Gran Proyecto de Urbanización. Plano Regulador de San Salvador. Anteproyecto del Centro del Gobierno." San Salvador, Boletín de fomento y obras públicas (1:1), October/December 1952, p. 30-35.

Guatemala

923 Guatemala. Laws, statutes, etc.
"Ley Preliminar de Urbanismo. Decreto Número 583." Guatemala, El Guatemalteco, February 29, 1956, p. 821-822.

924 Guatemala. Laws, statutes, etc.
"Reglamento para la Adquisición de las Tierras Ubicadas en el Area del Puerto Matías de Galvez (Santo Tomás), Su Indemnización y Bases para Su Explotación." Guatemala, El Guatemalteco (159:61), August 1, 1960, p. 761-763.

925 Peraza Sarausa, Fermín
"La Segunda Reunión Continental del Instituto Interamericano de Historia Municipal e Institucional (Guatemala)." México, Revista de historia de América, December 1946, p. 428-430.

Mexico

926 Carrasco, Lorenzo
"Proposiciones Urbanísticas para la Ciudad de Cuernavaca." México, Revista de economía (27:4), April 1964, p. 96-106; (27:5), May 1964, p. 148-154; (27:6), June 1964, p. 172-184.

927 Dotson, Floyd
"Urban Centralization and Decentralization in Mexico." Rural sociology (21:1), March 1956, p. 41-49.

928 Kubler, George A.
"Mexican Urbanism in the 16th Century." Art bulletin 24, 1942, p. 160-171.

929 Lazo, Carlos
"Planificación de Tampico." México, Espacios 11/12, October 1952, p. 87-110.

930 Nelson, H.J.
"Townscapes of Mexico: an Example of the Regional Variation of Townscapes." Economic geography 39, January 1963, p. 74-83.

931 Pani, M., & García Ramos, Domingo
"Plano Regulador de la H. Ciudad de Matamoros, Tamaulipas, México." México, Arquitectura México (16:70), June 1960, p. 62-82.

932 Pozas Arciniega, Ricardo
"Los Problemas Sociales en el Proceso Urbanístico de Ciudad Sahagún." México, Ciencias políticas y sociales (4:13), July-September 1958, p. 227-270.

933 Ramírez Vazquez, Pedro
"Urbanismo y Planificación en México." México, Cuadernos de bellas artes (4:10), October 1963, p. i-xi.

934 Rangel Coutu, H.
"La Socioplaneación Urbana en México." México, Estudios sociológicos, 1956, p. 303-320.

935 Rodríguez Sala, M. L.
La Regionalización de México." México, Revista mexicana de sociología (22:1), January-April 1960, p. 231-248.

936 Santacruz, Armando
"Planificación de Nuevo Laredo, Tamps." México, Revista de ingeniería, June 1939, p. 3-12.

Nicaragua

937 Nicaragua. Laws, statutes, etc.
"Ley de Urbanizaciones. Decreto No. 34-D." Managua, La Gaceta (60:70), March 23, 1956, p. 755-756.

Panama

938 Bermudez, R. J.
"La Ciudad de Panamá y los Fundamentos de su Planificación Futura." Panamá, Universidad Panamá 28, 2nd semester 1949, p. 103-118.

Paraguay

939 Albornoz, Miguel
"Town Planning in the Jungle." United Nations review (5:3), September 1958, p. 34-36.

Peru

940 Boza Ezeta, Salvador
"Problemas Técnicos y Legales de Urbanismo en el Perú." Lima, Informaciones y memorias de la Sociedad de Ingeniería del Perú (50:1), January 1949, p. 7-10.

941 Cole, John P.
"Some Town Planning Problems of Greater Lima." Liverpool, The town planning review (26:4), January 1956, p. 243-251.

942 Harth-Terré, E.
"Realidad Urbana del Perú." Lima, Economista peruano (40:98), April-July 1949, p. 776-783.

943 Ortiz de Zevallos, Luis
"La Creación Urbana en el Perú." Lima, El arquitecto peruano (20:237/239), April/June 1957, p. 17-27.

944 "El Plan Piloto de Lima." Lima, Arquitecto peruano, January/February 1950, p. 4-32.

945 Williams, Norman
"Peru Tackles Planned Urban Decentralization." The American city, September 1948, p. 98.

Uruguay

946 Jiménez, Asdrubal
"El Instituto de Urbanismo de la E. de Arquitectura Marca la Ruta para Embellecer Nuestro País." Montevideo, Mundo uruguayo, September 25, 1947, p. 4-5, 59.

947 Kirkpatrick, Malcolm
"A Landscape Architect Looks at Montevideo." Pan American Union bulletin 72, June 1938, p. 317-322.

948 Pan American Commission on Intermunicipal Cooperation
"La Ensenanza de la Urbanística en el Uruguay." Havana, Revista municipal interamericana (1:3/4), January/June 1951, p. 8-9.

Venezuela

949 Aristeguieta, Raimundo
"Ciudad Industrial." Caracas, Revista del Colegio de Ingenieros de Venezuela, April/June 1946, p. 68.

950 Armas Chitty, J.A. de
"Aventura de la Aldea Venezolana." Caracas, Revista Shell (1:3), June 1952, p. 49-51.

951 Sánchez Carillo, Jesús M.
"Mirando hacia el Futuro; la Reurbanización 'El Silencio' en la Capital de Venezuela." Lima, Pensamiento peruano, September-October 1946, p. 26-29.

952 Violich, Francis
"Caracas--Building for the Future." London, The South American journal (151:5), January 1952, p. 16-17.

953 Violich, Francis
"Crecimiento y Planeamiento Urbanos en Venezuela." New York, Servicios públicos (7:1), January/February 1960, p. 18-25.

954 Walker, D.
"City Astir." Travel 101, April 1954, p. 11-13.

955 Wright, H.
"$300,000,000 Avenida Bolivar Under Way." American city 67, July 1952, p. 124-125.

RECREATION
(including facilities)

Books

General

956 American Association for Health, Physical Education and Recreation
Completed research in health, physical education and recreation, including international sources, 1966. Ed. by A. W. Hubbard & R. A. Weiss. Washington, 1966, 158p.

957 American Association for Health, Physical Education & Recreation
Planning areas and facilities for health, physical education and recreation. Washington, 1966, 127p.

958 American Association for Health, Physical Education and Recreation
Research methods in health, physical education and recreation. 2d ed. Washington, 1959, 536p.

959 Butler, George D.
Introduction to community recreation. 3d ed. New York, McGraw-Hill, 1959, 577p.

960 Hjelte, George, & Jay S. Shivers
Public administration of park and recreational services. New York, Macmillan, 1963, 357p.

961 National Recreation Association
Recreation areas: their design and equipment, by George D. Butler. 2d ed. New York, Ronald Press, 1958, 174p.

962 Storey, Edward H.
Planning and developing public park and recreation systems; guidelines and current practices. Urbana, Dept. of Recreation and Municipal Park Administration, University of Illinois, 1964? variously paged.

Latin America

963 Deporte gráfico; una revista de México para Hispano América. México, 1950- .

Argentina

964 Argentine Republic. Dirección General de Parques Nacionales
Anales de parques nacionales. v. 6. Buenos Aires, 1956-

965 Argentine Republic. Dirección General de Parques Nacionales
Parques nacionales argentinos . . . Buenos Aires, 1959, unpaged.

966 Natura. v. 1-, Buenos Aires, 1954- , Annual.

967 Rey, Alfonso
El futbol argentino. Buenos Aires, Eds. Nogal, 1947, 250p.

968 Síntesis de deporte argentino. Buenos Aires? Servicio Internacional de Publicaciones Argentinas, 1952, 107p.

Brazil

969 Brasil. Conselho Nacional de Desportos
Anais. Rio de Janeiro, 1952- .

970 Brasil. Serviço de Recreação Operaria
Relatório. Rio de Janeiro. Annual.

971 Murgel, Angelo
Parques nacionais . . . Rio de Janeiro, Impr. Nacional, 1945, 27p.

Colombia

972 Colombia. Ministerio de Educación Nacional
Divulgación cultural. Bogotá, 1963- .

Mexico

973 González, Ambrosio, & Víctor M. Sánchez L.
Los parques nacionales de México; situación actual y problemas. 1st ed. México, Eds. del Instituto Mexicano de Recursos Naturales Renovables, 1961, 149p.

Peru

974 Perú. Comité Nacional de Deportes
Memoria. Lima. Annual.

Venezuela

975 Quintero, Rodolfo, et al
Como utilizan los caraqueños el tiempo libre. Caracas, Eds. del Cuatricentenario de la Fundación de Caracas, 1966, 91p.

Periodical Articles

General

976 Vaughn, G. F.
"In Search of Standards for Preserving Open Space." Public administration review 24, December 1964, p. 254-258.

977 Wolfe, R.I.
"Perspective on Outdoor Recreation; a Bibliographical Survey." Geographical review 54, April 1964, p. 203-238.

Latin America

978 "International Recreation: Pan America." Recreation 44, June 1950, p. 160-162.

Argentina

979 Anfossi, J.
"Parque 3 de Febrero." Buenos Aires, Revista geográfica americana, August 1948, p. 63-64.

980 Carrasco, B. J.
"Evolución de los Espacios Verdes." Buenos Aires, Boletín del H. Consejo deliberante (33, 34), 1942, p. 491-501.

981 Seguel S., V.J.
"Las Instituciones Deportivas de Buenos Aires." Santiago, Revista de educación, April 1944, p. 45-48.

Brazil

982 Architectural Record (periodical)
"Rio Sports Center: a Progress Report." (112:4), October 1952, p. 121-139.

983 Birkholz, L. Bastos, & B. Cyrino Bastos
"Areas Esportivas e Recreativas no Planejamento Municipal." Rio de Janeiro, Revista de administraçao municipal (12:68), January-February 1965, p. 18-22.

984 Medeiros, E. Bauzer
"Planejamento da Recreaçao Municipal; Plano para Brasilia." Rio de Janeiro, Revista de administraçao municipal (8:49), November-December 1961, p. 463-486.

985 Medeiros, E. Bauzer
"Plano Preliminar das Facilidades Materiais para a Recreaçao em Brasilia." Rio de Janeiro, Revista do serviço público (87:3), June 1960, p. 135-153.

986 Prochnik, R.E.
"Playground no Brasil." Sao Paulo, Habitat (14:77), May-June 1964, p. 31-32.

987 "Sao Paulo Opens its First Playgrounds." Pan American Union bulletin 65, April 1931, p. 445.

988 Stilwell, H.D.
"National Parks of Brazil: a Study in Recreational Geography." Annals of the Association of American Geographers 53, September 1963, p. 391-406.

Chile

989 "On July 20, 1929, the First Community Center for Workers to be Built in Chile Was Opened in Santiago." Pan American Union bulletin 63, December 1929, p. 1287.

990 "Plaza de Juegos Infantiles." Viña del Mar, Nuestra ciudad (I:7), April-May, 1931, p. 11.

991 Veliz, Claudio
"El Llamado Deporte Profesional Universitario." Santiago, Boletín de la Universidad de Chile 21, June 1961, p. 54-55.

Colombia

992 López Freyle, I.
"Como se Divierte Bogotá." Bogotá, Cromos, October 7, 1944, p. 8-9, 54-55.

993 Molano Campuzano, J.
"Parques Nacionales, Monumentos y Reservas de la Naturaleza en Colombia y en el Mundo." Bogotá, Boletín de la Sociedad Geográfica de Colombia, 1st quarter (22:81-82), 1964, p. 30-67.

994 Sánchez Grillo, G.
"Las Zonas Verdes en Bogotá." Bogotá, Registro municipal, October 31, 1943, p. 710-711.

Cuba

995 Sánchez Giquel, R.
"Un Nuevo Parque para la Ciudad de Matanzas." Havana, Boletín de obras públicas, July-September 1930, p. 14-16.

Dominican Republic

996 Vicioso P., S.
"Actividades Deportivas en el Distrito de Santo Domingo." Ciudad Trujillo, Revista municipal, May-June 1942, p. 25-29.

Ecuador

997 Rivadeneira C., J.
"Parques Nacionales en las Cercanías de Quito." Quito, Filosofía, letras y ciencias de la educación (15:31), December 1962, p. 64-66.

El Salvador

998 Alegría, Fernando
"Magical Parks: National Recreation Areas in El Salvador." Américas (10:1), January 1958, p. 6-10.

999 Argumedo, C.A.
"Paraíso Tropical para Obreros." San Salvador, Informaciones de El Salvador (4:56-57), April 14, 1955, p. 36-37.

Guatemala

1000 Gregersen, H.M.
"Wilderness City." American forests 68, December 1962, p. 28-29.

1001 Guatemala. Laws, statutes, etc.
"Créase la Dirección General de Recreación Popular Adscrita a la Secretaría General de la Presidencia de la República." Guatemala, El guatemalteco (153:45), June 6, 1958, p. 833.

Mexico

1002 Andrade, A.
"Arrancan! They're Off!" New York, Modern Mexico, February 1948, p. 14-15, 22.

1003 Compton, G.C.
"Little League Champs. Small Fry from Monterrey, Mexico, Take World Title." Américas (9:11), November 1957, p. 26-27.

1004 "'Grasshopper Hill', (Cerro del Chapulín)." México, Mexican-American review (22:8), August 1954, p. 14-15, 25-26.

1005 Hernández Ochoa, F.
"Por qué fué Vendido el Parque Mayor de la Colonia del Valle?" México, La nación, May 10, 1947, p. 11-13.

1006 Quevedo, M.A. de
"Los Jardines, Parques y Arboledas de la Ciudad de México." México, México forestal, May-June 1942, p. 35-41.

1007 Sesto, J.
"La Ciudad de los Deportes." New York, Norte, October 1947, p. 28-29.

1008 Solís Quiroga, H.
"Tipología del Ocio." México, Ensayos 3, March 1963, p. 65-75.

1009 Stevens, R. L.
"Mexico City Picnic Area: a Study in Recreational Geography." Annals of the Association of American Geographers 46, June 1956, p. 274.

1010 Taplin, G. W.
"National Parks of Mexico." National parks magazine 36, July 1962, p. 8-10.

1011 Vega, J. de la
"El Deporte en México." Américas (2:4), April 1950, p. 33-35, 44-45.

1012 Voigt, B.
"Sports: a Big Business." México, Mexican-American review, March 1948, p. 16-17, 43-47.

Peru

1013 "Jai Alai in Sumptuous Surroundings. New Building of the Frontón Nacional." Lima, West coast leader, February 10, 1931, p. 10.

1014 Morales Arnao, C.
"Los Parques Nacionales y Recreativos en el Perú." Lima, Boletín de la Sociedad Geográfica de Lima 80, January-April 1963, p. 37-40.

1015 "Proyectos de Amplicación del Parque Miraflores." Lima, Arquitecto, April 1944, p. 27-28.

Uruguay

1016 Pereira Rodríguez, J.
"Quebreda de los Cuervos." Américas 13, April 1961, p. 32-35.

1017 Ricossa, J. A.
"Parques de Montevideo." Buenos Aires, Revista geográfica americana, February 1945, p. 85-94.

1018 Solow, Anatole A.
"Case Study of Recreational Planning." American city 69, February 1954, p. 94-96.

Venezuela

1019 Carrillo Moreno, J.
"El Gusto por Nuestras Diversiones." Caracas, *El Farol*, April 1946, p. 22-23.

1020 López Ruiz, J.
"Los Parques de Caracas." Caracas, *Revista Shell*, December 1957, p. 79-81.

West Indies and the Caribbean

1021 James, C. L. R.
"Cricket in West Indian Culture." London, *New society* (1:36), June 6, 1963, p. 8-9.

1022 Walker, Grace
"Creative Recreation in Jamaica." *Recreation* 55, February 1962, p. 65.

RELIGION

Books

General

1023 Conférence Internationale de Sociologie Réligieuse. 5th, Louvain, 1956
Paroisses urbaines, paroisses rurales, by F. Boulard, et al. Paris, Casterman, 1958, 222p.

1024 Hackman, G.G., et al
Religion in modern life. New York, Macmillan, 1957, 480p.

1025 Houtart, François
La mentalidad religiosa y su evolución en las ciudades; conferencia. Bogotá, Universidad Nacional de Colombia, Depto. de Sociología, 1959, 22p.

1026 Lee, Robert, ed.
Cities and churches; readings on the urban church. Philadelphia, Westminister Press, 1962, 366p.

1027 Lutheran churches of the world. Minneapolis, Augsburg Publishing House, 1957, 333p.

1028 Mackay, John A.
Christianity on the frontier. London, Lutterworth, 1950, 205p.

1029 World Council of Churches
Man in community. Christian concern for the human in changing society. Ed. by E. DeVries, New York, Association Press, 1966, 382p.

1030 World Jewish Congress. Institute of Jewish Affairs
The Jewish communities of the world. Annual.

Latin America

1031 Arías Calderón, Ricardo
The intellectual challenge to the faith in Latin America (CICOP working paper C-16-66). Davenport, Latin America Bureau, National Catholic Welfare Conference, 1966, 15p.

1032 Bandeira, Marina
Christian social movements in Latin America (CICOP working paper C-6-65). Davenport, Latin America Bureau, Catholic Inter-American Cooperation Program, 1965, 20p.

1033 Barbieri, Sante U.
Land of Eldorado. New York, Friendship Press, 1961, 161p.

1034 Basic ecclesiastical statistics for Latin America. Maryknoll, Maryknoll Publications, 1954- .

1035 Christianity today (focus on Latin America). VII: 21, July 19, 1963- . (entire issue)

1036 Cohen, Jacob X.
Jewish life in South America. New York, Bloch Pub., 1941, 195p.

1037 Coleman, William J.
Latin American Catholicism: a self-evaluation; a study of the Chimbote report. New York, Maryknoll Publications, 1958, 105p.

1038 Considine, John J., ed.
The Church in the new Latin America. Notre Dame, Fides, 1964, 240p.

1039 Damboriena, Prudencio, & Enrique Dussel
El Protestantismo en América Latina. Bogotá, Oficina Internacional de Investigaciones Sociales de FERES, 1963, 287p.

1040 D'Antonio, William V., & Frederick B. Pike, eds.
Religion, revolution and reform; new forces for change in Latin America. New York, Praeger, 1964, 276p.

1041 Derby, Marian, & James E. Ellis
Latin American lands in focus. Ed. by D. McConnell. New York, Board of Missions of the Methodist Church, 1961, 152p.

1042 *Enciclopedia Judáica castellana; el pueblo judío en el pasado y el presente; su historia, su religión, sus costumbres, su literatura, su arte, sus hombres, su situación en el mundo.* 10v. México, Ed. Enciclopedia Judáica Castellana, 1948-51.

1043 Federbusch, Simon
World Jewry today. New York, Yoseloff, 1959, 747p.

1044 Gregory, Alfonso
Strengthening the Church in the city (CICOP working paper C-18-66). Davenport, Latin America Bureau, National Catholic Welfare Conference, 1966, 11p.

1045 Houtart, François
Pastoral planning in Latin America (CICOP working paper C-7-64). Davenport, Latin America Bureau, National Catholic Welfare Conference, 1964, 16p.

1046 *International review of missions.* New York, World Council of Churches, 1951- .

1047 Labelle, Yvan, & Adriana Estrada
Latin America in maps, charts, tables, no. 2: Socio-religious data (Catholicism). Cuernavaca, The Center of Intercultural Formation, 1964, 294p.

1048 *Latin America calls.* Davenport (3:7), Latin America Bureau, National Catholic Welfare Conference, November 1966- .

1049 Lee, Elizabeth M.
He wears orchids, and other Latin American stories. New York, Friendship Press, 1951, 181p.

1050 Lindsell, Harold, ed.
The church's worldwide mission. Waco, World Books, 1966, 276p.

1051 McGrath, Mark G.
The Church and social revolution in Latin America (CICOP working paper C-11-65). Davenport, Latin America Bureau, National Catholic Welfare Conference, 1965, 22p.

1052 McGrath, Mark G.
The role of the Church in the new Latin America (CICOP working paper C-1-64). Davenport, Latin America Bureau, National Catholic Welfare Conference, 1964, 24p.

1053 Mensaje. Santiago, # 143, October 1965- .

1054 Ortega, Alberto
The recognition of religious values in mass communications (CICOP working paper C-17-66). Davenport, Latin America Bureau, National Catholic Welfare Conference, 1966, 10p.

1055 Pardinas, Felipe
The contemporary religious challenges in Latin America and their historical origins (CICOP working paper C-21-66). Davenport, Latin America Bureau, National Catholic Welfare Conference, 1966, 51p.

1056 Pérez Ramírez, Gustavo
Urbanization and religious values (CICOP working paper C-15-66). Davenport, Latin America Bureau, National Catholic Welfare Conference, 1966, 19p.

1057 Rycroft, William S.
Religion and faith in Latin America. Philadelphia, Westminster Press, 1958, 208p.

1058 Shatzky, Jacob
Comunidades judías en Latinoamérica. Buenos Aires, American Jewish Committee, 1952, 179p.

1059 S.I.C.; revista venezolana de orientación. Caracas, 1938- .

1060 Sireau, Albert, et al
Terre d'angoisse et d'espérance, l'Amérique latine. Paris, Eds. Universitaires, 1959, 162p.

1061 Taylor, Clyde W., & Wade T. Coggins, eds.
Protestant missions in Latin America. Washington, Evangelical Foreign Missions Association, 1961, 314p.

1062 World Council of Churches. Commission on World Mission & Evangelism
The Christian ministry in Latin American and the Caribbean . . . Ed. by Wilfred Scopes. New York, 1962, 264p.

1063 Zañartú, Mario
Secular influences on religious values (CICOP working paper C-11-66). Davenport, Latin America Bureau, National Catholic Welfare Conference, 1966, 15p.

Argentina

1064 Instituto Judío Argentino de Cultura e Información
Comentario. Buenos Aires, 1953- .

Brazil

1065 Bastide, Roger
Les religions africaines au Brésil; vers une sociologie des interprétations de civilisations. 1st ed. Paris, Presses Universitaires de France, 1960, 578p.

1066 Brasil. Serviço de Estatística Demográfica, Moral e Política
Estatística do culto católico romano; províncias eclesiásticas do Brasil. Rio de Janeiro, Serviço Gráfico do Instituto Brasileiro de Geografia e Estatística, 1961- .

1067 Brasil. Serviço de Estatística Demográfica, Moral e Política
Estatística do culto protestante do Brasil. Rio de Janeiro, Servico Gráfico do Instituto Brasileiro de Geografia e Estatística, 1956- .

1068 Dornas, João
Capítulos da sociologia brasileira. Rio de Janeiro, Ed. da "Organização Simões," 1955, 249p.

1069 Shaull, M. R.
The new challenge before the younger churches. (In Rian, Edwin H., ed. Christianity and world revolution. New York, Harper, 1963, p. 190-206.)

1070 Verger, Pierre
Notes sur la culte des Orisa et Vodun à Bahia . . . Dakar, IFAN, 1957, 609p.

Chile

1071 Moore, Robert C.
Piety and poverty in Chile, a study of the economic and social effects of Roman Catholicism in Chile. Nashville, Broadman Press, 1946, 130p.

1072 Riesco, Gabriel
Así veo a Chile, notas de un periodista. Santiago, Impr. Universitaria, 1953, 146p.

1073 Vergara, Ignacio
El protestantismo en Chile. Santiago, Ed. del Pacífico, 1962, 259p.

Colombia

1074 Centro de Investigaciones Sociales. Depto. Socio-Religioso
Anuario de la Iglesia Católica en Colombia. Bogotá, 1927? Annual.

1075 Gómez, Antonio J.
Monografías eclesiástica y civil de Medellín . . . Medellín, Ed. Bedout, 1952, 782p.

1076 Haddox, Benjamin E.
Sociedad y religión en Colombia; estudio de las instituciones religiosas colombianas. 1st ed. Bogotá, Eds. Tercer Mundo & Facultad de Sociología, Universidad Nacional de Colombia, 1965, 180p.

1077 Ospina, Eduardo
The Protestant denominations in Colombia . . .
Bogotá, National Press, 1954, 211p.

Cuba

1078 Dewart, Leslie
Christianity and revolution, the lesson of Cuba.
New York, Herder, 1963, 320p.

1079 Sapir, Boris
The Jewish community of Cuba, settlement and growth. English translation by Simon Wolin.
New York, J. T. S. P. University Press, 1948, 94p.

Haiti

1080 Deren, Maya
Divine horsemen; the living gods of Haiti. New York, Thames & Hudson, 1953, 350p.

1081 Mortel, Roger
La mythanomie sociale en Haiti, essais de psychosociologie. Port-au-Prince, Impr. du Collège Vertières, 1947, 66p.

1082 Pressoir, Catts
Le protestantisme haïtien. v. 1- , Port-au-Prince, Impr. de la Société Biblique et de Livres Religieux d'Haiti, 1945- .

Mexico

1083 Carrión, Jorge
Mito y magia del mexicano. México, Porrúa y Obregón, 1952, 104p.

1084 Lerner, Ira T.
Mexican Jewry in the land of the Aztecs; a guide.
2d ed. México, Costa-Amic, 1963, 252p.

1085 McGavran, Donald, et al
Church growth in Mexico. Grand Rapids, Eerdmans, 1963, 136p.

1086 Ramos, Rutilio, et al
La Iglesia en Mexico; estructuras eclesiásticas.
Friburg, Oficina Internacional de Investigaciones Sociales de FERES, 1963, 119p.

1087 Rivera R., Pedro
Instituciones protestantes en Mexico. México, Ed. Jus, 1962, 186p.

Venezuela

1088 Felice Cardot, Carlos
La libertad de cultos en Venezuela. Madrid, Eds. Guadarrama, 1959, 183p.

Periodical Articles

General

1089 Barth, M.
"Latest Church Ideology; Response to Gibson Winter." Interpretation, a journal of Bible and theology 19, October 1965, p. 435-456.

1090 Considine, John J.
"The Missionary Approach to Urban Problems." Community development review (8:2), June 1963, p. 15-24.

1091 Ferkiss, V.C.
"Suburbia: a Religious Problem?" Social order (10:2), February 1960, p. 84-88.

1092 Leyburn, J.G.
"Idols We Bow Before." Christian century 77, August 31, 1960, p. 992-994.

1093 Opitz, E.A.
"The Battle for the Mind in Religion." Vital speeches 25, October 1, 1959, p. 744-748.

1094 Pusey, Nathan M.
"Secularism and Religion." Christian century 75, October 8, 1958, p. 1142-1143.

1095 Ryan, C.J.
"Democracy as a Religion." School & society 85, April 13, 1957, p. 133-134.

1096 Schuyler, J.B.
"The Parish Studied as a Social System." American Catholic sociological review (17:4), December 1956, p. 320-337.

Latin America

1097 Alvarez de Miranda, A.
"Caracter de las Religiones de México y Centroamérica." Madrid, Cuadernos hispanoamericanos (22:65), May 1955, p. 167-184.

1098 Andre-Vincent, Fr.
"Un Libro Curioso: L'Amérique Latine á la Croisée des Chemins." San Salvador, Estudios centroamericanos (20:203), April 1965, p. 88-91.

1099 Bainton, R.H.
"Mission in Latin America." Christian century 78, January 11, 1961, p. 41-44.

1100 Bistritzky, N.
"El Sionismo y el Judaismo en América Latina." Buenos Aires, Revista de la Cámara Argentina de Comercio 243, July 1949, p. 24-27.

1101 Boegner, M.
"Impressions of Latin America." Ecumenical review (II:2), 1950, p. 176-179.

1102 Botero Gómez, F.
"El Protestantismo y la América Espanola." Bogotá, Prometeo (3:15), June 1956, p. 197-208.

1103 Damboriena, Prudencio
"Génesis y Etapas de la Penetración Protestante en Iberoamérica." Madrid, Cuadernos hispanoamericanos (28:80), August 1956, p. 5-25.

1104 Frank, Waldo
"El Futuro de Israel en la América Hispana." México, Cuadernos americanos, March-April 1943, p. 24-34.

1105 Houtart, François
"Les Conditions Sociales de la Pastorale dans les Grandes Villes de l'Amérique Latine." The Hague, Social compass (5:6), 1957-58, p. 181-199.

1106 "La Invasión Protestante en Latinoamérica." San Salvador, Estudios centroamericanos (10:90), January-February 1955, p. 17-21.

1107 Lasaga, J.
"Responsabilidades de los Laicos en América Latina." Lima, Mercurio peruano (38:368), December 1957, p. 549-554.

1108 McCormack, A.
"Catholic Church in South America." Wiseman review 238, Autumn 1964, p. 226-260.

1109 Mol, J.J.
"La Disminución de la Fé Religiosa en los Migrantes." Geneva, Migraciones internacionales (3:3), 1965, p. 137-146.

1110 Murphy, E.
"La Invasión Protestante en Iberoamérica." Bogotá, Revista javierana, April 1946, p. 149-154.

1111 Powers, M.K.
"Legal Status of Non-Roman Catholic Mission Activities in Latin America." International review of missions 49, April 1960, p. 201-209.

1112 "Protestantism in Latin America." Religion in life 27, Winter 1957-58, p. 5-53.

1113 Rembao, A.
"Latin American Variations on the Protestant Theme." Religion in life (18:2), 1949, p. 199-210.

1114 Rembao, A.
"Protestant Latin America: Sight and Insight." International review of missions 46, January 1957, p. 30-36.

1115 Rossi, J.J.
"Encuentro entre Católicos y Protestantes Sudamericanos." Buenos Aires, Criterio (36:1427), May 9, 1963, p. 333-334.

1116 Schutz, R.
"Latin America, Testing Ground of Ecumenism." Catholic world 197, April 1963, p. 28-35.

1117 Stockwell, B. F.
"Protestantism in Latin America; Argentina and Uruguay: the Roman Catholic Church." Religion in life 27, Winter 1957-58, p. 15-17.

1118 "Triumph of Tolerance." Newsweek 59, February 26, 1962, p. 58-59.

1119 Tschuy, T.
"Latin American Protestantism: the Coming Crisis." Christian century 79, December 26, 1962, p. 1581-1583.

1120 Vallier, Ivan
"Challenge to Catholicism in Latin America." Trans-action (4:7), June 1967, p. 17-26, 60.

1121 Vallier, Ivan
"Religious Elites in Latin America: Catholicism, Leadership and Social Change.# Rio de Janeiro, América latina (8:4), October-December 1965, p. 93-115.

1122 Vekemans, Roger, & R.R. Huff
"Is the Church Losing Latin America?" Ave Maria 91, January 9, 1960, p. 5-10.

Argentina

1123 Alvarez Mejía, J.
"Panorama Religioso de Argentina." México, Latinamérica (5:59), November 1, 1955, p. 506-513.

1124 Caturelli, A.
"Responsabilidad de los Intelectuales Católicos Argentinos en la Actualidad." Buenos Aires, Estudios (49:519), November 1960, p. 710-715.

1125 Centeno, A. M.
"Notas sobre Penetración Protestante." Buenos Aires, Estudios 479, November 1956, p. 16-20.

1126 Franceschi, G. J.
"El Protestantismo en la Argentina." Buenos Aires, Criterio, February 1, 1945, p. 105-107.

1127 Frías, P.J.
"La Situación Actual del Catolicismo en Argentina." Madrid, Arbor (45:171), March 1960, p. 58-68.

1128 Horowitz, Irving L.
"The Jewish Community of Buenos Aires." Jewish Social studies 24, October 1962, p. 195-222.

1129 Pagura, F.J.
"Principales Sectas de Origen Protestante que Actuan en la Argentina." Buenos Aires, Criterio (36:1441-1442), December 25, 1963, p. 898-905.

1130 Schlesinger, G.
"Un Enfoque de la Comunidad Judía de la Argentina." Buenos Aires, Criterio (36:1441-1442), December 25, 1963, p. 910-911.

Bolivia

1131 Muñoz, H.
"La Iglesia en Bolivia." México, Latinoamérica (4:45), September 1, 1952, p. 412-415.

Brazil

1132 Azevedo, Thales de
"A Sociologiá da Religiao no Brasil." Petrópolis, Vozes (59:5), May 1965, p. 328-335.

1133 Castro, Josué de
"Paisagem Religiosa do Brasil." México, Latinoamérica (3:25), January 1, 1951, p. 24-28.

1134 Albein, J.
"Afro-Brazilian Rites." Américas 17, June 1965, p. 16-19.

1135 Gonçalves, A. de C.
"Evangelism in Brazil Today." International review of missions 48, July 1959, p. 302-308.

1136 Monk, A.
"Integración de Inmigrantes y Cambio Social." Rio de Janeiro, Boletim do Centro Latino-Americano de Pesquisas em Ciencias Sociais (3:4), November 1960, p. 13-23.

1137 "News of the Christian World." Christian century 80, April 3, 1963, p. 445-446.

1138 Rizzo, M.
"Brazil Welcomes Protestantism." Christian century, March 31, 1943, p. 391-392.

1139 Saunders, John V.D.
"Organizaçao Social de uma Congragaçao Protestante, Guanabara, Brasil." São Paulo, Sociologia (22:4), December 1960, p. 415-450.

1140 Weaver, B.H.C.
"Confederate Immigrants and Evangelical Churches in Brazil." Journal of southern history 18, November 1952, p. 446-468.

Central America

1141 Pike, Frederick B.
"The Catholic Church in Central America." Review of politics 21, January 1959, p. 83-113.

Chile

1142 "Enter the Catholic Left." Atlas 10, December 1965, p. 374-376.

1143 Fernández Aret, A.E.
"The Significance of the Chilean Pentecostals' Admission to the World Council of Churches." International review of missions 51, October 1962, p. 480-482.

1144 Muñoz, H.
"La Iglesia en Chile, 1953." México, Latinoamérica (5:59), November 1, 1953, p. 516-517.

1145 Tschuy, T.
"Shock Troops in Chile." Christian century 7, September 28, 1960, p. 1118-1119.

1146 Vergara T., I.
"Avance de los 'Evangélicos' en Chile." La nueva democracia (37:1), January 1957, p. 64-74.

Colombia

1147 Driver, W. R.
"Los Protestantes en Colombia." Bogotá, Prometeo (4:16), July 1956, p. 42-44.

1148 Newman, G.
"Jews in Colombia." American Hebrew, May 29, 1941, p. 11, 22.

1149 Rosenthal, C. S.
"Jews of Barranquilla; a Study of a Jewish Community in South America." Jewish social studies 18, October 1956, p. 262-274.

1150 Vega, M. I. de la
"La Acción de los Protestantes en Colombia." Bogotá, Prometeo (3:14), May 1956, p. 149-155.

Costa Rica

1151 Alvarez Mejía, J.
"La Iglesia en Costa Rica." México, Latinoamérica (5:53), May 1, 1953, p. 204-208.

Cuba

1152 Amigo, G.
"Los Protestantes en Cuba." México, Vida, November 10, 1946, p. 842-844.

1153 Sánchez Roig, M.
"Bibliografía Religiosa Cubana." Havana, Revista cubana, December 1945, p. 112-195.

1154 White, D.
"Cuba: Beautiful and Violent." Christian century 76, January 21, 1959, p. 74-76.

Ecuador

1155 Alvarez Mejía, J.
"La Iglesia en el Ecuador." México, Latinoamérica (2:19), July 1, 1950, p. 298-307.

1156 "Jewish Settlement in Ecuador." Lima, West Coast leader, April 20, 1937, p. 27-28.

El Salvador

1157 Alvarez Mejía, J.
"Esbozo Mínimo de la Iglesia en El Salvador." México, Latinoamérica (5:55), July 1, 1953, p. 316-320.

Guatemala

1158 Bollegüi, J.M.
"Protestantismo en Guatemala." San Salvador, Estudios centroamericanos (13:125), April 1958, p. 133-140.

1159 Paniagua S., B.
"La Cofradía." Guatemala, Nuestra Guatemala (6:16), March 1952, p. 18-19.

Haiti

1160 Breda, J.
"Life in Haiti: Voodoo and the Church." Commonweal 78, May 24, 1963, p. 241-244.

1161 Marcelin, M.
"Le Vodou: Religion Populaire." Port-au-Prince, Optique 14, April 1955, p. 37-44.

Honduras

1162 Valladares Rodríguez, J.
"Algunos Datos Sobre la Catedral de Tegucigalpa." Tegucigalpa, Honduras rotaria (ano XXIII:230), June-July 1966, p. 8-9.

Mexico

1163 Alvear Acevedo, C.
"El Catolicismo en México." Madrid, Arbor (36:136), April 1957, p. 489-508.

1164 Herrera, R.
"México Protestante?" México, Lectura (86:4), February 15, 1952, p. 114-126.

1165 Holmes, J.D.
"El Mestizaje Religioso en México." México, Historia mexicana (5:1), July-September 1955, p. 42-61.

1166 Kahan, Salomón
"The Jewish Community in Mexico." Contemporary Jewish record, May-June 1940, p. 253-263.

1167 Llano, C.
"El 'Católico Liberal' en México." México, Istmo 29, November/December 1963, p. 13-22.

1168 Marzal, M.M.
"The Religious Phenomenon in Oscar Lewis's 'The Children of Sánchez'; Religion in the Culture of Poverty." Cuernavaca, CIF reports, August 16, 1966, p. 121-126.

1169 Revitch, M.
"Mexico's Jews." American Hebrew, May 29, 1941, p. 14.

Panama

1170 Fitzpatrick, J.P.
"Parish of the Future." America 113, November 6, 1965, p. 521-523.

1171 Harari, Y.
"The Jews of Panama." Israel horizons 13, April 1965, p. 26-27.

Peru

1172 Chase, H.T.
"Peru Evangelicals Insist on Rights." Christian century 75, February 26, 1958, p. 258-260.

1173 "The Methodist Episcopal Church in Peru." Lima, West coast leader, July 11, 1933, p. 10-11, 14.

1174 Métraux, Alfred
"Living Ghosts of the Incas." Paris, The courier (8:9), February 1956, p. 14-16.

1175 Pike, Frederick B.
"Modernized Church in Peru: Two Aspects." Review of politics 26, July 1964, p. 307-318.

1176 Ruidíaz, J.
"El Protestantismo en el Perú." México, Latinoamérica (3:34), October 1, 1951, p. 453-454.

Uruguay

1177 Fitzgibbon, Russell H.
"Political Impact on Religious Development in Uruguay." Church history 22, March 1953, p. 21-32.

Venezuela

1178 Beller, Jacob
"Jews in Venezuela." Jewish frontier 33, June 1965, p. 24-28.

1179 Romero Gómez, M.
"La Iglesia y el Proletariado de Venezuela." México, Lectura (118:1), July 1, 1957, p. 16-32.

URBAN HISTORY
(including social life and customs)

Books

General

1180 Comhaire, Jean L. L., & Werner J. Cahnman
How cities grew; the historical sociology of cities. Madison, Florham Park Press, 1959, 141p.

1181 Gutkind, Erwin A.
International history of city development. New York, Free Press of Glencoe, 1964- .

1182 Handlin, Oscar, & John Burchard, eds.
The historian and the city. Cambridge, M.I.T. Press, 1963, 299p.

1183 Lavedan, Pierre
Histoire de l'urbanisme. 3v. Paris, Laurens, 1926-52.

1184 Mumford, Lewis
The city in history; its origins, its transformations, and its prospects. 1st ed. New York, Harcourt, Brace & World, 1961, 657p.

1185 Weber, Adna F.
The growth of cities in the nineteenth century; a study in statistics. Ithaca, Cornell University Press, 1963, 495p.

Latin America

1186 Bayle, C.
Los cabildos seculares en la América Española. Madrid, Sapientia, 1952, 814p.

1187 Casariego Fernández, Jesús E.
El municipio y las cortes en el imperio español de Indias. Madrid, Talleres Gráficos Masiega, 1946, 213p.

1188 Céspedes del Castillo, Guillermo
Lima y Buenos Aires; repercusiones económicas y políticas de la creación del Virreinato del Plata. Seville, Escuela de Estudios Hispano-Americanos, 1947, 214p.

1189 Curtis, William E.
The capitals of Latin America. New York, Harper, 1888, 715p.

1190 Gibson, John C.
A study of the relationship of settlement and socio-cultural patterns in urban Spanish America. Chapel Hill, University of North Carolina, Dept. of Sociology & Anthropology, 1953.

1191 Hoselitz, Bert F.
The role of the city in historical perspective. (In Cornell University. Latin American Program. Conference on the Role of the City in the Modernization of Latin America, November, 1965. Ithaca, Cornell University Press, 1967, p. 1-18).

1192 Instituto Interamericano de Historia Municipal e Institucional
Cuadernos. No. 1- , Havana, 1951- .

1193 Inter-American Municipal Historical Congress. 4th, Buenos Aires, 1949
Boletín informativo. Buenos Aires, 1949, 11p.

1194 Inter-American Municipal Historical Congress. 5th, Ciudad Trujillo, 1952
Memoria. 2v. Ciudad Trujillo, Ed. del Caribe, 1952.

1195 Kansas. University. Center of Latin American Studies
The community in revolutionary Latin America. Lawrence, 1964, 36p.

1196 Morse, Richard M., et al
The heritage of Latin America. (In Hartz, Louis, ed. The founding of new societies: Studies in the history of the United States, Latin America, South Africa, Canada and Australia. New York, Harcourt, Brace & World, 1964, p. 123-177.)

1197 Palm, E. W.
Los orígenes del urbanismo imperial en América. (In Instituto Panamericano de Geografía e Historia. Comisión de Historia. Contribuciones a la historia municipal de América. México, 1951, p. 239-268.)

1198 Pan American Institute of Geography & History. Commission on History
Contribuciones a la historia municipal de América, por Rafael Altamira y Crevea, et al. México, 1951, 298p.

1199 Urban life: section VI. (In Hanke, Lewis F., ed. History of Latin American civilization: sources and interpretations; the colonial experience, v. 1. Boston, Little, Brown, 1967, p. 276-379.)

Argentina

1200 Alurralde, Nicanor
Ubicación geográfica de la ciudad de Santa Fé de Luyando, fundada por Juan de Garay; un trabajo de investigación y de topografía historico-geográfica. Buenos Aires, 1950. 40p.

1201 Amico, Carlos d'
Buenos Aires, sus hombres, su política (1860-1890) . . . Buenos Aires, Ed. Americana, 1952, 306p.

1202 Arlt, Roberto
Nuevas aguafuertes portenas . . . Buenos Aires, Librería Hachette, 1960, 329p.

1203 Aunós y Pérez, Eduardo
Biografía de Buenos Aires. Madrid, El Grifón de Plata, 1956, 273p.

1204 Berenguer Carisomo, Arturo
Cuando Buenos Aires era colonia. Buenos Aires, Aguilar, 1960, 211p.

1205 Bischoff, Efraín U.
El general San Martín en Córdoba. Córdoba, Librerías Cervantes, 1950, 180p.

1206 Buenos Aires. Municipalidad
Evolución urbana de la Ciudad de Buenos Aires. Buenos Aires, (Cuadernos de Buenos Aires, XII), 1960, 68p.

1207 Buenos Aires. Universidad. Instituto de Investigaciones Históricas
Territorio y población. 3v. Buenos Aires, Peuser, 1919-55.

1208 Chaca, Dionisio
Breve historia de Mendoza, Argentina. Buenos Aires, 1961, 440p.

1209 Córdoba, Argentine Republic. Cabildo
Actas capitulares; libros cuadragésimo, quinto y cuadragésimo sexto. Córdoba, 1960, 630p.

1210 Ferrari Rueda, Rodolfo de
Historia de Córdoba. Córdoba, Biffignandi Eds., 1964- .

1211 Fitte, Ernesto J.
El motín de las trenzas. Buenos Aires, Ed. Fernández Blanco, 1960, 212p.

1212 Furlong Cardiff, Guillermo, ed.
Las ruinas de Cayastá son de la vieja ciudad de Santa Fé, fundada por Garay; informes de los miembros de número de la Academia Nacional de la Historia . . . el 31 de mayo de 1952. Buenos Aires, Eds. Arayú, 1953, 175p.

1213 Gandía, Enrique de
Buenos Aires colonial. 1st ed. Buenos Aires, Ed. Claridad, 1957, 205p.

1214 García, Juan A.
La ciudad indiana (Buenos Aires desde 1600 hasta mediados del siglo XVIII) . . . Santa Fé, Castellví, 1954, 286p.

1215 García Sanchiz, Federico
La pampa erguida (memorias de Buenos Aires). 1st ed. Madrid, Ed. Saso, 1950, 206p.

1216 Gerchunoff, Alberto
Buenos Aires, la metrópoli de mañana. Buenos Aires, 1960, 141p.

1217 Gianello, Leoncio
Historia de Santa Fé. Santa Fé, Ed. Castellví, 1949, 412p.

1218 González Arrili, Bernardo
Buenos Aires 1900. Buenos Aires, Kraft, 1951, 238p.

1219 Gori, Gastón
El camino de las nutrias. 1st ed. Santa Fé, Colmegna, 1949, 147p.

1220 Llanes, Ricardo M.
La Avenida de Mayo, media centuria entre recuerdos y evocaciones. Buenos Aires, Kraft, 1955, 340p.

1221 Luque Colombres, Carlos A.
Antecedentes documentales sobre la topografía del asiento urbano de Córdoba durante los siglos XVI y XVII. Córdoba, Dirección General de Publicidad de la Universidad Nacional de Córdoba, 1954, 19p.

1222 Marfany, Roberto H.
La semana de mayo; diario de un testigo. Buenos Aires, 1955, 62p.

1223 Montero Lacasa, José
Prototipos bonaerenses. Buenos Aires, Nalé, 1954, 206p.

1224 Olmedo, José I.
San Martín y Córdoba en la época de la campaña de los Andes. Buenos Aires, 1951, 192p.

1225 Pueyrredón, Carlos A.
1810. La revolución de mayo según amplia documentación de la época. Buenos Aires, Eds. Peuser, 1953, 670p.

1226 Razori, A.
Historia de la ciudad argentina. 3v. Buenos Aires, Impr. López, 1945.

1227 Sebreli, Juan J.
Buenos Aires, vida cotidiana y alienación. Buenos Aires, Eds. Siglo Veinte, 1964, 183p.

1228 Viggiano Esain, Julio
San Juan y San Pedro en Córdoba. Córdoba, Impr. de la Universidad, 1957, 109p.

1229 Wilde, José A.
Buenos Aires desde setenta años atrás, 1810-1880. Buenos Aires, Ed. Universitaria, 1960, 272p.

1230 Williams Alzaga, Enrique
La conspiración de Alzaga a la luz de una neuva documentación. Buenos Aires, 1962, 188p.

Bolivia

1231 Crespo R., Alberto
Historia de la ciudad de La Paz, siglo XVII. Lima, 1961, 211p.

1232 La Paz (Bolivia) Municipalidad
Actas capitulares de la Ciudad de La Paz, 1548-1554; 1555-1562. 2v. La Paz, 1965.

1233 Oropesa, Juan
Sucre. Santiago, 1937, 158p.

1234 Sanabria Fernández, Hernando, ed.
Cronistas cruceños del Alto Perú virreinal. Santa Cruz de la Sierra, 1961, 178p.

1235 Sanjinés G., Alfredo
Síntesis histórica de la ciudad de La Paz, 1548-1948. La Paz, 1948? 86p.

1236 Vidaurre, Enrique
Potosí, cuartel general de los guerreros de la independencia. La Paz, 1952, 210p.

Brazil

1237 Almeida, Theodoro Figueira de
Brasilia, a cidade histórica da América. Rio de Janeiro, Depto. de Impr. Nacional, 1960, 72p.

1238 Americano, Jorge
São Paulo naquele tempo, 1895-1915. São Paulo, Ed. Saraiva, 1957, 497p.

1239 Americano, Jorge
São Paulo nesse tempo, 1915-1935. São Paulo, Eds. Melhoramentos, 1962, 423p.

1240 Ammirato, Giacomo
Os galos de Dom Ambrósio; instantáneos do Rio e sua gente. Rio de Janeiro, Livraria São José, 1965, 384p.

1241 Araujo, José de Sousa Azevedo Pizarro e
Memórias históricas do Rio de Janeiro. 9v. Rio de Janeiro, Impr. Nacional, 1945-48.

1242 Barros, Maria Paes de
No tempo de Dantes. São Paulo, Ed. Brasiliense, 1946, 134p.

1243 Berger, Paulo
Copacabana. Rio de Janeiro, Depto. de História e Documentação da Prefeitura do Distrito Federal, 1959, 93p.

1244 Boletĩn internacional de bibliografĩa luso-brasileira. Lisbon. Fundação Calouste Gulbenkian (VI:2), April-June, 1965- .

1245 Boxer, Charles R.
Portuguese society in the tropics: The municipal councils of Goa, Macão, Bahia and Luanda, 1510-1800. Madison, University of Wisconsin Press, 1965, 240p.

1246 Brazil. Presidencia. Serviço de Documentação
Diário de Brasilia. Rio de Janeiro, 1960- .

1247 Bruno, Ernani Silva
História e tradições da cidade de São Paulo . . . 3v. Rio de Janeiro, Olympio, 1953-54.

1248 Castro, Josué de
Fatores de localização da cidade do Recife; um ensajo de geografia urbana. Rio de Janeiro, Impr. Nacional, 1948, 84p.

1249 Cortesão, Jaime
A fundação de São Paulo, capital geográfica do Brasil. Rio de Janeiro, Livros de Portugal, 1955, 275p.

1250 Costa, Luiz E. da
De um livro de memórias. 5v. Rio de Janeiro, 1958.

1251 Costa, Luiz E. da
O Rio de Janeiro no tempo dos vice-reis. 4th ed. rev. & annotated by the author. 3v. Rio de Janeiro, Conquista, 1956.

1252 Costa, Nelson
O Rio através dos séculos; a história da cidade em seu IV centenário. Rio de Janeiro, Eds. O Cruzeiro, 1965, 176p.

1253 Costa, Nelson
Rio de ontem e de hoje Rio de Janeiro, Leo Eds., 1958, 379p.

1254 Craveiro, Paulo F.
Prefácio da cidade; crónicas do Recife. Recife, Depto. de Documentação e Cultura, 1961, 210p.

1255 Dresser, Guy W.
Brazilian paradise. London, Lutterworth Press, 1960, 214p.

1256 Dunlop, Charles J.
Río antigo. Rio de Janeiro, Ed. Gráfica Laemmert, 1955- .

1257 Ender, Thomas
O velho Rio de Janeiro através das gravuras de Thomas Ender . . . São Paulo, Eds. Melhoramentos, 1956, 43p.

1258 Ferreira, Miguel A. Barros
Meio século de São Paulo. São Paulo, Eds. Melhoramentos, 1954, 95p.

1259 Freire, Francisco de Brito
Relação inédita de Francisco de Brito Freire, sobre a capitulação do Recife. Coimbra, Coimbra Ed., 1954, 17p.

1260 Gerson, Brasil
Botafôgo. Rio de Janeiro, Depto. de História a Documentação da Prefeitura do Distrito Federal, 195 ? 102p.

1261 Ivo, Ledo
A cidade e os dias; crónicas e histórias. Rio de Janeiro, Eds. O Cruzeiro, 1957, 234p.

1262 Latif, Miran Monteiro de Barros
Uma cidade nos trópicos, São Sabastião do Rio de Janeiro. São Paulo, Martins, 1948, 220p.

1263 Leite, Mario
Paulistas e mineiros, plantadores de cidades. São Paulo, Ed. Art, 1961, 292p.

1264 Leite, Serafim
Documentos inéditos sobre São Paulo de Piratininga, 1554-1555. Lisbon, 1953, 14p.

1265 Leite, Serafim
Fundador e "fundadores" do São Paulo, 1553-1554. Lisbon, 1953, 15p.

1266 Leite, Serafim
Nóbrega e fundação de São Paulo. Lisbon, Instituto de Intercámbio Luso-Brasileiro, 1953, 125p.

1267 Machado, José de Alcántara
Vida e morte do bandeirante. São Paulo, Martins, 1953, 260p.

1268 Menezes, Raimundo de
Histórias de história de São Paulo. São Paulo, Eds. Melhoramentos, 1954, 275p.

1269 Monbeig, Pierre
Pionniers et planteurs de São Paulo. Paris, Colin, 1952, 376p.

1270 Nascentes, Antenor
Efemérides cariocas. Rio de Janeiro, Prefeitura do Distrito Federal, Secretaria Geral de Educação e Cultura, 1957? 232p.

1271 Neme, Mario
Notas de revisão da história de São Paulo; século XVI. São Paulo, Ed. Anhembi, 1959, 396p.

1272 Omegna, Nelson
A cidade colonial . . . 1st ed. Rio de Janeiro, Livraria J. Olympio, 1961, 344p.

1273 Penteado, Jacob
Belenzinho, 1910; retrato de uma época. São Paulo, Martins, 1962, 322p.

1274 Rios, Adolfo M. de los
O Rio de Janeiro imperial . . . Rio de Janeiro, A Noite, 1946, 494p.

1275 Sarthou, Carlos
Relíquias da cidade do Rio de Janeiro. Rio de Janeiro, Gráfica Olimpica, 1961, 149p.

1276 Silveira, L.
Ensaio de iconografia das cidades portuguesas do ultramar. 4v. Lisbon [n.d.]

1277 Soeiro de Brito, Raquel
Agricultores e pescadores portugueses na cidade de Rio de Janeiro. Lisbon, Junta de Investigações do Ultramar, 1960, 96p.

1278 Stendardo, Alfredo
Visões de Rio de Janeiro . . . Rio de Janeiro, Pongetti, 1961, 68p.

1279 Tati, Miecio
O mundo de Machado de Assis. Rio de Janeiro, Livraria São José, 1961, 243p.

1280 Taunay, Affonso de Escragnolle
História da cidade de São Paulo. Sao Paulo, Eds. Melhoramentos, 1953, 272p.

1281 Travassos, Nelson Palma
No meu tempo de mocinho. Sao Paulo, Ed. Art. 1961, 255p.

1282 Zenha, Edmundo
O municipio no Brasil, 1532-1700. Sao Paulo, Instituto Progresso Editorial, 1948, 172p.

Chile

1283 Alemparte Robles, Julio
El cabildo en Chile colonial; orígenes municipales de las repúblicas hispanoamericanas. Santiago, Universidad de Chile, 1940, 451p.

1284 García Vergara, Lautaro
Novelario del 1900. Santiago, 1950, 166p.

1285 Santiago, Chile. Cabildo
Actas del Cabildo de Santiago durante el período llamado de la Patria Vieja (1810-1814). . . Labor literaria y científica de José Toribio Medina en 1910, por Guillermo Feliú Cruz. Santiago, Fondo Histórico y Bibliográfico José Toribio Medina, 1960, 367p.

1286 Silva Castro, Raúl
Asistentes al cabildo abierto de 18 de septiembre de 1810. 2d ed. Santiago, 1960, 96p.

1287 Vicuña Mackenna, Benjamín
Historia crítica y social de la ciudad de Santiago. 2v. Valparaíso, 1869.

Colombia

1288 Arboleda, Gustavo
Historia de Cali; desde los orígenes de la ciudad hasta la expiración del período colonial. 3v. Cali, Biblioteca de la Universidad del Valle, 1956-57.

1289 Arrazola, Roberto, ed.
Documentos para la historia de Cartagena, 1810-1812. Ed oficial. Cartagena, 1963- .

1290 Bogotá. Concejo Municipal del Distrito Especial
Cabildos de Santafé de Bogotá, cabeza del Nuevo Reino de Granada, 1538-1810. Bogotá, Empresa Nacional de Publicaciones, 1957, 297p.

1291 Caballero, José M.
Particularidades de Santafé, un diario. Bogotá, Ministerio de Educación de Colombia, 1946, 267p.

1292 Carrasquilla, Francisco de P.
Tipos de Bogotá . . . Bogotá, Pontón, 1886, 86p.

1293 Fals-Borda, Orlando, et al
Acción comunal en una vereda colombiana: su aplicación, sus resultados y su interpretación. 2d ed. Bogotá, Depto. de Sociología. Universidad Nacional de Colombia, 1961, 96p.

1294 Friede, Juan
Descubrimiento del Nuevo Reino de Granada y fundación de Bogotá, 1536-1539; según documentos del Archivo General de Indias, Sevilla (revelaciones y rectificaciones). Bogotá, Banco de la República, 1960, 342p.

1295 Friede, Juan
Vida y viajes de Nicolás Federman, conquistador, poblador y confundador de Bogotá, 1506-1542. Bogotá, Eds. Librería Buchholz, 1960, 290p.

1296 García Vasquez, Demetrio
Revalvaciones históricas para la ciudad de Santiago de Cali. 2v. Cali, Palau, Velásquez, 1924-51.

1297 Geonaga, Miguel
Lecturas locales; crónicas de la vieja Barranquilla, impresiones y recuerdos. Barranquilla, 1953, 452p.

1298 Ibanez, Pedro M.
Crónicas de Bogotá. 4v. Bogotá, Ministerio de Educación Nacional, 1952.

1299 Jiménez Molinares, Gabriel
Al paso de los siglos. Cartagena, Impr. Marina, 1961, 32p.

1300 Jiménez Molinares, Gabriel
Los mártires de Cartagena de 1816, ante el Consejo de Guerra y ante la historia. Ed. Oficial. Cartagena, Impr. Departamental, 1955- .

1301 Marco Dorta, Enrique
Cartagena de Indias; la ciudad y sus monumentos. 1st ed. Seville, Escuela de Estudios Hispano-Americanos, 1951, 322p.

1302 Marco Dorta, Enrique
Cartagena de Indias; puerto y plaza fuerte. Cartagena, Amadó, 1960, 369p.

1303 Ochoa, Lisandro
Cosas viejas de la villa de la Candelaria. Medellín, Escuela Tip. Salesiana, 1949, 304p.

1304 Otero Muñoz, Gustavo
Hombres y ciudades, antología del paisaje, de las letras y de los hombres de Colombia. Bogotá, 1948, 710p.

1305 Porras Troconis, Gabriel
Cartegena hispánica, 1533 a 1810. Bogotá, Ministerio de Educacion Nacional, Eds. de la Revista Bolívar, 1954, 342p.

1306 Tejado Fernández, Manuel
Aspectos de la vida social en Cartagena de Indias durante el seiscientos. 1st ed. Seville, Escuela de Estudios Hispano-Americanos, 1954, 345p.

1307 Vergara y Vergara, José M.
Un refresco en Santa Fé. Bogotá, 1948, 23p.

Cuba

1308 Arrate y Acosta, José M. F. de
Llave del Nuevo Mundo. 1st ed. México, Fondo de Cultura Económica, 1949, 264p.

1309 Cuba. Archivo Nacional
Nuevos papeles sobre la toma de la Habana por los ingleses en 1762. 1st ed. Havana, 1951, 281p.

1310 Franco, J. L.
Instituciones locales; urbanismo. Havana, Instituto Interamericano de Historia Municipal e Institucional, 1959, 94p.

1311 Gonzáles del Valle y Ramírez, Francisco
La Habana en 1841, obra póstuma ordenada y revisada por Raquel Catalá. Havana, Municipio de la Habana, 1947- .

1312 Roberts, Walter A.
Havana, the portrait of a city. New York, Coward-McCann, 1953, 282p.

Dominican Republic

1313 Rivera González, José A.
Trujillo y el Alcázar de Colón. Ciudad Trujillo, Ed. del Caribe, 1959, 110p.

1314 Utrera, Cipriano de
Isabel la Católica, fundadora de la ciudad de Santo Domingo. Ciudad Trujillo, Tip. Franciscana, 1952, 61p.

Ecuador

1315 Aspiazu, Miguel
Las fundaciones de Santiago de Guayaquil; primera etapa de la colonización española del Ecuador. Guayaquil, Impr. Casa de la Cultura Ecuatoriana, Núcleo del Guayas, 1955, 340p.

1316 Borrero, Manuel M.
La revolución quiteña, 1809-1812. Quito, Ed. "Espejo," 1962, 439p.

1317 Enríquez Bermeo, Eliecer, ed.
Guayaquil a través de los siglos . . . Quito, Talleres Gráf. Nacionales, 1946- .

1318 Enrïquez Bermeo, Eliecer, ed.
Guía espiritual de Quito; recopilación y notas bio-bibliográficas . . . Quito, Ed. "Los Andes"; dist.: Librería Universitaria, 1953, 244p.

1319 Quito. Cabildo
Libro de Cabildos de la Ciudad de Quito, 1610-1616. Version de Jorge A. Garcés G. Quito, Impr. Municipal, 1955, 600p.

1320 Quito. Cabildo
Libro de Cabildos de la Ciudad de Quito, 1638-1646. Versión de Jorge A. Garcés G. Quito, Impr. Municipal, 1960, 467p.

1321 El libro de la ciudad de San Francisco de Quito hasta 1950-51. Quito, Eds. Cegan, 1951, variously paged.

1322 Loor, Wilfrido
La victoria de Guayaquil. Quito, La Prensa Católica, 1960, 462p.

1323 Museo histórico. Quito, (I:1), 1949- .

1324 Navarro, José G.
La revolución de Quito del 10 de agosto de 1809. 1st ed. Quito, 1962, 532p.

1325 Pino Ycaza, Gabriel, ed.
Derecho territorial ecuatoriano. 2d ed. Guayaquil, Impr. de la Universidad, 1953- .

1326 Ponce Ribadeneira, Alfredo
Quito: 1809-1812; según los documentos del Archivo Nacional de Madrid. Madrid, 1960, 299p.

El Salvador

1327 Barón Castro, Rodolfo
Reseña histórica de la villa de San Salvador, desde su fundación en 1525, hasta que recibe el título de ciudad en 1546. Madrid, Eds. Cultura Hispánica, 1950, 323p.

1328 Lardé y Larín, Jorge
El grito de la Merced, 5 de noviembre de 1811. San Salvador, Ministerio de Cultura, Depto. Editorial, 1960, 132p.

Guatemala

1329 Chinchilla Aguilar, Ernesto
El ayuntamiento colonial de la Ciudad de Guatemala. Guatemala, Ed. Universitaria, 1961, 308p.

1330 Lanning, John T.
The eighteenth-century enlightenment in the University of San Carlos de Guatemala. Ithaca, Cornell University Press, 1956, 372p.

Honduras

1331 Ferrari de Harling, Guadalupe
Recuerdos de mi vieja Tegucigalpa. Comayagua, Impr. Libertad, 1953, 140p.

Mexico

1332 Academia de Ciencias Históricas de Monterrey
Memorias. #1- Monterrey, 1948- .

1333 Benítez, José R.
Como me lo contaron te lo cuento; por la calle de Juarez; relatos. Guadalajara, Eds. del Banco Industrial de Jalisco, 1963, 147p.

1334 Chávez Hayhoe, Arturo
Güadalajara en el siglo XVI. Guadalajara, Banco Refaccionario de Jalisco, 1953- .

1335 Cornejo Franco, José
Guadalajara. México, 1946, 130p.

1336 Covarrubias, Ricardo
Las calles de Monterrey. Monterrey, Tip. Garza y Jiménez, 1947- .

1337 González Ramírez, Manuel
México; litografía de la ciudad que se fué. México, 1962, 238p.

1338 Icaza, Alfonso de
Así era aquello . . . 60 años de vida metropolitana. 1st ed. México, Eds. Botas, 1957, 318p.

1339 Lemoine Villacena, Ernesto
Crónica de la ocupación de México por el Ejército de los Estados Unidos. México, 1950, 103 plus 7p.

1340 Lister, Florence C., & Robert H. Lister
Chihuahua: storehouse of storms. Albuquerque, University of New Mexico Press, 1966, 360p.

1341 Morales Díaz, Carlos
Quíen es quíen en la nomenclatura de la ciudad de México; apuntes biográficos de las personas cuyos nombres figuran en dicha nomenclatura. México, 1962, 582p.

1342 Ochoa Campos, Moisés
La reforma municipal; historia municipal de México. México, Escuela Nacional de Ciencias Políticas y Sociales, Universidad Nacional Autónoma de México, 1955, 538p.

1343 Páez Brotchie, Luis
Guadalajara capitalina y su cuarto centenario. Ed. del H. Ayuntamiento Constitucional. Guadalajara, 1961, 224p.

1344 Páez Brotchie, Luis
Guadalajara, Jalisco, México; su crecimiento, división y nomenclatura durante la época colonial, 1542-1821. Guadalajara, 1951, 208p.

1345 Pérez-Maldonado, Carlos
El Casino de Monterrey; bosquejo histórico de la sociedad regiomontana. Monterrey, Impr. Monterrey, 1950, 252p.

1346 Poniatowska, Elena
Todo empezó el domingo; dibujos de Alberto Beltrán, textos de Elena Poniatowska. 1st ed. México, Fondo de Cultura Económica, 1963, 260p.

1347 Reyes, Alfonso
Albores, segundo libro de recuerdos. 1st ed. México, El Cerro de la Silla, 1960, 160p.

1348 Saldaña, José P.
Episodios de ayer. Monterrey, Sistemas y Servicios Técnicos, 1959, 229p.

1349 Sánchez Fogarty, Federico
Vida y muerte del Tercer Imperio Mexicano, autoglorificación de Federico Sánchez Fogarty. 1st ed. México, 1960, 242p.

1350 Sánchez-Navarro y Peón, Carlos
Memorias de un viejo palacio (la Casa del Banco Nacional de México), 1523-1950. México, 1951, 316p.

1351 Testimonios tapatíos. Guadalajara, Eds. del Gobierno del Estado de México, 1959, 69p.

1352 Trens, Manuel B.
México de antaño. México, 1957, 164p.

1353 Vargas Martínez, Ubaldo
La Ciudad de México, 1325-1960. México, Depto. del Distrito Federal, 1961, 187p.

Nicaragua

1354 Cién años de Managua, D.N. Ed. by Ernesto Barahona López. Managua, 1946, 110p.

1355 Halftermeyer, Gratus
Complemento de la historia de Managua. Managua, Ed. Hospicio León, 1946? 188p.

1356 Halftermeyer, Gratus
Historia de Managua, data desde el siglo XVIII hasta hoy. Managua, 195- , 256p.

Panama

1357 Carles, Rubén D.
Cuando fueron fundados los pueblos y ciudades del Istmo de Panamá. Colón, Impr. El Independiente, 1959, 67p.

1358 Castillero Reyes, Ernesto de J.
Leyendas e historias de Panamá la Vieja. Panamá, Talleres de la Ed. Panamá Americana, 1950, 95p.

1359 García de Paredes, Luis E.
Mudanzas, traslado y reconstrucción de la Ciudad de Panamá en 1673 . . . Panamá, Concejo Municipal de Panamá, 1954, 40p.

1360 Miró, Rodrigo
La cultura colonial en Panamá; ensayos. México, 1950, 69p.

1361 Sosa, Juan B.
Panamá la vieja, con motivo del cuarto centenario de su fundación, 15 de agosto 1519-1919. 2d ed. Panamá, Impr. Nacional, 1955, 159p.

Paraguay

1362 Barredo Fernández, Georgiana, & José A. Tamayo y Avila
Asunción, la tierra del Guaraní. Tema presentado . . . en el II Congreso Histórico Municipal Inter-Americano con sede en la ciudad de New Orleans el 14 de abril de 1947 . . . Havana, González Impr., 1947, 18p.

1363 Zubizarreta, Carlos
Historia de mi ciudad. 1. Epopeya de la Asunción. Asunción, Ed. Emasa, 1964, 297p.

Peru

1364 Baudouin, Julio
Folklore de Lima, visión y síntesis. Lima, Eds. Biblioteca Peruanología, 1947, 73p.

1365 Capelo, Joaquín
Sociología de Lima. 4v. Lima, 1895-1902.

1366 Cobo, Bernabé
Obras. 2v. Madrid, Atlas, 1956.

1367 Lima. Universidad Nacional Mayor de San Marcos. Archivo Central "Domingo Angulo"
Catálogo . . . Lima, 1949- .

1368 Mariátegui Oliva, Ricardo
El Rímac, barrio limeño de abajo del puente; guía histórica y artística. Lima, 1956, 163p.

1369 Miró Quesada Sosa, Aurelio
Lima, tierra y mar. Lima, Mejía Baca, 1958, 151p.

1370 Moore, John P.
The cabildo in Peru under the Hapsburgs; a study in the origins and powers of the town council in the Viceroyalty of Peru, 1530-1700. Durham, Duke University Press, 1954, 309p.

1371 Palma, Ricardo
Tradiciones peruanas completas . . . 3d ed. Madrid, Aguilar, 1957, 1796p.

1372 Real, Alberto
Historia del Real Felipe del Callao, 1746-1900. Callao, 1961, 122p.

1373 Revoredo, César, ed.
Antología de la tradición, ofrenda a la ciudad de Lima. Lima, Mejía Baca, 1962? 285p.

1374 Rivera, Leónidas
Del vivir limeño de antaño, Lima, 1960, 127p.

1375 Rodil y Gayoso, José R.
Memoria del sitio del Callao. Seville, Escuela de Estudios Hispano-Americanos, 1955, 351p.

Uruguay

1376 Alvarez Daguerre, Andrés
Glorias del barrio Palermo, historia de Montevideo; con ilus. del artista Andrés Feldman. Montevideo? 1949, 130p.

1377 At home in Uruguay. Montevideo, Ghiga, 1957, 95p.

1378 Arredondo, Horacio
El transporte a sangre en el antiguo Montevideo y su extensión al interior. Montevideo? 1959, 245p.

1379 De-María, Isidoro
Montevideo antiguo; tradiciones y recuerdos. 2v. Montevideo, Ministerio de Instrucción Pública y Previsión Social, 1957.

1380 Iriarte, Tomás de
Memorias: El sitio de Montevideo y la política internacional en el Río de la Plata. Estudio preliminar de Enrique de Gandía. Buenos Aires, Eds. Argentina "S.I.A.," 1951, 409p.

1381 Marmier, Xavier
Buenos Aires y Montevideo en 1850. Buenos Aires, Dist. El Ateneo, 1948, 171p.

1382 Reyes de Viana, C.
El nacimiento de una ciudad: Trinidad o Porongos, 1804-1904, República Oriental del Uruguay. Montevideo, Ed. Minas, 1954, 346p.

1383 Zabala, Bruno M. de
Diario de Bruno de Zabala sobre su expedición a Montevideo. Montevideo, Barreiro y Ramos, 1950, 57p.

Venezuela

1384 Aracaya U., Pedro M.
El Cabildo de Caracas. Caracas, Eds. del Cuatricentenario de Caracas, 1965, 158p.

1385 Armas Chitty, José A. de
Origen y formación de algunos pueblos de Venezuela. Caracas, Tip. Americana, 1951, 205p.

1386 Crónica de Caracas. Caracas, (I:1), 1951- .

1387 Díaz, José D.
Recuerdos sobre la rebelión de Caracas. Caracas, Academia Nacional de la Historia, 1961, 600p.

1388 García de la Concha, José
Reminiscencias; vida y costumbres de la vieja Caracas. Caracas, Ed. Grafos, 1962, 236p.

1389 Historia de la creación del Distrito Federal. Caracas, Cuatricentenario de Caracas, Secretario General, 1965, 166p.

1390 Manzano, Lucas
Gentes de ayer y de hoy. Caracas, 1959, 184p.

1391 Nectario María
Los orígenes de Maracaibo. Maracaibo, Pubs. de la Universidad de Zulia, 1959, 540p.

1392 Nucete Sardi, José
La ciudad y sus tiempos. Caracas, Italgráfica, 1967, 180p.

1393 Pan American Institute of Geography & History. Commission on History. Committee on Origins of the Emancipation
Documentos relativos a la insurrección de Juan Francisco de León. Caracas, 1949, 243p.

1394 Perera, Ambrosio
Historia de la organización de pueblos antiguos de Venezuela. . . 3v. in 1. Madrid, 1964.

1395 Ponte, Andrés F.
La Revolución de Caracas y sus próceres . . . Caracas, Litografía Miangolarra, 1960, 172p.

1396 Royas, Arístides
Crónicas de Caracas, antología. Lima, Nuevo Mundo, 1962, 139p.

1397 Schael, Guillermo J.
Imagen y noticia de Caracas. Caracas, Tip. Vargas, 1958, 224p.

1398 Uslar Pietri, Arturo
Un rumor de ágora. Caracas, 1961, 37p.

West Indies and the Caribbean

1399 Carmona y Romay, Adriano G.
El gobierno municipal de las Antillas Mayores Españolas y la influencia que ha podido ejercer en su formación y desarrollo el de los Estados Unidos de América. Havana, Librería Martí, 1952, 15p.

Periodical Articles

General

1400 Davis, A. F.
"The American Historian vs. the City." Social studies 56, March 1965, p. 91-96.

1401 Davis, Kingsley
"The origin and Growth of Urbanization in the World." American journal of sociology (60:5), March 1955, p. 429-437.

Latin America

1402 Camargo, Paulo Teixeira de
"O Município na Fase de Colonizaçao das Américas." Rio de Janeiro, Revista brasileira dos municípios (6:22), April/June 1953, p. 121-127.

1403 Davis, Kingsley
"Colonial Expansion and Urban Diffusion in the Americas." Dharwar, International journal of comparative sociology (1:1), March 1960, p. 43-66.

1404 Domínguez Company, Francisco
Bibliografía de las instituciones locales de Hispanoamérica, época colonial. Revista interamericana de bibliografía (VI:3), July-September 1956, p. 209-223.

1405 "Expansión Urbana en la América Latina Durante el Siglo XIX." Seville, Estudios americanos XIII, April-May 1957, p. 67-68.

1406 Gomez Bustillo, Miguel R.
"Los Cabildos y la Independencia de Hispano-América." México, Justicia, February 1946, p. 7929-7935.

1407 Kubler, George A.
"Villes et Culture en Amérique Latine pendant la Période Coloniale." Paris, Diogenes 47, July-September 1964, p. 55-67.

1408 Morse, Richard M.
"Some Characteristics of Latin American History." Hispanic American historical review (67:2), January 1962, p. 317-338.

1409 Munoz Pérez, J.
"Una Descripción Comparativa de las Ciudades Americanas en el Siglo XVIII." Madrid, Estudios geográficos (15:54), February 1954, p. 80-120.

1410 Nuttall, Z.
"Royal Ordinances Concerning the Laying Out of New Towns." Hispanic American historical review (IV:4), November 1921, p. 743-753.

1411 Padula, E. L.
"Orígen de la Ciudad Hispanoamericana." Córdoba, Revista de la Universidad Nacional de Córdoba (4:3-4), July-October 1963, p. 357-377.

1412 Pike, Frederick B.
"Algunos Aspectos de la Ejecución de las Leyes Municipales en la América Española Durante la Epoca de los Austrias." Madrid, Revista de Indias (18:72), April/June 1958, p. 201-223.

1413 Pike, Frederick B.
"Municipality and the System of Checks and Balances in Spanish American Colonial Administration." Américas 15, October 1958, p. 139-158.

1414 Smith, R. C.
"Colonial Towns of Spanish and Portuguese America." Journal of the Society of Architectural Historians (XIV:4), 1955, p. 1-12.

1415 Veliz Lizarraga, José
"Cabildos Abiertos de Hispanoamérica." México, Humanismo (1:2), August 1952, p. 53-58.

1416 Villanueva, Carlos R.
"Creación de Ciudades y Leyes de Indias." Caracas, El farol (22:192), January-February 1961, p. 7-12.

Argentina

1417 Cánopa, Luis
"Las Construcciones en el Viejo Buenos Aires." Buenos Aires, Temas, June 1946, p. 413-416.

1418 Deheza, José A.
"La Fundación de la Ciudad de 'Ntra. Señora de los Buenos Aires.' (Algunos Factores Históricos Desconocidos que Intervinieron en la Fundación de Buenos Aires Sobre Todo en el Orden Económico)." Sucre, Boletín de la Sociedad Geográfica "Sucre," May 1945, p. 228-237.

1419 "Evolución de Buenos Aires en el Tiempo y en el Espacio." Buenos Aires, Revista de arquitectura (40:375), 1955, p. 25-92.

1420 Gandía, Enrique de
"Buenos Aires en Guerra con Napoleón." Madrid, Revista de las Indias (3:40), April/June 1950, p. 349-366.

1421 Gandía, Enrique de
"Buenos Aires en 1806. (Un Libro Editado en Londres, en 1818, Nos Trae las Imágenes de un Buenos Aires de Hace Poco Menos Siglo y Medio)." Buenos Aires, Revista geográfica americana, June 1947, p. 325-329.

1422 Gandía, Enrique de
"La Destrucción de Buenos Aires en el Año 1541." Buenos Aires, Revista geográfica americana, January 1938, p. 1-10.

1423 Gandía, Enrique de
"Las Dos Fundaciones de Buenos Aires." Madrid, Revista de las Espanas, January-March 1936, p. 3-8.

1424 González, Julio C.
"La Misión de Juan Manuel de Figueiredo a Buenos Aires en 1821." Montevideo, Revista histórica (28:82/84), July 1958, p. 193-233.

1425 Lumsden, E. W. H.
"Buenos Aires Childhood." Américas (5:9), September 1953, p. 9-11, 27.

1426 Lynch, John
"Intendants and Cabildos in the Viceroyalty of La Plata, 1782-1810." Hispanic American historical review 35, August 1955, p. 337-362.

1427 Martinez, Alvaro M.
"Buenos Aires." Buenos Aires, Liberalis 8, July/August 1950, p. 37-42.

1428 Mouchet, Carlos
"Alberdi y Sarmiento: Planificadores de Ciudades en Desarrollo Económico." Journal of inter-American studies (VIII:4), October 1966, p. 611-632.

1429 Orta Nadal, Ricardo
"La Historia de Nuestras Ciudades." Santa Fé, Universidad (Publicación de la Universidad Nacional del Litoral) 25, 1952, p. 137-155.

1430 "Buenos Aires Through Four Centuries." Pan American Union bulletin 70, May 1936, p. 384-391.

1431 Roldán, Belisario
"Amanece 1810 en Buenos Aires." Buenos Aires, Boletín de informaciones petroleras 321, January 1960, p. 3-12.

1432 Roque Gondra, Luis
"Primera Fundación de Buenos Aires." Buenos Aires, Hechos e ideas, May-June 1936, p. 205-223.

1433 Roussier, Paul
"Deux Mémoires Inédits des Frères Massiac sur Buenos Ayres en 1660." Paris, Journal de la Société des Américanistes 25, 1933, p. 219-249.

1434 Soiza Reilly, Juan José de
"Los Paraguayos, Fundadores de Buenos Aires." México, Genio latino (año XV, no. 112), 1945, p. 26.

1435 Torre Revello, J.
"La Casa y el Mobiliario en Buenos Aires Colonial." Buenos Aires, Revista de la Universidad de Buenos Aires, July/September 1945, p. 59-74.

1436 Torre Revello, J.
"El IV Centenario de la Fundación de Buenos Aires. Conferencia . . . 23 de junio de 1936." Cartagena, América espanola, September 1936, p. 26-37.

1437 Torre Revello, J.
"La Fundación de Buenos Aires." Buenos Aires, Revista de la municipalidad de la ciudad de Buenos Aires, January/March 1948, p. 15-20.

1438 Torre Revello, J.
"Moradas del Buenos Aires de Antaño." Buenos

Aires, Revista geográfica americana (42:247), February 1958, p. 261-264.

1439 Vedia y Mitre, Mariano de
"Cuarto Centenario de la Fundación de Buenos Aires." La Plata, Revista de Educación 4, 1936, p. 5-18.

1440 Vedia y Mitre, Mariano de
"Don Pedro de Mendoza, Fundador de Buenos Aires." Buenos Aires, Nosotros, September 1936, p. 3-44.

1441 Wilde, J.A.
"Del Buenos Aires de Antaño." Buenos Aires, Atica, August 1946, p. 16-17; August 1948, p. 14-15.

1442 Zabala, Rómulo
"Buenos Aires a Fines del Siglo XVIII." Buenos Aires, Revista geográfica americana, March 1938, p. 153-166.

1443 Zabala, Rómulo
"Buenos Aires en el Nacimiento de Montevideo." Montevideo, Revista nacional, February 1943, p. 249-278.

1444 Zapiola, José M.,
"El Primer Intendente Municipal de Buenos Aires." Buenos Aires, Revista informativa municipal, June 1944, p. 35-48.

Bolivia

1445 "IV Centenario de la Ciudad de La Paz en Homenaje a la República de Bolivia." Lima, Cahuide (11: 96/97), September/October 1948, p. 5-74.

1446 Díaz Arguedas, Julio
"Resúmen de la Historia de La Paz." La Paz, Revista de la Biblioteca Municipal "Mariscal de Santa Cruz" (1:1), January 1949, p. 35-41; (1:2), March 1949, p. 48-52.

1447 Feyles, Gabriel
"La Ciudad de La Paz y las Alteraciones de 1950."

La Paz, Kollasuyo (11:69), March 1952, p. 87-97.

1448 Iturry Nuñez, Nemasio
"La Fundación de La Paz." La Paz, Ultima, October 1941, p. 23, 25, 32.

1449 Llanos Aparicio, L.
"Nuevos Papeles Sobre el Descubrimiento y Fundación de la Ciudad de La Paz." La Paz, Revista "Ultima", April 1946, p. 21-22.

1450 Pasado y Presente de la Ciudad de La Paz (Síntesis Histórica Desde su Fundación Hasta la Batalla de Ayacucho)." Lima, Cahuide, October 1944, p. 50-54.

1451 Santa Cruz, Víctor
"La Fundación de la Ciudad de La Paz." Lima, Cahuide, October 1944, p. 79-80.

Brazil

1452 Barros, Valencio de
"São Paulo." São Paulo, Revista do arquivo municipal, October/November/December 1945, p. 25-39.

1453 Brancante, E.F.
"Nossa Antiga São Paulo." Rio de Janeiro, Habitat (4:13), December 1953, p. 35-42.

1454 Burns, E.B.
"Manaus, 1910: Portrait of a Boom Town." Journal of inter-American studies (VII:3), July 1965, p. 400-421.

1455 Carneiro, Daví
"São Paulo e Curitiba no Século 18." São Paulo, Investigaciones (3:30), June 1951, p. 50-80.

1456 Falção, Edgard de Cerqueira
"Dados Cronologicos Ligados à Fundação de São Paulo." São Paulo, Revista de história (3:7), July/September 1951, p. 215-216.

1457 Fernández y González, Eduardo
"A Fundação de São Paulo." São Paulo, Revista

de historia (11:21/22), January/June, 1955, p. 323-327.

1458 Ferreira, Jorge
"Tire o Chapéu a São Paulo: Bandeirantes em Festa." Rio de Janeiro, O Cruzeiro (27:3), October 30, 1954, p. 50-63.

1459 Ferreira, Tito L.
"A Propósito da Fundaçao da Cidade de Sao Paulo." Sao Paulo, Revista do Arquivo Municipal 140, June 1951, p. 27-38.

1460 Fortes, J.F. Blas
"A Formaçao dos Municípios Mineiros." Rio de Janeiro, Revista brasileira dos municípios (13: 49-52), January-December 1960, p. 23-26.

1461 Guimaraes, J.
"Marvelous City: Rio's 400th Anniversary." Americas 17, March 1965, p. 1-10.

1462 Lessa, Orígenes
"Sao Paulo de 1868. (Retrato de uma Cidade Através de Anúncios de Jornal)." Sao Paulo, Anhembi (10:28), March 1953, p. 26-52.

1463 Lima, Barbosa
"A Fundaçao de Sao Paulo." Rio de Janeiro, Revista da Academia Brasileira de Letras 87, January/June 1954, p. 52-54.

1464 Mateos, Francisco
"Presencia de Espana en la Fundación de Sao Paulo (Brasil)." Madrid, Razón y fé (148:668/ 669), September/October 1953, p. 160-171.

1465 Matos, O. Nogueira de
"A Cidade de Sao Paulo no Século XIX." Sao Paulo, Revista de história (11:21/22), January/ June 1955, p. 89-125.

1466 Matos, O. Nogueira de
"Contribuçao à História do Municipalismo no Brasil." Rio de Janeiro, Revista brasileira dos

municipios (15:59-60), July-December 1962, p. 105-137.

1467 Monteiro, Mozart
"Questões Relativas à Fundação de São Paulo." Rio de Janeiro, Revista do Instituto Histórico e Geográfico Brasileiro 224, July/September 1954, p. 371-391.

1468 Morse, Richard M.
"A Cidade de São Paulo no Período 1855-1870." São Paulo, Sociologia (13:3), August 1951, p. 230-251.

1469 Paula, E. Simões de
"A Segunda Fundação do São Paulo. (Da Pequena Cidade à Grande Metrópole de Hoje)." São Paulo, Revista de história (8:17), January/March 1954, p. 167-179.

1470 Petrone, Pasquale
"A Cidade de São Paulo no Século XX." São Paulo, Revista de história (11:21/22), January/June 1955, p. 127-170.

1471 Silva, Raul de Andrade e
"São Paulo nos Tempos Coloniais." São Paulo, Revista de história (11:21/22), January/June 1955, p. 55-88.

1472 Sousa, Thomas O. Marcondes de
"Algumas Considerações em Tôrno de uma Nova Lição do Padre Serafim Leite Relativa à Fundação de São Paulo." São Paulo, Revista de história (9:20), October/December 1954, p. 371-377.

1473 Viotti, H. Abranches
"Aspectos da Fundação de São Paulo Através de Escritos Nobreguenses." São Paulo, Revista do história (11:21/22), January/June 1955, p. 37-52.

1474 Viotti, H. Abranches
"A Fundação de São Paulo Pelos Jesuítas." São Paulo, Revista de história (8:17), January/March 1954, p. 119-133.

1475 Wilson, Betty
"Sao Paulo at 400. Founded in 1554, the Industrial Capital of Brazil is Devoting This Year to Celebration." Américas (6:6), June 1954, p. 9-12.

Chile

1476 Carranza, J. Rafael
"Santiago en el Año 1780. Desasea, Abandono y Misería. Un Documento del Gobernador Benávides." Santiago, Boletín municipal, October 17, 1930, p. 5-6.

1477 Illanes Adaro, Graciela
"Santiago Legendario y Artístico." Santiago, Anales de la Universidad de Chile, 1st & 2nd quarter 1944, p. 231-374.

1478 Lyon, Claude
"Santiago Half a Century Ago. Balmaceda's Presidency and the Civil War." Valparaiso, South Pacific mail, June 20, 1935, p. 9-11.

1479 Mesa Torres, Luis A.
"Informaciones Sobre la Antigua Vida Santiaguina." Santiago, Boletín municipal, June 12, 1931, p. 26-37.

1480 Molina Salas, Jorge
"El Raid a Santiago de Chile." Buenos Aires, Asociación Argentina de Fomento Equino (año IV, no. 26), 1944, p. 42-47.

1481 Pérez Rosales, Vicente
"Santiago de 1814 y 1860 (Recuerdos del Pasado)." Santiago, Campesino, September 1944, p. 483-487.

1482 Ugarte, B.R.
"Santiago Through Four Centuries." Pan American Union bulletin 75, April 1941, p. 235-245.

1483 Vicuña Mackenna, Benjamín
"Los Planes de la Ciudad de Santiago. A Raiz del Incendio de la Casa Consistorial en 1885. Interesante Bosquejo Histórico de Vicuña Mackenna." Santiago, Boletín municipal, December 31, 1930, p. 17-20.

Colombia

1484 Bayona Posada, Jorge
"La Ciudad y Su Historia: Los Misterios de Monserrate y Guadalupe." Bogotá, Registro municipal, June 15, 1945, p. 212-226.

1485 Bayona Posada, Jorge
"Los Fantasmas de Santa Fé." Bogotá, Registro municipal, September 15, 1943, p. 522-536.

1486 Bermúdez, José A.
"A Través de la Antigua Santafé. Leyendas Históricas." Bogotá, Boletín de historia y antigüedades (47:545/546), March/April 1960, p. 245-265.

1487 Carranza, Eduardo
"Evocación de la Vieja Santa Fé de Bogotá." Bogotá, Revista de América, August 1945, p. 311-313.

1488 Coester, Alfred L.
"The Bogotá Quadricentennial." Pan American Union bulletin 72, December 1938, p. 718-722.

1489 Coester, Alfred L.
"Santa Fé de Bogotá. [Brief Review of its Centennial Celebrations, 1938]." Hispania, October 1938, p. 191-196.

1490 Convers Fonnegra, C.
"La Ciudad y su Historia. Fundación de Bogotá." Bogotá, Registro municipal, July 31, 1937, p. 376-383.

1491 Convers Fonnegra, C.
"Ciudades Fundadas en Tierra Firme de 1525 a 1550. (Bogotá)." Bogotá, Boletín de historia y antigüedades, November 1936, p. 735-743.

1492 Cromos (periodical)
"Homenaje de Cromos a Bogotá en el IV Centenario 1538-1938." Bogotá, August 6, 1938, entire issue.

1493 Florez de Ocariz, Juan
"Santa Fé de Bogotá en 1672." Bogotá, Registro

municipal, March 1936, p. 176-178.

1494 Forero Durán, Luis
"Por qué Bogotá Llegó a Ser la Capital de la República." Bogotá, Revista javeriana, August 1952, p. 106-115.

1495 Gaitán, Luis A.
"Como se Celebró el III Centenario de la Fundación de Bogotá." Bogotá, Cromos, June 18, 1938, p. . . .

1496 El Gráfico (periodical)
"Homenaje de la Revista a Bogotá en su IV Centenario." Bogotá, August 6, 1938, entire issue.

1497 Guardia, Santiago de la
"Recuerdos Pintorescos. (Una Visita Aristocrática en el Bogotá de 1895)." Panamá, Lotería (3:28), March 1958, p. 51-56.

1498 Gutiérrez Ferreira, José A.
"Evocación de Santafé." Bogotá, Boletín de historia y antigüedades, June-July 1943, p. 607-622.

1499 Jiménez Romero, Luis H.
"La Capital bajo la Piqueta del Progreso. (Del Alero Colonial a las Azoteas Don Ascensor)." Bogotá, Cromos, February 17, 1945, p. 1-3, 58.

1500 Mark, Marcelo A.
"Santa Fé de Bogotá en su Cuatro Centenario." Buenos Aires, Revista geográfica americana, November 1938, p. 305-322.

1501 Martínez, Abraham
"Fourth Centenary of the Foundation of Bogotá. [Founded August 6, 1538]." Bogotá, Colombia, February 1935, p. 3-4.

1502 Miramón, Alberto
"La Vida Santaferena a Fines del Siglo XVIII." Bogotá, Universidad Nacional de Colombia, July/September 1946, p. 83-92.

1503 Monsalvo M., Manuel
"Bogotá y su Fundador. Reseña Biográfica de Don Gonzalo Jiménez de Quesada." Medellín, Universidad de Antioquia, October-November 1936, p. 463-478.

1504 Pardo, Ricardo
"Estampas de la Conquista: Santafé Fundada." Bogotá, Revista de América, September 1946, p. 354-359.

1505 Peñalosa Rueda, J.
"Santa Fé de Bogotá, (Biografía de la Ciudad)." Bogotá, Revista de América, April 1948, p. 11-16.

1506 Restrepo Canal, Carlos
"Bogotá y la Cultura Colombiana." Bogotá, Bolívar 24, October 1953, p. 605-625.

1507 Restrepo Canal, Carlos
"Erección del Virreinato de Santa Fé." Bogotá, Boletín de historia y antigüedades, September-October 1943, p. 982-1024.

1508 Sánchez, Luis C.
"Bogotá Ciudad del Futuro. (Desarrollo Urbano de la Capital. El Progreso Local a Través de la Historia)." Bogotá, Colombia, May 1944, p. 135-142.

1509 Schottelius, Justus W.
"Die Gründung der Stadt Santa Fe de Bogotá, am 6." Berlin, Ibero-Amerikanisches Archiv, July 1938, p. 167-195.

1510 Vasso, Lionel
"De Santafé a Bogotá." Panamá, Boletín de la Sociedad Boliviarana de Panamá 55, 1955, p. 43-62.

1511 Zarante Rhénals, S.
"Memorias de Santa Fé de Bogotá (A Manuel Zarante Rhénals, Bogotano Adoptivo y Literato de Verdad)." Cartagena, Boletín historial (de la Academia de la Historia de Cartagena de Indias), April 1946, p. 17-29.

Cuba

1512 Artiles, Jenaro
"La Habana Estuvo en Puentes Grandes." Havana, Carteles, September 30, 1945, p. 26-27.

1513 Artiles, Jenaro
"Historia Local de La Habana." Havana, Revista bimestre cubana, April 1945, p. 108-133.

1514 Bay Sevilla, Luis
"Costumbres Cubanas de los Siglos XVI al XIX." Havana, Arquitectura, October 1942, p. 393-404, 421-429.

1515 Bens Arrarte, José M.
"Apuntes Sobre La Habana del Siglo XVIII." Havana, Revista de arqueología (3:6/7), January/December 1948, p. 190-195.

1516 Bens Arrarte, José M.
"Los Avances Urbanísticos de La Habana." Havana, Arquitectura (23:261), April 1955, p. 188-197.

1517 Bens Arrarte, José M.
"Estudio Sobre La Habana del Siglo XVII." Havana, Arquitectura, November/December 1945, p. 376-380.

1518 Bens Arrarte, José M.
Estudios Sobre La Habana del Siglo XVI." Havana, Arquitectura, January 1945, p. 19-21, 36.

1519 Bens Arrarte, José M.
"La Habana del Siglo XVI y su Admirable Evolución Rural y Urbana (1519-1555)." Havana, Arquitectura, October 1942, p. 382-387, 409-420.

1520 Castro, Martha de
"Evocación de La Habana Colonial." Seville, Estudios americanos (12:63), December 1956, p. 417-434.

1521 Fernández y Simón, Abel
"Los Distintos Tipos de Urbanizaciones que Fueron Establecidos en la Ciudad de La Habana Durante

su Epoca Colonial. I-III." Havana, Ingeniería civil (7:8), August 1956, p. 559-577; (7:9), September 1956, p. 615-629; (7:10), October 1956, p. 679-696.

1522 González del Valle, F.
"La Habana en 1841." Havana, Revista nacional de la propiedad urbana, July 1948, p. 9-11.

1523 Lavín, Arturo G.
"Dos Escrituras del Archivo de Protocol." Havana, Revista de la Biblioteca Nacional (2:4), October/December 1951, p. 19-27.

1524 López Matoso, A.
"La Habana Vista por un Mexicano en 1817." Havana, Revista de la Biblioteca Nacional (6:1), January/March 1955, p. 27-41.

1525 Moreno Fraginals, M.
"Autobiografía de La Habana." Havana, Mensuario de arte, literatura, historia y crítica (1:5), April 1950.

1526 Pérez de la Riva, Francisco
"Panoramas de Ayer." Havana, Arquitectura, October 1944, p. 376-379.

1527 Planes, Juan M.
"La Habana Dentro de Cincuenta Años." Havana, Ingeniería civil (10:4), April 1959, p. 223-236.

1528 Portell Vilá, Herminio
"De la Otra Habana." Havana, Bohemia (43:3), January 21, 1951, p. 52-53.

1529 Russell, Nelson V.
"The Reaction in England and America to the Capture of Havana, 1762." Hispanic American historical review, August 1929, p. 303-316.

1530 Santovenia y Echaide, Emetrio S.
"El Destino Histórico de La Habana Antigua." Havana, Universidad de La Habana 8-9, March-June 1935, p. 57-67.

Dominican Republic

1531 Amiama, Manuel A.
"La Población de Santo Domingo." Ciudad Trujillo, Clio (Organo de la Academia Dominicana de la Historia) (27:115), July/December 1959, p. 116-134.

1532 Archivo General de Indias. Seville
"Documentos para la Historia Antigua de Esta Ciudad." Ciudad Trujillo, Revista municipal, July-September 1942, p. 37-40.

1533 Tejera, Apolinar
"Quid de Quisqueya?" Ciudad Trujillo, Boletín del Archivo General de la Nación, September/December 1945, p. 216-221.

1534 Utrera, Cipriano de
"El Estudio de la Ciudad de Santo Domingo." Ciudad Trujillo, Clio (16:82), July/December 1948, p. 145-177.

Ecuador

1535 Andrade Marín, L.
"Las Guerras de Guambras en Quito." Quito, Museo histórico (3:8), March 1951, p. 116-120.

1536 Azula Barrera, Rafael
"Los Secretos de Guayaquil." Quito, Continente, March 1, 1944, p. 12-13.

1537 Barrera, Isaac J.
"A Comienzos del Siglo XVII." Quito, Museo histórico (12:37/38), December 6, 1960, p. 118-120.

1538 Blanco, José M.
"Noticias Histórico-Económicas de Quito." Quito, Museo histórico (4:14/15), October 1952, p. 11-30.

1539 Castro Tola, María L.
"Guayaquil, a Través de los Siglos." Guayaquil, Cuadernos de historia y arqueología (6:16/18), December 1956, p. 136-141.

1540 "La Fundación de Quito." Quito, Gaceta municipal, December 6, 1944, p. I-XVI.

1541 Garcés, Víctor G.
"Quito Antiguo." Quito, Museo histórico (3:8), March 1951, p. 104-115.

1542 Garcés G., Jorge A.
"Relación de la Fiestas Reales, que Celebró la Muy Noble, y Muy Leal Ciudad de Quito, en la Augusta Proclamación del Señor Rey Don Carlos Quarto el Día 21 de Septiembre de 1789." Quito, Gaceta municipal, December 6, 1944, p. 39-55.

1543 Gómez, Diego M.
"La Ciudad del Guayas y Su Grandioso Congreso Eucarístico." Bogotá, Boletín de la Sociedad Geográfica de Colombia (16:60), 4th quarter, 1958, p. 230-240.

1544 "Homenaje a San Francisco de Quito." Quito, América, November-December 1934, p. 275-549.

1545 Huerta, Pedro J.
"La Querella Entre Rocafuerte y la Corte Superior de Justicia. I-IV." Guayaquil, Cuadernos de historia y arqueología (6:16/18), December 1956, p. 3-58.

1546 Jijón y Casamaño, Jacinto
"La Fecha de Fundación de Quito." Bogotá, Registro municipal, June 15, 1934, p. 350-353.

1547 Orbe, José E.
"Aspectos Históricos de la Fundación Española de la Ciudad de San Francisco de Quito." Quito, Educación, May-December 1934, p. 90-97.

1548 Pérez, Galo R.
"Viñeta del Guayaquil Antiguo." Quito, Ecuador (1:4), November-December 1949, p. 2-3.

1549 Pimental Garbo, Julio
Más Altos que Ellos, los Arboles." Guayaquil, Cuadernos de historia y arqueología (6:16/18), December 1956, p. 59-73.

1550 Rumazo, José
"Guayaquil Alrededor de 1908." Bogotá, Revista de Indias, October-December 1944, p. 631-680.

1551 Schottelius, Justus W.
"Die Gründung Quitos. Planung und Aufbau Einer Spanisch-Amerikanischen Kolonialstadt . . ." Berlin, Ibero-Amerikanisches Archiv, April 1936, p. 55-77.

1552 Stevenson, William B.
"La Ciudad de Quito en 1808-1810." Quito, Boletín del Archivo Nacional de Historia (1:2), July/December 1950, p. 425-442.

1553 Vargas, José M.
"Urbanismo Primitivo de las Ciudades Ecuatorianas." Quito, Casa de la Cultura Ecuatoriana (11:20), January/December 1958, p. 167-217.

1554 Vitcri, Atanasio
"Historia de Quito." Quito, Revista ecuatoriana de educación (6:22), July/August 1952, p. 106-151.

El Salvador

1555 "Actos Conmemorativos del IV Centenario de la Concesión del Título de Ciudad a la Villa de San Salvador." Madrid, Revista de Indias, October/December 1946, p. 1066-1090.

1556 "El IV Centenario de la Ciudad de San Salvador." San Salvador, Ateneo, April/June 1946, p. 1-48, entire issue.

1557 Lardé y Larín, J.
"Contestaciones a la Consulta del Ateneo de El Salvador para Establecer la Fecha en que Fué Ascendida a Ciudad La Villa de San Salvador." San Salvador, Ateneo, January/March 1946, p. 33-40.

1558 Lardé y Larín, J.
"IV Centenario de la Promoción de La Villa de San Salvador al Rango de Ciudad." San Salvador, Boletín de la Biblioteca Nacional, July/December 1946, p. 56-62.

1559 Lardé y Larín, J.
"Sucinta Historia de los Municipios Salvadoreños." San Salvador, Anales del Museo Nacional David J. Guzmán (2:8), October-December 1951, p. 45-79.

1560 "El San Salvador de Antes y el San Salvador de Ahora." San Salvador, Anales del Museo Nacional David J. Guzmán (2:6), April/June, 1951, p. 19-38.

1561 Urrutia, Carlos G.
"Teatro Histórico Escolar; Pasquine Espionaje." San Salvador, Correo escolar rural (4:20), October 1949, p. 31-57.

Mexico

1562 Alvarez Espinosa, Roberto
"Un Vistazo al Portentoso Desarrollo de la Capital Mexicana." México, Revista rotaria (38:2), February 1952, p. 9-12.

1563 Arregui, Domingo L. de
"Descripción de Guadalajara (1621)." México, Problemas educativos de México (3:15), May 1959, p. 49-54.

1564 Benítez, José R.
"I. Conquistadores de la Nueva Galicia. II. Fundadores de la Ciudad de Guadalajara. III. Primeros Vecinos Pobladores." Guadalajara, Boletín de la Junta Auxiliar Jalisciense de la Sociedad Mexicana de Geografía y Estadística, September 18, 1942, p. 277-331.

1565 Carrena Stampa, Manuel
"El Plano de la Ciudad de México en 1715 Hecho por Nicolás de Fer." México, Boletín de la Sociedad Mexicana de Geografía y Estadística, March/June 1948, p. 411-433.

1566 Chávez Hayhoe, A.
"Guadalajara de 1560 a 1600." Guadalajara, Boletín de la Junta Auxiliar Jalisciense de la Sociedad Mexicana de Geografía y Estadística, April 18, 1943, p. 13-49; October 18, 1943, p. 65-100.

1567 Cornejo Franco, J.
"Guadalajara Colonial." México, Arquitectura (14:61), March 1958, p. 3-10.

1568 Cornejo Franco, J.
"Orígenes de la Ciudad de Guadalajara." México, Problemas educativos de México (3:16), June 1959, p. 21-25.

1569 Díaz, Severo
"Guadalajara Actual." Guadalajara, Boletín de la Junta Auxiliar Jalisciense de la Sociedad Mexicana de Geografía y Estadística, August 1944, p. 127-185.

1570 Fernández, Justino
"Una Pintura Desconocida de la Plaza Mayor de México." México, Anales del Instituto de Investigaciones Estéticas (5:17), 1949, p. 27-35.

1571 Gallegos, J.I.
"Síntesis Histórica de la Ciudad de Durango." Monterrey, Humanitas, anuario del Centro de Estudios Humanísticos 8, Universidad de Nuevo León, 1967, p. 497-510.

1572 Galindo y Villa, Jesús
"México, la Ciudad Capital." México, Boletín de la Sociedad Mexicana de Geografía y Estadística, January 1934, p. 397-411.

1573 González Obregón, Luis
"Colonial Mexico City." México, Mexican Life, June 1946, p. 15-16, 68.

1574 "La Gran Tenochtitlan." México, Hoy, October 14, 1944, p. 19-23.

1575 Guerrero, Enrique
"Para una Biografía de la Ciudad." México, México en el arte 8, 1949, p. 3-40.

1576 Hernández Rodríguez, Rosaura
"Ciudades Prehispánicas de México." México, Memorias de la Academia Mexicana de la Historia

correspondiente de la Real de Madrid (17:2), April/June 1958, p. 218-231.

1577 Kaplan, D.
"City and Countryside in Mexican History." México, América indígena (24:1), January 1964, p. 59-69.

1578 Mora, Joaquín A.
"Origen y Cuna de la Ciudad de Monterrey." México, Universidad, Monterrey (8:9), July 1950, p. 189-201.

1579 Saldaña, José P.
"Monterrey en Fiestas." México, Intercambio, September 20, 1946, p. 6-7.

1580 Sánchez Santoreña, M.
"Meditación Sobre el Significado de lo Histórico en la Ciudad." México, Arquitectura México (22:86), June 1964, p. 67-78.

1581 Valle-Arizpe, Artemio del
"Biografía de un Viaje Paseo." México, Arquitectura (11:49), March 1955, p. 53-60.

Panama

1582 Arce, Enrique J.
"Fundación de Panamá. Cambia de Asiento." Panamá, Lotería, January 1948, p. 17-18.

1583 Caldwell, N. G.
"Panamá La Vieja. A Description of the First City of Panama in the Days of Its Glory, Before the Advent of Sir Henry Morgan and His Buccaneers." Panamá, The month in Panamá, March 1951, p. 8-9.

1584 Castillero Reyes, Ernesto de J.
"La Ciudad de Panamá. Su Pasado y su Presente." Panamá, Lotería (3:33), August 1958, p. 39-63.

1585 "Panamá en 1859." Panamá, Lotería 104, January 1950, p. 8-27.

1586 Rubio y Muñoz-Bocanegra, A.
"Algunos Datos Geográficos e Históricos Sobre la

Ciudad de Panamá." Panamá, Epocas, August 10, 1948, p. 20-21.

1587 "The Sack of Old Panama." Panamá, The month in Panama, January 1951, p. 12-13.

1588 Sosa, Juan B.
"La Antigua Ciudad de Panamá." Panamá, Lotería, May 1947, p. 5-9.

1589 Susto, Juan A.
"Un Portugués Precursor de la Fundación de la Nueva Ciudad de Panamá." Panamá, Lotería, January 1944, p. 5-7.

Paraguay

1590 Boccara, Augusto, & M.C. Repetto
"Compañía de Jesús: Planteo Urbano de las Misiones Jesuíticas Guaraníes." Buenos Aires, Nuestra arquitectura 368, July 1960, p. 48-50.

Peru

1591 Alvarado Sánchez, José
"Vida y Sonrisa de Lima." Bogotá, Revista de América, March 1945, p. 449-457.

1592 Arciniega, Rosa
"Pizarro y Lima." Lima, Fanal (10:43), 1955, p. 12-16.

1593 Belaunde Terry, Fernando
"La Evolución Urbana de Lima, una Obra de Juan Bromley y José Barbagelata." Lima, Arquitecto peruano, August 1945, entire issue.

1594 Feuillée, R.P.L.
"La Ciudad de Lima como Era en 1710." Buenos Aires, Revista geográfica americana, February 1940, p. 109-115.

1595 Fernández del Castillo, Antonio
"Lima." México, Memoria de la Academia Nacional de Historia y Geografía (14:6), 1955, p. 33-53.

1596 Fischer, Winifred
"Under the Dust of Lima." Lima, Peruvian times (20:1018), June 17, 1960, p. 4-6, 8-10; July 29, August 12, December 2, 1960.

1597 Gutiérrez Ferreira, Pedro P.
"Lima, Ciudad de los Reyes." Madrid, Cuadernos hispanoamericanos (41:121), January 1960, p. 83-95.

1598 "La Historia de Lima Acaso Es la de Nuestra Venerable Plaza Mayor, Tradicional y Legendaria, que Ahora Remoza con el Suntuoso Palacio Municipal." Lima, Cahuide, January-February 1944, p. 38, 40-41, 43-45.

1599 Longhurst, John E.
"Early Price Lists in Lima and a Petition for Redress." Hispanic American historical review (31:1), February 1951, p. 141-145.

1600 Miró Quesada Sosa, Aurelio
"La Ciudad en el Perú." Lima, Mercurio peruano, April 1942, p. 187-202.

1601 "Números Dedicados al IV Centenario de la Fundación de Lima." Madrid, Revista de las Españas, November-December 1934, p. 458-598.

1602 Ortiz de Zevallos, Luis
"La Creación Urbana en el Perú." Lima, El Arquitecto peruano (20:237/239), April/June 1957, p. 17-27.

1603 Pérez de Oleas Zambrano, L.
"Los Manos del Real de Lima." Quito, Museo histórico (12:37/38), December 6, 1960, p. 110-114.

1604 Perú. Archivo Nacional
"Descripción Anónima del Perú y de Lima a Principios del Siglo XVII." Lima, Revista del Archivo Nacional de Perú, January-June 1944, 3-44.

1605 Schaedel, Richard P.
"Incipient Urbanization and Secularization in Tiahuanacoid Peru." American antiquity, pt. 1 (31:3), January 1966, p. 338-344.

1606 Wiesse, Maria
"La Mujer Limeña en las 'Tradiciones.'" Lima, Hora del hombre, October 1944, p. 18-20.

1607 Zalamea, L.
"Farmer, City Founder and Poet; Founding and Construction of San Martín de Porres." Américas 15, November 1963, p. 35-39.

Venezuela

1608 Aguirre Elorriaga, Manuel
"La Instrucción en las Postrimerias de la Caracas Colonial. Un Interesante Documento Literario de 1788." Caracas, Boletín de la Academia Nacional de la Historia, April/June 1944, p. 113-120.

1609 Aragón, Víctor
"De la Caracas Vieja y Gloriosa." Caracas, Revista Shell (8:33), December 1959, p. 62-71.

1610 "Caracas a Través de los Siglos." Caracas, Boletín de la Academia Nacional de la Historia, January-March 1939, p. 21-185.

1611 "Conquista y Fundación de la Ciudad de Caracas." Caracas, Revista municipal del Distrito Federal, May 1940, p. 62-91.

1612 Jurado, Santos
"'El Milagro' o la Fundación de Santiago de León de Caracas." Caracas, Revista nacional de cultura, July/August 1945, p. 122-29.

1613 Martínez Pozueta, Juan A.
"Soliloquio de un Tranvía. Recuerdos de la Caracas Vieja." Caracas, Revista Shell (7:27), June 1958, p. 77-80.

1614 Millán, Blas
"Caracas bajo el Pontificado de Don Fray Mauro de Tovar." Caracas, Revista Shell (5:19), June 1956, p. 48-55.

1615 Nuñez, Enrique B.
"Los Pendones de Santiago de León de Caracas." Caracas, Revista nacional de cultura, March/April 1946, p. 26-50.

URBAN MATRIX FOR LITERATURE AND THE ARTS
(including Creative Writing; Learned Institutions; Music; Painting and Sculpture; Theater; and Intellectual Life generally)

Books

General

1616 Ghurye, Govind S.
Cities and civilization. Bombay, Popular Prakashan, 1962, 306p.

1617 Mumford, Lewis
The culture of cities. New York, Harcourt, Brace, 1938, 586p.

1618 Mumford, Lewis
The role of the creative arts in contemporary society; an address at the University of New Hampshire, February 28, 1957. Durham, University of New Hampshire, 1958, 23p.

Latin America

1619 Bastide, Roger
Arte y sociedad. México, Fondo de Cultura Económica, 1948, 231p.

1620 Boletín interamericano de música. Washington, # 54-, Division of Music, Dept. of Cultural Affairs, Pan American Union, July 1966- .

1621 Bueno, Miguel
Humanismo y universidad. México, Instituto de Investigaciones Sociales, Universidad Nacional Autónoma de México, 1960, 154p.

1622 Carpani, Ricardo
Arte y revolución en América Latina. Buenos Aires, Ed. Coyoacán, 1960? 79p.

1623 Chase, Gilbert
The artist. (In Johnson, John J., ed. Continuity

and change in Latin America. Stanford, Stanford University Press, 1964, p. 101-135.)

1624 Ellison, Fred P.
The writer. (In Johnson, John J., ed. Continuity and change in Latin America. Stanford, Stanford University Press, 1964, p. 79-100.)

1625 Franco, Jean
The modern culture of Latin America: society and the artist. New York, Praeger, 1967, 339p.

1626 Marinello, Juan
Meditación americana; cinco ensayos. Santa Clara, Dirección de Publicaciones, Universidad Central de Santa Clara, 1963, 241p.

1627 Mendieta y Núñez, Lucio
Sociología del arte. México, Instituto de Investigaciones Sociales, Universidad Nacional Autónoma de México, 1962, 326p.

1628 Mesa, José de, & Teresa Gisbert
Pintura contemporánea, 1952-1962. La Paz, Dirección Nacional de Informaciones de la Presidencia de la República, 1962, 50p.

1629 Mirador. New York (I:7), Inter-American Foundation for the Arts, 1966- .

1630 Teixeira, Anisio
A universidade e a liberdade humana. Rio de Janeiro, Ministério da Educação e Cultura, Serviço de Documentação, 1954, 76p.

Argentina

1631 Capdevila, Arturo
Tierra mia; Buenos Aires y las 14 provincias argentinas: la tierra y su alma. Buenos Aires, Espasa-Calpe Argentina, 1945, 166p.

1632 Carpani, Ricardo
La política en el arte. Buenos Aires, Ed. Coyoacán, 1962, 63p.

1633 Colón, Antonio
Contribución al estudio de la plástica santafesina. Santa Fé, Castellví, 1959, 67p.

1634 Comisión Nacional de la Reconquista y Defensa de Buenos Aires
La defensa de Buenos Aires en su 150 aniversario, 1807-1957, conferencias y discursos . . . Buenos Aires, 1962, 85p.

1635 Fajardo Terán, Florencia
Homenaje de la ciudad de Maldonado a la Ciudad de Buenos Aires en el CL aniversario de su gloriosa revolución. Maldonado, Concejo Departamental, 1960, 231p.

1636 Franchisena, César, et al
Las artes en la sociedad de masas. Ciudad Universitaria, Córdoba, República Argentina, Dirección General de Publicidad, 1961, 111p.

1637 Kreibohm, Enrique
Un siglo de cultura provinciana . . . Tucumán, Universidad Nacional de Tucumán, 1960, 176p.

1638 Lago, Catalina E.
Buenos Aires 1858: panorama artístico de la ciudad a través de sus diarios. Buenos Aires, 1961, 55p.

1639 Martínez Cuitiño Vicente
El café de Los Inmortales. Buenos Aires, Kraft, 1949, 393p.

1640 Otero Pedrayo, Ramón
Por os vieiros de saudade; lemblanzas e crónicas de um viaxe a Buenos Aires. Vigo, Ed. Galaxia, 1952, 203p.

1641 Pintos, J. M.
Así fué Buenos Aires: tipos y costumbres de una época, 1900-1950. Buenos Aires, Impr. Coni, 1954, 204p.

1642 Rottin, Luciano
Buenos Aires, ciudad, patria, mundo. Buenos

Aires, 1949, 113p.

Bolivia

1643 Beltrán Heredia, B. A.
El carnaval de Oruro. Oruro, Ed. Universitaria, 1956, 159p.

1644 Bolivia. Comité pro Cuarto Centenario de la Fundación de La Paz
La Paz en su IV centenario, 1548–1948. 4v. La Paz, 1948.

1645 Diez de Medina, Federico
Museos arqueológicos y colecciones de La Paz. La Paz, Impr. Artística, 1954, 58p.

1646 Velasco Franco, Antonio, ed.
Album conmemorativo del IV centenario de Santa Cruz de la Sierra, 1561-1961. 1st ed. Santa Cruz de la Sierra? 1961- .

1647 Villaroel Claure, Rigoberto
Arte contemporáneo . . . La Paz, 1952, 131p.

1648 Villaroel Claure, Rigoberto
Bolivia . . . Washington, Pan American Union, 1963, 86p.

Brazil

1649 Andrade, Mario de
Ensaio sôbre a música brasileira. São Paulo, Martins, 1962, 188p.

1650 Anuário de literatura brasileira. Rio de Janeiro, 1960- .

1651 Araujo, C. da S.
A cultura no Brasil colonial, vista através de sua literatura. Rio de Janeiro, Livraria São José, 1955, 71p.

1652 Azevedo, Luiz H. Correa de
Música do tempo desta casa. Rio de Janeiro, 194- , 58p.

1653 Bardi, P. M.
The arts in Brazil; a new museum at São Paulo.

Milan, Ed. del Milione, 1956, 296p.

1654 Brazil. Serviço de Estatística da Educação e Cultura
Aspectos estatísticos da vida cultural brasileira. 2v. Rio de Janeiro, 1956-8.

1655 Broca, José Brito
A vida literaria no Brasil-1900. Rio de Janeiro, Ministério da Educação e Cultura, Serviço de Documentação, 1956, 275p.

1656 Campos, Renato Carneiro
Arte, sociedade região; notas sôbre o movimento regionalista do Nordeste e sua projeção sôbre alguns escritores, artistas e outros intérpretes modernos do homem da sociedade da paisagem brásileiras . . . Salvador, Progresso, 1960, 118p.

1657 Carvalho, Edmea A.
O ballet no Brasil. Capa: Saulo L. Garrido. Rio de Janeiro, Pongetti, 1962? 195p.

1658 Castelo Branco, Lydia
Panorama bibliotecario do Recife, relatorio do estágio ao curso de biblioteconomia da U.R. Recife, Prefeitura Municipal do Recife, Depto. de Documentação e Cultura, 1955, 58p.

1659 Cortes, C.
Homens e instituições no Rio. Rio de Janeiro, 1957, 522p.

1660 Ferreira, José Ribamar
Cultura posta em questão. Rio de Janeiro, Ed. Civilização Brasileira, 1965, 126p.

1661 Galvão, Alfredo
Subsídios para a história da Academia Imperial e da Escola Nacional de Belas Artes. Rio de Janeiro, 1954, 142p.

1662 Girão, Raimundo
Geografia estética de Fortaleza. Fortaleza, Impr. Universitaria do Ceará, 1959, 360p.

1663 Jorge, Fernando
Vidas de grandes pintores do Brasil . . . São Paulo, Martins, 1954, 308p.

1664 Lima, Alceu Amoroso
A missão de São Paulo. Rio de Janeiro, Livraria AGIR, 1962, 42p.

1665 Martins, Luis
Homens e livros. São Paulo, Conselho Estadual de Cultura, Comissão de Literatura, 1962, 106p.

1666 Massaud, Moisés
Temas brasileiros. São Paulo, Conselho Estadual de Cultura, Comissão de Literatura, 1964, 142p.

1667 Milano, Miguel
Os fantasmas da São Paulo antiga; estudo histórico-literário da cidade de São Paulo. São Paulo, Ed. Saraiva, 1949, 111p.

1668 Monteiro Real, Regina
Casa de Rui Barbosa; resumo histórico de suas atividades. Rio de Janeiro, Casa de Rui Barbosa, 1957, 60p.

1669 Moraes, Eneida de
História do carnaval carioca. Rio de Janeiro, Ed. Civilização Brasileira, 1958, 315p.

1670 Negro, Carlos del
Contribuição ao estudo da pintura mineira. Rio de Janeiro, Publicações do Patrimônio Histórico e Artístico Nacional, 1958, 160p.

1671 Orquesta Sinfônica Brasileira
Relatório. Rio de Janeiro. Annual.

1672 Recife, Brazil. Direitoria de Documentação e Cultura
Teatro Santa Isabel; documentos para a sua história. Recife, 1950- .

1673 Ribeiro, Adalberto M.
Instituções brasileiras de cultura: Instituto Nacional do Livro, Casa de Ruy Barbosa, Museu Histórico

Nacional, Instituto Nacional do Cinema Educativo. Rio de Janeiro, 1945, 204p.

1674 Rio de Janeiro. Biblioteca Nacional
Rio musical; crônica de uma cidade. Exposição comemorativa do IV centenário da cidade do Rio de Janeiro. Rio de Janeiro, Biblioteca Nacional, Div. de Publicações e Divulgação, 1965, 51p.

1675 Rodrigues, José J.
A evolução a eficiência e a grandeza do Liceu Literário Português; artigos . . . Rio de Janeiro, Liceu Literário Português, 1948, 63p.

1676 Taunay, Affonso de Escragnolle
A missão artística de 1816. Rio de Janeiro, 1956, 351p.

1677 Torres, Heloisa A.
Museums of Brazil. Tr. by John Knox. Rio de Janeiro, Cultural Div., Ministry of Foreign Affairs, 1953, 82p.

1678 Vasconcelos, Ary
Panorama da música popular brasileira. São Paulo, Martins, 1964- .

Chile

1679 Abascal Brunet, Manuel, & Eugenio Pereira Salas
Pepe Vila. La zarzuela chica en Chile. Santiago, Impr. Universitaria, 1952, 225p.

1680 Alvarez Urquieta, Luis
La pintura en Chile. Santiago, Impr. La Ilustración, 1928, 90p.

1681 Chile. Universidad. Instituto de Extensión Musical
La temporada de conciertos de 1959. Santiago, 1959, 99p.

1682 Pereira Salas, Eugenio
Centenario del Teatro Municipal, 1857-1957. Santiago de Chile? 1957? unpaged.

1683 Romero, Antonio R.
Chile. Tr. by Ralph E. Dimmick and William

McL. Rivera. Washington, Pan American Union, 1963, 76p.

1684 Stuardo Ortiz, Carlos
El Liceo de Chile, 1828-1831. Antecedentes para su historia. Santiago, Impr. Universitaria, 1950, 146p.

Colombia

1685 García Valencia, Abel
Medellín en el mundo, en la poesía y en la historia . . . Medellín, Publicaciones de la Revista de la Universidad de Antioquia, 194- , 14p.

1686 Medellín, Colombia. Biblioteca Pública Piloto para la América Latina
Primer año de labores, 24 de octubre 1954-1955. UNESCO, Gobierno de Colombia. Medellín, Ed. Bedout, 1955, unpaged.

1687 Medellín, Colombia. Universidad de Antioquia
Algunos pintores antioqueños de todas las tendencias; publicación especial con motivo de los 25 años de labores. Medellín, 1958, 20p.

1688 Peñalosa Rueda, Juan
El Teatro Colón. Bogotá, Empresa Nacional de Publicaciones, 1956, 40p.

1689 Perdomo Escobar, José I.
Historia de la música en Colombia. 3d ed. Bogotá, ABC, 1963, 422p.

1690 Spain. Instituto de Cultura Hispánica
Arte de Colombia. Madrid, Eds. Castilla, 1963, 96p.

Costa Rica

1691 Araya Rojas, José R.
Vida musical de Costa Rica. San José, Impr. Nacional, 1957, 142p.

Cuba

1692 Betancourt, Juan R.
Mi lucha por los compositores. Havana, 1955, 89p.

1693 Carpentier, Alejo
La música en Cuba. Havana, 1961, 205p.

1694 Carreño Morales, Mario
Antillanas . . . Santiago, Cuadernos del Pacífico, 1949, 13p.

1695 Henríquez Ureña, Max
La Sociedad de Conferencias de la Habana y su época; conferencia pronunciada en el Ateneo de la Habana el 11 de noviembre de 1953. Havana, Oficina del Historiador de la Ciudad, 1954, 47p.

1696 Valderrama y Peña, Esteban, & Benigno Vásquez Rodríguez
La pintura y la escultura en Cuba. Pairting and sculpture in Cuba. La peinture et la sculpture à Cuba. Ed. homenaje del Cincuentenario de la Independencia de Cuba, 1902-1952. Havana, 1953, 351p.

Dominican Republic

1697 Coopersmith, Jacob R.
Music and musicians of the Dominican Republic. Washington, Pan American Union, 1949, 146p.

1698 Cordero, Armando
Panorama de la filosofía en Santo Domingo. 2v. Santo Domingo, Impr. Arte y Cine, 1962.

1699 García, Juan F.
Panorama de la música dominicana. Ciudad Trujillo, Secretaría de Estado de Educación y Bellas Artes, 1947, 46p.

Ecuador

1700 Carrión, Alejandro
Los poetas quiteños de "El Ocioso en Faenza." I: Historia y crítica. Quito, Casa de la Cultura Ecuatoriana, 1957, 372p.

1701 Filosofía y letras. Quito, 1950-

1702 Villasís Terán, Enrique M.
Quito y su progreso. Charlas hechas para la

Radioemisora Instituto Municipal de Cultura. Quito, Impr. Municipal, 1954, 96 plus 52p.

El Salvador

1703 García, Miguel A., ed.
San Salvador, desde la Conquista hasta el año de 1894. San Salvador, Impr. Nacional, 1952-

1704 San Salvador. Escuela Normal de Maestras "España"
Algunos maestros, pintores, músicos y escritores salvadoreños. San Salvador, 1953, 309p.

Guatemala

1705 Cifuentes, José L.
Algunos pintores contemporáneos de Guatemala. Guatemala? 1956, 106p.

1706 Guatemala (City) Museo del Libro Antiguo
Museo del Libro Antiguo. Ancient Book Museum. Antigua, 1959, 27p.

1707 Salazar, Ramón A.
Historia de desenvolvimiento intelectual de Guatemala: época colonial. 3v. Guatemala, Ministerio de Educación Pública, 1951.

Honduras

1708 Mariñas Otero, Luis
La pintura en Honduras. Tegucigalpa, Universidad Nacional Autónoma de Honduras, Depto. de Extensión Universitaria, 1959, 21p.

1709 Sánchez, Roberto M.
Significado de la Escuela Nacional de Bellas Artes de Honduras, 1940-1953. Tegucigalpa, Talleres Tip. Nacionales, 1953, 22p.

Mexico

1710 Campos, Rubén M.
El folklore músical de las ciudades. Investigación acerca de la música mexicana para bailar y cantar. México, Secretaría de Educación Pública, 1930, 455p.

1711 Cardoza y Aragón, Luis
Pintura mexicana contemporánea. México, Impr. Universitaria, 1953, 311p.

1712 Carnet musical. México, 1945-

1713 Chavez, Carlos
La música mexicana. México, 1949, 32p.

1714 Crabbe de Rubín, Madeleine
La ciudad de México en la novela mexicana del siglo XIX. México, 1951, 120p.

1715 Forster, Merlin H.
Los contemporáneos, 1920-1932; perfil de un experimento vanguardista México. México, Eds. De Andrea, 1964, 145p.

1716 Gómez, Enriqueta
Páginas musicales. Mexico, Ed. "Mi Mundo," 1956, 501p.

1717 Leal, Fernando
El derecho de la cultura . . . México, Organización Cultural Mexicana, 1952, 170p.

1718 Mendoza, Vicente T.
Vida y costumbres de la Universidad de México. México, Instituto de Investigaciones Estéticas, 1951, 71p.

1719 Mexico (City) Instituto Nacional de Bellas Artes. Depto. de Literatura
25 años del Palacio de Bellas Artes. México, 1959, 89 plus 69p.

1720 Rivera, Diego
My art, my life, an autobiography. New York, Citadel Press, 1960, 318p.

1721 Stewart, Virginia
45 contemporary Mexican artists; a twentieth-century renaissance. Stanford, Stanford University Press, 1951, 167p.

Panama

1722 Biesanz, John, & Mavis Biesanz
Panamá y su pueblo. Panamá, Ed. Letras, 1961, 308p.

1723 Díaz de Bosquez, Gilma
El estado actual de los servicios bibliotecarios en la ciudad de Panamá. Panamá, Universidad de Panamá, 1965, variously paged.

Peru

1724 Bermejo, Vladimiro
Panorama intelectual de Arequipa, 1540-1940. Arequipa? Tip. S. Quiroz, 1945, 242p.

Uruguay

1725 Ayestarán, Lauro
El centenario del Teatro Solís 1856-25 de agosto-1956. Montevideo, Comisión de Teatros Municipales, 1956, 15p.

1726 Ayestarán, Lauro
La música en el Uruguay. Montevideo, Servicio Oficial de Difusión Radio Eléctrica, 1953-

1727 Gallinal Heber, Alejandro
Camino de ronda. Montevideo, Instituto Uruguayo de Cultura Hispánica, 1956, 215p.

Venezuela

1728 Calcaño, José A.
La ciudad y su música; crónica musical de Caracas. Caracas, Conservatorio Teresa Carreño, 1958, 518p.

1729 Inter-American Conference. 10th, Caracas, 1954
La pintura en Venezuela. Caracas, Secretaría General de la Décima Conferencia Interamericana, 1954, 220p.

1730 Nazoa, Aquilés
Los humoristas de Caracas. Caracas, Comisión Nacional del Cuatricentenario de Caracas, 1966, 537p.

1731 Nucete Sardi, José
Notas sobre la pintura y la escultura en Venezuela. 2d ed. Caracas, Ed. Avila Gráfica, 1950, 111p.

1732 Stallbohm, Arnold
La música, sus intérpretes y el público de Venezuela. Caracas, Eds. Sursum, 1959, 182p.

1733 Suma universitaria. Caracas, Dirección de Cultura, 1955-

West Indies and the Caribbean

1734 Hill, Errol, ed.
The artist in West Indian society; a symposium. Mona, University of the West Indies, Dept. of Extra-Mural Studies, 1963? 79p.

Periodical Articles

General

1735 Almeida Prado, D. de
"Dramatic Renaissance." Atlantic 197, February 1956, p. 157-160.

1736 Campos, J.
"Realismo Mágico o Realismo Crítico?" México, Revista de la Universidad de México (15:5), January 1961, p. 4-8.

1737 Casais Monteiro, A.
"A Crítica Sociológica da Literatura." Sao Paulo, Revista brasiliense 45, January-February 1963, p. 38-51.

1738 Chaves Villa, H.
"Arte o Mensaje Social." Medellín, Universidad de Antioquia (35:138), July-September 1959, p. 199-207.

1739 Orrego Salas, Juan
"Rol de la Educación Musical en las Relaciones Entre la Creación Artística y el Público." Santiago, Revista musical chilena (18:87-88), January-June 1964, p. 46-56.

1740 Otero, L., et al
"Conversación Sobre el Arte y la Literatura." Havana, Casa de las Américas (4:22-23), January-February 1964, p. 130-138.

1741 Ovalles, C.
"Sobre Literatura de la Rebeldía." Bogotá, Espiral 86, March 1963, p. 61-78.

1742 Pacheco, J.E.
"Simpatías y Diferencias." México, Revista de la Universidad de Mexico (16:11), July 1962, p. 32.

1743 Passafarri de Gutierrez, C., & E.P. Castelli
"La Dinámica Socio-Cultural y la Expresión Literaria." Santa Fé, Universidad 54, October-December 1962, p. 231-243.

1744 Sanchez-Saez, B.
"Las Pasiones Como Problemas." Sao Paulo, Revista da Universidade Católica de Sao Paulo (24:43-44), September-December 1962, p. 467-471.

1745 Schechner, R.
"Blau and Irving at Lincoln Center." Tulane drama review 9, Summer 1965, p. 15-18.

1746 Silone, I.
"El Escritor y la Sociedad." Buenos Aires, Sur 280, January-February 1963, p. 5-7.

1747 "La Vida Actual." Newsweek 37, June 11, 1951, p. 90-91.

1748 Zambrano, M.
"Realismo y Realidad." México, Cuadernos de bellas artes (3:3), March 1962, p. 49-53.

Latin America

1749 Agramonte, R.
"La Moderna Civilización Lationoamericana y su Itinerario Histórico-Social." México, Revista mexicana de sociología (25:2), May-August 1963, p. 439-503.

1750 Anderson Imbert, Enrique
"Literatura Hispanoamericana de Posguerra." México, Revista de México (15:2), October 1960, p. 4-6.

1751 Anderson Imbert, Enrique
"Misión de los Intelectuales en Hispanoamérica." México, Cuadernos americanos (22:3), May-June 1963, p. 33-48.

1752 Angulo Iñiguez, D.
"Características Generales del Arte Hispano-Americano." Paris, Cahiers d'histoire mondiale (4:1), 1957, p. 59-82.

1753 Arciniegas, Germán
"Los Cuadros de Costumbres y las Malas Costumbres." Iowa City, Revista iberoamericana (21:41-42), January-December 1956, p. 245-259.

1754 Arciniega, Rosa
"La Literatura Hispanoamericana Vista Hace 59 Años." México, Cuadernos americanos (92:2), March-April 1957, p. 175-180.

1755 Arrom, Juan J.
"The flowering of Latin American Culture in Literature, Art and Music: an Aesthetic Approach." Brussels, Civilisations (5:4), 1955, p. 543-548.

1756 Bindhoff de Sigren, C.
"Informe Sobre el Estado Actual y la Organización de la Educación Musical en América Latina." Santiago, Revista musical chilena (18:87-88), January-June 1964, p. 5-8.

1757 Bueno, S.
"El Cuento en Hispano-América." San Salvador, Cultura 7, January-February 1956, p. 137-144.

1758 Bustamante, E. L.
"Ensayo Sobre la Música en Iberoamérica." Madrid, Arbor (43 bis:165-166), September-October 1959, p. 544-561.

1759 Caneva, R.
"El Realismo Crítico y la Novela en América." Medellín, Universidad de Antioquia, (36:140), January-March 1960, p. 21-32.

1760 Catlin, Stanton L.
"New Vistas in Latin American Art"; "Colonial Painting in Latin America," by M. Soria. Art in America (47:3), Fall 1959, p. 24-39.

1761 Chase, Gilbert
"Problema de la Música Americana Actual." San José, Brecha (4:9), May 1960, p. 17-19.

1762 Correa, G.
"El Nacionalismo Cultural en la Literatura Hispanoamericana." México, Cuadernos americanos (98:2), March-April 1958, p. 225-236.

1763 Gil Tovar, F.
"Pintura y Música Iberoamericanas de Hoy." Bogotá, Bolívar 36, January-February 1955, p. 171-176.

1764 González, M. P.
"Hispanic American Literature." México, Mexican life, July 1, 1948, p. 24, 46-48.

1765 Grossman, R.
"Dos Ensayos Sobre Latinoamérica I-II." Bogotá, Ideas y Valores (3:11-12), June-October 1954, p. 10-42.

1766 Latcham, Ricardo A.
"Perspectivas de la Literatura Hispanoamericana Contemporánea." Concepción, Atenea (131:380-381) April-September 1958, p. 305-336.

1767 Mander, John
"Mexico City to Buenos Aires." London, Encounter (XXV:3), September 1965, p. 5-14.

1768 Pachón Padilla, E.
"El 'Realismo Mágico' en la Narrativa Hispanoamericana." Bogotá, Boletín cultural y bibliográfico (6:8), 1963, p. 1170-1171.

1769 Pottier, B.
"La Langue des Capitales Latino-Américaines." Toulouse, Caravelle 3, 1964, p. 90-95.

1770 Ross, W.
"El Sentido de una Cosmovisión en la Literatura Latinoamericana." Bogotá, Bolívar 45, November-December 1955, p. 927-940.

1771 Santa Cruz, D.
"Realidad Musical de América Latina." Paris, Cuadernos 19, July-August 1956, p. 211-216.

1772 Teitelboim, Volodia
"Tendences de la Littérature en Amérique Latine." Paris, Nouvelle revue internationale (3:3), March 1960, p. 101-113.

Argentina

1773 Bastian, W.M.
"Famous American Theatres: Colón Theatre." Theatre arts 42, December 1958, p. 50-51.

1774 Caamaño, H.
"The Colón Theater in Buenos Aires." Inter-American music bulletin 54, July 1966, p. 1-9.

1775 Candee, M.D.
"Theatre Below the Equator." Theatre arts 37, August 1953, p. 65.

1776 Gimenez, A.E.
"Música: Posibilidades y Anhelos para 1964." Buenos Aires, Criterio (36:1443), January 9, 1964, p. 32-35.

1777 Gomez Blas, J.
"Theater in the Street: Buenos Aires Stages 18th-Century Venetian Comedy." Américas 10, June 1958, p. 12-17.

1778 Holbo, Paul S.
"José Ingenieros, Argentine Intellectual Historian: La Evolución de las Ideas Argentinas: Américas 21, July 1964, p. 20-35.

1779 Knepler, G.
"Verdi at the Colón." Opera news 28, December 21, 1963, p. 32-33.

1780 Lamuraglia, N.
"Ubicación de la Música en el Quehacer Argentino." Buenos Aires, Revista del Notariado (61:639), May-June 1958, p. 390-399.

1781 Nuñez, Solón
"Un Día de Arte Nacional en Buenos Aires." San José, Brecha (4:5), January 1960, p. 6-8.

1782 Pelazza, C.
"El Arte, 'lo Social,' la Nación Argentina." Buenos Aires, Dinámica social (7:80), June 1957, p. 17-20.

1783 Silva, M. N.
"Pioneer Theatres: Buenos Aires Independents." Américas 14, November 1962, p. 32-36.

1784 Spinedi, C.
"Along Calle Florida." Américas 8, June 1956, p. 8-11.

1785 Uribe, B.
"Arte Nuevo en la Argentina." Buenos Aires, Criterio (37:1448), March 26, 1964, p. 226-230.

1786 Vinacua, R.
"Speaking of Argentina: a Survey of Recent Cultural Trends." Américas 13, December 1961, p. 24-27.

1787 Vincent, J.
"New Opera in Buenos Aires." Américas 6, October 1964, p. 35-38.

Bolivia

1788 López Avila, H.
"La Música de Bolivia." La Paz, Educación boliviana (7:1), 1959, p. 22-44.

Brazil

1789 Azevedo, F. de
"Da Cultura Brasileira." São Paulo, Revista de

historia (29:60), October-December 1964, p. 369-382.

1790 Baker, E.C.
"Brazilian Bouillabaisse; Eighth Sao Paulo Bienal." Art news 64, December 1965, p. 30-31.

1791 Barroso, H.M. Jofre
"Brasil: Actual Prosa de Ficción." Buenos Aires, Ficción 39, September-October 1962, p. 71-79.

1792 Berkowitz, M.
"The Art in Brazil." Rio de Janeiro, Brazilian-American survey (11:22), 1st quarter 1964, p. 94-95.

1793 Brandão, O.
"Pelo Realismo Revolucionario." São Paulo, Revista brasiliense 35, May-June 1961, p. 95-119.

1794 Bruno, Ernani Silva
"Bibliotecas e Livreiros na Cidade de Sao Paulo." São Paulo, Boletím bibliográfico 15, 1950, p. 77-79.

1795 Castello, J.A.
"Aspectos do Realismo-Naturalismo no Brasil." São Paulo, Revista de historia (6:14), April-June 1953, p. 437-456.

1796 Corbisier, R.
"Situação e Alternativas da Cultura Brasileira." Sao Paulo, Digesto econômico (12:130), July-August 1956, p. 37-57.

1797 de Jong, G.
"Music in Brazil." Boletin interamericana de música 3, September 1962, p. 1-15.

1798 Fischer, E.
"O Problema do Real na Arte Moderna." Rio de Janeiro, Estudos sociais (4:16), March 1963, p. 412-432.

1799 Gómez-Sicre, José
"Today's Art at São Paulo." Américas 10, January 1958, p. 30-33.

1800 Gómez-Sicre, José
"World Art in Brazil; São Paulo Biennial." Américas 12, January 1960, p. 18-23.

1801 Konder, L.
"Alguns Problemas do Realismo Socialista." Rio de Janeiro, Estudos sociais (5:17), June 1963, p. 46-60.

1802 Landau, G.D.
"Patterns Underfoot." Américas 8, September 1956, p. 34-36.

1803 Mariz, V.
"A Renovação Artística e Literaria no Brazil Contemporâneo." Coimbra, Brasilia 5, 1950, p. 487-499.

1804 Martins, I.P. de
"Panorama y Sumario de la Vida Intelectual Brasileña en los Ultimos Diez Años." Rio de Janeiro, Brazilian American survey (4:21, special edition), December 1963, p. 8-9.

1805 Mortara, Giorgio
"Aspectos Culturais da Evolução e das Características Demográficas do Brasil." Rio de Janeiro, Revista brasileira de estatística (16:62), April-June 1955, p. 81-89.

1806 Muricy, J. de Andrade
"Music, Key to the National Psyche." Atlantic (197:2), February 1956, p. 109-111.

1807 "Museum in Rio Conceived as Fine Arts Center." Architectural record 133, March 1963, p. 149-152.

1808 Richards, S.
"Theatre." Theatre arts 47, February 1963, p. 64-65.

1809 Silva, F. Barbosa e
"São Paulo Art Center." Américas 6, October 1954, p. 20-23.

1810 Spanudis, T.
"Arte Moderna no Brasil." São Paulo, Habitat 76, March 1964, p. 94-102.

1811 Tobias, J.A.
"Contribuição à História da Filosofia da Arte no Brasil." São Paulo, Revista da Universidade Católica de São Paulo (17:30), June 1959, p. 143-175.

Chile

1812 Cruz-Coke Ossa, C.
"Santiago Story." Opera news 25, January 14, 1961, p. 33.

1813 Iturriaga, E.
"Algunas Experiencias en el Campo de la Difusión de la Música Contemporánea Entre los Estudiantes." Santiago, Revista musical chilena (18:87-88), January-June 1964, p. 41-45.

1814 Lafourcade, E.
"La Nueva Literatura Chilena." México, Cuadernos americanos (123:4), July-August 1962, p. 229-256.

1815 Melendez, L.
"Panorama de los Escritores Chilenos." (142:392), April-June 1961, p. 109-115.

Colombia

1816 Espinosa, G.
"Colombian Music and Musicians in Contemporary Culture." Boletín interamericano de música 27, January 1962, p. 1-4.

1817 Ferrán, J.
"Teatro de Arte Popular en Bogotá." Madrid, Mundo hispánico (18:213), December 1965, p. 36-37.

1818 Hoz, E. de la
"Música Contemporánea de Colombia." Madrid,

Cuadernos hispanoamericanos (31:93), September 1957, p. 338-354.

1819 Piñeros Corpas, J.
"Reflexiones Sobre el Estudio de la Literatura Colombiana." Bogotá, Boletín de la Academia Colombiana (13:47), April-May 1963, p. 81-93.

1820 Reid, John T.
"Cultural Bogotá." World affairs, June 1939, p. 110-112.

1821 Villa Esguerra, J.
"El Arte en la Arquitectura Moderna Colombiana." Bogotá, Revista de la Universidad de los Andes (2:3), September 1959, p. 52-62.

Costa Rica

1822 Ulloa Zamorano, A.
"La Mujer en la Literatura Costarricense." San José, Brecha (6:5), January 1962, p. 7-9.

Cuba

1823 Carreño Morales, Mario
"La Plástica Cubana de Hoy." Panorama (2:5), 1953, p. 76-95.

1824 Coulthard, Gabriel R.
"The Situation of the Writer in Contemporary Cuba." San Juan, Caribbean studies (7:1), April 1967, p. 23-35.

1825 Jerez Villareal, J.
"Una Revolución Literaria." Havana, Universidad de La Habana (27:164), November-December 1963, p. 171-183.

1826 Menton, Seymour
"La Novela de la Revolución Cubana." Havana, Casa de las Américas (4:22-23), January-February 1964, p. 150-156.

Dominican Republic

1827 Díaz Miese, R.
"Un Lustro de Esfuerzo Artístico." Ciudad Trujillo, Cuadernos dominicanos de cultura, July 1945, p. 3-124.

Ecuador

1828 Arbelaez Camacho, C.
"Arte Hispano-Americano: Ecuador." Bogotá, Arco (5:33), May 1963, p. 334-340.

1829 Arías Robalino, A.
"Letra Ecuatoriana y Conciencia Nacional." Caracas, Política 22, June-July 1962, p. 57-72.

1830 Cabezas Borja, Reinaldo
"Quito, Luz de América." Quito, El Libertador, January/March 1943, p. 29-32.

1831 Garcés Larrea, C.
"El Arte y la Literatura Ecuatorianos." Quito, Ateneo ecuatoriano (3:3-4), October 29, 1953, p. 140-145.

1832 Vargas, José M.
"El Arte Ecuatoriano en el Siglo Veinte." Quito, Letras del Ecuador (18:127), January-June 1963, p. 1-2, 14-15.

Guatemala

1833 Mariñas, L.
"La Revolución Intelectual de Guatemala." Madrid, Cuadernos hispanoamericanos (25:71), November 1955, pp. 137-152.

1834 Orive, M.C.
"Adonde Vamos; Actualidad Artística de Guatemala." Guatemala, Salón 13 (1:1), February 1960, p. 43-46.

Haiti

1835 Baqueiro Foster, G.
"Concurrencias Determinantes en la Música de Haiti." México, Humanismo (4:17-18), January-February 1954, p. 27-33.

1836 Ewald, M.
"Le Baneco: Nouvelle Forme d'Expression de l'Art Haïtien." Port-au-Prince, Conjonction 94-95, 1964, p. 59-61.

Honduras

1837 Mariñas Otero, L.
"Panorama de la Música Hondureña." Madrid, Cuadernos hispanoamericanos (35:103), July, 1958-

Mexico

1838 Brushwood, Joseph S.
"The Mexican Understanding of Realism and Naturalism." Hispania (43:4), December 1960, p. 521-528.

1839 Coss, J.A.
"En Busca de la Renovación de Nuestro Lenguaje Musical." México, Estaciones (3:10), Summer 1958, p. 230-236.

1840 "Living Temple; National Museum of Anthropology." Time 85, June 25, 1965, p. 76-78.

1841 Mayer Serra, Otto
"Notes from Abroad." High fidelity 12, January 1962, p. 22.

1842 Mendieta y Nuñez, Lucio
"Sociología del Arte." México, Revista mexicana de sociología (19:1), January-April 1957, p. 67-84.

1843 "Mexico's Artistic Revolution: the Gay Face of Her New University." London, Illustrated London news 245, October 10, 1964, p. 554.

1844 Monterde, Francisco
"Trayectoría de las Letras Mexicanas." México, Cuadernos de bellas artes (4:4), April 1963, p. 16-20.

1845 Muñoz, Peggy
"Mexico's Future Musicians. The Future of Mexican Music Lies in the Work Being Carried Out by the National Conservatory of Music." Mexico, Mexican-American review (20:2), February 1952, p. 18-26.

1846 Nelken, M.
"Arte Mexicano de Hoy." México, Cuadernos

americanos (22:3), May-June 1963, p. 237-249.

1847 Rivas, G.
"The New Universality in Mexican Art." México, Mexican life (35:1), January 1959, p. 30-32.

1848 Rivera, Diego
"La Cuestión del Arte en México." México, Indice (1:3), January-March 1952, p. 100-115.

1849 Schmidt, H.
"American Artist Looks at Mexico; Paintings." Look 22, September 2, 1958, p. 38-40.

1850 Weinstock, H.
"Music by Chavez." Américas 3, March 1951, p. 10-12.

1851 Wilder, E.
"Mexican Workshop: Taller de Gráfica Popular, a Workshop for Popular Graphic Art." Nation 159, September 9, 1944, p. 299.

1852 Willhelm, K.H., et al
"South of the Border." Opera news 29, December 12, 1964, p. 32-33.

Nicaragua

1853 Cuadra, P.A.
"Introducción a la Literatura Nicaragüense." San Salvador, Cultura 29, July-September 1963, p. 55-66.

Panama

1854 Brenes, G.
"La Música en Panamá." Panamá, Lotería (1:3), February 1956, p. 37-46.

Paraguay

1855 Pla, Josefina
"Contenido Humano y Social de la Narrativa." México, Panoramas (2:8), March-April 1964, p. 83-99.

Peru

1856 Raygada, C.
"Guía Musical del Perú." Lima, Fénix 14, 1964, p. 3-95.

Uruguay

1857 Benedetti, Mario
"Cambio de Sueños: Arraigo y Evasión en la Actual Literatura Uruguaya." México, Revista de la Universidad de México (16:7), March 1962, p. 10-17.

1858 Torres García, J.
"Recuerdos, Ideas, Doctrinas y Reacciones." Montevideo, Revista nacional (43:129), September 1949, p. 428-462.

Venezuela

1859 Díaz Seijas, P.
"Tres Generaciones Literarias Venezolanas." Caracas, Revista Shell (11:45), December 1962, p. 5-10.

1860 Fabbiani Ruiz, J.
"Realismo Grotesco y Realismo Lírico." Caracas, El farol, December 1947, p. 22-23.

1861 Freilich de Segal, A.
"El Niño en el Cuento Venezolano." Caracas, Revista nacional de cultura (24:153), July-August 1962, p. 126-163.

1862 Pineda, R.
"First Festival of Music; Lamas Foundation Festival, Caracas." Américas 7, March 1955, p. 33-36.

1863 Querol, M.
"De Nacionalismo Musical." Maracaibo, Ciencia y cultura (2:8), October-December 1957, p. 165-167.

West Indies and the Caribbean

1864 Crist, Raymond E.
"Changing Cultural Landscapes in Antigua, B.W.I."

American journal of economics & sociology (13:3), April 1954, p. 225-232.

1865 Drayton, A. D.
"West Indian Fiction and West Indian Society." _Kenyon review 25_, Winter 1963, p. 129-141.

URBAN SPEECH

Books

Latin America

1866 Alonso, Amado
Estudios lingüísticos; temas hispano-americanos. Madrid, Ed. Gredos, 1953, 446p.

1867 Alonso, Amado
Problemas de dialectología hispanoamericana. Buenos Aires, Instituto de Filología, Facultad de Filosofía, Universidad de Buenos Aires, 1930, 173p.

1868 Becerra, Marcos E.
Rectificaciones i adiciones al Diccionario de la Real Academia Espanola. México, 1954, 832p.

1869 Buenos Aires. Universidad. Instituto de Filología
Biblioteca de dialectología hispanoamericana. v. 1- . Buenos Aires, Impr. de la Universidad de Buenos Aires, 1930-

1870 Canfield, Delos L.
La pronunciación del espanol en América; ensayo histórico-descriptivo. Bogotá, Instituto Caro y Cuervo, 1963, 103p.

1871 Cuervo, Rufino José
El castellano en América. Bogotá, Ed. Minerva, 1935, 154p.

1872 Henríquez Urena, Pedro
Sobre el problema del andalucismo dialectal de América. Buenos Aires, Impr. de la Librería y Casa Edit. Hernando, 1932, 136p.

1873 Herrero Mayor, Avelino
Lengua y gramática; reflexiones sobre el bien

hablar y el mal decir. Buenos Aires, Ed. Fides, 1955, 126p.

1874 Kany, Charles E.
American-Spanish euphemisms. Berkeley, University of California Press, 1960, 249p.

1875 Kany, Charles E.
American-Spanish semantics. Berkeley, University of California Press, 1960, 352p.

1876 Malaret, Augusto
Los americanismos en el lenguaje literario. Santiago, Ed. Universitaria, 1953, 113p.

1877 Malaret, Augusto
Diccionario de americanismos. 3d ed. Buenos Aires, Emecé Eds., 1946, 835p.

1878 Malaret, Augusto
Semántica americana. Catano, Impr. San José, 1943, 128p.

1879 Malaret, Augusto
Voces afines. San Juan, Tip. San Juan, 1939? 101p.

1880 Martínez Vigil, Carlos
Arcaísmos españoles usados en América. Montevideo, Impr. Latina, 1939, 135p.

1881 Mead, Robert G.
Iberoamérica: sus lenguas y literaturas vistas desde los Estados Unidos. Antología de Hispania. México, Eds. de Andrea, 1962, 222p.

1882 Morínigo, Marcos A.
Programa de filología hispánica; artículos y reseñas. Buenos Aires, Ed. Nova, 1959, 162p.

1883 Navarro Tomás, Tomás
Cuestionario lingüístico hispano-americano . . . Buenos Aires, Instituto de Filología, Facultad de Filosofía y Letras, Universidad de Buenos Aires, 1945-

1884 Nichols, Madaline (Wallis)
A bibliographical guide to materials on American Spanish. Cambridge, Harvard University Press, 1941, 144p.

1885 Rona, José P.
Aspectos metodológicos de la dialectología hispano-americana. Montevideo, Instituto de Filología, Facultad de Humanidades y Ciencias, Universidad de la República, 1958, 36p.

1886 Rosenblat, Angel
El castellano de España y el castellano de América. Unidad y diferenciación. Caracas, Facultad de Humanidades y Educación, Universidad Central de Venezuela, 1962, 58p.

1887 Rosenblat, Angel
Lengua y cultura de Hispanoamérica; tendencias actuales. Caracas, Depto. de Publicaciones, Ministerio de Educación, 1962, 47p.

1888 Rubio, Darío
La anarquía del lenguaje en la América española. 2v. México, Confederación Regional Obrera Mexicana, 1925.

1889 Sucre Reyes, José L.
El futuro del castellano en Hispano-América. Caracas, Tip. La Nación, 1952, 60p.

Argentina

1890 Abeille, Luciano
Idioma nacional de los argentinos. Paris, Bouillon, 1900, 434p.

1891 Academia Argentina de Letras
Acuerdos acerca del idioma. Buenos Aires, 1947-

1892 Arrazola, Roberto
Diccionario de modismos argentinos. Buenos Aires, Ed. Colombia, 1943, 193p.

1893 Borges, Jorge L.
El idioma de los argentinos. El idioma de Buenos

<u>Aires, por José Edmundo Clemente.</u> Buenos Aires, Peña del Giudice, 1953, 59p.

1894 Canterell Dart, José
<u>Defendamos nuestro hermoso idioma; la expresión popular porteña . . .</u> Buenos Aires, "El Ateneo," 1944, 187p.

1895 Carriegos, Ramón C.
<u>El porvenir del idioma español en la República Argentina; frases i palabras criollas.</u> Tandil, F.C.S., "El Imparcial," 1928, 306p.

1896 Casullo, Fernando H.
<u>Diccionario de voces lunfardas y vulgares.</u> Buenos Aires, Ed. Freeland, 1964, 230p.

1897 Gandolfi Herrero, Arístides
<u>La poesía dialectal porteña, versos rantes, por Alvaro Yunque,</u> pseud. Buenos Aires, Peña Lillo, 1961, 75p.

1898 Malmberg, Bertil
<u>Etudes sur la phonétique de l'espagnol parlé en Argentine.</u> Lund, Gleerup, 1950, 290p.

1899 Moldenhauer, Gerhard
<u>Filología y lingüística; esencia, problemas actuales y tareas en la Argentina.</u> Rosario, Instituto de Filología, Facultad de Filosofía, Letras y Ciencias de la Educación, Universidad Nacional del Litoral, 1952, 74p.

1900 Monner Sans, Ricardo
<u>Notas al castellano en la Argentina.</u> Buenos Aires, Estrada y Cía., 1944, 391p.

1901 Murúa, Pedro O.
<u>Habla plebeya y habla vernácula.</u> Santa Fé, Instituto de Folklore del Litoral, Museo Municipal de Bellas Artes, 1944, 20p.

1902 Rossi, Vicente
<u>Folletos lenguaraces.</u> 29 nos. in 3v. Córdoba, Casa Ed. Impr. Argentina, 1927-41.

1903 Sánchez Garrido, Amelia
Indagación de lo argentino. Buenos Aires, Eds. Culturales Argentinos, 1962, 190p.

1904 Saubidet Gache, Tito
Vocabulario y refranero criollo . . . 5th ed. Buenos Aires, Kraft, 1958, 421p.

1905 Segovia, Lisandro
Diccionario de argentinismos, neologismos y barbarismos . . . Buenos Aires, Impr. de Coni Hnos., 1911, 1095p.

Bolivia

1906 Fernández Naranjo, Nicolás, & Dora Gómez de Fernández
Diccionario de bolivianismos . . . 1st ed. La Paz, Universidad Mayor de San Andrés, 1964, 251p.

Brazil

1907 Barbosa Lima, Alexander J.
A língua portuguêsa e a unidade do Brasil. Rio de Janeiro, Olympio, 1958, 202p.

1908 Cardoso, Armando Levy
Amerigenismos. Rio de Janeiro, Biblioteca do Exército, 1961-

1909 Castro, Aloysio de
Paroles françaises au Brésil. Rio de Janeiro, Briquiet, 1950, 149p.

1910 Castro, Eugenio de
Geographia linguística e cultura brasileira (ensaio). Rio de Janeiro, Gráphica Sauer, 1937, 277p.

1911 Elia, Silvio E.
O problema da língua brasileira. Rio de Janeiro, Instituto Nacional do Livro, Ministério da Educacão e Cultura, 1961, 180p.

1912 Fernandes, Francisco, & F. Marques Guimarães
Dicionário brasileiro contemporáneo. Rio de Janeiro, Ed. Glôbo, 1953, 1143p.

1913 Fortes, Herbert Parentes
A questão da língua brasileira. Rio de Janeiro, Ed. GRD, 196- , 221p.

1914 Houaiss, Antonio
Tentativa de descrição do sistema vocálico do português culto na área dita carioca. Rio de Janeiro, 1959, 137p.

1915 Jucá, Cándido
Língua nacional ¿As diferenciações entre o português de Portugal e o do Brasil autorizam e existencia de um ramo dialectal do português peninsular? Rio de Janeiro, Est. Gráphico Apollo, 1937, 135p.

1916 Jucá, Cándido
A pronúncia brasileira. Rio de Janeiro, Coed. Brasileira Coop., 1939, 70p.

1917 Leite, Solidonio A.
A lingua portuguêsa no Brasil. Rio de Janeiro, Leite, 1922, 115p.

1918 Lima, Hildebrando de
Dicionário popular brasileiro . . . São Paulo, Cía. Ed. Nacional, 1949, 582p.

1919 Machado, Aires da Mata
Portuguęs fora das gramáticas. Bêlo Horizonte, Ed. Liderosiana, 1964, 239p.

1920 Merryman, Montgomery
Portuguese, a portrait of the language of Brazil. Rio de Janeiro, Pongetti, 1945, 229p.

1921 Monteiro, Clóvis
Português da Europa e português da América, aspectos da evolução do nosso idioma. Rio de Janeiro, Leite, 1931? 253p.

1922 Monteiro, Mario Ypiranga
Aspectos evolutivos da língua nacional; ensaio. Manáus, 1946, 166p.

1923 Nascentes, Antenor
Dicionário de dúvidas e dificuldades do idioma nacional. 3d ed. Rio de Janeiro, Livraria Ed. Freitas Bastos, 1952, 220p.

1924 Nascentes, Antenor
A giria brasileira. Rio de Janeiro, Livraria Académica, 1953, 181p.

1925 Nascentes, Antenor
O linguajar carioca. 2d ed. rev. Rio de Janeiro, Ed. da "Organização Simões," 1953, 217p.

1926 Novo dicionário brasileiro ilustrado. 4v. São Paulo, Eds. Melhoramentos; distribuidora: Libroluz Divulgadora Cultural, 1961-63.

1927 Padua, Ciro T. de
O dialeto brasileiro . . . Curitiba, Ed. Guaira, 1942, 100p.

1928 Palhano, Herbert
A língua popular. Rio de Janeiro, Organização Simões, 1958, 68p.

1929 Revista brasileira de filologia. #1- , Rio de Janeiro, Livraria Académica, 1955-

1930 Ribeiro, João
Curiosidades verbais; estudos aplicáveis à língua nacional. 2d ed. Rio de Janeiro, Livraria São José, 1963, 244p.

1931 Sampaio, Bernardo Pedral
Língua portuguêsa no Brasil; modalidades de falar nos estados de Bahia e São Paulo. Salvador, Oficinas Gráficas da Imprensa Oficial da Bahia, 1961, 54p.

1932 Senna, Homero
O problema da língua brasileira . . . Rio de Janeiro, Ministério da Educação e Cultura, 1953, 45p.

1933 Seraine, Florival
Dicionário de termos populares (registrados no Ceará). Rio de Janeiro, Organização Simões, 1958, 276p.

1934 Silva Neto, Serafim
Guia para estudos dialectológicos. 2d ed. enl. Belem, Conselho Nacional de Pesquisas, Instituto Nacional de Pesquisas da Amazônia, 1957, 74p.

1935 Silveira Bueno, Francisco da
Tratado de semântica geral aplicada à língua portuguêsa do Brasil. 2d ed. enl. São Paulo, Saraiva, 1951, 239p.

1936 Soares, Antonio J. de Macedo
Estudos lexicográficos do dialeto brasileiro. Rio de Janeiro, Impr. Nacional, 1943, 269p.

1937 Sousa, Arlindo de
A língua portuguêsa no Brasil; aspectos léxicos e semânticos, alguns arcaísmos, folclore a linguagem. Rio de Janeiro, Ed. Fundo de Cultura, 1960, 269p.

1938 Tenorio d'Albuquerque, Acir
O nosso vocabulario. 2d ed. enl. Rio de Janeiro, Gráfica Ed. Aurora, 1953, 319p.

1939 Tenorio d'Albuquerque, Acir
Questões lingüísticas americanas. Rio de Janeiro, Ed. Aurora, 1949, 186p.

1940 Viana, Luiz
A língua do Brasil. 2d ed. Salvador, Progresso, 1954, 103p.

1941 Viotti, Manuel
Novo dicionário da gíria brasileira. 3d ed. rev., corr. & enl. . . Rio de Janeiro, Tupã, 1957, 476p.

1942 Vocabulário sul-rio-grandense . . . Rio de Janeiro, Ed. Glôbo, 1964, 489p.

Central America

1943 Bayo, Ciro
Manual del lenguaje criollo de Centro y Sudamérica. Madrid, Caro Raggeo, 1931, 273p.

1944 Costales Samaniego, Alfredo
Diccionario de modismos y regionalismos centroamericanos (Costa Rica, Nicaragua, Honduras, El Salvador, y Guatemala). Ciudad Universitaria "Rodrigo Facio," San José, 1962? 83p.

1945 Henríquez Ureña, Pedro, et al
El espanol en México, los Estados Unidos y la América Central. Buenos Aires, Impr. de la Universidad de Buenos Aires, 1938, 526p.

Chile

1946 Amunátegui, Miguel L.
Apuntaciones lexicográficas. 3v. Santiago, Impr. Barcelona, 1907-

1947 Lenz, Rudolf, et al
El español en Chile . . . (Biblioteca de dialectología hispanoamericana, vol. 6). Buenos Aires, Instituto de Filología, Facultad de Filosofía y Letras, Universidad de Buenos Aires, 1940, 374p.

1948 Medina, José T.
Chilenismos, apuntes lexicográficos. Santiago, Soc. Impr. y Lit. Universo, 1928, 383p.

1949 Meyer-Rusca, Walter
Voces indígenas del lenguaje popular sireño; 550 chilenismos. Padre Las Casas, Impr. "San Francisco," 1952, 100p.

1950 Rabanales O., Ambrosio
Introducción al estudio de español de Chile. Determinación del concepto de chilenismo. Santiago, Instituto de Filología, Sección del Instituto de Investigaciones Histórico-Culturales, Facultad de Filosofía y Educación, Universidad de Chile, 1953, 142p.

1951 Rojas Carrasco, Guillermo
Chilenismos y americanismos de la XVI edición del

Diccionario de la Academia Española. Valparaíso, Dirección General de Prisiones, Imprenta, 1943, 229p.

1952 Rojas Carrasco, Guillermo
Filología chilena; guía bibliográfica y crítica . . . Santiago, Impr. y Lit. Universo, 1940, 300p.

1953 Yrarrazaval Larrain, José M.
Chilenismos. Santiago, Impr. Cultura, 1945, 375p.

Colombia

1954 Alario di Filippo, Mario
Léxico de colombianismos. Cartagena, Ed. Bolívar, 1964, 391p.

1955 Buesa Oliver, Tomás, & Luis Florez
El Atlas lingüístico-etnográfico de Colombia (ALEC). Bogotá, Instituto Caro y Cuervo, 1956, 171p.

1956 Cuervo, Rufino J.
Apuntaciones críticas sobre el lenguaje bogotano, con frecuente referencia al de los países de Hispano-América. 9th ed. corr. Bogotá, Instituto Caro y Cuervo, 1955, 907p.

1957 Echeverry Mejía, Oscar
Nuestro idioma al día; un manual para quienes deseen enriquecer su vocabulario; texto auxiliar para la enseñanza del español. Bogotá, Espiral, 1965, 231p.

1958 Florez, Luis
Habla y cultura popular en Antioquia; materiales para un estudio. Bogotá, Instituto Caro y Cuervo, 1957, 489p.

1959 Florez, Luis
Lengua española. Bogotá, Instituto Caro y Cuervo, 1953, 299p.

1960 Florez, Luis
Léxico de la casa popular urbana en Bolívar, Colombia. Bogotá, Instituto Caro y Cuervo, 1962, 175p.

1961 González, Euclides J.
Contribución al vocabulario de colombianismos. [n.p., n.p.] 1959, 204p.

1962 González de la Calle, Pedro U.
Contribución al estudio del bogotano; orientaciones metodológicas para la investigación del castellano en América. Bogotá, 1963, 343p.

1963 Robledo, Emilio
Un millar de papeletas lexicográficas relativas a los departamentos de Antioquia y Caldas. Medellín, Impr. Oficial, 1934, 165p.

1964 Saitz, Robert L., & Edward J. Cervenka
Colombia and North American gestures, a contrastive inventory. Bogotá, Centro Colombo-Americano, 1962, 90p.

1965 Sánchez Camacho, Jorge
Diccionario de voces y dichos del habla santandereña. Bucaramanga, Impr. del Departamento, 1958, 340p.

1966 Tascón, Leonardo
Diccionario de provincialismos y barbarismos del Valle del Cauca y quechuismos usados en Colombia. Cali, Biblioteca de la Universidad del Valle, 1961, 458p.

1967 Tobón Betancourt, Julio
Colombianismos. 3d ed. Medellín, Impr. Departamental, 1962, 386p.

Costa Rica

1968 Gagini, Carlos
Diccionario de costarriqueñismos. 2d ed. San José, Impr. Nacional, 1919, 275p.

1969 Vocabulario de palabras-modismos y refranes ticos, por un salesiano. Cartago, Escuela Tip. Salesiana, 1938, 132p.

Cuba

1970 Castellanes y Bonilla, Isidoro
De cómo se habla el español en Cuba . . . Havana, Ed. Guerrero, 1950, 50p.

1971 Dihigo, Juan M.
Léxico cubano; contribución al estudio de las voces que lo forman. Havana, Impr. "El Siglo XX," 1928-

1972 Ortiz Fernández, Fernando
Glosario de afronegrismos. Havana, Impr. "El Siglo XX," 1924, 558p.

1973 Rodríguez Herrera, Esteban
Léxico mayor de Cuba. 2v. Havana, Ed. Lex, 1958-59.

1974 Suárez, Constantino
Vocabulario cubano . . . comprende, 6,828 voces o acepciones--321 frases--52 refranes. Havana, Veloso, 1921, 576p.

Dominican Republic

1975 Henríquez Ureña, Pedro
El español en Santo Domingo. Buenos Aires, Coni, 1940, 301p.

1976 Patín Maceo, Manuel A.
Dominicanismos. 2d ed. Ciudad Trujillo, Librería Dominicana, 1947, 206p.

1977 Rodríguez Demorizi, Emilio
Vicisitudes de la lengua española en Santo Domingo . . . Ciudad Trujillo, Ed. Montalvo, 1944, 25p.

Ecuador

1978 Canossa, Luis
Secretos y sorpresa del idioma. Buenos Aires, Ed. Atlántida, 1961, 149p.

1979 Toscano Mateus, Humberto
El español en el Ecuador. Madrid, Instituto Miguel de Cervantes, Patronato Menendez y Pelayo, C.S.I.C., 1953, 478p.

1980 Vásquez, Honorato
El idioma castellano en el Ecuador. Quito, Impr. y Encuad. Nacionales, 1925, 33p.

Guatemala

1981 Sandoval, Lisandro
Semántico guatemalense; o, Diccionario de guatemaltequismos. 2v. Guatemala, Tip. Nacional, 1941-42.

Haiti

1982 David, Odnell
Etude critique autour du Destin de la langue française en Haiti de Pradel Pompilus; ou, Le devenir du créole comme langue nationale. [n.p.] Impr. Les Presses Libres, 1952, 73p.

1983 Faine, Jules
Philologie créole; etudes historiques et étymologiques sur la langue créole d'Haiti. Port-au-Prince, Impr. de l'Etat, 1937, 320p.

1984 Goodman, Morris F.
A comparative study of Creole French dialects. The Hague, Mouton, 1964, 143p.

1985 Hall, Robert A., et al
Haitian creole: grammar, texts, vocabulary. Philadelphia, American Folklore Society, 1953, 309p.

1986 Hyppolite, Michelson P.
Le devenir du créole haïtien . . . Port-au-Prince, Impr. de l'Etat, 1952, 23p.

1987 Hyppolite, Michelson P.
Les origines du créole haïtien. Port-au-Prince, Impr. de l'Etat, 1949? 85p.

1988 Hyppolite, Michelson P.
Littérature populaire haïtienne. Port-au-Prince, Impr. de l'Etat, 1950, 135p.

1989 McConnell, H.O.
You can learn Creole: a simple introduction to Haitian Creole for English speaking people . . . 3d ed. Petit-Goâve, Impr. du Sauveur, 1957, 106p.

1990 Pompilus, Pradel
La langue française en Haiti. Paris, Institut des Hautes Etudes de l'Amérique Latine, 1961, 278p.

Honduras

1991 Membreño, Alberto
Hondureñismos. 3d ed. corr. and enl. México, Tip. Muller Hnos., 1912, 172p.

Mexico

1992 Boyd Bowman, Peter
El habla de Guanajuato. México, Impr. Universitaria, 1960, 411p.

1993 Chabat, Carlos G.
Diccionario de caló, el lenguaje del hampa en México. 2d ed. México, Méndez Oteo, Librería de Medicina, 1960, 120p.

1994 Donnell, Albert L.
El lenguaje del Pensador Mexicano. México, 1950, 111p.

1995 Gaarder, Alfred B.
El habla popular y la conciencia colectiva. México, 1954, 305p.

1996 Henríquez Ureña, Pedro, et al
El español en México, los Estados Unidos y la América Central . . . (Biblioteca de Dialectología Hispanoamericana, vol. 4). Buenos Aires, Impr. de la Universidad de Buenos Aires, 1938, 526p.

1997 Jiménez, A.
Picardía mexicana. 3d ed. México, Libro Mex, 1960, 268p.

1998 León, Aurelio de
Barbarismos comunes en México; solecismos, anglicismos, provincialismos del norte, voces forenses impropias. 2 pts. México, Impr. Mundial, 1936-37.

1999 Lope Blanch, Juan M.
Observaciones sobre la sintáxis del español hablado

en México. México, Instituto Hispano Mexicano de Investigaciones Científicas, 1953, 135p.

2000 Negrete Cárdenas, Daniel
El español de Jalisco; contribución a la geografía lingüística hispanoamericana. Ann Arbor, University Microfilms (Publication 6588), 1954.

2001 Ringo, Elbert W.
The position of the noun modifier in colloquial Mexican Spanish. Urbana, 1950, 10p.

2002 Rubio, Darío
Refranes, proverbios y dichos y dicharachos mexicanos. 2d ed. corr. & enl. 2v. México, Ed. Marquez, 1940.

2003 Santamaría, Francisco J.
Diccionario de mejicanismos, razonado; comprobado con citas de autoridades, comparado con el de americanismos y con los vocabularios provinciales de los más distinguidos diccionaristas hispanoamericanos. México, Porrúa, 1959, 1197p.

2004 Trejo Dueñes, Arnulfo
Una contribución al estudio del léxico de la delincuencia en México. México, 1959, 214p.

2005 Velasco Valdés, Miguel
Vocabularia popular mexicano. México, Ed. Olimpo, 1957, 139p.

Panama

2006 Aguilera Patiño, Luisita V.
El panameño vista a través de su lenguaje. Panamá, Ferguson & Ferguson, 194- , 415p.

2007 Blas Tejeira, Gil
El habla del panameño. Panamá, 1964, 171p.

Paraguay

2008 Malmberg, Bertil
Notas sobre la fonética del español en el Paraguay. Lund, Gleerup, 1947, 18p.

Peru

2009 Angeles Caballero, César A.
Los peruanismos en César Vallejo. Lima, Ed. Universitaria, 1958, 108p.

2010 Benvenutto Murrieta, Pedro M.
El languaje peruano . . . Lima, Talleres de Sanmartí y Cía., 1936-

2011 Bonilla Amado, José
Jerga del hampa. Lima, Ed. Nuevos Rumbos, 1956, 119p.

2012 Paz Soldán y Unánue, Pedro
Suplemento al Diccionario de peruanismos. Lima, Instituto de Literatura de la Facultad de Letras, Universidad Nacional Mayor de San Marcos, 1957, 28p.

2013 Ugarte, Miguel A.
Arequipeñismos. Arequipa, Tip. Portugal, 1942, 80p.

2014 Vargas Ugarte, Rubén
Glosario de peruanismos. Lima, Ed. San Marcos, 1953, 74p.

Uruguay

2015 Bermúdez, Washington P.
Lenguaje del Río de la Plata . . . v. 1. Buenos Aires, Talleres Gráficos Rosso, 1916? 212p.

2016 Laguarda Trías, Rolando A.
Historia semántica de dos uruguayismos: cuchilla y albardón. Montevideo, 1956, 28p. (Separate from Revista nacional 188, April-June 1956).

Venezuela

2017 Alvarado, Lisandro
Glosario de bajo español en Venezuela . . . 2v. Caracas, Ministerio de Educación, Dirección de Cultura y Bellas Artes, Comisión Editora de las Obras Completas de Lisandro Alvarado, 1954-55.

2018 Calcaño, Julio
El castellano en Venezuela; estudio crítico. Caracas, Ministerio de Educación Nacional, Dirección de Cultura, 1950, 571p.

2019 Müller, Inés de
Venezolanismos y otras palabras muy usadas. Caracas, 1961, 70p.

2020 Rosenblat, Angel
Buenas y malas palabras en el castellano de Venezuela. Caracas, Eds. EDIME, 1956-

2021 Wijk, Henri L.A. van
Contribución al estudio del habla popular de Venezuela. Amsterdam? 1946, 243p.

West Indies and the Caribbean

2022 Funk, Henry E.
The French Creole dialect of Martinique: its historical background, vocabulary, syntax, proverbs and literature; with a glossary. Ann Arbor, University Microfilms (Publication # 7961), 1954.

2023 Jourdain, Anne M. L. (Dujon)
Le vocabulaire du parleur créole du Martinique. Paris, Klincksieck, 1956, 303p.

2024 Zayas y Alfonso, Alfredo
Lexicografía antillana . . . 2d ed. 2v. Havana, Tip. Molina, 1931.

Periodical Articles

Latin America

2025 Arciniegas, Germán
"Vida del Lenguaje: Cuestiones Lexicográficas." Bogotá, *Boletín de la Academia Colombiana* (9:32), July-September 1959, p. 299-302.

2026 Baldinger, K.
"Designaciones de la Cabeza en la América Española." México, *Anuario de letras 4*, 1964, p. 25-56.

2027 Barrera Vásquez, Alfredo
"El Problema de las Lenguas Vernáculas en la Américan Latina." Quito, <u>Revista ecuatoriana de educación</u> (6:21), May/June 1952, p. 92-106.

2028 Bertens, Máximo
"Prognosis Lingüística de Latinoamérica." Concepción, <u>Atenea</u>, August 1944, p. 432-445.

2029 Dagatti, C.P. de
"Inmigración e Idioma Nacional." Santa Fé, <u>Universidad 63</u>, January-March 1965, p. 327-350.

2030 Farfán, J.M. B.
"Onomástica de Vehículos; el Chofer en los Nombres de sus Vehículos." Lima, <u>Folklore americano</u> (8:9), 1960-61, p. 285-286.

2031 Guitarte, C. L.
"Cuervo, Henríquez-Ureña y la Polémica Sobre el Andalucismo de América." Bogotá, <u>Thesaurus 14</u>, 1959, p. 20-81.

2032 Herrero Mayor, Avelino
"Preservación y Crecimiento del Idioma Hispanoamericano." Buenos Aires, <u>Veritas</u>, March 31, 1946, p. 214-217.

2033 Krauss, W.
"El Desarrollo del Castellano en España y del Español en América." Havana, <u>Universidad de La Habana</u> (28:170), November-December 1964, p. 23-29.

2034 Lazo, R.
"América y la Lengua Española." Havana, <u>Boletín de la Academia Cubana de la Lengua</u> (9:1-4), January-December 1960, p. 5-14.

2035 Malaret, Augusto
"Antología de Americanismos." Bogotá, <u>Boletín del Instituto Caro y Cuervo 5</u>, 1950, p. 214-226.

2036 Malaret, Augusto
"Generación Lingüística." Montevideo, <u>Boletín</u>

de filología (8:55/57), March, June, September 1959, p. 21-31.

2037 Wogan, Daniel
"Algunas Expresiones Populares en el Brasil e Hispanoamérica." Montevideo, Artigas-Washington, September 1947, p. 81-85.

Argentina

2038 Boggs, Ralph S.
"Sobre el 'Che' Ríoplatense." Montevideo, Boletín de filosofía, March-September 1943, p. 80-81.

2039 Devoto, Daniel
"Sobre Paremiología Musical Porteña." Buenos Aires, Filología (3:1/2), January/August 1951, p. 6-83.

2040 Herrero Mayor, Avelino
"El 'Vos' en la Educación Argentina." La Plata, Revista de educación 6, 3d quarter, December 1964, p. 59-65.

2041 Junco, A.
"Buenos Aires y la Lengua." México, Abside (29:1), January-March 1965, p. 96-102.

2042 Olivera, M.A.
"El Habla de Buenos Aires." Buenos Aires, Cursos y conferencias (44:262-264), January-March 1954, p. 435-454.

2043 Rona, José P.
"Sobre Algunas Etimologías Rioplatenses." México, Anuario de letras 3, 1963, p. 87-106.

2044 Villanueva, A.
"El Lunfardo." Santa Fé, Universidad de Santa Fé 52, April-June 1962, p. 13-42.

2045 Zilio, G.M.
"Curiosidades Onomásticas en el Río de la Plata." México, Anuario de letras 3, 1963, p. 221-232.

Bolivia

2046 Kany, Charles E.
"Some Aspects of Bolivian Popular Speech." Hispanic review January 1947, p. 193-205.

Brazil

2047 Colli, J. Pacini
"O Brasil Falando Brasileiro." São Paulo, Planalto, August 1, 1941, p. 14.

2048 Cunha, A. G.
"Modelos de Verbetes de um Dicionário Histórico dos Indigenismos da Língua Portuguêsa." Rio de Janeiro, Revista do livro (5:20), December 1960, p. 201-209.

2049 Hall, Robert A.
"Brazilian Portuguese Inflection." Hispanic review, July 1945, p. 231-242.

2050 Ihering, R. von
"Ensaio Geográfico Sôbre o Vocabulario Zoológico Popular do Brasil." Rio de Janeiro, Revista brasileira de geografia, July 1939, p. 73-88.

2051 Mariano, O.
"A Língua Brasileira." São Paulo, Planalto, May 15, 1941, p. 12-13.

2052 Melo, G. Chaves de
"A Língua Portuguêsa no Brasil." Petrópolis, Vozes, May-June 1943, p. 372-391.

2053 Monteiro, C.
"Denominação da Língua Nacional." Rio de Janeiro, Arquivos (1:2), March-April 1947, p. 13-26.

2054 Moser, G.
"A Gíria Académica: Portuguese Student Slang." Hispania (38:2), May 1955, p. 159-168.

2055 Nascentes, Antenor
"Divisão Dialectológica do Território Brasileiro." Rio de Janeiro, Revista brasileira de geografia

(17:2), April-June 1955, p. 213-219.

2056 Ricardo, C.
"A Academia e a Lîngua Brasileira." Rio de Janeiro, Revista da Academia Brasileira de Letras, January-June 1941, p. 326-387.

2057 Silva, I.
"O Linguajar Paulistano." Sao Paulo, Planalto, July 1, 1941, p. 4, 20; August 1, 1941, p. 16; February 1, 1942, p. 9-10.

2058 Silva, S. da
"Diferenciaçao e Unificaçao do Portugués no Brasil." Rio de Janeiro, Revista de cultura, August 1942, p. 63-70.

2059 Silveira, A.
"Anglicismos em Medicina." Petrópolis, Vozes (57:5), May 1963, p. 360-367.

2060 Sylveyra, Osvaldo de
"A Influéncia do Espanhol no Linguajar Paulista do Seiscentismo." Sao Paulo, Planalto, November 1, 1941, p. 14, 16.

2061 Spalding, W.
"Arcaîsmos Portugueses na Linguagem Popular do Rio Grande do Sul." Montevideo, Boletin de filologia, September 1947; p. 193-203.

2062 Teixeira, F.
"Vocabulário do Caipira Paulista." Sao Paulo, Revista do arquivo municipal, November-December 1946, p. 67-104.

2063 Tenorio d'Albuquerque, A.
"A Portuguès em Portugal e no Brasil. Sobrevivencias de Palavras e Construçoes." Rio de Janeiro, Revista brasileira (10:27), July-December 1959, p. 133-156.

2064 Vaz, L.
"A Lîngua Brasileira." Sao Paulo, Anhembi (23:68), July 1956, p. 247-252.

Central America

2065 Costales Samaniego, Alfredo
"Modismos y Regionalismos Centroamericanos." Rio de Janeiro, América latina (6:4), October-December 1963, p. 131-168.

2066 Menéndez Leal, A.
"El Voseo en los 'Cuentos de Barro' de Salarrué." San Salvador, Cultura 31, January-March 1964, p. 19-28.

Chile

2067 Araya, G.
"Conocimiento del Español de Chile." Santiago, Boletín de la Universidad de Chile 23, August 1961, p. 33-38.

2068 Cavada, F.J.
"Frases y Dichos de Uso Corriente en Chile." Santiago, Revista católica, July 14, 1934, p. 20-23.

2069 Di Lullo, Orestes
"Algunas Voces Santiagüeñas." Buenos Aires, Boletín de la Academia Argentina de Letras, January-June 1938, p. 145-204.

2070 Harris, Harriett
"Street Cries in Santiago." Grace Log, July-August 1934, p. 507-510, 518.

2071 Oroz, Rodolfo
"Metáforas Relativas a las Partes del Cuerpo Humano en la Lengua Popular Chilena." Bogotá, Boletín del Instituto Caro y Cuervo 5, 1949-1950, p. 85-100.

2072 Vicuña Mackenna, Carlos
"Chilenismos." Santiago, Boletín de la Academia Chilena (7:25-26), 1940, p. 48-57.

Colombia

2073 Academia Colombiana
"Vida del Lenguaje." Bogotá, Boletín de la Academia Colombiana (14:52), April-May 1964, p. 128-139.

2074 Acuna, Luis A.
"Diccionario de Bogotanismos." Bogotá, Revista de folklore 7, September 1951, p. 5-187.

2075 Alfonso, L.
"Colombianismos y Argentinismos." Bogotá, Boletín de la Academia Colombiana (14:53), June-July 1964, p. 197-204.

2076 Figueroa, J., & E. Camacho
"Léxico de la Carpintería en Bogotá." Bogotá, Thesaurus 14, 1959, p. 258-270.

2077 Florez, Luis
Algunas Fórmulas de Tratamiento en el Espanol del Departamento de Antioquia (Colombia)." Bogotá, Thesaurus (10:1/3), January/December 1954, p. 78-88.

2078 Florez, Luis
"Algunos Usos Bogotanos de la Preposición 'a'". Bogotá, Boletín de la Academia Colombiana (12:45), October-December 1962, p. 319-326.

2079 Florez, Luis
"Apuntes Sobre Léxico y Semántica en el Espanol Colombiano de Hoy." Bogotá, Boletín de la Academia Colombiana (12:43), April-June 1962, p. 94-98.

2080 Florez, Luis
"El Atlas Lingüístico-Etnográfico de Colombia (ALEC): Nota Informativa." Bogotá, Thesaurus (16:1), September-December 1961, p. 77-125.

2081 Florez, Luis
"Del Habla Popular en Santander (Colombia)." Bogotá, Revista colombiana de folclor (2:4), 1960, p. 9-14.

2082 Florez, Luis
"El Espanol Hablado en Colombia y su Atlas Lingüístico." Bogotá, Thesaurus (18:2), May-August 1963, p. 268-356.

2083 Florez, Luis
"El Espanol Hablado en Santander: Notas de Pronunciación." México, Anuario de letras 4, 1964, p. 71-94.

2084 Florez, Luis
"Muestra de Anglicismos y Galicismos en el Español de Bogotá, 1964." Bogotá, Boletín de la Academia Colombiana (14:55), October-November 1964, p. 260-278.

2085 Fontanella, M.B.
"Algunas Observaciones Sobre el Diminutivo en Bogotá." Bogotá, Thesaurus (17:3), September-December 1962, p. 556-573.

2086 León Rey, J.A.
"Sobre los Colombianismos: Corbatear, Solapear, Gollatear y Cachetear." Bogotá, Boletín de la Academia Colombiana (11:41), November-December 1961, p. 319-320.

2087 Lopez Cruz, F.
"Del Vocabulario Hípico en Bogotá." Bogotá, Thesaurus 15, 1960, p. 294-299.

2088 Montes G., J.J.
"Algunas Voces Relacionadas con los Animales Domésticos." Bogotá, Thesaurus (20:1), January-April 1965, p. 1-47.

2089 Montes G., J.J.
"Sobre la Perífrasis 'ir' en el Español de Colombia." Bogotá, Thesaurus (18:2), May-August 1963, p. 384-403.

2090 Montoya, W.
"Colombianismos." Medellín, Universidad de Antioquia, June/August 1947, p. 395-410; January/February 1948, p. 115-30; March/May 1948, p. 287-298.

2091 Montoya, W.
"Comentarios y Adiciones a la Obra 'Bogotanismos' del Dr. Luis Alberto Acuña." Medellín, Univer-

sidad de Antioquia (41:157), April-June 1964, p. 303-325.

2092 Mora Naranjo, A.
"El Castellano en Antioquia." Medellín, Universidad Pontificia Bolivariana (27:96), 1st quarter 1965, p. 159-176.

2093 Otero D'Costa, Enrique
"Mestizajes del Castellano en Colombia." Bogotá, Boletín del Instituto Caro y Cuervo, January/April 1946, p. 166-175; (6:1), January/April 1950, p. 15-80.

2094 Poloniato de Partnoy, A.
"Algunos Usos de las Preposiciones A, Bajo, Con, De, Desde, En, Hasta, Por, Sobre, en la Prensa de Bogotá." Bogotá, Thesaurus (19:2), May-August 1964, p. 221-247.

2095 Robledo, Emilio
"Habla y Cultura Popular en Antioquia de Luis Florez. Materiales para un Estudio." Medellín, Universidad de Antioquia (34:134), July/September 1958, p. 394-406.

2096 Robledo, Emilio
"Un Millar de Papeletas Lexicográficas Relativas a los Departamentos de Antioquia y Caldas." Medellín, Repertorio histórico, November 1934, p. 1-164.

2097 Robledo, Emilio
"Orígenes Castizos del Habla Popular de Antioquia y Caldas." Bogotá, Boletín del Instituto Caro y Cuervo 5, 1949-1950, p. 176-191.

2098 Simbaquebra R., L. R.
"Apuntes Lexicográficos Sobre la Industria del Ladrillo en Bogotá." Bogotá, Thesaurus 13, 1958, p. 57-82.

2099 Tobón Betancourt, Julio
"Colombianismos." Medellín, Universidad de Antioquia, January/March 1946, p. 449-458.

2100 "Vocabulario de Lenguaje Popular Colombiano." Bogotá, Boletín de la Academia Colombiana (9: 33), October/December 1959, p. 367-394.

2101 Wagner, Max L.
"Apuntaciones Sobre el Caló Bogotano." Bogotá, Boletín del Instituto Caro y Cuervo (6:2), May-August 1950, p. 181-213.

2102 Wills Pradilla, Jorge
"Concordancias de las Apuntaciones Críticas Sobre el Lenguaje Bogotano con el Diccionario de la Academia Espanola." Bogotá, Boletín de la Academia Colombiana (8:26), January/March 1958, p. 5-14.

2103 Yepes, Jesús M.
"Neologismos de Construcciones en el Lenguaje Bogotano." Medellín, Universidad de Antioquia (35:138), July/September 1959, p. 347-355.

Costa Rica

2104 Zamora Elizondo, Hernán
"Los Diminutivos en Costa Rica." Bogotá, Boletín del Instituto Caro y Cuervo, September/December 1945, p. 541-546.

Cuba

2105 Almendros, N.
"Estudio Fonético del Espanol en Cuba." Havana, Boletín de la Academia Cubana de la Lengua (7: 1-2), January-June 1958, p. 138-176.

2106 Alzola, C. T.
"Habla Popular Cubana." Havana, Universidad de La Habana (27:159), January-February 1963, p. 95-107.

2107 Gonzalez del Campo, L.
"Una Versión del Rico Slang Habanero." Havana, Bohemia (42:4), January 22, 1950, p. 22-23, 122-123.

2108 Padrón, Alfredo F.
"Giros Sintácticos Usados en Cuba." Bogotá,

Boletín del Instituto Caro y Cuervo 5, 1949-1950, p. 163-175.

Dominican Republic

2109 Patín Maceo, Manuel A.
"Americanismos en el Lenguaje Dominicano." Ciudad Trujillo, Anales de la Universidad de Santo Domingo, July/December 1940, p. 409-423.

Ecuador

2110 Boyd-Bowman, Peter
"Sobre la Pronunciación del Español en el Ecuador." México, Nueva revista de filología hispánica (7: 1-2), January-June 1953, p. 231-233.

2111 Jarrín Paez, J.
"Timbre Cerrado de la Vocal Ecuatoriana." Quito, Filosofía, letras y ciencias de la educación (15:31), December 1962, p. 26-56.

El Salvador

2112 Canfield, Delos L.
"Andalucismos en la Pronunciación Salvadoreña." Hispania (36:1), February 1953, p. 32-33.

2113 Tovar y Ramírez, Enrique D.
"Contribución al Estudio del Lenguaje Salvadoreño: Algo Sobre el Léxico de Flora." Bogotá, Boletín del Instituto Caro y Cuervo, September/December 1946, p. 421-459.

2114 Tovar y Ramírez, Enrique D.
"Un Puñado de Gentilicios Salvadoreños." Bogotá, Boletín del Instituto Caro y Cuervo, September/December 1945, p. 547-557.

Guatemala

2115 Predmore, Richard L.
"Dobletes Modernos en el Español Guatemalteco." Hispania, May 1946, p. 214-215.

Haiti

2116 Bellegarde, Dantes
"Le Créole Haïtien, Patois Français." Panorama (3:11), 1954, p. 56-63.

2117 David, Odnell
"Origine, Formation et Structure de la Langue Créole." Port-au-Prince, Bulletin du Bureau d'Ethnologie 15, May 1958, p. 58-79.

2118 Efron, E.
"French and Creole Patois in Haiti." Port-of-Spain, Caribbean quarterly (3:4), August 1954, p. 199-213.

2119 Faine, Jules
"Contribution à l'Etude du Créole." Port-au-Prince, Le temps, April 14, 1934, p. 5-8.

2120 Faine, Jules
"Phonétique du Créole." Port-au-Prince, La relève, January 1936, p. 21-32.

2121 Hall, Robert A.
"Haitian Creole: Grammar, Texts, Vocabulary." American anthropologist (55:2), April-June 1953, p. 1-309.

2122 Jacobs, H. P.
"The Creole Language of Haiti." Kingston, West Indian review, May 1937, p. 41-44.

2123 Martin, A.
"La Langue Française en Haiti: Thèse pour le Doctorat ès Lettres." Port-au-Prince, Conjonction 84-85, 1962, p. 35-52.

2124 Pompilus, Pradel
"Destin de la Langue Française en Haiti." Port-au-Prince, Conjonction 37, February 1952, p. 5-16.

2125 Pompilus, Pradel
"La Langue Française en Haiti." Port-au-Prince, Optique 11, January 1955, p. 19-27.

2126 Pompilus, Pradel
"Quelques Particularités Grammaticales du Français Parlé en Haiti." Port-au-Prince, Conjonction 72, 1958, p. 5-12.

2127 Pompilus, Pradel
"Les Taches Nouvelles du Professeur de Français

en Haiti." Port-au-Prince, Conjonction 99, August 1965, p. 67-69.

2128 Saint-Victor, R.
"La Crise du Français en Haiti." Port-au-Prince Optique 22, December 1955, p. 71-73.

2129 Schwartz, W. L.
"Langue Américaine et Français Haïtien." Port-au-Prince, Revue de la Société Haïtienne d'Histoire, de Géographie et de Géologie (22:82), July 1951, p. 68-73.

Honduras

2130 Clavos, E.
"Lingüística Hondureña." Tegucigalpa, Boletín de la Academia Hondureña (6:7), May 1961, p. 79-84.

2131 Isaguirre, Carlos, comp.
"Hondureñismos." Tegucigalpa, Boletín de la Academia Hondureña (1:1), July 1955, p. 55-138.

Mexico

2132 Alatorre, Antonio
"El Idioma de los Mexicanos. Pt. I-II." México, Universidad de México (10:2), October 1955, p. 1-2, 11-15; (10:3), November 1955, p. 7-13.

2133 Canellada de Zamora, M.J., & A. Zamora Vicente
"Vocales Caducas en el Español Mexicano." México, Nueva revista de filología hispana (14:3-4), July-December 1960, p. 221-241.

2134 Frenk Alatorre, Margit
"Designaciones de Rasgos Físicos Personales en el Habla de la Ciudad de México." México, Nueva revista de filología hispánica (7:1/2), January/June 1953, p. 134-156.

2135 Guerrero de la Rosa, R.
"El 'Slang' Americano y la Jerga Mexicana." México, Revista iberoamericana, November 1939, p. 365-374.

2136 Magaña Esquivel, A.
"Lenguaje y Modismos." Mérida, Revista de la

Universidad de Yucatán (5:30), November-December 1963, p. 99-101.

2137 Marcom, A.J.
"Mexican Slang." Modern Mexico, February 1937, p. 7.

2138 Matluck, Joseph H.
"La é Trabajada en la Ciudad de México: Estudio Experimental." México, Anuario de letras 3, 1963, p. 5-34.

2139 Menton, Seymour
"Mexican Baseball Terminology: an Example of Linguistic Growth." Hispania (37:4), December 1954, p. 458-481.

2140 Mora, E. Cortichs
"Aspectos del Habla de Tepoztlan." México, Nueva revista de filología hispánica (8:2), April-June 1954, p. 137-155.

2141 Ramírez Flores, J.
"Los 'Tochos' de Jalisco, Semántica de un Vocablo." Monterrey, Humanitas 5, 1964, p. 433-438.

2142 Rosaldo, R.
"A List of Slang and Colloquial Expressions of Mexico City." Hispania (31:4), November 1948, p. 437-445.

Nicaragua

2143 Academia Nicaragüense de la Lengua
"Vocablos Usados en Nicaragua y Otras Partes que Merecen Lugar en el Diccionario Oficial . . ." Managua, Boletín de la Academia Nacional de la Lengua, June 1940, p. 46-56.

2144 Castrillo Gómez, Manuel
"Vocablos, Modismos y Refranes Nicaragüenses." Managua, Revista comercial de Nicaragua (18:224), November 1954- , November 1958-

2145 Lacayo, H.
"Apuntes Sobre la Pronunciación del Español de Nicaragua." Hispania (37:3), September 1954, p. 267-268.

2146 Lacayo, H.
"Cômo Pronuncian el Espanol en Nicaragua." Managua, Educación (4:21), July-September 1962, p. 19-31.

Panama

2147 Herrero Fuentes, I.
"El Castellano en Panamá." Panamá, Universidad 22, 1944, p. 81-100.

2148 Nunez O., R.
"El Lenguaje Lugareno y sus Modalidades." Panamá, Tierra y dos mares (5:26), 1965, p. 18.

Peru

2149 Benvenutto Murrieta, P.M.
"Ecuatorianismos y Peruanismos." Lima, Revista de la Universidad Católica del Perú, May-June 1939, p. 141-150.

2150 Russell, D.I.
Peruanismos." Lima, Idea, artes y letras (7:29), July-September 1956, p. 5.

Uruguay

2151 Berro García, A., et al
"Repertorio o Vocabulario de Uruguayismos." Montevideo, Revista nacional (46:137), May 1950, p. 271-284.

2152 Rusconi, A.
"Breve Historia de Algunos Anglicismos Usuales en Nuestro Medio." Montevideo, Boletín de la Asociación de Profesores de Ensenanza Secundaria y Preparatoria del Uruguay, March 1945, p. 7-9.

2153 Silva Valdés, F.
"Vocabulario Popular del Uruguay." Montevideo, Revista nacional (46:138), June 1950, p. 385-397.

2154 Vásquez, W.
"El Fonema /s/ en Espanol del Uruguay." Montevideo, Revista de la Facultad de Humanidades y Ciencias 10, August 1953, p. 87-94.

Venezuela

2155 Alonso, M.R.
"Angel Rosenblat y el Español de Venezuela." Caracas, Cultura universitaria 64, July-September 1958, p. 74-78.

2156 Hauser, G.
"La Pronunciación del Castellano en Venezuela." Caracas, Educación, August 1947, p. 95-104.

2157 Martínez, M.A.
"Notas Sobre la Idea de Alboroto y Desorden en Venezuela." Caracas, Archivos venezolanos de folklore (4-5:5), 1957-58, p. 7-100.

2158 Rosenblat, Angel
"Notas Sobre el Español de Venezuela: Incorrección o Creación?" Caracas, Revista del Instituto Pedagógico Nacional, May-June 1947, p. 79-86.

Part II

ECONOMICS - INDUSTRY - COMMERCE

COST AND STANDARD OF LIVING

Books

General

2159 Bhagwati, J.
L'économie des pays sous-développés. Paris, Hachette, 1966, 250p.

2160 Clark, Colin
Conditions of economic progress. 3d ed. New York, St. Martin's Press, 1957, 720p.

2161 Melman, Seymour
Our depleted society. New York, Holt, Rinehart & Winston, 1965, 366p.

2162 Perlman, Mark, ed.
Human resources in the urban economy. Baltimore, Johns Hopkins Press, 1963, 265p.

2163 United Nations. Dept. of Economic & Social Affairs. Statistical Office
Handbook of household surveys: a practical guide for inquiries on levels of living: #ST/STAT/SER. F/10. New York, 1964, 172p.

2164 U.S. Dept. of Labor. Bureau of Labor Statistics
Computation of cost-of-living indexes in developing countries. Washington, 1964, 43p.

2165 U.S. Dept. of Labor. Bureau of Labor Statistics
U.S. Department of State indexes of living costs abroad. Washington, reprinted from Labor developments abroad, October 1966, p. 17-22.

Latin America

2166 Inter-American Statistical Institute
Costo de la vida y materias afines: lista de referencias bibliográficas escogidas sobre trabajos metodológicos. Washington, Unión Panamericana, 1956-

2167 Lannoy, Juan L. de
Los niveles de vida en América Latina; vivienda alimentación y salud. Friburg, Oficina Internacional de Investigaciones Sociales de FERES, 1963, 235p.

2168 National Planning Association
Latin America and the freedom from want. 2v. Washington, 1942.

2169 Pan American Union
Consumer price (cost-of-living) indexes of the American nations, 1955- March 1963, #14. Washington, 1963, 24p.

2170 Pan American Union. Dept. of Statistics
Consumer price (cost-of-living) indexes of the American nations. Indices de precios al consumidor (costo de la vida) de las naciones americanas. Washington, 1959-

2171 Poblete Troncoso, Moisés
El standard de vida de las poblaciones de América (Problemas sociales y económicos de América Latina, v. 2). Santiago, Eds. de la Universidad de Chile, 1942.

Argentina

2172 Argentine Republic. Dirección de Estadística Social
Nivel de vida de la familia obrera. Evolución durante la Segunda Guerra Mundial, 1939-1945. Buenos Aires, 1945, 161p.

2173 Instituto para el Desarrollo de Ejecutivos en la Argentina. División de Investigaciones
Indice de costo de vida de IDEA. Buenos Aires, 1966-

Brazil

2174 Brazil. Serviço de Estatística da Previdencia e Trabalho
Levantamento do custo de vida no Brasil. Rio de Janeiro, 1946-

2175 Brazil. Serviço de Estatística da Previdencia e Trabalho
Meio circulante e custo de vida. Rio de Janeiro, 1948, 23p.

British Honduras

2176 International Labor Office
Report to the Government of British Honduras on a survey of family expenditures, 1958, and on new consumer price indices. Geneva, 1959, 141p.

Colombia

2177 Munoz Vila, Cecilia
El nivel de vida de los trabajadores ferroviarios (Via Paipa-Bogotá-El Espinal). Bogotá, 1963, 44p.

2178 Prieto Durán, Rafael
Evolución de una urbanización en Bogotá. Bogotá, Centro de Estudios sobre Desarrollo Económico, Universidad de Los Andes, 1960, 32 plus 3 p.

2179 Usandizaga, Elsa, & A.E. Havens
Tres barrios de invasión: estudio de nivel de vida y actitudes en Barranquilla. Bogotá, Eds. Tercer Mundo, 1966, 94p.

Costa Rica

2180 Costa Rica. Dirección General de Estadística y Censos
Ingresos y gastos de las familias del área metropolitana de San José, según encuesta preliminar de 1958. San José, 1960, 57p.

2181 Santoro, Gustavo
Algunos aspectos de la vida urbana en San José, tres problemas apremiantes; investigación dirigida por Gustavo Santoro. Jefes de los equipos de barrio: Ricardo Esquivel, et al. San José, Universidad de Costa Rica, 1962, 62p.

Honduras

2182 Tosco, Manuel, et al
Indice de precios al pormenor para familias de ingresos moderados en Tegucigalpa, D.C. Tegucigalpa, 1952, 5p.

Jamaica

2183 Jamaica. Dept. of Statistics
Household expenditure survey, 1953-54. Kingston, 1955, 46p.

2184 Moser, Claus A.
The measurements of levels of living: with special reference to Jamaica. London, H.M.S.O., 1957, 106p.

Mexico

2185 Ferrocarriles Nacionales de México
Un estudio del costo de vida en México. México, Ed. Cultura, 1931, 104p.

2186 James, Daniel
How to invest and live in Mexico. México, Ross, 1960, 278p.

2187 México. Secretaría de Industria y Comercio. Depto. de Muestreo
Las 16 ciudades principales de la República Mexicana: ingresos y egresos familiares. México, 1962, 231p.

Panama

2188 Paro, Pauline B.
Estudio de los ingresos, gastos y costo de la vida, Ciudad de Panamá, 1952-1953 . . . Panamá, 1954, 99p.

Paraguay

2189 González Ruiz, Z.
Informe al gobierno del Paraguay sobre presupuestos familiares y estadísticas de los precios del consumo. Geneva, International Labor Office, 1966, 79p.

Peru

2190 Arrus, Oscar F.
El costo de la vida en Lima y causas de su carestía. Lima, La Opinión Nacional, 1925, 40p.

2191 Perú. Servicio de Empleo y Recursos Humanos
Estructura salarial y ocupacional de la industria textil de Lima y Callao. Lima, 1966, 58p.

Uruguay

2192 Uruguay. Asesoría en Estadigrafía y Economía . . . Costo de la vida; estudio de los precios y salarios a través de los años 1943-1952. Montevideo, Impr. Nacional, 1953, 819p.

Venezuela

2193 Universidad Central, Caracas. Instituto de Investigaciones Económicas
Análisis de presupuestos familiares. Caracas, 1960-

2194 Universidad de Los Andes. Facultad de Economía. Instituto de Investigaciones Económicas
Condiciones y costo de vida en la Ciudad de Mérida. Mérida, 1962, 76 plus 5p.

Periodical Articles

General

2195 Beckerman, W., & R. Bacon
"International Comparisons of Income Levels: a Suggested New Measure." London, Economic journal (76:303), September 1966, p. 519-536.

2196 Cummings, L.D.
"Employed Poor: Their Characteristics and Occupations." Monthly labor review 88, July 1965, p. 828-835.

2197 "The Income Needs of the City Worker's Family." AFL-CIO American federationist 72, May 1965, p. 16-19.

2198 Kloek, T., & H. Theil
"International Comparisons of Prices and Quantities Consumed." Econometrica 33, July 1965, p. 535-556.

2199 Lamale, Helen H.
"Poverty: the Word and the Reality." Monthly labor review 88, July 1965, p. 822-827.

2200 Niewiaroski, D. H.
"The Level of Living of Nations: Meaning and Measurement." Estadística (23:86), March 1965, p. 3-31.

Latin America

2201 "Facts and Figures of the Americas." Américas 14, November 1962, p. 43-44.

2202 "Facts and Figures of the Americas, Consumer Price Indexes, Monthly Average, 1961 and 1963." Américas 16, June 1964, p. 47.

2203 Galarza, Ernesto
"The Cost of Living in Latin America." México, Mexican-American review (16:12), December 1948, p. 8-43.

2204 Maison de l'Amérique Latine
"Le Standard de Vie des Populations en Amérique Latine." Brussels, Belgique Amérique Latine, April 20, 1948, p. 19-20.

2205 Montesino Samperio, José V.
"El Costo de la Vida en las Capitales Americanas en los Ultimos Anos." Caracas, Producción, August 20, 1946, p. 40-43.

Argentina

2206 Argentine Republic. Ministerio de Relaciones Exteriores y Culto
"Cost of Living Indexes, Argentina, During the First and Second World Wars." Monthly labor review, March 1942, p. 710.

2207 "Austerity for Dinner." Time 73, June 23, 1959, p. 33.

2208 Belaunde, César H.
"El Costo de la Vida y los Salarios Industriales." Buenos Aires, Revista de economía argentina, September 1942, p. 274-277.

2209 "Cheaper Living or Higher Wages?" Buenos Aires, The review of the River Plate, July 9, 1948, p. 33.

2210 "Income and Expenditure of a Laborer's Family in Buenos Aires in 1929." Monthly labor review, March 1931, p. 236.

2211 "Income Distribution in Argentina." Economic bulletin for Latin America (XI:1), April 1966, p. 106-131.

2212 International Labour Office
"Wages and the Cost of Living in Argentina." Geneva, Industry and labour (7:7), April 1, 1952, p. 285-286.

2213 "Resúmenes Estadísticos y su Expresión Gráfica: Estadísticas Sociales. Costo de la Vida." Buenos Aires, Revista de economía, November 1945, p. 514-518.

2214 Siri, Emilio
"La Campaña Contra la Carestía de la Vida." Buenos Aires, Revista de información municipal Boca y Barracas (Ano XIII:69-70), 1946, p. 5-7.

2215 Tella, Torcuato di
"La Población Ocupada y las Rentas Individuales en la Argentina." Buenos Aires, Revista de economía argentina, June 1945, p. 256-267.

2216 U.S. Department of Labor
"Cost of Living and Retail Prices in Buenos Aires May, 1940." Monthly labor review, December 1940, p. 1567-1568.

Bolivia

2217 Pomcranz, Rodolfo
"Costo de Vida." La Paz, Protección social, March 1940, p. 31-38.

2218 Trueblood, Edward G.
"Living and Office Operating Costs in Bolivia." Bureau of Foreign and Domestic Commerce Special Circular No. 179, May 31, 1929.

Brazil

2219 Almeida, V. Unzer de
"A Pesquisa Social do Indice de Preços ao Con-

sumidor. Notas para Estudo, Organização e Estabelecimento de um Indice de ao Consumidor para São Paulo." São Paulo, Sociologia (23:4), December 1961, p. 315-328.

2220 Araújo, Oscar E. de
"Pesquisa de Padrão de Vida." São Paulo, Sociologia (21:3), August 1959, p. 247-273.

2221 Azevedo, Aldo M.
"Problemas Brasileiros." São Paulo, Idort (Revista de Organização Científica), December 1946, p. 3-6.

2222 Azevedo, Osvaldo B. de
"As Causas do Encarecimiento do Custo da Vida." São Paulo, Digesto econômico, December 1945, p. 109-118.

2223 Azevedo, Osvaldo B. de
"O Custo da Vida." Rio de Janeiro, Boletim da Associação Comercial do Rio de Janeiro, April 19, 1944, p. 18-19.

2224 Azevedo, Osvaldo B. de
"Estudos Sobre: Custo da Vida; Salarios e Seus Aumentos Compulsorios . . ." São Paulo, Idort (Revista de Organização Científica), July 1948, p. 157-162.

2225 Bastos, Humberto
"O Problema da Carestia." Rio de Janeiro, O observador econômico e financeiro, October 1942, p. 49-55.

2226 Brown, W. D.
"Cost of Living for Americans in Brazil." Rio de Janeiro, Brazilian business, September 1929, p. 19 & 26.

2227 "Cost of Living: an Analysis of its Behavior (Rio de Janeiro)." Rio de Janeiro, Conjuntura econômica internacional), June 1961, p. 33-39.

2228 "Cost of Living: Analysis of its Behavior." Rio de Janeiro, Conjuntura econômica internacional 10,

January 1963, p. 63-70.

2229 "Cost of Living at Rio de Janeiro. Average Wholesale and Retail Prices of Principal Articles and Foodstuffs." Rio de Janeiro, Wileman's Brazilian review, March 13, 1930, p. 335-337.

2230 "Cost of Living in Rio de Janeiro (1937-1939)." Brazilian bulletin, June 14, 1944, p. 5.

2231 "Cost of Living: Record Increase in 1959." Rio de Janeiro, Conjuntura econômica internacional, January 1960, p. 39-44.

2232 Costa, Aguinaldo
"O Sempre Crescente Custo da Vida." São Paulo, Revista Brasiliense 25, September/October 1959, p- 23-44.

2233 Costa, L. Nery da
"Indice de Preços de Gêneros Alimentícios no Comércio Varejista da Guanabara." Rio de Janeiro, SUNAB--Boletim técnico 2, April 1965, p. 47-55.

2234 "Costs of Living in Brazil." Brazil, January 1936, p. 12-13 & 16.

2235 Desenvolvimento e Conjuntura (periodical)
"A Batalha dos Preços." Rio de Janeiro (7:5), May 1963, p. 32-40.

2236 Duncan, Julian S.
"Rice and Feijoada." Inter-American, October 1943, p. 10-14.

2237 Heare, Gertrude E.
"Living Costs in Brazil." Foreign commerce weekly, August 3, 1946, p. 11, 41-42.

2238 "Os Indices do Custo da Vida." Rio de Janeiro, Desenvolvimento e conjuntura (6:4), April 1962, p. 51-55.

2239 "Living Costs in Brazil." London, The South American journal, October 12, 1946, p. 172-174.

2240 Macedo, E. de F.
"Meios de Pagamento e o Padrão da Vida." Rio de Janeiro, Revista de finanças públicas (20:212), March-April 1960, p. 18-23.

2241 "A Marcha dos Preços em 1960." Rio de Janeiro, Desenvolvimento e conjuntura (4:9), September 1960, p. 93-100.

2242 Medeiros, Octavia Virinto de
"O Custo da Vida e os Salários." Rio de Janeiro, Revista do comercio, January 1948, p. 26-28.

2243 "New Cost of Living Index." Rio de Janeiro, Conjuntura econômica internacional (XIII:7), July 1966, p. 43-54.

2244 "New Cost of Living Index for Pôrto Alegre." Rio de Janeiro, Conjuntura econômica internacional (XIII:9), September 1966, p. 77-78.

2245 Prado, Hamilton
"Causas do Encarecimento da Vida." Rio de Janeiro, O observador econômico e financeiro (20: 239), January 1956, p. 35-41.

2246 Prado, Hamilton
"O Estado, o Cidadão e o Custo da Vida." Rio de Janeiro, O observador econômico e financeiro (23:267), May 1958, p. 8-12.

2247 Rollemberg, Luiz Dias
"Padrão de Vida e Nivel de Consumo." Rio de Janeiro, O observador econômico e financeiro (16:192), January 1952, p. 68-82.

Chile

2248 Abrisqueta e Iraculis, Francisco de
"Costo de la Vida y Salarios." Bogotá, Anales de economía y estadística (III:46), August 25, 1940, p. 30-32.

2249 Benítez, Fernando
"El País de los Problemas." Santiago, Boletín minero, Sociedad Nacional de Minería, January 1945, p. 17-20.

2250 Boal, Sam
"Bargain paradise . . . Chile." Holiday (10:5), November 1951, p. 16-22, 121.

2251 Crocco F., Juan
"El Consumo en Nuestro País." Santiago, Panorama económico, March 1948, p. 9-13.

2252 Harris, Harriet
"It's Cheaper in Chile." The Grace Log, May-June 1934, p. 465-467.

2253 Hartard Ebert, Mauricio
"Producción Circulante, Emisiones y Costo de la Vida." Santiago, Economía y finanzas, August 1947, p. 7, 9.

2254 International Labour Office
"Los Salarios y el Costo de la Vida." Madrid, Revista internacional del trabajo, May 1936, p. 550-552 & 553-555.

2255 Kent, Francis B.
"Latin Slum Way of Life for Uncounted Millions." Los Angeles times, September 18, 1965, pt. 1, p. 9.

2256 Pan American Union
"Chilean Consumers and the Cost of Living." Pan American Union bulletin 81, November 1947, p. 641-642.

2257 U.S. Dept. of Labor
"Expenditures for Food and Housing by Urban Families in Chile." Monthly labor review, February 1937, p. 520.

2258 U.S. Dept. of Labor
"Working Conditions and Cost of Living in Chile, 1937-44." Monthly labor review, April 1945, p. 789-796.

2259 Szulc, Tad
"Chile's Nightmare; Case Study of Inflation." New York times magazine, October 13, 1957, p. 37.

Colombia

2260 Abrisqueta, Francisco de
"El Problema de los Arrendamientos de Viviendas en Bogotá." Bogotá, Anales de economía e estadística, July/August 1945, p. 99-103.

2261 Abrisqueta, Francisco de
"Las Condiciones y el Costo de la Vida de la Clase Obrera en Medellín. I-VII." Bogotá, Anales de economía y estadística (III:6), October 25, 1940, 153p.

2262 "Ante la Carestía de la Vida." Bogotá, Revista Javeriana (61:302), March 1964, p. 133-139.

2263 Brooks, Clarence C.
"Living and Office Operating Costs in Colombia." Bureau of Foreign and Domestic Commerce. Division of Regional Information. Special circular no. 353, February 4, 1936, 10p.

2264 "Las Condiciones Económico-Sociales y el Costo de la Vida de la Clase Obrera en la Ciudad de Barranquilla." Bogotá, Anales de economía y estadística 4 (supl. to nos. 40 to 42:V-IX), December 1948, p. 1-169.

2265 Castro Torrijos, Rodolfo
"Evolución de los Salarios y del Costo de la Vida en Medellín." Bogotá, Seguridad social 17/20, January/December 1953, p. 29-34.

2266 Colombia. Depto., Admin., Nacional de Estadística
"Memoria de las Encuestas Sobre Ingresos y Gastos de las Familias de Emleados y de Obreros de Bogotá, Barranquilla, Cali, Medellín, Bucaramanga, Manizales y Pasto, Metodología Aplicada para Actualizar las Bases de los Indices del Costo de la Vida." Bogotá, Economía y estadística (14:85), November 1958, p. 1-350.

2267 Díaz Granados C., Manuel J.
"Costo de Vida y Precios de Víveres." Bogotá, El mes financiero y económico, August 1945, p. 135-39.

2268 Díaz Granados C., Manuel J.
"Costo de la Vida en Bogotá." Bogotá, El mes financiero y económico, July 1945, p. 123-127.

2269 Hermberg, Paul
"El Costo de la Vida de la Clase Obrera en Bogotá." Bogotá, Anales de economía y estadística (I:1), 1937, p. 1-82.

2270 Ibero, Mario
"De Como es Escandaloso el Costo de la Vida." Bogotá, El mes financiero e económico, January 1945, p. 142-148.

2271 International Labour Office
"The Colombian Family Budget Enquiry of 1936 in Bogota." Geneva, International labour review, September 1958, p. 425-433.

2272 Martínez Cabana, Carlos
"De Uno en Fondo." Bogotá, Cromos, December 21, 1946, p. 3-5, 56.

2273 Ortiz C., Luis
"El Costo de la Vida. Síntesis de una Conferencia Dictada en el Instituto de Acción Social." Bogotá, Información económica y estadística de Colombia, June 15, 1936, p. . .

2274 Polo, Pepe
"La Vida Cara." Bogotá, Cromos, March 15, 1947, p. 3-5, 49-50.

2275 "El Precio de los Viveres en Bogotá." Bogotá, Anales de economía y estadística, November 5, 1942, p. 65-66.

2276 Restrepo Restrepo, Fabián
"Algunos Aspectos del Nivel de Vida del Campesino Colombiano." Medellín, Revista de ciencias económicas (1:3), March 1954, p. 503-509.

Costa Rica

2277 "La Carestía de Productos de Primera Necesidad Trae Graves Consecuencias al País." San José, El agricultor costarricense, June 1947, p. 193-194.

2278 Pan American Union
"Cost of Living and Wages in Costa Rica." Pan American Union bulletin 74, May 1940, p. 414-415.

2279 U.S. Dept. of Labor
"Family Expenditures: San José, Costa Rica, 1949." Monthly labor review (71:4), October 1950, p. 443-445.

2280 Unckles, Roderick W.
"Living and Office Operating Expenses in Costa Rica." Bureau of Foreign and Domestic Commerce, Division of Regional Information, January 15, 1933, Special Circular no. 88, 5p.

Cuba

2281 Alvarez Acevedo, J.M.
"Editorial: Abastecimiento y Producción Local." Havana, Revista nacional, September 1946, p. 3.

2282 Crau Agüero, Vicente
"El Precio del Azúcar (La Tragedia de Cuba)." Havana, Tierra libre, November 1944, p. 16.

2283 Isern, J.
"Cómo Han Subido los Precios." Havana, Carteles (31:34), October 9, 1950, p. 31-32.

2284 Knox, Charles F.
"Living and Office Operating Costs in Cuba." Bureau of Foreign and Domestic Commerce, Division of Regional Information, Special circular no. 352, January 15, 1936, 12p.

2285 "Niveles de Precios y de Costo de Vida." Havana, Cuba económica y financiera, November 1943, p. 19.

2286 Raggi y Ageo, Carlos M.
"Niveles de Vida en Cuba: Presupuesto Familiar." Havana, Revista nacional, November 1943, p. 19-20.

2287 Riccardi, Antonio
" Por Qué Encarece Más Cada Día el Costo de la Vida en Cuba?" Havana, Carteles, August 1, 1948, p. 46-48.

Dominican Republic

2288 Johnson, Albion W.
"Living and Office Operating Expenses in the Dominican Republic." Bureau of Foreign and Domestic Commerce, Division of Regional Information, Special Circular no. 65, September 15, 1932, 5p.

Ecuador

2289 Pan American Union
"Fighting Living Costs in Ecuador." Pan American Union bulletin 81, March 1947, p. 166.

El Salvador

2290 El Salvador. Departamento Nacional del Trabajo
"Indice del Costo de la Vida." San Salvador, Revista de trabajo (1:1), March/May 1950, p. 182-201.

2291 "How a Family Lives in Middle America." Pan American magazine, December 1945, p. 30-32.

2292 Suay, José E.
"El Problema de las Subsistencias en El Salvador." San Salvador, Boletín de la Cámara de Comercio e Industria de El Salvador, July/August 1945, p. 10-12.

Guatemala

2293 Orellana G., R. A.
"Variaciones en el Costo de la Vida en Guatemala, y el Poder Adquisitivo de la Moneda." Guatemala, Universidad de San Carlos 56, January-April 1962, p. 127-164.

2294 Orellana G., R. A.
"Variaciones en el Costo de la Vida en Guatemala." San Salvador, ECA (16:166), December 1961, p. 646-655.

2295 Roux, Rómulo
"Approach to Minimum Wage Fixing in Guatemala." Geneva, International labor review 71, January 1955, p. 1-33.

Haiti

2296 Haiti. Dept. du Travail
"Coût de la Vie dans les Familles à Faibles Revenus." Port-au-Prince, Revue du travail 1, June 1951, p. 108-118.

2297 Haiti. Dept. du Travail et du Bien-être Social
"Indices du Coût de la Vie, 1952-1959." Port-au-Prince, Revue du travail 9, May 1960, p. 193.

2298 Hyppolite, B.
"La Notion de 'Coût de la Vie.'" Port-au-Prince, Revue du travail 6, May 1, 1956, p. 17-22.

Honduras

2299 Spaña Valladares, Emilio
"Como Abaratar el Precio de la Vivienda en Tegucigalpa." Tegucigalpa, Honduras rotaria, March 1945, p. 10, 28.

Jamaica

2300 Hoyt, E.E.
"Voluntary Unemployment and Unemployability in Jamaica with Special Reference to the Standard of Living." London, The British journal of sociology 11, June 1960, p. 129-136.

Mexico

2301 Bach, Federico
"El Costo de la Vida de la Clase Obrera." México, Revista de economía y estadística, November 1934, p. 20-23.

2302 Buelink, Juan H.
"El Problema de la Vivienda y el Crédito Recíproco." Mexico, El economista, January 1948, p. 55-60.

2303 Castellano, Pablo
"El Costo de la Vida en el Año 1946." México, Carta semanal, May 3, 1947, p. 5-6.

2304 "Costo de la Vida." México, Estadística nacional, April 1, 1929, p. 121-122.

2305 "Datos Estadísticos para Estudiar el Encarecimiento." México, Carta semanal, May 1943, p. 5-7.

2306 Eddy, D.
"On the Road to Utopia." American magazine 162, July 1956, p. 34-37.

2307 "Guillotina para los Hambreadores. Imponente Manifestación de Hombres y Mujeres Exigiendo el Descenso de los Precios . . ." México, Hoy, October 18, 1947, p. 9-11.

2308 Guisa y Acevedo, Jesús
"A Propósito del Aumento del Costo de la Vida Nadie Entiende a Nadie." México, Lectura (101: 3), October 1, 1954, p. 67-72.

2309 Hernández, Manuel A.
"El Costo de la Vida en México." México, Vida, October 10, 1947, p. 727-734.

2310 Huerta Maldonado, M.
"El Nivel de Vida en México." México, Revista mexicana de sociología (22:2), May-August 1960, p. 463-527.

2311 "Indices de Precios y del Costo de la Vida." México, Revista de estadística, September 1944, p. 795-798.

2312 Instituto de Estudios Económicos y Sociales
"Estudios y Declaraciones Sobre el Alto Costo de la Vida." México, El economista, November 16, 1939, p. 6-13.

2313 Joseph, R.
"Luxury Living on $45 a Week." Coronet 40, October 1956, p. 102-106.

2314 Kemp, L.
"Perils of Paradise." House & Garden 111, April 1957, p. 172-174.

2315 Maldonado S., G.
"Indice del Costo de Vida del Obrero en Monterrey." Monterrey, Revista de la Escuela de Contabilidad,

Economía y Administración, January 1962, p. 1-25.

2316 Mallo, Jerónimo
"El Problema del Nivel de Vida de la Clase Trabajadora." México, Carta semanal, June 30, 1945, p. 77-79.

2317 Mexico. Instituto de Orientación Económica
"El Problema de los Salarios y Subsistencias." México, Problemas de México, August/September 1946, p. 1-81.

2318 Newman, R.E.
"Current Living Costs in Mexico City." International markets, September 1952, p. 35-37.

2319 Rivera Marín, G.
"La Mano de Obra, el Nivel de Vida y los Salarios en la Ciudad de Oaxaca." México, El trimestre económico (24:4), October/December 1957, p. 363-398.

2320 Zamora, Clementina
"Costo de Vida, Problema Trascendente de México." México, Revista de económia (15:6), June 1952, p. 193-195.

Panama

2321 "Costo de la Vida." Panamá, Estadística panameña, September 1943, p. 10-14.

Paraguay

2322 "Paraguay, País Aislado y de Lucha." México, Datos y cifras (4:1/2), January/February 1955, p. 1-10.

Peru

2323 Joseph, R.
"Paradise, on $200 a Month." Coronet 26, June 1949, p. 44-47.

2324 "Números Indicadores de Precios al por Mayor y del Costo de Vida en Lima." Lima, Revista de hacienda, no. 18, 1944, p. 277-287.

2325 Nuñez del Prado Tío, G.
"Números Indices Mensuales de Artículos de Primera Necesidad para la Provincia del Cuzco." Cuzco, Revista universitaria (49:119), 2nd quarter 1960, p. 29-37.

2326 Nuñez del Prado Tío, G., comp.
"Números Indices Mensuales de Artículos de Primera Necesidad al Por Menor, para la Ciudad del Cuzco." Cuzco, Revista universitaria (50:120), 1st quarter 1961, p. 141-157.

2327 Osorio Zamalloa, Adriel
"Ensayo de Investigación Socio-Económica Sobre Condiciones de Vida de los Trabajadores Obreros de la Ciudad del Cuzco, en Función de sus Presupuestos Familiares." Lima, Revista de la Facultad de Ciencias Económicas y Comerciales 58, January/June 1958, p. 154-285.

2328 Palacios, L.M.
"Gastos y Consumo de Artículos Alimenticios por Familias Obreras de Lima y Callao." Lima, Revista de la Facultad de Ciencias Económicas y Comerciales 62, January-June 1961, p. 87-92.

2329 Palacios, L.M.
"Indice de Precios al por Menor de Artículos Alimenticios en la Ciudad de Lima, 1940-1954." Lima, Revista de la Facultad de Ciencias Económicas y Comerciales 53, July/December 1955, p. 176-222.

2330 Shearer, L.
"Bargain Paradise." Holiday 9, February 1951, p. 16-18.

Uruguay

2331 U.S. Dept. of Labor
"Cost of Living of Worker's Family in Montevideo, Uruguay, 1937-44." Monthly labor review, June 1945, p. 1299-1301.

2332 Wells, H.B.
"Living and Office Operating Costs in Uruguay."

Bureau of Foreign and Domestic Commerce, Division of Regional Information, Special circular no. 363, May 30, 1936, 10p.

Venezuela

2333 Bengoa, J.M., et al
"Variaciones de los Costos de Alimentación en Caracas en los Ultimos 20 Años." Caracas, Archivos venezolanos de nutrición 5, 1954, p. 113-131.

2334 "Busy Bs." Time 62, September 21, 1953, p. 44.

2335 Moore, O.E.
"Policy Measures and Food Production in Venezuela." Foreign agriculture, June/July 1946, p. 96-104.

2336 Recao, Manuel F.
"Estructura y Métodos de Funcionamiento de la Comisión Especial para el Estudio del Costo de la Vida en Venezuela." Estadística (Journal of the Inter-American Statistical Institute) (12:42), March 1954, p. 113-115.

2337 Venezuela. Ministerio de Relaciones Exteriores
"El Costo de la Vida en Venezuela." Caracas, Informaciones Dadas por el Ministerio de Relaciones Exteriores de los EE. UU. de Venezuela 32, January 15, 1951, p. 10-11.

INDUSTRIALIZATION

Books

General

2338 Andersen, Nels
Our industrial urban civilization. New York, Asia Pub. House, 1964, 113p.

2339 Inter-Regional Seminar on Development Policies and Planning in Relation to Urbanization, University of Pittsburgh, Pittsburgh, Pa., 24 October-7 November 1966.
Background and working papers. New York, United Nations, 1966, variously paged.

2340 ISSUE (Information sources in urban economics). #1. Washington, Communication Service Corp., January 1967-

2341 Reissman, Leonard
The urban process; cities in industrial societies. New York, Free Press, 1964, 255p.

2342 Schneider, Eugene V.
Industrial sociology: the social relations of industry and the community. New York, McGraw-Hill, 1957, 559p.

Latin America

2343 Inter-American Seminar on Area and Industrial Development. 1st, La Guaira, Venezuela, 1965
El desarrollo regional e industrial. Atlanta, Conway Research Inc., 1965, 123p.

2344 Leiserson, Alcira
Notes on the process of industrialization in Argentina, Chile and Peru. Berkeley, Institute of International Studies, University of California, 1966, 99p.

2345 Medina Echavarría, José
Consideraciones sociológicas sobre el desarrollo económico de América Latina. Buenos Aires, Solar-Hachette, 1964, 171p.

Bolivia

2346 Canelas O., A.
Mito y realidad de la industrialización boliviana. La Paz, 1966, 478p.

Brazil

2347 Costa Pinto, Luiz Aguiar de, & T. P. Accioly Borges
O comércio metropolitano do Distrito Federal. Rio de Janeiro, 1957, 65p.

2348 Freitas, Norma, et al
O sub-distrito de Nazaré; estudo de geografia urbana. Salvador, Pubs. da Universidade da Bahia, 1959, 22p.

2349 Lima, Heitor Ferreira
Evolução industrial de São Paulo; esboço histórico. São Paulo, Martins, 1954, 196p.

2350 Lopes, Juarez R. Brandão
Sociedade industrial no Brasil. São Paulo, Difusão Européia do Livro, 1964, 186p.

2351 Survey of the Brazilian economy, 1965. Washington, Brazilian Embassy, 1966, 254p.

Chile

2352 Butler, Joseph H.
Manufacturing in the Concepción region of Chile... Washington, National Research Council, 1960, 106p.

2353 Hoffman, Rodolfo, & Debuyst, Frederic
Chile, una industrialización desordenada. Santiago, DESAL, 1966, 279p.

2354 Ljubetic G., René A.
Industrialización de Magallanes. Santiago, Editorial Universitaria, Universidad de Chile, 1955, 109p.

2355 Villanueva Barra, L. H.
La población de Valdivia y su influencia en la provincia. Santiago, Ed. Universitaria, Universidad de Chile, 1955, 99p.

Colombia

2356 Asociación Nacional de Industriales
Bucaramanga, development and perspectives. Bucaramanga, 1962, 92p.

2357 Asociación Nacional de Industriales
Cali and the Cauca Valley, a guide for the industrial investor. Cali, 1961, 48p.

2358 Asociación Nacional de Industriales
Medellín and surrounding area, a guide for the industrial investor. Medellín, 1961, 67p.

2359 Lipman, Aaron
El empresario bogotano. Bogotá, Eds. Tercer Mundo, 1966, 190p.

El Salvador

2360 Reynolds, D. R.
Rapid development in small economies: the example of El Salvador. New York, Praeger, 1967, 124p.

Mexico

2361 Bassols Batalla, Angel
La ciudad de México y su region económica. (In International Geographical Union. Proceedings of the First Latin American Regional Conference, Mexico City, August 2-8, 1966. v. 4. Mexico, 1966, p. 113-136).

2362 Guanajuato: industrial vein of Mexico. Guanajuato, Secretaría de Fomento Económico, 1965, 24p.

2363 Puebla, factores de localización industrial, 1966. Puebla, Comisión de Promoción Industrial y Turística, Estado de Puebla, 1966, 54p.

2364 Soza Valderrama, H.
Planificación del desarrollo industrial. México, Siglo 21 Eds., 1966, 370p.

Peru

2365 Arequipa: paraíso de inversionistas. Arequipa, Junta de Rehabilitación y Desarrollo de Arequipa, 1964, 23p.

2366 Chaplin, David
Industrialization and the distribution of wealth in Peru. Madison, Land Tenure Center, University of Wisconsin, 1966, 18p.

Venezuela

2367 Friedmann, John R.
Regional development policy: a case study of Venezuela. Cambridge, M.I.T. Press, 1966, 183p.

2368 Labouisse, Henry R., et al
The economic development of Venezuela. Baltimore, Johns Hopkins Press, 1961, 494p.

2369 Maza Zavala, D. F.
Condiciones generales del área metropolitana de Caracas para su industrialización. Caracas, Eds. de Cuatricentenario de Caracas, 1966, 145p.

West Indies and the Caribbean

2370 Aruba. Dept. of Economic Development
General information on Aruba as an industrial area. Oranjestad, 1962, 20p.

2371 Farley, R.
Nationalism and industrial development in the British Caribbean. Georgetown, Daily Chronicle, 1957, 58p.

Periodical Articles

General

2372 Agulla, Juan C.
"Aspectos Sociales del Proceso de Industrialización en una Comunidad Urbana." México, Revista mexicana de sociología (XXV:2), May-August 1963, p. 747-772.

2373 Davis, Kingsley, & H. Hertz
"Urbanization and the Development of Preindustrial Areas." Economic development & culture change 3, October 1954, p. 6-26.

2374 Nash, Manning
"Industrialization in a Non-Western Civilization." Geographical review 49, October 1959, p. 564-566.

2375 Reeb, D.J.
"An Inquiry into the Economic Goal Structure of Urban Areas." Urban affairs quarterly, December 1966, p. 36-48.

2376 Ventre, Francis T.
"Local Initiatives in Urban Industrial Development." Urban affairs quarterly, December 1966, p. 49-62.

Latin America

2377 Germani, Gino
"Urbanización, Secularización y Desarrollo Económico." México, Revista mexicana de sociología (25:2), May-August 1963, p. 625-646.

2378 Huneeus, A.
"Las Reformas Estructurales." Santiago, Finis terrae (10:39), 3rd quarter 1963, p. 3-14.

2379 James, Preston E.
"The Significance of Industrialization in Latin America." Economic geography 26, 1950, p. 159-161.

2380 Landin, D.F.
"Urban Growth and Economic Strategy in Latin America." Development digest (IV:4), January 1967, p. 9-12.

2381 MacEoin, Gary
"Latin America Industrializes." Commonweal 60, April 16, 1954, p. 31-34.

2382 Wythe, George A.
"Progress in Industrialization of Latin America." Annals of the American Academy of Political &

Social Science 255, January 1948, p. 48-57.

Argentina

2383 Agulla, Juan C.
"Poder, Comunidad y Desarrollo Industrial: la Estructura de Poder en una Comunidad Urbana en Desarrollo: Córdoba." Paris, Aportes # 2, October 1966, p. 80-105.

2384 Schumacher, E.
"El Gran Buenos Aires." Buenos Aires, Revista geográfica americana, año 20 (XXXVI: 216), 1953, p. 97-108.

Brazil

2385 Bazzanella, Waldemiro
"Industrialização e Urbanização no Brasil." Rio de Janeiro, América latina (VI:1), January-March 1963, p. 3-26.

2386 Campos, W.
"Recordes da Indústria Paulista." Rio de Janeiro, O observador (15:179), December 1950, p. 42-49.

2387 Cardoso, Fernando H.
"A Estructura da Indústria de São Paulo (a Partir de 1930)." Rio de Janeiro, Educação e ciências sociais (7:13), February 1960, p. 28-42.

2388 Cardoso, Fernando H., & Octavio Ianni
"Condiciones y Efectos de la Industrialización de Sao Paulo." México, Ciencias políticas y sociales (5:18), October-December 1959, p. 577-584.

2389 Costa, Aguinaldo
"Algunas Indústrias de São Paulo." São Paulo, Revista brasiliense 6, July/August 1956, p. 167-185.

2390 Cruls, Gastão
"O Comércio no Velho Rio de Janeiro." Rio de Janeiro, Revista do comércio, July 1947, p. 24-26.

2391 Ianni, Octavio
"Factores Humanos de la Industrialización en

en Brasil." México, Ciencias políticas y sociales (6:20), April-June 1960, p. 325-338.

2392 Juillard, E.
"Europa Industrial e Brasil; Dois Tipos de Organização do Espaço Pernambucano." Salvador, Boletim baiano de geografia 4, 1961, p. 3-10.

2393 Lima, Heitor Ferreira
"Contribuiçao Italiana à Indústria de S. Paulo. Estudo Histórico." Rio de Janeiro, O observador econômico e financeiro (24:276), February 1959, p. 24-30.

2394 Lima, Heitor Ferreira
"Sao Paulo. Evoluçao Industrial em Meio Século." Rio de Janeiro, O observador econômico e financeiro (17:200), September 1952, p. 70-81.

2395 MacQuarrie, L.W.
"São Paulo City Expands. A report on 1946 Accomplishments." Rio de Janeiro, Brazilian business, January 1947, p. 36-39.

2396 Morse, Richard M.
"Sao Paulo in the Nineteenth Century: Economic Roots of the Metropolis." Inter-American economic affairs (V:3), 1951, p. 3-39.

2397 "O Parque Industrial Guanabarino." Rio de Janeiro, Desenvolvimento e conjuntura 3, 1963, p. 18-31.

2398 Petrone, Pasquale
"As Indústrias Paulistanas e os Fatores de sua Expansao." Sao Paulo, Boletim paulista de geografia 14, 1953, p. 26-37.

2399 Simao, A.
"Industrializaçao e Sindicalizaçao no Brasil." Belo Horizante, Revista brasileira de estudos políticos 13, January 1962, p. 87-101.

Central America

2400 Baranson, J.
"Industrialization and Regionalism in Central America." Inter-American economic affairs 16, Autumn 1962, p. 87-95.

Colombia

2401 Acevedo Latorre, Eduardo
"Panorama Geo-Económico del Distrito Especial de Bogotá." Bogotá, Economiá y estadística (14: 84), July 1958, p. 5-83.

2402 "Las Actividades Comerciales e Industriales en Bogotá Durante el Ano de 1945." Bogotá, Boletín de la Cámara de Comercio de Bogotá, January 30, 1946, p. 1-5.

2403 Lipman, Aaron
"Social Background of the Bogotá Entrepreneur." Journal of Inter-American studies (7:2), April 1965, p. 227-235.

2404 Lleras Camargo, Alberto
"Problemas Econômicos em Bogotá." Rio de Janeiro, O observador (4:167), December 1949, p. 20-28.

2405 Pan American Union
"Progress of Industrialization in Bogotá, Colombia." Pan American Union bulletin 79, February 1945, p. 86-87.

2406 Pérez Ramirez, Gustavo
"La Urbanización y el Cambio Social en Colombia." Río Piedras, Revista de ciencias sociales (IX:2), June 1965, p. 203-220.

Cuba

2407 Maruri Guilló, Carlos M.
"La Habana de 1956." Havana, Arquitectura (25: 282), January 1957, p. 35-42.

2408 Pérez, R. R.
"La Habana También Crece Horizontalmente." Havana, Carteles (39:22), June 1, 1958, p. 80-82.

Ecuador

2409 Linke, Lilo
"What's Happening to Guayaquil?" Américas (9:6), June 1957, p. 3-8.

2410 Walker, Guild
"Guayaquil, Ecuador's Leading Port Undergoing Vast Changes." Lima, Peruvian times (16:802), May 4, 1956, p. 7-8; (16:803), May 11, 1956, p. 9-10.

El Salvador

2411 Tricart, Jean
"Un Exemple du Déséquilibre Villes--Campagnes dans une Economie en Voie de Développement, le Salvador." Brussels, Développement et civilisations 11, 1962, p. 80-102.

Haiti

2412 "Le Développement de l'Industrialisation à Haiti." Paris, Industrie et travail d'outre-mer 10, September 1954, p. 535-537.

Mexico

2413 Bird, Richard M.
"The Economy of the Mexican Federal District." Inter-American economic affairs 17, Autumn 1963, p. 19-51.

2414 Brown, William
"Monterrey: City of Progress." México, Mexican-American review (20:12), December 1952, p. 25-26, 74-80.

2415 Cipnic, Dennis J.
"Industrial Monterrey." Américas (12:6), June 1960, p. 3-8.

2416 "Distrito Federal. Promoción Industrial." México, Revista industrial (10:138), January 10, 1954, p. 31-32.

2417 Flores, Edmundo
"El Crecimiento de la Ciudad de México: Causas y Efectos Económicos." La Plata, Economía (5: 17-20), July 1958-June 1959, p. 181-210.

2418 Gildea, R.Y.
"Geographic Aspects of Industrial Growth in the Monterrey Region of Mexico." Journal of geography 1, 1960, p. 34-41.

2419 Hernandez Moreno, J., & S. Nahmad
"La Política Económica del Estado como Factor del Desarrollo Social Regional." México, Revista mexicana de sociología (23:1), 1961, p. 147-167.

2420 Horn, A. B.
"Guadalajara: Economic Hub of a Fast-Growing Region." México, Mexican-American review 32, October 1964, p. 14-17.

2421 Mauro, Frédéric
"Le Développement Economique de Monterrey (1890-1960)." Toulouse, Caravelle 2, 1964, p. 35-126.

2422 Megee, Mary C.
"Some Postwar Aspects of Industrial Development in Monterrey, Mexico." Rio de Janeiro, Revista geográfica del Instituto Panamericano de Geografía y Historia (XXVIII:54), 1961, p. 29-34.

2423 "Monterrey." México, Todo 958, January 17, 1952, p. 40-63.

2424 Nuevo Leon. Universidad. Centro de Investigaciones Económicas
"La Actividad Económica en el Area Metropolitana de Monterrey en 1966." Monterrey, Boletín bimestral (V:25), February 1967, p. 1-5.

2425 Salazar, Rubén
"Mexican Stock Market Turns to Small Investor for Growth." Los Angeles times, March 27, 1967, pt. 3, p. 9, 13.

2426 Todd-Amsden, Mary
"Sultana of the North." México, Mexican-American review, July 1945, p. 60-62, 144.

Peru

2427 Dollfus, Olivier
"Quelques Remarques sur le Poids de la Capitale dans l'Economie Péruvienne." Toulouse, Caravelle 3, 1964, p. 289-297.

2428 Harth-Terré, Emilio
"A Glance at Lima in the Year 1955." Lima, Peruvian times (15:757), June 24, 1955, p. 2, 33.

2429 León, H. M.
"Las Zonas Industriales; Análisis de los Problemas Creados por la Presencia de la Fábrica Dentro de la Ciudad." Lima, El arquitecto peruano (279-281), October-December 1960, p. 45-46.

2430 Woolley, G. A.
"Boom Town S. A.: the Story of Tingo María." Foreign agriculture (XVI:4), April 1952, p. 67-71.

Venezuela

2431 Urdaneta, Heberto
"Breves Consideraciones sobre la Economía Urbana." Caracas, Economía y ciencias sociales (7:2), 2a. época, April-June 1965, p. 93-120.

West Indies and the Caribbean

2432 "Jamaica's Ten Years Plan." London, Commonwealth development (5:2), 1958, p. 30-31.

POVERTY
(including Unemployment)

Books

General

2433 American Jewish Committee
The tyranny of poverty: a selected bibliography of books, pamphlets, articles and memoranda on government and community action, employment, education, legal and social services, economic and social problems. New York, 1966, 18p.

2434 Bogue, Donald J.
Skid row in American cities. Chicago, Community & Family Study Center, University of Chicago, 1963, 521p.

2435 Clinard, Marshall B.
Slums and community development. New York, Free Press, 1966, 384p.

2436 Devine, E. J.
A frame work for the analysis of depressed areas: report #MR-7. Los Angeles, Institute of Government & Public Affairs, University of California, 1964, 26p.

2437 Dunne, G. H., ed.
Poverty in plenty. New York, Kenedy, 1964, 142p.

2438 Ferman, L. A., et. al
Poverty in America . . . Ann Arbor, University of Michigan Press, 1965, 832p.

2439 Lamale, Helen H.
Levels of living among the poor; report #MR-42. Los Angeles, Institute of Government & Public Affairs, University of California, 1965, 36p.

2440 Miller, Herman P.
Changes in the number and composition of the poor; report #MR-32. Los Angeles, Institute of Government & Public Affairs, University of California, 1965, 19p.

2441 Miller, Herman P.
Major elements of a research program for the study of poverty; report #MR-14. Los Angeles, Institute of Government & Public Affairs, University of California, 1964, 34p.

2442 Miller, Herman P., ed.
Poverty American style. Belmont, Wadsworth, 1966, 304p.

2443 Miller, Herman P.
What is poverty--who are the poor? Report #MR 31. Los Angeles, Institute of Government & Public Affairs, University of California, 1965, 110p.

2444 Nelson, Richard R.
Economic growth and poverty; report #MR-45. Los Angeles, Institute of Government and Public Affairs, University of California, 1965, 12p.

2445 Paltiel, F.L.
Poverty; an annotated bibliography and references. Ottawa, Canadian Welfare Council, 1966, 136p.

2446 Pearl, Arthur, & Frank Reissman
New careers for the poor; the non-professional in human service. New York, Free Press, 1965, 273p.

2447 Poverty and human resources abstracts. Ann Arbor (I:1), Institute of Labor and Industrial Relations, University of Michigan, January 1966-

2448 Schorr, Alvin L.
Slums and social insecurity. London, Nelson, 1964, 172p.

2449 Seligman, Ben B., ed.
Poverty as a public issue. New York, Free Press of Glencoe, 1965, 359p.

2450 Weisbrod, B. A., ed.
The economics of poverty; an American paradox. Englewood Cliffs, Prentice-Hall, 1966, 180p.

Latin America

2451 Ahumada, Jorge C.
En vez de la miseria. 5th ed. Santiago, Ed. del Pacífico, 1965, 183p.

2452 DESAL
Marginalidad en América Latina: ensayo de diagnóstico. Santiago, 1966, 126p.

2453 Frank, Andrew G.
Urban poverty in Latin America (studies in comparative international development, II:019). St. Louis, Social Science Institute, Washington University, 1966, 47p.

2454 Hunter, David R.
The slums: challenge and response. New York, Free Press, 1964, 307p.

Argentina

2455 Pablo, V.E. de
Investigación social en agrupaciones de "villas miserias" de la ciudad de Buenos Aires. Buenos Aires, Comisión Nacional de la Vivienda, 1958, 64p.

Brazil

2456 Bonilla, Frank
Rio favelas: the rural slum within the city. New York, American Universities Field Staff reports service, East Coast South American Series (v. 8, # 3), 1961, 15p.

2457 Goulart, José Alipio
Favelas do Distrito Federal. Rio de Janeiro, Serviço de Informação Agrícola, Ministerio de Agricultura, 1957, 80p.

2458 Jesus, Carolina M. de
Child of the dark. New York, Dutton, 1962, 190p.

2459 Louzeiro, José, ed.
Assim marcha a família; onze dramáticos flagrantes da chamada sociedade cristã e democrática, no ano do IV centenário da cidade do Rio de Janeiro. Rio de Janeiro, Ed. Civilização Brasilera, 1965, 177p.

2460 Medina, Carlos A. de
A favela e o demagôgo. São Paulo, Martins, 1964, 101p.

2461 Minas Gerais. Secretaria de Estado do Trabalho e Cultura Popular
Levantamento da população favelada de Bêlo Horizonte . . . Bêlo Horizonte, 1966, 63p.

2462 Rio de Janeiro (Federal District). Depto. de Geografia e Estatística
Censo das favelas; aspectos gerais. Rio de Janeiro, 1949, 33p.

Chile

2463 DESAL
Poblaciones marginales y desarrollo urbano, el caso chileno. Santiago, 1966, 114p.

2464 Rivano, Juan
El punto de vista de la miseria. Santiago, Facultad de Filosofía y Educación, Universidad de Chile, 1965, 175p.

2465 Antequera Stand, Miguel A.
Ocupación y desocupación en Bogotá: Los Alcázares, Quiroga, Las Ferias. Bogotá, Centro de Estudios sobre Desarrollo Económico, Universidad de los Andes, 1962, 68p.

2466 Jaramillo Q., Stella
Estudio de los ranchos de lata y cartón de la ciudad de Medellín. Medellín, 1957, 31p.

Ecuador

2467 Brooks, Rhoda, & Earle Brooks
The barrios of Manta: a personal account of the Peace Corps in Ecuador. New York, New American Library, 1965, 366p.

Guatemala

2468 Coronado Iturbide, Jorge
Sugestiones para la eradicación del Campamento San Diego (tugurio) en la ciudad de Guatemala. Guatemala, 1955, 40p.

Mexico

2469 Dromundo, Baltasar
Mi barrio de San Miguel. México, Antigua Libraría Robredo, 1951, 136p.

2470 Instituto Nacional de la Vivienda
Herradura de tugurios; problemas y soluciones. México, 1958, 28p.

2471 Lewis, Oscar
The children of Sánchez; autobiography of a Mexican family. New York, Random House, 1961, 499p.

2472 Lewis, Oscar
Five families: Mexican case studies in the culture of poverty. New York, Basic Books, 1959, 351p.

2473 Rubio, Darío
El Nacional Monte de Piedad. 3d. ed. México, 1949, 80p.

Panama

2474 Gutierrez, Samuel A.
El problema de las "barriadas brujas" en la ciudad de Panamá. Panamá, 1961, 85p.

Peru

2475 Berckholtz Salinas, Pablo
Barrios marginales; aberración social. Lima, 1963, 100p.

2476 Patch, Richard W.
Life in a callejón; a study of urban disorganization. New York, American Universities Field Staff (Reports Service: West Coast South America Series, volume 8, # 6), 1961, 24p.

Uruguay

2477 Bon Espasandín, Mario
Cantegriles; familia, educación, niveles económicos-

laborales, vivienda y aspectos generales de las poblaciones que componen el "collar de miserias" de Montevideo. Montevideo, Ed. Tupac Amarú, 1963, 113p.

2478 Bon Espasandín, Mario
Panorama de los cantegriles; conferencia pronunciada en la Facultad de Derecho de la Universidad de Córdoba. [n.p.] 1960, 16p.

2479 Uruguay. Servicio de Empleo
Informe estadístico anual. Montevideo, 1956-58- . Annual.

Venezuela
2480 Instituto Venezolano de Acción Comunitaria
Barrio Gran Colombia; estudio sociológico. Caracas, 1967, 97p.

Periodical Articles

General
2481 Lewis, W. A.
"Unemployment in Developing Countries." London, World today (23:1), January 1967, p. 13-22.

Latin America
2482 Artiles, M. F.
"Concilio, Pobreza, Iglesia." Buenos Aires, Criterio (36:1426), April 25, 1963, p. 286-292.

2483 Castro, Josué de
"Subdesarrollo y Hambre en América Latina." Paris, Cuadernos 71, April 1963, p. 6-14.

2484 Folliet, J.
"Para una Economía de la Santa Pobreza." Buenos Aires, Criterio (35:1457), August 13, 1964, p. 566-571.

2485 Gross, J.
"As the Slum Goes, so Goes the Alliance." New York Times magazine, June 23, 1963, p. 12-13.

2486 Johnson, La Verne D.
"Slums--The Crippling Pain of Latin America!" The Pan American (9:8), January 1949, p. 11-14.

2487 Magaña, M. T.
"Cooperación Interamericana a Través de los Organismos Interamericanos." Montevideo, Boletín del Instituto Interamericano del Nino (23:4), December 1959, p. 647-651.

2488 "Misery Village." Economist 199, April 22, 1961, p. 330.

2489 Montini, J. B.
"El Espíritu de Pobreza." Santiago, Finis terrae (10:38), 2nd quarter, 1963, p. 14-18.

2490 Ramos, G.
"Pauperismo e Medicina Popular." São Paulo, Sociología (13:3), August 1951, p. 252-273.

2491 Savage, C. H.
"Let's Listen to Latin America." Harvard business review 39, July 1961, p. 103-109.

2492 Sanabria, Tomás J.
"Los Ranchos, Aflicción Urbana." Desarrollo ecónomico (3:1), 1st quarter 1966, p. 22-26.

2493 Suavet, T.
"Ser con los Pobres." Montevideo, Cuadernos latinamericanos de economía humana (3:8), 1960, p. 111-117.

2494 Trusso, A.
"La Iglesia y la Pobreza." Buenos Aires, Criterio (36:1439), November 14, 1963, p. 790-792.

Argentina

2495 Elena, I. V., & E. Palermo
"Las 'Villas Miserias' y el Desarrollo Industrial en la Republica Argentina." Cuadernos americanos (123:4), July-August 1962, p. 67-85.

Brazil

2496 Bonilla, Frank
"Rio's Favelas: the Rural Slum Within the City." American Universities Field Staff (East Coast South America Series, 8:13), 1961, p. 1-15.

2497 Duprat, A. L.
"O Problema da Favela." Rio de Janeiro, Revista do serviço público (79:2), May 1958, p. 168-189.

2498 Kent, Francis B.
"Rio's Peasants Resist Urban Renewal Plan." Los Angeles times, pt. 1, July 27, 1967, p. 27.

2499 "Padrao de Vida de Operários em Sao Paulo." Rio de Janeiro, O observador, October 1941, p. 39-54.

2500 Parks, G.
"Freedom's Fearful Foe: Poverty." New York, Life 50, June 16, 1961, p. 86-96.

2501 "Radiografia da Favela." Rio de Janeiro, Síntese política, econômica, social (6:21), January-March 1964, p. 60-73.

2502 Ribeiro, Adalberto M.
"A Defesa da Criança no Brasil." Rio de Janeiro, Revista do Serviço Público, March 1943, p. 84-115.

2503 Silveira, G. P.
"Down with Shantytowns: Brazilian Students Lead the Way." Community development review (8:2), June 1963, p. 7-9.

2504 Teulières, R.
"Bidonville au Brésil: les Favelles de Belo-Horizonte." Bordeaux, Cahiers d'outre-mer (8:29), January-March 1955, p. 30-55.

Chile

2505 "Ocupación y Desocupación." Santiago, Banco Central de Chile 444, February 1965, p. 167-173.

2506 Pisculich R., E.
"Contribución al Estudio del Problema de la Vagancia." Lima, Servicio social, December 1946, p. 119-134.

2507 Chile. Universidad. Instituto de Economía
"5% de Desocupación Señaló Ultima Encuesta Ocupacional." Santiago, Panorama económica (15:227), January 1962, p. 7-10.

Colombia

2508 Duque Gómez, L.
"Los Problemas Antropo-Geográficos de Colombia." Ciencias sociales (5:29), October 1954, p. 194-206.

2509 Jerez, H.
"Un Oculto Valor Colombiano: La Ciudad del Niño." Bogotá, Revista javeriana (54:270), November 1960, p. 695-703.

2510 Powelson, John P.
"The Land-Grabbers of Cali." The reporter, January 16, 1964, p. 30-31.

2511 Schulman, Sam
"Latin American Shantytown." New York times magazine, January 16, 1966, p. 30-31.

Cuba

2512 Ruiz, G.G.
"Grandeza y Miseria del 'Albergue del Necesitado.'" Havana, Carteles (31:25), June 18, 1950, p. 25-28.

2513 Zamora, C.A.
"La Sierra da Nadie." Havana, Carteles (31:26), June 25, 1950, p. 14-15.

Dominican Republic

2514 Corten, A.
"Como Vive la Otra Mitad de Santo Domingo: Estudio de Dualismo Estructural." Río Piedras, Caribbean studies (IV:4), January 1965, p. 3-19.

2515 Hernandez R., L.E.
"Crecimiento y Desarrollo Normal del Niño Pobre

Dominicano." Boletín de la Oficina Sanitaria Panamericana (61:1), July 1966, p. 27-39.

Mexico

2516 Argüelles, C.
"Una Vez Fuimos Humanos." México, Mañana (39:393), March 10, 1951, p. 44-51.

2517 Cicognani Cardeal, A. G.
"La Urgencia de Elevar el Nivel de Vida." México, Doctrina 12/13, 1965, p. 48-62.

2518 Georges, S.
"En el Corazón de la Cuidad Perdida." México, Hoy, February 1, 1947, p. 12-18.

2519 Georges, S.
"En el Mundo de los Niños: Constructores de Almas." México, Hoy, January 4, 1947, p. 46-50.

2520 Lewis, Oscar
"The Culture of Poverty in Mexico City." Bombay, The economic weekly, June 1960, p. 965-972.

2521 Lewis, Oscar
"Manuel in the Thieves' Market." Harper's 222, June 1961, p. 66-68.

2522 Lewis, Oscar
"Tender Violence of Pedro Martinez: Excerpts ..." Harper's 228, February 1964, p. 54-60.

2523 Masdeu, J.
"Los Olvidados de Noche Buena." Havana, Bohemia (42:52), December 24, 1950, p. 40-42.

2524 "El Problema Económico de la Desnutrición Infantil." México, Comercio mexicano 4, January 10, 1952, p. 34-39.

2525 Romero, Don
"Dr. Ragpicker Finds the Forgotten Ones." Reader's Digest 60, May 1952, p. 117-120.

2526 Sánchez Sosa, J.
"La Penitenciaria Abre sus Fauces para Tragar tan Sólo Carne de Pobres." México, Todo 899, November 30, 1950, p. 8-9.

Panama

2527 Gutierrez, Samuel A.
"El Problema de las 'Barriadas Brujas' en la Ciudad de Panamá." Panamá, Lotería (6:66), May 1961, p. 33-51.

Peru

2528 Caravedo, Baltasar
"Algunas Consideraciones Sobre el Problema de la Vagancia en Lima." Lima, Boletín del Depto. de Protección Materno-Infantil, 1st semester 1946, p. 41-47.

2529 Cruchaga, Miguel
"El Fenómeno de los Barrios Marginales." Lima, El arquitecto peruano 306-308, January-March, 1963, p. 120-121.

2530 Hammel, E.A.
"Family Cycle in a Coastal Peruvian Slum and Village." American anthropologist 63, October 1961, p. 989-1005.

2531 Palacio de Habich, E.
"Investigación Socio-Económica y Etnólogo-Educacional de los Moradores de los Cerros Circunvencinos y Arrabales de la Ciudad de Lima." Lima, Servicio social (7:7), December 1949, p. 56-95.

2532 "Residents of Lima Dump Are Adopted." The Times of the Americas (XI:26), June 28, 1967, p. 2.

2533 "Slum Clearance in Lima." Américas 6, May 1954, p. 35.

2534 Turner, John F.C.
"Lima's Barriadas and Corralones: Suburbs vs. Slums." Athens, Ekistics (19:112), 1965, p. 47-71.

Uruguay

2535 Bon Espasandín, Mario
"Aspectos Socio-Económicos del Cantegril." Sao Paulo, Sociologia (24:2), June 1962, p. 107-115.

2536 González Penelas, W.
"El Problema del Rancherío." Montevideo, Boletín uruguayo de sociologia (1:2), 1959, p. 5-29.

2537 Olimar
"Un Cinturón de Miseria Circunda a Montevideo; el Pueblo Reconoce con Emoción el Esfuerzo del Gobierno por Mitigar Estos Males." Montevideo, Mundo libre, September-October 1946, p. 8, 10.

2538 "Veinte Años del 'Boletín del Instituto Psicopedagógico Nacional', 1942-1965." Lima, Boletín bibliográfico (33:3-4), July-December 1962, p. 87-109.

Venezuela

2539 Bracho Acuna, J.A.
"Estudio Sobre el Pauperismo en Maracaibo." Maracaibo, Revista de la Universidad de Zulia (2:2), January-April 1950, p. 75-91.

2540 Brisseau, J.
"Les 'Barrios' de Petare, Faubourgs Populaires d'une Banlieue de Caracas." Bordeaux, Cahiers d'outre-mer (16:61), January-March 1963, p. 5-42.

West Indies and the Caribbean

2541 Simpson, G.E.
"Begging in Kingston and Montego Bay." Mona, Social & economic studies (3:2), September 1954, p. 197-211.

TRANSPORTATION

Books

General

2542 Ad Hoc Committee for Sources of Information in Transportation
Sources of information in transportation. Compiled by Ruth F. Blaisdell, et al . . . Evanston . . . Northwestern University Press, 1964, 262p.

2543 Berry, Donald S., et al
The technology of urban transportation. Evanston, Transportation Center, Northwestern University, 1962, 145p.

2544 Bone, Alexander J., et al
Principals and techniques of predicting future demand for urban area transportation. Cambridge, M.I.T. Press, 1966, 91p.

2545 Buchanan, C.D.
Traffic in towns. Baltimore, Penguin Books, 1963, 263p.

2546 Danielson, M.N.
Federal-metropolitan politics and the commuter crisis. New York, Columbia University Press, 1965, 244p.

2547 Foster, C.D.
The transport problem. London, Blackie, 1963, 354p.

2548 Gwilliam, K.M.
Transport and public policy. London, Allen & Unwin, 1964, 255p.

2549 International Road Transport Union
Discours et résolutions du 10e Congrès, Londres,

5-9 Juin, 1966. Geneva, 1966, 103p.

2550 Lang, Albert S., & Richard M. Soberman
Urban rail transit; its economics and technology. Cambridge, M.I.T. Press, 1964, 139p.

2551 Martin, Brian V., et al
Principals and techniques of predicting future demand for urban area transportation. Cambridge, M.I.T. Press, 1965, 215p.

2552 Meyer, John R., et al
The urban transportation problem. Cambridge, Harvard University Press, 1965, 427p.

2553 Mumford, Lewis
The highway and the city; essays. New York, Harcourt, Brace & World, 1963, 246p.

2554 National Committee on Urban Transportation
Better transportation for your city. Chicago, Public Administration Service, 1958, 96p.

2555 Northwestern University. Transportation Center. Library
Current Literature in traffic and transportation. Evanston, January-February 1960-

2556 Northwestern University. Transportation Center. Library
A reference guide to metropolitan transportation. Evanston, 1964, 101p.

2557 Oi, Walter Y., & P. Shuldiner
Analysis of urban travel demands. Evanston, Transportation Center, Northwestern University, 1966, 141p.

2558 Owen, Wilfred
The metropolitan transportation problem. Rev. ed. Washington, Brookings Institution, 1966, 266p.

2559 Real Estate Research Corporation, Chicago
The influence of highway improvements on urban land use patterns. Prepared for the Bureau of

of Public Roads, U.S. Dept. of Commerce. Chicago, 1958, 69p.

2560 Smerk, G.M.
Urban transportation: the federal role. Bloomington, Indiana University Press, 1965, 336p.

2561 Soberman, Richard M.
Transport technology for developing regions. Cambridge, M.I.T. Press, 1966, 177p.

2562 Stewart, J.W.M.
A pricing system for roads. Edinburgh, Oliver & Boyd, 1965, 80p.

2563 Tetlow, J., & A. Goss
Homes, towns and traffic. London, Faber & Faber, 1965, 286p.

2564 U.S. Dept. of Health, Education & Welfare
Urban public transportation: selected references; HUD-MP-3. Washington, U.S. Government Printing Office, 1966, 17p.

2565 Wilson, G. L.
Transportation and communications. New York, Appleton-Century-Crofts, 1954, 757p.

2566 Wingo, Lowdon
Transportation and urban land. Washington, Resources for the Future, 1961, 132p.

Latin America

2567 Argentina. República. Empresa Nacional de Transportes. Servicio de Bibliotecas y Publicaciones de Transportes
Bibliografía ferroviaria. Buenos Aires, 1955, 131p.

2568 Pan American Union
Guide to institutions in the Washington, D.C.-New York area containing bibliographical references on transportation in Latin America. Washington, 1961, 107p.

2569 Pan American Union
Problemas generales del transporte en América Latina. (#OEA/ser. H/x.3. Doc. 18-A). Washington, 1963, 41p.

2570 Transportation research. v. 1- New York, Pergamon Press, 1967-

Argentina

2571 Humet, Enrique
Estudio de la red primaria, secundaria y total de caminos de la Provincia de Buenos Aires. La Plata, Dirección de Vialidad, 1958, 29p.

2572 López Airaghi, Antonio C.
Acceso a las ciudades; plan orgánico para Tucumán. Tucumán, Instituto de Vías de Comunicación, Universidad Nacional de Tucumán, 1951, 45p.

2573 Roigt, Honorio
Presente y futuro de los ferrocarriles argentinos. Buenos Aires, Hachette, 1956, 237p.

2574 Romero Villanueva, Horacio
Política nacional de transportes. Buenos Aires, Asociación de Economistas Argentinos, 1965, 22p.

Bolivia

2575 Upham, Charles M., Associates (firm)
Highway program review for Bolivia. Washington, 1962, 80p.

Brazil

2576 Azevedo, Murillo Nunes de
Transportes sem rumo; o problema dos transportes no Brasil. Rio de Janeiro, Ed. Civilização Brasileira, 1964, 141p.

2577 Brazil. Conselho do Desenvolvimento
Report on Brazilian railways. Rio de Janeiro, 1956, 98p.

2578 Bernardes, L.M. Cavalcanti
Circulação e rêde urbana no nordeste do Brasil.

(In International Geographical Union. Proceedings of the First Latin American Regional Conference. Mexico City, August 2-8, 1966. v. 2. 1966, Mexico, p. 505-514).

2579 Joint Brazil-United States Economic Development Commission
Projetos. 14v. Rio de Janeiro, 1953-54.

2580 Ottoni, Homero B.
Viação férrea brasileira; planejamento. São Paulo, 1948, 70p.

2581 Rio de Janeiro (State) Depto. Estadual do Estatística
Tábuas itinerárias do Estado do Rio de Janeiro. Rio de Janeiro, 1953-54.

2582 Wanderley, Alberto
Transportes no Brasil. Bêlo Horizonte, 1959, 132p.

2583 Wilhelm, Jorge
São Paulo: metropole 65. São Paulo, Difusão Européia do Livro, 1965, 170p.

Chile

2584 Chile. Inspección Superior de Ferrocarriles
Servicio nacional de transportes; estado actual y dificultades que afrontan nuestros transportes por tierra, agua y aire . . . Santiago, Impr. de los FF. CC. del E., 1947, 483p.

2585 Hurtado Ruiz-Tagle, Carlos, & Arturo Israel P.
Tres ensayos sobre el transporte en Chile. Santiago, Instituto de Economía, Universidad de Chile, 1964, 149p.

Colombia

2586 Ortega Díaz, Alfredo
Ferrocarriles colombianos. 4v. Bogota, Impr. Nacional, 1920-49.

2587 Parson, Brinckerhoff, Quede & Douglas (firm)
Plan for improvements in national transportation. New York, 1961, 25p.

2588 Restrepo Castro, Jorge
El transporte colectivo en el Distrito Especial de Bogotá. Bogotá, 1960, 63p.

2589 Rojas, P.J., & Hijos, Caracas (firm)
Ferrocarril de Maracaibo a Bogotá i túnel de La Guaira a Caracas; estudio. Caracas, Tip. Americana, 1949, 20p.

Ecuador

2590 Empresa de Ferrocarriles del Estado
Una etapa en la administración de los ferrocarriles, 1957-1960. Quito, 1960? 535p.

El Salvador

2591 Clarke, John H.T.
Inland transportation in El Salvador. New York, United Nations (Document ST/TAA/K/El Salvador/11), 1954, 88p.

Honduras

2592 Honduras. Consejo Nacional de Economía
Plan bienial de transportes. Tegucigalpa, 1960-

Mexico

2593 Escobedo, José G.
Tres años de realizaciones ferrocarrileras; síntesis gráfica. México, 1950, 160p.

2594 Gurria Lacroix, Jorge
Bibliografía mexicana de ferrocarriles. México, Ferrocarriles Nacionales, 1956, 499p.

2595 Higgins Industries, Inc., New Orleans
Estudio sobre México; economía, transportes, navegación. 2v. Mexico, 1949.

2596 Rejón Núñez, Manuel
El crecimiento de la ciudad de México y su relación con algunos problemas de la circulación. (In International Geographical Union. Proceedings of the First Latin American Regional Conference, Mexico City, August 2-8, 1966. v. 5. Mexico, 1966, p. 197-204).

2597 Salazar Viniegra, Guillermo
El problema del tránsito en el Distrito Federal. México, Banco de México, 1950, 74p.

Panama

2598 Rubio y Muñoz-Bocanegra, Angel
La evolución portuaria en Panamá . . . publicación #6. Panamá, Banco de Urbanización y Rehabilitación, 1946, 78p.

Paraguay

2599 Bejarano, Ramón C.
Vías y medios de comunicaciones de Paraguay. Asunción, Ed. Toledo, 1963, 262p.

Peru

2600 Drewes, Wolfram U.
The economic development of the western Montaña of central Peru as related to transportation . . . Lima, Peruvian Times 1958, 44p.

2601 Peru. Ministerio de Fomento
Registro oficial de fomento. Ferrocarriles, Caminos y Puentes. Lima, 1950-

Venezuela

2602 Bingham, Sidney H.
A study of traffic problems within the city of Caracas . . . New York, 1959, 194p.

2603 Delgado Dugarte, Carlos
El transporte colectivo. Caracas, Instituto Municipal de Transporte Colectivo del Distrito Federal Cuatricentenario de Caracas, 1964, 66p.

2604 Ibec Technical Services Corp.
Estudio de transporte y tráfico para la cuidad de Caracas, Venezuela. New York, 1948, 65p.

2605 Segundo Orta, Celio
El sistema de transporte interno y en el área metropolitana. Caracas, Eds. del Cuatricentenario de la Fundación de Caracas, 1966, 115p.

Periodical Articles

General

2606 Doxiadis, Constantinos A.
"Ekistics and Traffic." Traffic quarterly 17, July 1963, p. 439-457.

2607 Khanna, T.
"The Traffic Problem and City Government." New Delhi, Indian journal of public administration (5:3), July-September 1959, p. 333-341.

2608 Lieper, J. McC.
"Transportation Planning in a Mature Metropolis." Urban affairs quarterly (I:2), December 1965, p. 22-38.

2609 Modern cities via transportation. Pittsburgh, Eutter Pubs., (I:1), 1966-

Latin America

2610 "A Associação Latino-Americana de Livre Comercio e os Problemas de Transportes." Rio de Janeiro, Desenvolvimento e conjuntura (7:10), October 1963, p. 49-57.

2611 Alig, W. B.
"Hemisphere on Wheels." Américas 7, February 1955, p. 27-29.

2612 "Les Chemins de Fer en Amérique Latine." Paris, Revue générale des chemins de fer, December 1956, p. 613-618.

2613 Margariños de Melo, M.
"El Problema del Transporte en la ALALC y sus Vinculaciones con el Desarrollo Económico General de la Zona." México, Trimestre económico (29: 116), October-December 1962, p. 531-564.

2614 "Railroads: Progress in Mexico; the Other Latin American Countries." Américas, December 1954, p. 2.

2615 "Les Transports et les Communications au Guatemala et en Bolivie." Paris, Revue des transports et des communications (III:1), January-March 1950, p. 38-54.

Argentina

2616 "Un Aspecto Fundamental del Problema del Transporte." Buenos Aires, Veritas, June 15, 1946, p. 747-48.

2617 "Buenos Aires Transport Service." Buenos Aires, Review of the River Plate (131:3452), March 13, 1962, p. 375-377.

2618 "Buenos Aires City Transport Services." Buenos Aires, The review of the River Plate, September 8, 1944, p. 19, 21.

2619 Buenos Aires. Universidad. Instituto de Economía de los Transportes.
"La Empresa Nacional de Transportes." Buenos Aires, Revista de la Facultad de Ciencias Económicas (5:41-42), March/April 1952, p. 106-112.

2620 "A Central Railway Station for Buenos Aires." Buenos Aires, Review of the River Plate, January 25, 1946, p. 18-21.

2621 Delfino, Pedro
"Política y Economía de los Transportes." La Plata, ECA (Revista de la Escuela Superior de Ciencias Administrativas) (1:2), April/June 1959, p. 28-35.

2622 "Estadística de 50 Años de Tracción Eléctrica en la Ciudad de Buenos Aires." Buenos Aires, Boletín de la Asociación Permanente, January-February 1948, p. 107-110.

2623 Fugier, A.
"Buenos Ayres et ses Problèmes de Croissance." Bordeaux, Cahiers d'outre-mer (II:6), 1949, p. 97-111.

2624 "Gremios, Patronos y Gobierno." Buenos Aires, Review of the River Plate (132:3465), July 20, 1962,

p. 73-77.

2625 Johnson, Victor L.
"Edward A. Hopkins and the Development of Argentine Transportation and Communication." Hispanic American historical review, February 1946, p. 19-37.

2626 Lopez Abuin, A.
"Transporte y Urbanismo." Córdoba, Revista de la Universidad Nacional de Córdoba (4:3-4), July-October 1963, p. 661-693.

2627 Montagne, V.
"Vinculaciones Interprovinciales Catamarca-Tucumán." Buenos Aires, Revista geográfica americana, March 1946, p. 121-130.

2628 Moreiras Marque, Carlos
"La Coordinación de los Transportes en la Argentina." Córdoba, El ingeniero, June 1942, p. 73-90.

2629 Narizzano, Hugo
" Coordinación o Competencia Entre el Camino y el Ferrocarril?" Santiago, Economía y finanzas, July 1946, p. 5-14; August 1946, p. 21-26; September 1946, p. 23-26.

2630 "Plan Ferroviario Después de la Huelga; Railway Programme After the Strike." Buenos Aires, Review of the River Plate (13:3444), December 20, 1961, p. 9-15.

2631 Sánchez de Bustamante, T.
"Historia de la Ingeniería Argentina." Buenos Aires, Caminos (27:208), June 1960, p. 32-38.

2632 "The Social and Labor Aspects of the Long-Range Plan for Transport in Argentina." Geneva, International labour review 88, December 1963, p. 621-626.

2633 "Trains and Meat." Economist 201, November 18, 1961, p. 640.

2634 "El Transporte Urbano de Pasajeros en la Ciudad de Buenos Aires." Santigao, Revista municipalidades de la República, nos. 150-155, January/June 1943, p. 112-114.

2635 Veitch, Robert
"The Port of Buenos, Past and Present." Buenos Aires, The times of Argentina, April 1943, p. 23-25.

2636 Vercellana, Juan F.
"El Organismo Centralizador de los Transportes." Buenos Aires, La Información, May 1946, p. 6-8.

Bolivia

2637 Voimuller, J.
"Les Transports en Bolivie." Paris, Revue des transports et des communications des Nations Unies (VII:2) 1954, p. 17-32.

Brazil

2638 Baer, Werner, et al
"Transportation and Inflation: a Study of Irrational Policy Making in Brazil." Economic development & culture change 13, January 1965, p. 188-202.

2639 Bernard, John H.
"O Brasil e o seu Sistema de Transporte." Rio de Janeiro, Boletim geográfico (6:66), September 1948, p. 571-580

2640 "Best in Brazil: O Estado de Sao Paulo." Newsweek 63, February 3, 1964, p. 75.

2641 Brasil. Conselho Nacional de Economía
"Precariedade do Sistema de Transporte no Brasil." Rio de Janeiro, Revista do Conselho Nacional de Economía (7:4), July/August 1958, p. 232-239.

2642 "Brazilian Railways: Brief History." Rio de Janeiro, Conjuntura econômica internacional 4, October 1957, p. 39-45.

2643 Brown, L.
"Sursan Pushes Ahead Projects to Ease Rio's

Traffic, Sewage Problems." Rio de Janeiro, Brazilian business (40:12), December 1960, p. 30-34, 64-65.

2644 Desenvolvimento e Conjuntura (periodical)
"Estudo Especial: Um Método para Determinação dos Fluxos de Tráfego." Rio de Janeiro (6:6), June 1962, p. 85-101.

2645 Duncan, Julian S.
"The Improvement of Railroad Transport in Brazil." Inter-American economic affairs, Winter 1954, p. 83-95.

2646 Ebacher, L.
"Bread, Butter and Jam." Américas 10, February 1958, p. 34.

2647 Ebling, F.
"Metropolitano do Rio de Janeiro." Rio de Janeiro, Engenharia, mineração e metalurgia (XVI:94), November-December 1951, p. 277-280.

2648 "Faixa Rio-Santos: Area Econômica Vital." Rio de Janeiro, Conjuntura econômica 11, 1963, p. 79-84.

2649 "Green is for Go in São Paulo." Rotarian 78, January 1950, p. 42-43.

2650 Lima, Heitor Ferreira
"Ferrovias no Brasil." São Paulo, Revista brasiliense 37, September-October 1961, p. 47-61.

2651 Freitas, Gibson Cortines de
"Os Sistemas de Transportes do Brasil." Rio de Janeiro, Revista do IRB (Instituto de Reseguros do Brasil) (11:62), June 1950, p. 65-75; (11:62), August 1950, p. 123-137; (11:63), October 1950, p. 106-130.

2652 Marcal, Joseph N.
"Problemas de Transporte no Brasil." Rio de Janeiro, Revista do serviço público (67:1), ano XVII, April 1955, p. 56-62.

2653 Meira, Lucio
"Transporte e Indústria: Problema Atual de Brasil." Rio de Janeiro, O observador econômico e financiero (19:220), June 1954, p. 34-48.

2654 Meira, Lucio
"Visão Geral do Problema dos Transportes no Brasil." Rio de Janeiro, O observador econômico e financeiro (22:261), November 1957, p. 32-39.

2655 Moreira, A. L.
"Considerações Sôbre a Ligação Rio-Niterói." Rio de Janeiro, Revista do serviço público (94:4), October-December 1962, p. 62-94.

2656 Paim, E.
"Panorama de Infra-Estrutura." Rio de Janeiro, O observador econômico e financeiro (27:311), June-July 1962, p. 21-24.

2657 "O Problema dos Transportes no Rio de Janeiro." Rio de Janeiro, Revista do comércio, August 1946, p. 9-20.

2658 Reis, José de Oliveira
"Engenharía de Tráfego e as Municipalidades; Caso do Rio de Janeiro." Rio de Janeiro, Revista de administração municipal (9:54), September-October 1962, p. 355-366.

2659 Sodrê, Nelson Werneck
"O Problema Ferroviário." Rio de Janeiro, Boletim geográfico (21:172), January-February 1963, p. 39-43.

2660 Spinelli, Paulo A.
"Os Transportes no Estado da Guanabara." Rio de Janeiro, Brazilian-American survey (8:13), 1960, p. 78-85.

2661 Tischendorf, A.
"Recife and São Francisco Pernambuco Railway Company." Inter-American economic affairs 13, Spring 1960, p. 87-94.

2662 "Transportation (1949-1958) and Utilities in São Paulo." Rio de Janeiro, Conjuntura econômica internacional 6, March 1959, p. 57-63.

2663 Vieira, F. "Linhas Integrantes do Sistema Ferroviário Brasileiro." Rio de Janeiro, Boletim geográfico (8: 86), May 1950, p. 133-150.

Central America

2664 Roper, George S. "TACA Makes History over Central America." Inter-American quarterly 3, January 1941, p. 36-51.

Chile

2665 Gazitúa Navarrete, Víctor "Consideraciónes Generales Sobre Política de Transportes." Santiago, Anales de la Facultad de Ciencias Jurídicas y Sociales (13:52/59), 1948, 1949, p. 5-12.

2666 Hardy, O. "El Ferrocarril Sud-Pacífico." Pacific historical review 20, August 1951, p. 261-269.

2667 "La Crisis en el Sistema de Transportes de Chile." Santiago, Panorama económico (6:61), August 29, 1952, p. 509-522.

2668 Marizzano, F. "Situación de la Empresa de los Ferrocarriles." Santiago, Economía y finanzas (17:199), May 1953, p. 21-24.

2669 Navarro, O., & R. Escobar "Caminos de Acceso a Santiago de Chile." Santiago, Revista de caminos, 4th quarter 1955, p. 196-199.

2670 Orozco Tobón, F. "Los Ferrocarriles y las Carreterras de Chile." Medellín, Dyna (16:61), May 1948, p. 43-48.

2671 "La Red Caminera de la Provincia de Concepción." Santiago, Revista de caminos, 1st quarter 1955, p. 46-48.

2672 Wagemann W., Günter
"Chile y el Problema del Transporte y Comunicaciones." Santiago, Economía y finanzas (15:172), February 1951, p. 9-12.

Colombia

2673 Bailey, J.H.
"Colombia's Transportation Plans." Ottawa, Foreign trade, Canada 117, January 13, 1962, p. 12-14.

2674 Barnhart, Donald S.
"Colombian Transport and the Reforms of 1931: an Evaluation." The Hispanic American historical review (38:1), February 1958, p. 1-24.

2675 Camacho Gamba, Guillermo
"Coordinación de Transportes." Medellín, Estudios de derecho (12:35), August 1950, p. 261-297.

2676 Ospina B., Sebastián
"Problemas Viales de Colombia." Bogotá, Anales de ingeniería (57:627), 3rd quarter 1950, p. 225-255.

2677 Restrepo Castro, Jorge
"El Transporte Colectivo en el 'Distrito Especial de Bogotá.'" Bogotá, Universitas 19, December 1960, p. 65-119.

2678 Rincón, Ovidio
"Necesidad de una Reforma: Nacionalización del Transporte." Bogotá, Economía colombiana (7: 18), October 1955, p. 103-109.

2679 Salazar Montoya, Jaime
"El Transporte en Colombia." Bogotá, Economía colombiana (17:50), June 1958, p. 525-530.

Costa Rica

2680 Adeane, R.
"Costa Rica Railway Company, Ltd.; Statement by Chairman." London, Economist 215, April 10, 1965, p. 246.

Cuba

2681 Gómez Riopelle, María A.
"Los Transportes, su Presente y su Futuro en Cuba." Havana, Contabilidad y finanzas (12:2), August 1955, p. 59-67.

Ecuador

2682 Meyer, S.
"Streetcar Named Autoferro Ecuatoriano; a Ride from Quito to Guayaquil." Saturday review 46, October 12, 1963, p. 94.

2683 Murgueytio D., J.A.
"Ecuador: El Ferrocarril Quito-San Lorenzo." Buenos Aires, Boletín de la Asociación Permanente (36:127), March-April 1952, p. 67-72.

El Salvador

2684 Escoto, Ricardo
"Hacia la Municipalización del Servicio de Transportes Urbanos de San Salvador." San Salvador, Economía salvadoreña (1:1), 1952, p. 55-59.

Honduras

2685 "Le Honduras et ses Transportes." Paris, Vie du rail, June 24, 1962, p. 15-27.

Jamaica

2686 Maunder, W. F.
"Notes on the Development of Internal Transportation in Jamaica." Mona, Social & economic studies 3, University College of the West Indies, September 1954, p. 161-185.

Mexico

2687 Asociación Regional de Caminos de Puebla
"El Tránsito en Puebla." México, Más caminos (2:22), August 1951, p. 48-50.

2688 Cruz, O.R.
"La Importancia Relativa del Sistema Ferroviario." México, Revista de economía (23:3), March 1960, p. 95-99.

2689 Fuentes Delgado, Rubén
"Los Transportes Urbanos Nacionales." México, Revista de economía (15:4), April 1952, p. 130-132.

2690 Gajdusek, D.C.
"Sierra Tarahumara: Transportation into the Sierra." Geographical review 43, January 1953, p. 21-27.

2691 Gómez Sicre, José
"A Través del Lente." Américas, June 1950, p. 24-28, 44.

2692 Idosaga, René
"La Organización del Tránsito en la Ciudad de México." México, Todo, February 27, 1947, p. 38-39, 58.

2693 López de la Parra, M.
"Significado y Desarrollo Actual de los Caminos Vecinales y en General de las Vías de Comunicaciones del País." México, Investigación económica (18:72), 4th quarter, 1958, p. 675-698.

2694 Medina Urbizu, E.
"Aspectos de los Transportes Nacionales." México, Investigación económica (22:85), 1st quarter, 1962, p. 81-113.

2695 Moyo Porras, Edmundo
"Transportes." México, Revista de economía (17:12), December 15, 1954, p. 326-334; (18:5), May/June 1955, p. 131-153.

2696 Muñoz Pérez, J.
"Los Ferrocarriles Mexicanos." Madrid, Estudios geográficos 82, 1961, p. 122-126.

2697 Pletcher, David M.
"General William S. Rosecrans and the Mexican Transcontinental Railroad Project." Mississippi Valley historical review 38, March 1952, p. 657-678.

2698 Quint, B.
"Railroad Through the Wilderness: Chihuahua-Pacific Railroad; History and Importance of this Railroad That Took 90 Years to Build." México, Mexican-American review 29, December 1961, p. 14-17.

2699 "Streetcar Named Tortoise." Time 63, April 5, 1954, p. 43.

2700 Tamayo López Portillo, J.
"Coordinación de los Transportes Nacionales." México, Revista de economía (12:2), February 15, 1949, p. 59-67.

2701 Tamayo López Portillo, J.
"La Función Económica de los Transportes." México, Revista de economía (33:7), July 1960, p. 192-200.

2702 Torre, E. de la
"El Ferrocarril de Tacubaya." Historia mexicana (9:35), January-March 1960, p. 377-393.

2703 Torre, E. de la
"La Capital y sus Primeros Medios de Transporte: Prehistoria de los Tranvías." México, Historia mexicana (9:2), October-December 1959, p. 215-248.

2704 Widdison, J.G.
"Mexico's Trans-Sierran Railroad." Geographic review 51, July 1961, p. 429-431.

Panama

2705 Porras, Demetrio A.
"Sociología del Desarrollo del Istmo de Panamá." Quito, Ensayos 4, August 1963, p. 61-71.

Peru

2706 Fawcett, B.
Switchbacks to the Sky." Trains, January 1955, p. 48-57.

2707 Heredia, F.D.
"Vilcabamba-Apurimac." Cuzco, Revista del Museo e Instituto Arqueológico (9:15), September 1953, p. 95-118.

Uruguay

2708 Maggi, A.
República Oriental del Uruguay: Los Ferrocarriles en la Economía Nacional." Buenos Aires, Boletín de la Asociación Permanente (36:127), March-April 1952, p. 86-95.

2709 Snyder, David E.
"Commercial Passenger Linkages and the Metropolitan Nodality of Montevideo." Economic geography 38, April 1962, p. 95-112.

Venezuela

2710 Boccalandro, A.
"El Metro de Caracas." Caracas, Revista del Colegio de Ingenieros de Venezuela 286, January-March 1960, p. 3-12.

2711 "Los Transportes Terrestres en Venezuela." Caracas, Cuadernos de información económica (2:2), February-March 1950, p. 32-59.

2712 Viteri-Huerta, L.
"Venezuela Shapes a Railway System: Plans for a National Railway Network Move Forward." Ottawa, Foreign trade, Canada 112, December 5, 1959, p. 16-18.

URBAN EMPLOYMENT
(including Labor Unions)

Books

General

2713 Florence, P. S.
Economics and sociology of industry. London, Watts, 1964, 258p.

2714 Hammond, J. L., & B. Hammond
The town laborer, 1760-1832: the new civilization. London, Longmans, 1966, 329p.

2715 Segal, M.
Wages in the metropolis. Cambridge, Harvard University Press, 1960, 211p.

Latin America

2716 Alba, Víctor. (pseud.)
Historia del movimiento obrero en América Latina. México, Libreros Mexicanos Unidos, 1964, 598p.

2717 Alvarez Pereira, C.
La evolución del sindicalismo; estudio comparativo de la organización sindical en América. Bogotá, 1962, 106p.

2718 Bernate deKanter, María D.
Summary of the Report on the economic status of working women in the American republics presented by the Inter-American Commission of Women (Chapter III, topic 27 of the agenda). Washington, Pan American Union, 1962, 61p.

2719 Bonilla, Frank
The urban worker (In Johnson, John J., ed. Continuity and change in Latin America. Stanford, Stanford University Press, 1964, p. 186-205.)

2720 Bourricaud, François, & A. Simão
El sindicalismo en Latinoamérica: los casos de Perú y Brasil. Barcelona, Ed. Nova Terra, 1965, 59p.

2721 Debuyst, Frédéric
La población en América Latina: demografía y evolución de empleo. Brussels, Center of Socio-Religious Research, 1961, 188p.

2722 Doherty, William C.
Christians and workers' movements in Latin America (CICOP working paper C-9-65). Davenport, Latin America Bureau, National Catholic Welfare Conference, 1965, 21p.

2723 Galenson, Walter, comp.
La clase obrera y el desarrollo económico. México, Ed. Limusa-Wiley, 1964, 405p.

2724 Galvin, M.E.
Unionism in Latin America. Ithaca, New York State School of Industrial & Labor Relations, Cornell University, 1962, 58p.

2725 Inter-American Regional Organization of Workers of the ICFTU
On the tenth anniversary of ORIT . . . Mexico City, ORIT Press & Publications Dept., 1961, 65p.

2726 International Labour Office
The role of labour ministries in the improvement of labour-management relations in Latin America. Geneva, 1964, 43p.

2727 Jones, Gavin W.
The problem of unemployment and underemployment in Latin America and its relations to demographic trends (Meeting on population policies in relation to development in Latin America); UP/Ser.H/V/REPO/I/7. Washington, Pan American Union, 1966, 22p.

2728 Quintero, Rodolfo
Elementos para una sociología del trabajo. Caracas, Eds. de la Biblioteca, Universidad Central de Venezuela, 1963, 271p.

2729 U.S. Dept. of Labor. Bureau of Labor Statistics
Labor developments abroad. Washington, 1956-

Argentina

2730 Argentine Republic. Ministerio de Trabajo y Seguridad Social. Dirección General de Estudios e Investigaciones
Conflictos del trabajo. Buenos Aires, 1961, 108p.

2731 Belaunde, C.H.
Los convenios colectivos de trabajo en la Argentina. Buenos Aires, Selección Contable, 1958, 135p.

2732 Cerrutti Costa, Luis B.
El sindicalismo; las masas y el poder, con una historia del movimiento obrero argentino. Buenos Aires, Trafac, 1957, 203p.

2733 Cochran, Thomas C., & Rubén E. Reina
Entrepreneurship in Argentine culture. Philadelphia, University of Pennsylvania Press, 1963, 338p.

2734 Dimase, L., et al
La situación gremial en la Argentina. Buenos Aires, Eds. Libera, 1964, 63p.

2735 Di Tella, Torcuato S.
El sistema político argentino y la clase obrera. Buenos Aires, Instituto Torcuato di Tella, 1964, 92p.

2736 Imaz, José L. de
Los que mandan. Buenos Aires, EUDEBA, 1964, 250p.

2737 Instituto Torcuato di Tella. Centro de Investigaciones Económicas
Los recursos humanos de nivel universitario y técnico en la República Argentina. 2d ed. 2v. Buenos Aires, 1965.

2738 Iscaro, R.
Orígen y desarrollo del movimiento sindical argentino. Buenos Aires, Ed. Anteo, 1958, 287p.

2739 Marotta, S.
El movimiento sindical argentino; su génesis y su desarrollo. Buenos Aires, Eds. Lacio, 1960, 313p.

Bolivia

2740 Ericson, A. S.
Labor law and practice in Bolivia. Washington, Bureau of Labor Statistics, U. S. Dept. of Commerce, 1962, 38p.

2741 Patiño Mines & Enterprises Consolidated, Inc.
Los conflictos sociales en 1947: I. Documentos. II. Notas finales por José E. Rivera. La Paz, 1948, 416p.

Brazil

2742 Brazil. Laws, statutes, etc.
Consolidação das leis do trabalho e legislação complementar. 14th ed. Sao Paulo, Ed. Atlas, 1966, 460p.

2743 Brazil. Serviço de Estatística da Previdencia e Trabalho
Inquérito do salário mínimo. 4v. Rio de Janeiro, 1949-50.

2744 Cardoso, Fernando H.
Empresário industrial e desenvolvimento econômico no Brasil. São Paulo, Difusão Européia do Livro, 1964, 196p.

2745 Cormier, Gerald H., & Louise E. Butt
Labor in Brazil. Washington, Bureau of Labor Statistics, U. S. Dept. of Labor, 1962, 35p.

2746 Governmental Affairs Institute
Brazilian labor: a management survey. Washington, 1960, 59p.

2747 Rio de Janeiro. Centro Brasileiro de Pesquisas Educacionais
Mobilidade e trabalho: um estudo na cidade de São Paulo. . . por Bertram Hutchinson, et al. Rio de Janeiro, 1960, 451p.

2748 Rodrigues, Leôncio Martins
Conflicto industrial e sindicalismo no Brasil. São Paulo, Difusão Européia do Livro, 1966, 224p.

Central America

2749 Ducoff, Louis J.
Human resources of Central America, Panama and Mexico, 1950-1980, in relation to some aspects of economic development. New York, United Nations Economic Commission for Latin America, 1960, 155p.

Chile

2750 Barría Serón, Jorge I.
Los movimientos sociales de Chile desde 1910 hasta 1926; aspecto político y social. Santiago, Ed. Universitaria, 1960, 440p.

2751 Chile. Universidad
Ocupación y desocupación: Gran Santiago. Santiago, Instituto de Economía, Universidad de Chile, 1965, 35p.

2752 Chile. Universidad, Valparaíso. Escuela de Economía. Centro de Investigaciones
Ocupación y desocupación en Valparaíso. Valparaíso, 1961, 12p.

2753 Humeros Magnan, Héctor
La huelga. 1st ed. Santiago, Ed. Jurídica de Chile, 1957, 267p.

2754 Kaempffer Villagrán, Guillermo
Así sucedió, 1850-1925; sangrientos episodios de la lucha obrera en Chile. Santiago, 1962, 265p.

2755 Lauterbach, Albert
Management attitudes in Chile. Santiago, Instituto de Economía, Universidad de Chile, 1961, 196p.

2756 Morris, J.O., et al
Afiliación y finanzas sindicales en Chile, 1932-1959. Santiago, Facultad de Ciencias Económicas, Universidad de Chile, 1962, 100p.

2757 Silva Pena y Lillo, Hugo
El paro forzoso. Chile, 1952, 57p.

2758 Vivanco Guerra, Graciela
Bosquejo del problema social en Chile. Santiago, 1951, 169p.

Colombia

2759 Braun, Kurt
Labor in Colombia. Washington, Bureau of Labor Statistics, U.S. Dept. of Labor, 1962, 54p.

2760 Camacho Pardo, Armando
Las huelgas de trabajadores. Bogotá, Ed. Diana, 1962, 95p.

2761 Colombia. Laws, statutes, etc.
El trabajo de la mujer; disposiciones legales. Bogotá, Impr. Nacional, 1953, 51p.

2762 Colombia. Ministerio de Trabajo
Memoria, 1946/47- Bogotá, Impr. Nacional. Annual.

2763 Daza Pérez, Antonio
La huelga. Bogotá, Ed. Granadina, 1956, 150p.

2764 Suárez Fajardo, Alfonso
Estudio del mercadeo de las principales frutas cítricas en la ciudad de Bogotá. Bogotá, Centro de Estudios sobre Desarrollo Económico, Universidad de los Andes, 1961, 54 plus 13p.

2765 Torres Restrepo, Camilo
La proletarización de Bogotá; ensayo de metodología estadística. Bogotá, Facultad de Sociología, Universidad Nacional de Colombia, 1961, 30p.

Costa Rica

2766 Friedman, J. A.
Labor law and practice in Costa Rica. Washington,

Bureau of Labor Statistics, U.S. Dept. of Commerce, 1962, 43p.

Cuba

2767 Clavijo Aguilera, F.
Los sindicatos en Cuba. Havana, Ed. Lex, 1954, 128p.

2768 Cuban Economic Research Project
Labor conditions in Communist Cuba. Coral Gables, University of Miami Press, 1963, 158p.

2769 Prado Pérez, L.
Clasificación ocupacional de Cuba. Havana, Tribunal de Cuentas, 1955, 103p.

Dominican Republic

2770 Gomez Cerda, J.
El sindicalismo cristiano. Santiago, Dominican Republic, 1966, 112p.

Ecuador

2771 Brackett, J.A.
Labor law and practice in Ecuador. Washington, G.P.O., 1963, 41p.

2772 Pérez Patino, Carlos
El derecho de huelga. Quito, Ed. Casa de la Cultura Ecuatoriana, 1958, 235p.

Guatemala

2773 Friedman, J.A.
Labor law and practice in Guatemala. Washington, Bureau of Labor Statistics, U.S. Dept. of Commerce, 1963, 32p.

Honduras

2774 Honduras. Secretaría de Trabajo, Asistencia Social y Clase Media
Memoria. Tegucigalpa, Cía. Ed. Nacional, 1954-55- . Annual.

Jamaica

2775 Jamaica. Ministry of Labour
Report. Kingston, Government Printer, 1953- . Annual.

2776 Jamaica. Ministry of Labour & National Insurance
Guide to industrial relations in Jamaica. Kingston, 1966, 59p.

2777 Maunder, W. F.
Employment in an underdeveloped area; a sample survey of Kingston, Jamaica. New Haven, Yale University Press, 1960, 215p.

Mexico

2778 Basurto, Jorge
La influencia de la economía y del estado en las huelgas; el caso de México. México, Escuela Nacional de Ciencias Políticas y Sociales, U.N.A.M., 1962, 146p.

2779 Galenson, Walter
La clase obrera y el desarrollo económico. Tr. into Spanish by Eduardo Escalona. 1st ed. México, Ed. Limusa-Wiley, 1964, 405p.

2780 Gasio Campuzano, Alfonso
La abolición del derecho de huelga en las empresas de servicios públicos. México, 1963, 97p.

2781 Guzmán Rodríguez, R. G.
El éxodo de los trabajadores mexicanos y su relación con la reforma agraria. México, 1963, 138p.

2782 Jaffe, Abram J.
People, jobs and economic development; a case history of Puerto Rico, supplemented by recent Mexican experience. Glencoe, Free Press, 1959, 381p.

2783 López Aparicio, A.
El movimiento obrero en México; antecedentes, desarrollo y tendencias. México, Ed. Jus, 1958, 280p.

2784 Melchor Pérez, Jesús
Inexistencia de la huelga que sobreviene por desaparición de la mayoría de trabajadores; posibilidad de un segundo recuento. México, 1957, 109p.

2785 Moore, Wilbert E.
Industrialization and labor; social aspects of economic development. Ithaca . . . Cornell University Press, 1951, 410p.

2786 Neef, Arthur F.
Labor in Mexico. Washington, U.S. Bureau of Labor Statistics, 1963, 108p.

2787 Neef, Arthur F.
Labor law and practice in Mexico. Washington, G.P.O., 1963, 70p.

2788 Ortega Ramos, Virginia
Protección a la mujer en el derecho del trabajo. México, 1955, 121p.

2789 Quiroz Cuarón, Alfonso
Psicología del funcionario bancario. México, Banco de México, 1954, 27 plus 7p.

2790 Solano, Tomás
Estudio sobre los conflictos de orden económico. México, 1956, 130p.

2791 Trueba Urbina, Alberto
Evolución de la huelga. México, Eds. Botas, 1950, 342p.

Panama

2792 Servicio Cooperativo Inter-Americano de Educación. Panamá
An industrial occupational survey, a study of the needs of industry for skilled and semi-skilled workers with proposals for the development of the vocational education program in the city of Panama. Panama, 1949, 120p.

2793 Servicio Cooperativo Inter-Americano de Educación. Panamá
Investigación sobre las ocupaciones industriales de la República (i.e., Ciudad) de Panamá, estudio que consulta la necesidad que tienen las industrias panameñas, de trabajadores especializados y semi-especializados . . . Panamá, 1953, 192p.

Peru

2794 Briones, Guillermo, & José Mejía Valera
El obrero industrial: aspectos sociales del desarrollo económico en el Perú. Lima, Instituto de Investigaciones Sociológicas, Universidad Nacional Mayor de San Marcos, 1964, 109p.

2795 Chaplin, David
The Peruvian industrial labor force. Princeton, Princeton University Press, 1967, 277p.

2796 Conferencia Obrera Regional del Sur. 1st, Arequipa, Peru, 1947
Conclusiones y resoluciones. Arequipa, Eds. Sindicales Amauta, 1947, 23p.

2797 León de Izaguirre, Virginia
Legislación del trabajo; la mujer trabajadora; apuntes de su curso sobre legislación de trabajo dictado en la Escuela Sindical Autónoma de Lima en el ciclo acelerado de educación sindical para mujeres. Lima, 1960, 33p.

2798 Lima. Universidad Nacional Mayor de San Marcos. Facultad de Ciencias Económicas y Comerciales. Instituto de Investigaciones Económicas
Ocupación y desocupación en Gran Lima . . . Lima, 1966, 84p.

2799 Peru. Laws, statutes, etc.
Legislación del empleado: leyes, reglamentos, decretos, resoluciones. Lima, 1964, 513p.

2800 Romero, Fernando
La industria peruana y sus obreros . . . Lima, Impr. de Politécnico Nacional "José Prado," 1958, 74p.

Venezuela

2801 Ericson, A. S.
Labor law and practice in Venezuela. Washington, Bureau of Labor Statistics, U. S. Dept. of Commerce, 1962, 39p.

West Indies and the Caribbean

2802 Grenada, West Indies. Labour Dept. Report. St. George's, Government Printer. Annual.

2803 Harewood, J. Employment in Trinidad and Tobago in 1960. Mona, Institute of Social & Economic Research, University of the West Indies, 1964, 81p.

2804 Knowles, W.H. Trade union development and industrial relations in the British West Indies. Berkeley, University of California Press, 1959, 214p.

2805 Trinidad and Tobago. Central Statistical Office Labour force by sex, age, industry, occupation, type of worker. Port-of-Spain, 1966, 23p.

Periodical Articles

General

2806 Karpik, L. "Urbanisation et Satisfaction au Travail." Paris, Sociologie du travail (8:2), April-June 1966, p. 179-204.

2807 "Rural-Urban Employment Relationship." International labour review 74, December 1956, p. 568-575.

Latin America

2808 Alba, Víctor (pseud.) "Un Sindicalismo Latino-Americano para la Era Atómica." México, Cuadernos americanos (16:1), January-February 1957, p. 42-58.

2809 Anderson, M. "What the Americas Are Doing for the Woman Worker." Pan American Union bulletin 69, July 1935, p. 521-535.

2810 "Aspects of Industrial Relations in Latin America." Industrial & labor relations review 17, April 1964, p. 357-425.

2811 Bianchi, E., ed.
"Latin American Labor Union: Interviews." Catholic world 191, July 1960, p. 225-231.

2812 Borges, M. A.
"Labor Relations in Latin America." Ohio State law journal (17:3), Summer 1956, p. 290-301.

2813 Briones, Guillermo
"La Calificación y Adaptación de la Fuerza de Trabajo en las Primeras Etapas de la Industrialización." Rio de Janeiro, América latina (6:4), October-December 1963, p. 13-25.

2814 Cannon, M. M.
"La Mujer que Trabaja y la Legislación Social." Noticias de la Oficina de Información Obrera y Social, April 1946, p. 3-5.

2815 Cannon, M. M.
Women Workers in Argentina, Chile and Uruguay." Pan American Union bulletin 76, March 1942, p. 148-154.

2816 Cannon, M. M.
"Women's Organizations in Ecuador, Paraguay and Peru." Pan American Union bulletin 77, November 1943, p. 601-607.

2817 Cárdenas Ojeda, M., & C. Valiente Vallejo
"Las Relaciones Laborales, la Opinión Dentro de la Fábrica y la Calificación de Méritos de los Trabajadores." México, Estudios sociológicos 1955, p. 155-168.

2818 "Changes in Employment Structure in Latin America, 1945-55." New York, Economic bulletin for Latin America 2, February 1957, p. 15-42.

2819 "Emploi des Femmes en Amérique Latine." Geneva, Revue internationale du travail (73:2), February 1956, p. 196-214.

2820 Fischlowitz, Estanislao
"Manpower Problems and Prospects in Latin America." Monthly labor review 83, September 1960, p. 909-916.

2821 Fischlowitz, Estanislao
"Las Migraciones Internas." México, Panoramas 5, September-October 1963, p. 53-63.

2822 Fox, J.S.
"Administración del Trabajo en América Latina." Buenos Aires, Revista textil, January 1957, p. 9-23.

2823 Guillén, C.
"How Labor is Learning," ed. by K. Walker. Américas 9, May 1957, p. 3-6.

2824 International Labour Office
"Technical Conference on Manpower in Latin America." Geneva, Industry and labour, March 1-15, 1953, p. 150-156.

2825 International Labour Office
"Women's Employment in Latin America." Geneva, International labour review (73:2), February 1956, p. 177-193.

2826 Inter-American Conference of Ministers of Labor of the Alliance for Progress. 2nd, Caraballeda, Venezuela, 1966
"Formulación de una Política Laboral para el Desarrollo Nacional." Revista Interamericana de ciencias sociales (4:1), 1966, p. 51-62.

2827 Kalijarvi, T.V.
"U.S. Business and Labor in Latin America." Vital speeches 28, July 15, 1962, p. 595-601.

2828 Lambert, Denis
"L'Urbanisation Accélérée de l'Amérique Latine et la Formation d'un Secteur Tertiaire Refuse." Brussels, Civilisations (XV:3), 1965, p. 309-325.

2829 Lauterbach, Albert
"Executive Training and Productivity: Managerial Views in Latin America." Industrial & labor relations review (17:3), April 1964, p. 357-379.

2830 Owen, E.D.
Sources of Information on Social and Labor Problems in Latin America." Inter-American bibliographical review (1:2), 1941, p. 91-97.

2831 Pagés, Pedro
"Un Problema Social: Libre Circulación de Trabajadores." La Paz, Nova 4, November 1962, p. 4.

2832 Pérez Salinas, P.B., & V.G. Reuther
"Two Labor Leaders Speak: Role of Unions." Américas 13, October 1961, p. 27-36.

2833 Rottenberg, Simon
"Problems in a Latin American Factory Society." Monthly labor review 77, July 1954, p. 756-760.

2834 Rubio, J.L.
"Notas Sobre las Centrales Sindicales Iberoamericanas." Madrid, Revista de política internacional (56-57), July-October 1961, p. 161-184.

2835 Sturmthal, A., & D. Felix
"U.S. Firms as Employers in Latin America: Excerpt from United States Business and Labor in Latin America." Monthly labor review 83, May 1960, p. 479-485.

2836 "Youth and Work in Latin America." Geneva, International labour review 90, July-August 1964, p. 1-23, 150-179.

2837 Zañartu, Mario
"Le Syndicalisme Chrétien en Amérique Latine." Paris, Revue d'action populaire 125, February 1959, p. 193-209.

Argentina

2838 Di Pietro, E.G.
"La Baja del Esfuerzo Laboral en la Industria Argentina." Rosario, Estudios (2:3), September-October 1952, p. 112-134.

2839 Dorrego, R.
"Perspectivas de Regularización de la C.G.T."

Buenos Aires, Estudios 531, January-February 1962, p. 16-18.

2840 Knox, J.
"Absenteeism and Turnover in an Argentine Factory." American sociological review (26:3), June 1961, p. 424-428.

2841 "Labor Relations in Latin America--III: Argentina's Unions Sizzle with Politics." Business Latin America, February 16, 1967, p. 50-54.

Bolivia

2842 Bolivia. Laws, statutes, etc.
"Employment of Women in the Bolivian Mining Industry." Montreal, International labor review, June 1944, p. 678.

2843 "Ocupaciones Industriales y Mano de Obra." La Paz, Industria (3:25), October 1954, p. 35-39.

Brazil

2844 Bueno, L. de Freitas
"Padrão de Vida do Operário Industrial de Porto Alegre." Pôrto Alegre, Revista da Facultad das Ciências Econômicas (5:5), December 1958, p. 7-42.

2845 Cardoso, Fernando H.
"Le Prolétariat Brésilien: Situation et Comportement Social." Paris, Sociologie du travail (3:4), October-December 1961, p. 50-65.

2846 Castaldi, C.
"Mobilidade Ocupacional de um Grupo Primário de Imigrantes Italianos na Cidade de São Paulo." Rio de Janeiro, Educação e ciências sociais (2:4), March 1957, p. 135-172.

2847 Conjuntura Econômica (periodical)
"Wage Structure in the State of Guanabara." Rio de Janeiro (13:3), March 1966, p. 37-42.

2848 Debes, C.S.
"A Remuneração do Trabalhador Menor." São

Paulo, IDORT (31:365-366), May-June 1962, p. 21, 27, 38.

2849 Diegues, Manoel
"Urban Employment in Brasil." Geneva, International labour review (93:6), June 1966, p. 643-657.

2850 Gusmao, W. de
"Indústria, Mão-de-Obra e Ensino Industrial." Rio de Janeiro, O observador econômico e financiero (21:246), August 1956, p. 48-54.

2851 Hillman, J.S.
"Economic Development and the Brazilian Northeast; What is Economic Development?" Inter-American economic affairs 10, Summer 1956, p. 84-86.

2852 Hutchinson, Bertram
"The Migrant Population of Urban Brasil." Rio de Janeiro, América latina (6:2), April-June 1963, p. 41-71.

2853 Jochmann, J.
"Tamanho das Cidades e Padrao de Vida do Operário Industrial." Rio de Janeiro, Revista brasileira dos municipios (7:27), July-September 1954, p. 125-132.

2854 Johnston, H.T.
"Ladies Can so Count Cruzeiros." Rio de Janeiro, Brazilian business (43:12), December 1963, p. 34-37.

2855 Jordao, A.
"Barreiras no Contrôle da Mobilidade Occupacional e Espacial do Imigrante Espanhol." São Paulo, Sociologia (24:2), June 1962, p. 117-119.

2856 Kahl, Joseph A., ed.
"Mobilidade e Trabalho: um Estudo na Cidade de São Paulo, by B. Hutchinson." American journal of sociology 66, November 1960, p. 303-305.

2857 Lenhard, R.
"Atividades Econômicas na Cidade de São José do Rio Prêto." São Paulo, Sociologia (26:2), June 1964, p. 171-182.

2858 Lopes, J.R. Brandão
"A Fixação do Operário de Origem Rural na Industria." Rio de Janeiro, Educação e ciências sociais (2:6), November 1957, p. 293-322.

2859 Martins Rodrigues, L.
"Sindicalismo y Desarrollo en el Brasil." Buenos Aires, Revista latinoamericana de sociología (II:1), March 1966, p. 27-42.

2860 Moraes, Eneida de
"A Regulamentação das Relações de Trabalho no Brasil." Rio de Janeiro, Revista brasileira de ciências sociais (3:2), July 1963, p. 3-30.

2861 Novaes, Menandro
"Migrações Internas." Rio de Janeiro, Estudos sociais (4:16), March 1963, p. 341-362.

2862 Pereira, L.
"Mulher e Trabalho." Rio de Janeiro, Educação e ciências sociais (8:15), September 1960, p. 143-158.

2863 "A População Ativa Feminina e o Recenseamento." Rio de Janeiro, Conjuntura econômica, September 1953, p. 64-70.

2864 Resi, H. Corrêa dos
"Fatos do Movimento Operário no Brasil." São Paulo, Revista brasiliense 35, May-June 1961, p. 70-78.

2865 Rodrigues, J.A.R.
"Condições Econômico-Sociais da Mão de Obra em São Paulo." São Paulo, Anhembi (35:103), June 1959, p. 44-63.

2866 Rodrigues, Leôncio Martins
"Sindicalismo y Desarrollo en el Brasil." Buenos

Aires, Revista latinoamericana de sociología (2:1), March 1966, p. 27-42.

2867 Saito, H.
"Mobilidade de Ocupação e de Status de un Grupo de Imigrantes." São Paulo, Sociologia (22:3), September 1960, p. 241-253.

2868 Touraine, A.
"Industrialisation et Conscience Ouvrière à São Paulo." Paris, Sociologie du travail (III:4), October-December 1961, p. 77-95.

2869 "U.S. Launches Road Show in Rio: Sponsorship of Worker-to-Worker Program." Business week, February 12, 1966, p. 98-100.

2870 "Wages Structure in São Paulo." Rio de Janeiro, Conjuntura econômica internacional (XII: # 10), October 1966, p. 31-38.

2871 "Wage Trends in the Industries of Rio de Janeiro." Rio de Janeiro, Conjuntura econômica internacional (XIII: # 10), October 1966, p. 39-43.

Chile

2872 Barrera Romero, M.
"Acerca de los Sindicatos Industriales Chilenos." Santiago, Economía 21, 3rd quarter, 1963, p. 57-80.

2873 Casanova, H.V.
"Estratificación Social de la Población Trabajadora en Chile y su Participación en el Ingreso Nacional, 1940-1954." Santiago, Economía (18:62), 1st quarter, 1959, p. 75-78.

2874 Garmendia, I.I.
"Estudio Comparativo del Trabajo de la Mujer en la Fábrica en el Año 1939." Santiago, Servicio social, January-March 1940, p. 1-58.

2875 Landsberger, Henry A., et al
"The Chilean Union Leader: a Preliminary Report on his Background and Attitudes." Industrial &

labor relations review (17:3), April 1964, p. 399-420.

2876 Poblete Troncoso, Moisés
"El Movimiento Sindical Chileno." San José, Combate 23, July-August 1962, p. 25-34.

2877 Robinson, C.
"Concepción, Chile: South American Microcosm." Yale review (42:4), June 1953, p. 580-589.

Colombia

2878 Camacho Pardo, Armando
"Las Investigaciones Estadísticas en el Servicio Nacional de Aprendizaje 'SENA'." Bogotá, Revista javeriana (54:266), July 1960, p. 415-420.

2879 "Casabe." Bogotá, Economía grancolombiana (5:14), 1961, p. 240-247.

2880 Duque de Carbonell, M., & I. Monsalve Cuellar
"La Capacidad de la Mujer Casada Mayor de Edad para Ejecer el Comercio." Bogotá, Universitas 26, June 1964, p. 100-104.

2881 Lozano Henao, J.
"Empleo y Salarios en el Valle del Cauca." Bogotá, Economía grancolombiana (2:5), 1960, p. 213-220.

2882 Rincón, Ovidio
"El Trabajo Femenino en Colombia." Bogotá, Economía colombiana (3:8), December 1954, p. 299-307.

2883 Sánchez, A.M.
"Mujeres que Trabajan." Bogotá, Economía colombiana (12:35), March 1957, p. 443-454.

Cuba

2884 Leitz, P.S.
"Cuba: Sugar and Social Justice." America 90, January 16, 1954, p. 391.

2885 Masó, C.
"El Movimiento Obrero Cubano." México, Pano-

ramas (2:9), May-June 1964, p. 69-94.

2886 O'Connor, J.
"The Labour Force, Employment and Unemployment in Cuba, 1957-61." Kingston, Social and economic studies (15:2), June 1966, p. 85-91.

2887 Woodward, Robert L.
"Urban Labor and Communism: Cuba." Río Piedras, Caribbean studies (3:3), October 1963, p. 17-50.

El Salvador

2888 Guillén, C.
"Labor Learns the Way." Américas 5, November 1953, p. 30-31.

2889 Velásquez, J.H.
"El Trabajo y el Ocio en la Población Estudiantil Universitaria de El Salvador." México, Estudios sociológicos 12, 1961, p. 273-295.

Guatemala

2890 Graham, D.
"Liberated Guatemala." Nation 183, July 14, 1956, p. 34-37.

2891 Woodward, Robert L.
"Octubre: Communist Appeal to the Urban Labor Force of Guatemala, 1950-1953." Journal of Inter-American studies 4, July 1962, p. 75-82.

Haiti

2892 Antoine, M.A.
"La Situation Syndicale en Haiti." Port-au-Prince, Revue du travail (10:10), May 1961, p. 3-6.

2893 Plummer, Y.
"Le Travail des Enfants." Port-au-Prince, Revue du travail 11, May 1962, p. 83-93.

2894 Poitevien, L.
"Enquête sur les Salaires, l'Emploi, le Placement et la Qualification Professionelle à Port-au-Prince." Port-au-Prince, Revue du travail (9:9), May 1960, p. 101-160.

Honduras

2895 Valerio, A. de
"La Situación de la Mujer Obrera en Honduras." Tegucigalpa, The Pan-América (7:86), July 1951, p. 10-11.

Jamaica

2896 Phelps, O. W.
"Rise of the Labour Movement in Jamaica." Mona, Social & economic studies (9:4), December 1960, p. 417-468.

Mexico

2897 Castoreña y Bringas, J. L.
"Trabajo y Técnica." México, Revista mexicana de trabajo (5:7-8), July-August 1958, p. 7-42.

2898 Castorena Zavala, J. J.
"La Huelga y el Contrato de Trabajo." México, Boletín del Instituto de Derecho Comparado de México (6:18), September-December 1953, p. 49-61.

2899 Castoreña Zavala, J. J.
"La Integración Social del Trabajador." México, Revista mexicana del Trabaho (10:7-8), July-August 1963, p. 35-58.

2900 Castro de la Lama, C.
"El Mercado de Mano de Obra en México." San Salvador, Revista del trabajo (6:21), April-June 1955, p. 103-115.

2901 Cavazos Flores, B.
"La Capacitación Obrera y el Futuro Industrial de México." México, Revista ITAT 8, 1959, p. 102-105.

2902 Cepeda Villareal, R.
"El Contrato Colectivo de Trabajo en Italia y en México." México, Revista de la Facultad de Derecho de México (12:46), April-June 1962, p. 237-256.

2903 Colorado, B.
"El Salario Familiar." México, Estudios socio-

lógicos, 1956, p. 235-236.

2904 Gómez R., G.
"Atribuciones y Funcionamiento del Depto. de Protección al Trabajo de Mujeres y Menores." México, Revista mexicana de trabajo 1, January-March 1965, p. 31-34.

2905 Guerrero del Castillo, E.
"El Mercado de Trabajo y el Servicio Social." México, Ciencias políticas y sociales (7:23), January-March 1961, p. 91-110.

2906 Kahl, Joseph A.
"Tres Tipos de Trabajadores Industriales Mexicanos." México, Ciencias políticas y sociales (5:16), April-June 1959, p. 193-201.

2907 López Malo, E.
"El Problema de los Trabajadores Mexicanos." México, Universidad de México (8:6), February 1954, p. 1-2, 17-18.

2908 Merino, M. del C.
"Lineamientos Sociológicos del Trabajo en México." México, Revista del ITAT 9, 1959, p. 79-114.

2909 Moreno Contreras, C.
"Consideraciones Generales Sobre la Mano de Obra Feminina en México." México, Revista del ITAT 8, 1959, p. 106-121.

2910 O'Connor, A. D.
"Informe Sobre los Estudios Verificados en la Ciudad de México, D. F., en Relación a la Oficina Investigadora Sobre la Situación de la Mujer y de los Menores Trabajadores." San Salvador, Revista de trabajo (3:11), October-December 1952, p. 43-90.

2911 Randall, L.
"La Migración Laboral y el Desarrollo Económico de México." México, Comercio exterior (13:6), June 1963, p. 409-413.

2912 Rivera Marín, G.
"Los Conflictos de Trabajo en México, 1937-1950." México, Trimestre económico (20:2), April-June 1955, p. 181-208.

2913 Rivera Marín, G.
"La Mano de Obra, el Nivel de Vida y los Salarios en la Ciudad de Oaxaca." México, Trimestre económico (24:4), October-December 1957, p. 363-398.

2914 Rojas P. Palacios, A.
"El Salario de la Madre." México, Puericultura (6:3), May-June 1955, p. 85-87.

2915 Salazar, Rubén
"El Movimiento Sindical de México." San José, Combate 13, November 1960, p. 27-31.

2916 Tello, Manuel
"La Evolución Social de México Durante el Presente Siglo." México, Revista internacional y diplomática 52, February 28, 1955, p. 50-52.

Panama

2917 Pereira Burgos, C. A.
"Socialismo y Sindicalismo en Panamá." Caracas, Política 13, January 1961, p. 64-74.

Peru

2918 Bourricaud, François
"Syndicalisme et Politique: le Cas Péruvien." Paris, Sociologie du travail (3:4), October-December 1961, p. 33-49.

2919 Briones, Guillermo
"Movilidad Ocupacional y Mercado de Trabajo en el Perú." Rio de Janeiro, América latina (6:3), July-September 1963, p. 63-76.

2920 Hague, J. L.
"El Salario de la Mujer en el Perú." Lima, Voz rotaria, August 16, 1941, p. 115-128.

2921 Llosa Larrabure, J.
"'Cooperación Popular', a New Approach to Community Development in Peru." Geneva, International labour review (94:3), September 1966, p. 221-236.

Uruguay

2922 Alfonso, P.H.
"El Problema de la Unidad Sindical." Montevideo, Cuadernos latinoamericanos de economía humana (3:8), 1960, p. 143-159.

2923 Wood, J.R., & E.A. Weinstein
"Industrialization, Values and Occupational Evaluation in Uruguay." American journal of sociology (72:1), July 1966, p. 47-57.

Venezuela

2924 Almoina de Carrera, P.
"Apuntes Sobre Formas Tradicionales Populares de Trabajo de la Mujer Venezolena." Caracas, Archivos venezolanos de folklore (10-11:7), 1961-62, p. 269-275.

2925 Creole Petroleum Corporation
"La Industria y el Hombre." Caracas, El farol (21:188), May-June 1960, p. 32-43.

2926 Lander M., C.
"El Progreso del Trabajador Venezolano." Caracas, El farol (25:209), April-June 1964, p. 12-16.

2927 Quintero, Rodolfo
"Las Bases Económicas y Sociales de una Aristocracia Obrera en Venezuela." Caracas, Economía y ciencias sociales (5:2), April-June 1963, p. 90-100.

West Indies and the Caribbean

2928 Ahiram, E.
"Distribution of Income in Trinidad-Tobago and Comparison with Distribution of Income in Jamaica." Mona, Social & economic studies (15:2), June 1966, p. 103-120.

2929 Cumper, G.E.
"Labour and Development in the West Indies: the Worker and his Social Background." Mona, Social & economic studies (10:3), September 1961, p. 278-305.

2930 Harewood, J.
"Overpopulation and Underemployment in the West Indies." International labor review (82:2), 1960, p. 103-137.

2931 Knowles, W.H.
"Trade Unionism in the British West Indies." Monthly labor review (79:12), December 1956, p. 1394-1400.

Part III

GOVERNMENT - LAW

MUNICIPAL FINANCE

Books

General

2932 Conference on Urban Public Expenditures. 2d, New York, 1964
The public economy of urban communities; papers . . . Ed. by Julius Margolis. Washington, Resources for the Future; distributed by Johns Hopkins Press, Baltimore, 1965, 264p.

2933 Drummond, J.M.
Finance of local government. Mystic, Conn., Lawrence Verry, 1966, 277p.

2934 Hardacre, W.S., & N.D.B. Sage
Local authority capital finance. London, C. Knight, 1965, 411p.

2935 Heikoff, Joseph M.
Planning and budgeting in municipal management. Chicago, International City Managers' Association, 1965, 39p.

2936 Hillhouse, Albert M., & S.K. Howard
Revenue estimating by cities. Chicago, Municipal Finance Officers' Association of the United States and Canada, 1965, 16p.

2937 Hirsch, Werner Z.
State and local program budgeting; report # MR-66. Los Angeles, Institute of Government & Public Affairs, University of California, 1966, 28p.

2938 Lichfield, N.
Cost-benefit analysis in urban redevelopment. Berkeley, University of California Press, 1962, 52p.

2939 Lindman, Eric L.
State school support and municipal government costs, a local tax allocation correction factor for use in apportioning state school funds; report #MR-27. Los Angeles, Institute of Government & Public Affairs, University of California, 1964, 24p.

2940 Mace, Ruth (Lowens), comp.
Costing urban development and redevelopment . . . Chapel Hill, 1964, 21p.

2941 Mao, J. C. T.
Efficiency in public urban renewal expenditures through capital budgeting. Berkeley, Institute of Urban & Regional development, University of California, 1965, 118p.

2942 Moody's municipal and government manual, American and foreign. New York, Moody, 1964-

2943 Schaller, H. G., ed.
Public expenditure decisions in the urban community. Washington, Resources for the Future, 1964, 198p.

2944 Ulmer, Melville J.
Capital in transportation, communications, and public utilities. Princeton, Princeton University Press, 1960, 548p.

2945 Urban Land Institute
Open space land, planning and taxation: a selected bibliography. Washington, Superintendent of Documents, G. P. O., 1965, 58p.

2946 Young, Harold H.
Forty years of public utility finance. Ed by L. R. Johnston. Charlottesville, University of Virginia Press, 1965, 205p.

Latin America

2947 Inter-American Development Bank
Reunión sobre financiamiento municipal en Latinoamérica, Washington, D. C., 23-26 de enero de 1966. 3v. Washington, 1966.

2948 Conference on Fiscal Policy, Santiago de Chile, 1962
Fiscal policy for economic growth in Latin America; papers and proceedings . . . Baltimore, Published for the Joint Tax Program by Johns Hopkins Press, 1962, 462p.

2949 Hardoy, Jorge E.
Bases de un programa de asistencia técnica y financiera para el desarrollo urbano; extracto del trabajo preparado para la Reunión sobre Financiamiento Municipal en Latinoamérica, enero de 1966. (In Fundación para el Desarrollo de la Comunidad y Fomento Municipal. Biblioteca. Boletín bibliográfico de divulgación municipal 11.) Caracas, January-March 1966, p. 3-7).

Brazil

2950 Brasil. Conselho do Desenvolvimento
Financiamento dos serviços municipais de abastecimento de agua. Rio de Janeiro, 1957, 116p.

2951 Leite, Antonio de Oliveira
Impostos na Guanabara; estudo econômico-financeiro dos impostos estaduais e municipais. Rio de Janeiro, Eds. Financeiras, 1961, 257p.

2952 Olivetti, Benedicto
Municipalismo caótico. Sao Paulo, Atena Ed., 1955, 131p.

Central America

2953 United Nations. Economic Commission for Latin America. Committee of Economic Cooperation of the Central America Isthmus
La política tributaria y el desarrollo económico en Centroamérica . . . Washington, Dept. of Economic & Social Affairs, United Nations, 1956, 141p.

2954 Workshop on Budgetary Classification and Management on Central America and Panama, San José, Costa Rica, 1963
Report; document ST/TAO/ser. C/6; E/CN.12/692; E/CN.12/CCE/312. New York, United Nations, 1964, 83p.

Chile

2955 Chile. Laws, statutes, etc.
Ley de rentas municipales; concordancias, jurisprudencia, ordenanzas, reglamentos. Santiago, Ed. Ordili, 1953, 550p.

2956 Varas Guzmán, Eugenio
Estudio jurídico-administrativo sobre economía y finanzas municipales. Santiago, Impr. Relámpago, 1944, 110p.

Colombia

2957 Álvarez Cardona, Javier
Finanzas públicas departamentales y municipales comparadas en Colombia, 1957. Bogotá, Universidad de los Andes, Centro de Estudios sobre Desarrollo Económico, 1960, 52p.

2958 Casas Morales, Carlos
Régimen tributario de los pequeños municipios colombianos. Bogotá, 1952, 111p.

2959 García, Antonio
Planificación municipal y presupuesto de inversiones; esquema de una reforma municipal en Colombia. Bogotá, Impr. Municipal, 1949, 280p.

2960 Harvard University. Law School. International Program in Taxation
Taxation in Colombia. New York, Commerce Clearing House, 1964, 586p.

2961 Joint Tax Program of the Organization of American States & the Inter-American Development Bank. Fiscal Mission to Colombia
Fiscal survey of Colombia; a report . . . Baltimore . . . Johns Hopkins Press, 1965, 276p.

2962 Martner, Gonzalo
El desarrollo de las finanzas públicas de Colombia, 1950-1960. Bogotá, 196- , 116p.

Cuba

2963 Cuba. Laws, statutes, etc.
Ley de contabilidad municipal. Havana, Tribunal de Cuentas, 1954, 44p.

Ecuador

2964 Riofrío Villagómez, Eduardo
Teoría presupuestaria municipal y aplicación en el mundo hispánico . . . Quito, Impr. Municipal, 1958, 364p.

Guatemala

2965 Adler, John H., et al
Las finanzas públicas y el desarrollo económico de Guatemala . . . Tr. by Carlos A. d'Ascoli. México, Fondo de Cultura Económica, 1952, 338p.

2966 Instituto de Fomento Municipal
Memoria de las labores desarrolladas por el Instituto de Fomento Municipal . . . 1 de julio de 1964 al 30 de junio de 1965. Guatemala, 1965, 42p.

Haiti

2967 Lamy, Amilcar F.
Affaires communales; tableau des attributions de l'édilité suivi du tarif communal et d'un répertoire de législation. Manuel préparé à l'intention des préfectures et des communes d'Haiti . . . Port-au-Prince, 1950, 150p.

Honduras

2968 Tosco, Manuel, & M. Napley
Ingresos del gobierno local, 1924-25/ 1951-52. Tegucigalpa, Banco Central de Honduras, 1953, 70p.

Mexico

2969 Guizar Zamora, Rafael
La hacienda municipal. México, 195- , 111p.

2970 Tamaulipas, Mexico. Laws, statutes, etc.
Ley general de arbitrios de los municipios del Estado de Tamaulipas. Ciudad Victoria, Talleres Linotipográficos del Gobierno, 1956, unpaged.

2971 Moore, O.E.
Evolución de las instituciones financieras en Mexico. México, Centro de Estudios Monetarios Latinoamericanos, 1963, 413p.

2972 Oldman, Oliver
Financial urban development in Mexico City. Cambridge, Harvard University Press, 1967, 217p.

2973 Orantes Durazo, Teodoro
Crédito municipal. México, 1947, 55p.

Panama

2974 Joint Tax Program of the Organization of American States & the Inter-American Development Bank. Fiscal Mission to Panama
Fiscal survey of Panama: problems and proposals for reform. Ed. by M. Ballesteros. Baltimore, Johns Hopkins Press, 1964, 212p.

Venezuela

2975 Comisión Encargada de Estudiar el Sistema Fiscal del Distrito Federal
El sistema fiscal de Caracas; informe. Caracas, Talleres Gráf. "Mersifrica," 1962, 254p.

2976 Shoup, Carl S., et al
The fiscal system of Venezuela; a report. Baltimore, Johns Hopkins Press, 1959, 491p.

Periodical Articles

General

2977 Hirsch, Werner Z.
"Administrative and Fiscal Considerations in Urban Development." Annals of the American Academy of Political & Social Science, March 1964, p. 48-61.

2978 Massotti, L.H., & D.R. Bowen
"Communities and Budgets: the Sociology of Municipal Expenditures." Urban affairs quarterly (I:2), December 1965, p. 39-58.

Argentina

2979 "The Province of Buenos Aires." London, South American journal, August 2, 1930, p. 105-106.

Brazil

2980 Azevedo, E. de Andrade
"Empréstimo e Financiamentos aos Municípios." Rio de Janeiro, Revista brasileira dos municípios (16:63-64), July-December 1963, p. 209-210.

2981 "Balanços Municipais de 1960." Rio de Janeiro, Revista de finanças públicas (22:222), April-June 1962, p. 48-52.

2982 Botelho, C. de Paula
"Aspecto Financeiro dos Municípios Brasileiros." Rio de Janeiro, Revista brasileira dos municípios (13:49-52), January-December 1960, p. 63-65.

2983 Bueno, C.
"Bancos Municipais". Rio de Janeiro, Revista brasileira dos municípios (13:49-52), January-December 1960, p. 27-42.

2984 Burkinski, Francisco
"Distribuição das Rendas Fiscais e Aproveitamento dos Recursos Locais." Rio de Janeiro, Revista brasileira dos municípios (14:55-56), July-December 1961, p. 134-137.

2985 Donald, C. L.
"The Politics of Local Government Finance in Brazil." Inter-American economic affairs (13:1), Summer 1959, p. 21-37.

2986 Dumont, C.
"A Fiscalização da Administração Financeira do Município: a Experiência Mineira." Bêlo Horizonte, Revista brasileira de estudos políticos 9, July 1960, p. 252-291.

2987 "The Finances of the Municipality of San Paulo." London, South American journal, July 26, 1930, p. 81-82.

2988 Froomkin, J.
"Fiscal Management of Municipalities and Economic Development." Economic development & culture change 3, July 1955, p. 309-320.

2989 Gatto, H.
"Escrituraçao da Receita e da Despresa Pública." Rio de Janeiro, Revista de administraçao municipal (11:62), January-March 1964, p. 24-32.

2990 Improta, M.
"O Drama Econômico-Financeiro do Município de São Paulo." Rio de Janeiro, Revista da administraçao municipal (9:51), March-April 1962, p. 107-121.

2991 Improta, M.
"Receitas Municipais e Inflaçao." Rio de Janeiro, Revista brasileira dos municípios (17:65-66), January-June 1964, p. 66-75.

2992 Improta, M., & W. Christianini
"Discriminação das Receitas Públicas." Rio de Janeiro, Revista de finanças públicas (22:223), July-September 1962, p. 17-30.

2993 Instituto Brasileiro de Administraçao Municipal
"Estrutura do Orçamento de Capital para os Municípios." Rio de Janeiro, Revista da administraçao municipal (8:46), May-June 1961, p. 229-244.

2994 Machado, A. Ramos
"Creditos Adicionais." Rio de Janeiro, Revista de administraçao municipal (12:70), May-June 1965, p. 182-188.

2995 Machado, J. Teixeira
"Encerramento das Contas do Exercicio com Base na Lei 4. 320/64." Rio de Janeiro, Revista de administraçao municipal (12:69), March-April 1965, p. 101-107.

2996 Mello, D. Lordello de
"O Problema das Finanças Municipais no Brasil." Rio de Janeiro, Revista da Administraçao municipal (8:48), September-October 1961, p. 412-414.

2997 Mendanha, D. da Carvalho
"A Fiscalizaçao dos municípios pelos Tribunais de

Contas Estaduais." Bêlo Horizonte, Revista brasileira de estudos políticos 13, January 1962, p. 249-274.

2998 "Orçamentos Municipais para 1961." Rio de Janeiro, Revista de finanças públicas (22:221), January-March 1962, p. 36-41.

2999 Pierrot, A. Ogdes
"Municipal Budget for 1931." Rio de Janeiro, Brazilian business, January 1931, p. 15-16 & 31.

3000 Silva, D.
"As Receitas Municipais e os 30% do Excesso da Arrecadaçao Estadual." Rio de Janeiro, O observador (13:156), January 1949, p. 29-32.

3001 Soares, G.A. Dillon, & A.M. Carvalho
"Urbanizaçao e Dispersao Eleitoral." Rio de Janeiro, Revista de direito público e ciencia política (3:2), July-December 1960, p. 258-270.

Chile

3002 Alfaro Olivares, A.
"Presupuestos Municipales de 1936." Santiago, Boletín municipal de la República, March 1936, p. 6-14.

3003 Chile. Departamento de Municipalidades
"Instrucciones para la Confección, Aprobación y Manejo de los Presupuestos Municipales." Santiago, Revista de las municipalidades, April-June 1940, p. 35-54.

3004 Chile. Departamento de Municipalidades
"Presupuestos Municipales de 1940." Santiago, Revista de las municipalidades, July-September 1940, p. 18-32.

Colombia

3005 Bogotá (Colombia) Laws, statutes, etc.
"Acuerdo . . . Sobre Presupuestos de Rentas y Gastos Comunes . . . 1935." Bogotá, Registro municipal, December 31, 1934, p. 329-363.

3006 "Contrato Sobre Emisión y Servicio de un Empréstito en Bonos de las Empresas Municipales de Bogotá." Bogotá, Registro municipal, June 30, 1937, p. 333-344.

3007 García Rojas, B.
"Los Presupuestos Departamentales y Municipales." Bogotá, Economía grancolombiana (1:1), August 1959, p. 169-175; (1:2), September 1959, p. 279-288.

3008 Mira Restrepo, J.
"La Situación Fiscal de los Municipios." Bogotá, Economía (1:2), 1964, p. 216-221.

Guatemala

3009 Guatemala. Dirección General de Estadística
"Memoria de Labores de la Dirección General de Estadística Durante el Año 1956." Guatemala, Boletín mensual de la Dirección General de Estadística 1, January 1937, p. 1-6.

Mexico

3010 Alisky, Marvin
"Mexico's Special Districts: Municipal Civic Betterment Boards."
Public affairs bulletin (IV:2), Arizona State University, 1965, p. 1-4.

3011 Bird, Richard M.
"The Economy of the Mexican Federal District." Inter-American economic affairs (17:2), Autumn 1963, p. 19-51.

3012 "As Rendas Federais do México em 1941." Portuguese bulletin 44, Pan American Union, November 1942, p. 559-562.

MUNICIPAL GOVERNMENT AND LEGAL MATTERS

Books

General

3013 Altshuler, Alan A.
The city planning process: a political analysis. Ithaca, Cornell University Press, 1965, 217p.

3014 Baker, Benjamin
Urban government. Princeton, Van Nostrand, 1957, 572p.

3015 Baulina, Angel V.
El gobierno municipal . . . Córdoba, Ed. Assandri, 1941, 387p.

3016 Booth, David A., comp.
Council-manager government, 1940-64, an annotated bibliography. Chicago, International City Managers' Association, 1965, 38p.

3017 Berkman, Herman G.
Our urban plant; essays in urban affairs. Madison, University of Wisconsin Extension, 1964, 66p.

3018 Bollens, John C., & Henry J. Schmandt
The metropolis: its people, politics and economic life. New York, Harper & Row, 1965, 643p.

3019 Cannon, Mark W.
Impacto de la administración municipal en el desarrollo económico del país. Caracas, Fundación para el Desarrollo de la Comunidad y Fomento Municipal, 1965, 14p.

3020 Current municipal problems. Mundelein, v.-1- , Callaghan, 1959- .

3021 Duhl, Leonard J., & John Powell, eds.
The urban condition; people and policy in the metropolis. New York, Basic Books, 1963, 410p.

3022 East, John P.
Council-manager government; the political thought of its founder, Richard S. Childs. Chapel Hill, University of North Carolina Press, 1965, 183p.

3023 Gobierno Municipal de la Capital del Estado Libre Asociado de Puerto Rico
Boletín municipal. San Juan (año 9, #12), December 1966- .

3024 Government Affairs Foundation, Inc.
Metropolitan communities: a bibliography with special emphasis on government and politics: 1955-57. Chicago, Public Administration Service, 1960, 229p.

3025 Guzmán Botero, Carlos A., & Alberto Jimenez B.
Organización municipal. Bogotá, Impr. Departamental "Antonio Nariño," 1964, 511p.

3026 Halasz, D.
Metropolis; a selected bibliography on administrative and other problems of metropolitan areas throughout the world. The Hague, Nijhoff, 1961, 45p.

3027 Hamlin, Herbert M.
Citizen participation in local policy making for public education. 2d ed. Urbana, College of Education, University of Illinois, 1960, 35p.

3028 International City Managers' Association
Municipal year book. Chicago, 1934- . Annual.

3029 International City Managers Association
Post-entry training in the local public service. Chicago, 1963, 82p.

3030 International Union of Local Authorities
Local government in the 20th century. The Hague, Nijhoff, 1963, 491p.

3031 Journal of urban law. #1-, Detroit, University of Detroit, 1966- .

3032 Kaplan, H.
Urban renewal politics. New York, Columbia University Press, 1964, 219p.

3033 Kneier, Charles M.
City government in the United States. 3rd ed. New York, Harper, 1957, 611p.

3034 Landis, James M.
The administrative process. New Haven, Yale University Press, 1966, 339p.

3035 Local government throughout the world. The Hague, International Union of Local Authorities, 1961- .

3036 Lordello de Mello, Diogo
Curso de administraçao municipal (programa e justificaçao). Rio de Janeiro, Escola Brasileira de Administraçao Pública, Fundaçao Getulio Vargas, 1955, 56p.

3037 Los Angeles. Public Library. Municipal Reference Library
Government of metropolitan areas: a bibliography. Los Angeles, 1947, variously paged.

3038 Martin, Roscoe C.
The cities and the federal system. New York, Atherton Press, 1965, 200p.

3039 Nigro, F. A.
Modern public administration. New York, Harper & Row, 1965, 531p.

3040 Revers, H. J. D.
International Union of Local Authorities, 1913-1963: the story of fifty years of international municipal cooperation. The Hague, Nijhoff, 1964, 86p.

3041 Robson, William A., ed.
Great cities of the world; their government, politics and planning. New York, Macmillan, 1955, 693p.

3042 Sharpe, L.J.
Research in local government. London, London School of Economics and Political Science, 1965, 19p.

3043 Tennessee. University. Municipal Technical Advisory Service
Selective bibliography on municipal government from the files of the library of the Service. Knoxville, 1963, 40p.

3044 U.S. Advisory Committee on Intergovernmental Relations
Metropolitan social and economic disparities; implications for intergovernmental relations in central cities and suburbs. Washington, G.P.O., 1965, 253p.

3045 Urban problems and prospects. Robinson O. Everett & Richard H. Leach, special editors for this symposium. Durham, School of Law, Duke University, 1965, 229p.

3046 Valdivia, Manuel A.
Autonomía municipal. León, 1948, 28p.

3047 Wall, Ned L.
Municipal reporting to the public. Chicago, International City Managers Association, 1963, 71p.

3048 Warren, Robert O.
Government in metropolitan regions. Davis, Institute of Governmental Affairs, University of California, Davis, 1966, 77p.

3049 Wilhelm, S.M.
Urban zoning and land-use theory. New York, Collier-Macmillan, 1963, 243p.

Latin America

3050 Albi, Fernando
Derecho municipal comparado del mundo hispánico . . . Madrid, Aguilar, 1955, 678p.

3051 Angulo y Pérez, Andrés
La democracia en los concejos municipales; raíces de la democracia en América. Tesis presentada al VI Congreso Histórico Municipal Interamericano, Madrid, España, octubre 5-12 de 1957. Havana, Ed. Selecta, 1957, 23p.

3052 Arratia Vidal, Alejandro
Control jurídico de los actos municipales; estudio histórico-positivo. Santiago, Ed. Universitaria, 1959, 314p.

3053 Bayle, Constantino
Cabildos de indios en la América Española. Madrid, Ed. Jura, 1951, 35p.

3054 Bueno, Antonio S. C.
Angulos práticos do municipalismo. 2d ed. Rio de Janeiro, IBGE, Conselho Nacional de Estatística, 1957, 86p.

3055 Calcaprina, Cino, & Enrique Tedeschi
Urbanismo con legislación; el problema legislativo de la planificación urbana y rural. Tucumán, Instituto de Arquitectura y Urbanismo, Universidad Nacional de Tucumán, 1950, 94p.

3056 XI Interamerican Congress of Municipalities and V University Seminar. November 13-19, 1966. Final act. Caracas, 1966, 117p.

3057 Gabaldón Márquez, Joaquín
El municipio, raíz de la república; ponencia. Caracas, Instituto Panamericano de Geografía e Historia, 1961, 136p.

3058 Galvão de Sousa, José P.
Política e teoría do estado. São Paulo, Ed. Saraiva, 1957, 263p.

3059 Garza Lewels, Joaquín
Gobierno de la ciudad. México, 1953, 89p.

3060 Montes, René
Temas para una legislación sobre urbanismo. Guatemala, 1951, 45p.

3061 Mouchet, Carlos
Municipal government. (In Davis, Harold E., ed. Government and politics in Latin America. New York, Ronald Press, 1954, p. 368-392).

3062 Onsari, Fabián
Gobierno municipal. Buenos Aires, Ed. Claridad, 1941, 227p.

3063 Paraná, Brazil (State) Laws, statutes, etc.
Lei orgânica dos municípios (Lei no. 64, de 21 de fevereiro de 1948). Curitiba, Impr. Oficial do Estado, 1953, 32p.

3064 Revista municipal interamericana. Inter-American municipal review. Havana, 1950- .

3065 Ribeiro, Manoel
O município na federação. Salvador, Universidad da Bahia, 1959, 104p.

3066 Rodríguez O., José
Ciudad y zonificación. Guatemala, 1950, 39p.

3067 The Second Caribbean Seminar on Municipal Administration, November 14 to 19, 1965
Proceedings. Maracaibo, Fundación para la Comunidad y Desarrollo Municipal, 1966, 124p.

Argentina

3068 Argentina Republic. Congreso. Biblioteca
Derecho municipal. Buenos Aires, Biblioteca del Congreso de la Nación, Sección Referencia Legislativa, 1951, 29p.

3069 Berardo, Rodolfo
El actual régimen argentino. Córdoba, Dirección de Publicadad de la Universidad Nacional de Córdoba, 1952, 15p.

3070 Buenos Aires. Municipalidad.
Boletín municipal. 1950-

3071 Caldúmbide, Alberto G.
Administración municipal. La Plata, 1942, 310p.

3072 Canal Feijóo, Bernardo
Teoría de la ciudad argentina. Buenos Aires, Ed. Sudamericana, 1951, 265p.

3073 Gómez Forgues, Máximo I.
La municipalidad de Buenos Aires y la reforma constitucional de 1949. Buenos Aires, Librería y Casa Ed. de E. Perrot, 1952, 91p.

3074 Mazzocco, Angel R.
Las descentralizaciones en la municipalidad de la Capital Federal y las reparticiones autárquicas de la Nación; estudio legal, económico, y financiero de su regimen . . . Buenos Aires, Ed. Alfa, 1957, 148p.

3075 Mouchet, Carlos
Pasado y restauración del régimen municipal. Buenos Aires, Ed. Perrot, 1957, 74p.

3076 Rositto, Diego B.
Córdoba, artería de la democracia argentina. Chivilcoy, Eds. Populares Reparación, 1958, 231p.

3077 Selecciones municipales. Buenos Aires, Instituto Argentino de Estudios Municipales (I:2), August 1965- .

3078 Millares Carlo, Agustín
Los archivos municipales de Latinoamérica; libros de actas y colecciones decomentales; apuntes bibliográficos. Maracaibo, 1961, 220p.

3079 Onsari, Fabían
Gobierno municipal. Buenos Aires, Ed. Claridad, 1941, 288p.

3080 Vigo, Salvador C.
El régimen municipal de la constitución y las leyes orgánicas municipales. Santa Fé, Impr. de la Universidad Nacional del Litoral, 1944, 35p.

3081 Zalduendo, Eduardo
Geográfia electoral de la Argentina. Buenos Aires, Eds. Ancora, 1958, 238p.

Brazil

3082 Alves, Francisco M. Rodrigues
Um homem ameaça o Brasil; a história secreta e espantosa da "caixinha" de Adhemar de Barros. São Paulo, 1954, 216p.

3083 Barros, Adhemar Pereira de
Pensamento e ação. São Paulo, 1948, 189p.

3084 Bueno, Antônio S. Cunha
Angulos práticos do municipalismo. 2d ed. Rio de Janeiro, Conselho Nacional de Estatística, I.B.G.E., 1957, 86p.

3085 Burkinski, Francisco
A administração municipal e seus serviços fundamentais. Rio de Janeiro, Coelho Branco, 1951, 189p.

3086 Cavalcanti, Araújo
Desenvolvimento econômico e social dos municipios-novos rumos administração para as comunas Brasileiras. Rio de Janeiro, Departamento Administrativo del Servicio Público (DASP), 1959, 701p.

3087 Curitiba, Brazil. Prefeitura Municipal
Decreto-leis e decretos de 1942. Curitiba, Empr. Gráf. Paranaense, 1944, 179p.

3088 Daland, Robert T., ed., et al
Perspectives of Brazilian public administration. Rio de Janeiro, Brazilian School of Public Administration, Getulio Vargas Foundation, 1963, variously paged.

3089 Divisão territorial do Brasil; quadro vigente em 1.º-VII - 1955. Rio de Janeiro, Conselho Nacional de Estatística, I.B.G.E., 1955, 269p.

3090 Fina, Wilson Maia
Paço Municipal de São Paulo; sua história nos quatro séculos de sua vida. São Paulo, Anhembi, 1962, 174p.

3091 Gomes, Francelino de A.
Operação Município; fundamentos do Plano Nacional de Obras e Serviços Municipais . . . Rio de Janeiro, Instituto Internacional de Ciências Administrativas, Seção Brasileira, 1955, 200p.

3092 Instituto Brasileiro de Administração Municipal
Roteiro dos programas federais de assistência aos municípios. Rio de Janeiro, 1957, 41p.

3093 Leal, Victor Nunes
Coronelismo, enxada e voto; o município e o regime representativo no Brasil. Rio de Janeiro, 1948, 311p.

3094 Lessa, Gustavo
O distrito na organização municipal. Rio de Janeiro, Fundação Getúlio Vargas, 1952, 64p.

3095 Macedo, Roberto
Henrique Dodsworth. Rio de Janeiro, Serviço de Documentação, 1955, 108p.

3096 Medeiros, Ocelio de
Problemas fundamentais dos municípios brasileiros; planejamentos intergovernamentais como instrumentos de solução; política da valorização de áreas e projetos da Operação-Município. Rio de Janeiro, 1956, 123p.

3097 Neto, Antônio Delorenzo
Problemas fundamentais na organização dos municípios. A reforma da Lei orgânica . . . São Paulo, Fundação Escola de Sociologia e Política de São Paulo, Instituto de Estudos Municipais, 1958, 73p.

3098 Oliveira, Yves O. T. de
Curso de derecho municipal. Buenos Aires, Abeledo-Perrot, 1960, 238p.

3099 Pauperio, A. Machado
O município e seu regime jurídico no Brasil. Rio de Janeiro, Dis. Récord Edit., 1959, 89p.

3100 Pôrto Alegre, Brasil. Prefeitura Municipal
Relatório. Pôrto Alegre. Annual.

3101 Prata, Alaor
Recordações de vida pública. Rio de Janeiro, Ed. Borsoi, 1958, 409p.

3102 Quadros, Jânio
Bilhetinhos de Jânio. São Paulo, 1959, 165p.

3103 Quaglia, Vicente Celso
Fundamentos de administração municipal; guia teórico-prático do vereador e do prefeito. 2d ed. rev. plus enl. Catanduva, Boso, 1964, 494p.

3104 Revista brasileira dos municipios. Rio de Janeiro, 1947-

3105 Rio de Janeiro (Federal District)
Diário municipal. ano 1-4, no. 89; 14 nov. 1957-20 abril 1960. Rio de Janeiro, Irregular.

3106 Rio de Janeiro (Federal District) Prefeito
Mensagem ao Conselho Municipal. Rio de Janeiro. Annual.

3107 São Paulo, Brazil (City) Universidade
Publicações. no. 1- 1947-

3108 São Paulo, Brazil (State)
Plano de ação do governo, 1959-1963; administração estadual e desenvolvimento econômico-social. São Paulo, Impr. Oficial de Estado, 1959, 143p.

3109 Sergipe e seus municipios. Aracajú, Instituto Brasileiro de Geografia e Estatística, 1944, 211p.

3110 Severo, Archibaldo
O moderno município brasileiro; uma contribução aos estudos de municipalismo. Pôrto Alegre, Ed. Thurmann, 1946, 195p.

3111 Sherwood, Frank
Brazil's municipalities: a comparative view. San Francisco, Chandler Pub., 1967, 192p.

3112 Siegel, Gilbert B.
The vicissitudes of governmental reform in Brazil. Los Angeles, University of Southern California International Public Administration Center, 1966, 227p.

3113 Xavier, Rafael
Campanha municipalista. Rio de Janeiro, Serviço Gráfico do Instituto Brasileiro de Geografia e Estatística, 1950, 234p.

3114 Xavier, Rafael
Pela revitalização do município brasileiro. Rio de Janeiro, Serviço Gráfico do Instituto Brasileiro de Geografia e Estatística, 1948, 204p.

3115 Zenha, Edmundo
O municipio no Brasil, 1532-1700. Sao Paulo, Instituto Progresso Editorial, 1948, 172p.

Chile

3116 Arratia Vidal, Alejandro
Control jurídico de los actos municipales; estudio histórico-positivo. Santiago, Ed. Universitaria, 1959, 314p.

3117 Bernaschina González, Mario
Administración municipal: El gran Santiago; bases para una reforma. Santiago, 1957, 20p.

3118 Moraga Ramos, Carlos
De la responsibilidad en las municipalidades. Valparaíso, Impr. Aurora de Chile, 1944, 154p.

3119 Tapia Moore, Astolfo
Legislación urbanística de Chile, 1818-1959. Santiago, Instituto de Vivienda, Urbanismo y Planeación, Facultad de Arquitectura, Universidad de Chile, 1961, 89p.

Colombia

3120 Cardozo, Antonio M.
Derecho municipal colombiano. Bogotá, Libr. Camacho Roldán, 1944, 240p.

3121 Cooperativa de Municipalidades de Antioquia, Ltda.
Documentos sobre su fundación. Medellín, Impr. Departamental, 1939, 67p.

3122 Galvis Gaitán, Fernando
El municipio colombiano; bases históricas, sociológicas y jurídicas para un cambio de la estructura municipal de Colombia. Bogotá, Impr. Departamental "Antonio Nariño," 1964, 442p.

3123 Piñeros Corpas, Joaquín
Síntesis del conflicto entre la ciudad y la provincia de Colombia. Roma, Instituto Internacional de Sociología, 1951, 30p.

3124 Restrepo, Alonso
El municipio ladrón; artículos publicados en El Diario de Medellín. Medellín, Ed. Bedout, 1949- .

3125 Romero Velazco, Fernando
La reforma del régimen municipal. Bogotá, Ed. Retina, 1962, 158p.

Costa Rica

3126 Portocarrero A., Alfonso
Estado de la opinión pública de Costa Rica sobre el gobierno municipal; trabajo de campo, VI curso de aplicación 1958. San José, 1959, 39p.

3127 Quesada Picado, Máximo, ed.
Disposiciones legales relacionadas con el gobierno municipal. San José, Impr. Nacional, 1939, 332p.

3128 Revista municipal de Costa Rica. San José (I:1), 1940- .

Cuba

3129 Díaz Padilla, Antonio O.
Las instituciones locales y las reforma constitucional. Havana, Impr. de la Universidad, 1947, 31p.

3130 Franco, José L.
Instituciones locales: urbanismo. Havana, Instituto Interamericano de Historia Municipal e Institucional, 1959, 94p.

3131 Havana. Municipalidad
Datos estadísticos acerca de la administración municipal de la Habana. Havana, 1947- (Annual.)

3132 Sánchez Roca, Mariano
Legislación municipal de la República de Cuba . . . Havana, Ed. Lex, 1941, 584p.

Dominican Republic

3133 Santo Domingo. Ayuntamiento
Memoria. Santo Domingo, 1960-

Ecuador

3134 Castillo, Abel R.
Olmedo, el político; discurso parlamentario pronunciado en la sesión solemne del 6 de marzo de 1945 . . .Guayaquil, Impr. de la Universidad, 1946, 28p.

3135 Muñoz Chavez, Ricardo
Defensa de los trabajadores municipales. Cuenca, Casa de la Cultura Ecuatoriana, Núcleo del Azuay, 1964, 87p.

El Salvador

3136 Public Administration Service
Strengthening municipal government in El Salvador. Chicago, 1955, 71p.

3137 San Salvador. Alcaldía Municipal
Segundo congreso de municipalidades. República de El Salvador, 1943. San Salvador, Ed. Ahora, 1944, 48p.

Guatemala

3138 Montes, René
Temas para una legislación sobre urbanismo. Guatemala, 1951, 45p.

3139 Specher Bonnato, Luis
Necesidad de una conveniente legislación urbanística

para la República de Guatemala. Guatemala, 1954, 29p.

Guyana

3140 Young, Allan
The approach to local self-government in British Guiana. London, Longmans, Green, 1958, 246p.

Haiti

3141 Aristide, Achille
Mémoire sur la municipalité en Haiti, présenté au 5ème Congrès interaméricain d'histoire municipale et institutionnelle le 24 avril 1952 à Ciudad Trujillo, République Dominicaine. Port-au-Prince, Impr. de l'Etat, 1952, 54p.

3142 Craan, Jacques A.
La commune, son rôle, son importance. Port-au-Prince, Impr. de l'Etat, 1956, 59p.

3143 Haiti (Republic) Service d'Information de Presse et de Propagande
Décentralization et renaissance des provinces; l'application du programme Magloire. Port-au-Prince, Impr. de l'Etat, 1952, 32p.

Honduras

3144 Hernández, F.E.
Oficio o profesión de secretario municipal, observaciones sobre actuaciones municipales. San Pedro Sula, 1948, 162p.

Mexico

3145 Barrera Fuentes, Florencio
Historia y destino del municipio en México. México, 1950, 106p.

3146 Cárdenas, Leonard
The municipality in northern Mexico. El Paso, Texas Western College, 1963, 37p.

3147 Carneiro, Levi
Organização dos municipios e do Distrito Federal. Rio de Janeiro, Revista Forense, 1953, 323p.

3148 Carvajal Moreno, Gustavo
El municipio mexicano. México, 1963, 125p.

3149 Colin, Mario
El municipio en México. Toluca, Cámara de Diputados, 1949, 101p.

3150 D'Antonio, William V., & William H. Form
Influentials in two border cities: a study in community decision making. Notre Dame, University of Notre Dame Press, 1965, 273p.

3151 Gaxiola, Francisco J.
El Distrito Federal. México, 1956, 38p.

3152 González Lobo, Salvador
El municipio mexicano; antecedentes, naturaleza, funciones. Tésis. México, Universidad Nacional Autónoma de México, 1941, 111p.

3153 Instituto de Estudios Sociales de Monterrey, A.C.
Apuntes para el plan regulador de la ciudad de Monterrey. Monterrey, 1950, 34p.

3154 Lomeli Crezo, Aurelio
Breve estudio del Departamento del Distrito Federal. México, 1952, 74p.

3155 Medina Villanueva, Alberto
Historia de la propiedad territorial en México y algunos problemas de la Zona Federal. México, 1952, 100p.

3156 México. Dirección General de Estadística
División municipal de las entidades federativas en diciembre de 1946. México, 1947, 96p.

3157 México. Dirección General de Estadística
División municipal de las entidades federativas, 30 de junio de 1954. México, 1954, 165p.

3158 México. Dirección General de Estadística
Integración territorial de los Estados Unidos Mexicanos. Séptimo censo general de población, 1950. México, 1952, 734p.

3159 México (Federal District) Depto. del Distrito Federal
Résumen de actividades. México. Annual.

3160 Ochoa Campos, Moisés
La reforma municipal; historia municipal de México. México, 1955, 538p.

3161 Ojeda Ortega, Concepción
El municipio en México desde el punto de vista constitucional. México, 1946, 93p.

3162 Pier Gonzalez, Rogelio
El gobierno del Distrito Federal y su evolución histórica. México, 1957, 111p.

3163 Puente Arteaga, Martín
El municipio en México; génesis y evolución. México, Eds. Studium, 1954, 128p.

3164 Vega Mireles, Carlos
El municipio libre en el Distrito Federal; artículo 73, fracción VI de la Constitución política de los Estados Unidos Mexicanos. México, 1955, 81p.

3165 Villegas Ayala, José
La organización municipal en México. México, 1955, 128p.

Nicaragua

3166 Castillo Rodríguez, Alejandro
El municipio. Managua, 1946, 25p.

3167 Managua (National District)
Veintidos meses de gobierno local, del 23 de marzo de 1944 al 23 de enero de 1946. Managua, 1946, 61p.

Peru

3168 Alianza AP DC de Miraflores
Estudio técnico urbano: plan gobierno municipal. Lima, Librería Juan Mejía Baca, 1964, 86p.

3169 Austin, Allan
Estudio sobre el gobierno municipal del Perú. Lima, Oficina Nacional de Racionalización y Capacitación de la Administración Pública, 1965, 93p.

3170 Lima (Dept.). Junta Departamental
Memoria. Lima. Annual.

3171 Moore, John P.
The cabildo in Peru under the Hapsburgs; a study in the origins and powers of the town council in the viceroyalty of Peru, 1530-1700. Durham, Duke University Press, 1954, 309p.

3172 Peru. Congreso. Cámara de Diputados. Biblioteca
Municipalidades; bibliografía y guía legislativa. Lima, 1958, 125p.

3173 Peru. Laws, statutes, etc.
Compilación de disposiciones legales y reglamentarias sobre urbanizaciones 1900-1953, por Ernesto Sandoval Cerná. Con inclusión del Nuevo reglamento de construcciones para Lima y balnearios . . . Lima, 1953, 434p.

3174 Peru. Laws, statutes, etc.
Municipalidades; la Ley orgánica de municipalidades en concordancia con las disposiciones vigentes en materia de legislación comunal y con el proyecto y anteproyectos del gobierno local . . . Arequipa, Ed. Universitaria, 1962-

Trinidad

3175 Trinidad
District administration reports. Port-of-Spain. Annual.

Uruguay

3176 Canelones. Uruguay. Junta Departamental
Normas para la formación de centros poblados. Canelones, 1962, 64p.

3177 Ganón, Isaac
Municipalización de servicios públicos. Montevideo, 1952, 169p.

3178 Montevideo (Dept.) Concejo Departamental
Registro oficial. Montevideo (I:1), 1955-

3179 Montevideo. Intendencia Municipal
Boletín mensual. Montevideo, 1950-

Venezuela

3180 Boletín bibliográfico de divulgación municipal. Caracas, Fundación para el Desarrollo de la Comunidad y Fomento Municipal, Depto. de Programas Municipales, # 12, April-May, 1966-

3181 Cabildo. Caracas, Concejo Municipal del Distrito Federal, # 12, September-October 1965-

3182 Caracas, Venezuela. Consejo Municipal del Distrito Federal
Caracas y su régimen municipal. 1960, 288p.

3183 Convención Nacional de Municipalidades. 2d, Caracas, 1960
Actuaciones. Caracas, Publicaciones de la Secretaría General de la Presidencia de la República, Impr. Nacional, 1961-

3184 Fundación para el Desarrollo de la Comunidad y Fomento Municipal. Biblioteca
Boletín bibliográfico de divulgación municipal. Caracas, # 11, March-April 1966-

3185 Relations of nation, states and municipalities in the government of the Republic of Venezuela; a survey report. Chicago, Public Administration Service, 1960, 93p.

Periodical Articles

General

3186 Daland, Robert T.
"Political Science and the Study of Urbanism; Bibliographical Article." American political science review 51, June 1957, p. 491-509.

3187 Garcini y Guerra, Heitor J.
"A Organização Administrativa das Grandes Concentrações Urbanas." Rio de Janeiro, Revista brasileira dos municípios (11:43/44), July/December 1958, p. 127-131.

3188 Morlan, R. L.
"Foreign Local Government: a Bibliography." American political science review (LIX:1), March 1965, p. 120-136.

3189 Mouchet, Carlos
"Florentino González, un Jurista de América: Sus Ideas Sobre el Régimen Municipal." Journal of Inter-American Studies (2:1), January 1960, p. 83-101.

3190 Oliveira, Yves O. T. de
"Direito e Urbanismo." Havana, Boletín, January 1947, p. 1-13.

3191 Ostrom, V., & E. Ostrom
"Behavioral Approach to the Study of Intergovernmental Relations." Annals of the American Academy of Political & Social Science 359, May 1965, p. 137-146.

3192 Quintero, César A.
"Los Medios Económicos de los Municipios en Relación con la Autonomía Municipal y la Necesidad de Asegurar y Ampliar Está Dentro de los Límites Propios." Panamá, Comercio, industria y turismo 139, September 1956, p. 3-11.

Latin America

3193 Brasil. Câmara de Deputados
"Projeto no. 4. 656-58 Sôbre o Convenio Interamericano de Cooperação Intermunicipal." Rio de Janeiro, Revista do serviço público (88:1), July 1960, p. 50-68.

3194 Cavalcanti, Araújo
"O Desenvolvimento Planificado dos Municípios do Continente." Rio de Janeiro, Revista do serviço público, año XXII (82:1/3), January/March 1959, p. 78-118.

3195 Greca, Alcides
"El Derecho Municipal Americano." Buenos Aires, Revista de derecho y administración municipal, September 1947, p. 657-662.

3196 Fitzgibbon, Russell
"Our Municipal Neighbors to the South . . ." National municipal review 30, February 1941, p. 80-84.

3197 Horowitz, Irving L.
"Electoral Politics, Urbanization and Social Development in Latin America." Urban affairs quarterly (II:3), March 1967, p. 3-35.

3198 Johnson, John J.
"The Latin American Municipality Deteriorates." Inter-American economic affairs (5:1), Summer 1951, p. 24-35.

3199 Johnson, John J.
"Middle Groups in National Politics in Latin America (Strengthened by the Growth of Cities)." Hispanic American historical review 37, August 1957, p. 313-329.

3200 Lambert, Jacques
"Le Rôle Politique des Capitales en Amérique Latine." Toulouse, Caravelle 3, 1964, p. 130-138.

3201 Lepawsky, Albert
"Municipal Cooperation in the Americas." Inter-American quarterly, July 1941, p. 72-79.

3202 Pessoa, A.
"A Propaganda dos Municipios." Rio de Janeiro, Cultura política (2:11), January 1942, p. 27-34.

3203 Rowe, Leo S.
"Cooperation Between the Municipalities of the American Continent." National municipal review 13, February 1924, p. 69-70.

3204 Seminario Interamericano de Registro Civil, 2o. Reunión Preparatoria, 1961
"Informe del Comité Para el Mejoramiento del Registro Civil en las Américas." Montevideo, Boletín del Instituto Interamericano del Niño (35:138), September 1961, p. 175-186.

3205 "Seminario Universitario Interamericano Sôbre Asuntos Municipales, 3°; Montevideo, 1962. Conclusões." Rio de Janeiro, Revista de administração municipal (10:59), July-August 1963, p. 314-316.

3206 Tercero, José
"City Government in Spanish American Capitals." Pan American Union bulletin 67, March 1933, p. 172-180.

Argentina

3207 Dana Montaño, S.M.
"La Participación de los Técnicos en el Gobierno Local." Buenos Aires, Revista de administración pública (3:9-10), April-September 1963, p. 108-113.

3208 Gómez Forgues, Máximo I.
"El Régimen Municipal en la Capital Federal." Buenos Aires, Revista de la Facultad de Derecho y Ciencias Sociales, January/April 1949, p. 138-171.

3209 Greca, Alcides
"Experiencias y Alternativas del Régimen Municipal Metropolitano." Santa Fé, Revista de ciencias jurídicas (8:38), 1943, p. 99-114.

3210 Korn Villafañe, Adolfo
"La República Representativa Municipal." Buenos Aires, Boletín de la Biblioteca del Congreso, July-August 1941, p. 1031-1108.

3211 Miller, D.C., et al
"The Power Structure of an Argentine City." Buenos Aires, Cuadernos 76, October 1964, p. 229-249.

3212 Mouchet, Carlos
"Alberdi y Sarmiento, Planificadores de Ciudades y Precursores de Programas de Desarrollo Económico." Buenos Aires, Revista de administración pública (2:7), October-December 1962, p. 11-29.

3213 Mouchet, Carlos
"Análisis de las Relaciones Entre el Gobierno Municipal y el Desarrollo de la Comunidad." Buenos Aires, Revista de administración pública (2:5), April-June 1962, p. 20-36.

3214 Mouchet, Carlos
"Las Ideas Sobre el Município en el Período Hispano-Indiano." Buenos Aires, Revista de la Facultad de Derecho y Ciencias (10:44) July/August 1955, p. 751-763.

3215 Oliveira, Yves O. T. de
"Influencia Doctrinaria de la Argentina en la Evolución de la Ciencia Municipal Americana." Rosario, Revista de la Facultad de Ciencias, Económicas, Comerciales y Políticas 60/61, September 1949-April 1950, p. 618-636.

3216 Reyes, César
"Los Alcaldes Coloniales y los de la Revolución." Rosario, Revista de la Facultad de Ciencias Económicas, Comerciales y Políticas, September-December 1940, p. 566-600.

3217 Spota, Alberto G.
"La Colaboración Administrativa y la Denuncia de Bienes Municipales." Buenos Aires, Revista de derecho y administración municipal, February 1944, p. 109-134.

3218 Tello, Roberto
"El Plan Quinquenal y el Gobierno de la Ciudad de Buenos Aires." Buenos Aires, Revista argentina de estudios políticos, March 1947, p. 297-302.

3219 Vivante, Amando
"La Formación de un Pueblo Argentino." Buenos Aires, Revista geográfica americana (39:233/234), May/June 1955, p. 199-204.

3220 Zorraquín Becú, Ricardo
"Los Cabildos Argentinos." Buenos Aires, Revista de la Facultad de Derecho y Ciencias Sociales (11: 47), January/March 1956, p. 95-156.

Brazil

3221 "Administração Municipal de Recife." Rio de Janeiro, O economista, March 1945, p. 80-82.

3222 Andre, A.
"Males da Administração Municipal." Rio de Janeiro, Revista de administração municipal (8:47), July-August 1961, p. 349-353.

3223 Anglade, Christian
"Une Tentative de Repartition du Phénomène de la Capitale: le Municipe Brésilien." Toulouse, Caravelle 3, 1964, p. 228-250.

3224 Aragão, J. G. de
"Município e Administração." Rio de Janeiro, Revista brasileira dos municípios (12:47-48), July-December 1959, p. 105-113.

3225 Araujo Cavalcanti, J. M. dos Santos
"Reorganização Geral do Serviço de Documentação do Estado da Guanabara." Rio de Janeiro, Revista do serviço público (88:3), September 1960, p. 234-242.

3226 "Associação Brasileira de Municipios." Rio de Janeiro, Revista do serviço público, April 1946, p. 78-80.

3227 Backhouser, Everardo
"Crescimento da Cidade de Rio-de-Janeiro." Rio de Janeiro, Boletim geográfico, August 1945, p. 734-736.

3228 Bauer Novelli, F.
"Considerações Sôbre a Organização Municipal da Guanabara." Rio de Janeiro, Revista de direito público e ciência política (4:1), January-April 1961, p. 17-29.

3229 Brazil. Senado. Câmara dos Deputados. Biblioteca.
"Administração Municipal." (Bibliografia.) Brasilia, Boletim da Biblioteca da Câmara dos Deputados (9:1), January/June 1960, p. 101-162.

3230 Brazil. Consultor Geral da República.
"Autonomia dos Municipios." Rio de Janeiro, Revista de administração pública (9:53), July-August 1962, p. 326-331.

3231 Burkinski, Francisco
"Administração Municipal." Rio de Janeiro, Revista do serviço público, April 1946, p. 16-20.

3232 Burkinsky, Francisco
"O Municipio e a Assistência Social." Rio de Janeiro, Revista do serviço público, July 1946, p. 52-57.

3233 Carvalho, Orlando M.
"O atual Regime dos Municipios." Rio de Janeiro, Cultura política (I:1), March 1941, p. 24-33.

3234 Carvalho, Orlando M.
"O Município na Estructura Política do Brasil." Rio de Janeiro, Revista forense (147:599/600), May/June 1953, p. 20-23.

3235 Carvalho, Orlando M.
"A Política Constitucional dos Municípios no Brasil." Rio de Janeiro, Revista forense, September 1945, p. 435-441.

3236 Cavalcanti, Araújo
"Emancipação Global e Desenvolvimento Planificado dos Municípios." Rio de Janeiro, Revista do serviço público, ano XXIII (87:3), June 1960, p. 170-200.

3237 Cavalcanti, Araújo
"Presença do Brasil no II Congresso Ibero-Americano de Municípios." Rio de Janeiro, Revista do serviço público, ano XXIII (86:3), March 1960, p. 191-203.

3238 "La Cooperación Intermunicipal en la Práctica."
Havana, Boletín, January-March 1948, p. 2-9.

3239 Cunha, M. Wagner Vicira da
"Características Gerais da Administração Municipal no Estado de São Paulo." São Paulo, Revista de administração (I:3), September 1947, p. 3-44.

3240 Delorenzo Neto, Antônio
"O Aglomerado Urbano de São Paulo." Bêlo Horizonte, Revista brasileira de estudos políticos (3:6), July 1959, p. 111-143.

3241 Delorenzo Neto, Antônio
"A Condificação do Direito Municipal." Rio de Janeiro, Revista do serviço público, ano XVII (66: 3), March 1955, p. 518-526.

3242 Delorenzo Neto, Antônio
"A Evolução do Municipalismo no Brasil." Rio de Janeiro, Revista do serviço público, ano XX (74:1), January 1957, p. 76-94.

3243 Delorenzo Neto, Antônio
"Problemas Fundamentais na Organização dos Municípios." São Paulo, Sociologia (2:2), May 1958, p. 255-265.

3244 Dillon Soares, G.A., & M.A. Carvalho de Noronha
"Urbanização e Dispersão Eleitoral." Rio de Janeiro, Revista de direito público e ciência política (3:2), July-December 1960, p. 258-270.

3245 Donald, C.L.
"Brazilian Local Self-Government: Myth or Reality?" Western political quarterly 13, December 1960, p. 1043-1055.

3246 Guimaraes, Admar
"O Município e seu Governo." Rio de Janeiro, Revista de administração municipal (10:61), November-December 1963, p. 467-471.

3247 Hardy, G.N.
"O Aperfeiçoamento do Sistema de Govêrno Municipal no Brasil." Bêlo Horizonte, Revista Brasileira de Estudos Políticos (1:1), December 1956, p. 101-115.

3248 Hardy, G.N.
"Course Held for Brazilian Officials." American city 70, May 1955, p. 165.

3249 Instituto Brasileiro de Administração Municipal
"Assistencia Técnica aos Municípios." Rio de Janeiro, _Revista do serviço público_ (95:1), January-March 1963, p. 105-123.

3250 "Linhas Fundamentais do Município." Rio de Janeiro, _Revista do serviço público,_ July 1946, p. 135-139.

3251 Lopes, T. de Vilanova Monteiro
"A Capacitação Técnica dos Governos Municipais e os Conceitos de Territorio, Pôvo e Administração." Rio de Janeiro, _Revista do serviço público_ (87:1-2), April-May 1960, p. 39-41.

3252 Machado, J. Teixeira
"Autonomia e Centralização." Rio de Janeiro, _Revista de administração dos municípios_ (9:51), March-April 1962, p. 129-132.

3253 Machado, J. Teixeira
"Interpretação do Artigo 141 Parágrafo 34 da Constitução Federal à Luz de Julgados do S. T. F." Rio de Janeiro, _Revista de administração pública_ (9:55), November-December 1962, p. 466-476.

3254 Medeiros, Ocelio de
"A Constituição do Direito Municipal Brasileiro na Organização do Império." Rio de Janeiro, _Revista do serviço público,_ July/August 1947, p. 44-56.

3255 Medeiros, Ocelio de
"Reorganização Municipal Brasileira." Rio de Janeiro, _Revista do serviço público,_ August/September 1946, p. 51-61.

3256 Meirelles, H. Lopes
"Arruamento, Alinhamento e Nivelamento." Rio de Janeiro, _Revista de administração municipal_ (10:59), July-August 1963, p. 293-296.

3257 Meirelles, H. Lopes
"Autarquias Intermunicipais." Rio de Janeiro, _Revista de administração pública_ (9:54), September-October 1962, p. 374-384.

3258 Meirelles, H. Lopes
"Fiscalização de Construções." Rio de Janeiro, Revista de administração municipal (11:62), January-February 1964, p. 5-8.

3259 Meirelles, H. Lopes
"O Regime Municipal Brasileiro em Confronto com o de Outros Países." Rio de Janeiro, Revista de direito administrativo 42, October/December 1955, p. 30-45.

3260 Meirelles, H. Lopes
"Regimento das Câmaras Municipais." Rio de Janeiro, Revista de administração municipal (10: 59), July-August 1963, p. 305-313.

3261 Meirelles, H. Lopes
"A Responsabilidade Civil dos Prefeitos. Rio de Janeiro, Revista de administração municipal (12:69), March-April 1965, p. 121-123.

3262 Mello, D. Lordello de
"Competência dos Municípios." Rio de Janeiro, Revista de administração municipal (11:62), January-February 1964, p. 40-52.

3263 Mello, D. Lordello de
"Podêres Municipais." Rio de Janeiro, Revista de administração municipal (11:63), March-April 1964, p. 110-113.

3264 Mello, D. Lordello de
"Racionalização do Governo Municipal no Brasil." Rio de Janeiro, Revista brasileira dos municípios (10:39/40), July/December 1957, p. 151-160.

3265 Melo, L. de Anhaia
"Elementos para o Planejamento Territorial dos Municípios." Rio de Janeiro, Revista do serviço público (78:1-3), January-March 1958, p. 85-109.

3266 Melo, Manuel Caetano Bandeira de
"Relatório Geral do V Congresso Nacional de Municípios." Rio de Janeiro, Revista do serviço público, ano XXIII, (86:1/2), January/February 1960, p. 76-79.

3267 Menezes, Djacir
"A Democracia, o Município e a Evolução Económica." Rio de Janeiro, Revista do serviço público, July 1946, p. 60-65.

3268 Moreira, João R.
"A Administração Municipal e o Ruralismo Pedagógico." Rio de Janeiro, Revista do serviço público, July 1946, p. 66-72.

3269 Nogueira, Carlos Rodrigues
"A Administração da Cidade de São Paulo em 1835." São Paulo, Investigações (3:31), July 1951, p. 71-78.

3270 Oliveira, R.R. de
"Organização Municipal Brasileira." Rio de Janeiro, Revista brasileira dos municípios (15: 57-58), January-June 1962, p. 1-5.

3271 Oliveira, Yves O. T. de
"Síntese da Formação de Nosso Espírito Municipal." Rio de Janeiro, Revista brasileira dos municipios (88:1), July 1960, p. 31-49.

3272 Omegna, Nelson
"Municipalismo e Descentralização Administrativa." Rio de Janeiro, Revista do serviço público (87:1-2), April-May 1960, p. 42-60.

3273 Passos, Edison
"Melhoramentos do Rio de Janeiro." Rio de Janeiro, Revista do Clube de Engenharia, May/June 1941, p. 3-22.

3274 Passos, Edison
"Plano de Melhoramentos da Cidade de Rio de Janeiro." Rio de Janeiro, Revista municipal de engenharia, July 1941, p. 212-223.

3275 Paupério, A. Machado
"O Governo Municipal na Monarquia." Rio de Janeiro, Revista do serviço público, ano XXI (79:1), April 1958, p. 61-72.

3276 Peçanha, Celso
"Recuperação e Desenvolvimento dos Municípios Brasileiros." Rio de Janeiro, Revista do serviço público, ano XXII (83:2), May 1959, p. 189-196.

3277 Pereira, R. de Mattos
"Meios para Planificar a Administraçao Municipal." Rio de Janeiro, Revista brasileira dos municípios (13:49-52), January-December 1960, p. 73-74.

3278 Pereira, R. de Mattos
"Organizaçao para o Planejamento Municipal." Rio de Janeiro, Revista de administração municipal (10:59), July-August 1963, p. 271-292.

3279 Pezzolo, Antônio
"Organizaçao Municipal no Brasil." Havana, Revista municipal interamericana (2:3), January/March 1952, p. 4-10.

3280 Reis, José de Oliveira
"Uma Síntese Sôbre as Principais Vías do Plano Diretor." Rio de Janeiro, Revista municipal de engenharia, July 1942, p. 204-209.

3281 Rosso, H. Z. de
"Obras Sôbre Municípios Brasileiros Existentes na Biblioteca Waldemar Lopes do Conselho Nacional de Estatística." Rio de Janeiro, Boletím Bibliográfico (1:7), November 1957, p. 111-137.

3282 "Seminario Universitario Interamericano Sôbre Asuntos Municipales 3º; Montevideo, 1962. Conclusões." Rio de Janeiro, Revista de administraçao municipal (10:59), July-August 1963, p. 314-316.

3283 Soares, S. de P.
"Organizaçao de uma Secretaria Municipal." Rio de Janeiro, Revista brasileira dos municípios (16:63-64), July-December 1963, p. 199-201.

3284 Xavier, Rafael
"O Movimento Municipalista e os Problemas Nacionais." Salvador, Revista de direito municipal (12:33/34), May/August 1951, p. 37-52.

3285 Xavier, Rafael
"O Município no Brasil." Rio de Janeiro, *Revista brasileira dos municípios* (6:21), January/March 1953, p. 1-6.

3286 Xavier, Rafael
"A Organização Nacional e o Município." Rio de Janeiro, *Revista do serviço público,* May 1946, p. 56-71.

Chile

3287 Charlín Ojeda, Carlos
"Síntesis Histórica de la Legislación Orgánica Municipal de Chile." Santiago, *Acción social,* December 1935, p. 87-91.

3288 Muñoz Maluchka, Luis
"Manual de Urbanismo. Para Uso de los Alcaldes y Directores de Obras Municipales." Santiago, *Boletín municipal de la República,* April 1933, p. 19-32; May 1933, p. 19- ; July 1933, p. 21-25.

3289 Tapia Moore, Astolfo
"Legislación Urbanística de Chile, 1818-1959." Santiago, *Anales de la Universidad de Chile* (118: 119), 3d quarter 1960, p. 177-203.

Colombia

3290 Cuellar, José M.
"El Municipio Colombiano." Havana, *Revista municipal interamericana* (2:1), July/September 1951, p. 1-3.

3291 Escobar Barrazabal, M.
"El Desarrollo de Bogotá." Bogotá, *Registro municipal,* April 15, 1937, p. [169] 173.

3292 García Samudio, Nicolás
"La División Departamental y los Orígenes del Municipio en Colombia." Bogotá, *Boletín de historia y antigüedades,* February 1933, p. 1-14.

3293 Giraldo Zuluaga, Enrique
"El Municipio Colombiano Frente a la Reforma Constitucional." Medellín, *Estudios de derecho* (14:40), November 1952, p. 85-92.

3294 Moreno Clavijo, Jorge
"Bogotá se Va a Transformar el Plan Soto-Bateman." Bogotá, Cromos, August 26, 1944, p. [8], [9], 60-62.

3295 "Municipios y Corregimientos de Colombia." Bogotá, Boletín de la Sociedad Geográfica de Colombia (10:3), 3d quarter 1952, p. 157-172; (10:4), 4th quarter 1952, p. 209-219.

3296 Puyo Delgado, Carlos
"Las Ciudades y el Campo." Bogotá, Cromos, August 3, 1946, p. 3-5.

3297 "Reconstrucción de Bogotá. Primera Etapa: Remodelación del Sector Central, Plano Piloto, Reparcelaciones." Bogotá, Proa, June 1948, p. 11-17.

3298 Unión de Municipios. Bogotá
"La Intermunicipalidad en la República de Colombia." Havana, Boletín de la Comisión Panamericana de Cooperación Intermunicipal, May 1941, p. 14-20.

Costa Rica

3299 Costa Rica. Laws, statutes, etc.
"Leyes y Disposiciones Relacionadas con el Gobierno Municipal." San José, Revista municipal de Costa Rica, September 1942, p. 610-616.

Cuba

3300 Carrera Jústiz, F.
"El Régimen Municipal ante la Convención Constituyente." Havana, América (8:1), October 1940, p. 49-59.

3301 Roig de Lauchsenring, Emilio
"Las Casas del Cabildo Habanero." Havana, Policía, October 10, 1944, p. 9, 47.

3302 Schwerert Ferrer, Arnaldo
"El Régimen Municipal en la Constitución de 1940." Havana, Revista del Colegio de Abogados de la Habana, January/March 1947, p. 5-10.

3303 Téllez de la Torre, A.
"Economía Municipal Cubana." Havana, Contabilidad y finanzas, March 1946, p. 175-189.

Dominican Republic

3304 Amiama, Manuel A.
"Las Instituciones Municipales en el Nuevo Mundo y en Santo Domingo. Trabajo Presentado al I. Congreso de Municipios Dominicanos." Ciudad Trujillo, Revista municipal del Distrito de Santo Domingo, April 1942, p. 27-36.

3305 Cruz Ayala, Hernán
"Evolución de las Instituciones Municipales en la República Dominicana en la Era de Trujillo." Ciudad Trujillo, Renovación (1:4), October/December 1953, p. 5-25.

Ecuador

3306 "La Intermunicipalidad es ya Parte Integrante de la Ley de Régimen Municipal Ecuatoriano." Havana, Boletín, June 1946, p. 15-17.

3307 Oquendo H., Juan L.
"Codificación de Leyes y Ordenanzas Municipales." Quito, Anales de La Universidad Central, April-June 1936, p. 445-548.

3308 "Reglamento de los Trabajos de Higiene Municipal." Cuenca, El tres de noviembre, November 1945, p. 40-44.

3309 Villacreces I., Juan B.
"Plan Regulador de la Ciudad de Quito." Quito, Boletín de obras públicas, no. 63-65, año 1947-1948, p. 110-121.

Guatemala

3310 Guatemala. Laws, statutes, etc.
"Apruébanse los Estatutos de la 'Asociación Nacional de Municipalidades de la República de Guatemala'; y Reconócese su Personalidad Jurídica." Guatemala, El Guatemalteco (160:35), November 4, 1960, p. 313-314.

3311 Guatemala. Laws, statutes, etc.
"Ley Municipal de la República de Guatemala." Guatemala, Diario de Centro América, August 10, 1935, p. 245-250.

3312 Guatemala. Laws, statutes, etc.
"Reglamento para la Administración, Contabilidad y Control de las Municipalidades de la República." Guatemala, Diario de Centro América, October 19, 1939, p. 913-929.

Haiti

3313 Haiti. Laws, statutes, etc.
"Décret-loi Pourvoyant les Communes de la République d'un Conforme à la Constitution Actuelle." Port-au-Prince, Le moniteur, September 23, 1937, p. 601-604.

3314 Pan American Commission on Intermunicipal Cooperation
"El Municipio en Haiti." Havana, Boletín de la Comisión Panamericana de Cooperacion Intermunicipal, July 1943, p. 3-6.

Honduras

3315 Honduras. Laws, statutes, etc.
"Ley Orgánica de los Distritos Departamentales, Seccionales y Locales." Tegucigalpa, La Gaceta, April 19, 1940, p. 1-4.

3316 Mendoza, Julio C.
"Organización y Funcionamiento de la Dirección de Municipalidades." Tegucigalpa, La Gaceta (83:16.618), October 31, 1958, p. 1-2.

Mexico

3317 Cárdenas Renteria, O.
"Régimen Legal de la Planificación Urbana." México, Revista del Instituto Técnico y de Administración del Trabajo 16, January-April 1962, p. 63-145.

3318 "Cuadros Sinópticos de Futurismo Político." México, Mañana (37:375), November 4, 1950, p. 28-29.

3319 Gibson, Charles
"Rotation of Alcaldes in the Indian Cabildo of Mexico City." The Hispanic American historical review (33:2), May 1953, p. 212-223.

3320 Herrera y Lasso, Manuel
"Que el Gobierno de los Estados Se Subordine a los Municipios." México, La Nación, March 1, 1947, p. 6-7, 21.

3321 Klapp, O.E., & L.V. Padgett
"Power Structure and Decision-Making in a Mexican Border City." American journal of sociology (65: 4), January 1960, p. 400-406.

3322 México. Comisión Nacional Organizadora de los Municipios en México
"El Municipio en México." Havana, Boletín de la Comisión Panamericana de Cooperación Intermunicipal, August 1943, p. 3-15.

3323 "El Primer Anillo de Circunvalación." México, Hemisferio, November 20, 1944, p. 96-97.

3324 "V Convención de Acción Nacional para el Estudio de Problemas Municipales." México, La nación, February 15, 1947 (entire issue).

3325 "Vast Improvements for Mexico City. An Ample Water Supply and Modern Sewage. More Paved Highways and Streets for the Federal District. Schools, Markets and Public Buildings." México, Mexican news digest, December 1942, p. 2-3.

3326 Vieyra, Aurelio S.
"Deudas de la Revolución: El Municipio Libre." México, Todo, May 2, 1946, p. 20.

Nicaragua

3327 "Managua Changes its Form of Government." Pan American Union bulletin 64, February 1930, p. 174.

Panama

3328 Luciani J., René
"The Municipalities of Panama." Havana, Revista municipal interamericana (8:3/4), January/June

1958, p. 32-43.

3329 Fabrega, Edwin E.
"La Ciudad de Panamá y el Problema de los Municipios." Panamá, Presente 4, October 1965, p. 6-8.

Peru

3330 Bourricaud, François
"Lima en la Vida Política Peruana." Rio de Janeiro, América latina (7:4), October-December 1964, p. 89-95.

3331 "Lima Municipality. Review of 1942 Activities." Lima, Peruvian times, February 26, 1943, p. 21-22.

3332 Mimbela de los Santos, Eduardo
"Las Municipalidades en el Perú." Havana, Boletín April 1946, p. 20-22.

3333 Zea, Leopoldo
"El Peru, Lima y Belaunde." México, Foro internacional (4:3), January-March 1964, p. 429-452.

Venezuela

3334 Henríquez Rojas, J.A.
"Fundación para el Desarrollo de la Comunidad y Fomento Municipal." Caracas, Política (3:28), November 1963, p. 140-141.

West Indies and the Caribbean

3335 Rodrigues, M.R.
"Local Government in Jamaica." London, Journal of local administration overseas (1:2), April 1962, p. 102-111.

PUBLIC UTILITIES

Books

General

3336 Branco, Plínio A.
Serviços de utilidade pública. A doutrina do custo de reprodução e suas absurdas consequencias . . . São Paulo, Pub. da Prefeitura Municipal de São Paulo, 1942, 83p.

3337 Daley, Robert
World beneath the city. Philadelphia, Lippincott, 1959, 223p.

3338 Garfield, Paul, & Wallace Lovejoy
Public utility economics. Englewood Cliffs, Prentice-Hall, 1964, 505p.

3339 Paz Maroto, José
Urbanismo y servicios urbanos. 3v. Madrid, 1947.

3340 Shepherd, William G., & T.G. Gies
Regulations of public utilities. New York, Random House, 1966, 284p.

3341 U.S. Bureau of Foreign Commerce
Electric currents abroad. Revision. Washington, 1959, 77p.

Latin America

3342 Cavers, David F., & James R. Nelson
Electric power regulation in Latin America. Baltimore, Johns Hopkins Press, 1959, 279p.

3343 Puga, William B., ed.
Directory of Latin America electric utilities. New York, McGraw-Hill, 1965, 115p.

3344 United Nations. Economic Commission for Latin America
Energy in Latin America; publication E/CN, 12/384. Geneva, 1957, 268p.

Argentina

3345 Anaya, Laureano O.
La nacionalización de los transportes y servicios públicos, su significado desde el punto de vista de la defensa nacional . . . Buenos Aires, Tall. Gráf. D. Cersosimo, 1951, 49p.

3346 Argentine Republic. Comisión Especial de Coordinación de Transportes de la Ciudad de Buenos Aires
Informe elevado al poder ejecutivo de la nación. 2v. Buenos Aires, Talleres Gráficos Argentinos Rosso, 1938.

3347 Argentine Republic. Laws, statutes, etc.
Plan técnico integral de trabajos públicos, año 1949 . . . Decreto no. 26.055 del 19 de octubre de 1949. Buenos Aires, 1949? 753p.

3348 Cámara Argentina de la Construcción
Las actividades de la Cámara Argentina de la Construcción en favor de la industria de la construcción en la República Argentina, 1936-1947. Buenos Aires, 1947, 247p.

3349 Construcciones. Buenos Aires, Cámara Argentina de la Construcción, 1957- .

3350 Iñigo Carrera, Héctor
El engaño de las nacionalizaciones totalitarias; una estafa al descubierto. Buenos Aires, Gure, 1955, 146p.

3351 Oyhanorte, Julio
La expropriación y los servicios públicos . . . Buenos Aires, Ed. Perrot, 1957, 162p.

3352 Seminario sobre Diseño de Abastecimientos de Agua, Buenos Aires, Argentina, 1962
Seminario sobre diseño de abastecimientos de agua, Buenos Aires, Argentina, 20-29 de septiembre de

1962. Washington, Oficina Sanitaria Panamericana, 1964, 211p.

Bolivia

3353 Avis S., Julio A. d'
Apropiación privada de los servicios públicos . . . Cochabamba, Impr. Universitaria, 1950, 56p.

Brazil

3354 Assis Ribeiro, C.J. de
Financiamento de obras públicas. Rio de Janeiro, Eds. Financeiras, 1956, 272p.

3355 Branco, Plínio A.
A experiência da municipalidade de São Paulo como subsídio para a regulamentação dos serviços públicos concedidos. São Paulo, Prefeitura do Município, 1942, 17p.

3356 Brasil constroi. año 1- Rio de Janeiro, 1948- .

3357 Brazil. Ministério da Viação e Obras Públicas. Serviço de Documentação
Atividades do Ministério. 1949- .

3358 Brazil. Serviço de Estatística da Educação e Cultura
Melhoramentos urbanos. Rio de Janeiro, Instituto Brasileiro de Geografia e Estatística. Annual.

3359 Maranhão, Jarbas
Municipalismo e ruralismo; plano nacional de obras e serviços municipais . . . Rio de Janeiro, Depto. Administrativo do Serviço Público e Instituto Brasileiro de Ciências Administrativas, 1960, 298p.

3360 Oliveira, Américo Barbosa de
Exploração dos serviços públicos. Recife, Comissão de Desenvolvimento Econômico de Pernambuco, 1963, 82p.

Chile

3361 Raurich Cooke, Mario
El contrato de concesión de obra pública. Temuco, 1946, 34p.

3362 United Nations. Economic Commission for Latin America
Los servicios públicos en una población de erradicación. Santiago, 1965, 121p.

Colombia

3363 Arias Aristazabal, Arturo
De las indemnizaciones por trabajos públicos. Bogotá, 1954, 168p.

3364 Bogotá. Secretaría de Hacienda
Proyectos y realizaciones. Bogotá, 1953- .

3365 Colombia. Dirección de Información y Propaganda
Un país que trabaja. Bogotá, 1954, 332p.

3366 Ellis, Cecil A.
Public utilities in Colombia . . . New York, United Nations (Document ST/TAA/K/Colombia/1), 1953, 65p.

3367 Giraldo Lozano, Hernando
Concesiones administrativas. Bogotá, 1951, 89p.

3368 Piedrahíta Arango, Rubén
Una política en obras públicas. Bogotá, Gobierno de las Fuerzas Armadas, 1955, 167p.

3369 Restrepo Daeghsel, José M.
Servicio público a través de concesión. Bogotá, 1956, 89p.

Costa Rica

3370 Costa Rica. Ministerio de Obras Públicas
Informe. San José, 1951- .

Cuba

3371 Portocarrero y Montero, Jesús A.
Exposición al mayor general Fulgencio Batista y Saldívar C. de H., honorable señor Presidente de la República. Re: Aplicación práctica del plan para el desarrollo económico-social de Cuba (Ley-Decreto 1589 de 1954); informe. Havana, 1955, 218p.

Dominican Republic

3372 García Bonnelly, Juan U.
Las obras públicas en la era de Trujillo. 2v. Cuidad Trujillo, Impr. Dominicana, 1955.

3373 Henríquez y Carvajal, Francisco
El contrato. Ciudad Trujillo, Ed. del Caribe, 1955, 48p.

Ecuador

3374 Ecuador. Comisión Nacional de Valores
Informe. Quito. Annual.

3375 Ecuador. Laws, statutes, etc.
El sucre del patriotismo. Ley de progreso local por iniciativa cívica. Quito, Tall. Gráf. Nacionales, 1951, 16p.

3376 Muñoz Chavez, Ricardo
Defensa de los trabajadores municipales. Cuenca, Casa de la Cultura Ecuatoriana, Núcleo del Azuay, 1964, 87p.

3377 Rolando, Carlos A.
Conozca Vd. lo que fué el general Sr. don Eloy Alfaro. Guayaquil, Universidad de Guayaquil, Depto. de Publicaciones, 1958, 147p.

Guatemala

3378 Guatemala. Ministerio de Comunicaciones y Obras Públicas
Memoria. Guatemala, 1954- .

Honduras

3379 Honduras. Oficina de Cooperación Intelectual
Obra material del Gobierno del Dr. Galvez; 2 años y medio de administración pública. Tegucigalpa, Talleres Tipo-Litográficos 'Ariston,' 1951, 150p.

Mexico

3380 Alarcón Zaragoza, David
Los ferrocarriles como servicio público. México, 1950, 147p.

3381 Banco Nacional Hipotecario Urbano y de Obras Públicas, S. A., México
Obras y servicios públicos. México, 1959- .

3382 *Boletin.* No. 1- , México, Comisión Federal de Electricidad, 1950-

3383 Bermúdez Limón, Carlos
Las obras públicas y el desarrollo económico de México. México, 1960, 236p.

3384 Campo Carballo, María E. del
La concesión de servicio público. México, 1956, 118p.

3385 Galván Escobedo, José
El crédito para obras públicas. México, 1947, 317p.

3386 Gasio Campuzano, Alfonso
La abolición del derecho de la huelga en las empresas de servicios públicos. México, 1963, 97p.

3387 López Rosado, Diego G.
La política de obras públicas en México. México, 1948, 347p.

3388 México (Federal District) Depto. del Distrito Federal
Informe de las obras públicas realizadas. México, 1956-

3389 Ortiz Gutiérrez, Leonel
La concesión de servicio público. México, 1956, 118p.

3390 Serna Maciel, José M.
La Comisión Federal de Electricidad y la nacionalización de la industria eléctrica. México, 1961, 166p.

3391 Serrano Rebeil, Ernesto
La huelga en los servicios públicos. México, 1951, 84p.

3392 Solano Yañez, Delfino
Las características de la reglamentación de los servicios públicos. México, 1952, 69p.

3393 Transmisiones. 2a. época. v. 15- México, 1955-

Nicaragua

3394 Jiménez Castillo, Francisco J.
Servicios públicos. León, 1946, 28p.

3395 Nicaragua. Ministerio de Fomento y Obras Públicas
Boletín de fomento. Managua, 1951- .

Panama

3396 Panamá. Ministerio de Obras Públicas
Memorias. Panamá, 1957- .

3397 Rangel M., Carlos
Historia del Cuerpo de Bomberos de Panamá: bodas de brillantes, 1887-1962. Panamá, Impr. Nacional, 1962, 528p.

Paraguay

3398 Peña Villamil, Manuel
La concesión de servicios públicos: doctrina y legislación. Asunción, Ed. Lapacho, 1957, 246p.

Peru

3399 Peru. Ministerio de Fomento y Obras Públicas
Boletín. año 1 . Lima, 1956- .

Uruguay

3400 Congreso de Integración Eléctrica Regional. 1st, Montevideo, 1964
Documentos. Montevideo, Comisión para la Integración Eléctrica Regional, 1965, 275p.

3401 Ganón, Isaac
Municipalización de servicios públicos. Montevideo, 1952, 169p.

3402 Montevideo. Intendencia Municipal. Depto. de Arquitectura
Memoria. Montevideo, 1951- .

3403 Uruguay. Ministerio de Obras Públicas
Boletín oficial. año 1, no. 1- , Montevideo, 1951-

Venezuela

3404 Asociación Venezolana de Ingenieros Eléctricos & Mecánicos. Sociedad Venezolana de Ingenieros de Petróleo. Sociedad Venezolana de Planificación
Mesa redonda; la utilización de los recursos energéticos en Venezuela, Caracas, Octubre 1964. Caracas, La Comisión Organizadora de la Mesa Redonda, 1965, 68p.

3405 Venezuela. Junta de Gobierno
Aspectos fundamentales de una obra de gobierno, 1950-1951 . . . Caracas, 1951? 24p.

3406 Venezuela. Ministerio de Obras Públicas
Exposición de obras públicas, 1950. Caracas, 1950? unpaged.

3407 Venezuela. Ministerio de Obras Públicas
Obras públicas nacionales. Caracas, 1949-1950- .

3408 Venezuela
Obras dadas el servicio durante le segundo año de gobierno del coronel Marcos Pérez Jiménez e inauguraciones que se efectuarán entre el 2 y 9 de diciembre de 1954. Caracas, Impr. Nacional, 1954, 149p.

Periodical Articles

General

3409 Koeb, B.A.
"The Rise and Fall of Public Utilities: an Appraisal of Risk." Journal of business 37, October 1964, p. 329-345.

3410 Lam, W.M.C.
"The Lighting of Cities." Architectural record 137, June 1965, p. 210-214.

3411 MacMeekin, J.W.
"Utility Dividend Pay-out Policy." Public utilities fortnightly 75, March 1, 1965, p. 17-23.

Latin America

3412 Carlson, E.
"La Renovación Urbana y los Servicios Públicos en América Latina. Los Casos de Cali, Bogotá, y Maracaibo." Servicios públicos (7:1), January/February 1960, p. 38-44.

3413 Ortega Mata, R.
"La Electrificacion Planificada y sus Consecuencias Sociales en los Países Poco y Subdesarrollados de Latinoamérica." Río Piedras, Revista de ciencias sociales (8:1), March 1964, p. 79-102.

3414 Ortega Mata, R.
"Los Servicios Públicos en Relación con la Economía y el Derecho en los Países Poco Desarrollados." México, Revista mexicana de sociología (23:2), 1961, p. 385-402.

Argentina

3415 Frondizi, Arturo
"Retrenchment and Reorganization in the Public Services." Buenos Aires, Review of the River Plate (131:3448), January 30, 1962; p. 141-143, 160-163.

3416 Greca, Alcides
"Servicios Públicos Intermunicipales." Santa Fé, Revista de ciencias jurídicas y sociales 47, 1946, p. 21-40.

3417 Orencio Anaya, Laureano
"La Nacionalización de los Transportes y Servicios Públicos. Su Significado Desde el Punto de Vista de la Defensa Nacional." Buenos Aires, Hechos e ideas (12:94), January 1952, p. 391-429.

3418 Pinedo, F.
"The Proposed Unification of Electricity Services in Greater Buenos Aires Zone." Buenos Aires, Review of the River Plate (130:3436), September 30, 1961, p. 21-23- .

3419 Santa Cruz, Juan M.
"Estatización o Actividad Privada?" Rosario,

Revista del Instituto de Derecho Público y Ciencias Sociales 1, 1st semester 1958, p. 69-77.

3420 U.S. Chamber of Commerce in Argentina
"Argentine Power Production." Buenos Aires, Comments on Argentine trade (31:9), April 1952, p. 37-41.

3421 Wolfes, C.
"La Provisión de Energía Eléctrica en la Zona de la Gran Buenos Aires Durante la Guerra." Buenos Aires, Camoatí, April 1946, p. 23-24.

Brazil

3422 Centrais Elêtricas Brasileiras, S.A. (firm)
"Estrutura e Política de Investimentos da Eletrobras." Rio de Janeiro, Brazilian-American survey (4:23), 3d quarter 1964, p. 42-45.

3423 Cotrim, J.
"O Problema da Energia Elêtrica no Brasil." Rio de Janeiro, Revista do Conselho Nacional da Economia 3, 1960, p. 99-110.

3424 Fundaçao Getulio Vargas, Rio de Janeiro
"Eletrificação na Area São Paulo Paraná." Rio de Janeiro, Conjuntura econômica (XII:9), 1958, p. 69-71.

3425 "General Electric in Brazil--Forty Years Mutual Benefits." Rio de Janeiro, Brazilian business (35:4), April 1955, p. 22-26.

3426 Gomes, Pedro Andrade
"Os Serviços de Utilidade Pública no Brasil." Rio de Janeiro, Revista forense (135:576), June 1951, p. 371-375.

3427 Guimarães, Josué
"Energia Elétrica, um Problema." Rio de Janeiro, O observador econômico e financeiro (24:283), September 1959, p. 36-39.

3428 Maranhão, J.
"Plano Nacional de Obras, Empreendimentos e

Serviços Municipais." Rio de Janeiro, Revista do serviço público (88:3), September 1960, p. 256-295.

3429 Martins, A. Feitosa
"Distribuição Municipal de Energia Elêtrica." São Paulo, Revista brasiliense 37, September-October 1961, p. 28-46.

3430 Medeiros, Ocelio de
"Avaliação das Emprêsas de Serviço Público para Fins Tarifários." Rio de Janeiro, O observador econômico e financeiro (22:252), February 1957, p. 50-60.

3431 Monserrat, J.
"Economia, Estudo do Mes, Considerações Sôbre a Produção de Energia Elêtrica no Brasil." Pôrto Alegre, Intercâmbio (3:3/4), March/April 1955, p. 14-19.

3432 Oliveira, Américo Barbosa de
"O Planejamento Governamental e o Setor de Energia Elêtrica." Rio de Janeiro, O observador econômico e financeiro (23:264), February 1958, p. 6-14.

3433 "Programa de Melhoramentos Públicos para a Cidade de São Paulo. São Paulo, Engenharia (9:103), March 1951, p. 285-292.

3434 Reis, Hugo Regis dos
"Por uma Política Brasileira de Energia Elêtrica." São Paulo, Estudos sociais (3:7), March 1960, p. 267-279.

3435 Silva Monteiro, J. da
"O Problemà de Distribuição de Energia Elêtrica." Pôrto Alegre, O observador econômico e financeiro 277, 1959, p. 14-15.

Chile

3436 Compañía Chilena de Electricidad
"Plan de Progreso de Chilectra." Santiago, Panorama económico (16:234), November-December 1962, p. 282-283.

3437 Del Rio Aldunate, Hernán
"El Racionamiento de Energía Eléctrica y su Influencia en la Producción Industrial y en Algunos Servicios de Utilidad Pública." Santiago, Industria, May 1948, p. 312-322.

3438 Mardones, Francisco
"Plano Regulador de Santiago." Santiago, Boletín municipal October 1934, p. 25-39.

3439 Sáez, R.
"El Problema Eléctrico." Santiago, Revista chilena de ingeniería y anales del Instituto de Ingenieros (LXX:1-2), 1957, p. 3-12.

Colombia

3440 Colombia. Laws, statutes, etc.
"Creada la Corporación Nacional de Servicios Públicos. Decreto No. 2956 de 1955 (Nov. 10)." Bogotá, Diario oficial, Nov. 22, 1950, p. 708.

3441 Colombia. Laws, statutes, etc.
"Decreto No. 1653 de 1960 (Julio 15) por el Cual se Crea la Superintendencia de Regulación Económica y se Fijan sus Funciones." Bogotá, Diario oficial (97:30301), August 10, 1960, p. 389-390.

3442 Osorio, Armando
"La Producción de Energía Eléctrica en Colombia." Bogotá, Economía colombiana (3:8), December 1954, p. 439-442.

3443 Rippy, J. Fred
"The Development of Public Utilities in Colombia." Hispanic American historical review, February 1945, p. 132-137.

3444 Zúñiga, Miguel Angel
"Servicios Públicos." Popayán, Revista de la Universidad del Cauca 26, March 1960, p. 39-51.

Cuba

3445 "La Remodelación de La Habana. Las Obras del Ministro de Obras Públicas Ing. Manuel Febles Valdés: El Futuro Centro Civico." Havana,

Arquitectura (13:207), October 1950, p. 449-454.

Ecuador

3446 Miño Terán, L. A.
"Servicio de Agua Potable, Canalización, Luz y Fuerza Eléctrica en el Ecuador." Quito, *Boletín de obras públicas* 63-65, 1947-48, p. 133-147.

El Salvador

3447 Piloña Araujo, Gabriel
"Cooperativa Redistribuidora de Energía Eléctrica Salvadoreña. (C.R.E.E.S.)." San Salvador, *Económia salvadoreña* (2:2), 1953, p. 57-60.

Guatemala

3448 Santa Cruz, Enrique
"Camino a Seguir para la Electrificación Nacional." Guatemala, *Universidad de San Carlos* 44, January/April 1958, p. 105-124.

Mexico

3449 Compañía Mexicana de Luz y Fuerza
"Informe." México, *Investigación económica* (22: 87), 3d quarter 1962, p. 825-830.

3450 Galarza, Ernesto
"Electrical Public Utilities in Mexico." *Modern Mexico*, September 1936, p. 8-12.

3451 Hiriart B., Fernando
"El Problema Fundamental de la Ciudad de México. Hundimiento, Provisión de Aguas. Proyecto de las Obras Necesarias y Programa para su Realización." México, *Arquitectura* (11:52), December 1955, p. 196-199.

3452 Lama, M. de la
"L'Industrie Elèctrique au Méxique." Paris, *Revue générale de l'hydraulique* 78, 1957, p. 115-123.

3453 Lara Beautell, Cristóbal
"Desarrollo Económico y Electrificación." México, *Comercio exterior* (8:2), February 1958, p. 94-99.

3454 Maza, F. de la
"Informe Sobre la Pavimentación de la Ciudad de San Luis Potosí." México, Anales del Instituto de Investigaciones Estéticas 32, 1963, p. 148-152.

3455 Navarro Vásquez, A.
"La Electricidad y el Progreso de México." México, Temas contemporáneos (2:13-14), July 15, 1956, p. 1-14.

3456 Ortega Mata, R.
"La Electrificación del País y el Actual Período Gubernamental." México, Revista de economía 6, June 1965, p. 192-199.

3457 Ortega Mata, R.
"Necesidad de la Nacionalización Progresiva de la Industria de Servicios Eléctricos Públicos." México, Investigación económica, 3d quarter 1955, p. 335-352.

3458 Ortega Mata, R.
"Los Servicios en Relación con la Tecnología, la Economía y el Derecho en los Países Poco Desarrollados." México, Revista mexicana de sociología (23:2), May-August 1961, p. 385-402.

3459 Saint Albans, Mary
"Big Boom in Paradise. (Jalisco with its Capital City)." Modern Mexico, February 1945, p. 5-9.

Nicaragua

3460 "La Electrificación en Nicaragua." Managua, Revista conservadora de pensamiento centroamericano (10:54), March 1965, p. 3-6.

3461 "Expansión de la Industria Eléctrica de Nicaragua." Managua, El desarrollo económico nicaragüense (2:13), May 31, 1954, p. 4-8.

Panama

3462 Panama. Laws, statutes, etc.
"Decreto No. 15 de 13 de Mayo de 1953, por el Cual se Aprueba un Proyecto de Decreto-Ley

que Declara la Disposición Contenida en el Artículo 24 de la Ley No. 2 de 19 de Enero, 1953." Panamá, Gaceta oficial (50:12,099), June 13, 1953, p. 1-2.

Peru

3463 Belaunde Terry, Fernando
"La Evolución Urbana de Lima, una Obra de Juan Bromley y José Barbagelata." Lima, Arquitecto peruano, August 1945, entire issue.

3464 Caballero, Jorge E.
"La Electrificación del Perú." Lima, Fanal (13: 50), 1957, p. 7-11.

3465 Cole, John P.
"Some Town Planning Problems of Greater Lima." Liverpool, The town planning review (26:4), January 1956, p. 243-251.

3466 González Loli, Alejandro
"Los Servicios Eléctricos de Lima y el Perú." Lima, Revista de la Facultad de Ciencias Económicas y Comerciales 51, July/December 1954, p. 140-155.

3467 Mariotti, Carlos
"Economía del Desarrollo Eléctrico en el Perú." Lima, Boletín de la Sociedad Nacional de Minería y Petróleo 68, July/August 1959, p. 130-137.

3468 Peru. Laws, statutes, etc.
"Reglamentación de Impuesto a las Utilidades. Decreto Supremo." Lima, El Peruano 5468, July 6, 1959, p. 1.

3469 Peru. Laws, statutes, etc.
"Se Suspende en Arequipa, por el Año 1960, el Pago del Adelanto de Impuesto a las Utilidades. Decreto Supremo No. 14." Lima, El Peruano 5649, February 15, 1960, p. 1.

3470 Wunenburger, Gastón
"Estado Actual de la Producción de Energía Eléctrica en el Perú." Lima, Boletín de la Universidad Nacional de Ingeniería (33:4), April/June 1960, p. 57-76.

Venezuela

3471 Compañía Anónima de Administración y Fomento Electrico, Caracas
"El Programa de Electrificación de Venezuela." Caracas, Política (3:25), August 1963, p. 183-191.

3472 Corporación Venezolana de Fomento
"Plan Nacional de Electrificación." Caracas, Cuadernos de información económica (8:1), January/February 1956, p. 1-16.

3473 "El Programa de Electrificación." Caracas, Cuadernos de información económica venezolana (1:3), September/October 1949, p. 66-82.

3474 Páez Pumar, Mauro
"Características Jurídico-Económicas de los Bonos de la Avenida Bolívar." Caracas, Temas Económicos (1:3), March 1951, p. 77-89.

Part IV

SOCIOLOGY

COMMUNICATIONS
(including Moving Pictures; Newspapers; Publishing; Radio and Television)

Books

General

3475 Arons, Leon, & Mark A. May, eds.
Television and human behavior: tomorrow's research in mass communication. New York, Appleton-Century-Crofts, 1963, 307p.

3476 Blum, Eleanor
Reference books in the mass media; an annotated, selected booklist covering book publishing, broadcasting, films, newspapers, magazines and advertising. Urbana, University of Illinois Press, 1962, 103p.

3477 Bray, T.C.
The newspaper's role in modern society. St. Lucia, University of Queensland Press, 1965, 27p.

3478 Bryson, Lyman, ed.
Communication of ideas. New York, Cooper Square Publishers, 1964, 427p.

3479 Dizard, Wilson P.
Television: a world view. Syracuse, Syracuse University Press, 1966, 349p.

3480 Kahn, A.J.
Neighborhood information centers: a study and some proposals. New York, School of Social Work, Colombia University, 1966, 150p.

3481 Lawrence, Robert de T.
Rural mimeo newspapers; a guide to the production of low-cost community newspapers in developing countries. Paris, Unesco, 1965, 42p.

3482 McLuhan, H. M.
Understanding media; the extensions of man. New York, McGraw-Hill, 1964, 359p.

3483 Merrill, John C., et al
The foreign press. 2d ed. Baton Rouge, Louisiana State University Press, 1963, 256p.

3484 Park, Robert E.
Society. New York, Free Press, 1955, 358p.

3485 Schramm, Wilbur
Urbanization and the spread of information. Buenos Aires, Centro de Sociología Comparada, Instituto Torcuato di Tella, 1965, 125p.

3486 Siepmann, Charles A.
Radio, television and society. New York, Oxford University Press, 1950, 140p.

3487 Siller, B., et al
Television and radio news. New York, Macmillan, 1960, 227p.

3488 Unesco. Dept. of Mass Communications
World communications: press, radio, television, film. 4th ed. Paris, 1964, 380p.

3489 World radio handbook for listeners. Copenhagen, O. L. Johansen. Annual.

Latin America

3490 Centro Internacional de Estudios Superiores de Periodismo para América Latina
Dos semanas en la prensa de América Latina. Quito, 1967, 250p.

3491 Centro Internacional de Estudios Superiores de Periodismo para América Latina
La radio y la televisión frente a la necesidad cultural en América Latina. Quito, 1966, 392p.

3492 Chilcote, Ronald H.
The press in Latin America, Spain and Portugal; a summary of recent development. Stanford,

Institute of Hispanic American & Luso Brazilian Studies, Stanford University, 1963, 68p.

3493 Otero, G. A.
La cultura y el periodismo en América. Quito, Ed. Liebmann, 1953, 545p.

3494 Primera Mesa Redonda Centroamericana de Enseñanza de Periodismo: informe final, Managua, 18 al 22 de abril de 1966. Quito, Eds. CIESPAL, 1966, 130p.

3495 Sánchez, Rodrigo
Situación de la documentación y comunicación en Centro América. San José, Programa Interamericano de Información Popular, 1965, 21p.

3496 Unesco
Meeting of experts on development of information media in Latin America, Santiago, Chile, 1-13 February, 1961: report of the meeting; Unesco/MC/41. Paris, 1961, 37p.

3497 Valtierra, Angel
Las fuerzas que forjan la opinión pública: prensa, cine, radio, televisión. Bogotá, Ed. Pax, 1964, 558p.

3498 Waisanen, F. B.
Communication flow to traditional social systems. San José, Programa Interamericano de Información Popular, 1963, 6p.

3499 Waisanen, F. B.
Some perspectives for research in communication and development. San José, Programa Interamericano de Información Popular, 1965, 8p.

Argentina

3500 Castro Estevez, R. de
Historia de las comunicaciones argentinas. Buenos Aires, Ministerio de Comunicaciones, 1958, 530p.

3501 López Airagho, Antonio C.
Función social y económica de las vías de comuni-

cación, su importancia en la Argentina. Tucumán, Instituto de Vías de Comunicación, Universidad Nacional de Tucumán, 1950, 58p.

3502 Mulleady, Ricardo T.
Breve historia de la telefonía argentina: 1886-1956. Buenos Aires, Kraft, 1957, 70p.

3503 Petit de Murat, Ulises
Este cine argentino. Buenos Aires, Eds. del Carro de Tespis, 1959, 78p.

Brazil

3504 Nobre, F. Silva
A margem do cinema brasileiro. Rio de Janeiro, Pongetti, 1963, 158p.

3505 Rêde Paranaense de Rádio
Dados e informações. Curitiba, 1962? unpaged.

3506 Rocha, Glauber
Revisão crítica do cinema brasileiro. Rio de Janeiro, Ed. Civilização Brasileira, 1963, 147p.

3507 Viany, Alex, pseud.
Introdução ao cinema brasileiro. Rio de Janeiro, Instituto Nacional do Livro, 1959, 487p.

Chile

3508 Baros González, Mario
Ministerio de Telecomunicaciones. Santiago, 1957, 63p.

Colombia

3509 Castro, José F.
Estructura de la radiofusión. Bogotá, Ed. Cultura, 1962, 324p.

Costa Rica

3510 Instituto Costarricense de Electricidad
National telecommunications project, Costa Rica; feasibility study: first stage, 1965 . . . San José, 1962, 75p.

3511 McNelly, John T., & Augusto Torres
El uso de los medios de comunicación en una capital latinoamericana. San José, Programa Interamericano de Información Popular, 1963, 116p.

Cuba

3512 Valdés Rodríguez, José M.
Ojeada al cine cubano, 1906-1958. Havana, 1963, 15p.

Ecuador

3513 Centro Internacional de Estudios Superiores de Periodismo para América Latina
Utilización de los medios de información en Quito. Quito, 1966, 106p.

Mexico

3514 Amado G., Francisco, & Alicia Echeverría M.
El cine en México; estudio sociológico. México, 1960, 219p.

3515 Blanco Moheno, R.
Autopsia del periodismo mexicano. México, Libro Mex, 1961, 357p.

3516 García Riera, Emilio
El cine mexicano. México, Eds. Era, 1963, 237p.

3517 México. Secretaría de Comunicaciones y Transportes
Comunicaciones y transportes. México (época 2:1), January-March 1966- .

3518 México. Secretaría de Gobernación
Adolfo López Mateos y la función social de la radiodifusión (AIR). México, 1961, 28p.

3519 Musik Kolis, Guillermo A.
El servicio público postal mexicano. México, 1956, 109p.

3520 Ruiz Castañeda, M. del C.
. . . historia de la imprenta y la prensa jalisciences. (In Estudios sociológicos. Segundo Congreso Nacional de Sociología, 1951. México, Universidad Nacional, 1953, p. 103-116.)

3521 Salas Soto, Virginia
Radiodifusoras comerciales en México. México, 1953, 156p.

Panama

3522 Panama (City) Universidad. Instituto Panameño de la Opinión Pública
Boletín. Panamá, 1949-

Paraguay

3523 Bejarano, Ramón C.
Vías y medios de comunicaciones del Paraguay, 1811-1960. Asunción, Ed. Toledo, 1963, 262p.

Peru

3524 Waples, Douglas
Public communication in Peru. (In Chicago. University. Committee on Communication. Studies in public communication, Summer, 1959. Chicago, 1959, p. 61-65).

Periodical Articles

General

3525 Deutsch, K.W.
"On Social Communication and the Metropolis." Daedalus, Winter 1961, p. 99-110.

3526 Edelstein, A.S., & O.N. Larsen
"The Weekly Press Contribution to a Sense of Urban Community." Journalism quarterly (37:4), Autumn 1960, p. 489-498.

3527 Wilson, E.C.
"Problems of Survey Research in Modernizing Areas." Public opinion quarterly (22:3), Fall 1958, p. 230-234.

Latin America

3528 Aguiar, C.L.
"Struggles for Christ and Life." Catholic press annual 3, 1962, p. 9-11.

3529 Bastide, Roger
"L'Amérique Latine Vue à Travers le Miroir de son Cinéma." Le Havre, Revue de psychologie des peuples (15:4), 4th quarter, 1960, p. 366-379.

3530 Bogart, L.
"Changing Markets and Media in Latin America." Public opinion quarterly (23:2), Summer 1959, p. 159-167.

3531 Castaño, L.
"El Desarrollo de los Medios de Información en América Latina y la Crisis de la Libertad de Expresión." México, Ciencias políticas y sociales (8:28), April-June 1962, p. 291-306.

3532 Deutschmann, Paul K., et al
"Mass Media Used by Sub-Elites in 11 Latin American Countries." Journalism quarterly (38:4), Autumn 1961, p. 460-472.

3533 Fabregat Cúneo, R.
"Principales Influencias del Cine Sobre el Público." México, Revista mexicana de sociología (20:1), January-February 1958, p. 27-55.

3534 Gabel, E.
"Report on the Second Congress of the Latin American Catholic Press Union." Catholic journalist 13, September 1962, p. 15.

3535 Hopper, Rex D., & J.W. Harris
"Culture de Masas en Latinoamérica." México, Revista mexicana de sociología (24:3), September-December 1962, p. 735-750.

3536 Knopp, R.
"How We Look to Latin Americans." America 100, March 7, 1959, p. 662-664.

3537 Ortega Mata, R.
"La Electrificación Planeada y sus Consecuencias Sociales en los Países Poco y Subdesarrollados de Latino-América." Rio Piedras, Revista de de ciencias sociales (8:1), March 1964, p. 79-102.

3538 "The Press in Latin America: Catholic Press Association Program." America 105, September 2, 1961, p. 678-679.

3539 Unesco. Secretariat
"El Desarrollo de los Medios de Información en Hispanoamérica." México, Ciencias políticas y sociales (5:15), January-March 1959, p. 113-121.

Argentina

3540 Gardner, Mary A.
"The Argentine Press Since Perón." Journalism quarterly 37, Summer 1960, p. 426-430.

3541 Patin, T.
"Un Problema de la Radio y la TV Argentinas." Buenos Aires, Estudios 552, March-April 1964, p. 127-132.

3542 Potenze, J.
"Argentine Movies. River Plate Film Industry is Rich in Beauty and Talent." Américas (6:8), August 1954, p. 20-23, 44-46.

Brazil

3543 Fenin, G.N.
"Film Progress in Brazil." Quarterly of film, radio & television 10, Spring 1956, p. 253-256.

3544 "Hot Line: Demand for Telephones." Newsweek 62, October 21, 1963, p. 8-10.

3545 Matos, O. Nogueira de
"Evolução das Vias de Comunicação no Estado do Rio de Janeiro." São Paulo, Boletím paulista de geografia 3, 1949, p. 51-75.

3546 Pires, A.S.
"Ads Infinitum: Between the Lines of the Classified in Brazil and United States." Américas 7, May 1955, p. 7-9.

3547 "Reorganization of Communications Services in Brazil." Rio de Janeiro, Conjuntura econômica internacional 8, March 1961, p. 29-39.

3548 Silva, F. Barbosa e
"On the Brazilian Screen." Américas 5, June 1953, p. 13-16.

3549 Silveira, T.
"Brazil's Biggest Daily, 'Estado de São Paulo,' Basks in World Fame." Rio de Janeiro, Brazilian business (40:9), September 1960, p. 28-29, 58-59.

Central America

3550 Alisky, Marvin
"Central American Radio." Quarterly of film, radio and television 10, Fall 1955, p. 59-61.

3551 "Television in Central America." Latin American report (VI:5), March-April 1967, p. 25-28.

Chile

3552 Carter, Roy E., & Orlando Sepúlveda
"Some Patterns of Mass Media Use in Santiago de Chile." Journalism quarterly 41, Spring 1964, p. 216-224.

3553 Matas, R.
"Chile on the Air." Américas 7, October 1955, p. 6-9.

3554 Rojas Castro, A.
"Iniciación y Desarrollo de la Cinematografía Educativa en Chile." Santiago, Revista de educación (15:64), May 1955, p. 59-62.

Colombia

3555 O'Hara, H.
"Voice of the Andes." Américas 13, September 1961, p. 27-30.

3556 Scully, M.
"Adventure in Inspiration: Radio Broadcasting in Sutatenza, Colombia." Reader's digest 65, September 1954, p. 25-28.

Costa Rica

3557 Edwards, H.T.
"Power Structure and its Communication Behavior

in San José, Costa Rica." Journal of Inter-American studies (IX:2), April 1967, p. 236-247.

3558 McNelly, John T., & E. Fonseca
"Media Use and Political Interest at the University of Costa Rica." Journalism quarterly 41, Spring 1964, p. 225-231.

3559 McNelly, John T., & Paul J. Deutschmann
"Media Use and Socioeconomic Status in a Latin American Capital." Gazette (9:1), 1963, p. 1-15.

Cuba

3560 Bueno Montoya, M.
"La Prensa Cubana en el Régimen de Fidel Castro." Madrid, Nuestro tiempo (14:81), March 1961, p. 315-328.

Ecuador

3561 Hernández Alonso, F.
"Las Comunicaciones en un País Andino: Ecuador." Madrid, Estudios geográficos (17:64), August 1956, p. 415-441.

3562 O'Hara, H.
"The Voice of the Andes: Station Reaches Four Corners of Ecuador as World Listens In." Américas 13, September 1961, p. 27-30.

Honduras

3563 Gardner, Mary A.
"The Press of Honduras: a Portrait of Five Dailies." Journalism quarterly (40:1), Winter 1963, p. 75-82.

Mexico

3564 Alisky, Marvin
"Early Mexican Broadcasting." Hispanic American historical review 34, November 1954, p. 513-526.

3565 Alisky, Marvin
"Growth of Newspapers in Mexican Provinces." Journalism quarterly 37, Winter 1960, p. 75-82.

3566 Alvarado, Rafael
"Mejor en Sumo Grado el Servicio de Transportes Eléctricos del F. F." México, Todo, December 4, 1947, p. 30-31.

3567 Bataillon, Claude
"Communications de Masse et Vie Urbaine au Mexique." Paris, Communications 3, March 1964, p. 19-35.

3568 Erlandson, E.H.
"The Press in Mexico: Past, Present and Future." Journalism quarterly 41, Spring 1964, p. 232-236.

3569 Figueroa, José
"Nuestras Vías de Comunicación." México, Revista de economía (23:10), October 1960, p. 283-288.

3570 Morton, S.
"Expanding Mexico's Communication Network." México, Mexican life (38:1), January 1962, p. 27-29.

3571 Morton, S.
"Widening Mexico's Routes of Communication." México, Mexican life (37:3), March 1961, p. 27-29.

3572 Nicholson, I.
"Mexican Films, Their Past and Their Future." Quarterly of film, radio & television 10, Spring 1956, p. 248-252.

3573 Rodríguez Sala de Gomez Gil, M. L.
"Incremento de las Comunicaciones en México e Influencia en Algunos Aspectos Socio-económicos." México, Revista mexicana de sociología (25:1), January-April 1963, p. 189-202.

3574 Rosaldo, R.
México y sus Películas." Ann Arbor, The modern language journal (36:2), February 1952, p. 84-86.

Peru

3575 Alisky, Marvin
"The Peruvian Press and the Nixon Incident."

Journalism quarterly 35, Fall 1958, p. 411-419.

3576 Barreda Bustamante, J. F.
"Forum Sobre el Desarrollo Económico del Perú y las Vías de Comunicacion." Lima, Boletín de la Universidad Nacional de Ingeniería 31, April-June 1958, p. 3-14.

3577 Barreda Bustamante, J. F.
"Vías de Comunicación para el Desarrollo Económico del País." Lima, Boletín de la Sociedad Geográfica de Lima 79, May-August 1962, p. 22-40.

3578 "Economic Position of the Peruvian Corporation Railways." Lima, Andean airmail & Peruvian times 18, September 5, 1958, p. 6-8.

Venezuela

3579 Lluch S. de Mons, H.
"Ensayo Sobre la Cinematográfia Nacional." Caracas, Cultura universitaria 30, March-April 1952, p. 63-70.

3580 Venezuela. Consejo Nacional de Vialidad
"Historia de las Vías de Comunicación en Venezuela." Caracas, Temas económicos (1:12), December 1951, p. 1-12.

West Indies and the Caribbean

3581 Richardson, W.
"The Place of Radio in the West Indies." Port-of-Spain, Caribbean quarterly 7, December 1961, p. 158-162.

COMMUNITY DEVELOPMENT

Books

General

3582 American Universities Field Staff
Expectant peoples; nationalism and development. Ed. by K.H. Silvert. New York, Random House, 1963, 489p.

3583 Batten, T.R.
Training for community development: a critical study of method. London, Oxford University Press, 1962, 192p.

3584 Community development abstracts. Washington, U.S. Dept. of State, Agency for International Development, Office of Technical Cooperation & Research, Rural & Community Development Service, 1963? 281p.

3585 Community development review. v. 1- , Washington, 1956-

3586 International Conference of Social Work. 11th, Rio de Janeiro, 1962
Urban and rural community development: proceedings. Rio de Janeiro, 1963, 351p.

3587 International Seminar on the Role of Voluntary Agencies in the Development of the Community. 3d, Haifa, 1963
. . . Discussions and lectures. Haifa, Mt. Carmel International Training Center for Community Services, 1964, 305p.

3588 King, Clarence
Working with people in community action: an international casebook for trained community workers and volunteer community leaders. New York, As-

sociation Press, 1965, 192p.

3589 New York (State) Dept. of Commerce. Division of Economic Development
Your home town's future; a manual for community development. Albany, New York State Dept. of Commerce, 1945, 32p.

3590 Osborn, F.J., & A. Whittick
The new towns: the answer to megalopolis. London, Hill, 1963, 376p.

3591 Sehnert, F.H.
A functional framework for the action process in community development. Carbondale, Southern Illinois University Press, 1964? 182p.

3592 United Nations
Approaches to community development in urban areas; notes on recent experience in 24 countries and territories; (document ST/SOA/ser.O/32). New York, 1959, 19p.

3593 United Nations. Secretariat
Social aspects of urban development; report. Document A/AC. 35/L. 335. New York, 1961, 150p.

3594 United Nations. Ad Hoc Group of Experts on Community Development
Community development and national development; report by an ad hoc group of experts appointed by the Secretary-General of the United Nations; document E/CN.5/379/rev. 1. New York, 1963, 78p.

3595 United Nations. Secretary-General, 1953-1961 (Hammarskjold)
Community development in urban areas; report. Document ST/SOA/43, E/CN.5/356/rev. 1. New York, Dept. of Economic & Social Affairs, 1961, 44p.

3596 United Nations. Secretary General
The applicability of community development to urban areas. New York, 1961, 53p.

Latin America

3597 Acción en Venezuela
Los problemas que enfrentan hoy a América Latina. Caracas, 1962, 8p.

3598 Albano, M.J.R.
El factor humano en los programas de rehabilitación de tugurios. Bogotá, Centro Interamericano de Vivienda, 1957, 19p.

3599 Association for Latin American Studies. Mid-West Council
The community in revolutionary Latin America; selected papers presented at the annual conference . . . October 24-26, 1963, Western Michigan University, Kalamazoo. Lawrence, Center of Latin American Studies, University of Kansas, 1964, 36p.

3600 Carley, Verna A., & Elmer A. Starch
Report on community development programs in Jamaica, Puerto Rico, Bolivia and Peru. Washington, International Cooperation Administration, 1955, 76p.

3601 Chamber of Commerce of the United States of America. Construction & Community Development Dept.
Case studies in community development. Comp. by S.H. Evans. Washington, 1963, 412p.

3602 Inter-American Development Bank
Community development: theory and practice. Round Table, Inter-American Development Bank, Mexico City, April 1966. Washington, 1967? 280p.

3603 Inter American Seminar on Municipal Studies. 2d, San Diego, California, 1960
Community development in the Western Hemisphere; selected papers. San Diego, Public Affairs Research Institute, San Diego State College, 1961, 88p.

3604 International Labor Office
The Andean programme. Geneva, 1958, 103p.

3605 Mezirow, J.D.
The literature of community development: a biblio-

graphic guide. Washington, Training Division, Peace Corps, 1964, 177p.

3606 Stevenson, Rafael, et al
La planificación agraria; su inter-relación con los problemas de urbanización y una reforma agraria como su instrumento. Bogotá, Fundación Universidad de América, Centro de Planificación Integral, 1960, 94p.

3607 United Nations
Programa de desarrollo de la comunidad rural en el Brasil, el Ecuador y Perú: informe. Washington, Economic Development Institute, International Bank for Reconstruction & Development, 1964, 37p.

3608 United Nations. Secretariat
Report of the United Nations study tour on community development to Mexico, Costa Rica, Jamaica and Puerto Rico. New York, 1958, 43p.

3609 Violich, Francis
Bibliography on community development applied to urban areas in Latin America. Eugene, Council of Planning Librarians, 1963, 20p.

3610 Ware, Carolyn (Farrar)
Organización de la comunidad para el bienestar social. Washington, Unión Panamericana, 1962, 260p.

Bolivia

3611 Rubio Orbe, Gonzalo
Educación fundamental. Quito, Casa de la Cultura Ecuatoriana, 1954, 103p.

Brazil

3612 Willems, Emilio
Uma vila brasileira; tradição e transição. São Paulo, Difusão Européia do Livro, 1961, 222p.

3613 Wisdom, Robert W.
Community development in Brazil. Rio de Janeiro, U.S. Operations Mission, Public & Business Adminstration Division, 1959, 19p.

Colombia

3614 Bogotá, Colombia. Consejo Municipal del Distrito Especial
La acción comunal en el Distrito Especial de Bogotá. Bogotá, 1959, 58p.

3615 CARE & Federación Nacional de Cafeteros de Colombia
Acción comunal en Colombia. Bogotá, 1962, 175p.

3616 Centro Interamericano de Vivienda y Planeamiento
Bello Horizonte: proyecto de rehabilitación urbana. Bogotá, 1958, 94p.

3617 Corporación Nacional de Servicios Públicos. Depto. de Vivienda
Centros comunales rurales: plan integral de mejoramiento rural, centro piloto de La Chamba. Bogotá, 1956, 73p.

3618 Fondo Nacional de Caminos Vecinales
Hacia un mejoramiento social. Bogotá, 1962, 40p.

Ecuador

3619 Estupiñán Tello, Julio
La educación fundamental. Quito, Casa de la Cultura Ecuatoriana, 1957, 199p.

Guyana

3620 British Guiana. Ministry of Community Development & Education
Community development in British Guiana. Report on pilot projects. Georgetown. Annual.

Haiti

3621 Antoine, Charles
Quelques considérations sur le milieu rural à Déseaux, une expérience de développement communautaire dans la vallée de l'Artibonite. Port-au-Prince, Théodore, 1959, 59p.

Mexico

3622 Campos, C.M., & J. Arroyo Riestra
Desarrollo de las comunidades rurales. México, Costa-Amic, 1963, 159p.

3623 Edmonson, Munro S., et al
Synoptic studies of Mexican culture. New Orleans, Middle American Research Institute, Tulane University, 1957, 240p.

3624 Leet, Glen
Computer-aided community development reporting in Mexico. New York, Community Development Foundation, 1964, 37p.

3625 México. Dirección General de Alfabetización y Educatión Extraescolar
Informe de labores y nuevos lineamientos; memoria, 1944-1955. México, Secretaría de Educación Pública, 1956, 90p.

Peru

3626 Bazán, F.M.
El indio y la cooperativa agrícola. Lima, Impr. Torres Aguirre, 1936, 55p.

3627 Dobyns, Henry F., & Mario C. Vásquez
The Cornell Peru Project bibliography and personnel. Ithaca, Dept. of Anthropology, Cornell University, 1964, 55p.

Uruguay

3628 Silveira, Víctor E.
Las misiones sociopedagógicas en el Uruguay. Washington, Unión Panamericana, 1960, 51p.

Venezuela

3629 Fundación para el Desarrollo de la Comunidad y Fomento Municipal
Programa para el desarrollo del Distrito Falcón. Caracas, 1962, 21p.

3630 Schaedel, Richard, & Robert W. Wisdom
Community development in Venezuela. Caracas, U.S. Agency for International Development, 1962, 28p.

Periodical Articles

General

3631 Adams, L. W.
"Urban Community Development: its Role in Developing Countries." Community development review (8:1), March 27-29, 1963, p. 27-29.

3632 Chatterjee, B.
"Some Issues in Urban Community Development." Rome, International review of community development 9, 1962, p. 113-124.

3633 Groeman, S.
"Community Development in Urban Areas." Rome, International review of community development 7, 1961, p. 61-69.

3634 Meister, A.
"Urbanization and Community Development." Community development review (6:3), September 1961, p. 1-3.

3635 Milligan, F. S.
"Community Development in the Urban Neighborhood." Rome, International review of community development 5, 1960, p. 177-185.

3636 Provinse, J.
"Community Development Research and Evaluation." Community development review (5:4), December 1960, p. 31-50.

3637 Ranade, S. N.
"Urban Community Development: its Nature and Scope." London, Community development bulletin (11:3), June 1960, p. 67-71.

3638 Stensland, P. G.
"Urban Community Development." Community development review 8, March 1958, p. 32-39.

3639 Ulrey, O.
'Training and Development Centers in Urban Com-

munities.' (In his "Training and Development Centers in Patterns of National Development." _Agricultural economics report #12_, Dept. of Agricultural Economics, Michigan State University, June 1965, p. 40).

Latin America

3640 Adams, Richard N.
"Una Nota Sobre el Mito de la Comunidad." Rio de Janeiro, _América latina_ (6:4), October-December 1963, p. 125-127.

3641 Anderson, David C., & Alex Zipperer
"Two Aspects of Urban Community Development: an Operating Philosophy, an Operational Criticism." _Peace Corps volunteer_ (IV:11), September 1966, p. 22-25.

3642 Chávez Nuñez, F.
"El Papel de las Cooperativas en los Programas de Desarrollo de la Comunidad Rural en América." Bogotá, _Economía gran-colombiana_ (4:12), 1961, p. 347-356.

3643 Diegues, Manoel
"Transformações na Comunidade Rural da América Latina." Rio de Janeiro, _América latina_ (7:3), July-September 1964, p. 25-36.

3644 Engl, C.P., & J.N. Parmer
"The Peace Corps." _Annals of the American Academy of Political & Social Science 365_, May 1966, p. 1-146.

3645 Konig, R.
"Interrogantes Relativas a la Tipología de las Comunidades Rurales y Urbanas." México, _Revista mexicana de sociología_ (20:3), September-December 1958, p. 679-685.

3646 Pastor, José M. F.
"La Liberación de las Fuerzas Internas de la Comunidad." México, _Panoramas_ (2:9), May-June 1964, p. 105-121.

3647 Pozas Arciniega, Ricardo
"La Planificación Regional y el Desarrollo de la Comunidad." México, Revista de economía (27:7), July 1964, p. 203-206.

3648 Smith, Thomas L.
"Una Sugestión para la Planeación de las Comunidades Rurales en América Latina." México, Revista mexicana de sociología (22:2), May-August 1960, p. 441-447.

3649 Stavenhagen, Rodolfo
"The Community in Latin America: a Changing Myth." Rio de Janeiro, América latina (6:2), April-June 1963, p. 131-132.

3650 Whitten, Norman E.
"Power Structure and Sociocultural Change in Latin American Communities." Social forces (43:3), March 1965, p. 320-329.

Bolivia

3651 Schweng, L. D.
"An Indian Community Development Project in Bolivia." México, América indígena (22:2), April 1962, p. 155-168.

Brazil

3652 Beemer, Chris
"Fighting Apathy in a Rio Suburb." Peace Corps volunteer (IV:11), September 1966, p. 10-11.

3653 Miocque, R.
"Les Cités Expérimentales du Brésil." Paris, Société des Ingénieurs Civiles de France, Memoires (113:11), November 1960, p. 41-51.

3654 Paulson, Belden
"Difficulties and Prospects for Community Development in Northeast Brazil." Inter-American economic affairs 17, Spring 1964, p. 37-58.

3655 Ries, A. F. Pereira
"O Desenvolvimento e a Organização da Comunidade como Instrumento do Desenvolvimento Nacional."

Montevideo, Cuadernos latinoamericanos de economía humana (4:10), 1961, p. 76-87.

3656 Ríos, José A.
"La Cooperación y la Integración en el Desarrollo de la Comunidad: La Experiencia del Brasil." Pátzcuaro, Boletín trimestral (9:2), Spring 1957, p. 91-99.

Central America

3657 Huizer, G.
"A Community Development Experience in a Central American Village." Rome, International review of community development 12, 1963, p. 161-187.

Chile

3658 Levy, G.
"Lo Valledor, una Provechosa Experiencia Estudiantil en el Desarrollo de una Comunidad." Santiago, Boletín de la Universidad de Chile 23, August 1961, p. 54-58.

3659 Severino Mauna, N.
"El Centro de Educación Fundamental de Ancud, Chile." Montevideo, Boletín del Instituto Interamericano del Niño (34:4), December 1960, p. 372-390.

Colombia

3660 "Air Force as Welfare Worker." Time 83, February 21, 1964, p. 43.

3661 Alderfer, E.G.
"The People, Sí." Américas 13, May 1961, p. 2-9.

3662 Kelley, Joseph B.
"Community Organization in Colombia, S.A." Catholic charities review 48, March 1964, p. 13-16.

3663 McNamee, M.B.
"Barrio in Bogotá." Américas 108, January 19, 1963, p. 95-97.

3664 Morales Velandia, H.
"Necesidad de la Acción Comunal." Medellín, Ciencias económicas (6:17), October 1960, p. 177-184.

3665 Ware, Carolyn (Farrar)
"Community Development in Urban Areas, Initial Experience in Bogotá, Colombia." Community development review (7:1), June 1962, p. 43-61.

Ecuador

3666 Cowan, P.
"A Program Dies in the City." Peace Corps volunteer (V:7), May 1967, p. 2-5.

3667 Luea, Michael
"Taking a 'Broad Shotgun Approach' to Development." Peace Corps volunteer (IV:11), September 1966, p. 29-31.

El Salvador

3668 Huizer, G.
"A Community Development Experience in a Central American Village." México, América indígena (24:3), July 1964, p. 221-231.

Guyana

3669 Grant, C.H.
"The Politics of Community Development in British Guiana, 1954-57." Mona, Social & economic studies 14, June 1965, p. 170-182.

3670 Rosane, R.E.
"Mackenzie in Metamorphosis: the Emerging Need for Institutions of Social Authority in Guayana's Second Community." Geneva, Bulletin of the International Institute for Labor Studies 1, October 1966, p. 65-79.

Haiti

3671 Bretones, G.J.
"Expériences de Développement Communautaire en Haiti." Rome, International review of community development 10, 1962, p. 76-87.

3672 Delmas, G.
"Le Mouvement se Prouve en Marchant." Port-au-Prince, Revue du travail (10:10), May 1961, p. 38-49.

3673 Lubin, Maurice A.
"Quelques Aspects des Communautés Rurales d'Haiti." Rio de Janeiro, América latina (5:1-2), January-June 1962, p. 3-22.

Jamaica

3674 Reveley, Bob
"He Was 'White Trash Boy' in the Slum." Peace Corps volunteer (IV:11), September 1966, p. 32-33.

Mexico

3675 Belshaw, Michael
"Aspects of Community Development in Rural Mexico." Inter-American economic affairs 15, Spring 1962, p. 71-94.

3676 Caso, Antonio
"Les Buts de la Politique Indigéniste au Méxique." Geneva, Revue internationale du travail (72:6), December 1955, p. 568-576.

3677 Castillo Pérez, Isidoro
"Problemas Educativos de México." México, Ideario de la educación fundamental 25, March-April 1960, p. 1-76.

3678 Cornejo Cabrera, E.
"Necesidad de Enmarcar los Programas de Mejoramiento Agrario en una Planificación Regional." México, Revista mexicana de sociología (24:2), May-August 1962, p. 401-436.

3679 Foster, George M.
"The Dyadic Contact: a Model for the Social Structure of a Mexican Peasant Village." American anthropologist (63:6), December 1961, p. 1173-1192.

3680 Kunkel, J. H.
"Economic Autonomy and Social Change in Mexican Villages." Economic development and cultural

change (10:1), October 1961, p. 51-63.

3681 Pozas Arciniega, Ricardo
"Niveles del Desarrollo y la Dinámica en la Comunidad." México, *Ciencias políticas y sociales* (9:34), October-December 1963, p. 539-553.

3682 Ríos Díaz, A.
"Los Problemas de Desarrollo Regional y el Desarrollo de la Comunidad." México, *Revista de economía* (27:5), May 1964, p. 141-147.

3683 Stother, R. S.
"Golden Eggs of Pátzcuaro." *Reader's digest 80*, April 1962, p. 238-245.

3684 Varela Resendez, S.
"Aspectos de la Educación Fundamental en México." Montevideo, *Boletín del Instituto Interamericano del Niño* (35:2), June 1961, p. 85-106.

Peru

3685 Dobyns, Henry F., et al
"Desarrollo Comunal y Regional; Experimento Conjunto del Proyecto 'Perú-Cornell.'" Lima, *Perú indígena* (9:20-21), January-June 1961, p. 133-139.

3686 Faron, Louis C.
"The Formation of Two Indigenous Communities in Costal Peru." *American anthropologist* (62:3), June 1960, p. 437-453.

3687 Holmberg, Allan R.
"The Changing Values and Institutions of Vicos." *American behavioral scientist 8*, March 1965, p. 3-8.

3688 Lear, John
"Reaching the Heart of South America; Vicos Project." *Saturday review 45*, November 3, 1962, p. 55-58.

3689 Vasallo Bedoya, S.
"La Función Social de la Escuela Rural en la

Educación de la Familia Campesina." Montevideo, Boletín del Instituto Interamericano del Niño (34:3), September 1960, p. 312-332.

Uruguay

3690 Gandara, L.W.
"Como Iniciar Experiencias de Educación Fundamental en el Medio Rural." Montevideo, Anales del Consejo Nacional de Enseñanza Primaria y Normal (23:4-6), April-June 1960, p. 109-111.

3691 Holz, V.R.
"Community Development Needs in Uruguay." Rome, International review of community development 112, 1963, p. 133-143.

3692 Wiles, Christopher
"The Curious Marriage of Basketball and Urban Community Development." Peace Corps volunteer (IV:11), September 1966, p. 26-28.

Venezuela

3693 Culhane, E.K.
"Big, Bad Businessmen; Venezuelan Institute of Community Action." America 110, March 14, 1964, p. 331.

3694 Ozaeta, P.M.
"Iniciativa y Desarrollo de la Comunidad." Caracas, El farol (25:208), January-March 1964, p. 35-40.

3695 Pérez, J.L., & E. Caldera
"Estudio Sociométrico de la Comunidad Campo Ayacucho." Caracas, Sociología (1:2), December 1961, p. 28-51.

3696 Silva Michelena, José A.
"Estudio Sociológico de dos Comunidades Rurales del Oriente Venezolano." Caracas, Sociología (1:1), April 1961, p. 44-79.

3697 Thelen, J.
"Almost Like Home." Peace Corps volunteer (IV: 11), September 1966, p. 6-7.

CRIME AND JUVENILE DELINQUENCY

Crime

Books

General

3698 Bajarlía, Juan J.
Sadismo y masoquismo en la conducta criminal. Buenos Aires, Abeledo-Perrot, 1959, 133p.

3699 Cajías K., Huáscar
Criminología. 1st ed. 2v. La Paz, Librería Ed. Juventud, 1955-57.

3700 Cancino, Luis A.
La psique o personalidad del delincuente. México, 1963, 180p.

3701 Castiglione, Teodolindo
Lombroso perante a criminologia contemporânea. São Paulo, Saraiva, 1962, 295p.

3702 Excerpta criminologica. v. 1- #1, Amsterdam, 1961-

3703 Henriques, Fernando
Prostitution in Europe and the Americas. New York, Citadel, 1965, 378p.

3704 Hernández Hernández, Santos
La muchedumbre delincuente y el delito. México, 1955, 49p.

3705 Jones, H.
Crime in a changing society. Baltimore, Penguin Books, 1965, 173p.

3706 López-Rey y Arrojo, Manuel
Cuestiones penológicas. Tucumán, Ed. Richardet, 1955, 94p.

3707 Meade, J.G., & A.S. Parkes, eds.
Biological control of social problems. Edinburgh, Oliver & Boyd, 1965, 226p.

3708 Pérez, Luis C.
Criminología, la nueva concepción naturalista del delito. Bogotá, Universidad Nacional de Colombia, 1950, 415p.

3709 Raab, E., & G.J. Selznick
Major social problems. New York, Harper & Row, 1964, 594p.

3710 Ribeiro, Leonidio
Criminologia. 2v. Rio de Janeiro, Ed. Sul Americana; distribuidora: Livraria Freitas Bastos, 1957.

3711 Sousa Neto, Joaquim de
A mentira e o delinqüente. Rio de Janeiro, 1947, 80p.

3712 Spergel, I.
Racketville, slumtown, haulburg: an exploratory study of delinquent subcultures. Chicago, University of Chicago Press, 1964, 211p.

3713 Tabío Evelio
Criminología. Havana, Montero, 1960, 438p.

3714 Toca Cangas, Amador
Las aberraciones sexuales desde el punto de vista criminológico. México, 1956, 96p.

Latin America

3715 Alfaro González, Anastasio
Arqueología criminal americana. San José, Ed. Costa Rica, 1961, 226p.

3716 Dipp Muñoz, Alejandro
Ensayos de criminología. León, Ed. "Los Hechos," 1946, 59p.

3717 Estudios de derecho penal y criminología. Buenos Aires, Bibliográfica Omega, 1961-

3718 Ferrara, Floreal
Alcoholismo en América Latina. Buenos Aires, Ed. Palestra, 1961, 263p.

3719 Laplaza, Francisco P.
Objeto y método de la criminología. Buenos Aires, Eds. Arayú, 1954, 150p.

3720 Latin American Seminar on the Prevention of Crime and the Treatment of Offenders, Rio de Janeiro, 1953
Proceedings; document ST/TAA/ser.C/13. New York, United Nations, 1954, 89p.

3721 Ruiz-Funes García, M.
A crise nas priseõs. Tr. by H. Veiga Carvalho. São Paulo, Saraiva, 1953, 207p.

3722 Wolff, Pablo O.
La marihuana en América Latina. Buenos Aires, El Ateneo, 1948, 55p.

Argentina

3723 Aftalión, Enrique R.
La delincuencia en Argentina. Buenos Aires, Impr. de la Universidad, 1955, 101p.

3724 Bernardi, Humberto P.J., & Rodolfo G. Pessagno
Temas de penología y de ciencia penitenciaria. Buenos Aires, Librería y Casa Edit. de E. Perrot, 1952, 275p.

3725 Blarduni, Oscar C.
Progreso técnico y delincuencia. La Plata, Instituto de Investigaciones y Docencia Criminológicas, Ministerio de Gobierno, Provincia de Buenos Aires, 1961, 48p.

3726 Buenos Aires. Argentine Republic (Province). Instituto de Investigaciones y Docencia Criminológicas
Política penitenciaria. El código de ejecución penal. Buenos Aires? 1950, 179p.

3727 Bunster, Enrique
Motín en Punta Arenas, y otros procesos célebres.

2d ed. Santiago, Ercilla, 1962, 193p.

3728 Casiello, Luis
Carceles y encarcelados. Rosario, Librería y Ed. Ciencia, 1949, 313p.

3729 Ciafardo, Roberto
Criminología. Eva Perón, Arg., Eds. Nuevo Destino, 1953, 359p.

3730 Ciattino, Oreste
La delincuencia en Buenos Aires. New ed., enl. Buenos Aires, 1954, 208p.

3731 _Estudios penitenciarios_. v. 1- , La Plata, 1957-

3732 Fontán Balestra, Carlos
Delitos sexuales; artículos 118 a 133 de Código penal argentino. 2d ed. Buenos Aires, Eds. Arayú, 1953, 353p.

3733 Gusmão, Chrysolito de
Delitos sexuales. Buenos Aires, Ed. Bibliográfica Argentina, 1958, 316p.

3734 Jiménez de Asúa, Luis
El criminalista. 10v. Buenos Aires, La Ley, 1941-51.

3735 Lamas, Raúl
Los torturadores; crímenes y tormentos en las cárceles argentinas. Buenos Aires, Ed. Lamas, 1956, 203p.

3736 Luder, Italo A.
La política penitenciaria en la reforma constitucional. La Plata, Instituto de Investigaciones y Docencia Criminológicas, 1952, 77p.

3737 Pagano, José L.
Criminalidad argentina. Buenos Aires, Eds. Depalma, 1964, 326p.

Brazil

3738 Barbosa, Ruy
A obra de Ruy Barbosa em criminologia e direito criminal; seleções e dicionário de pensamentos. Rio de Janeiro, 1949, 265p.

3739 Carvalho, Beni
Sexualidad anômala no direito criminal. 2d ed. corr. plus enl. Rio de Janeiro, Ed. Revista Forense, 1957, 266p.

3740 Gusmão, Chrysolito de
Dos crimes sexuais, estupro, atentado violento ao pudor, sedução, e corrupção de menores. 4th ed. . . . Rio de Janeiro, Livraria Freitas Bastos, 1954, 330p.

3741 Investigações. ano 1, São Paulo, 1949- .

3742 Louzeiro, José, ed.
Assim marcha a familia; onze dramáticos flagrantes da chamada sociedade cristã e democrática no ano do IV centenário da cidade do Rio de Janeiro. Rio de Janeiro, Ed. Civilização Brasileira, 1965, 177p.

3743 Macedo, J. S. B.
O delinquente e o cárcera, sugestões para uma reforma de base do sistema penitenciário brasileiro. Maceió, 1954, 50p.

3744 Menezes, Raimundo de
Crimes e criminosos célebres. São Paulo, Livraria Martins, 1950, 261p.

3745 Montenegro, Abelardo F.
História do cangaceirismo no Ceará. Fortaleza, 1955, 129p.

3746 Pereira, Armando
Mulheres deitadas. 2d ed. Rio de Janeiro, Gráfica Record Ed.; dist.: Irmãos Pongetti, 1961? 256p.

3747 Pinto, Herondino Pereira
Nos subterraneos do Estado Novo. Rio de Janeiro, 1950, 110p.

3748 Ramos, Graciliano
Memórias do cárcere; obra póstuma. 4v. Rio de Janeiro, Olympio, 1953.

3749 Rio de Janeiro. Penitenciaria Central
Relatório das actividades. Irregular.

Chile

3750 Cea Quiroz, Waldo
La prostitución y el delito de contágio venéreo. Santiago, 1950, 62p.

3751 Criminología. Santiago, 1951- .

3752 Cuevas Torrealba, Sergio
Estudio crítico sobre la organización y régimen de la Penitenciaría de Santiago. Santiago, 1949, 92p.

3753 Gurrieri, A.
Situación y perspectivas de la juventud en una población urbana popular. Santiago, Economic Commission for Latin America, United Nations, 1965, 93p.

3754 Jackson, Christopher
Manuel. New York, Knopf, 1964, 251p.

3755 Orrego, Regina
Escándalo. Santiago, Ed. Guía, 1962, 96p.

3756 Ríos Ruy-Pérez, Carlota
El régimen correccional chileno y sugerencias para su modificación. Santiago, 1946, 133p.

3757 Zamorano Hernández, Manuel, & Carlos Munizaga Aguirre
Crimen y alcohol. Santiago, Universidad de Chile, 1963, 122p.

Colombia

3758 Acevedo Villamizar, A.
Los estados antisociales, vagancia, malvivencia y ratería. Bucaramanga, 1954, 108p.

3759 Barrera Domínguez, Humberto
Delitos sexuales. Bogotá, Ed. Temis, 1963, 362p.

3760 Bejarano, Jorge
La derrota de un vicio; orígen e historia de la chicha. Bogotá, Iqueima, 1950, 114p.

3761 Cadena Farfán, Augusto
La indagotoria en el proceso penal colombiano. Bogota, 1963? 143p.

3762 Guerrero Pérez, Arcesio
Estudios penitenciarios y problema colombiano. Madrid, 1954, 98p.

3763 Hernández Carrillo, Jorge
La mujer delincuente en Colombia. Bogotá, Ed. Centro-Instituto Gráfico, 1947, 208p.

3764 Paz Otero, G.
Alcohol y delito: de la embriaguez voluntaria y de la grave anomalía psíquica. Popayán, Universidad del Cauca, 1953, 114p.

3765 Ramírez Alonso, Leonor
Causas del aumento de la criminalidad femenina en nuestro medio. Bogotá, Ed. Minerva, 1960, 106p.

3766 Toro Escobar, Carlos del
Comentarios a la legislación sobre estados antisociales. Bogotá, 1955, 70p.

3767 Toro O., Luis A.
Apuntes sobre régimen penitenciario; plan general para una reforma penitenciaria en Colombia. 3d ed. Manizales, Impr. Departamental, 1953, 79p.

Costa Rica

3768 Costa Rica. Ministerio de Gobernación, Policía, Justicia y Gracia
Reforma penitenciaria. San José, Impr. Nacional, 1961, 126p.

3769 Jinesta, R.
La evolución penitenciaria en Costa Rica. San José, Impr. Falco Hnos., 1940, 286p.

Cuba

3770 Aparicio Laurencio, Angel
La reforma penitenciaria en Cuba . . . Havana, Ruiz-Castañeda, 1956, 71p.

Ecuador

3771 Perez, Galo R.
Formas del hecho delictivo. Quito, Impr. de la Universidad, 1953, 94p.

El Salvador

3772 Masferrer, Alberto
El dinero maldito. San Salvador, Impr. Nacional, 1950, 80p.

Guatemala

3773 Barreda Avila, Rubén
Guaridas infernales; mi drama vivido durante 1096 días en las mazmorras penitenciarias, en el período en el que Carlos Castillo Armas detentó poder y ultrajó la dignidad nacional. Guatemala, 1960, 176p.

3774 Juárez y Aragón, Luis A.
El problema del alcoholismo y la delincuencia en Guatemala. Guatemala, 1951, 32p.

3775 Paiz Ayala, Luis R.
Breve ensayo sobre criminología guatemalteca. Guatemala, 1950, 60p.

Guyana

3776 British Guiana
Report on the treatment of offenders. Georgetown, Annual.

Mexico

3777 Aguilar de la Torre, Manuel
Las cárceles y los sistemas penitenciarios. México, 1954, 132p.

3778 Aguirre Enríquez, Armando
Política criminal mexicana. México, 1948, 55p.

3779 Almada Santini, Enrique
La prostitución en sus relaciones con la criminalidad. México, 1957, 61p.

3780 Arredondo Vilchis, Conrado
La evolución de los delitos según las edades y los sexos. México, 1954, 113p.

3781 Bernaldo de Quirós y Pérez, Constancio
El bandolerismo en España y México. México, Ed. Jurídica Mexicana, 1959, 411p.

3782 Cabello Valdés, Rafael
El delincuente, sus causas y medios de combatirlo. México, 1949, 65p.

3783 Carrancá y Trujillo, Raúl
Principios de sociología criminal y de derecho penal. México, Escuela Nacional de Ciencias Políticas y Sociales, 1955, 247p.

3784 Falcón Cámara, Dimas
La delincuencia sectaria. México, 1958, 80p.

3785 Flores Navarro, Hirla
La delincuencia en Veracruz; estudio social. México, 196- ? 66p.

3786 Franco Guzmán, María de la L.
Criminalidad feminina. México, 1954, 116p.

3787 García Calderón, Francisco
Breve estudio sobre el problema de la delincuencia en México. México, 1952, 102p.

3788 González Pérez, Beatriz
Problema de la prostitución en México. México, 1949, 57p.

3789 Granados, Mariano
El crimen: causas, psicología del criminal, métodos de investigación. 1st ed. México, Ed. Alameda, 1954, 296p.

3790 Guitron Fuentevilla, Julián
El delito de atendados al pudor, estudio dogmático. México, Facultad de Derecho, Universidad Nacional Autónoma de México, 1961, 131p.

3791 Jiménez Perez, Jesús
Los sistemas penitenciarios. México, 1946, 73 plus 27p.

3792 Marcos, Ramón
Hacia una arquitectura penal mexicana; ponencia al primer Congreso Nacional Penitenciario. México? 195- ? unpaged.

3793 Mejía Ramírez, Xavier
La profilaxis criminal en la ciudad de México. México, 1956, 169p.

3794 Mendivil Martínez, Cirino
El problema de la prostitución en México. México, 1949, 84p.

3795 Millán Morales, Román
La criminalidad en la decimatercera delegación del Ministerio Público. México, 1963, 78p.

3796 Moctezuma Santos, Arturo
Sistemas penitenciarios. México, 1955, 122p.

3797 Quiróz Cuarón, Alfonso
La criminalidad en la República Mexicana. México, Instituto de Investigaciones Sociales, Universidad Nacional Autónoma de México, 1958, 110p.

3798 Rodríguez Sala de Gómez Gil, María L.
El suicidio en México, D. F. México, Instituto de Investigaciones Sociales, Universidad Nacional, 1963, 118p.

3799 Sodi, Federíco
El jurado resuelve; memorias. México, Trillas, 1961, 312p.

3800 Verea Palomar, Jorge
El problema penitenciario. Guadalajara, Eds. de

la Universidad de Guadalajara, 1954, 111p.

3801 Villareal de Sánchez, María A.
Defensa de la seguridad sexual de menores. México, 1948, 122p.

Nicaragua

3802 Centeno Sequeira, Esperanza
Delincuencia de la mujer en Nicaragua. Granada, 1949, 39p.

3803 Jirón Icaza, Arnoldo
El alcohol como factor primordial de la delincuencia en Nicaragua. León, 1950, 73p.

Peru

3804 Jiménez León, Max
Por qué fué delincuente . . . Lima, Eds. Biblioteca Penalogía, 1948, 100p.

Uruguay

3805 Gómez Folle, Juan C.
Instituciones penales del Uruguay; antecedentes y notas sobre un proceso de evolución en marcha. Montevideo, Tall. Graf. de Institutos Penales, 1947, 377p.

3806 Gómez Folle, Juan C.
La responsibilidad técnica de una función especializada. Montevideo, 1951, 93p.

3807 Luisi, Paulina
Otra voz clamando en el desierto (proxenetismo y reglamentación). 2v. Montevideo, 1948.

3808 Montevideo (Dept.) Jefatura de Policía
Memoria. Montevideo, 1949-

3809 Rovira, Alejandro
Prostitución y proxenetismo. Montevideo, 1951, 318p.

3810 Uruguay. Dirección General de Institutos Penales
Resúmen estadístico de la criminalidad feminina en el Uruguay durante el decenio 1940-49. Montevideo, 1951, 52p.

Venezuela

3811 Aguilar Mawdsley, Andrés
La delincuencia en Venezuela; su prevención. Caracas, Tip. Vargas, 1961, 85p.

3812 Fontiveros, A.
Factores predominantes de la criminalidad en Venezuela y sus estadísticas; ponencia que presenta el Dr. Alfonso Fontiveros a la primera convención nacional de la Comisión de Prevención de la Delincuencia. Caracas, Ministerio de Justicia, 1956, unpaged.

3813 Gómez Grillo, Elio
Introducción a la criminología; con especial referencia al medio venezolano. Caracas, Publicaciones de la Facultad de Derecho, Universidad Central de Venezuela, 1964, 460p.

3814 Mendoza, José R.
Estudio de sociología criminal venezolana; trabajo presentado al II Congreso internacional de Criminología reunido en París en septiembre de 1950. Caracas, 1952, 58p.

3815 Rísquez, Fernando
Investigación integral de un grupo representativo de la delincuencia feminina en Venezuela. Caracas, 1960, 459 plus 329p.

3816 Unda Briceño, Hugo, & Domingo Ricovery López
Bases para un estudio criminógeno del Departamento Libertador del Distrito Federal; homicidios y lesiones en hechos de sangre, suicidios consumados y frustrados, años 1951-1953. Caracas, Eds. del Ministerio de Justicia, 1955, 85p.

West Indies and the Caribbean

3817 Trinidad. Superintendent of Prisons
Administration report. Port of Spain, 1946- Annual.

Periodical Articles

General

3818 Alves, Roque de Brito
"Uma Orientação na Bibliografia Recente de Criminologia." Recife, Revista pernambucana de direito penal e criminologia (3:9), January/March 1956, p. 57-71.

3819 Castellanos, Israel
"El Gabinete Nacional de Identificación: lo que Era y lo que Es." Havana, Revista de identificación y asuntos generales, December 1932, p. 617-714.

3820 Medrano Ossio, José
"Tercer Congreso Continental de Criminología." Potosí, Revista de criminología y ciencia penales, January 1946, p. 5-7.

Latin America

3821 Gutiérrez Anzola, J.E.
"Seminario Latinoamericano Sobre la Prevención del Delito y Tratamiento del Delincuente." Bogotá, Universitas 4, 1953, p. 123-134.

3822 Hoover, John E.
"The First Pan American Congress on Criminology." Pan American Union bulletin 78, November 1944, p. 605-608.

3823 Martínez-Espinoso O., Felix
"El Primer Congreso Panamericano de Criminalística." Caracas, Identidad y derecho, July 23, 1944, p. 6-16.

3824 Navarrete A., Hector I.
"Publicaciones Periódicas de Criminología que Aparecen en América." Lima, Boletín de la Biblioteca, Universidad Nacional Mayor de San Marcos (12:3-4), December 1942, p. 272-275.

3825 Seminario Latinoamericano sobre la Prevención del Delito y Tratamiento del Delincuente, Rio de Janeiro, 1953
"Actas . . ." São Paulo, Revista interamericana

do Ministério Público (1:1), May 1956, p. 45-48.

3826 Solís Quiroga, H.
"Industrialización y Delincuencia." México, Criminalia (30:3), March 31, 1964, p. 204-216.

3827 "Tercer Congreso Panamericano de Criminología." México, Criminalia, February 1, 1947, p. 45.

Argentina

3828 Aftalión, Enrique R.
"Manifestaciones Predominantes de Criminalidad en Argentina." Paris, Revue internationale de police criminelle 6, July 1954, p. 18-24.

3829 Argentine Republic. Dirección Nacional de Institutos Penales
"Actas del Segundo Congreso Penitenciario Justicialista 'Eva Perón.'" Buenos Aires, Revista penal y penitenciaria (19:74), December 1954, p. 1-579.

3830 Dichio, J.J.
"El Estudio de los Delincuentes en la República Argentina." México, Criminalia (26:10), October 1960, p. 736-744.

3831 Ocampo, V.
"Testimonio." Buenos Aires, Sur 267, November-December 1960, p. 30-35.

3832 Ortiz, Eduardo A.
"Acción Penitenciaria Argentina." Buenos Aires, Boletín del Museo Social Argentino, January-February 1945, p. 3-14.

Bolivia

3833 Durán, Manuel
"Algunas Notas para el Estudio de la Sociología Criminal en Bolivia." Sucre, Revista del Instituto de Sociología Boliviana, July/December 1941, p. 69-82.

3834 Durán, Manuel
"La Sociología Criminal en Bolivia." Havana, América, January 1946, p. 26-34.

Brazil

3835 Araujo, A. Placeres de
"A Identificação Dactiloscópica no Brasil." São Paulo, Investigações (4:39), March 1952, p. 33-43.

3836 Brazil. Laws, statutes, etc.
"Business Regulation, Crimes Against Social Economy." Comparative law series, February 1939, p. 98-101.

3837 Chaves, P.
"Memórias de um Capelão de Presídio." Rio de Janeiro, Síntese política econômica social (3:12), October-December 1961, p. 27-37.

3838 López-Rey y Arrojo, Manuel
"Instituto Latinoamericano de Criminología da ONU em São Paulo." São Paulo, Anhembi (35:103), June 1959, p. 4-8.

3839 Menezes, Raimundo
"O Famoso 'Processo Pinto' da Campinas." São Paulo, Investigações (3:35), November 1951, p. 63-81.

3840 Pitta, G. Rocha
"Um Quarto de Milhão de Homens e Mulheres Fora da Lei." Rio de Janeiro, Intercambio, March/April 1946, p. 49-53.

3841 Saito, H.
"O Suicídio Entre os Imigrantes Japonêses e seus Descendentes no Estado de São Paulo." São Paulo, Sociología (15:2), May 1953, p. 109-130.

3842 Salgado, José A. C.
"Pesquisa Sobre as Formas Predominantes da Criminalidade na América Latina." São Paulo, Revista interamericana do Ministério Público (1:2), November 1956, p. 149-161.

Chile

3843 Cubillos, L. L.
"El Problema Médico-Social y Legal de Nuestra

Delincuencia." Santiago, Servicio social, September-December 1934, p. 258-277.

3844 Drapkin S., Israel, & L. Sandoval S.
"Grupos Sanguíneos de la Población Penitenciaria de Santiago." Santiago, Revista de ciencias penales, January/March 1945, p. 5-18.

3845 Novella, Eneas
"Las Doctrinas Penales ante la Prevención del Crimen." Santiago, Revista de criminología y policía científica (9:121), June 1949, p. 53-56.

Colombia

3846 Aguilar, Juan M.
"La Criminalidad en el Departamento de Santander." Bogotá, Anales de economía y estadística (3:1), February 25, 1940, p. 29-41.

3847 Amaya González, Víctor
"La Estadística y la Criminalidad." Bogotá, Anales de economía y estadística, June/July 1941, p. 41-43.

3848 Colombia. Laws, statutes, etc.
"Decreto no. 720 por el Cual se Crea la Comisión de Reformas Penales." Bogotá, Diario oficial, March 8, 1947, p. 839.

3849 Colombia. Laws, statutes, etc.
"Decreto no. 0014 de 1955 (Enero 12) por el Cual se Dicta Disposiciones Sobre Prevención Social." Bogotá, Diario oficial, January 19, 1955, p. 49-55.

3850 Montoya Canal, Aníbal
"Estadística de la Delincuencia en Colombia." Bogotá, Anales de economía y estadística, February 1945, p. 37-53.

3851 Pérez, Luis C.
"Apuntes para una Interpretación de la Delincuencia Feminina en Colombia." Bogotá, Universidad Nacional de Colombia, September/November 1947, p. 209-228.

3852 Rodríguez, Jorge
"La Criminalidad en Colombia." Bogotá, Anales de economía y estadística, March/April 1941, p. 27-32.

3853 Samper, Darío
"Interpretación de la Estadística de la Criminalidad en Colombia." Bogotá, Anales de economía y estadística (3:1), February 25, 1940, p. 1-28.

3854 Uribe Cualla, Guillermo
"El Abuso del Alcohol como Factor de Delincuencia en Colombia." Bogotá, Universitas 9, November 1955, p. 59-83.

Costa Rica

3855 Costa Rica. Laws, statutes, etc.
"No. 57 [Refórmase el Artículo 6º del Decreto Ejecutivo No. 1 de 13 de Enero de 1942 (Reglamento del Registro Judicial de Delincuentes)]." San José, La Gaceta (82:207), September 14, 1960, p. 3357.

Cuba

3856 D'Estefano Pisani, Miguel A.
"La Estadística Criminal en Cuba." Havana, Revista del Colegio de Abogados de La Habana, November/December 1944, p. 633-637.

3857 "Es Descubierta por la Policía Nacional, la Existencia de una Banda de Delincuentes Internacionales, que Operaban en Europa, y Actualmente lo Estaban Haciendo en Cuba, Centro y Sur América." Havana, Revista de la Policía November 1945, p. 16-17, 29.

Ecuador

3858 Borja y Borja, R.
"Consideraciones Relativas al Artículo Segundo del Código Penal Ecuatoriano Vigente." Quito, Ensayos 1, March 1962, p. 33-38.

El Salvador

3859 El Salvador. Laws, statutes, etc.
"Ley de Estado Peligroso. Decreto No. 1028."

San Salvador, Diario oficial, May 25, 1953, p. 3882-3885.

Honduras

3860 Gálvez, José M.
"Criminalidad Hondureña." Tegucigalpa, Foro hondureño, June/July 1946, p. 17-18.

Mexico

3861 Aguirre Pequeño, E.
"La Medicina Geriátrica y la Prevención de la Delincuencia Senil." México, Estudios sociológicos, 1954, p. 198-203.

3862 Argüelles, Benjamín
"La Delincuencia de la Postguerra en México." México, Prevención social, November/December 1945, p. 7-15.

3863 Bernaldo de Quirós, Constancio
"Criminología y Derecho Penal en Cuba y México." Ciudad Trujillo, Anales de la Universidad de Santo Domingo, January/June 1946, p. 318-356.

3864 Braddy, Haldeen
"Running Contraband on the Rio Grande." Southern folklore quarterly 25, June 1961, p. 101-112.

3865 Carrancá y Rivas, R.
"Las Causas Generadoras del Crímen." México, Criminalia (28:3), March 1962, p. 174-179.

3866 Carrancá y Trujillo, Raúl
"Criminalidad y Legislación en México." México, Criminalia, January 1, 1947, p. 25-30.

3867 Carrancá y Trujillo, Raúl
"Vicios Sociales y Criminalidad." México, Estudios sociológicos, 1954, p. 23-29.

3868 Ceniceros, J.A., & J. Piña Palacios
"Las Prisiones en México: Sus Problemas en el Distrito Federal." México, Estudios sociológicos 1954, p. 325-335.

3869 Flores, Anselmo M.
"La Criminología y una Nueva Técnica de Craneología Constitucionalista." México, Revista mexicana de estudios antropológicos, January/December 1945, p. 113-149.

3870 Franco Sodi, C.
"Artículos Escritos Entre 1942 y 1961." México, Criminalia (28:4), April 1962, p. 182-291.

3871 García Ramírez, S.
"El Derecho Penitenciario y Su Situación en México." México, Criminalia (30:4), April 30, 1964, p. 254-262.

3872 Gómez Viveros, C., et al
"El Centro de Reclusión Número 2 del Distrito Federal." México, Criminalia (31:3), March 1965, p. 100-123.

3873 Gonzalez Bustamante, J.J.
"La Delincuencia Feminina." México, Estudios sociológicos 1954, p. 281-293.

3874 Grave, D.
"La Delincuencia en las Fronteras." México, Estudios sociológicos 1954, p. 309-326.

3875 Hayner, Norman S.
"Criminogenic Zones in Mexico City; with Discussion by E.H. Sutherland." American sociological review 11, August 1946, p. 428-438.

3876 Mendoza, José R.
"La Delincuencia y la Economía." México, Estudios sociológicos 1955, p. 233-248.

3877 P. Moreno, A. de
"Los Grupos Sociales y la Delincuencia." México, Estudios sociológicos, 1954, p. 61-116.

3878 Piña Palacios, J.
"Situación de las Prisiones en México." México, Criminalia (27:4), April 1961, p. 175-293.

3879 Quiróz Cuarón, Alfonso
"El Crímen en México." México, Criminalia (26:1), January 1960, p. 8-20.

3880 Quiróz Cuarón, Alfonso
"Datos Cuantitativos de la Criminalidad en la República Mexicana." México, Criminalia (26:4), April 1960, p. 293-296.

3881 Quiróz Cuarón, Alfonso
"El Régimen Penitenciario en las Entidades Federativas." México, Ciencias políticas y sociales (9:33), July-September 1963, p. 339-357.

3882 Quiroga, H.
"El Fenómeno Criminal en México." México, Revista mexicana de sociología (23:1), 1961, p. 203-213.

3883 Reyes Tayabas, Jorge
"La Responsibilidad Penal de las Personas Morales en el Derecho Positivo Mexicano." México, Criminalia (19:4), April 1953, p. 186-203.

3884 Solís Quiroga, H.
"El Fenómeno Criminal en México." México, Revista mexicana de sociología (23:2), May-August 1961, p. 545-554.

3885 Solís Quiroga, H.
"La Prostitución en México Hasta 1957." México, Criminalia (30:4), April 30, 1964, p. 271-277.

3886 Vela, Alberto R.
"Vagancia y Malvivencia." México, Estudios sociológicos 1954, p. 295-307.

Peru

3887 Rotondo, H.
"Conducta Antisocial en una Area Urbana en Estado de Desorganización." México, Criminalia (26:10), October 1960, p. 763-778.

Uruguay

3888 Duarte Gonzalez, A.
"Análisis Estadístico de 120 Casos de Menores

Delincuentes en el Uruguay." Montevideo, Boletín del Instituto Interamericano del Niño (35:138), September 1961, p. 227-249.

Venezuela

3889 Alvarez, V.M.
"Aspectos Sobre el Problema de la Delincuencia en Venezuela." Caracas, Boletín de la Academia de Ciencias Políticas y Sociales 20, April-June 1961, p. 163-170.

3890 Cova García, Luis
"Grafología, Iridología y Odontología Legal, para el Estudio de los Factores Criminógenos en Venezuela." Caracas, Revista nacional de cultura (11:77), November/December 1949, p. 80-95.

3891 "El Hampa y la Metrópoli." Caracas, Política 15, April-May 1961, p. 98a-98d.

3892 García Maragna, A.
"Algunas Consideraciones Sobre el Problema Sexual de los Penados." Panamá, Lotería (6:71), October 1961, p. 42-44.

3893 Mendoza, José R.
"Estudios Acerca del Recidivismo en Venezuela." Caracas, Revista de la Facultad de Derecho 9, October 1956, p. 137-199.

3894 "La Reforma Penitenciaria en la Venezuela Democrática." Caracas, Política 10, June 1960, p. 109a-109c.

Juvenile Delinquency

Books

General

3895 Goldstein, Bernard
Low income youth in urban areas. New York, Holt,

Rinehart & Winston, 1967, 416p.

3896 Gottlieb, D., & J. Reeves
Adolescent behavior in urban areas. New York, Free Press of Glencoe, 1963, 244p.

3897 Jones, Howard
Crime in a changing society. Baltimore, Penguin Books, 1965, 173p.

3898 Kvaraceus, William C.
Juvenile delinquency, a problem for the modern world. Paris, Unesco, 1964, 85p.

3899 Mays, J.
Growing up in the city. New York, Wiley, 1964, 225p.

3900 Rubenfeld, Seymour
Family of outcasts: a new theory of delinquency. New York, Free Press, 1965, 350p.

3901 Sherif, Muzafer, & Carolyn W. Sherif
Problems of youth: transition to adulthood in a changing world; modern applications in psychology. Chicago, Aldine, 1965, 218p.

3902 Tunley, Roul
Kids, crime and chaos; a world report on juvenile delinquency. New York, Harper & Row, 1962, 250p.

3903 United Nations. Dept. of Economic & Social Affairs
The young adult offender; a review of current practices and programmes in prevention and treatment. New York, 1965, 135p.

Argentina

3904 Caballero, José S.
Regulación de la tutela y de la represión de los menores delincuentes en la República Argentina. Buenos Aires, Bib. Omeba, 1963, 186p.

3905 Landó, Juan C.
Protección al menor: teoría práctica, soluciones.

Buenos Aires, Depalma, 1957, 168p.

3906 Pierris, Carlos A. de
Delincuencia juvenil. Buenos Aires, Bibliográfica Omeba, 1963, 164p.

Bolivia

3907 Saavedra, María J.
Régimen jurídico de la menor edad en Bolivia; estudios, informes, proyectos, legislación. La Paz, Ed. U.M.S.A., 1950, 119p.

British Honduras

3908 British Honduras. Prison Dept.
Report. Belize. Annual.

Chile

3909 Dumay Deremond, Alejandro
El discernimiento en nuestra legislación penal de menores. Santiago, 1946, 68p.

3910 Gajardo Contreras, Samuel
Protección de menores. 1st ed. Santiago, Ed. Jurídica de Chile, 1955, 124p.

Colombia

3911 Abello Lobo, Fernando
El problema de la delincuencia en los menores. Barranquilla, 1951, 141p.

3912 Bermúdez Hernández, Ventura
El niño delincuente en Colombia; las disposiciones legales y ensayo psico-pedagógico. Bogotá, 1950, 72p.

Guatemala

3913 Rodríguez González, Horacio
La legislación de menores, una jurisdicción privativa. Guatemala, 1952, 107p.

Haiti

3914 Gourgue, Gérard
Le problème de la délinquance juvénile et l'institution du juge des enfants. Port-au-Prince, Impr. de l'Etat, 1955, 168p.

Mexico

3915 Báez Santoyo, Rosario
El trabajo social y la readaptación del menor infractor. México, 1953? 77p.

3916 Carrasco Morgan, Daniel
Los menores delincuentes en México. México, 1954, 80p.

3917 Islas Allende, Vela
Escuela de rehabilitación infantil. Mexico? 1954? 20p.

3918 Martínez Schmid, Carmen
Apuntes sobre delincuencia infantil y juvenil. México, 1952, 24p.

3919 Paredes y Delgado, Alma
Menores delincuentes. México, 1947, 128p.

3920 Ruiz de Chávez P., Leticia
La delincuencia juvenil en el Distrito Federal. México, 1959, 71p.

Uruguay

3921 Reyes, Reina
Psicología y reeducación; informe presentado al Consejo del Niño del Uruguay. Buenos Aires, Ed. Americalee, 1947, 123p.

Venezuela

3922 Ramírez Sánchez, Alfredo
Etiologie de la délinquance juvénile, le statut des mineurs au Venezuela, 1949. Paris, Editions Cujas, 1955, 183p.

Periodical Articles

General

3923 Philippon, O.
"El Problema de la Delincuencia Juvenil." México, Latino-américa (3:28), April 1, 1951, p. 173-175.

Latin America

3924 Altmann Smythe, Julio
"Juvenile Delinquency in Latin American Countries." International review of criminal policies 5, January 1954, p. 9-18.

3925 Buentello y Villa, E.
"Una Hipótesis Patogénica de la Delincuencia Juvenil." México, Criminalia (28:1), January 1962, p. 17-37.

3926 Cucullu, G., & E. Gargalione
"Delincuencia y Clase Social." Buenos Aires, Revista latino-americana de sociología (I:3), November 1965, p. 314-332.

3927 Escardo y Anaya, V.
"La Cooperación Interamericana y la Conducta Antisocial del Menor." Montevideo, Boletín del Instituto Interamericano del Niño (37:147), December 1963, p. 296-299.

3928 Estudios Centroamericanos (periodical)
"Como Hacer Frente a la Inmoralidad Juvenil." San Salvador (18:187), November 1963, p. 331-333.

3929 González de Behringer, Clara
"Why Juvenile Delinquency?" Américas 9, November 1957, p. 21-25.

3930 Graue, D.
"Consideraciones Sobre los Menores Socialmente Inadaptados." Río Piedras, Revista de ciencias sociales (6:3), September 1962, p. 291-306.

3931 Klimpel, Felicitas
"La Delincuencia Infantil en las Américas. Las Medidas Más Adecuadas para Evitarlas." Santiago, Revista de criminología y policía científica, April 1948, p. 59-63.

3932 Landó, Juan C.
"La Conducta Antisocial del Menor en América." Montevideo, Boletín del Instituto Interamericano del Niño (38:1), March 1964, p. 33-61.

3933 Llach, Guillermina
"Delincuencia Infantil y Defensa Social." México, Continente January/February 1941, p. 57-58.

3934 Mira y López, E.
"Patogenía de la Delincuencia Juvenil." Caracas, Política 8, April 1960, p. 56-65.

3935 Mendoza, José R.
"Peculiaridad del Problema Americano de la Delincuencia Infantil." Lima, Nueva educación (6:32), August 1950, p. 24-28.

3936 Morey Otero, Sebastián
"Educación Correctiva del Delincuente." Montevideo, Anales de instrucción primaria (13:3), March 1950, p. 31-34.

3937 Peña Nuñez, J.
"La Prevención de la Delincuencia." México, Criminalia (29:11), November 1963, p. 757-767.

3938 Sajón, Rafael
"La Legislación Americana y la Conducta Antisocial del Menor." Montevideo, Boletín del Instituto Interamericano del Niño (38:1), March 1964, p. 86-94.

3939 Saldún de Rodríguez, M. L.
"La Salud en Relación con la Conducta Antisocial del Menor." Montevideo, Boletín del Instituto Interamericano del Niño (37:147), December 1963, p. 283-292.

3940 Serrano Linuesa, O.
"Juventud en Crisis." Bogotá, Arco 14, May-June 1961, p. 188-193.

3941 Solís Quiroga, H.
"La Legislación de los Países Americanos en Relación con el Menor Infractor." México, Criminalia (30:3), March 31, 1964, p. 228-232.

3942 Sucupira Kenworthy, Z.
"La Prevención de la Delincuencia Juvenil." México, Criminalia (29:11), November 1963, p. 720-733.

3943 Urbina Pinto, R.
"La Prevención de la Delincuencia Juvenil." México, Criminalia (29:11), November 1963, p. 734-744.

3944 Vethencourt B., J. L.
"La Prevención de la Delincuencia." México, Criminalia (29:11), November 1963, p. 745-756.

Argentina

3945 Aftalión, Enrique R., & J. A. Alfonsín
"Memoria Sobre la Ejecución de las Sanciones Penales en la República Argentina." Buenos Aires, Revista penal y penitenciaria (14:51/54), January/December 1949, p. 101-145.

3946 Rojas, Héctor
"La Colonia Hogar 'Ricardo Gutiérrez' y la Delincuencia Infantil." Cochabamba, Revista jurídica, June 1946, p. 147-155.

Bolivia

3947 Durán P., Manuel
"La Reforma Penal en Bolivia y el Problema de la Delincuencia." Buenos Aires, Revista del Colegio de Abogados de Buenos Aires (30:3), September/December 1952, p. 165-172.

3948 Ferrufino S., Eduardo
"Delincuencia Infantil y Medios de Prevenirla." Cochabamba, Revista jurídica (13:49), September 1949, p. 68-71.

3949 Pérez, Julio C.
"El Reformatorio de Menores de Arocagua." Montevideo, Boletín del Instituto Internacional Americano de Protección a la Infancia, September 1945, p. 422-430.

Brazil

3950 Lima, A. Saboia
"Criminalidade Infantil no Brasil e em Especial, no Rio de Janeiro." Rio de Janeiro, Revista de serviço social, September 1945, p. 4-8.

3951 Lima, A. Saboia
"O Problema dos Menores Abandonados." Rio de Janeiro, Formação (16:181), August 1953, p. 33, 47-56.

3952 Martins, João
"60 Milhões de Cruzeiros para Forzar Criminosos. S.A.M. 'Seu Amor nem Misericórdia.'" Rio de Janeiro, O cruzeiro (24:51), October 4, 1952, p. 66-70.

3953 Martins, Wilson
"Notas Sobre o Problema dos Menores do Paraná." Curitiba, Divulgações de serviço social (3:7), April/June 1951, p. 3-5.

3954 Pennino, Joaquín B.
"Contribuição no Estudo da Delinquencia Infante-Juvenil." São Paulo, Boletim do serviço social dos menores 11, October 1952, p. 9-18.

Chile

3955 Huici, Matilde
"Delincuencia de Menores, sus Causas. Reeducación de Jovenes Delincuentes." Santiago, Acción social, November 1940, p. 24-27.

3956 Huici, Matilde
"La Vagancia Infantil." Santiago, Acción social, July 1947, p. 41-44.

Colombia

3957 Briñón Mercant, M.
"Delincuencia Juvenil." Bogotá, Arco 13, March-April 1961, p. 96-105.

3958 "La Delincuencia Infantil en Colombia. 'Los Hijos del Viento.' La Investigación Obligatoria de la Paternidad Es Base para la Redención del Niño." Bogotá, Yo, October 3, 1953, p. 17-23.

3959 Gómez, Eduardo
"Gaminos. Los Niños Vagabundos que Trata de Rescatar una Hermosa Mujer en la Capital de Colombia." Bogotá, Cromos (87:2160), October 20, 1958, p. 14-20.

3960 Jiménez Fandiño, P. J.
"Delincuencia Juvenil." México, Criminalia (28:5), May 1962, p. 296-308.

3961 Medina Madroñero, Edmundo
"Causas de la Delincuencia Infantil." Pasto, Anales de la Universidad de Nariño (4:34/35), January/April 1951, p. 36-43.

3962 Pérez, Luis C.
"La Infancia Delincuente." Popayán, Revista de la Universidad del Cauca, June 1946, p. 39-56.

3963 Pérez Roldán, Gabriel
"El Problema del Menor Delincuente." Medellín, Estudios de derecho, July 1948, p. 255-278.

3964 Rincón, Ovidio
"Delincuencia Infantil." Medellín, Universidad de Antioquia (26:104), September/November 1951, p. 641-644.

3965 Ruiz Funes García, M.
"El Menor y la Criminologia." Bogotá, Universidad Nacional de Colombia 14, May 1949, p. 83-99.

Cuba

3966 Blanco, Leandro
"Como Castiga la Sociedad a los Niños Delincuentes." Havana, Bohemia (42:22), May 28, 1950, p. 32-34, 104-105.

3967 Esparza González, Oscar
"Importancia de la Educacion Fisica en la Prevención de la Delincuencia Juvenil." Santa Clara, Islas (2:1), September/December 1959, p. 217-230.

3968 Henríquez, Enrique C.
"Orientación Infantil y Prevención Social en Cuba. (Ideas Generales para un Plan de Reorganización)." Havana, Policía Secreta Nacional, September 1944, p. 105-121.

3969 Pérez, R. R.
"El Año Judicial: La Delincuencia en Cuba." Havana,

Carteles (37:44), October 30, 1955, p. 64-65, 99-100.

Dominican Republic

3970 Guzmán, Olagario Helena
"La Delincuencia Infantil. Grado de Desarrollo en la República." Ciudad Trujillo, Revista del trabajo (1:1), January/March 1956, p. 49-51.

3971 Mejía Felid, Juan T.
"Prevención y Corrección de la Delincuencia Juvenil en la Era de Trujillo." Ciudad Trujillo, Renovación (2:12), January-June 1956, p. 5-18.

3972 Paillerest, M. B. de
"Un Experimento con Niños Delincuentes." Ciudad Trujillo, Prevision social, September 1948, p. 25-27.

3973 Torino y Roldán, Fernando
"La Delincuencia Infantil y los Tribunales para Niños." Ciudad Trujillo, Revista jurídica dominicana, April 1, 1940, p. 66-72.

Ecuador

3974 Castro, Manuel J.
"Casos Delictivos de Menores Sobre Datos Estadísticos, en Quito, Capital della República del Ecuador." México, Criminalia (20:2), February 1954, p. 60-63.

Guatemala

3975 Guatemala. Laws, statutes, etc.
"Reglamento General de los Centros de Observación y Reeducación de Menores." Guatemala, El Guatemalteco (150:87), July 29, 1957, p. 1169-1171.

Haiti

3976 Noel, U. J.
"Facteurs de l'Inadaptation Juvenile dans un Pays Afro-Latin." Port-au-Prince, Revue de la Faculté d'Ethnologie 11, 1966, p. 9-21.

Mexico

3977 Arilla Baz, Fernando
"El Menor ante la Ley Penal Mexicana." México,

Criminalia (19:8), August 1953, p. 434-436.

3978 Beard, B.D.
"Mexico's Way with Children." Journal of the American Association of University Women, Fall 1944, p. 15-18.

3979 Cardona, Sara A.
"Escuela para los Padres de Niños Delincuentes." México, Economista, March 1945, p. 43-45.

3980 Lavalle Urbina, M.
"Delincuencia Infantil." México, Criminalia (15:4), April 1949, p. 134-146.

3981 Lavalle, Urbina, M.
"Los Menores Infractores y su Tratamiento por el Departamento de Prevención Social de la Secretaría de Gobernación." México, Criminalia (28:12), December 1962, p. 716-723.

3982 Lizarriturri, J.
"Los Trabajadores Sociales Frente a los Problemas de la Delincuencia Infantil y Juvenil." México, Asistencia 8, April 1942, p. 69-83.

3983 Menéndez Díaz, C.
"El Problema de los Menores Infractores." Mérida, Revista de la Universidad de Yucatán (6:33), May-June 1964, p. 16-23.

3984 "Mesa Redonda Sobre la Delincuencia Juvenil en México, 1962. Trabajos." México, Criminalia (28:12), December 1962, p. 692-715.

3985 Mexico. Secretaría de Salubridad
"La Niñez, la Juventud y los Vicios." México, Carta semanal, May 17, 1947, p. 18-19.

3986 Navarro Zimbrón, E.
"El Niño Delincuente." México, Vida, October 22, 1947, p. 30-33.

3987 Palmero Zilveti, O.
"Estudio de la Delincuencia Juvenil en los Tribunales

de Menores de la Ciudad de México." México, Criminalia (28:9), September 1962, p. 568-578.

3988 "Causes of Delinquency Among Children." Pan American Union bulletin 64, June 1930, p. 635-636.

3989 Ruiz de Chavez P., Leticia
"La Delincuencia Juvenil en el Distrito Federal." México, Criminalia (25:12), December 1959, p. 704-742.

3990 Saenz, M. A.
"Breves Consideraciones Acerca de la Delincuencia Infantil y del Funcionamiento del Tribunal para Menores del Estado de Nuevo León." México, Estudios sociológicos 1954, p. 265-280.

3991 Solís Quiroga, Roberto
"La Delincuencia Juvenil en México." México, Criminalia (20:1), January 1954, p. 8-24.

3992 Solís Quiroga, Roberto
"Los Grandes Problemas de la Tercera Infancia, de la Adolescencia y la Profiláxis de la Delincuencia Juvenil." México, Estudios sociológicos 1954, p. 247-254.

3993 Urzaiz, R. E.
"Delincuencia Precoz." México, Estudios sociológicos 1954, p. 125-131.

3994 Vela, Alberto R.
"El Niño y la Delincuencia." México, Prevención social, March/April 1946, p. 3-18.

3995 Zendejas, Adelina
"La Guerra, la Delincuencia Infantil y la Delincuencia Juvenil." México, Criminalia (17:11), November 1951, p. 608-623.

Panama

3996 Campbell, Carolina de
"Delincuencia Infantil." Panamá, Boletín del Instituto Panameño de la Opinión Pública 9, August 1950, p. 1-7.

Peru

3997 Altmann Smythe, Julio
"Nuevas Modalidades de la Antisociabilidad de los Menores Peruanos." México, Criminalia (30:5), May 1964, p. 315-326.

3998 Fenton, Ronald
"The Teacher Who Tamed the 'Fruit Birds' of Lima." Paris, Courier (6:1), January 1953, p. 12.

3999 Herrera Orrego, J.M.
"Delincuencia Infantil." Lima, La revista del foro, January-March 1945, p. 154-159.

4000 Oneto G., M.
"El Problema de la Delincuencia Infantil y los Principios Rotarios." Lima, Rotario peruano, September-October 1944, p. 358-369.

4001 Peru. Laws, statutes, etc.
"Créase el Establecimiento de Infractores Juveniles y Primarios, en lo que Fué el Penal de Comisarías. Decreto Supremo." Lima, El peruano 5762, July 2, 1960, p. 1.

4002 Tamayo Vargas, Manuel
"Causas de la Conducta Antisocial de los Menores en Nuestro País." Lima, Información social (15:3), July-September 1960, p. 10-15.

4003 Tamayo Vargas, Manuel
"La Protección Jurídica de los Menores." Lima, Revista del foro (40:2), May/August 1953, p. 323-336.

Uruguay

4004 Achard, José P.
"Aspectos de una Reforma en la Judicatura de Menores y de la Legislación Atinente a los Mis-Mos." Montevideo, Boletín del Instituto Internacional Americano de Protección a la Infancia (29:3), September 1955, p. 719-725.

4005 Duarte Gonzalez, A.
"Análisis Estadístico de 120 Casos de Menores Delincuentes en el Uruguay." Montevideo, Boletín del

Instituto Interamericano del Niño (35:138), September 1961, p. 227-249.

4006 Knox, Estelle F.
"Treatment of the Juvenile Delinquent in Montevideo, Uruguay." Montevideo, Boletín del Instituto Internacional Americano de Protección a la Infancia (27:106), September 1953, p. 320-328.

Venezuela

4007 Consejo Venezolano del Niño
"Un Niño que Encontró su Camino." Caracas, El farol (10:118), March 1949, p. 20-24.

4008 García Melendez, P.
"La Delincuencia Juvenil en Venezuela." San Juan, Revista de la Asociación de Maestros (10:5), October 1951, p. 138-139, 157-159.

4009 Demestre de Landaez, María
"El Problema de la Delincuencia Infantil." Caracas, Infancia y adolescencia (1:2), March/April 1949, p. 16-17.

4010 Machado, Gustavo H.
"Factores Sociales como Causas Comunas de Mortalidad y Abandono Infantiles. Sus Orígenes y sus Consecuencias." Caracas, Infancia y adolescencia (3:11), December 1951, p. 11-48.

4011 Santos Mendoza, E.
"La Lucha Contra el Peligro de la Infancia Abandonada, Delincuente y Predelincuente de Venezuela." Caracas, Revista del Ministerio de Justicia (4:12/13), January/June 1955, p. 13-27.

4012 Pollitz, Paul.
"La Delincuencia Juvenil." Caracas, Guardia Nacional (3:13), March 1949, p. 11-13.

DEMOGRAPHY

Books

General

4013 American Academy of Arts and Sciences Seminar, 1963
Human fertility and population problems; proceedings. Ed. by R.O. Greep. New York, Schenkman, 1964, 278p.

4014 Ashley Montague, M. F., ed.
The concept of race. New York, Free Press, 1964, 270p.

4015 Carter, Robert L., et al
Equality. New York, Pantheon, 1965, 191p.

4016 Coon, Carleton S., & Edward E. Hunt
The living races of man. New York, Knopf, 1965, 344p.

4017 Durán Ochoa, Julio
Población. México, Fondo de Cultura Económica, 1955, 277p.

4018 Eldridge, H. T.
The materials of demography, a selected and annotated bibliography. New York, Colombia University Press, 1959, 222p.

4019 Gutman, Robert
Urban sociology; a bibliography. New Brunswick, Urban Studies Center, Rutgers, the State University, 1963, 44p.

4020 Hertzler, J.O.
The crisis in world population; a sociological examination, with special reference to the underdeveloped areas. Lincoln, University of Nebraska Press, 1956, 279p.

4021 Levi-Strauss, Claude
Race and history. Paris, Unesco, 1958, 47p.

4022 National Academy of Sciences
The growth of world population. Washington, 1963, 38p.

4023 Population index. Princeton, Office of Population Research, Princeton University, 1934- .

4024 Population Investigation Committee
Population studies: a journal of demography. London (20:1), July 1966- .

4025 Schnore, Leo F.
The urban scene; human ecology and demography. New York, Free Press, 1965, 374p.

4026 United Nations
Demographic yearbook. New York, 1950- . Annual.

Latin America

4027 Comas, Juan
Relaciones inter-raciales en América Latina: 1940-1960. 1st ed. México, Universidad Nacional Autónoma de México, 1961, 77p.

4028 Ferguson, J.H.
Latin America: the balance of race redressed . . . New York, Oxford University Press, 1961, 101p.

4029 Harris, Marvin
Patterns of race in Latin America. New York, Walker, 1964, 154p.

4030 Pérez de Barradas, José
Los mestizos de América. Madrid, Cultura Clásica y Moderna, 1948, 204p.

4031 Poviña, Alfredo
Nueva historia de la sociología latinoamericana. Córdoba, Impr. de la Universidad, 1959, 492p.

4032 Texas. University. Population Research Center
International population census bibliography: Latin America and the Caribbean. Austin, Bureau of Business Research, University of Texas, 1965, 240p.

Argentina

4033 Cervera, Felipe J.
Estudio de la población de Santa Fé: relación con factores económicos; colección "Extensión Universitaria" no. 101. Santa Fé, Depto. de Extensión Universitaria, Universidad Nacional del Litoral, 1966, 61p.

4034 Miatello, Roberto A.
Población de la provincia de Córdoba: estudio de las poblaciones departamentales. Córdoba, Impr. Universitaria, 1959, 57p.

Brazil

4035 Azevedo, Thales de
As elites de côr; um estudio de ascensão social. São Paulo, Cia. Ed. Nacional, 1955, 203p.

4036 Azevedo, Thales de
Les élites de couleur dans une ville brésilienne. Paris, Unesco, 1953, 107p.

4037 Bastide, Roger, & Florestan Fernandes, eds.
Brancos e negros em São Paulo; ensaio da formação, manifestações atuais e efeitos do preconceito de Côr na sociedade paulistana. 2d ed. rev. São Paulo, Cia. Ed. Nacional, 1959, 371p.

4038 Bastide, Roger, & Florestan Fernandes
O preconceito racial em São Paulo. São Paulo, Publicações do Instituto de Administração no. 118, 1951, 49p.

4039 Cardoso, Fernando H., & Octavio Ianni
Côr e mobilidade social em Florianopolis; aspectos das relações entre negros e brancos numa comunidade do Brasil meridional. São Paulo, Cia. Ed. Nacional, 1960, 286p.

4040 Chacon, V.
O antisemitismo no Brasil: tentativa de interpretação sociológica. Recife, Clube Hebráico, 1955, 34p.

4041 Diegues, Manoel
Etnias e culturas no Brasil. Rio de Janeiro, Ministério da Educação e Saúde, 1952, 79p.

4042 Freyre, Gilberto
The mansions and the shanties . . . the making of modern Brazil . . . 1st American ed. New York, Knopf, 1963, 431p.

4043 Freyre, Gilberto
Problemas brasileiros de antropologia. 3d ed. Rio de Janeiro, Olympio, 1962, 323p.

4044 Freyre, Gilberto
Sobrados e mucambos; decadencia do patriarcado rural e desenvolvimento do urbano. 2d ed. rev. 3v . . . Rio de Janeiro, Olympio, 1951.

4045 Gordon, Eugene
An essay on race amalgamation. Rio de Janeiro, Service of Publications, 1951, 52p.

4046 Lambert, Jacques
Le Brésil, structure sociale et institutions politiques. Paris, Cahiers de la Fondation Nationale des Sciences Politiques no. 44, 1953, 166p.

4047 Lang, Irmgard
Die rassenverhältnisse Brasiliens: eine soziologische und sociolgeschichtliche studie. 2v. Mainz? 1955?

4048 Lima, Jorge de
Patologia social do "branco" brasileiro. Rio de Janeiro, Jornal do Comercio, 1955, 28p.

4049 Marais, B. J.
Colour: unsolved problem of the West. Capetown, Timmins, 1953, 329p.

4050 Melo, A. da Silva
Estudos sôbre o negro. Rio de Janeiro, Olympio, 1958, 231p.

4051 Mortara, Giorgio
Pesquisas sôbre populações americanas. Rio de Janeiro, Kosmos, 1947, 228p.

4052 Pierson, Donald
Negroes in Brazil: a study in race contact at Bahia. Chicago, University of Chicago Press, 1942, 392p.

4053 Ramos, Arthur
Le métissage au Brésil . . . Paris, Hermann, 1952, 142p.

4054 Ribeiro, R.
Religião e relações raciais. Rio de Janeiro, Ministério da Educação e Cultura, Serviço de Documentação, 1956, 241p.

4055 Wiznitzer, Arnold
Jews in colonial Brasil. New York, Columbia University Press, 1960, 227p.

Central America

4056 Goldrich, Daniel
Sons of the establishment: elite youth in Panama and Costa Rica. Chicago, Rand, McNally, 1966, 139p.

Chile

4057 Chile. Universidad. Instituto de Economía
La población del gran Santiago; fuerza de trabajo, educación, ingresos, migración. Santiago, 1959, 173p.

4058 Tabah, L., & R. Samuel
Preliminary findings of a survey on fertility and attitudes toward family formation in Santiago, Chile. (In Kiser, C.V., ed. Research in family planning. Princeton, Princeton University Press, 1962, p. 263-304).

Colombia

4059 Escalante Angulo, C.
El problema racial en Colombia. Bogotá, Instituto Etnológico Nacional, 1952, 7p.

4060 Lipman, A.
La clase social del impresario Bogotano. (In Primer Congreso Nacional de Sociología, 8-10 marzo, 1963. Memoria. Bogotá, Asociación Colombiana de Sociología, 1963, p. 39-54).

Costa Rica

4061 Amador Guevara, José, et al
Nuestro problema demográfico. San José, Ministerio de Salud Pública, 1966, 26p.

Cuba

4062 Entralgo, Elías J.
La liberación étnica cubana. Havana, 1953, 272p.

4063 Martínez, Marcial
Cuba, la verdad de su tragedia. México, 1958, 173p.

4064 Ortiz Fernández, Fernando
Martí y las razas. Havana, Comisión Nacional Organizadora de los Actos y Eds. del Centenario y del Monumento de Martí, 1953, 33p.

Guatemala

4065 Linares Montúfar, Aquiles
El problema indígena en Guatemala en función de la democracia. Guatemala, 1950, 45p.

4066 Skinner-Klee, Jorge
Consideraciones en torno a la clase media emergente en Guatemala. Guatemala, Depto. Editorial "José de Pineda Ibarra," Ministerio de Educación, 1965, 25p.

Haiti

4067 Devauges, Roland, & Maurice A. Lubin
Population et activités commerciales et artisanales à Port-au-Prince. Port-au-Prince, Impr. de l'Etat, 1955, 10p.

4068 Mellon, Roger
Construcción de una tabla abreviada de vida activa masculina para Haiti y la ciudad de Puerto Príncipe en base a los datos censales de 1950. Santiago, CELADE, 1961, 45p.

4069 Viau, Alfred
Negroes, mulatos, blanco; o, Sangre, nada más que sangre. Ciudad Trujillo, Ed. Montalvo, 1955, 223p.

Jamaica

4070 Henriques, Fernando
Family and colour in Jamaica. London, Eyre & Spottiswoode, 1953, 196p.

4071 Roberts, George W.
The population of Jamaica, an analysis of its structure and growth. Cambridge, Cambridge University Press, 1957, 356p.

4072 Stycos, J.M.
The control of human fertility in Jamaica. Ithaca, Cornell University Press, 1964, 377p.

Mexico

4073 Gyves Falcón, Zaida de
Evolución demográfica de la ciudad de Puebla. (In International Geographical Union. Proceedings of the First Latin American Regional Conference, Mexico City, August 2-8, 1966. v. 1. México, 1966, p. 675-691).

4074 Morrison, Paul C.
Population changes in Mexico, 1950-60. (In Loomis, R.A., ed. Papers of the Michigan Academy of Science, Arts and Letters. Ann Arbor, University of Michigan Press, 1964, p. 351-366.)

4075 Patch, Richard W.
La Parada, Lima's market: a study of class and assimilation. 3pts. New York, West Coast South America series, American Universities Field Staff, 1967.

Uruguay

4076 Carvalho Neto, Paulo de
El negro uruguayo. Quito, Ed. Universitaria, 1965, 345p.

Venezuela

4077 Venezuela. Dirección General de Estadística y Censos Nacionales
IX (nono) censo nacional de población; población urbana, intermedia y rural, censos de 1961, 1950, 1941 y 1936. Caracas, 1962, 87p.

West Indies and the Caribbean

4078 Leiris, Michel
Contacts de civilisations en Martinique et en Guadeloupe. Paris, Gallimard, 1955, 192p.

4079 Richmond, A. H.
The colour problem: a study of racial relations. Baltimore, Penguin, 1955, 371p.

Periodical Articles

General

4080 Axelrod, M.
"Urban Structure and Social Participation." American sociological review (21:1), February 1956, p. 13-18.

4081 Buitrón, Aníbal
"Discriminación y Transculturación." México, América indígena (18:1), January 1958, p. 7-15.

4082 Centro de Estudios y Documentación Sociales
"Hipocresía y Discriminación Raciales." México, Panoramas (3:16), July-August 1965, p. 3-39.

4083 Lafforgue, J. R.
"El Racismo." Buenos Aires, Revista de la Universidad de Buenos Aires (7:2), April-June 1962, p. 323-340.

4084 Myers, G. C., et al
"Metropolitan Area Mobility: a Comparative Analysis of Family Spatial Mobility in a Central City and Selected Suburbs." Social forces 42, March 1964, p. 310-314.

Latin America

4085 Bastide, Roger
"Ethnologie des Capitales Latinoaméricaines."

Toulouse, Caravelle 3, 1964, p. 73-82.

4086 Birou, A.
L'Amérique Latine en Ebullition." Caluire et Cuire, Economie et humanisme 137, 1962, p. 21-35.

4087 Comas, Juan
"La Discriminación Racial en América." México, América indígena (5:1), January 1945, p. 73-89; (5:2), April 1945, p. 161-170.

4088 Comas, Juan
"¿Otra Vez el Racismo 'Científico'?" México, América indígena (21:2), April 1961, p. 99-140.

4089 Comas, Juan
"Relaciones Inter-Raciales en América: 1940-1960." México, Cuadernos del Instituto de Historia Antropológica 12, 1961, p. 5-75.

4090 Davis, M.
"Centres of Jewry in the Western Hemisphere: a Comparative Approach." Jewish journal of sociology (5:1), June 1963, p. 4-26.

4091 Germani, Gino
"La Clase Como Barrera Social: Algunos Resultados de un Test Proyectivo." Buenos Aires, Revista latinoamericana de sociología (I:3), November 1965, p. 431-434.

4092 Goldman, Frank P.
"Big Metropole, América do Sul." Journal of inter-american studies 7, October 1965, p. 519-540.

4093 Hecht, W.
"The Population of the Latin American Republics." Rome, Bulletin international de l'Institut de Statistiques 35, 1957, p. 291-305.

4094 Konetzke, R.
"Sobre el Problema Racial en la América Española." Madrid, Revista de estudios políticos 60, September 1960, p. 113-114; December 1960, p. 179-213.

4095 MacLean y Esteños, Roberto
"Plantamientos y Soluciones del Problema Indígeno." México, América indígena (18:3), July 1958, p. 205-336.

4096 Mendieta y Núñez, Lucio
"Les Tensions Sociales de Caractère Racial et Culturel en Amérique Latine." Paris, Bulletin international des sciences sociales (4:3), Autumn 1952, p. 467-476.

4097 Rama, Carlos M.
"Enfoque Sociológico del Antisemitismo." México, Revista mexicana de sociología (25:2), May-August 1963, p. 705-720.

4098 Smith, Thomas L.
"Current Population Trends in Latin America." American journal of sociology 63, January 1967, p. 399-406.

4099 Stycos, J.M.
"Survey of Research and Population Control in Latin America." Public opinion quarterly (28:3), Autumn 1964, p. 367-372.

4100 Terra, J.P., et al
"Situación y Perspectivas Demográficas de América Latina." Montevideo, Cuadernos latinoamericanos de economía humana (1:1), 1958, p. 34-59.

Argentina

4101 Alvo, Florencio E.
"La Población de la Ciudad de Buenos Aires a Través del Cuarto Censo General de la Nación." Buenos Aires, Revista de la ciudad de Buenos Aires, August 1948, p. 61-74.

4102 Barral Souto, J.
"Características Demográficas de la República Argentina." Rome, Bulletin international de l'Institut de Statistiques (XXXV:3), 1957, p. 359-367.

4103 Medina Gómez, José
"Buenos Aires: En 1580, 69 Habitantes, en 1956, 5 Millones y Medio en la Ciudad, Más Extensa que Nueva York, Hay Más Extranjeros que Argentinos." Madrid, Mundo hispánico (9:102), September 1956, p. 61-62.

4104 "La Población de la Ciudad de Buenos Aires." Havana, Boletín, April 1946, p. 9-10.

4105 Rosenswaike, I.
"Jewish Population of Argentina: Census and Estimate, 1887-1947." Jewish social studies 22, October 1960, p. 195-214.

4106 Vidal, Alfredo
"Génesis y Perfil de los Pueblos Coloniales Bonaerenses." La Plata, Revista de educación (90:2), February 1949, p. 39-64.

4107 Viñas, D.
"'Gauchos Judíos' y Xenofobia." México, Revista de la Universidad de México (18:3), November 1963, p. 14-19.

Barbados

4108 Lowenthal, David
"The Population of Barbados." Mona, Social & economic studies (6:4), 1957, p. 445-501.

Bolivia

4109 Leonard, Olen E.
"La Paz, Bolivia: its Population and Growth." American sociological review 13, 1948, p. 448-454.

4110 Mangan, S.
"Storm Clouds Over the Bolivian Refuge; South America's New Pattern of Anti-Semitism." Commentary 14, August 1952, p. 99-106.

4111 Villanueva Llano, J.
"El 'Problema del Indio' en Bolivia." Madrid, Cuadernos hispanoamericanos (29:84), December 1956, p. 314-338.

Brazil

4112 Araujo, José Ribeiro de
"Alguns Aspectos da População da Cidade de São Paulo." São Paulo, Revista de história (12:25), January/March 1956, p. 3-21.

4113 Araujo, Oscar E. de
"Estatística Predial. I-III." São Paulo, Revista do arquivo municipal, March 1945, p. 7-43.

4114 Azevedo, Aldo M.
"A Vida dos Paulistas e dos Cariocas." São Paulo, IDORT, January 1947, p. 3-7.

4115 Azevedo, Thales de
"Imagens e Esterotipos Raciais e Nacionais." Salvador, Arquivos da Universidade da Bahia 2, 1953, p. 102-116.

4116 Bastide, Roger
"Introduction à l'Etude de Quelques Complexes Afro-Brésiliens." Port-au-Prince, Bulletin du Bureau d'Ethnologie, July 1948, p. 3-41.

4117 Bastide, Roger
"Stéréotypes et Préjugés de Couleur." São Paulo, Sociologia (18:2), May 1956, p. 141-171.

4118 Bastide, Roger, & P. Van den Berghe
"Stereotypes, Norms and Inter-Racial Behavior in São Paulo, Brazil." American sociological review (22:6), December 1957, p. 689-694.

4119 Borges, T. Poumpeu Accioly
"Censo Demográfico de Brasília, a Nova Capital do Brasil." Rio de Janeiro, Boletim do Centro Latino-Americano de Pesquisas em Ciências Sociais (3:2), May 1960, p. 30-37.

4120 Cascudo, Luiz da Câmara
"Considerações Sôbre as Relações de Vizihança." São Paulo, Sociologia (17:4), October 1955, p. 348-354.

4121 Christopher, R. A.
"The Human Race in Brazil." Américas (5:7), July 1953, p. 3-5, 30-31.

4122 Curtis, María L. Lessa de
"Distribuição da População no Estado do Ceará em 1950." Rio de Janeiro, Revista brasileira de geografía (XVII:3), July-September 1955, p. 111-124.

4123 Diegues, Manoel
"Relações de Raça e de Cultura no Brasil." Rio de Janeiro, Boletim do Ministério do Trabalho, Indústria e Comércio (1:3), July-September 1951, p. 9-22.

4124 Egler, E. Gonçalves
"Distribuição da População no Estado de Minas Gerais em 1940." Rio de Janeiro, Revista brasileira de geografía (XV:1), January-March 1953, p. 123-149.

4125 Freyre, Gilberto
"Ethnic Democracy: the Brazilian Example." Américas 15, December 1963, p. 1-6.

4126 Hammond, H. R.
"Race, Social Mobility and Politics in Brazil." Race (4:2), May 1963, p. 3-13.

4127 Harris, Marvin, & C. Kottak
"The Structural Significance of Brazilian Racial Categories." São Paulo, Sociologia (25:3), September 1963, p. 203-208.

4128 Holanda, Sergio Buarque de
"Movimentos da População em São Paulo no Século XVIII." São Paulo, Revista do Instituto de Estudos Brasileiros 1, 1966, p. 55-111.

4129 Ianni, Octavio
"A Ideologia Racial do Negro e do Mulato em Florianópolis." São Paulo, Sociologia (20:3), August 1958, p. 352-365.

4130 Izumi, S., & H. Saito
"Pesquisas Sôbre a Aculturação dos Japoneses no Brasil." São Paulo, Sociologia (15:3), August 1953, p. 195-209.

4131 Leão, Mario L.
"Crescimento da População da Cidade de São Paulo." Rio de Janeiro, Boletim do Ministério do Trabalho, Indústria e Comércio, November 1945, p. 237-247.

4132 "The Legal Condition of the Indians in Brazil." Brussels, Civilisations (4:2), 1954, p. 241-254.

4133 Manchester, A.K.
"Racial Democracy in Brazil." South Atlantic quarterly 64, Winter 1965, p. 27-35.

4134 Meyer Ginsberg, A.
"Relações Raciais Entre Negros e Brancos em São Paulo." São Paulo, Anhembi (13:39), February 1954, p. 443-464; (14:40), March 1954, p. 22-52.

4135 Oberg, Kalervo
"Race Relations in Brazil." São Paulo, Sociologia (20:3), August 1958, p. 340-351.

4136 "Race Relations in Brazil." Paris, Courier (5:8-9), August-September 1952, p. 6-15.

4137 Ribeiro, D.
"L'Intégration des Aborigènes au Brésil." Geneva, Revue internationale du travail (85:4), April 1962, p. 351-376.

4138 Santos, Milton
"População da Bahia." Rio de Janeiro, Boletim geográfico 146, 1958, p. 622-625.

4139 Soares, M.T. de Segadas
"O Conceito Geográfico de Bairro e su Exemplificação na Cidade de Rio de Janeiro." Rio de Janeiro, Boletim carioca de geografía 3-4, 1958, p. 47-68.

4140 Souza Keller, E. Coelho de
"Distribuição da População no Estado de Mato Grosso em 1940." Rio de Janeiro, Revista brasileira de geografía (XV:2), April-June 1953, p. 123-131.

Chile

4141 Abasoal H., Manuel
"Las Ciudades del Mundo con Más de un Millón de Habitantes." Santiago, Boletín del Instituto Nacional, May 1941, p. 29.

4142 Gabello, O.
"The Demography of Chile." London, Population studies (9:3), March 1956, p. 237-250.

4143 León-Portilla, Miguel
"The Indian Problem in Chile." México, América indígena, July 1957, p. 247-259.

Colombia

4144 Arboleda, J. R.
"La Historia y la Antropología del Negro en Colombia." Rio de Janeiro, América latina (5:3), July-September 1963, p. 3-15.

4145 Colombia. Dirección Nacional de Estadística
"Series Demográficas de Bogotá." Bogotá, Boletín informativo (1:10), December 1951, p. 4.

4146 Escobar Barrazabal, M.
"El Desarrollo de Bogotá." Bogotá, Registro municipal, April 15, 1937, p. [169]-173.

4147 "The Legal Condition of the Indians in Colombia."
Brussels, Civilisations (4:2), 1954, p. 255-258.

Cuba

4148 Fernández y Simón, Abel
"Estudios Sobre la Población, las Areas Urbanas y la Densidad de Población de la Ciudad de La Habana, en su Epoca Colonial. I-II." Havana, Ingeniería civil (6:3), August 1955, p. 627-636; (6:9), September 1955, p. 679-688.

4149 Foyaca, M.
"Razas y Trabajo en Cuba." México, Latino-américa (3:31), July 1, 1951, p. 308-310.

4150 Muller, Carlos
" De Qué Se Muere en La Habana?" Havana, Carteles, November 9, 1947, p. 64-65.

4151 Pérez de la Riva, J.
"La Population de Cuba et ses Problèmes." Paris, Population (22:1), January-February 1967, p. 99-110.

4152 Poviña, Alfredo
"Un Problema Social en Santiago de Cuba." México, Universidad de México (13:7), March 1959, p. 34.

Dominican Republic

4153 Amiama, Manuel A.
"La Población de Santo Domingo." Ciudad Trujillo, Clio (27:115), July/December 1959, p. 116-134.

4154 Dyer, D.R.
"Distribution of Population on Hispaniola." Economic geography 30, 1954, p. 337-346.

4155 Ucko, E.
"La Fusión de los Sefardís con los Dominicanos: Cuestiones Raciales." Ciudad Trujillo, Cuadernos dominicanos de cultura, November 1944, p. 55-82.

Ecuador

4156 "Population of the City of Quito on December 31, 1930, at 91,641." Pan American Union bulletin 65, June 1931, p. 667.

Guatemala

4157 Nash, Manning
"Political Relations in Guatemala." Mona, Social & economic studies (7:1), March 1958, p. 65-75.

Guyana

4158 Fried, Morton H.
"Some Observations on the Chinese in British Guiana." Mona, Social & economic studies (5:1), March 1956, p. 54-73.

4159 Halperin, Ernst
"Racism and Communism in British Guiana." Journal of inter-American studies 7, January 1965, p. 95-134.

4160 Nair, K.S.K.
"Indians in British Guiana." New Delhi, Indo-Asian culture (6:4), April 1958, p. 417-421.

4161 "Reds' Own War in Guiana: Signs of Another 'Congo'." U.S. news & world report 56, June 15, 1964, p. 60-61.

Haiti

4162 Aristide, A.
"Los Problemas Demográficos de Haití." México, América indígena (16:1), 1956, p. 35-39.

Honduras

4163 Lang, J.
"Espectro Racial de Honduras." México, América indígena, July 1951, p. 209-217.

Jamaica

4164 Ellis, R.A.
"Color and Class in a Jamaican Market Town." Sociology & social research 41, May-June 1957, p. 345-360.

4165 Kerr, M.
"Some Areas in Transition: Jamaica." Phylon (14:4), 1953, p. 410-412.

4166 Lind, A.W.
"Adjustment Patterns Among the Jamaican Chinese." Mona, Social & economic studies (7:2), June 1958, p. 144-164.

Mexico

4167 Burnright, R.G., et al
"Differential Rural-Urban Fertility in Mexico." American sociological review 21, February 1956, p. 3-8.

4168 Cacho, R.
"La Ciudad de México." México, Revista económica (24:4), April 1961, p. 123-133.

4169 Dotson, Floyd
"A Note on Participation in Voluntary Associations in a Mexican City." American sociological review (18:4), August 1953, p. 381-386.

4170 Rivera Marín, G.
"El Crecimiento de la Población y el Problema de la Mano de Obra Industrial." México, Revista de economía (29:10), October 1966, p. 298-304.

Panama

4171 Biesanz, John
"Race Relations in Panama and the Canal Zone." American journal of sociology (57:1), July 1951, p. 7-14.

4172 Westermann, George W.
"School Segregation on the Panama Canal Zone." Phylon (15:3), 1954, p. 276-287.

Paraguay

4173 Barreiro-Saguier, R.
"Le Paraguay, Nation de Métis." Le Havre, Revue de psychologie des peuples (18:4), 4th quarter, 1963, p. 442-463.

4174 Carvalho Nêto, Paulo de
"Contribución al Estudio de los Negros Paraguayos." Rio de Janeiro, América latina (5:1-2), January-June 1962, p. 23-40.

Peru

4175 Area Parro, Alberto
"La Ciudad Capital de la República y el Censo Nacional de 1940." Lima, Estadística peruana, January 1945, p. 24-29.

4176 Cavanaugh, Joseph A.
"Método para Estimar la Población de Lima, Perú." Lima, Informaciones sociales (10:1), January/March 1955, p. 11-24.

4177 García Frías, Roque
"Crecimiento de la Población de Lima, Ciudad Capital." Lima, Estadística peruana, January 1945, p. 32-50.

4178 Mason, P.
"Gradualism in Peru; Some Impressions on the Future of Ethnic Group Relations." London, Race (8:1), July 1966, p. 43-61.

4179 Matos Mar, J.
"El Caso del Perù: Consideraciones Sobre su Situación Social como Marco de Referencia al Problema de Lima." Toulouse, Caravelle 3, 1964, p. 111-124.

4180 Oyagüe, Víctor M.
"Area, Densidad y Población de la Ciudad de Lima a Través de Cuatro Siglos." Lima, Boletín de la Sociedad Geográfica 53, 2d-3d quarter, 1936, p. 175-185.

4181 Uriarte, Carlos A.
"Un Ensayo de la Distribución de los Habitantes de Lima, Ciudad Capital, por Grupos Socio-Económicos; Algo Sobre el Método de la 'Muestra.'" Lima, Estadística peruana, March 1948, p. 40-56.

Venezuela

4182 Henry, L.
"La Population du Venezuela." Paris, Population (4:1), 1949, p. 155-156.

4183 Marchand, B.
"Etude Géographique de la Population du Venezuela." Paris, Annales de geographie (72:394), November-December 1963, p. 734-745.

4184 Montesino Samperio, José V.
"La Población del Area Metropolitana de Caracas. Factores de Crecimiento y Tendencia Futura." Caracas, Cuadernos de información económica (9:3), May/June 1957, p. 55-108.

4185 Michalup, E.
"Algunos Aspectos Demográficos de la Población de Venezuela." Rome, Bulletin international de l'Institut de Statistiques (XXXV:3), 1957, p. 325-331.

West Indies and the Caribbean

4186 Pellier, J.
"La Région des Caraïbes: Problèmes de Population." Paris, Etudes et conjoncture 10, 1958, p. 973-984.

4187 Roberts, George W.
"Recent Demographic Trends in Cuba, Haiti and the British Caribbean." Population bulletin 5, July 1956, p. 42-50.

4188 Rubin, Vera
"Social and Cultural Pluralism in the Caribbean." Annals of the New York Academy of Science (83:5), 1960, p. 763-916.

4189 Williams, E.E.
"The Contemporary Pattern of Race Relations in the Caribbean." Phylon 16, 4th quarter 1955, p. 367-379.

EDUCATION

Books

General

4190 Bloom, Benjamin S., et al
Compensatory education for cultural deprivation. A report based on working papers contributed by participants in the Research Conference on Education and Cultural Deprivation. New York, Holt, Rinehart & Winston, 1965, 179p.

4191 Conference on the Impact of Urbanization on Education, Washington, D.C., 1962
The impact of urbanization on education; summary report . . . Washington, U.S. Office of Education, 1962, 12p.

4192 Dobbins, C.G., ed.
The university, the city and urban renewal. Washington, American Council on Education, 1964, 58p.

4193 Gittell, Marilyn, ed.
Educating an urban population. Beverly Hills, Sage Publications, 1966, 224p.

4194 Havighurst, Robert
Education in the metropolis. Boston, Allyn & Bacon, 1966, 307p.

4195 Hunnicutt, Clarence W., ed.
Urban education and cultural deprivation. Syracuse, Div. of Summer Sessions, Syracuse University, 1964, 126p.

4196 Kerber, August, & Barbara Bommarito, eds.
The schools and the urban crisis; a book of readings. New York, Holt, Rinehart & Winston, 1963, 367p.

4197 Klotsche, J.M.
The urban university and the future of our cities. New York, Harper & Row, 1966, 149p.

4198 Mays, J.B.
Education and the urban child. Liverpool, Liverpool University Press, 1962, 208p.

4199 Reiss, Albert J., ed.
Schools in a changing society. New York, Free Press, 1965, 224p.

4200 Symposium on Library Functions in the Changing Metropolis, Dedham, Massachusetts, 1963
The public library and the city . . . Ed. by Ralph W. Conant. Cambridge, M.I.T. Press, 1965, 216p.

4201 Urban education. v. 1- Buffalo, University of Buffalo Foundation, 1964-

Latin America

4202 AACTE Conference on International Understanding. 6th, University of Pittsburgh, 1964
Education for national development, focus: Latin America . . . Washington, American Association of Colleges for Teacher Education, 1964, 72p.

4203 Aguirre Beltrán, Gonzalo
La universidad latinoamericana, y otros ensayos. 1st ed. Xalapa, Universidad Veracruzana, 1961, 203p.

4204 Bergström Lourenço, Manoel
Primary school curricula in Latin America. Paris, Unesco, 1957, 36p.

4205 Cardoso, Manoel, ed.
Higher education in Latin America, a symposium. Washington, Catholic University of America Press, 1961, 68p.

4206 La educación. (Año 1, no. 1-) Washington, División de Educación, Depto. de Asuntos Culturales, Unión Panamericana, 1956-

4207 Harner, Evelyn L.
Changing patterns of education in Latin America. Santa Barbara, Technical Military Planning Operation, General Electric Company, 1960, 63p.

4208 Havighurst, Robert J., et al
La sociedad y la educación en América Latina. Buenos Aires, Ed. Universitaria de Buenos Aires, 1962, 335p.

4209 Inter-American Meeting of Ministers of Education. 3d, Bogotá, 1963.
Final act, and appendices. 4v. Washington, Pan American Union, 1964.

4210 Inter-American Seminar on Overall Planning for Education, Washington, D.C., 1958
Documentos de trabajo. 5v. Washington, Unión Panamericana, 1959.

4211 Inter-American Seminar on Secondary Education, Santiago de Chile, 1954-1955
La educación secundaria en América; memoria. Washington, Division of Education, Pan American Unión, 1956, 466p.

4212 Palacín Iglesias, Gregorio B.
La educación en Latinoamérica. Coral Gables, University of Miami, 1952, 135p.

4213 Pan American Union. Dept. of Cultural Affairs. Division of Education
Education in Latin America: a partial bibliography. Washington, 1958, 50p.

4214 Pan American Union. Division of Education
Estado actual de la educación en la América Latina . . . 2d ed. rev. Washington, 1957, 206p.

4215 Pan American Union. Section of Labor, Migration & Social Security
Serie sobre educación social del trabajador. Washington, 1949-

4216 Reissig, Luis
Problemas educativos de América Latina. Buenos Aires, EUDEBA, 1963, 100p.

4217 Silvert, Klaman H.
The social origins and political commitment of the Latin American university student. Paris, International Political Science Association, 1964, 34p.

4218 Zanetti, Juan E.
Las bibliotecas públicas de Latinoamérica al servicio de la educación popular. Córdoba, Federación Argentina de Bibliotecas Populares, 1951, 28p.

Argentina

4219 Alvarez Rojas, Federíco E.
La escuela popular argentina; su defensa. Buenos Aires, El Ateneo, 1964, 327p.

4220 Argentine Republic. Dirección General de Enseñanza Secundaria Normal y Especial
Cuadernos para la escuela media. Buenos Aires, 1953-

4221 Argentine Republic. Secretaría de Educación. Dirección General de Informaciones, Biblioteca y Estadística
Anuario estadístico. Buenos Aires, Annual.

4222 No entry

4223 Argentine Republic. Secretaría de Educación. Dirección General de Informaciones, Biblioteca y Estadística
Ministerio de Educación de la Nación, sus dependencias al 15 de junio de 1949. Buenos Aires, Depto. de Informaciones, Biblioteca y Estadística, 1949, 39p.

4224 Candioti, Alberto M.
Escuelas hogares, rurales y urbanas . . . Buenos Aires, 1949, 127p.

4225 Dana Montaño Salvador M.
La crisis argentina y la educación común y superior. Buenos Aires, Emecé Eds., 1963, 160p.

4226 Lapalma, M.M. & E.M. Rivas
Youth in Argentine politics. Paris, International Political Science Association, 1964, 28p.

4227 Mignone, Emilio F.
Política educacional y organización política argentina; responde a los programas en vigencia. Buenos Aires, Ed. Dallas, 1955, 214p.

4228 Reissig, Luis
La educación del pueblo. Buenos Aires, Ed. Losada, 1952, 125p.

4229 Sánchez, V.
Cultura nacional o cultura liberal; la batalla por la enseñanza libre. Buenos Aires, Eds. Arayú, 1963, 187p.

4230 Solari, Manuel H.
Política educacional argentina; política, legislación y organización escolar de la República Argentina. 2d ed. Buenos Aires, El Ateneo, 1950, 251p.

Bolivia

4231 Arce Vargas, Mario
Estadística de la división política administrativa de Bolivia . . . La Paz, Ed. "Kollasuyo," 1954, 71p.

4232 Bolivia. Ministerio de Educación
Plan de fomento de la educación nacional presentado en el gobierno del Excmo. Sr. Presidente Dr. Hernán Siles Zuazo y bajo la gestión ministerial del Sr. Fernando Díez de Medina. La Paz, 1958, 163p.

4233 Carpio de McQueen, Aurora del
Reforma educacional. Cochabamba, Ed. "Atlantic," 1962, 29p.

4234 Donoso Torres, Vicente
Bases para una reforma integral de la educación . . . La Paz, Ed. Don Bosco, 1953, 55p.

4235 Donoso Torres, Vicente
Filosofía de la educación boliviana. Buenos Aires, Ed. Atlántida, 1946, 205p.

4236 Ibañez López, Mario
Fundamentos para un régimen autónomo de la educación pública en Bolivia. Santa Cruz, Universidad Gabriel René Moreno, 1961, 104p.

4237 Salinas, José M.
Historia de la Universidad Mayor de San Andrés. 2v. La Paz, Ed. U.M.S.A., 1949.

4238 Suárez Arnez, Faustino, et al
Hacia la nueva educación nacional. La Paz, 1953, 198p.

4239 Sucre, Bolivia (City) Escuela Normal
Nuevos rumbos. Sucre. Irregular.

Brazil

4240 Azevedo, Fernando de
Brazilian culture, an introduction to the study of culture in Brazil; tr. by William Crawford. New York, Macmillan, 1950, 562p.

4241 Berlinck, Eodoro Lincoln
Fatores adversos na formação brasileira . . . 2d ed. São Paulo, 1954, 303p.

4242 Brazil. Depto. Nacional de Educação
Relatorio. Rio de Janeiro. Irregular.

4243 Campos, Ernesto de Souza
Temas universitarios. São Paulo, Depto. de Cultura e Ação Social da Reitoria da Universidade de São Paulo, Div. de Difusão Cultural, Secção de Publicações, 1952, 216p.

4244 Faust, Augusto P.
Brazil: education in an expanding economy. Washington, U.S. Office of Education, 1959, 142p.

4245 Havighurst, Robert J., & João R. Moreira
Society and education in Brazil. University of Pittsburgh Press, 1965, 263p.

4246 Lamparelli, Celso M., & Luiz L. Rivera
Análise da situação educacional; ensino fundamental e médio no Estado de São Paulo. São Paulo, Comissão Interestadual da Bacia Paraná-Uruguai, 1964, 71p.

4247 Lemme, Paschoal
Educação democrática e progressista. São Paulo, Ed. Pluma, 1961, 268p.

4248 Mascaro, Carlos Corrêa
O municipio de São Paulo e o ensino primário; ensaio de administração escolar. São Paulo, Faculdade de Filosofia, Ciências e Letras, Universidade de São Paulo, 1960, 397p.

4249 Mascaro, Carlos Corrêa
Município e ensino no Estado de São Paulo. São Paulo, Faculdade de Filosofía, Ciencias e Letras, Universidade de São Paulo, 1959, 308p.

4250 Mello, José A. Gonsalves de
A Universidade do Recife e a pesquisa histórica. Recife, Impr. Universitaria, 1959, 31p.

4251 Moreira, João R.
Educação e Desenvolvimento no Brasil. Rio de Janeiro, 1960, 298p.

4252 Motta, Cándido
Servindo à educação. Rio de Janeiro, Serviço de Documentação, 1955, 130p.

4253 Rio de Janeiro (Federal District), Secretaria Geral de Educação e Cultura
Programas do ensino normal. Rio de Janeiro, 1950, 86p.

4254 Rio de Janeiro. Instituto Nacional de Estudos Pedagógicos
O ensino superior e médio no Brasil; relação dos estabelecimentos de ensino em funcionamento no pais no 2º semestre de 1948. Rio de Janeiro, 1949, 297p.

4255 Díaz Sánchez, D.
La educación en Brasil. Friburg, Feres, 1961, 114p.

4256 São Paulo, Brazil (State) Directoria Geral da Instrucção Pública
Annuario do ensino do Estado de São Paulo. São Paulo, 1945-

4257 Werebe, María J. García
Grandezas e miserías do ensino brasileiro. São Paulo, Difusão Européia do Livro, 1963, 152p.

Central America

4258 Consejo Superior Universitario Centroamericano. Comisión Centroamericana en pro de los Estudios Generales Los estudios generales en Centroamérica. San José, Ciudad Universitaria "Rodrigo Facio," 1963, 402p.

4259 Reunión de Ministros de Educación de Centroamérica y Panamá. 1st, Guatemala, 1955
Primera Reunión de Ministros de Educación de Centro América y Panamá, junio de 1955. Guatemala, Ed. del Ministerio de Educación Pública, 1956, 289p.

Chile

4260 Gill, Clark C.
Education and social change in Chile; bulletin 1966, no. 7. Washington, U.S. Office of Education, Dept. of Health, Education & Welfare, 1966, 143p.

4261 Hamuy, Eduardo
Educación elemental, analfabetismo y desarrollo económico. Santiago, Ed. Universitaria, 1960, 87p.

4262 Ossa S.M., Gastón
La mitad de los niños chilenos no se educan, con otros artículos y discursos sobre problemas educacionales, relaciones internationales, administración pública. Valparaíso, Fundación Educacional del Rotary Club de Valparaíso, 1948, 95p.

4263 Pino Batory, Martín
La educación pública y el desarrollo de Chile. Santiago, Sociedad Cooperativa de Cultura y Publicaciones, 1961, 58p.

4264 Riquelme Rodríguez, Vicente A.
El valor económico de la educación pública. Santiago, 1948, 122p.

4265 Saavedra I., Enrique
La educación no en una comuna de Santiago: comuna de San Miguel. Tercera parte/plan de educación regular. Santiago, Instituto de Educación, Facultad de Filosofía y Educación, 1965, 246p.

4266 Samper, Armando
A case study of cooperation in secondary education in Chile . . . Washington, National Planning Association, 1957, 83p.

4267 Vega, Julio
La racionalización de nuestra enseñanza. Santiago, Eds. de la Universidad de Chile, 1954, 277p.

4268 Vivanco Mora, H.
El problema básico, nuestra educación primaria. Santiago, Ed. Hiram, 1953, 149p.

Colombia

4269 Atlántico, Colombia (Dept.) Dirección de Educación Pública
Informe. Barranquilla. Annual.

4270 Bernal Jiménez, Rafael
La educación, he ahí el problema. Bogotá, Prensas del Ministerio de Educación Nacional, 1949, 317p.

4271 Bohórquez Casallas, Luis A.
La evolución educativa en Colombia. Bogotá, Pubs. Cultural Colombiana, 1956, 555p.

4272 Colombia. Ministerio de Educación Nacional
Planes y programas de la enseñanza primaria, rural y urbana. Bogotá, 1950, 138p.

4273 Nieto Caballero, Agustín
La segunda enseñanza y reformas de la educación. Bogotá, 1964, 269p.

4274 Pinto L., Luis E.
Reflexiones de un educador; ensayo sobre sociología educativa. Bogotá, Ed. Kelly, 1946, 261p.

Costa Rica

4275 Asociación Nacional de Educadores
Conferencia anual de educación. No. 1-, San José, 1945- .

4276 Consejo Superior Universitario Centroamericano
El sistema educativo en Costa Rica, situación actual y perspectivas. Ciudad Universitaria, San José, Universidad de Costa Rica, 1964, 242p.

4277 Cortés Chacón, Rafael
Necesidad de una reorganización del sistema educativo costarricense. San José, Escuela Superior de Administración Pública de América Central, 1957, 199p.

4278 Costa Rica. Junta de Educación
Informe. San José. Annual.

4279 Costa Rica. Secretaría de Educación Pública
Estadísticas de educación. San José. Annual.

4280 Karsen, Sonia
Educational development in Costa Rica with UNESCO's technical assistance, 1951-1954. San José, Ministerio de Educación Pública, 1954, 167p.

4281 Liceo de Costa Rica
Anales. San José, 1950- .

Cuba

4282 Centro Asturiano, Havana. Sección de Instrucción
Memoria. Havana, 1951-

4283 Le-Roy y Gálvez, Luis F.
La Universidad de la Habana; síntesis histórica. El escudo de la Universidad; su simbolismo. Havana, Impr. de la Universidad de la Habana, 1960, 24p.

4284 Pérez, Emma
La educación en el siglo XX. Havana, Impr. de la Universidad de la Habana, 1945, 126p.

4285 U.S. Office of Education. Division of International Studies & Services
Educational data: Cuba. Washington, 1962, 18p.

Dominican Republic

4286 Báez Soler, Osvaldo
Realidades dominicanas modernas. Ciudad Trujillo, Sánchez Andújar, 1948, 42p.

4287 Dominican Republic. Secretaría de Educación Pública y Bellas Artes
Programas de la educación primaria. Ciudad Trujillo, 1951, 217p.

4288 Nivar Ramírez, Consuelo
Sistema educativo en la República Dominicana. Ciudad Trujillo, 1949, 119p.

4289 Pacheco, Armando O.
La obra educativo de Trujillo. 2v. Ciudad Trujillo, Impr. Dominicana, 1955.

4290 Sánchez, Juan F.
La universidad de Santo Domingo. Ciudad Trujillo, Impr. Dominicana, 1955, 414p.

4291 Santo Domingo. Instituto Profesional
Anales del Instituto Profesional de Santo Domingo. Santo Domingo, 1947-

Ecuador

4292 Alberola, V., et al
Cinco siglos de historia; centenario del Colegio San Gabriel, 1863-1962. Quito, Prensa Católica, 1962, 258p.

4293 Alemán, Hugo
Transito de generaciones; el Instituto Nacional "Mejía"; medio siglo de educación democrática. Quito, Casa de la Cultura Ecuatoriana, 1947, 271p.

4294 Chávez, Ligdano
Educación y nacionalidad. Quito, Casa de la Cultura Ecuatoriana, 1952, 141p.

4295 Ecuador. Ministerio de Educación Pública
Reglamento general de segunda educación. Quito, Tall. Gráf. Nacionales, 1947, 46p.

4296 Olaizola, Sabás
El plan de maestros asociados o de ambientes especializados; una nueva estructura de la escuela primaria. Tegucigalpa, Ministerio de Educación Pública de la República de Honduras, 1956, 257p.

4297 Romo Dávila, Carlos
El proyecto educativo en el Ecuador y en Latinoamérica . . . Quito, Ed. Casa de la Cultura Ecuatoriana, 1956, 68p.

El Salvador

4298 San Salvador. Universidad Nacional
Guíon histórico de la Universidad Autónoma de El Salvador. San Salvador, Ed. Ahora, 1949, 84p.

Guatemala

4299 Castañeda Paganini, Ricardo
Historia de la Real y Pontificia Universidad de San Carlos de Guatemala. Guatemala, 1947- .

4300 Consejo Superior Universitario Centroamericano
El sistema educativo en Guatemala; situación actual y perspectivas. Ciudad Universitaria, San José, 1964, 283p.

4301 Guatemala. Secretaría de Educación Pública
Programas para la escuela primaria urbana. Guatemala, 1950, 156p.

4302 Martínez Durán, Carlos
Discursos universitarios, 1958-1962. Prólogo: Alberto Velázquez. Guatemala, Universidad de San Carlos de Guatemala, 1962, 229p.

4303 Martini Orozco, Margarita
Hacia la escuela activa en la educación guatemalteca.

Guatemala, Universidad de Guatemala, Facultad de Humanidades, 1951, 126p.

4304 Mata Gavidia, José
Fundación de la Universidad en Guatemala: 1548-1688. Guatemala, Ed. Universitaria, 1954, 388p.

4305 Zapata Castañeda, Adrián
Forjando vidas; memorias. 2v. Guatemala, 1949-50.

Guyana

4306 Bone, Louis W.
Secondary education in the Guianas. Chicago, Comparative Education Center, University of Chicago, 1962, 70p.

Haiti

4307 Auguste, C. A.
Pour une éducation haitienne. Port-au-Prince, Presses Libres, 1954, 132p.

4308 Dale, George A.
Education in the Republic of Haiti. Washington, Office of Education, U.S. Dept. of Health, Education and Welfare, 1959, 180p.

4309 Lamy, Amilcar F.
Le Lycée Alexandre Pétion, 1816-1950. Port-au-Prince, Impr. de l'Etat, 1950, 50p.

4310 L'effort du gouvernement dans le domaine de l'education nationale. Port-au-Prince, Impr. Théodore, 1956, 198p.

4311 Haiti (Republic) Dept. du Travail
Education ouvrière. Port-au-Prince, 1955, unpaged.

4312 Mirville, S.
L'école primaire et la lutte contre l'analphabétisme en Haiti; étude statistique. Port-au-Prince, La Phalange, 1959, 58p.

Honduras

4313 Bardales B., Rafael
La educación en Honduras. Madrid, Oficina de Educación Iberoamericana, Instituto de Cultura Hispánica, 1953, 54p.

4314 Consejo Superior Universitario Centroamericano
El sistema educativo en Honduras; situación actual y perspectivas. San José? Depto. de Publicaciones, Universidad de Costa Rica, 1965, 119p.

4315 Honduras. Dirección General de Educación Primaria
Planes y programas de estudio para la educación primaria . . . Tegucigalpa, Talleres Ariston, 1951, 362p.

4316 International Labor Office
Informe sobre educación obrera en la República de Honduras. Geneva, 1964, 17p.

4317 Lara Cerrato, Fausto, ed.
Aspectos culturales de Honduras. Tegucigalpa, 1951, 484p.

4318 Thompson, M. W.
Education in Honduras. Washington, U.S. Office of Education, 1955, 33p.

Mexico

4319 Brito, Luis C.
Educación democrática en la adolescencia. México, Ed. Buena Prensa, 1950, 86p.

4320 Bueno, Miguel
Estudios sobre la universidad. 1st ed. México, Instituto de Investigaciones Sociales, Universidad Nacional Autónoma de México, 1962, 196p.

4321 El Cuarto Centenario de la Universidad. México, Ed. Ruta, 1951, 29p.

4322 García Ruz, Ramón
Hombres y rutas de México. Guadalajara, Eds. El Estudiante, 1953, 136p.

4323 Garrido, Luis
Palabras universitarias, 1951-1953. 1st ed. México, Eds. Botas, 1954, 222p.

4324 Johnston, Marjorie C.
Education in Mexico. Washington, U.S. Office of Education, 1956, 135p.

4325 Kneller, George F.
The education of the Mexican nation. New York, Columbia University Press, 1951, 258p.

4326 Larroyo, Francisco
Historia comparada de la educación en México. 4th ed. corr. & enl. México, Ed. Porrúa, 1956, 437p.

4327 Magisterio; revista de educación y orientación sindical. México, 1945-

4328 México (City) Instituto Nacional de Pedagogía
Revista. México (I:1), 1947- .

4329 México (City) Universidad Nacional
Pensamiento y destino de la Ciudad Universitaria de México. México, Impr. Universitaria, 1952, 155p.

4330 México. Dirección General de Estadística Educativa
Estadística educativa; boletín. v. 1-, México, 1947- .

4331 Reyes Rosales, J.J.
Historia de la educación en Veracruz. Xalapa, 1959, 241p.

4332 Rosa, Agustín de la
La instrucción en México. Guadalajara, Eds. I.T.G., 1952, 171p.

4333 Tirado Benedí, Domingo
Problemas de la educación mexicana; nueva época. México, Secretaría de Educación Pública, 1955, 110p.

Panama

4334 Panama (City) Universidad. Escuela de Temporada
La educación en Panamá. Mesa redonda sobre los problemas de la educación nacional, celebrada del 18 al 22 de marzo de 1957 en el paraninfo de la Universidad. Panamá, Impr. Nacional, 1957, 334p.

4335 Panamá. Ministerio de Educación. Depto. Estadística, Personal y Archivos
Estadística cultural. Panamá, Impr. Nacional. Annual.

4336 Rodríguez Bou, Ismael
Estudio del sistema de la República de Panamá; informe para el plan de desarrollo económico. Panamá? 1956, 241p.

Paraguay

4337 Paraguay. Ministerio de Educación y Culto
Reforma de la educación secundaria en el Paraguay. Asunción, Impr. Nacional, 1957, 105p.

4338 Revista de educación. Asunción (I:1), 1945-

4339 Uzcátegui García, Emilio
Panorama de la educación paraguaya. 2d ed. corr. & enl. Asunción, Impr. Nacional, 1959, 229p.

Peru

4340 Alzamora Valdez, Marco
La educación peruana: crisis y perspectiva; errores de una política educativa. Lima, Ed. Universitaria, 1960, 53p.

4341 Amézaga, M.
Problemas de la educación peruana. Lima, Facultad de Educación, Universidad Nacional Mayor de San Marcos, 1952, 108p.

4342 Astete Abrill, M. A.
Significado de la educación en la vida del pueblo peruano. Cuzco, Ed. Rozas, 1956, 162p.

4343 Bazán, Juan F.
La escuela y la comunidad. 2d ed. Lima, 1964, 145p.

4344 Eguiguren, Luis A., ed.
Historia de la Universidad. Lima, Impr. Santa María, 1951-

4345 Encinas, José A.
Un ensayo de escuela nueva en el Perú. 2v. 2d ed. Lima, 1959.

4346 Freeburger, Adela R., & Charles E. Hauch
Education in Peru. Washington, Office of Education, U.S. Dept. of Health, Education, and Welfare, 1964, 69p.

4347 Guardia Mayorga, César A.
El problema de la reforma universitaria: conferencia. Lima, 1947, 48p.

4348 International Labor Office
Informe al Gobierno del Perú sobre la educación obrera. Geneva, 1959, 20p.

4349 Mendoza Rodríguez, Juan
Nuevo potencial para la educación peruana. Lima, 1956, 426p.

4350 Nueva educación. Lima, 1952-

4351 Peña de Calderón, Isabel de la, ed.
Noches peruanas; un ensayo de escuela activa. Lima, 1958, 239p.

4352 Perú. Dirección de Enseñanza Secundaria
Instrucción primaria; programas. Lima, 1950- .

4353 Perú. Ministerio de Educación Pública
Inventario de la realidad educativa del Perú. 4v. Lima, 1957-58.

4354 Perú. Ministerio de Educación Pública
Plan de educación nacional, aprobado por decreto supremo del 13 de enero de 1950. Lima, 1950, 179p.

4355 Revista de educación nacional. Lima, 1948- .

4356 Salazar Larraín, Arturo
San Marcos: entre la ley y el caos; ensayo de interpretación. Lima, Baca y Villaneuva, 1956, 139p.

4357 Valcárcel Esparza, Carlos D.
Reformas virreinales en San Marcos. Lima, Impr. de la Universidad Nacional Mayor de San Marcos, 1960, 94p.

4358 Valcárcel Esparza, Carlos D.
San Marcos, la más antigua universidad real y pontificia de América. Lima, 1959, 103p.

Uruguay

4359 Congreso Nacional de Apoyo a la Escuela Pública. 1st, Montevideo, 1960
A las autoridades al pueblo. Montevideo, Movimiento Nacional de Apoyo y Defensa a la Escuela Pública, 1960, 32p.

4360 Montevideo. Universidad. Instituto de Investigaciones Históricas
Fuentes para la historia de la Universidad. Serie 1, tomo primero; Actas del Consejo Universitario, 1849-1870. Montevideo, 1949, 545p.

4361 Morey Otero, Antonio
Contralor del rendimiento en la escuela uruguaya, acorde a los nuevos programas y unidades de trabajo. Montevideo, Ed. Bibliográfica Uruguaya, 1961, 76p.

4362 Oddone, Juan A., & M. B. París de Oddone
Historia de la Universidad de Montevideo. Montevideo, Universidad de la República, Depto. de Publicaciones, 1963 - .

4363 Verdesio, Emilio
Reforma de la enseñanza primaria. Montevideo, 1957, 158p.

Venezuela

4364 Beltrán Prieto Figueroa, Luis
De una educación de castas a una educación de masas; conferencias pronunciadas en la Facultad de Educación de la Universidad de la Habana en el mes de abril de 1950. Havana, Ed. Lex, 1951, 251p.

4365 Briceño-Iragorry, M.
Problemas de la Juventud Venezolana; temas acerca de la presente crisis universitaria. Madrid, Eds. Bitacora, 1953, 61p.

4366 López Graff, Hilda
La escuela venezolana, una institución en conflicto. Caracas, Pensamiento Vivo, 1962, 268p.

4367 Uslar Pietri, Arturo
De una a otra Venezuela. Caracas, Eds. Mesa Redonda, 1950? 171p.

4368 Venezuela. Ministerio de Educación Nacional
Informe sobre educación y adiestramiento para el progreso económico y social de Venezuela; documento que presenta el Gobierno de Venezuela a la III Reunión Interamericana de Ministros de Educación, Bogotá, agosto de 1963. Caracas, Impr. del Ministerio de Educación, 1963, 141p.

West Indies and the Caribbean

4369 Houle, C.O.
Adult education in the British West Indies. Chicago, Center for the Study of Liberal Education for Adults, 1960, 36p.

4370 Howes, H.W.
Fundamental, adult, literacy and community education in the West Indies; a study prepared for the West Indian Conference (6th Session), Puerto Rico, 1955. Paris, Unesco Caribbean Commission, 1955, 79p.

4371 Trinidad. Education Dept.
Administration report. Port-of-Spain, 1945- . Annual.

4372 Wilgus, A.C., ed.
The Caribbean: contemporary education. Gainesville, School of Inter-American Studies, University of Florida, 1960, 290p.

Periodical Articles

Latin America

4373 Abreu, J., & Robert J. Havighurst
"El Problema de la Educación Secundaria en América Latina." Caracas, Política 19, December 1961, p. 81-96.

4374 Bakke, E.W.
"Students on the March: the Cases of Mexico and Colombia." Sociology of education (37:3), Spring 1964, p. 200-228.

4375 Bellegarde, Dantes
"Mass Education in Latin America." IIE News bulletin (30:7), April 1955, p. 19-23, 67.

4376 Bergstrom Lourenço, M.
"Relaciones entre la Enseñanza Media en América Latina." La educación (9:33), January-March 1964, p. 5-28.

4377 Davis, T.B.
"A Survey of Elementary and Secondary Education in Latin America." Journal of inter-American studies 3, January 1961, p. 97-120.

4378 "L'Education en Amérique Latine." Brussels, Civilisations (XVI:3), 1966, p. 409-415.

4379 Frondizi, Risieri
"Universidad y Desarrollo." Buenos Aires, Revista de la Universidad de Buenos Aires (6:1), January-March 1961, p. 126-132.

4380 Havighurst, Robert J., et al
"La Sociedad y la Educación en América Latina." Paris, Revue internationale des sciences sociales (16:1), 1964, p. 165-166.

4381 "Inter-American Seminar on Overall Planning for Education, Washington, D.C., 1958. Resoluciones y Recommendaciones." Rubio, Educación rural 2, July-September 1958, p. 98-187.

4382 Iutaka, Sugiyama
"Estratificación Social y Oportunidades Educacionales en Tres Metrópolis Latinoamericanas: Buenos Aires, Montevideo, São Paulo." Rio de Janeiro, América latina (5:4), October-December 1962, p. 53-72.

4383 Iutaka, Sugiyama
"Mobilidade Social e Oportunidades Educacionais em Buenos Aires e Montevideo: uma Análise Comparativa." Rio de Janeiro, América latina (6:2), April-June 1963, p. 21-39.

4384 Kandel, Isaac L.
"Education in Latin America." Hispania, May 1947, p. 163-174.

4385 Kaulfers, W.V.
"Latin American Education in Transition." Educational record 42, April 1961, p. 91-98.

4386 Labarca Hubertson, A.
"La Educación en la América Latina." Paris, Cuadernos 19, July-August 1956, p. 74-81.

4387 León, O. de
"Sobre la Educación Media y Secundaria." La educación (9:35-36), July-December 1964, p. 17-31.

4388 Mayagoitia, D.
"La Enseñanza Láica." México, Estudios sociológicos 1953, p. 171-180.

4389 Miró Quesada, F.
"The University South and North. Two Views of Higher Education in Latin America and in the United States." Américas (12:12), December 1960, p. 2-10.

4390 Moreira, João R.
"Educación y Desarrollo." Buenos Aires, Revista

de la Universidad de Buenos Aires (6:1), January-March 1961, p. 99-125.

4391 Oliveira e Silva, O. de
"A Falta de Docentes Qualificados: Alguns Aspectos do Problema em Quatro Paises Latino-Americanos." Rio de Janeiro, América latina (6:1), January-March 1963, p. 65-78.

4392 Otero, G.A.
"La Deserción Escolar y el Problema de la Educación Democrática en Latino América." Quito, Anales de la Universidad Central del Ecuador (86:341), March 1957, p. 337-354.

4393 Pinto, F.A.
"Rol de la Universidad en el Desarrollo Económico de Latino-América." Santiago, Economía (19:72-73), 3rd quarter 1961, p. 24-33.

4394 Prieto, L.B.
"Una Educación para América Latina." Rio de Janeiro, América latina (5:3), July-September 1962, p. 17-32.

4395 Reindorp, R.C.
"Idioma, Cultura y Educación." Quito, Revista ecuatoriana de educación (6:28), September-December 1953, p. 3-236.

4396 Ruiz, M.A.
"Estadísticas de la Educación en América Latina." La educación (9:35-36), July-December 1964, p. 40-58.

Argentina

4397 Aizicson, B.
"Reflexiones sobre la Educación Primaria en la Argentina." Quito, Nueva era 24, 1958, p. 81-88.

4398 Bacas, C.
"Antecedentes de la Creación y Desenvolvimiento del Colegio de Huérfanas en Buenos Aires." Buenos Aires, Estudios (76:414), December 1946, p. 445-467.

4399 Borquez, Y.
"La Deserción Escolar Incide sobre la Profesión." Rio de Janeiro, Boletim do Centro Latinoamericano de Pesquisas em Ciências Sociais (3:4), November 1960, p. 25-29.

4400 Caturelli, A.
"La Reforma de la Enseñanza Media." Buenos Aires, Estudios (48:512), March-April 1960, p. 99-106.

4401 Cowes, H. W.
"Nuestra Enseñanza Secundaria." Buenos Aires, Sur 237, November-December 1955, p. 121-124.

4402 Cristía, P. J.
"La Enseñanza Secundaria y los Barrios de Rosario." Buenos Aires, Revista parlamentaria, June 1948, p. 1-10.

4403 García Cone, R. R.
"La Educación Pública y Su Sostenimiento." La Plata, Revista de educación, March-April 1964, p. 61-67.

4404 Mantovani, J.
"150 años de Educación Argentina." Buenos Aires, Revista de la Universidad de Buenos Aires (5a. época, 5:4), October-December 1960, p. 585-600.

4405 Olivera Lahore, C. E.
"Diez Preguntas sobre la Enseñanza de Iniciativa Privada." Bogotá, Revista interamericana de educación (24:128), May-June 1964, p. 111-125.

4406 Olivera Lahore, C. E.
"Escuela Oficial, Escuela Privada, Escuela Argentina." Buenos Aires, Criterio (33:1371), January 1961, p. 25-28.

4407 Reissig, Luis
"El Ciclo Industrial y Urbano en la Educación Argentina." Caracas, Cultura universitaria 66-67, January-June 1959, p. 80-90.

Bolivia

4408 Arzo, J. A.
"Fines y Medios de la Reforma Educacional Boliviana." Oruro, Universidad (2:3), 2nd quarter 1953, p. 50-84.

4409 Carrero, G.
"Bolivia; una Experiencia de Nuevo Plan y Programa." La Paz, Revista interamericana de educación (24:128), May-June 1964, p. 153-160.

4410 Donoso Torres, V.
"La Instrucción Secundaria en Bolivia." Valparaíso, Semana internacional, January 27, 1940.

4411 Rico Quiroga, H.
"Análisis de la Situación Actual en la Educación Boliviana." La Paz, Educación boliviana (8:24), June 1960, p. 4-15.

Brazil

4412 Abreu, J.
"A Educação Secundaria no Brasil." Rio de Janeiro, Revista brasileira de estudos pedagógicos (23:58), April-June 1955, p. 26-104.

4413 Abreu, J.
"Ensino no Brasil." Rio de Janeiro, Educação e ciências sociais (8:14), June 1960, p. 105-108.

4414 Almeida, A. de
"Escola Pública e Escola Particular." São Paulo, Anhembi (39:115), June 1960, p. 4-16.

4415 Brazil. Serviço de Estatística de Educação e Cultura
"Ensino Médio 1962." Rio de Janeiro, Revista brasileira dos municípios (16:61-62), January-June 1963, p. 11-91.

4416 Canduro, R.
"O Esfôrço Educacional do Rio Grande do Sul." Rio de Janeiro, Revista brasileira de estudos pedagógicos (39:89), January-March 1963, p. 79-88.

4417 Cardoso, Fernando H.
"Educação para o Desenvolvimento." São Paulo, Anhembi (39:115), June 1960, p. 35-43.

4418 Centro Brasileiro de Pesquisas Educacionais
"Bibliografia em Língua Inglêsa Sobre Educação no Brasil." Rio de Janeiro, Revista brasileira de estudos pedagógicos (33:77), January-March 1960, p. 144-152.

4419 "Cidade Universitária do Rio de Janeiro." São Paulo, Habitat 15, March-April 1954, p. 2-28.

4420 Dorin, L.
"Análise de uma Educação em Constante Crise." São Paulo, Revista brasiliense 32, November-December 1960, p. 97-115.

4421 "Education in Brasil." Paris, Education abstracts 10, November 1958, p. 1-35.

4422 Fernandes, Florestan
"Dados Sôbre a Situação do Ensino." São Paulo, Revista brasiliense 3, July-August 1960, p. 67-119.

4423 Fernandes, Florestan
"A Democratização do Ensino." São Paulo, Anhembi (39:115), June 1960, p. 24-34.

4424 Fernandes, Florestan
"A Educação Popular no Brasil." São Paulo, Revista brasiliense 39, January-February 1962, p. 128-138.

4425 Fernandes, Florestan
"Em Defensa da Escola Pública." Rio de Janeiro, Revista Brasileira de estudos pedagógicos (33:77), January-March 1960, p. 3-15.

4426 Freyre, Gilberto
"Sugestões para uma Nova Política no Brasil: a Rurbana." Rio de Janeiro, Revista brasileira de estudos pedagógicos (27:65), January-March 1957, p. 65-82.

4427 Hutchinson, Bertram
"Aspectos da Educação Universitaria e Status Social em São Paulo." Rio de Janeiro, Educação e ciências sociais (2:4), March 1957, p. 39-76.

4428 Kimball, Solon T.
"Uma Appreciação do Ensino Primario." Rio de Janeiro, Revista brasileira de estudos pedagógicos (33:77), January-March 1960, p. 16-33.

4429 Lopes, J.R. Brandão
"Escolha Ocupacional e Origem Social de Ginacianos em São Paulo." Rio de Janeiro, Educação e ciências sociais (1:2), August 1956, p. 43-62.

4430 Lopes, J.R. Brandão
"Estructura Social e Educação no Brasil." Rio de Janeiro, Educação e ciências sociais (4:10), April 1959, p. 53-77.

4431 Lowrie, S.H.
"Social Science Instruction in Brazil." American sociological review 2, April 1937, p. 262-265.

4432 Moreira, João R.
"A Escola Primaria Brasileira." Rio de Janeiro, Educação e ciências sociais (2:6), November 1957, p. 133-184.

4433 Oliveira, M.L. Barbosa de
"Articulação do Ensino no Brasil." Rio de Janeiro, Revista brasileira de estudos pedagógicos (34:79), July-September 1960, p. 101-107.

4434 "As Origens da Cidade Universitária." Rio de Janeiro, Revista do serviço público (4:2), November 1950, p. 20-30.

4435 Padín, D. Cándido
"Diretrizes e Bases da Educação Nacional." Rio de Janeiro, Síntese política econômica social (2:5), January-March 1960, p. 27-38.

4436 Penido, P.P.
"Discurso do Posse do Ministro." Rio de Janeiro,

Revista brasileira de estudos pedagógicos (34:79), July-September 1960, p. 58-62.

4437 Pretto, H. M.
"O Problema da Escola Brasileira numa Comunidade Holandesa de São Paulo." São Paulo, Revista de antropologia (1:1), June 1953, p. 29-33.

4438 Rabello, O.
"Alguns Aspectos Sociais da Educação no Meio Rural Paulista." São Paulo, Sociologia (25:1), March 1963, p. 65-76.

4439 Saffioti, H.I. Bongiovani
"A Educação no Brasil como Problema Social." São Paulo, Sociologia (25:2), June 1963, p. 155-161.

4440 Scully, M.
"São Paulo's Mackenzie University." Américas 7, February 1955, p. 18-23.

4441 Silva, O. Sampaio
"A Escola Pública e a Escola Particular em Face do Projeto de Diretrizes e Bases da Educação." São Paulo, Revista brasiliense 34, March-April 1961, p. 56-59.

4442 Stewart, S.
"Some Aspects of Brazilian Education." Peabody journal of education (30:1), July 1952, p. 16-21.

4443 Teixeira, A.
"A Escola Brasileira e a Estabilidade Social." Bêlo Horizonte, Revista brasileira de estudos políticos (3:5), January 1959, p. 97-128.

4444 Villalôbos, João E.R.
"A Luta Pela Escola Pública e Seu Significado Histórico." São Paulo, Anhembi (39:117), August 1960, p. 562-575.

Central America

4445 Schmidt, K.M.
"Primers for Progress: the Alianza in Central

America." Inter-American economic affairs 18, Summer 1964, p. 87-94.

Chile

4446 Calvo, G.
"La Tendencia Aristocratizante de Nuestra Educación." Santiago, Boletín de la Universidad de Chile 56, May 1965, p. 13-16.

4447 Cortés W.
"Problemas que Abarcó el Seminario de Educación." Santiago, Boletín de la Universidad de Chile 47, May 1964, p. 18-20.

4448 Dulanto, R.
"La Educación Secundaria en Chile." Lima, Educación (8:17), 1953, p. 60-72.

4449 Grassau, E.
"Desarrollo de la Educación Chilena desde 1940." Santiago, Boletín estadístico de la Universidad de Chile (3:1), 1959, p. 1-84.

4450 Gutierrez Roldán, H.
"Estimación de las Necesidades de Profesores en la Enseñanza Secundaria en Chile, 1957-1982." Santiago, Boletín de la Universidad de Chile 11, May 1960, p. 24-25.

4451 Gutierrez Roldán, H.
"Proyección de la Población Escolar de Chile, 1957-1982." Santiago, Boletín de la Universidad de Chile 12, June 1960, p. 36-39.

4452 Hamuy, Eduardo
"El Problema de los Bajos Niveles de Educación del Pueblo de Chile." Santiago, Economía (18:67), 2nd quarter 1960, p. 10-19.

4453 Jobet Borquez, J.C.
"El Problema Educacional en Chile." Caracas, Política 17, August-September 1961, p. 79-102.

4454 Ranstead, C.
"Nido de Aguilas; Art Program." School arts 65,

February 1966, p. 5-8.

4455 Rocha, R.
"La Educación Privada en Chile en el Decenio 1950-1960." Santiago, Panorama económico (17: 238), August 1963, p. 113-117.

4456 Salas S., I.
"Education in Chile." International house quarterly 16, Spring 1952, p. 68-75.

4457 Salas S., I., & Enrique Saavedra I.
"La Educación en una Comuna de Santiago." Santiago, Boletín de la Universidad de Chile 31, July 1962, p. 16-26.

Colombia

4458 Arias Osorio, E.
"Desarrollo y Tendencia de la Educación Superior en Colombia." Bogotá, Arco 48, September 1964, p. 575-578.

4459 Betancourt, B.
"Educación, la Nueva Frontera." Popayán, Revista de la Universidad del Cauca 29, June 1961, p. 29-47.

4460 Llobell Escobar, T.
"Bibliografía Colombiana Sobre Educación." Bogotá, Boletín cultural y bibliográfico (4:7&8), July-August 1961, p. 650-658, 707-717.

4461 Morales, H.
"Severo Análisis de la Crisis del Bachillerato." Bogotá, Revista interamericana de educación (24: 127), March-April 1964, p. 103-106.

4462 Tapias H., G.
"Qué es Nuestro Bachillerato?" Medellín, Universidad de Antioquia (35:139), October-December 1959, p. 524-530.

Costa Rica

4463 Martén, Teodoro
"City within a City." Américas (11:11), November 1959, p. 14-17.

Cuba

4464 Rego, Oscar F.
"Cincuenta Años de Escuela Pública Republicana." Havana, Carteles (31:13), March 26, 1950, p. 38-40.

4465 Reissig, Luis
"La Educación: Primer Problema Nacional e Internacional." Havana, Revolución cubana 26, January-June 1950, p. 245-270.

4466 Vicente Aja, P.
"La Crisis de la Universidad de La Habana." Quito, Ensayos 2, August 1962, p. 39-46.

Ecuador

4467 Ecuador. Junta Nacional de Planificación y Coordinación Económica
"Programas de Educación." Quito, Revista ecuatoriana de educación (2a. época, 1:1), January-June 1961, p. 23-76.

4468 Mena Soto, J.
"El Movimiento Educativo en el Ecuador y sus Problemas." Hamburg, International review of education (6:2), 1960, p. 188-206.

4469 Paredes, A.M.
"La Reforma de la Educación Secundaria Ecuatoriana." Quito, Revista de educación 123, April 1952, p. 71-77.

4470 Tobar, J.
"Evolución de las Ideas Pedagógicas en el Ecuador." Quito, Filosofía, letras y educación (6:17), January-March 1953, p. 5-124.

4471 Uzcátegui García, Emilio
"A Comparison between Education in the State of California and in the Republic of Ecuador." Quito, Filosofía, letras y ciencias de la educación (5:16), October-December 1952, p. 77-110.

4472 Velasco, E.N.
"Estructuración Actual de la Escuela Ecuatoriana

y Algunos Datos del Escolar Ecuatoriano." Quito, Revista ecuatoriana de educación (6:21), May-June 1952, p. 107-127.

4473 Velasco, E.N.
"Realidad Estadística de la Educación Ecuatoriana." Quito, Revista ecuatoriana de educación (18:54-55), July 1964-June 1965, p. 141-150.

4474 Wirth, A.
"Observaciones sobre Algunos Problemas de Educación Secundaria en el Ecuador." Quito, Revista de educación 125, 1953, p. 190-195.

El Salvador

4475 Landarech, A.M.
"La Educación Media en El Salvador." El Salvador, Estudios centroamericanos (14:135), March 1959, p. 70-77.

4476 Moran, F.
"Problemas Educacionales de El Salvador." San Salvador, Cultura (21:45-49), July-September 1961, p. 45-49.

4477 "La Universidad Autónoma de El Salvador." Guatemala, Nuestra Guatemala (7:18), September 1952, p. 50-51.

Guatemala

4478 MacVean, R.B.
"Educational Reorganization in Guatemala." Comparative education review (1:3), February 1958, p. 18-23.

4479 "Seminario Nacional sobre la Educación en Guatemala, 1o, 1961." Guatemala, Antropología e historia de Guatemala (13:1), January 1961, p. 52-54.

Haiti

4480 Brice, C.
"Le Nouvel Aspect du Programme d'Education Ouvrière." Port-au-Prince, Revue du travail (10:10), May 1961, p. 20-27.

4481 Florez, P. L.
"Organisation de l'Enseignement Primaire en République d'Haiti." Montevideo, Boletín del Instituto Internacional Americano de Protección a la Infancia (27:106), September 1953, p. 264-278.

4482 Mars, L.
"L'Education des Enfants en Haiti." Port-au-Prince, Optique 19, September 1955, p. 18-22.

4483 Pompilus, Pradel
"Les Problèmes de l'Enseignement Supérieur en Haiti." Port-au-Prince, Conjonction 46, August 1953, p. 10-17.

Honduras

4484 Honduras. Dirección General de Educación Secundaria
"La Educación Secundaria en Honduras." Tegucigalpa, Boletín de la Secretaría de Educación Pública (5:24), November-December 1954, p. 30-38.

4485 "Progresos de la Educación en Honduras." Caracas, Política 15, April-May 1961, p. 102-104.

Mexico

4486 Bailey, B.
"Bookmobile Fiesta in Mexico." Wilson library bulletin 25, April 1951, p. 610-611.

4487 Bueno, M.
"Finalidad y Orientación Socioeducativas del Bachillerato." México, Revista mexicana de sociología (22:3), September-December 1960, p. 869-892.

4488 Candiani, G.
"El Rescate de los Bienes Culturales en Beneficio del Trabajador Mexicano." México, Revista mexicana del trabajo (7:11-12), November-December 1960, p. 17-21.

4489 Cano, C.
"La Educación Primaria en México." La educación (9:33), January-March 1964, p. 69-82.

4490 Castillo Pérez, Isidoro
"Cómo Dar Educación Primaria a Todos los Niños de México." México, Problemas educativos de México (3:11), January 1959, p. 26-39.

4491 Castro, E.
"Ideología de la Educación Mexicana." México, Estudios sociológicos 1953, p. 215-224.

4492 Gallo Gonzales, V.
"La Deserción Escolar: Causas y Proyecciones Sociales." México, Estudios sociológicos, 1953, p. 125-140.

4493 Gaos, José
"Opinión acerca de la Segunda Enseñanza Mexicana." México, Educación 2, September 1959, p. 177-185.

4494 García Barna, F.
"Profesores y Alumnos Universitarios Deben Llevar el Saber a las Masas." Mérida, Revista de la Universidad de Yucatán (6:33), May-June 1965, p. 85-90.

4495 Gil Bevía, R.
"México y los Problemas Educativos." Seville, Estudios americanos (7:32), May 1954, p. 449-463.

4496 González Irigoyen, Rómulo
"Importancia del Instituto Tecnológico de Monterrey." México, Economista, September 1945, p. 69-70.

4497 González Irigoyen, Rómulo
"Monterrey Tech. A Revolution in Mexican Education." Américas (7:5), May 1955, p. 16-19.

4498 Gutiérrez Eskildsen, R. M.
"La Educación Moral en los Diversos Grados de la Educación Mexicana." México, Estudios sociológicos 1953, p. 167-170.

4499 Holmes, Lula T.
"Educating Mexican Masses." Headline series 94, July-August 1952, p. 55-62.

4500 Jimenez C., M.R.
"Alumnos Irregulares en la Escuela Nacional de Ciencias Políticas y Sociales." México, Ciencias políticas y sociales (8:29), July-September 1962, p. 445-457.

4501 Larroyo, F.
"Half a Century of Education in Mexico." Texas quarterly 2, Spring 1959, p. 113-125.

4502 México. Consejo Nacional Técnico de la Educación. Comité Directivo
"Informe." México, Educación 4, June 1960, p. 31-372.

4503 Moreno Díaz, D.A.
"Datos Demográficos para la Educación Mexicana." México, Educación (época 2:1), July 1959, p. 101-113.

4504 Moreno Díaz, D.A.
"Demografía y Educación." México, Educación (1:3), October 1958, p. 57-65.

4505 Torres Bodet, Jaime
"Ideario Educativo del Régimen." México, Educación (época 2:1), July 1959, p. 11-60.

4506 Torres Bodet, Jaime
"Nuevo Concepto de la Educación Pública." Mérida, Revista de la Universidad de Yucatán (4:24), November-December 1962, p. 10-20.

4507 Treviño, V.L., & R. Gonzáles Montemayor
"La Educación del Obrero Manual en México." México, Estudios sociológicos, 1953, p. 381-388.

4508 Zavala, L.J.
"El Problema de la Literatura Vulgar y Otras Influencias Negativas en la Educación Infantil y Popular." México, Estudios sociológicos, 1953, p. 153-158.

Nicaragua

4509 Grimberg Villaroel, A.
"Educación en Nicaragua." León, Cuadernos uni-

versitarios 19, January 1962, p. 46-50.

4510 Schick, R.
"Informe sobre el Estado de la Educación Fundamental y de la Alfabetización de Adultos en Nicaragua." Montevideo, Boletín del Instituto Interamericano del Niño (35:2), June 1961, p. 85-106.

Panama

4511 Domínguez Caballero, D.
"La Educación Panameña." Panamá, Revista de educación (2:9), July 1959, p. 33-38.

4512 Gudiño Bazán, L.
"La Educación Panameña en la Ciudad y en el Campo." Madrid, Estudios geográficos (26:101), November 1965, p. 519-539.

4513 Panamá. Dirección de Estadística y Censo
"Características Educacionales de la Población de la Ciudad de Panamá." Panamá, Lotería (8:97), December 1963, p. 49-59.

4514 Westerman, George W.
"School Segregation on the Panama Canal Zone." Phylon (15:3), 1954, p. 276 287.

Paraguay

4515 Morínigo, M.
"Características Sociales y Culturales del Paraguay y sus Consecuencias en Relación a la Educación Primaria Gratuita y Obligatoria." Asunción, Boletín de educación paraguaya (2:18), February 1958, p. 12-20.

4516 Uzcátegui García, Emilio
"Evaluación de las Labores de la Misión de la Unesco en el Paraguay: 1955-1959." Asunción, Boletín de educación paraguaya (3:36), August 1959, p. 1-51.

Peru

4517 Arenas Delgado, A.
"La Educación en el Perú: Características de los Programas de Educación Primaria de 1943, Vigentes." Lima, Educación 14-15, 1951, p. 50-76.

4518 Basadre, Jorge
"La Educación Peruana: Problemas y Posibilidades." Lima, Nueva educación (29:148), April 1962, p. 6-9.

4519 Lima. Pontificia Universidad Católica del Perú
"Bibliografía Selecta sobre el Proceso Educacional Peruano (1900-1950)." Lima, Revista de la Facultad de Educación (1:1), July 1950, p. 39-42.

4520 Prado, J.
"Las Condiciones Sociológicas del Perú y el Problema de la Educación." Lima, Revista de la Facultad de Educación (2:4), December 1951, p. 17-20.

4521 Rojas Dias, B.
"Un Aspecto de los Problemas de la Educación Nacional." Cuzco, Revista universitaria (41:102), 1st quarter 1952, p. 83-119.

Uruguay

4522 Carlos, M. de
"La Escuela Pública Uruguaya." Montevideo, Anales de instrucción primaria, September 1947/March 1948, p. 40-60.

4523 Cortinas Pelaez, L.
"La Nouvelle Structure Administrative de l'Université en Uruguay: le Co-gouvernement des Etudiants." Paris, Revue du droit public et de la science politique en France et à l'étranger (79:1), January-February 1963, p. 20-47.

Venezuela

4524 Abellanas Alfonso, A.
"El Sistema Educacional en Bancarrota?" Caracas, Arco (44-45), May-June 1964, p. 292-296; 369-376.

4525 Corta, J. F.
"La Injusta Distribución del Presupuesto Escolar." Bogotá, Revista interamericana de educación (20:112), May-June 1961, p. 154-173.

4526 Gonzalez Reyes, E.
"La Universidad de Oriente y sus Perspectivas de Desarrollo." Cumaná, *Ciencias sociales* (1:1), December 1963, p. 5-10.

4527 Mora, R. L.
"Palabras." Caracas, *Política 20*, January-March 1962, p. 187-193.

4528 Uslar Pietri, Arturo
"La Impostergable Reforma de Nuestra Educación." Caracas, *Boletín de la Academia Nacional de la Historia* (46:182), April-June 1963, p. 270-278.

4529 Velásquez de Rojas, N.
"Relaciones Socio-Económicas en el Problema del Abandonado Escolar en Cumaná." Cumaná, *Ciencias sociales* (1:2), June 1964, p. 168-182.

West Indies and the Caribbean

4530 Braithwaite, Lloyd E.
"The Role of the University in the Developing Society of the West Indies." Mona, *Social & economic change 14*, March 1965, p. 76-87.

4531 Sherlock, Philip
"Evolución Dinámica de la Educación Superior en el Caribe Británico." Santiago, *Boletín de la Universidad de Chile 20*, May 1961, p. 27-30.

4532 Sherlock, Philip
"University Education in the British Caribbean." Manchester, *Science & freedom 17*, December 1960, p. 16-21.

4533 Smith, Michael G.
"Education and Occupational Choice in Jamaica." Mona, *Social & economic studies* (9:3), September 1960, 332-354.

HOUSING

Books

General

4534 Abrams, Charles
Man's struggle for shelter in an urbanizing world. Cambridge, M.I.T. Press, 1964, 307p.

4535 The Appraisal Journal (periodical)
Urban renewal and development; articles from the Appraisal Journal. Chicago, American Institute of Real Estate Appraisers, 1963, 172p.

4536 Foley, D., et al
Housing trends and related problems. Berkeley, Centre for Planning & Development Research, University of California, 1963, 230p.

4537 Frieden, Bernard J.
The future of old neighborhoods; rebuilding for a changing population. Cambridge, M.I.T. Press, 1964, 209p.

4538 Garner, J. F.
Slum clearance and compensation. London, Oyez Publications, 1965, 248p.

4539 International Seminar on Urban Renewal. 1st, The Hague, August 22-29, 1958
Urban renewal, report. The Hague, International Federation for Housing and Planning, & Netherlands Housing & Town Planning Institute, 1958, 120p.

4540 Merrett, A.J., & A. Sykes
Housing finance and development: an analysis and a programme for reform. London, Longmans, 1965, 127p.

4541 Pretoria. State Library
Town planning and housing; a select list of U.S.

Government publications. Pretoria, 1952, 18p.

4542 United Nations. Economic Commission for Europe
Report of the Seminar on Housing Surveys and Programmes with particular reference to problems in the developing countries. Geneva, 1962, 170p.

4543 United Nations. Economic Commission for Europe
Techniques for surveying a country's housing situation including estimating of current and future housing requirements. Geneva, 1962, 46p.

4544 U.S. Housing & Home Finance Agency. Office of International Housing
Catalog of programs of international cooperation in housing & town & country planning . . . Washington, Office of the Administrator, International Housing Service, U.S. Housing & Home Finance Agency, 1958, 67p.

4545 U.S. Housing & Home Finance Agency. Library
60 books on housing and community planning. Washington, Office of the Administrator, 1963, 21p.

4546 Wheaton, William L.C., et al, eds.
Urban housing. New York, Free Press, 1966, 544p.

4547 Wilner, D.M., et al
The housing environment and family life: a longitudinal study of the effects of housing on morbidity and mental health. Baltimore, Johns Hopkins, 1962, 338p.

4548 World Planning and Housing Congress. 28th, Tokyo, 1966
Proceedings. 2v. Tokyo, International Federation for Housing & Planning, 1966.

Latin America

4549 Banco Nacional Hipotecario Urbano y de Obras Públicas, S.A.
Cartilla de la vivienda . . . Bogotá, Centro Interamericano de Vivienda, Servicio de Intercambio Científico, 1956- .

4550 Harris, Walter DeS., & James Gillies, eds.
La formación de capitales para la vivienda en América Latina/Capital formation for housing in Latin America. Washington, Unión Panamericana, 1963, 176p.

4551 Inter-American Housing & Planning Center
Informe. Washington, Div. of Housing & Planning, Pan American Union, 1953- Annual.

4552 Inter-American Housing & Planning Center
Vivienda y planeamiento: suplemento informativo. Bogota, 1966- .

4553 Inter-American Housing & Planning Center
Vivienda y urbanismo, ensayos preparados durante el curso básico de 1952. Bogotá, 1952, 147p.

4554 Inter-American Housing & Planning Center. Library
Lista de nuevas adquisiciones. Current Acquisitions list. Bogotá, Annual.

4555 Inter-American Statistical Institute
La situación de la vivienda en América. Washington, Unión Panamericana, 1962, 261p.

4556 Koth, Marcia N., et al
Housing in Latin America. Cambridge, M.I.T. Press, 1965, 259p.

4557 Latin American Seminar on Housing and Statistics Programmes, Copenhagen and Stockholm, 1962
Report. New York, United Nations, 1963, 87p.

4558 Mantilla Bazo, Víctor
Vivienda y planeamiento en América Latina; bibliografía preliminar. Washington, Div. de Vivienda y Planeamiento, Depto. de Asuntos Económicos y Sociales, Unión Panamericana, 1952, 112p.

4559 Pan American Union. Dept. of Social Affairs
Centro Interamericano de Vivienda y Planeamiento, 1952-1962. Washington, 1962, 54p.

4560 Pan American Union. Division of Housing & Planning
The problem of low-cost housing in Latin America; report . . . Washington, 1953, 148p.

4561 Pan American Union. Division of Housing & Planning
Renovación urbana . . . 2d ed. Washington, 1958, 53p.

4562 Pan American Union. Division of Labor & Social Affairs
Informe final, seminarios regionales de asuntos sociales: vivienda y urbanismo. Resúmen de las discusiones de Mesa Redonda de Vivienda y Urbanismo, Quito, Ecuador, mayo de 1950, San Salvador, El Salvador, noviembre de 1950, Pôrto Alegre, Brasil mayo de 1951. Washington, 1952, 140p.

4563 Pan American Union. Inter-American Economic & Social Council
Problems of housing of social interest. Washington, 1954, 232p.

4564 Primer Congreso Interamericano de la Vivienda, 10 al 15 de Octubre de 1966, Santiago de Chile
Antecedentes y resoluciones. 2v. Santiago, Cámara Chilena de la Construcción, 1967.

4565 Stycos, J.M., & J. Arias, eds.
Population dilemma in Latin America. Washington, Potomac Books, 1966, 249p.

4566 United Nations. Economic Commission for Latin America
Housing and building materials industry: Central America economic integration programme. New York, 1960, 96p.

4567 U.S. Dept. of Housing & Urban Development. Division of International Affairs
Housing market analysis in Latin America . . . 2v. Washington, 1966.

Argentina

4568 Argentina. Comisión Nacional de la Vivienda
Informe sobre la actuación y plan integral. Buenos

Aires, 1957, 614p.

4569 Argentina. Congreso. Biblioteca. Sección Referencia Legislativa
Locación urbana; legislación de emergencia. Buenos Aires, 1949, 26p.

4570 Babini, Nicolás
Realidad y destino de la vivienda. Buenos Aires, Ed. Raigal, 1954, 156p.

4571 Cámara Argentina de la Construcción
El problema de la vivienda; conferencias y debates . . . Buenos Aires, 1950, 296p.

4572 Del Giudice, J. C.
La vivienda, un problema insoluble? Buenos Aires, Eds. Intercooperativas, 1958, 107p.

4573 Wilson, L. A.
Voice of the villas, socio-economic analysis of the residents of villas in Parque Almirante Brown, Buenos Aires, Argentina. Washington, F. C. H. Co., & Foundation for Cooperative Housing, Inc., 1965, 72p.

Brazil

4574 Brazil. Presidencia. Serviço de Documentação
Diário de Brasilia, 1956, 1957, 1958, 1960. 3v. Rio de Janeiro, 1960.

4575 Condicões de habitação em Fortaleza. Fortaleza, Instituto de Pesquisas Econômicas, Universidade do Ceará, 1963, 66p.

Central America

4576 Pan American Union. Division of Housing & Planning
Reunión sobre Problemas de Vivienda, Industrias de Edificación y de Materiales de Construcción en Centroamérica y Panamá . . . Washington, 1957, 39p.

Chile

4577 Chile. Universidad. Instituto de Economía
Un aspecto de la situación habitacional de Chile:

estudios sobre deficiencias habitacionales. Santiago, 1958, 28p.

4578 Daroch de Vergara, Adriana
Hacia un futuro mejor. Towards a better future. Santiago, Fundación Viviendas de Emergencia, 1950, 63p.

Colombia

4579 Colombia. Contraloría General de la República. Estadística Nacional. División General de Censos
Primer censo nacional de edificios, efectuado el 20 de abril de 1938. Bogotá, Impr. Nacional, 1939, 393p.

4580 Instituto de Crédito Territorial
Una política de vivienda para Colombia. Bogotá, 1955, 308p.

4581 Instituto de Crédito Territorial
El problema de la vivienda en Colombia; planeamiento y soluciones. Bogotá, 1958, 27p.

4582 Instituto de Credito Territorial
Una política de vivienda para Colombia; Primer Seminario Nacional de Vivienda, 1955. Bogotá, 1956, 315p.

4583 Inter-American Housing & Planning Center
Bibliografía colombiana de vivienda de interés social; construcción y planeamiento. Bogotá, 1954- .

4584 Inter-American Housing & Planning Center
Ensayo en evaluación de barrios: Quiroga, 1956. Bogotá, 1957, 78 plus 8p.

4585 Inter-American Housing & Planning Center
Estudios para la rehabilitación del barrio inglés, en la ciudad de Bogotá. Bogotá, 1952, 76p.

4586 Inter-American Housing & Planning Center
Proyecto de rehabilitación urbana: barrio Bello Horizonte-Bogotá, Colombia. Bogotá, Centro Interamericano de Vivienda y Planeamiento, Servicio de Intercambio Científico, 1958, variously paged.

4587 Inter-American Housing & Planning Center
Siloé; el proceso de desarrollo comunal aplicado a un proyecto de rehabilitación urbana. Bogotá, Centro Interamericano de Vivienda y Planeamiento, Servicio de Intercambio Científico, 1958, 91p.

4588 South American Gulf Oil Company
Plan de préstamos para vivienda, manual de instrucciones, anexas formas y modelos, relaciones industriales. Bogotá, 1962, variously paged.

4589 Turner, C.B.
Squatter settlements in Bogotá, Bogotá, Inter-American Housing & Planning Center, 1964, 51p.

Costa Rica

4590 Instituto Nacional de Vivienda y Urbanismo
Memoria. San José. Annual.

Dominican Republic

4591 Sobá, J.G.
Algunos programas sociales y construcción de viviendas realizados en los últimos 30 años en la República Dominicana, 1930-1961. Ciudad Trujillo, 1961, 50p.

El Salvador

4592 Pachano, W.G.
Estudio sobre la vivienda en El Salvador. New York, United Nations, 1954, 85p.

4593 Pan American Union. Division of Social Affairs
La vivienda en El Salvador . . . Washington, 1950, 36p.

Guatemala

4594 Antillón Enríquez, Carlos E.
El problema de la vivienda en la ciudad de Guatemala. Guatemala, 1951, 46p.

4595 Solow, Anatole A.
Housing in Guatemala: a study of the problem, with recommendations for the program and organization of the Housing Department . . . Washington, Section of Housing & City Planning, Div. of Labor

& Social Affairs, Pan American Union, 1950, 110p.

Haiti

4596 Haiti (Republic). Dept. du Travail et du Bien-être Social
Logement ouvrier populaire. Port-au-Prince, 1958, 20p.

Honduras

4597 Harris, Walter DeS., & H.A. Hossé
Housing in Honduras. Washington, Pan American Union, 1964, 295p.

Mexico

4598 Audirac Garcés, Armando
Estudio económico sobre la industria de la construcción en México. México, 1956, 119p.

4599 Banco Nacional Hipotecario Urbano y de Obras Públicas, S.A.
Memoria de las conferencias sobre habitación popular. México, 1950, 231p.

4600 México. Instituto Mexicano del Seguro Social
Algunos aspectos de la habitación obrera en el Distrito Federal. México, Depto. de Prestaciones Sociales y Divulgación, 1957, 63p.

4601 México. Instituto Nacional de la Vivienda
Colonias proletarias; problemas y soluciones. México, 1958, 24p.

4602 México. Instituto Nacional de la Vivienda
Tacubaya, problemas y soluciones. México, 1958, 23p.

4603 Ramírez Moguel Goyzueta, Leonor
El problema de la vivienda en el Distrito Federal referido al arrendamiento. México, 1963, 237p.

4604 Solorio Suárez, Alicia
Habitaciones obreras. México, 1957, 126p.

Nicaragua

4605 U.S. Housing & Home Finance Agency. Office of International Housing

Colonial Managua: an aided self-help housing project in Nicaragua (IME-58). Washington, 1962, 15p.

Peru

4606 Berckholtz Salinas, Pablo
Barrios marginales, aberración social. Lima, 1963, 100p.

4607 Harris, Walter DeS., et al
Housing in Peru: a research study. Washington, Pan American Union, 1963, 713p.

4608 Montero Bernales, Manuel
Crisis en el Perú; conjunto de artículos sobre política, economía y finanzas. Lima, 1961, 57p.

4609 Pimental Benites, Elio
Arrendamiento urbano . . . Trujillo, Peru, 1967, 662p.

Venezuela

4610 Banco Obrero
Estudio de evaluación de los superbloques. Caracas, 1960, 94p.

4611 Carlson, Eric
Política y programación de la vivienda en Venezuela . . . Bogotá, Centro Interamericano de Vivienda y Planeamiento, 1958? 35p.

4612 Fundación para el Desarrollo de la Comunidad y Fomento Municipal
Memoria y cuenta, 1963. Caracas, 1963, 114p.

4613 Grooscors, Rolando
Problemas de vivienda urbana en Venezuela. (In VI Congreso Latinoamericano de Sociología. Memoria. 2v. Caracas, 1961, p. 47-51).

4614 Inter-American Housing & Planning Center
Proyecto de evaluación de los superbloques. 2d ed. Caracas, Banco Obrero, 1961, 196p.

4615 Venezuela
Housing and social security; report presented by the Republic of Venezuela. Caracas, General Secretariat, 1955, 92p.

West Indies and the Caribbean

4616 Caribbean Commission. Central Secretariat
Aspects of housing in the Caribbean. Port-of-Spain, 1951, 236p.

4617 Trinidad and Tobago. Central Statistical Office
Housing, 1957-1958: a preliminary report on the housing census. Port-of-Spain, 1960, 17p.

Periodical Articles

General

4618 García, H.
"Aided Self-Help Housing." London, Community development bulletin (6:2), March 1955, p. 36-38.

4619 Turner, John F.C., & R. Goetze
"Environmental Security and Housing Input." Athens, Ekistics, February 1967, p. 120-122.

4620 Umrath, H.
"The Promotion of Low-Cost Housing." The Hague, Local Government Throughout the World 4, January-February 1965, p. 3-7.

Latin America

4621 Alvarez Lezarra, F.U.
"El Urbanismo y la Sociología Económica." México, Estudios sociológicos, 1955, p. 295-314.

4622 Balcero, I. de, & L. Balcero Gómez
"Un Problema Social: La Vivienda Sub-Normal." Bogotá, Boletín mensual de la Sociedad de Estudios Latinoamericanos (II:18), November 1966, p. 1-13.

4623 Carter, M.
"Alliance for Progress Makes Housing Instrument of American Foreign Policy." Journal of Housing 19, January 1962, p. 22-27.

4624 Compton, G. C.
"To House a Hemisphere." Américas 3, May 1951, p. 13-15.

4625 Crane, Jacob
"City Building in Latin America. I-II." Pan American, October 1945, p. 15-18; November 1945, p. 23-24.

4626 Figueroa Román, Miguel
"La Política de la Habitación en la América Latina." Rosario, Estudios (1:3), September/October 1951, p. 125-129.

4627 Frankenhoff, Charles A.
"Low-Cost Housing in a Latin American Economy." Inter-American economic affairs (17:4), Spring 1964, p. 79-86.

4628 "Housing Problems and Policies in Latin America." Geneva, International labour review 65, March 1952, p. 348-378.

4629 Inter-American Conference of Ministers of Labor of the Alliance for Progress. 2nd, Caraballeda, Venezuela, 1966
"La Vivienda para los Trabajadores." Revista interamericana de ciencias sociales (4:1), 1966, p. 63-73.

4630 Mora Rubio, R.
"El Problema Habitacional y las Cooperativas de Vivienda en América Latina." Lima, Información social (15:4), October-December 1960, p. 3-37.

4631 "Needed: Millions of Houses." Américas 13, July 1961, p. 19-23.

4632 Poblete Troncoso, Moisés
"Too Many People?" Américas 12, September 1960, p. 11-15.

4633 "Le Problème et la Politique du Logement dans les Pays d'Amérique Latine." Geneva, Revue internationale du travail (65:3), March 1952, p. 365-399.

4634 Puig, A. J.
"El Problema de la Vivienda en América Latina." Bogotá, Arco (5:30), February 1963, p. 106-110.

4635 Solow, Anatole A.
"Urban Progress in Latin America: Housing and City-Planning Developments." American city 67, April 1952, p. 120-122.

4636 Solow, Anatole A.
"Housing and Urban Progress in Latin America. 'Point IV' Technical Assistance to Help People Help Themselves. The Hague, News sheet of the International Federation for Housing and Town Planning 25, August 1952, p. 25-27.

4637 Turner, John F. C.
"Asentamientos Urbanos no Regulados." Caracas, Cuadernos de la Sociedad Venezolana de Planificación 36, December 1966, p. 1-86.

4638 Turner, John F. C.
"Squatters and Urban Policy." Urban affairs quarterly (II:3), March 1967, p. 111-115.

4639 Vaughn, Jack H.
"Housing and Urban Development in Latin America." Dept. of State bulletin 53, July 12, 1965, p. 66-70.

4640 Violich, Francis
"Visitando Nuevamente las Ciudades de la América Latina." Lima, El arquitecto peruano (20: 243/244), October/November 1957, p. 33-34.

Argentina

4641 Alsogaray, A.
"Government's Plan for Housing." Buenos Aires, Review of the River Plate 128, August 12, 1960, p. 19-22.

4642 Balista, J.
"Análisis del Plan Federal de Vivienda." Buenos Aires, Estudios 542, March-April 1963, p. 97-104.

4643 Blasi Brambilla, Alberto
"Acostaciones al Problema de la Vivienda Argentina." Buenos Aires, Estudios (48:512), March/April 1960, p. 88-98.

4644 Bunge, Alejandro E.
"Un Importante Problema de la Ciudad de Buenos Aires." Buenos Aires, La habitación popular, July-September 1938, p. 281-283.

4645 Cánepa, T.A., & A.G. Varsi
"El Cooperativismo y la Vivienda en la República Argentina." Buenos Aires, Revista de ciencias económicas (47:7), July-September 1959, p. 283-294.

4646 LoValo, J.
"La Propiedad Horizontal y el Urbanismo." Santa Fé, Revista de ciencias jurídicas y sociales 48-49, 1946, p. 151-195.

4647 Morea, Alberto, & Luis M. Morea
"Vivienda Multifamiliar." Buenos Aires, Nuestra arquitectura (28:334), September 1957, p. 33-60.

4648 Morea, Luis M.
"Vivienda y Desarrollo Económico." Córdoba, Revista de la Universidad Nacional de Córdoba (4:3-4), July-October 1963, p. 727-742.

4649 "Primer Congreso Argentino de Planeamiento y Vivienda Realizado en Tucumán en Octubre de 1957; (Resoluciones)." Buenos Aires, Nuestra arquitectura (28:338), January 1958, p. 40-51.

4650 Ricur, A., & Luis M. Morea
"Política de la Vivienda en Argentina y Desarrollo Integral-Armónico." Montevideo, Cuadernos latinoamericanos de economía humana (4:11), 1961, p. 162-181.

4651 Scott, W.H.
"Congreso Argentino de Financiación de la Vivienda, Mar del Plata, 1960." Buenos Aires, Nuestra arquitectura (30:371), 1960, p. 45-48.

Bolivia

4652 Quiroga Pereira, H.
"Informe Sobre los Proyectos de Construcción de Viviendas Populares Baratas para los Trabajadores Mineros." Oruro, Universidad (4:6/7), 1st and 2nd semester, 1955, p. 249-265.

Brazil

4653 Associação de Dirigentes Cristãos de Emprêsa da Guanabara.
"O Problema Nacional de Habitação Popular." Rio de Janeiro, Síntese política econômica social (5:20), October-December 1963, p. 86-91.

4654 "The Building Industry in Brazil." Rio de Janeiro, Conjuntura econômica internacional 8, July 1961, p. 57-64.

4655 "Casas Para os Industriários." Rio de Janeiro, Brasil construi (3:5), 1950, p. 28-31.

4656 Duprat, L. A.
"Habitação e Previdencia Social." Rio de Janeiro, Revista de administração municipal (9:54), September-October 1962, p. 385-389.

4657 "Favelas Cariocas." Rio de Janeiro, Desenvolvimento e conjuntura 12, 1961, p. 75-85.

4658 "Huge Slums Crowd in on Brazilian Dream City." The Times of the Americas (XI:50), December 20, 1967, p. 2.

4659 Lagenest, H. D. Barruel de, et al
"Os Cortiços de São Paulo." São Paulo." Anhembi (12:139), June 1962, p. 5-17.

4660 Lebret, Louis J.
"Le Logement de la Population de São Paulo, Brésil." Paris, Economie et humanisme, cahiers d'économie humaine 2-3, 1951, p. 82-90.

4661 Mackenzie, E.
"Exploding Population Makes Latin Beauty Lift Her Face." Engineering news 174, January 28, 1965, p. 74-77.

4662 Mendonça, M. Larangeira de
"O Plano Habitacional e a Expansão das Areas Urbanas." Rio de Janeiro, Revista de administração municipal (11:70), May-June 1965, p. 155-175.

4663 Oliveira, F. Baptista de
"A Casa Popular como Problema Urbanístico." São Paulo, Boletím do Instituto de Engenharia, January-July 1941, p. 77-90.

4664 "A População das Favelas Cariocas." Rio de Janeiro, Conjuntura econômica (VI:5), May 1952, p. 34-42.

4665 "Seminario de Habitaçao e Reforma Urbana, "1º, Brazil, 1963. Conclusões." Rio de Janeiro, Revista de administração municipal (11:62), January-February 1964, p. 9-23.

4666 Teulières, R.
"Bidonvilles du Brésil: les 'Favelles' de Bêlo Horizonte." Bordeaux, Cahiers d'outre-mer 8, 1955, p. 1-28.

4667 "Urbanismo e Habitação Popular." São Paulo, Habitat (13:74), December 1963, p. 39-46.

4668 Violich, Francis
"Urban Growth and Planning in Brazil." São Paulo, Sociologia (21:4), October 1959, p. 361-384.

4669 Watanabe, H., et al
"Contribuição para a Análise do Problema Habitacional e da Ordenação Territorial." Bêlo Horizonte, Revista brasileira de estudos políticos 22, January 1967, p. 71-123.

4670 "The World Above Rio." Maryknoll 58, February 1964, p. 56-61.

Central America

4671 Solow, Anatole A.
"Cambio en el Paisaje Centroamericano." Américas (2:5), May 1950, p. 28-31, 39-40.

Chile

4672 Aguirre Tupper, Fernando
"Un Programa de Fomento a la Construcción de Viviendas." Santiago, Panorama económico (10: 154), September 28, 1956, p. 617-621.

4673 Alexander, Robert J.
"Housing in Chile." Land economics (25:2), 1949, p. 146-154.

4674 Alvarez, Olga Freddy de
"Aporte de Fundación Viviendas de Emergencia a la Solución del Problema de Habitación en Chile." Santiago, Servicio social (28:2), May/August 1954, p. 13-18.

4675 Carvallo Hederra, S.
"Building Their Own: Chilean Workers Turn to Co-Ops." Américas 10, August 1958, p. 14-17.

4676 Donoso Carrasco, Rafael
"Posibilidades y Dimensiones de un Plan de Construcción de Viviendas." Santiago, Panorama económico (8:105), July 30, 1954, p. 521-523.

4677 Kusnetzoff K., F.
Dimensiones de una Política Habitacional para el Sexenio, 1964-1970." Santiago, Planificación 1, October 1964, p. 13-50.

4678 Labadia, A.
"El Plan Habitacional Chileno." Santiago, Finis terrae (7:27), 3d quarter 1960, p. 51-53.

4679 Lorca F., F.
"La Planificación del Desarrollo y el Problema Metropolitano." Santiago, Economía (20:75-76), 2d-3d quarter 1962, p. 45-54.

4680 Opaz Tagle, J.
"Estadísticas del Plan Habitacional Chileno." Santiago, Panorama económico (16:236), April-May 1963, p. 45-49.

4681 Raposo, A.
"La Familia Habitante y su Vivienda." Santiago, Planificación 2, December 1965, p. 63-86.

4682 Rivera A., H.
"Impacto de Localizaciones Habitacionales en el Suelo Urbano." Santiago, Planificación 3, June 1966, p. 71-82.

4683 Ruíz Luján, S.
"Cooperative Approach to Housing Problems in Latin America: the Example of Chile." International labour review 91, May 1965, p. 406-419.

4684 "La Vivienda: Problema con Solución." Santiago, Panorama económico (8:105), July 30, 1954, p. 521-524.

Colombia

4685 Abad-Gómez, H.
"La Vivienda y los Servicios Públicos." Medellín, Revista de ciencias económicas (5:12), May 1959, p. 85-95.

4686 Andrade Valderrama, V.
"Es Urgente la Reforma Urbana." Bogotá, Revista javeriana (62:306), July 1964, p. 12-13.

4687 Bustamante, R.
"Las Asociaciones de Ahorro y Crédito para la Vivienda." Bogotá, Arco (5:35), July 1963, p. 502-504.

4688 "Las Habitaciones Colectivas en Bogotá." Bogotá, Proa 38, August 1950, p. 5-21.

4689 Mallol de Recasens, M.R., & José de Recasens Tuset
"Estudio Comparativo de los Niveles de Vivienda en Buenaventura y Puerto Colombia." Bogotá, Revista colombiana de antropología (XII: año 1963), 1965, p. 293-328.

4690 Robledo Uribe, F.
"Planes Sociales de Vivienda en Colombia." Bogotá, Arco 23-24, July-August 1962, p. 444-447.

4691 Uribe Uribe, Leonardo
"Las Actuales Necesidades de Colombia Respecto a la Vivienda." Medellín, Universidad Pontificia Bolivariana (21:75), February/March 1956, p. 16-33.

4692 Utria, Rubén D.
"La Vivienda, un Problema Nacional." Medellín, DYNA (Organo de los Estudiantes de la Facultad de Minas) (21:70), November 1954, p. 83-90.

Costa Rica

4693 "El Problema de la Vivienda." Tegucigalpa, Boletín mensual de información 9/10, May/June 1950, p. 2-11.

Cuba

4694 Bravo Heitmann, L.
"La Vivienda en el Campo del Planeamiento." Havana, Arquitectura-Cuba (28:327-329), October-December 1960, p. 454-464.

4695 Colete, Honorato
"Un Caso Concreto de Rehabilitación Urbana en La Habana Intramuros." Havana, Revista de la propiedad urbana, April 1948, p. 11-14.

4696 Dyer, D.R.
"Urbanism in Cuba." Geographical review (47:2), April 1957, p. 224-233.

4697 Krasnopolsky, V.
"Cuba in Construction." Moscow, New times 38, September 20, 1961, p. 14-16.

4698 Vera Rojas, Luis
"Vivienda y Planeamiento: Renovación Urbana." Havana, Revista nacional de la propiedad urbana (24:275), January 1957, p. 13-15; (24:276), February 1957, p. 11-12; (24:277), March 1957, p. 26-27; (24:280), June 1957, p. 14-15.

Ecuador

4699 Linke, Lilo
"Houses, not Hovels: Ambato, Ecuador." Américas

8, August 1956, p. 3-7.

El Salvador

4700 "El Salvador's Laboratory for Better Living." United Nations bulletin 15, December 15, 1953, p. 600-602.

4701 Picó Rafael, et al
"La Vivienda en El Salvador." San Salvador, Revista de economía (1:1/4), January/December 1950, p. 197-231.

4702 "Vivienda para Todos." San Salvador, Avance 2, January 1952, p. 15-17.

4703 Zúñiga Idiáquez, M.
"La Vivienda Multifamiliar en El Salvador." San Salvador, Síntesis (2:17), August 1955, p. 93-103.

Guatemala

4704 Méndez Escobar, P. F.
"Bancos de Ahorro y Préstamo como Solución al Problema de la Vivienda Familiar en Guatemala." Guatemala, El mes económico y financiero (4:4), April 1951, p. 9-16.

Guyana

4705 Drayton, E.
"L'Habitat en Guyane Brittannique." Port-of-Spain, Caraïbe (8:10), May 1955, p. 5-7, 20-21.

Haiti

4706 Sterlin, F.
"Logement, Facteur du Progrès Economique et Social." Port-Au-Prince, Revue du travail (10:10), May 1961, p. 31-37.

Honduras

4707 Dominguez A., Roberto
"Sobre la Vivienda y sus Problemas en Tegucigalpa." Tegucigalpa, May 4, 1947, p. 3.

Mexico

4708 Aaron, Henry
"Rent Controls and Urban Development: a Case

Study of Mexico City." Mona, *Social & economic studies* (15:4), December 1966, p. 314-328.

4709 "Arquitectura México: Número Dedicado a la Unidad de Servicios Sociales y de Habitación 'Independencia' del Instituto Mexicano del Seguro." México, *Arquitectura México* (17:73), March 1961, p. 3-46.

4710 "Banco Nacional Hipotecario Urbano y de Obras Públicas, S.A., México." México, *Estudios 6,* 1952, p. 1-267.

4711 Carmona, F.
"El Problema de la Vivienda en México." México, *Investigación económica* (18:69), 1958, p. 79-101.

4712 Carrasco, Lorenzo
"Proposiciones Urbanísticas para la Ciudad de Cuernavaca." México, *Revista de economía* (27:4), April 1964, p. 96-106.

4713 Covantes, H.
"La Vivienda Popular en México." México, *Istmo 24,* January-February 1963, p. 35-39.

4714 Domínguez E., Félix F.
"Una Ciudad Nueva para una Nueva Vida del Trabajador, en las Lomas de Santa Fé, en el Distrito Federal, Fué Inaugurada por el Señor Presidente de la República." México, *Todo 1217,* July 25, 1957, p. 34-39.

4715 Frieden, Bernard J.
"The Search for Housing Policy in Mexico City." London, *The town planning review* (36:2), July 1965, p. 75-94.

4716 Gutiérrez, J.M., et al
"Desarrollo de las Colonias Proletarias de la Ciudad de México." México, *Boletín de la Sociedad Mexicana de Urbanismo 2,* 1962, p. 23-27.

4717 López, María del S.
"El Problema Nacional de la Vivienda." México, *Revista de economía* (26:11), November 1963, p. 310-317.

4718 Noriega Herrera, A.
"Comentarios en Torno a la Vivienda." México, Revista de economía (20:11), November 15, 1957, p. 293-299.

4719 "Housing Plans for the Mexico City Area." Pan American Union bulletin 82, February 1948, p. 116-117.

4720 Pani, M.
"Renovación Urbana." México, Arquitectura México (20:81), March 1963, p. 5-10.

4721 Ramírez G., Ramón
"El Problema de la Habitación en sus Aspectos Generales y en la Ciudad de México." México, Estudios 1, January 1952, p. 62-67.

4722 Seijas R., G., & J. Villareal
"Estudio Sobre el Problema de la Vivienda Popular en Monterrey." Monterrey, Revista de la Escuela de Contabilidad, Economía y Administración (14:55), July 1962, p. 163-184.

4723 "Up From the Slums; La Laja Shanty Dwellers Get Government Aid." Newsweek 66, November 15, 1965, p. 70.

4724 Villegas, M.C., & María del S. López
"El Problema Nacional de la Vivienda." México, Revista de economía (26:11), November 1963, p. 310-317.

Nicaragua

4725 Argüello Peñalba, Ramiro
"Estado Actual de la Vivienda en Nicaragua y Programas en Desarrollo." León, Cuadernos universitarios 15, June 1960, p. 37-43.

4726 Peña, Horacio
"El Problema de la Vivienda en Nicaragua." San Salvador, ECA (Estudios centro-americanos) (14: 138), June 1959, p. 267-271.

Panama

4727 Gordon, A.
"El IVU y sus Proyecciones Sociales." Panamá, Lotería (5:57), August 1960, p. 52-58.

4728 Gutiérrez, Samuel A.
"El Problema de las 'Barriadas Brujas' en la Ciudad de Panamá." Panamá, Lotería (6:66), May 1961, p. 33-51.

4729 Navarro, H.
"Una Política Nacional de Vivienda." Panamá, Universidad 38, 1960, p. 101-119.

Paraguay

4730 Paraguay. Dirección General de Estadísticas y Censos
"Censo de Población y Vivienda de 1962." Asunción, Paraguay industrial y comercial (19:222-223), March-April 1963, p. 90-95.

Peru

4731 Alcocer, Francisco
"La Vivienda en Lima. Problema y Solución." México, Latinoamérica (6:65), May 1, 1954, p. 225-228.

4732 Belaunde Terry, Fernando
"Casas para el Pueblo." Américas (2:12), December 1950, p. 19-22, 46.

4733 Neira Alva, Eduardo
"El Problema de la Vivienda en el Perú." Lima, El arquitecto peruano (20:224/225), March/April 1956, p. 39-46.

4734 Smirnoff, V.
"25 Años de Vivienda en el Perú." Lima, El arquitecto peruano (20:83), September 1963, p. 177-182.

4735 Turner, John F.C.
"Barriers and Channels for Housing Development in Modernizing Countries." Journal of the American Institute of Planners (23:3), May 1967, p. 167-180.

4736 Valdivia Pezo, E.
"El Proceso de Reconstrucción del Cuzco y la Legislación Vigente." Cuzco, Revista universitaria (49; 118), 1st quarter, 1960, p. 115-124.

Uruguay

4737 Rama, Carlos M.
"La Vivienda y las Clases Sociales en el Uruguay." São Paulo, Sociología (20:1), March 1958, p. 67-83.

4738 Saxlund, R.H.
"Crisis de Vivienda en el Uruguay." Montevideo, CEDA (Centro de Estudiantes de Arquitectura) 27, February/September 1956, p. 1-3.

Venezuela

4739 "Caracas Pushes Low-Rent Housing Program." American city 72, November 1957, p. 167.

4740 Carlson, Eric
"Evaluación de Proyectos y Programas de Vivienda Sobre Venezuela." Caracas, Revista del Colegio de Ingenieros de Venezuela 287, April/June 1960, p. 43-58.

4741 Corporación Venezolana de Fomento
"La Vivienda y la Construcción en Venezuela." Caracas, Cuadernos de información económica (4:3), May/June 1952, p. 3-34.

4742 Ferris, J.
"La Vivienda en las Areas Industriales." Caracas, El farol (22:192), January-February 1961, p.55-62.

4743 "El Gobierno Democrático y el Problema de la Vivienda." Caracas, Política (3:26), September 1963, p. 187-197.

4744 González, P.J.
"Problèmes d'Habitation à Caracas." Paris, Vie urbaine 2, 1961, p. 117-149.

4745 López, Francisco
"Algunos Aspectos del Problema de la Vivienda en Venezuela." Caracas, Integral 7, May 1957, p. 5-11.

4746 Pérez Olivares, L.
"La Vivienda en Venezuela." Bogotá, Arco (2:6), January-February 1960, p. 59-60.

West Indies and the Caribbean

4747 Hanson, Donald R.
"Caribbean Housing." Port-of-Spain, The Caribbean (8:6), January 1955, p. 116-119.

4748 Piegeay, M.
"Le Problème des Matériaux de Construction aux Antilles." Paris, Industrie et travail d'outre-mer 12, November 1954, p. 689-691.

4749 Safa, H. I.
"From Shanty Town to Public Housing." Rio Piedras, Caribbean studies (IV:1), April 1964, p. 3-11.

PUBLIC HEALTH

Public Health (General)

Books

General

4750 Andrzejewski, A., et al
Housing programmes: the role of public health agencies; public health papers # 25. Geneva, World Health Organization, 1964, 197p.

4751 Gregory, P.
Polluted homes. London, Bell, 64p.

4752 Health services research. Chicago (I:1), Hospital Research & Educational Trust, 1966- .

4753 Lilienfeld, A.
Chronic diseases and public health. Baltimore, Johns Hopkins Press, 1966, 271p.

4754 London. University. Centre for Urban Studies
Public health and urban growth. London, 1964, 108p.

4755 National Commission on Community Health Services
Health is a community affair: a report . . . Cambridge, Harvard University Press, 1966, 252p.

4756 Olivero Aycinena, Humberto
Basic sanitary services in shanty towns: migration and urbanization (scientific publication # 123). Washington, Pan American Health Organization, 1965, 66p.

4757 Pan American Health Organization
Catálogo de publicaciones. Washington, 1955- .

4758 Pan American Health Organization
Health in the Americas and the Pan American Health Organization, program of the Pan American Health Organization and the World Health Organization in the Americas . . . Washington, G.P.O., 1960, 105p.

4759 Pan American Health Organization
Official documents. Washington, 1949-

4760 P.A.H.O. quarterly. Washington, Pan American Sanitary Bureau, 1956- .

4761 Pan American Sanitary Bureau
Informe financiero del director e informe del auditor externo. Washington, 1949- .

4762 Paz Soldán, Carlos E.
La OMS y la soberanía sanitaria de las Américas. Lima, Instituto de Medicina Social de la Universidad Mayor de San Marcos, 1949, 262p.

4763 Phelps, Earle B.
Public health engineering. New York, Wiley, 1948, 276p.

4764 Porterfield, John D., ed.
Community health; its needs and resources. New York, Basic Books, 1965, 250p.

4765 Seminar on Community Development, University of North Carolina, 1963
Professional preparation of public health personnel; proceedings of the seminar, May 5-9, 1963. Chapel Hill, 1963, 110p.

4766 Stirrup, F.L.
Public cleansing: refuse disposal. New York, Pergamon, 1965, 145p.

4767 Suchman, Edward A.
Sociology and the field of public health. New York, Russell Sage Foundation, 1963, 182p.

4768 Techniques et sciences municipales. Paris, Association Génerale des Hygiénistes et Techniciens Municipaux, 1958-

4769 World Health Organization
Environmental health aspects of metropolitan planning and development. Technical report series # 297. Geneva, 1965, 66p.

Latin America

4770 Morgan, Murray C.
Doctors to the world. New York, Viking Press, 1958, 271p.

4771 U.S. Institute of Inter-American Affairs
Report on cooperative health program of the governments of Bolivia, Brazil, Chile, Colombia, Guatemala, Haiti, Honduras, Nicaragua, Peru, El Salvador, Uruguay and the United States. 11 pts. in 13. Washington, Health & Sanitation Div., Institute of Inter-American Affairs, 1947-48.

4772 U.S. Public Health Service. Bureau of State Services
10 years of cooperative health programs in Latin America . . . Washington, 1953, 175p.

Argentina

4773 Almanaque de la salud. Buenos Aires, Secretaría de Salud Pública. Annual.

4774 Argentine Republic. Ministerio de Salud Pública
Bases para la organización de los distritos sanitarios de la Nación; instrucciones para los jefes de distritos sanitarios. Buenos Aires, 1952, 204p.

4775 Argentine Republic. Ministerio de Salud Pública
Memoria. Buenos Aires, June 1946/May 1952- .

4776 Carrillo, Ramón
Contribuciones al conocimiento sanitario. Buenos Aires, Ministerio de Salud Pública de la Nación, 1951, 511p.

4777 Carrillo, Ramón
Política sanitaria argentina. 2v. Buenos Aires, Ministerio de Salud Pública de la Nación, Depto. de Publicaciones y Talleres Gráf., 1949.

4778 Ferrara, F.
La villas miserias: aspectos médicos y sociales. La Plata, 1958, 16p.

4779 Grau, Carlos A.
La sanidad en las ciudades y pueblos de la Provincia de Buenos Aires. Eva Perón, Dirección de Impresiones Oficiales, 1954, 174p.

4780 Revista de sanidad, asistencia social y trabajo. v. 1- Santa Fé, 1945-

Bolivia

4781 Servicio Cooperativo Interamericano de Salud Pública. Bolivia
Diez años de cooperación sanitaria, 1942-1952. La Paz? 1952? 140p.

Brazil

4782 Bahia, Brasil (State) Direitoria Geral de Saúde Pública
Relatorio. Bahia, Impr. Official do Estado, 1959-

4783 Brasil. Ministerio da Educação e Saúde Pública. Serviço de Documentação
Arquivos. ano 1- , Rio de Janeiro, 1947-

4784 Brasil. Ministério da Saúde
Programa de trabalho. Rio de Janeiro, 1966? 84p.

4785 Brasil. Serviço Especial de Saúde Pública
Quinze anos de cooperação Brasil-Estados Unidos no campo de saúde pública, 17 de julho de 1957. Rio de Janeiro, 1957, 66p.

4786 Pinotti, Mario
Vida e morte do brasileiro; saúde e doença do Brasil. Rio de Janeiro, Ed. Civilização Brasileira, 1959, 164p.

Chile

4787 Chile. Servicio Médico Nacional de Empleados
Boletín. Santiago, 1946-

4788 Chile. Servicio Nacional de Salud
Revista. v. 1- Santiago, 1956-

4789 Chile. Servicio Nacional de Salud. Departamento de Parasitología
Memoria anual. Santiago. Annual.

4790 Viel Vicuña, Benjamín
La medicina socializada y su aplicación en Gran Bretaña, Unión Soviética y Chile. Santiago, Eds. de la Universidad de Chile, 1961, 195p.

Colombia

4791 Colombia. Ministerio de Salud Pública
Memoria al Congreso Nacional. Bogotá, Impr. Nacional, 1947- Annual.

4792 Colombia. Ministerio de Salud Pública. División Técnica de Bio-Estadística
Boletín epidemiológico. Bogotá? Annual.

4793 Instituto Nacional de Abastecimientos
Informe presentado al Sr. Presidente de la República. Bogotá. Annual.

4794 Instituto Nacional de Fomento Municipal
Plan bienal 1962-1963; primer informe de labores, enero 1962-julio 1963. 5v. Bogotá, 1963?

4795 Servicio Cooperativo Interamericano de Salud Pública. Colombia
Informe general de labores. Bogotá. Irregular.

Costa Rica

4796 Costa Rica. Ministerio de Salubridad Pública
Informe de la labor de salubridad pública. San José. Annual.

Dominican Republic

4797 Dominican Republic. Secretaría de Salud Pública
Boletín de salud pública. Ciudad Trujillo. Irregular.

Ecuador

4798 Plan decenal de salud pública para el Ecuador; resúmen general. [n.p.] 1964? 56p.

El Salvador

4799 Salvador. Ministerio de Salud Pública y Asistencia Social
Memoria. San Salvador? Annual.

4800 U.S. Treaties, etc. 1961-1963 (Kennedy)
Health and sanitation: cooperative program . . . Washington, G.P.O., 1963, 3p.

Guatemala

4801 Olivero Aycinena, Humberto
Un programa de saneamiento, experiencias y resultados. II Congreso Interamericano de Ingeniería Sanitaria. Guatemala, Universidad de San Carlos de Guatemala, Facultad de Ingeniería, 1950, 23p.

4802 Soto Avendaño, José A.
Salmonelosis, su proyección nacional como problema de salud pública. Guatemala, 1956, 76p.

4803 Valladores Ortiz, Oscar
Necesidad de una división infantil de rehabilitación para Guatemala. Guatemala, 1954, 58p.

Haiti

4804 Charmant, Rodolphe
Vers les sommets par l'éducation et la santé. Port-au-Prince, Impr. de l'Etat, 1953, 294p.

4805 Haiti (Republic) Département de la Santé Publique et de la Population
Le Président Magloire et la santé publique. Port-au-Prince? 1951? 24p.

4806 Haiti (Republic) Service National d'Hygiène Publique
The health of Haiti. Port-au-Prince. Annual.

Honduras

4807 Servicio Cooperativo Interamericano de Salud Pública
Informe. Tegucigalpa. Annual.

4808 Servicio Cooperativo Interamericano de Salud Pública
Sanidad y salud pública en Honduras; primeros seis años . . . Tegucigalpa, 1948, 110p.

Mexico

4809 Alvarez Amézquita, José, et al
Historia de la salubridad y de la asistencia en México. México, Secretaría de Salubridad y Asistencia, 1960-

4810 México (Federal District) Distrito Sanitario No. 3
Informe. México. Annual.

4811 México. Ministerio de Communicaciones y Obras Públicas. Depto. Médico
Reglas y procedimientos del sistema médico S.C.O.P. México, 1958, 565p.

4812 Salud pública de México. v. 1- México, 1959- .

4813 México
La seguridad social en México. Programa nacional de construcción de unidades médicas, sociales y administrativas, 1958-1964. 5v. México, Instituto Mexicano del Seguro Social, 1964.

Nicaragua

4814 Nicaragua. Ministerio de Salud Pública
Boletín sanitario. v. 1- Managua, 1954- .

Panama

4815 Canal Zone. Health Bureau
History and information guide. Mt. Hope, Panama Canal Press, 1946- .

4816 Falk, Isidore S.
Health in Panama, a survey and a program . . . Stonington, 1957, 406p.

4817 Falk, Isidore S.
A survey of health services and facilities in the Canal Zone. Stonington, 1958, 264p.

4818 Panamá. Ministerio de Trabajo, Previsión Social y Salud Pública
Memoria. Panamá. Irregular.

4819 Panama (Republic). Depto. de Salud Pública. Sección de Bioestadística y Educación Sanitaria
Educación y estadísticas sanitarias; informe bienal.

Panamá. Semi-annual.

Paraguay

4820 Gagliardone, César
Organicemos una nación. Inquietudes políticas de la época presente. 2d ed. Asunción, El Arte, 1959- .

Peru

4821 Salud y bienestar social. v. 1- , no. 1- , Lima, 1953- .

Trinidad

4822 Trinidad. Health Dept.
Medical and sanitary report of the director of medical services. Port-of-Spain. Annual.

Venezuela

4823 Archila, Ricardo
Historia de la sanidad en Venezuela . . . 2v. Caracas, Impr. Nacional, 1950.

4824 Briceño Romero, Gabriel
Socialización de la medicina en Venezuela. Caracas, Academia Nacional de Medicina, 1963, 337p.

4825 Oropeza, Pastor
Puericultura y administración sanitaria. Caracas, 1955, 475p.

4826 Venezuela. Comisión de Programas de Edificaciones Sanitarias
Documentos de la Comisión de Programas de Edificaciones Sanitarias . . . 2v. Caracas, Impr. Nacional, 1952-55.

West Indies and the Caribbean

4827 McCulloch, William E.
Your health in the Caribbean. Kingston, Pioneer Press, 1955, 149p.

Periodical Articles

General

4828 Barnhart, G. R.
"Note on the Impact of Public Health Service Re-

search on Poverty." Journal of social issues 21, January 1965, p. 142-149.

4829 Carson, D.H., & B.L. Driver
"An Ecological Approach to Environmental Stress." American behavioral scientist (10:1), September 1966, p. 8-11.

4830 Miller, H.H., ed.
"Health: Are We the People Getting our Money's Worth? A Symposium." New republic 149, November 9, 1963, p. 5-43.

4831 Paul, B.D.
"Anthropological Perspective on Medicine and Public Health." Annals of the American Academy of Political & Social Science 346, March 1963, p. 34-43.

4832 Roemer, Milton I.
"Changing Patterns cf Health Service: Their Dependence on a Changing World." Annals of the American Academy of Political & Social Science 346, March 1963, p. 44-56.

4833 Taylor, C.E.
"Medical Care for Developing Countries." The Atlantic 213, January 1964, p. 75-76.

4834 Watt, J.
"International Cooperation for Health: a Modern Imperative." Dept. of State bulletin 53, September 6, 1965, p. 412-418.

Latin America

4835 Dunham, George C.
"The Cooperative Health Program of the American Republics." American journal of public health, August 1944, p. 817-827.

4836 Dunham, George C.
"Health Makes Economic Wealth." Foriegn commerce weekly, December 2, 1944, p. 3-5, 37-38.

4837 Fermoselle Bacardí, Joaquín
"Las Unidades Sanitarias en las Américas." Boletín de la Oficina Sanitaria Panamericana (30:5), May 1951, p. 686-689.

4838 Croel, John N.
"La SCISP--Lesson in Cooperation." The Pan American, July/September 1947, p. 23-26.

4839 Horwitz, Abraham
"Health and Development." Américas 17, April 1965, p. 54-58.

4840 Martin, Edwin M.
"The Public Health Program of the Alliance for Progress." Dept. of State bulletin (47:1203), July 16, 1962, p. 120-124.

4841 Noriega, C.G.
"El Hábito de la Coca en Sud América." México, América indígena (12:2), April 1952, p. 111-120.

4842 Ros, E.
"El Nivel Sanitario de América Latina." México, Panoramas (2:10), July-August 1964, p. 147-151.

4843 Rubén Acuña, H.
"Algunas Consideraciones Sobre la Introducción de Nuevos Métodos de Enseñanza en al Adiestramiento de Personal Sanitario." Guatemala, Universidad de San Carlos 54, May-August 1961, p. 53-57.

4844 "Segunda Conferencia Latinoamericana de Escuelas de Salud Pública." Caracas, Política 18, October-November 1961, p. 105-107.

4845 Williams, M.W.
"Health and Social Progress in Latin America." Dept. of State bulletin 51, November 23, 1964, p. 747-751.

Argentina

4846 Argentine Republic. Laws, statutes, etc.
"Normas para el Ingreso al País de Pasajeros Enfermos. Dec. No. 19, 168." Buenos Aires, Boletín oficial, August 19, 1949, p. 1.

4847 "Argentine Public Health Office." Pan American Union bulletin 79, April 1945, p. 245.

4848 Argentine Republic. Laws, statutes, etc. "Salud Pública: Convenios. Apruébase el Celebrado con el Gobierno de Salta Sobre la Conducción Técnica de Establecimientos Asistenciales. Decreto No. 7.700." Buenos Aires, Boletín oficial (67: 18.971), June 27, 1959, p. 1.

4849 Argentine Republic. Laws, statutes, etc. "Salud Pública. Convenios. Apruébase el Suscripto con el Gobierno de Santa Cruz Sobre Conducción Técnica de Establecimientos Asistenciales. Decreto No. 7.701." Buenos Aires, Boletín oficial (67:18.972), June 29, 1959, p. 4.

4850 Argentine Republic. Laws, statutes, etc. "Salud Pública: Convenios. Apruébase el Celebrado con el Gobierno de la Pampa Sobre Conducción Técnica de Establecimientos Asistenciales. Decreto No. 7.703." Buenos Aires, Boletín oficial (67: 18.974), July 1, 1959, p. 4.

4851 Argentine Republic. Laws, statutes, etc. "Salud Pública. Convenios. Apruébase el Celebrado con la Provincia de San Juan Sobre Dirección Técnica de Establecimientos Asistenciales. Decreto No. 12.254." Buenos Aires, Boletín oficial (67: 19.063." October 17, 1959, p. 1.

4852 Besselievre, E.B. "Skeptics and the Septic Tanks." Public works 95, April 1964, p. 70.

4853 "Secretaría de Salud Pública Argentina." Pan American Union bulletin 81, February 1947, p. 117.

4854 Lazarte, J. "Panorama Sanitario y Asistencial del País." Santa Fé, Universidad 46, October-December 1960, p. 241-270.

Bolivia

4855 Arian, E.
"La Reorganización de los Servicios Departamentales de Profilaxis e Higiene en Bolivia." La Paz, Protección social, pt. 2, June 1941, p. 17-27.

4856 Bloomfield, J.J.
"Problemas de Higiene Industrial en Bolivia." La Paz, Protección social (13:145/146), March/April 1950, p. 7-113.

4857 Bolivia. Laws, statutes, etc.
"Código Sanitario de la República de Bolivia. D.S. 5006 de 24 de julio de 1958. Se Pone en Vigencia, a Partir de los Noventa Días del Presente Decreto." La Paz, Anales de legislación boliviana (10:38), July/September 1958, p. 31-32.

4858 Bolivia. Laws, statutes, etc.
"Consejo Nacional de Salubridad Pública. Decreto Supremo No. 04694." La Paz, Seguridad social (18:234), November 1957, p. 88-90.

4859 Bolivia. Laws, statutes, etc.
"Decree Issued by President Siles Placing the General Sanitary Bureau in Charge of the Investigation of Hygienic Conditions in Industrial Establishments." Pan American Union bulletin 63, December 1929, p. 1286.

4860 Bolivia. Laws, statutes, etc.
"Departamento de Higiene Pública. D.S. 4664 de 29 de Mayo de 1957. Dispónese su Organización por las HH. Alcaldías Municipales en las capitales de Departamento." La Paz, Anales de legislación boliviana (9:33), April/June 1957, p. 70-71.

4861 Fernández M., E.
"Política Sanitaria Boliviana." Sucre, Boletín de la Sociedad Geográfica e Histórica Sucre (48:449), 1964, p. 158-173.

4862 La Paz (Bolivia) City
"La Acaldía Municipal Proyecta la Solución del Problema de la Salubridad de la Población." La Paz, Ultima, May 1943, p. 22-24.

4863 Peru. Treaties, etc.
"Convenio de Salud Entre la República Peruana y la República de Bolivia. [May 2, 1959]." Lima, El Peruano 5425, May 14, 1959, p. 1.

Brazil

4864 Abel, J. F.
"The National Ministry of Education and Public Health in Brazil." School and society, July 2, 1932, p. 17-18.

4865 American Chamber of Commerce for Brazil
"Better Health for Brazil's Millions." Rio de Janeiro, Brazilian business (33:3), March 1953, p. 24-28.

4866 Brazil. Laws, statutes, etc.
"Aprova o Regulamento da Escola Nacional de Saúde Pública, do Ministério da Saúde. Decreto No. 46.258--de 23 de junho de 1959." Rio de Janeiro, Diário oficial (98:141), June 24, 1959, p. 14488-14491.

4867 Brazil. Laws, statutes, etc.
"Decreto No. 49.464--de 7 de Dezembro de 1960. Aprova os Estatutos da Fundação Serviço Especial da Saúde Pública." Brasilia, Diário oficial (99: 285), December 16, 1960, p. 16013-16017.

4868 Carneiro, Jarduny
"Os Problemas de Saúde no Plano Salte." Rio de Janeiro, Trabalho e seguro social (21:73/74), January/February 1949, p. 137-139.

4869 Faria, A. de
"Saúde e Desenvolvimento Econômico." São Paulo, Revista brasiliense 35, May-June 1961, p. 79-90.

4870 Farias, R. Cordeiro de
"Usage du Maconha (Cannabis Sativa) au Brésil. Mesures Prises par les Autorités Sanitaires et la Police pour Mettre Fin a Cet Usage." Bulletin des stupéfiants (7:2), May-August 1955, p. 6-21.

4871 Iutaka, Sugiyama
"Social Status and Illness in Urban Brazil." Milbank Memorial Fund quarterly (XLIV:2, pt. 2), April 1966, p. 97-110.

4872 "Mortalidade Infantil nas Capitais Brasileiras, 1940-1953." Rio de Janeiro, Conjuntura econômica (IX: 4), April 1955, p. 63-67.

4873 "Mortalidade Infantil: Retrato do Desenvolvimento Econômico de São Paulo." Rio de Janeiro, Desenvolvimento e conjuntura 5, 1961, p. 91-97.

4874 Novaes, Menandro
"Diretrizes de um Programa de Saúde para a Bahia." São Paulo, Revista brasiliense 49, September-October 1963, p. 91-104.

4875 Nunes Guimaraes, J.
"A Margem de Alguns Problemas Brasileiros. 1-3." Petrópolis, Vozes de Petrópolis, November/December 1945, p. 759-767.

4876 Pessôa, Samuel Barnsley
"Educação Sanitaria." São Paulo, Revista brasiliense 16, March/April 1958, p. 105-117.

4877 Pessôa, Samuel Barnsley
"Os Municipios e a Proteção e Saúde Da Criança." São Paulo, Revista brasiliense 26, November/December 1959, p. 130-140.

4878 Pessôa, Samuel Barnsley
"As Tarefas Fundamentais de Saúde Pública no Brasil." São Paulo, Revista brasiliense 32, November-December 1960, p. 93-96.

4879 "Problemas Sociais e de Saúde no Brasil." Curitiba, Divulgações de serviço social, January/March 1949, p. 33-47.

4880 Ribeiro, Jonas D.
"Emílio Ribas." São Paulo, Anhembi (39:115), June 1960, p. 93-102.

4881 Ribeiro, P. de Assis
"A Saúde e o Planejamento." Rio de Janeiro, _Revista brasileira de economia_ (16:4), December 1962, p. 45-81.

4882 Sampaio, G. Ferreira
"Saneamento das Cidades Brasileiras." Rio de Janeiro, _Revista de serviço público,_ July-August 1962, p. 109-124.

4883 Santos, N.R. dos
"O Problema da Saúde no Brasil." São Paulo, _Revista brasiliense 42,_ July-August 1962, p. 121-135.

4884 "VII Congresso Brasileiro de Higiene." São Paulo, _R.A.E._ July 1949, p. 115-123.

4885 Silveira, M. Magalhaes da
"Desenvolvimento Econômico e Saúde." São Paulo, _Revista brasiliense 48,_ July-August 1963, p. 27-37.

Chile

4886 Durán, Hernan, & Miguel Solar
"La Organización Local del Servicio Nacional de Salud." Santiago, _Revista del Servicio Nacional de Salud_ (1:1), October 1956, p. 19-22.

4887 Flores, A., & Manuel de Viado
"Organized Medical Care in Chile." Montreal, _International labour review,_ March 1945, p. 302-329.

4888 International Labor Office
"Enseñanza de Higiene y Seguridad Industrial en Chile." Montreal, _Revista internacional del trabajo,_ March 1944, p. 450.

4889 Laval, M. Enrique
"Síntesis del Desarrollo Histórico de la Salubridad en Chile." Santiago, _Revista del Servicio Nacional de Salud_ (1:1), October 1956, p. 23-29.

4890 San Martín, H.
"La Salud de la Población y el Desarrollo." Santiago, _Panorama económico_ (15:231), June 1962, p. 169-175.

4891 Sepúlveda, Orlando
"Algunos Problemas de la Salud en el Area Metropolitana del Gran Santiago." Santiago, Boletín de la Universidad de Chile 15, September 1960, p. 41-43.

4892 Verdugo Binimelis, D.
"Problemas Sanitarios en la Provincia de Arauco." Santiago, Previsión social 89, 1962, p. 8-10.

Colombia

4893 Aguilera Ballesteros, A.
"Estudios de los Aspectos de Salud Circunvecina del Recinto Simón Bolívar del Centro de Salud No. 27." Bogotá, Revista de la Facultad de Medicina 31, October-December 1963, p. 99-107.

4894 Bejarano, Jorge
"Nuevos Conceptos Sobre el Cocaísmo en Colombia." México, América indígena (13:1), January 1953, p. 15-46.

4895 Bejarano, Jorge
"Progresos de la Salubridad Pública en Colombia." Boletín de la Oficina Sanitaria Panamericana (25:10), October 1949, p. 1024-1026.

4896 Colombia. Laws, statutes, etc.
"Decreto No. 1371 de 1953 (Mayo 27) por el Cual se Establece el Código Sanitario Nacional." Bogotá, Diario oficial (90:28229), June 23, 1953, p. 1269-1289.

4897 Cruz, Eliseo
"La Sanidad en Colombia." Boletín de la Oficina Sanitaria Panamericana (27:9), September 1948, p. 806-813.

4898 Reichel-Dolmatoff, Gerardo, & Alicia Reichel-Dolmatoff
"Nivel de Salud y Medicina Popular en una Aldea Mestiza Colombiana." Bogotá, Revista colombiana de antropologia 7, 1958, p. 199-249.

4899 Sánchez, A. M.
"La Salud Pública y la Economía de los Colombianos." Bogotá, Economía colombiana (6:16), August 1955, p. 345-375.

Costa Rica

4900 Costa Rica. Laws, statutes, etc.
"Decreto No. 7. [Medidas de Prevención Contra la Introducción de la Fiebre Aftosa y de la Peste Bovina en el País. Sept. 27, 1951]." San José, Gaceta (73:254), November 9, 1951, p. 2805.

4901 Costa Rica. Laws, statutes, etc.
"Decreto No. 8. Reglamento para la Inspección Sanitaria de la Carne. [Junio 28, 1954]." San José, La Gaceta (76:178), August 10, 1954, p. 2053-2054.

4902 Costa Rica. Laws, statutes, etc.
"Decreto No. 9. Reglamento para la Industrialización Sanitaria de la Carne. [Julio 9, 1954]." San José, La Gaceta (76:195), August 29, 1954, p. 2249-2271.

4903 Costa Rica. Laws, statutes, etc.
"Decreto No. 1206. [Sobre Cursos de Capacitación para Dentistas. Refórmanse Algunos Artículos del Código Sanitario. Oct. 10, 1950]." San José, Gaceta (52:239), October 22, 1950, p. 2043.

4904 Costa Rica. Presidente. (Calderón)
"Salubridad Pública." San José, Salud, January-December 1943, p. 12-23.

4905 "Costa Rica: Programa de Asistencia Enfermera de Higiene Pública." Madrid, Revista del trabajo 4, April 1951, p. 381.

Cuba

4906 "El Nuevo Código Sanitario." Havana, Revista Nacional de la propiedad urbana (19:215), January 1952, p. 5.

Dominican Republic

4907 Thomén, L. F.
"La Sanidad en la República Dominicana." Boletín

de la Oficina Sanitaria Panamericana (27:10), October 1948, p. 881-884.

Ecuador

4908 Ecuador. Laws, statutes, etc.
"Sanitary Campaigns in Ecuador." Pan American Union bulletin 68, July 1934, p. 533-534.

4909 Léon, L. A.
"Historia y Extinción del Cocaísmo en el Ecuador; sus Resultados." México, América indígena (12:1), January 1952, p. 7-32.

El Salvador

4910 Castro, Ranulfo
"La Sanidad en El Salvador." Boletín de la Oficina Sanitaria Panamericana (27:9), September 1948, p. 814-818.

4911 El Salvador. Laws, statutes, etc.
"Acuerdo No. 524.--Autorízase al Señor Ministro de Salud Pública y Asistencia Social, para que en Nombre del Gobierno de El Salvador Firme con el Representante Autorizado del Gobierno de los Estados Unidos de América el Acuerdo Sobre Contribuciones Financieras al Programa Cooperativo de Salud y Saneamiento en El Salvador para 1956." San Salvador, Diario oficial, January 4, 1956, p. 41.

4912 El Salvador. Treaties, etc.
"Canje de Notas Celebrado Entre el Ministerio de Relaciones Exteriores de El Salvador y la Embajada de los Estados Unidos de Norte América, por el Cual se Extiende Hasta el 30 de Junio de 1960 el Programa Cooperativo de Salud y Saneamiento y Convenio Sobre las 'Contribuciones Financieras' al Programa Cooperativo de Salud y Saneamiento para 1956 . . ." San Salvador, Diario oficial, March 15, 1956, p. 2158-2160.

4913 El Salvador. Treaties, etc.
"Convenio Sobre Contribuciones al Programa Cooperativo de Salud y Saneamiento en El Salvador para Desarrollo de un Programa de Enseñanza Médica en la Escuela de Medicina de El Salvador para 1956.

Acuerdo del Ministerio de Relaciones Exteriores No. 209, Aprobándolo y Decreto Legislativo No. 2121 Ratificándolo en Todas sus Partes." San Salvador, Diario oficial, June 12, 1956, p. 4684-4685.

4914 "Review of Public Health and Social Welfare in El Salvador." Pan American Union bulletin 65, July 1931, p. 790-791.

4915 "Sanitary Campaign for Promoting Better Health." Pan American Union bulletin, February 1929, p. 212.

4916 "Social-Welfare Activities of the Government of El Salvador." Pan American Union bulletin 66, September 1932, p. 668-671.

Guatemala

4917 Stutsky, H. L.
"Ecological Study of Total Mortality Among Guatemalan Pre-school Children, with Special Emphasis on Protein Malnutrition and Kwashiorkor." Annals of the Association of American Geographers 50, September 1960, p. 347.

Haiti

4918 Haiti.
"Contributions Financières au Programme Coopératif de Santé en Haiti pour l'Année 1953." Port-au-Prince, Le Moniteur, December 22, 1952, p. 888.

4919 Haiti. Laws, statutes, etc.
"Décret Revisant la Loi du 12 Février 1958 Organisant sur de Nouvelles Bases le Département de la Santé Publique et de la Population." Port-au-Prince, Le moniteur 114 (special no. 22), January 31, 1959, p. 117-118.

4920 Sam, André
"Unités Sanitaires dans la République d'Haiti." Boletín de la Oficina Sanitaria Panamericana (30:5), May 1951, p. 638-639.

Honduras

4921 Alonzo de Quesada, A.
"Prolimpieza de la Capital y Mejoramiento Vecinal." Tegucigalpa, Honduras rotaria (20:216), August-September 1963, p. 12.

4922 "Servicio Interamericano de Salud Pública en Honduras." La Ceiba, Voz de Atlántida, April 1946, p. 9, 16.

Mexico

4923 Barrales Valladares, J.
"La Higiene y la Seguridad en el Trabajo en México es Obra de la Revolución Mexicana." México, Revista mexicana del trabajo (5a. época, 8:3-4), March-April 1961, p. 9-18.

4924 Blayne, Thornton
"La Casa del Pueblo. National Regeneration Through Education in Mexico." Hispania, December 1941, p. 451-458.

4925 Bustamante, Miguel E.
"Public Health and Medical Care." Annals of the American Academy of Political & Social Science, March 1940, p. 153-161.

4926 Carrasco, G.
"Datos Sobre el Desarrollo de la Conducta en Niños de la Ciudad de México." México, Anales del Instituto Nacional de Antropología e Historia (13:42), 1961, p. 189-203.

4927 Espinosa y de Los Reyes, Isidro
"Labor de los Centros de Higiene de México." Pan American Union bulletin 66, July 1932, p. 486-494.

4928 Garza Brito, Angel de la
"La Enseñanza de la Higiene en las Escuelas Técnicas y Superiores." México, Salubridad y asistencia, September/October 1945, p. 57-68.

4929 Garza Brito, Angel de la
"Escuela de Salubridad y Higiene." México, Salubridad y asistencia, September/October 1945, p. 103-115.

4930 González Rivera, Manuel
"Educación Higiénica y Lucha Contra el Alcoholismo." México, Carta semanal, May 10, 1947, p. 519-520.

4931 "Health Education for Workers in Mexico." Pan American Union bulletin 78, June 1944, p. 353-354.

4932 León, Alberto P.
"Análisis Estadístico de las Causas de Mortalidad. Problemas Principales de Salud Pública en México." México, Boletín de la Sociedad Mexicana de Geografía y Estadística (77:2/3), March/June 1954, p. 345-361.

4933 Martínez Lavalle, A.
"Toxicomanías y Criminalidad." México, Estudios sociológicos 1954, p. 31-50.

4934 Medellín Sánchez, Roberto
"La Ingeniería Sanitaria en la Salubridad Industrial. Saneamiento Industrial e Higiene Industrial." México, Revista mexicana de ingeniería y arquitectura, May 1943, p. 223-243.

4935 Mendez Becerril, R.
"Los Riesgos Profesionales Dentro de la Seguridad social." México, Revista del ITAT 12, 1960, p. 37-65.

4936 México. Instituto de Higiene
"Mexico's Institute of Hygiene." Translated from the Spanish by Marian Keefer. Pan American Union bulletin 63, June 1929, p. 568-574.

4937 Millán, Verna C.
"Mobilizing for Health. Mexico Marshals All Her Tremendous Resources in Bitter War Against Her Oldest Enemy." Interamerican, May 1943, p. 15-18.

4938 Montanari, Francis W.
"Joint Battle Against Disease." México, Mexican-American review (18:9), September 1950, p. 21-24, 64.

4939 Moreno, Fabián
"Cooperación Interamericana. Se Establece un Plan para Evitar Enfermedades." México, Hoy 723, December 30, 1950, p. 46.

4940 Pan American Sanitary Office
"Sexta Reunión Anual. Asociación Fronteriza Mexicana-Estadounidense de Salubridad." Boletín de la Oficina Sanitaria Panamericana, August 1948, p. 681-784.

4941 "El Progreso de la Salubridad y Asistencia en México." Pan American Union Spanish bulletin 81, January 1947, p. 29-34.

4942 Payne, George C., et al
"Estudios Sobre Desplojamiento." México, Salubridad y asistencia, September/October 1945, p. 69-78.

4943 Reissmann, Ricardo
"El Problema de la Higiene y la Desnutrición en México." México, Higiene y seguridad, August 1946, p. 378-379.

4944 Sordo Noriega, Antonio
"Las Labores de los Centros de Higiene y Asistencia Infantiles y su Coordinación con la Maternidad de las Lomas." México, Salubridad y asistencia, March/April 1947, p. 183-189.

Nicaragua

4945 Nicaragua. Laws, statutes, etc.
"Decreto No. 101, Ley de Sanidad Animal. [Oct. 19, 1954]." Managua, La gaceta (58:242), October 27, 1954, p. 2207-2208.

4946 Pan American Sanitary Office
"Las Unidades Sanitarias de Nicaragua." Boletín de la Oficina Sanitaria Panamericana (30:5), May 1951, p. 617-621.

Panama

4947 Candanedo, César A.
"Informe Final de los Trabajos Realizados por la

Brigada Curativa No. 2 en San Blas." Panamá, Universidad, 1st semester 1947, p. 127-141.

4948 Chiodi, Hugo
"La Campaña Sanitaria del Canal de Panamá." Buenos Aires, Ciencia e investigación (5:4), April 1949, p. 135-139.

4949 Roux, Rómulo
"Las Unidades Sanitarias de Panamá." Boletín de la Oficina Sanitaria Panamericana (30:5), May 1951, p. 583-607.

Paraguay

4950 Buongermini, Gerardo
"La Salud Pública en Paraguay." Asunción, Paraguay industrial y comercial, May 1946, p. 8-9.

4951 Luna, Joaquín de
"The Organization of Public Hygiene in Paraguay." Pan American Union bulletin 63, February 1929, p. 157-163.

4952 "Textos de los Acuerdos Suscritos con los Estados Unidos de Norte América." Asunción, Paraguay industrial y comercial (11:215), January 1955, p. 18-20.

Peru

4953 Bernales Chienda, L.
"Hacia un Plan Nacional de Salud Pública." Lima, Informaciones sociales (17:2), April-June 1962, p. 3-11.

4954 Kuon Cabello, J.
"Realidad Sanitaria en los Pueblos Serranos." Cuzco, Revista universitaria, 1st semester 1948, p. 221-225.

4955 Peru. Treaties, etc.
"Convenio de Salud Entre la República Peruana y la República de Bolivia. [May 2, 1959]." Lima, El peruano 5425, May 14, 1959, p. 1.

4956 Peru. Laws, statutes, etc.
"Se Crea el Cargo de Consultor de Salud Pública. Decreto Supremo." Lima, El peruano, October 16, 1957, p. 1.

4957 Rebagliati, Edgardo
"Las Unidades Sanitarias del Perú." Boletín de la Oficina Sanitaria Panamericana (30:5), May 1951, p. 633-637.

4958 Ricketts, C.A.
"El Cocaísmo en el Perú." México, América indígena (12:4), October 1952, p. 309-322.

4959 Ugarte, Luis A.
"Organización Regional de Salud Pública en el Perú." Lima, Salud y bienestar social (3:8), March/April 1954, p. 17-22.

4960 Westphal, Edward A.
"A Survey of the Public Health Work Being Carried Out in Peru by the Institute of Inter-American Affairs." Lima, Peruvian times, September 15, 1944, p. 11-14.

Uruguay

4961 Cappeletti, Ricardo
"Unidades Sanitarias del Uruguay." Boletín de la Oficina Sanitaria Panamericana (30:5), May 1951, p. 628-632.

4962 Etchepare, Alberto
"El Doctor Scoseria y su Fecunda Vida al Servicio de la Salud Pública." Montevideo, Mundo uruguayo, June 1, 1944, p. 4-5, 49, 57.

4963 Gomensoro, Javier
"La Educación Sanitaria en el Uruguay." Montevideo, Boletín del Instituto Internacional Americano de Protección a la Infancia (24:2), June 1950, p. 181-192.

4964 Saralegui, J.
"La Educación Sanitaria en el Uruguay." Boletín de la Oficina Sanitaria Panamericana (38:1), January 1955, p. 1-9.

Venezuela

4965 "Aporte del I. N. O. S. a la Transformación Socio-Económica de la Cuenca del Lago Maracaibo." Caracas, Política 10, June 1960, p. 94a-94e.

4966 "Breve Historia de la Sanidad en Venezuela." Caracas, El farol, June 1948, p. 22-24.

4967 González, C. L.
"Progreso Sanitario en Venezuela 1946-50." Caracas, Revista de sanidad y asistencia social (15:6), November-December 1950, p. 359-380.

4968 Venezuela. Ministerio de Agricultura
"Matadouros Industriais." Rio de Janeiro, Revista de administração municipal (8:47), July-August 1961, p. 341-348.

4969 Zuñiga Cisneros, M.
"Seguridad Social y Servicios Médicos en Venezuela." Montevideo, Boletín del Instituto Internacional Americano de Protección a la Infancia (23:1), March 1949, p. 65-70.

West Indies and the Caribbean

4970 Floch, H.
"La Lutte Contre la Fièvre Jaune en Guyane Française." Port-of-Spain, Le caraïbe (VIII:9), 1955, p. 12-14.

4971 Hyronimus, D. R.
"L'Amélioration des Conditions Sanitaires dans les Départements Français d'Amérique au Cours des Années 1954 et 1955." Port-of-Spain, Le caraïbe (XI:8), 1958, p. 2-5.

Air Pollution

Books

General

4972 Farber, Seymour M., & Roger H.L. Wilson, eds. The air we breathe: a study of man and his environment. Springfield, Thomas, 1960, 414p.

4973 Herber, Lewis Crisis in our cities. Englewood Cliffs, Prentice-Hall, 1965, 239p.

4974 Magill, Paul L., et al, eds. Air pollution handbook. New York, McGraw-Hill, 1956-

4975 National Society for Clean Air Clean air yearbock, 1965-1966. London, 1965- . Annual.

4976 Smith, Alan R. Air pollution: a survey; Society of Chemical Industry monograph no. 22. New York, Pergamon Press, 101p.

4977 U.S. Dept. of Health, Education & Welfare National conference on air pollution, 1962: proceedings. Washington, G.P.O., 1963, 436p.

4978 World Health Organization Air pollution. Geneva, 1961, 442p.

4979 World Health Organization. Expert Committee on Atmospheric Pollutants Atmospheric pollutants; report. Geneva, World Health Organization, 1964, 18p.

Mexico

4980 Bravo A. H., & A.P. Baez Approach to the characterization of airborne organic matter, benzene soluble, in the atmosphere of Mexico City; proceedings of the 54th annual meeting, APCA, New York, N.Y., 1961. Pittsburgh, Air Pollution Control Association, 1961, 3p.

Periodical Articles

General

4981 Goldsmith, J.R.
"Air Pollution and Health: Report on Seventh Annual Air Pollution Medical Research Conference." Science 145, July 10, 1964, p. 184-186.

4982 Griffin, C.W.
"The Air Around Us." Reporter 33, September 10, 1964, p. 39-43.

4983 "Man and His Habitat: Problems of Pollution; Symposium." Bulletin of the atomic scientists 21, March 1965, p. 18-30.

4984 Wolman, A.
"Metabolism of Cities." Scientific American 213, September 1965, p. 178-188.

Latin America

4985 Fournier d'Albe, E.M.
"'Smog' en los Trópicos." Paris, El correo (12:3), March 1959, p. 15-19.

4986 Haddad, R., & J.J. Bloomfield
"La Contaminación Atomosférica en América Latina." Boletín de la Oficina Sanitaria Panamericana 57, September 1964, p. 241-249.

4987 Francis, B.
"Air Pollution Perils South American Cities." Los Angeles times, February 6, 1967, pt. 1, p. 16.

Argentina

4988 Rubin, M.
"The Problem of Smoke in Buenos Aires." Air repair 2, November 1952, p. 20-21.

4989 Sánchez Díaz, A.
"El Problema Higiénico del Aire y del Humo en la Ciudad de Buenos Aires." Buenos Aires, Boletín del honorable Consejo deliberante, May 1941, p. 151-160.

Brazil

4990 Haddad, R.
"Air Pollution in the Metropolitan Area of São

Paulo, Brazil." Boletín de la Oficina Sanitaria Panamericana 56, March 1964, p. 243-256.

4991 Lima, A.O., et al
"Incidência dos Fungos no Atmôsfera de Algumas Cidades Brasileiras." Rio de Janeiro, Hospital 63, May 1963, p. 1045-1054.

Chile

4992 Bloomfield, J.J.
"El Instituto de Higiene Industrial y de Contaminación del Aire en Santiago de Chile." Córdoba, Revista medica de la Universidad de Córdoba 51, January-March 1963, p. 75-81.

Costa Rica

4993 Armbrister, T.
"The Sky is Falling: Irazú Eruption." Saturday evening post 237, April 11, 1964, p. 20-25.

4994 Cordero, C.J.
"Spectacular Irazú." Americas 16, April 1964, p. 21-27.

4995 Horton, R.J.M., & R.O. McCaldin
"Observations on Air Pollution Aspects of Irazú Volcano, Costa Rica." Public health reports 79, October 1964, p. 925-929.

Mexico

4996 Baez, A.P.
"La Medición de la Concentración del Bióxido de Carbono del Aire y el Estudio de su Difusión, como un Medio para Evaluar la Contaminación Atmosférica." México, Ingeniería química 4, February 1959, p. 22-26.

4997 Baez, A.P., & H. Bravo A.
"Air Pollution in Mexico City." México, Mexican-American review (33:6), June 1965, p. 24-31.

4998 Bravo A., H.
"Variación de Contaminadores Diferentes en el Atmósfera de la Ciudad de México." Journal of the Air Pollution Control Association 10, December 1960, p. 447-449.

4999 Guilmant, P.
"Mexico's Smog Menace." México, Mexican-American review (31:5), May 1963, p. 13-14.

5000 McCabe, L.C., & G.D. Clayton
"Air Pollution by Hydrogen Sulfide in Poza Rica, Mexico." Archives of industrial hygiene & occupational medicine 6, September 1952, p. 199-213.

5001 "Mexico City Newspaper Predicts End of Pollution." New York times, August 22, 1965, p. 36.

5002 Vignola, L., et al
"Hongos Atmosféricos en la Ciudad de Veracruz, Ver., México." México, Revista médica del Hospital General 26, October 1963, p. 755-761.

5003 Viniegra G., & H. Bravo A.
"Polución Atmosférica en la Ciudad de México; Informe Preliminar." México, Prensa médica mexicana (24:2), February 1959, p. 73-80.

Hospital and Medical Care

Books

General

5004 Association of Teachers of Preventive Medicine. Committee on Medical Care Teaching
Readings in medical care. Chapel Hill, University of North Carolina Press, 1958, 708p.

5005 Evang, Karl
Health service, society and medicine. New York, Oxford University Press, 1960, 171p.

5006 Saunders, Lyle
Cultural difference and medical care. New York, Russell Sage Foundation, 1954, 317p.

Latin America

5007 Roemer, Milton I.
Medical care in Latin America. Washington, Pan American Union, 1963, 329p.

5008 San Martín Ferrari, Hernán, et al
Salud y enfermedad; problemas de medicina social en América Latina. 2v. Havana, Comisión Editora, Confederación Médica Panamericana, 1964.

5009 Seminar on the Training of Nursing Auxiliaries, Cuernavaca, Mexico, 1963.
Guide for the training of nursing auxiliaries in Latin America . . . Washington, Pan American Health Organization, 1964, 36p.

Brazil

5010 Perrone, Oberdam Revel
Armamento hospitalar no Brasil. Rio de Janeiro, 1958, 127p.

Chile

5011 Laval M., Enrique
Historia del Hospital San Juan de Dios de Santiago, apuntes. Santiago, Asociación Chilena de Asistencia Social, 1949, 333p.

5012 Neghme Rodríguez, Amador
Reflexiones sobre la medicina y la salubridad en Chile. Santiago, Impr. Universitaria, 1950, 28p.

5013 Pimentel Orellana, Manuel
La medicina preventiva en sus aspectos económico y social. Santiago, Impr. "Relámpago," 1948, 56p.

Colombia

5014 Cartagena, Colombia. Hospital de Manga
Balance e informes. Cartagena, 1955-

Cuba

5015 Lage, Guillermo
El primer hospital de la Habana. Havana, Ministerio de Salubridad y Asistencia Social, 1952, 41p.

5016 Le Roy y Cassá, Jorge E.
Historia del Hospital San Francisco. . . Havana, 1958, 553p.

Ecuador

5017 Urbina, José M.
Organización hospitalaria y educación médica para el Ecuador. Quito, Impr. de la Universidad, 1949, 44p.

Guatemala

5018 Barascout, Jorge E.
Monografía económica sobre el problema hospitalario de Guatemala. Guatemala, 1949, 152p.

5019 Congreso Médico Hospitalario Nacional
Congreso Médico Hospitalario: anales. Guatemala, 1946-

5020 Ortega Avila, Moisés
Mortalidad materna y mortenatalidad en la ciudad de Guatemala. Guatemala, 1948, 47p.

Mexico

5021 Barba Rubio, J.
La lepra; problema social en Jalisco. (In Estudios sociológicos. Segundo Congreso Nacional de Sociología, 1951. México, Universidad Nacional, 1953, p. 233-252).

5022 Cooper, Donald B.
Epidemic disease in Mexico City, 1761-1813. Austin, University of Texas Press, 1965, 236p.

5023 Cruz, Francisco S.
Los hospitales de México y la caridad de don Benito. México, Ed. Jus, 1959, 118p.

5024 Mexico (City) Hospital de San Lázaro
Ordenanzas del Hospital de San Lázaro de México, año de 1582. México, Porrúa, 1956, 42p.

5025 Muy y Mendoza, Raúl
Programa de organización contable y auditoria interna del Hospital de Zona Número Uno "La Raza." México, 1957, 114p.

5026 Sánchez Márquez, J.
Asistencia social en lepra: su estado actual en

Jalisco. (In Estudios sociológicos. Segundo Congreso Nacional de Sociología, 1951. México, Universidad Nacional, 1953, p. 253-260).

5027 Sodi de Pallares, María E.
Historia de una obra pía, el Hospital de Jesús en la historia de México. 1st ed. México, Eds. Botas, 1956, 343p.

Panama
5028 Susto, Juan A.
Historia de la actividad hospitalaria en Panamá, 1514-1924; el Hospital de Santo Tomás de Villanueva. Panamá, 1958, 36p.

Peru
5029 Kuczynski-Godard, Maxime H.
Estudios médico-sociales en Ayacucho. Lima, Ministerio de Salud Pública y Asistencia Social, 1946-

Periodical Articles

General
5030 "Doctors, Patients and Society: Symposium." Nation 200, May 3, 1965, p. 464-481.

5031 "Medical Care Protection Under Social Security Schemes: a Statistical Study of Selected Countries." International labour review 89, June 1964, p. 570-593.

5032 Trussell, R.E.
"The Quality of Medical Care as a Challenge to Public Health." American journal of public health 55, February 1965, p. 173-182.

Latin America
5033 Horwitz, Abraham
"The Positive and Negative of Health Care in Latin America." Milbank Memorial Fund quarterly (42: 1), January 1964, p. 67-81.

5034 "Inter-American Hospital Construction Program." Lima, Cahuide, June 1943, p. 58.

5035 Roemer, Milton I. "Medical Care and Social Class in Latin America." Milbank Memorial Fund quarterly (42:3), 1964, p. 54-64.

Argentina

5036 "Ampliación de Servicios Hospitalarios." Buenos Aires, Continente, May 15, 1948, p. 122-123.

5037 Carrillo, R. "La Arquitectura Hospitalaria en la Argentina." Buenos Aires, Yapeyú 61, January/March 1950, p. 43-56.

5038 Fernández, José B. "El Hospital Regional Español de Bahia Blanca." Bahia Blanca, Ibero-América, August 1945, p. 18-19.

5039 "La Inauguración del Hospital en Tucumán." Buenos Aires, La fraternidad, September 5, 1946, p. 2-6.

5040 Sobel, R. "Capacitación del Personal de un Hospital." Buenos Aires, Revista de administración pública (4:14-15), July-December 1964, p. 271-283.

5041 Wolaj, I. F. "El Problema Médico-Sanitario y Social de los Tugurios. Resultados de un Estudio de 2 Areas en la Ciudad de Córdoba." Córdoba, Revista médica de Córdoba 47, May-June 1959, p. 352-361.

Bolivia

5042 Schenone, H. H. "Acerca del Hospital de Sucre, Bolivia." Buenos Aires, Anales del Instituto de Arte Americano e Investigaciones Estéticas 15, 1962, p. 125-127.

Brazil

5043 Alvarenga, L. de Melo "Santa Casa de Misericordia de São João del Rei." Petrópolis, Vozes (58:1), January 1964, p. 25-28.

5044 Amaral, Julio Marcondes do
"As Enfermarias de Marinha." Rio de Janeiro, Revista marítima brasileira, January-March 1944, p. 565-586.

5045 Broos, H.
"Hospital Osvaldo Cruz, São Paulo." São Paulo, Habitat (14:77), May-June 1964, p. 23-30.

5046 Campos, E. de Sousa
"Santa Casa de Misericórdia, de São Paulo." São Paulo, Revista do Instituto Histórico Geográfico de São Paulo 44, 2nd part, 1949, p. 9-50.

5047 Clark, Oscar
"A ler. Escola Hospital no Distrito Federal." Rio de Janeiro, Revista de educação pública, January-March 1943, p. 32-40.

5048 Daniel, C.
"Hospital Pedro Ernesto." Rio de Janeiro, Revista do serviço público, March/April 1947, p. 74-91.

5049 "O Govêrno Dutra e as Realizações do I.A.P.C. no Setor Médico-Hospitalar." Rio de Janeiro, Rio 129, March 1950, p. 86-91.

5050 Navarro, E. Ferraz
"Santa Casa de Santos, a Mais Antiga da América do Sul." São Paulo, IDORT (31:367-368), July-August 1962, p. 18-20.

5051 Pan American Union
"Hospital Facilities in the State of Rio Grande do Sul, Brazil." Pan American Union bulletin 71, January 1937, p. 73.

5052 Roach, G.E.
"Strangers' Hospital." Rio de Janeiro, Brazilian-American survey (9:17), April-June 1962, p. 75-77.

Chile

5053 Romero, H.
"El Proceso de Conformación de la Medicina y de la Salubridad en Chile." Santiago, Anales de la Universidad de Chile (118:119), 3rd quarter,

1960, p. 155-176.

5054 Romero, H.
"El Proceso de Conformación de la Medicina y de la Salubridad en Chile." Santiago, Anales de la Universidad de Chile (119:123), 3rd quarter, 1961, p. 104-126.

Colombia

5055 Bayona Posada, Jorge
"El Hospital de San Juan de Dios." Bogotá, Cromos, January 26, 1946, p. 4, 54.

5056 Lee Lopez, A.
"Cuarto Centenario de la Fundación del Hospital de San Juan de Dios." Bogotá, Boletín de historia y antigüedades (51:600/602), October-December 1964, p. 501-522.

5057 Muñoz, L.
"Homenaje al Médico y al Ciudadano." Medellín, Universidad de Antioquia (38:148), January-March 1962, p. 120-139.

Cuba

5058 Canalejo, Armando
"Una Hermosa Labor Humanitaria y Científica se Está Realizando en el Hospital de Guanabacoa." Havana, Policía, October 10, 1944, p. 24-25.

5059 "Nuevos Hospitales Nacionales." Madrid, Revista iberoamericana de seguridad social (9:1), January/February 1960, p. 75-76.

5060 Portell Vilá, Herminio
"Hospitales Municipales." Havana, Bohemia, (42:35), August 27, 1950, p. 56-57, 91.

Dominican Republic

5061 Mencia Lister, Rafael
"El Nuevo Hospital de Maternidad." Ciudad Trujuillo, Boletín de sanidad y asistencia pública (5:3), July/August/September 1949, p. 204-206.

5062 Pan American Union
"Hospital Services in Santo Domingo Have Been Greatly Improved by the Completion and Opening of the New Building of the International Hospital in February." Pan American Union bulletin 66, April 1932, p. 301.

5063 "Primer Hospital de América se Fundó en Santo Domingo." Ciudad Trujillo, Boletín de salud pública, January/June 1953, p. 3-9.

5064 Saladín Vélez, Manuel E.
"La Obra Hospitalaria en la Era de Trujillo." Ciudad Trujillo, Renovación (6:22), July/September 1959, p. 45-56.

5065 Utrera, Cipriano de
"El Hospital de San Andrés." Ciudad Trujillo, Clio (19:89), January/April 1951, p. 1-14.

Ecuador

5066 Martínez, A.
"Santo Domingo de los Colorados y el Hospital 'Dunham.'" Quito, Previsión social, July 1944, p. 116-122.

5067 Urbina, J.M.
"Organización Hospitalaria y Educación Médica para el Ecuador." Quito, Previsión social 22, September/December 1948, January 1949, p. 88-122.

Guatemala

5068 Guatemala. Dirección General de Estadística
"Estadísticas Hospitalarias de la República de Guatemala, 1955 y 1956." Guatemala, Boletín mensual 11, November 1957, p. 3-36.

5069 Pan American Union
"Roosevelt Hospital in Guatemala." Pan American Union bulletin 77, August 1943, p. 474-475.

5070 "Segundo Instituto Regional de Organización y Administración de Hospitales." Guatemala, Boletín sanitario de Guatemala, January/December 1944, p. 132-139.

Mexico

5071 Asenjo, A.
"México, Hernan Cortés y el Hospital de Jesús." Concepción, Atenea (140:390), October-December 1960, p. 30-47.

5072 Baz, Gustavo
"El Plan de Hospitales de una Nación, México." México, Salubridad y asistencia, November/December 1944, p. 15-22.

5073 Calvo, José
"El Hospital de Enfermedades de la Nutrición de la Ciudad de México." Boletín de la Oficina Sanitaria Panamericana (28:12), December 1949, p. 1241-1246.

5074 "Centenario del Hospital Juarez." México, Salubridad y asistencia, May/June 1947, p. 371-373.

5075 Cervera Andrade, A.
"Apuntes para la Historia del Hospital O'Horan de la Ciudad de Mérida, Yucatán." Merida, Revista de la Universidad de Yucatán (6:36), November-December 1964, p. 11-29.

5076 Chacón, M.
"Centro Hospitalario '20 de Noviembre'; la Obra Estelar del ISSTE." México, Arquitectura mexicana (17:75), September 1961, p. 120-134.

5077 "Children's Hospital, First Unit of New Medical Center." Architectural record 96, October 1944, p. 60- 67.

5078 "La Construcción de Hospitales en México." México, Higiene y seguridad, February 1946, p. 89-91.

5079 "El Hospital Infantil de México Inaugura sus Servicios." Farmacéutico, May 1944, p. 46-48.

5080 "El Hospital de Jesús." México, Salubridad y asistencia, November/December 1944, p. 45-57.

5081 "Hospitales de México." México, Intercambio, May 1945, p. 16-17, 78.

5082 "It Happened at Taxco." The rotarian (74:3), March 1949, p. 42-43.

5083 Jiménez, Antonio
"El Hospital 'Alcalde' de Guadalajara. Honra y Prez de Instituciones Benéficas." México, Todo, June 26, 1947, p. 54-57.

5084 McHenry, P.
"The New American British Cowdray Hospital." México, Mexican-American review (31:12), December 1963, p. 50-52.

5085 "La Maternidad Número 2, del Seguro Social." México, Vida, August 22, 1947, p. 38-39.

5086 Moncada, Raúl
"Ayuda a la Niñez Desvalida; los Servicios de Asistencia Medico-Social del Hospital Infantil Necesitan Urgente Ayuda para Crear Nuevas Casas de Recuperación." México, Hoy, September 21, 1946, p. 28-31.

5087 "Un Nuevo Hospital en la Provincia." México, Hoy, November 23, 1946, p. 78.

5088 "Obra Magna: La Construcción de Hospitales." México, Hoy, December 9, 1944, p. 34.

5089 Ocampo, Antonio
"Hospital para Empleados del Gobierno del Distrito Federal." México, Todo, May 16, 1946, p. 48-50.

5090 Vives, S.A.A.
"El Seguro Social de Enfermedad y la Profesión Médica." México, Seguridad social (11:14), March-April 1962, p. 43-63.

Nicaragua

5091 Lautoing, M.T.
"Algunos Datos Históricos del Hospital de León." León, Cuadernos universitarios 20, April 1962, p. 22-28.

5092 Pérez-Valle, E.
"Esbozo Histórico del Hospital de El Realejo e História Remota del Hospital de León." León, Cuadernos universitarios 21, September 1962, p. 15-19.

Panama

5093 Arango Carbone, R.E.
"Las Quejas y los Hospitales." Panamá, Lotería (7:83), October 1962, p. 39-44.

5094 Arango Carbone, R.E.
"Servicios Sociales: Capacidad Profesional Artesana." Panamá, Lotería (10:110), January 1965, p. 66-72.

Peru

5095 Harth-Terré, Emilio
"Hospitales Mayores, en Lima, en el Primer Siglo de su Fundación." Buenos Aires, Anales del Instituto de Arte Americano e Investigaciones Estéticas 16, 1963, p. 34-47.

5096 Hogg Peralta Ramos, R., & A.H. Medina
"Organización y Funcionamiento de los Hospitales Obreros del Perú." Buenos Aires, Archivo de la Secretaria de Salud Pública de la Nación (4:6), December 1948, p. 535-542.

5097 "Hospital and Clinic for Employees and Workmen Recently Inaugurated in Piurá by the National Office of Social Security." Lima, Peruvian times (11:562), September 28, 1951, p. 10-12.

5098 Levene, K.C.
"The Central Social Security Hospital for Employees." Lima, Peruvian times (11:564), October 12, 1951, p. 2.

5099 "Lima Benevolent Society--Its History and Operations." Lima, West Coast leader, June 21, 1938, p. 5-6.

5100 Marroquín, J.
"Trazos Culturales de la Población del Sur del Perú en Relación con la Salud, la Enfermedad y los Servicios Médico-Sanitarios." Lima, Perú indígena (8:18-19), January-June 1959, p. 48-90.

5101 "El Seguro Social del Empleado Inicia una Gran Obra." Lima, El arquitecto peruano (15:168/169), July/August 1951, p. 6-15.

5102 "A Social Security Hospital Project in Peru." London, The South American journal (149:13), March 31, 1951, p. 150.

Uruguay

5103 Jiménez, Asdrubal
"El Hospital de Clínicas Podría Ser Fundamental para la Medicina Uruguaya." Montevideo, Mundo uruguayo, October 16, 1947, p. 3-5.

5104 "Realidad Hospitalaria de Nuestro País." Montevideo, CEDA, November 1953, p. 3-15.

Venezuela

5105 Bruni Celli, B.
"El Hospital San Juan de el Tocuyo." Caracas, Boletín de la Academia Nacional de la Historia (44:176), October-December 1961, p. 574-587.

5106 "Hospitales, Baluarte de la Salud." Caracas, El farol, April 1948, p. 2-5.

5107 "Instituciones Sanitario-Asistenciales." Caracas, El mes financiero y económico 9, February 1951, p. 25-56.

Mental Hygiene

Books

General

5108 California. Dept. of Mental Hygiene. Bureau of Planning
Bibliographic, indexing, abstracting, and current activity sources: a guide for their uses in mental health program planning, by Marian P. Anderson,

planning staff consultant. Sacramento, 1964, 17p.

5109 Conference on Community Mental Health. 5th, Washington University, St. Louis, 1963. Mobility and mental health; proceedings . . . Ed. by Mildred B. Kantor . . . Springfield, Thomas, 1965, 247p.

5110 David, Henry P., ed. International trends in mental health. New York, McGraw-Hill, 1966, 366p.

5111 International Study Group on Mental Health Report of an international and interprofessional study group . . . Ed. by Kenneth Soddy & Robert H. Ahrenfeldt with the assistance of Mary C. Kidson. Philadelphia, Lippincott, 1965-

5112 Mangin, William P. Mental health and migration to cities. (In Annals of the New York Academy of Science, vol. 84, article 17. New York, 1960, p. 911-917).

5113 Riessman, Frank, et al, eds. Mental health of the poor; new treatment approaches for low income people. New York, Free Press, 1964, 663p.

5114 Taylor, Lord, & S. Chave Mental health and environment. London, Longmans, 1964, 228p.

5115 World Federation for Mental Health Mental health aspects of urbanization; report of a panel discussion conducted in the Economic and Social Council Chamber, United Nations, New York, 11 March 1957. London, 1957, 45p.

Latin America

5116 Adis-Castro, Gonzalo, & F.B. Waisanen Attitudes toward mental illness: some socio-economic and modernication oorrelatives. San José, Programa Interamericano de Informacion Popular, 1965, 56p.

Argentina

5117 Fénix, Victoria
Veintiún días en el Asilo San Miguel. Buenos Aires, 1955, 92p.

5118 Ingenieros, J.
La locura en la Argentina. Buenos Aires, Eds. Meridión, 1954, 158p.

Chile

5119 Ahumada Pacheco, Hermes
Plan nacional de defensa de la salud mental. Santiago, Ed. Jurídica de Chile, 1954, 238p.

Costa Rica

5120 Adis-Castro, Gonzalo, & F.B. Waisanen
El contexto socioeconomico de las actitudes hacia el enfermo mental. San José, Centro de Investigaciones Psicológicas, Universidad de Costa Rica, & Programa Interamericano de Información Popular, 1965, 25p.

5121 Adis-Castro, Gonzalo, & F.B. Waisanen
Modernidad y tolerancia: el caso de las actitudes hacia la enfermedad mental. San José, Centro de Investigaciones Psicológicas, Universidad de Costa Rica & Programa Interamericano de Información Popular, 1965, 56p.

El Salvador

5122 Salinas, J.I.
5 años entre los locos. San Salvador, 1963, 72p.

Mexico

5123 Torres Cornejo, Ernestina
Importancia del trabajo social en el Manicomio General. México, 1951, 53p.

Peru

5124 Caravedo, Baltasar, et al
Estudios de psiquiatría social en el Peru. Lima, Eds. del Sol, 1963, 400p.

Periodical Articles

General

5125 Barton, Walter F.
"The Role of the State Mental Hospital in the Community Mental Health Program." State government 37, Autumn 1964, p. 231-234.

5126 French, J.R.P.
"Social Environment and Mental Health." Journal of social issues 19, October 1963, p. 39-56.

5127 Lagmanovich, D.J.
"Mental Health." Américas 15, March 1963, p. 1-5.

5128 Lieberman, E.J., & Leonard J. Duhl
"Physical and Mental Health in the City." Annals of the American Academy of Political & Social Science 352, March 1964, 13-24.

5129 Meier, R.L.
"Some Thoughts on Conflict and Violence in the Urban Setting." American behavioral scientist (10:1), September 1966, p. 11-12.

Latin America

5130 Mitscherlich, A.
"Gran Ciudad y Neurosis." Bogotá, Arco (9:50), June 1964, p. 199-227.

5131 Reca, T.
"La Relación Familia-Escuela en América Latina y sus Implicaciones para la Salud Mental." México, Criminalia (18:4), April 1952, p. 176-191.

Brazil

5132 Dantas, P. da Silva
"Perspectiva da Assistencia Psiquiátrica no Brasil." São Paulo, Revista brasiliense 44, November-December 1962, p. 82-91.

5133 Roxo, H.
"Problemas de Higiene Mental." Rio de Janeiro, Arquivos brasileiros de higiene mental, November

1944, p. 5-8.

5134 Santana, E.T.
"Higiene Mental para o Negro Brasileiro." São Paulo, Anhembi (19:56), July 1955, p. 289-301.

Chile

5135 Sirvent, I.B.
"Actitud Psico-Biológico del Escolar Chileno y su Influencia en la Higiene Mental." Santiago, Servicio social, January-April 1944, p. 4-47.

Haiti

5136 Mars, L.
"L'Hygiene Mentale et la Communauté Haïtienne." Port-au-Prince, Projection 1, March 1951, p. 31-40.

Uruguay

5137 Lizano Vargas, E.
"Hygiene Mental: Algunos de sus Aspectos en el Uruguay." Montevideo, Boletín del Instituto Internacional Americano de Protección a la Infancia (27:106), September 1953, p. 229-240.

Venezuela

5138 Avila Girón, R.
"Consideraciones Sobre la Asistencia Psiquiátrica en Venezuela." Maracaibo, Revista de la Universidad de Zulia (3:9), January-March 1960, p. 47-51.

West Indies and the Caribbean

5139 Schaffner, B.
"Progress in Mental Health in the Caribbean." Trinidad, The Caribbean (13:2), February 1959, p. 26-29, 44.

Nutrition

Books

General

5140 Bavly, S.
Levels of nutrition in Israel, 1963-64: urban wage and salary earners. Jerusalem, Central Bureau of Statistics, 1966, 97p.

5141 Bourne, Geoffrey H., ed.
World review of nutrition and dietetics. 5v. New York, Hafner, 1960-1964.

5142 Castro, Josué de
Geografía del hambre. Tr. by Inés Carrasco. Santiago, Ed. Universitaria, 1961, 240p.

5143 Centennial Nutrition Conference
Century of nutrition progress. Ed. by Lowell Brandner, et al. Kansas City, Midwest Feed Manufacturers' Association, 1961, 283p.

5144 Institute of Social and Historical Medicine
Human nutrition: historic and scientific; monograph no. 3, ed. by Iago Galdston. New York, International Universities Press, 1960, 321p.

5145 Mitchell, H.H., & Marjorie Edman
Nutrition and climatic stress, with particular reference to man. Springfield, Thomas, 1951, 234p.

5146 Moomaw, I.W.
To hunger no more: a positive reply to human need. New York, Friendship Press, 1963, 163p.

5147 Nicholls, Lucius
Tropical nutrition and dietetics. 4th ed., rev. by H.M. Sinclair & D.B. Jelliffe. Baltimore, Williams & Wilkins, 1961, 457p.

5148 World food program studies. # 1- , Rome, Food & Agriculture Organization of the United Nations, 1965-

Latin America

5149 Castro, Josué de
Le problème de l'alimentation en Amérique du Sud. Paris, Dunod, 1950, 39p.

5150 Conference on Nutrition Problems in Latin America. 3d. Caracas, 1953
Informe. Washington, Pan American Sanitary Bureau, 1954, 54p.

5151 Latin American Regional Meeting of the Food and Agriculture Organization of the United Nations, 2nd Montevideo, 1950
Agriculture in Latin America: current development and prospects, two reports. Washington, Food and Agriculture Organization of the United Nations, 1951, 169p.

5152 Symposium on Infantile Nutrition in South America, Cali, Colombia and La Paz, Bolivia, 1958
Simposios sobre nutrición infantil en América del Sur, Cali, Colombia, febrero 17-21, La Paz, Bolivia, febrero 27-marzo 3, 1958. Montevideo, 1958, 181p.

Argentina

5153 Pierangeli, Enrique
El problema de la alimentación popular. Buenos Aires, Instituto Nacional de la Nutrición, 1952, 66p.

Brazil

5154 Amaral, Francisco Pompeo do
O problema da alimentação; aspectos médico-higiênico-sociais. 2v. Rio de Janeiro, Olympio, 1963.

5155 Arquivos brasileiros de nutrição. v. 1. Rio de Janeiro, 1952-

5156 Gonçalves, Antonio C., et al
Problemas do abastecimento alimentar no Recife. Recife, Ministerio da Educação e Cultura, 1962, 442p.

5157 Mello, Antonio da Silva
Alimentação humana e realidade brasileira. São Paulo, Olympio, 1950, 86p.

5158 Paula, Alvino de
Na alimentação o futuro do Brasil. Rio de Janeiro, Empr. Gráfica "O Cruzeiro," 1950, 172p.

5159 Scott, John
Hunger: must we starve? New York, Time, Inc., 1966, p. 55-70.

Chile

5160 Chile. Dirección General de Bibliotecas, Archivos y Museos
Chile: su futura alimentación . . . Santiago, Biblioteca Nacional, 1963, 233p.

5161 Santa María, Julio V.
La alimentación como problema de salubridad. Santiago, Impr. Universitaria, 1946, 190p.

Colombia

5162 Bejarano, Jorge
Alimentación y nutrición en Colombia. 3d ed. Bogotá, Ed. Iqueima, 1950, 239p.

5163 Inter-Departmental Committee on Nutrition for National Defense
Nutrition survey: Colombia. Washington, U.S. Dept. of Defense, 1961, 263p.

5164 Palacio del Valle, Guillermo
Por una mejor alimentación para el pueblo colombiano. Bogotá, Ed. Minagricultura, 1953, 45p.

Cuba

5165 Mears, Leon G.
Agriculture and food situation in Cuba. Washington, Economic Research Service, U.S. Dept. of Agriculture, 1962, 22p.

5166 Neblett, Myrtle H.
Tablas de composición de los alimentos de mayor consumo en Cuba, expresadas en medidas comunes. Havana, 1946, 54p.

Ecuador

5167 Inter-Departmental Committee on Nutrition for National Defense
Nutrition survey: Ecuador. Washington, U.S. Dept. of Defense, 1960, 230p.

Guatemala

5168 Viteri Echeverría, Fernando E.
La deficiencia de vitamina A en Guatemala como problema de salud pública. Guatemala, 1955, 83p.

Mexico

5169 Gómez Aldecoa, Enriqueta
El problema de la subalimentación de la clase campesina en México y sus relaciones con el derecho agrario. México, 1957, 84p.

5170 Lira Porragas, Gonzalo
El abastecimiento nacional de productos agrícolas alimenticios. México, 1951, 110p.

Paraguay

5171 Ciancio, Pedro N.
La soja y el problema alimentario del Paraguay. Asunción, Ed. "El Gráfico," 1951, 502p.

Peru

5172 Collazos Chiriboga, Carlos, et al
La alimentación y el estado de nutrición en el Perú. Lima, Ministerio de Salud Pública y Asistencia Social, Servicio Interamericano Cooperativo de Salud Pública, Instituto de Nutrición, 1960, 343p.

5173 Malpica, C.
Crónica del hambre en el Perú. Lima, Francisco Moncloa, 1966, 285p.

5174 Perú. Departamento de Nutrición
La familia peruana; suma y resta de su nutrición. Lima, Depto. de Nutrición de Ministerio de Salud Pública y Asistencia Social, 1954, 151p.

5175 Perú. Ministerio de Salud Pública
La alimentación y el estado de nutrición en el Perú. Lima, Anales de la Facultad de Medicina, 1960, 344p.

Uruguay

5176 Inter-American Council of Commerce & Production
Encuesta continental sobre el consumo de productos de alimentación y vestido sobre la vivienda popular; respuesta referente a la República Oriental del Uruguay. Redactor: Roberto Graña. 2d ed. Montevideo, 1945, 221p.

Venezuela

5177 Archivos venezolanos de nutrición. v. 1- , Caracas, 1950-

5178 Guevara, Arturo
El poliedro de la nutrición, aspectos económico y social del problema de la alimentación en Venezuela. Caracas, Ed. Grafolit, 1946, 180p.

5179 Vélez Boza, Fermín
Bibliografía venezolana de alimentación y nutrición. Caracas, Ministerio de Sanidad y Asistencia Social, Instituto Nacional de Nutrición, 1961, 453p.

West Indies and the Caribbean

5180 Floch, H.
Etude du problème de l'alimentation en Guyane Française. Cayenne, Archives de l'Institut Pasteur de Guyane no. 298, October 1953, 7p.

5181 Inter-Departmental Committee on Nutrition for National Defense
Nutrition survey August-September 1961: the West Indies: Trinidad and Tobago, St. Lucia, St. Christopher, Nevis and Anguilla. Washington, U.S. Dept. of Defense, 1962, 187p.

5182 Steenmeijer, F.
Food and nutrition of the Arubans. Utrecht, 1957, 139p.

Periodical Articles

General

5183 "The Hungry World." Montreal, Royal Bank of Canada monthly letter 45, June 1964, p. 1-4.

5184 King, C. G.
"International Nutrition Programs." Science 147, January 1, 1965, p. 25-29.

5185 Maddox, G.
"Better Nutrition Through Research and Education." Today's health 43, October 1965, p. 42-45.

5186 Ros-Zanet, J. G.
"La Desnutrición Como Producto del Desequilibrio Económico-Social de la Familia." Panamá, Lotería (9:107), October 1964, p. 72-77.

Latin America

5187 Avdalov de Rossemblatt, F.
"Seminario Sobre Educación en Nutrición en Sud América, Rio de Janeiro, 1960." Montevideo, Boletín del Instituto Interamericano del Niño (34:2), June 1960, p. 276-281.

5188 Ayensa, A.
"El Deterioro de las Condiciones Alimenticias y Sanitarias en América Latina." México, Comercio exterior (12:1), January 1962, p. 47-49.

5189 Brister, William C.
"Increasing the Food Supply of the Western Hemisphere." Pan American Union bulletin 79, July 1945, p. 383-390.

5190 Brister, William C.
"Latin America's Food--'Servicios' Aid Advance." Foreign commerce weekly, May 25, 1946, p. 10-13, 19.

5191 Burton, B.
"What's in a Meal?" Americas 15, February 1963, p. 1-6.

5192 Castro, Josué de
"El Combate Contra el Hambre en América Latina." México, Revista de la Universidad de México (17:2), October 1962, p. 22-26.

5193 Enochs, E.S.
"A Mass Attack on a Basic Problem: a Child Nutrition Project in Latin America." Annals of the American Academy of Political & Social Science 329, May 1960, p. 115-122.

5194 Heysen, Luis E.
"Necesidades y Perspectivas Alimentarias en América Latina." México, Humanismo (5:38), July/August 1956, p. 57-63.

5195 MacDonagh, Emiliano J.
"Un Ataque 'Biológico' a la América Latina." Buenos Aires, Dinámica social (3:29), January 1953, p. 7-8.

5196 Schultz, G.M.
"More Children, More Hunger." Today's health 43, October 1965, p. 18-23.

5197 Scrimshaw, N.S.
"Estudios Sobre los Problemas de la Nutrición en la América Latina." Boletín de la Oficina Sanitaria Panamericana 28, 1949, p. 1201-1214.

5198 Seminarios de Nutrición, La Paz, Santa Fé, Mendoza, 1962.
"Crónica; Reglamento; Recomendaciones." Montevideo, Boletín del Instituto Interamericano del Niño (36:140), March 1962, p. 7-60.

Argentina

5199 Escudero, Adolfo
"La Racionalización de la Distribución de Alimentos como Directiva de la Política Alimentaria del Futuro." Buenos Aires, Revista de economia argentina, March 1945, p. 87-95.

5200 Rivadeneira, Milton
"El Instituto de Nutrición de Buenos Aires." Quito, Boletín del Departamento Médico del Seguro Social, April 1945, p. 49-56.

Bolivia

5201 Tichauer, R.
"The Aymara Children of Bolivia." Journal of

pediatrics 62, 1963, p. 399-412.

Brazil

5202 "Abastecimento: Sugestões para um Plano de Contenção de Preços de Produtos Básicos da Alimentação." Rio de Janeiro, *Desenvolvimento e conjuntura* (6:7), July 1962, p. 86-90.

5203 Borges, T. Pompeu Accioly
"Alimentação e Desenvolvimento Econômico." Rio de Janeiro, *Estudos sociais* (5:17), June 1963, p. 61-68.

5204 Borges, T. Pompeu Accioly
"Aspectos Demográficos, Econômico-Sociais e Estruturais do Problema Alimentar no Brasil e em Outras Areas Subdesenvolvidas." Rio de Janeiro, *Arquivos brasileiros de nutrição 16*, 1960, p. 91-109.

5205 Borges, T. Pompeu Accioly
"Desnutrição e Subdesenvolvimento." São Paulo, *Revista brasiliense 48*, July-August 1963, p. 38-44.

5206 Brum, H. de Almeida
"O Abastecimento no Quadro da Conjuntura Nacional." Rio de Janeiro, *Desenvolvimento e conjuntura* (7:12), December 1963, p. 62-68.

5207 Castro, Josué de
"La Alimentación en el Area Amazónica." México, *América indígena* (9:2), April 1949, p. 113-142.

5208 Castro, Josué de
"Política Alimentar no Brasil de Após-Guerra." Rio de Janeiro, *Boletim do Ministério do Trabalho, Industria e Comercio*, December 1945, p. 167-185.

5209 Castro, Josué de, et al
"Relatório do Brasil a 3a. Conferencia Latino-Americana de Nutrição, 1953." Rio de Janeiro, *Arquivos brasileiros da nutrição 10*, 1954, p. 9-43.

5210 Costa, Dantes
"Deficiencias Nutritivas de Crianças em Idade Escolar." Rio de Janeiro, *Boletim do Ministerio do*

Trabalho, Indústria e Comércio, November 1954, p. 185-199.

5211 Costa, Dantes
"La Política Nacional de la Alimentación en el Brasil." Montevideo, Boletín del Instituto Internacional Americano de Protección a la Infancia (22:4), December 1948, p. 478-483.

5212 Cunha, T. Ferreira da
"Problema do Abastecimento de Gêneros Alimenticios." Rio de Janeiro, Desenvolvimento e conjuntura (6:10), October 1962, p. 65-93.

5213 Duncan, Julian S.
"Beef and Milk for Urban Brazil." Inter-American economic affairs (9:1), Summer 1955, p. 3-16.

5214 Duque, Guimarães
"A Política de Abundância de Alimentos." Rio de Janeiro, Boletím do Ministerio do Trabalho, Industria e Comércio, August 1946, p. 169-177.

5215 Fraga, Constantino Carneiro
"O Plano de Emergencia e a Produção de Gêneros Alimenticios."' São Paulo, Colheitas e mercados, January/February 1948, p. 49-50.

5216 Gandra, Y.R.
"Inquérito Sôbre o Estado de Nutrição de um Grupo da População da Cidade de São Paulo." São Paulo, Arquivos da Faculdade de Higiene de São Paulo 8, 1954, p. 193-216.

5217 Guimarães, L. Ribeiro, & E. Pechnik
"Contribuição ao Estudo dos Alimentos da Região Amazônica." Rio de Janeiro, Arquivos brasileiros da nutrição 12, 1956, p. 7-40.

5218 Joviano, R.
"Problemas de Abastecimento do Rio de Janeiro em Leite e Carne." Rio de Janeiro, Revista brasileira de geografia (22:3), July/September 1960, p. 433-464.

5219 Lopes, N.
"Inquérito Alimentar em Maceió." Rio de Janeiro, Arquivos brasileiros da nutrição 18, 1962, p. 131-154.

5220 Lowenstein, F.W.
"Panorama Alimentar no Brasil." Rio de Janeiro, Arquivos brasileiros de nutrição 15, 1959, p. 25-41.

5221 Lowenstein, F.W.
"Some Observations on the Nutritional Status of Medical Students in the Brasilian Amazon." American journal of clinical nutrition 8, 1960, p. 870-874.

5222 Miranda, Nicanor
"A Alimentação nos Parques Infantis de São Paulo." Rio de Janeiro, Revista brasileira de estudos pedagógicos, October 1945, p. 71-86.

5223 Pokrovsky, Ivan
"Possibilidades de Expansão do Mercado do Gêneros Alimenticios da Região Econômica Convergente para a Praça de São Paulo. I-." São Paulo, IDORT, June 1948, p. 18-20.

5224 Siqueira, R. de
"Notas para um 'Planning' Alimentar Brasileiro." Rio de Janeiro, Arquivos brasileiros da nutrição 8, 1951, p. 31-62.

Central America

5225 Béhar, M.
"Death and Disease in Infants and Toddlers of Preindustrial Countries." American journal of public health 54, 1964, p. 1100-1105.

5226 Harris, Robert S.
"Progresos de la Nutrición en Centro América." Boletín de la Oficina Sanitaria Panamericana (27:10), October 1948, p. 902-911.

5227 León Méndez, R. de
"Evaluación del Estado Nutricional de la Población

de Centro América y Panamá." México, Salud pública 7, 1965, p. 229-234.

5228 Manchester, H.C.
"New Food for Hungry Children." Reader's digest 83, September 1963, p. 137-141.

5229 Reh, E., et al
"Estudio de Dieta en Centro América." Guatemala, Revista del Colegio Médico (2:4), 1951, p. 2-22.

Chile

5230 Arteaga, A., et al
"Encuesta Sobre Tendencia de Consumo en 100 Familias de Clase Media Urbana." Santiago, Nutrición, bromatología, toxicología 3, 1964, p. 78-85.

5231 Barja, I., & Julio V. Santa María
"Dietas en Estudiantes Universitarios Chilenos." Santiago, Nutrición, bromatología, toxicología 2, 1963, p. 180-184.

5232 Cornejo, R.R.
"Consumo Nacional de Carne por Estratos Sociales." Santiago, Nutrición, bromatología, toxicología 2, 1963, p. 126-133.

5233 Dragoni, Carlo
"Report on Popular Nutrition in Chile." Geneva, Bulletin of the Health Organisation, June 1937, p. 299-370.

5234 Escobar M., Humberto
"Campaña de Producción de Alimentos." Santiago, Acción social, January/February 1948, p. 32-39.

5235 Morales Beltrami, Guillermo
"Alimentación Infantil en Chile." Montevideo, Boletín del Instituto Internacional Americano de Protección a la Infancia, July 1943, p. 27-36.

5236 Santa María, Julio V.
"Nueva Organización de las Actividades Alimentarias en Chile." Caracas, Archivos venezolanos de nutrición (5:2), December 1954, p. 327-342.

5237 Schatan W., Jacobo
"El Abastecimiento de Productos Alimenticios en Santiago." Santiago, Revista economía (12:39), July 1952, p. 45-68; (12:40), October 1952, p. 46-67.

5238 Viveros S., R.
"Abastecimiento Alimenticio del Gran Santiago y su Relación con la Comunidad." Santiago, Mapocho (2:1), 1964, p. 136-156.

5239 Weinstein Rodoy, F.
"Contribución del Mar Chileno a Nuestra Alimentación." Santiago, Revista chilena de educación física (31:124), April 1965, p. 51-55.

Colombia

5240 Bejarano, Jorge
"La Alimentación en Colombia." Medellín, Universidad de Antioquia 101, January/February 1951, p. 7-11.

5241 Comas Calvet, Pedro
"La Producción y el Consumo de Alimentos en Colombia." Pan American Union bulletin 79, October 1945, p. 582-589.

5242 "Necesidades Alimenticias del Pueblo Colombiano." Bogotá, Anales de economía y estadística (2:21/22), November 1946, p. 1-24.

5243 Nel Gómez, Pedro
"Algunas Ideas Sobre el Abastecimiento de Nuestras Ciudades." Bogotá, Universidad Nacional de Colombia, October 1944, p. 231-238.

5244 Romero-Rojas, B.
"El Consumo de Bebidas Alcohólicas en Colombia." Bogotá, Economía y estadística 82, 1956, p. 49-76.

5245 Socarrás, José F.
"Alimentación de la Clase Media en Bogotá. Análisis Fisiológicos." Bogotá, Anales de economía y estadística, March 5, 1943, p. 21-28.

5246 Socarrás, José F.
"Alimentación de la Clase Obrera en Bogotá." Bogotá, Anales de economía y estadística, September 1939, p. 1-77.

5247 Socarrás, José F.
"Alimentación de la Clase Obrera en Medellín--Análisis Fisiológico." Bogotá, Anales de economía y estadística, November 5, 1942, p. 16-28.

Cuba

5248 Jolliffe, N., et al
"Nutrition Status Survey of the Sixth Grade School Population of Cuba." Journal of nutrition 64, 1958, p. 355-398.

5249 Sentmanat, Rafael M.
"El Problema de la Alimentación en Cuba." Havana, Revista bimestre cubana, July-August 1944, p. 16-26.

Dominican Republic

5250 Cuevas Alvarez, Luis E.
"La Alimentación del Pueblo Dominicano." Ciudad Trujillo, Anales de la Universidad de Santo Domingo (26:93-96), January-December 1960, p. 103-149.

5251 Cuevas Alvarez, Luis E.
"La Alimentación del Pueblo Dominicano. Nociones de Nutrología." Ciudad Trujillo, Anales de la Universidad de Santo Domingo (20:73/76), January/December 1955, p. 99-148; (23:87/88), July/December 1958, p. 363-386.

Ecuador

5252 Dávila, Carlos
"Los Alimentos que se Consumen en el Ecuador." Quito, Boletín de informaciones científicas nacionales (6:59), January/February 1954, p. 498-502.

5253 Portilla, J.M.
"Síndrome Pluricarencial Infantil." Caracas, Archivos venezolanos de nutrición 5, 1954, p. 463-467.

5254 Thomason, M. J., et al
"Dietary Studies in Ecuador." American journal of clinical nutrition 5, 1957, p. 295-304.

El Salvador

5255 Cabezas, A.
"Introducción a los Problemas Nutricionales de El Salvador." San Salvador, Sanidad en El Salvador 2, 1951, p. 298-303.

5256 Sogandares, L., et al
"Estudios Dietéticos de Grupos Urbanos y Rurales de la República de El Salvador." Boletín de la Oficina Sanitaria Panamericana, 1953, suplemento 1, p. 27-37.

Guatemala

5257 Beaton, G. H., et al
"Alterations in Serum Proteins During Pregnancy and Lactation in Urban and Rural Populations in Guatemala." American journal of clinical nutrition 14, 1964, p. 269-279.

5258 Flores, M., et al
"Estudio de Hábitos Dietéticos en Poblaciones de Guatemala." Guatemala, Revista del Colegio Médico de Guatemala 8, 1957, p. 84-90.

5259 Goubaud Carrera, A.
"Estudio de la Alimentación en Guatemala." Guatemala, Boletín del Instituto Indigenista Nacional, March/June 1946, p. 31-45.

5260 Mendez Dominguez, A.
"Organización Social y Prevalencia de la Malnutrición Proteica en una Comunidad de Guatemala." Guatemala, Guatemala indígena (2:2), April-June 1962, p. 5-16.

5261 "Mezclas Vegetales como Fuentes de Proteína en la Alimentación Humana. Desarrollo de la Incaparina." Guatemala, Revista del colegio médico 12, 1961, p. 1-29.

5262 Moen, M. L.
"Consumo de Alimentos de 13 Familias de los Em-

pleados de una Fábrica de Textiles en Quezaltenango, Guatemala, C.A." Boletín de la Oficina Sanitaria Panamericana, 1953, suplemento no. 1, p. 37-49.

5263 Solien de Gonzalez, Nancy L.
"Beliefs and Practices Concerning Medicine and Nutrition Among Lower-Class Urban Guatemalans." American journal of public health 54, 1964, p. 1726-1734.

Guyana

5264 Nicholson, C.C.
"Assessment of the Nutritional Status of Elementary School Children of British Guiana by Periodic Sampling Surveys and Evaluation of the Beneficial Effects of Supplementary Feeding." Kingston, West Indian medical journal 5, 1956, p. 240-246.

Haiti

5265 Beghin, I.
"Le Problème de l'Alimentation et de la Nutrition en Haiti." Port-au-Prince, Conjonction 99, August 1965, p. 40-57.

5266 Comhaire-Sylvain, Suzanna, & J. Comhaire-Sylvain
"La Alimentación en la Región de Kenscoff, Haiti." México, América indígene (12:3), July 1952, p. 177-203.

5267 Grant, F.W., & D. Groom
"A Dietary Study in Haiti." Journal of the American Dietetic Association 34, 1958, p. 708-716.

5268 Jelliffe, D.B., & E.F.P. Jelliffe
"The Prevalence of Protein-Calorie Malnutrition in Haitian Pre-School Children." Kingston, West Indian medical journal 9, 1960, p. 260-272.

5269 Pan American Union
"Extension of Food Supply Agreement with Haiti." Pan American Union bulletin 81, March 1947, p. 168-169.

5270 Sebrell, W.H., et al
"Appraisal of Nutrition in Haiti." American journal

of clinical nutrition 7, 1959, p. 538-584.

Jamaica

5271 Fox, H.
"The Composition of Food Stuffs Commonly Used in Jamaica." Kingston, West Indian medical journal 7, 1958, p. 84-92.

5272 Mackay, I. F. S., et al
"Dietary Survey of Jamaican Children." Journal of the American Dietetic Association 34, 1958, p. 603-610.

Mexico

5273 Barriga, A.
"El Problema de la Leche en México." Boletin de la Oficina Sanitaria Panamericana 33, 1952, p. 405-409.

5274 Brown, E. L.
"Mexico's Family Dining Room." Survey 79, December 1943, p. 336-337.

5275 Díaz Barriga, Jesús
"La Nutrición en México." México, Reinvindicación 17, August 1950, p. 8, 23.

5276 Kaplan, S.
"Food for a City." México, Mexican life (38:10), October 1962, p. 17-18, 64-65.

5277 Ochoa Campos, Moisés
"Un Problema Nacional: la Alimentación del Pueblo." México, Hoy, October 26, 1946, p. 48-50.

5278 Ornelas, Manuel
"Las Levaduras Alimenticias: una Solución al Problema de la Escasez de Carne en México." Jalapa, Universidad veracruzana (3:2), April/June 1954, p. 8-30.

5279 Prado Vértiz, Antonio
"El Problema Económico de la Alimentación Infantil en México." México, El trimestre economía (18:4), October/December 1951, p. 601-616.

5280 Ramos Espinosa, A.
"Dietética Popular: el Maíz en la Alimentación Mexicana." México, Puericultura (6:1), January/February 1955, p. 22-26.

5281 Sepúlveda, B., et al
"Malnutrition and Liver Disease in Mexico." Gastroenterology 33, 1957, p. 249-257.

5282 Suarez del Real, E.
"El Problema Alimenticio en México; Datos Bioquímicos y Planteamientos Socio-Políticos." México, Revista mexicana de sociología (24:2), May-August 1962, p. 367-381.

5283 Venezuela. Instituto Nacional de Nutrición
"La Educación Alimentaria en México." Caracas, Archivos venezolanos de nutrición (4:2), December 1953, p. 291-297.

5284 Wylie, Kathryn H.
"Food Consumption in Mexico." Foreign agriculture (19:8), August 1955, p. 162-164.

5285 Zubirán, S., & A. Chavez
"Algunos Datos Sobre la Situación Nutricional en México." Boletín de la Oficina Sanitaria Panamericana 54, 1963, p. 101-113.

Panama

5286 Noriega, T.A.
"Consumos Básicos en la Alimentación Panameña." Panamá, Carta del I.F.E. 15, January 1960, p. 30-34.

5287 Scrimshaw, N.S., et al
"Nutritional Problems of Children in Central America and Panama." Pediatrics 16, 1955, p. 378-397.

5288 Sogandares, L., et al
"Estudios Diéteticos en Panamá, 2: Barrio El Chorrillo, Ciudad de Panamá." Boletín de la Oficina Sanitaria Panamericana, suplemento no. 2, 1955, p. 47-53.

Peru

5289 Collazos Chiriboga, Carlos, et al
"La Composición de los Alimentos Peruanos." Caracas, Archivos venezolanos de nutrición 8, 1957, p. 126-166.

5290 Ferrero, Rómulo A.
"Bases Económicos para una Política de Alimentación en el Perú." Lima, Vida agraria, March 1946, p. 201-208.

5291 Guzmán Barrón, A.
"Deficiencia a las Vitaminas B en el Perú." Caracas, Archivos venezolanos de nutrición 9, 1958, p. 81-103.

5292 Guzmán Barrón, A.
"Estudios de Nutrución en el Perú." Caracas, Archivos venezolanos de nutrición (5:2), December 1954, p. 263-284.

5293 Klinge, Gerardo
"Las Condiciones del Medio Peruano y el Régimen Alimenticio Nacional." Lima, Agronomía, April/May 1946, p. 21-32.

5294 "El Problema de la Alimentación Nacional." Lima, Vida agraria, May 1945, p. 403-418.

5295 Servicio Cooperativo Interamericano de Producción de Alimentos, Perú
"Estudios y Publicaciones del SCIPA." Lima, Boletín del Proyecto Bibliográfico 3, January/March 1959, p. 59-86.

5296 Vera Bravo, Max
"El Problema Nacional de la Papa." Lima, Agronomía (17:72), October/December 1952, p. 133-141.

Uruguay

5297 Chmielnicki de Herszhorn, C.
"Síndromo Policarencial Infantil (Kwashiorkor) en Dos Niñas de Montevideo." Montevideo, Archivos de Pediatría del Uruguay 32, 1961, p. 209-219.

5298 Collazo, Juan A.
"El Problema Alimenticio en el Uruguay." Montevideo, Boletin del Instituto Internacional Americano de Protección a la Infancia, July 1943, p. 125-135.

5299 "Conferencia de Nutrición." Montevideo, Boletín del Instituto Internacional Americano de Protección a la Infancia, September 1948, p. 337-356.

5300 Peluffo, E., et al
"La Desnutrición Infantil. Patología y Aspectos Clínicos." Montevideo, Archivos de pediatría del Uruguay 27, 1956, p. 767-777.

5301 Ramón Guerra, A. U., et al
"La Desnutrición en Primera Infancia. Su Proyección en la Población Hospitalaria." Montevideo, Archivos de Pediatría del Uruguay 34, 1963, p. 525-540.

5302 Saldún de Rodríguez, M. L.
"Simposios Sobre Nutrición del Niño y de la Familia." Montevideo, Boletín del Instituto Interamericano del Niño (33:1), March 1959, p. 75-85.

5303 Yanuzzi de Lassabe, E. S.
"Alimentación de Escolares." Montevideo, Archivos de pediatría del Uruguay 30, 1959, p. 425-438.

Venezuela

5304 Bengoa, J. M., et al
"Hojas de Balance de Alimentos en Venezuela en 1951." Caracas, Archivos venezolanos de nutrición 5, 1954, p. 95-111.

5305 "Estimación de las Necesidades Nutritivas de la Nación." Caracas, Producción 37, 1947, p. 51-55.

5306 Gonzalez, H.
"The Venezuelan Accomplishment. I. Food Supply." Inter-American economic affairs (XI:3), 1957, p. 83-91.

5307 Gonzalez S., M.
"Una Encuesta Alimentaria en 103 Familias de la

Parroquia de El Valle, Distrito Federal. Complemento de una Investigación Médico-Nutricional." Caracas, Archivos venezolanos de nutricion 7, 1956, p. 167-209.

5308 González S., M.
"Hojas de Balance de Alimentos--Venezuela: 1952-1957." Caracas, Archivos venezolanos de nutrición 10, 1960, p. 39-64.

5309 Hickey, John
"The Venezuelan Food Supply." Inter-American economic affairs (7:4), Spring 1954, p. 23-35.

5310 Jaffe, Werner
"Algunas Proposiciones para el Mejoramiento de la Alimentación en Venezuela." Caracas, Revista de sanidad y asistencia social, February 1946, p. 1-14.

5311 Jaffé, Ilse
"Alimentación Popular en Venezuela a Través de un Estudio de 71 Familias del Barrio 'Lidice' en Caracas." Caracas, Servicio social, June 1946, p. 7-40.

5312 Liendo Coll, P., et al
"Las Necesidades Venezolanas en Nutrientes y en el Consumo Actual." Caracas, Archivos venezolanos de nutrición 6, 1955, p. 127-137.

5313 Rodríguez Cabrera, J.H.
"Educación Alimentaria en Venezuela." Caracas, Archivos venezolanos de nutrición 5, 1954, p. 179-195.

5314 Rodríguez Cabrera, J.H.
"La Protección Alimentaria del Trabajador en Venezuela." Lima, Informaciones sociales (10:1), January/March 1955, p. 39-51.

5315 Romero Briceño, José A.
"Vida y Alimentación en Venezuela." Caracas, Revista Shell (2:6), March 1953, p. 20-25.

5316 Vélez Boza, Fermín
"La Alimentación en Colectividades, sus Características, Importancia, Estudio y Orientación." Caracas, Archivos venezolanos de nutrición 9, 1959, p. 171-183.

5317 Vélez Boza, Fermín
"Estudio de la Alimentación en un Grupo de Colectividades de Caracas Durante los Años de 1953-54." Caracas, Archivos venezolanos de nutricion 6, 1955, p. 35-47.

5318 Vêlez Boza, Fermín, & A.B. Braunstein
"Encuestas de Hábitos Alimenticios en un Grupo de Escolares." Caracas, Archivos venezolanos de nutrición 3, 1952, p. 419-431.

5319 Vélez Boza, Fermín, & M. González
"Los Alimentos Básicos Utilizados en Algunas Poblaciones de Venezuela." Caracas, Archivos venezolanos de nutrición 11, 1961, p. 31-54.

5320 Vélez Boza, Fermín, & M. González
"Reconocimiento de Costumbres Alimenticias de Niños Pre-escolares de Familias de Recursos Económicos Modestos en un Barrio de Caracas." Caracas, Archivos venezolanos de nutrición 12, 1962, p. 7-25.

5321 Zamorani, V.
"Investigaciones Sobre Escorbuto Latente en Ambiente Tropical." Caracas, Archivos venezolanos de puericultura y pediatría 21, 1958, p. 3-14.

West Indies and the Caribbean

5322 "Nutritional Research in the Caribbean Area." Pan American Union bulletin 80, April 1946, p. 235-236.

5323 Van der Saar, A., & T.A.J. Kroon
"Avitaminosis A and Subclinical Vitamin C Deficiency in Curação." Amsterdam, Documenta medica geographica et tropica 8, 1956, p. 144-150.

Sanitary Engineering

Books

General

5324 American Public Works Association. Committee on Refuse Disposal
Municipal refuse disposal . . . Chicago, Public Administration Service, 1961, 506p.

5325 Ehlers, V.M., & E.S. Steel
Municipal and rural sanitation. 6th ed. New York, McGraw-Hill, 1965, 663p.

5326 Logan, John A., et al, eds.
Environmental engineering and metropolitan planning. Evanston, Northwestern University Press, 1962, 430p.

5327 Mitchell, George E.
Sanitation, drainage and water supply. 6th ed. rev. by S.E. Thrower. London, Newnes, 1960, 208p.

5328 Salvato, Joseph A.
Environmental sanitation. New York, Wiley, 1958, 660p.

Latin America

5329 Ingeniería sanitaria. México, v. 7, 1953-

5330 International Sanitary Conference of American Republics
Transactions of the Fourth International Sanitary Conference . . . Washington, Pan American Union, 1910, 209p.

Mexico

5331 Estudios y Proyectos (firm) Mexico City
Los desperdicios urbanos: análisis de las soluciones actuales; aplicación al problema del Distrito Federal. México, 1955, 97p.

5332 México (Federal District) Dirección de Salubridad
Un año de labor sanitaria en el Distrito Federal, diciembre de 1946 a diciembre de 1947. México, 1948, 76p.

Venezuela

5333 Foro Libre Sobre Problemas Sanitarios del Valle de Caracas, Caracas, 1964
Acta final. Caracas, Depto. de Ingeniería Sanitaria, Universidad Central de Venezuela, 1964, 33p.

5334 Venezuela. División de Ingeniería Sanitaria
Trabajos sobre edificios sanitarios. Caracas, Ed. Grafolit, 1946, 87p.

West Indies and the Caribbean

5335 Fortas, André D.
Problèmes sanitaires et de sous-développement à la Martinique. Toulouse, Imp. Boisseau, 1962, 162p.

5336 Magoon, Estus H.
Drenaje y salud en la zona del Caribe. Drainage for health in the Caribbean area . . . Havana? 1945? 556p.

5337 Seminario de Ingeniería Sanitaria del Area del Caribe
Memorias. San Juan, 1955-

Periodical Articles

General

5338 Edelman, S.
"Legal Aspects of Sanitation Programs." "Environmental Sanitation Controls," by C. L. Senn. Public health reports 79, August 1964, p. 676-688.

5339 Horton, J. P.
"Street-Cleaning Revolution." American city 78, March 1963, p. 106-108.

Latin America

5340 Ruiz, P.
"Observaciones Sobre Servicios Públicos Sanitarios

en Latinoamérica." Boletín de la Oficina Sanitaria Panamericana, May 1966, p. 423-429.

5341 Steel, Ernest W.
"El Problema de Obtener Servicios Ingenieros Competentes en Latinoamérica." Boletin de la Oficina Sanitaria Panamericana 55, September 1963, p. 309-311.

Argentina

5342 Gando, A. R.
"El Canal Sanitario de Buenos Aires." Buenos Aires, Hechos e ideas (24:103), October 1952, p. 167-176.

Brazil

5343 Besselievre, E.B.
"Beginning of Waste Treatment." Public works 95, March 1964, p. 74.

5344 Congresso Brasileiro de Engenharia Sanitária 2º, Pôrto Alegre, 1963
"Planejamento de Sistemas de Abastecimento de Agua." Rio de Janeiro, Revista de administração municipal (11:63), March-April 1964, p. 83-102.

5345 Kitover, J.
"Tratamento de Lixo no Recife." Rio de Janeiro, Revista de Administração municipal (10:57), March-April 1963, p. 85-99.

Chile

5346 "Motor Garbage Collection Starts." American city 68, March 1953, p. 104.

Ecuador

5347 Parks, Lois F.
"The Sanitation of Guayaquil." Hispanic American historical review, May 1943, p. 197-221.

5348 "The Sum of 30,000, 000 Sucres Has Been Appropriated for the Sanitation of Guayaquil." Pan American Union bulletin 63, April 1929, p. 421.

El Salvador

5349 Valdivieso, J. A.
"Operaciones de Compuestos en El Salvador: Problemas e Estado Actuales." Boletín de la Oficina Sanitaria Panamericana 50, January 1961, p. 14-18.

Mexico

5350 "Despite Sandbagging of Sewer Walls Sewage Inundates Mexico City Streets." Engineering news 161, October 2, 1958, p. 23.

5351 González Navarro, M.
"México en una Laguna." México, Historia mexicana (4:4), April-June 1955, p. 506-522.

5352 Montes de Oca, M.
"Depuración de Aguas Fecales en México." Boletín de la Oficina Sanitaria Panamericana 52, April 1962, p. 287-292.

5353 Montes de Oca, M., et al
"Depuración de Basura Sólida en la Ciudad de Matamoros, México." Boletín de la Oficina Sanitaria Panamericana 57, December 1964, p. 572-578.

5354 Rolland, M. C.
"La Ciudad de México y los Problemas de Previsión de Agua, Hundimento y Drenaje, y un Olvido del Ing. Oribe de Alba." México, Revista industrial (6:70), July 1, 1952, p. 57-61.

Uruguay

5355 Gianoni, A.
"Plan Quinquenal de Obras de Saneamiento en el Uruguay." Organo oficial de la Asociación Interamericana de Ingeniería Sanitaria (3:1-4), December 1951, p. 88-105.

Venezuela

5356 Berti, L. A., et al
"Estudio y Conocimiento General Sobre el Problema de Desperdicios en Venezuela." Caracas, Revista venezolana de sanidad y asistencia social, suplemento no. 3, September 1961, p. 201-289.

5357 Osorio Struve, L.A.
"Estudio Sobre el Problema de la Recolección y Disposición de las Basuras en Caracas." Caracas, Revista de sanidad y asistencia social, April 1947, p. 165-214.

Water Supply

Books

General

5358 Dieterich, J.H., & J.M. Henderson
Urban water supply conditions and needs in 75 developing countries. Geneva, World Health Organization, 1966, 371p.

5359 Hirshleifer, Jack, et al
Water supply. Chicago, University of Chicago Press, 1960, 378p.

5360 Marais, Gerrit V.R., & Frederick E. McJunkin
Water supply and sanitation in developing countries. Chapel Hill, Dept. of Environmental Sciences & Engineering, University of North Carolina, 1967-

5361 Water Pollution Control Federation
Proceedings of the Third International Conference on Water Pollution Research, Munich, Germany, September 5-9, 1966. 3v. Washington, 1967.

Latin America

5362 Seminario Sobre Diseño de Abastecimientos de Agua, Buenos Aires, 1962
Seminario Sobre Diseño de Abastecimientos de Agua, Buenos Aires, Argentina, 20-29 de septiembre de 1962. Washington, Oficina Sanitaria Panamericana, 1964, 211p.

5363 United Nations. Economic Commission for Latin America
Water resources and their utilization in Latin America . . . [n.p.] 1959, 40p.

Bolivia

5364 Flores, Domingo
Las aguas potables de Potosí. Potosí, Ed. Universitaria, 1950, 61p.

Cuba

5365 Fernández y Simón, Abel
Memoria histórico-técnica de los acueductos de la ciudad de La Habana. Havana, 1950-

5366 García Hernández, Manuel
Abastecimiento de agua en la Habana; desde el punto de vista histórico. Havana? 1956, 28p.

Guatemala

5367 Gálvez Sobral, Jorge
Consideraciones sobre la dotación de agua potable necesaria en poblaciones de la República de Guatemala. Guatemala, 1951, 34p.

5368 Municipalidad de la Ciudad de Guatemala. Dirección de Aguas
Proyecto Pixcaya: Informe sobre el abastecimiento municipal de agua en la ciudad de Guatemala. Guatemala, 1966, 135p.

Haiti

5369 U.S. Geological Survey
Reconnaissance investigations of public water supplies of Port-au-Prince . . . Washington, 1960, 105p.

Mexico

5370 Aragonés, Ruiperez R. de
El sistema actual de drenaje de la ciudad de México como substitución al sistema hidrológico del valle. (In International Geographical Union. Proceedings of the First Latin American Regional Conference, Mexico City, August 2-8, 1966. v. 4, Mexico, 1966, p. 100-112).

5371 Guía, exposición internacional, agua para la paz/ Guide, international exposition on water for peace. México? [n.d.] unpaged.

5372 Mexico (Federal District) Depto. del Distrito Federal
Las obras de Lerma. México, 1949, 72 plus 89p.

Uruguay

5373 Uruguay. Comision Honoraria para Estudiar el Régimen de Explotación de Servicio de Abastecimiento de Agua a Montevideo
Informe elevado al M.O.P. Montevideo, 1946, 216p.

West Indies and the Caribbean

5374 Martin-Kaye, P.H.A.
Water supplies of the British Virgin Islands. Georgetown, Demerara, 1954, 73p.

Periodical Articles

General

5375 Hilburg, C.J.
"El Abastecimiento de Agua Potable y Desarrollo Económico-Social." Boletín de la Oficina Sanitaria Panamericana 54, January 1963, p. 11-17.

5376 Nogueira Garcez, L.
"El Financiamiento de Servicios para Abastecimiento de Agua y Alcantarillado." Boletín de la Oficina Sanitaria Panamericana 53, November 1962, p. 419-425.

5377 Trancart, G.
"Planejamento Financeiro do Serviço de Agua." Rio de Janeiro, Revista da administração municipal (8:48), September-October 1961, p. 390-400.

5378 Vallejo, N.
"Información Públ ica e Educación de la Comunidad en Programas de Agua Potable." Boletín de la Oficina Sanitaria Panamericana 55, August 1963, p. 202-206.

Latin America

5379 Casanueva del Canto, R.
"El Financiamiento de Programas de Abastecimento de Agua Potable." Boletín de la Oficina Sanitaria

Panamericana 60, February 1966, p. 120-132.

5380 Hernández, A.E.
"El Trabajo del BID en el Campo de Abastecimiento de Agua y Depuración de Aguas Fecales en Latinoamérica." Boletín de la Oficina Sanitaria Panamericana 60, February 1966, p. 133-138.

5381 Jezler, H.
"Ayuda Técnica de la Organización Panamericana de Salud en el Campo de Abastecimiento de Agua." Boletín de la Oficina Sanitaria Panamericana 58, May 1965, p. 424-427.

5382 Olivero Aycinena, Humberto
"Antecedentes Históricos de Sistemas Urbanos de Abastecimiento de Agua y Consideraciones Generales Sobre Estos en Latinoamérica." Boletín de la Oficina Sanitaria Panamericana 51, September 1961, p. 195-205.

5383 Olivero Aycinena, Humberto
"Desarrollo de Sistemas de Abastecimiento de Agua y Alcantarillado en América Latina." Boletín de la Oficina Sanitaria Panamericana 55, August 1963, p. 180-185.

5384 Wagner, E.G.
"Comentarios Sobre el Financiamento de Sistemas de Abastecimiento de Agua y Alcantarillado en América Latina." Boletín de la Oficina Sanitaria Panamericana 55, August 1963, p. 189-195.

Argentina

5385 Bodenbender, Otto E.
"El Abastecimiento de Agua Potable en la República Argentina." Buenos Aires, Revista de obras sanitarias de la nación (17:152), April/May 1953, p. 166-175.

5386 "Consolidated Waterworks of Rosario." London, South American journal, August 12, 1944, p. 81.

5387 Durieux, Santiago
"El Problema del Agua en la Provincia de Córdoba, Argentina." Ingeniería internacional, April 1946, p. 54-58, 98.

5388 Flores, Mario
"Del Molino 'San Francisco' a los 'Rios' Subterráneos!" Buenos Aires, Revista geográfica americana (39:229), January 1955, p. 1-14.

5389 Lombardi, Rafael R.
"Los Servicios de Provisión de Agua y Desagüe Colocal en la República Argentina y su Influencia en el Progreso de los Pueblos, 1869-1941." Buenos Aires, La ingeniería, March 1943, p. 173-178.

5390 Marzinelli, M.A.
"El Abastecimiento de Agua a Buenos Aires." Buenos Aires, Saneamiento, revista de obras sanitarias de la nación, 1963, p. 29-38.

5391 Olmos Castro, Amalio
"El Problema del Agua en Santiago del Estero." Buenos Aires, Veritas, April 1945, p. 235-236.

Bolivia

5392 Rudolph, William
"The Lakes of Potosí." Geographical review, October 1936, p. 528-554.

Brasil

5393 Alcântara, Ulysses M.A. de
"As Primeiras Galerias de Aguas Pluviais do Rio de Janeiro." Rio de Janeiro, PDF, Revista municipal de engenharia (20:1), January/March 1953, p. 18-28.

5394 Carmargo, José Piratininga de
"Taxa de Agua para a Cidade de São Paulo." São Paulo, Engenharia (7:73), September 1948, p. 19-26.

5395 Castelo Branco, Z.
"Administração de Sistemas de Abastecimento de Agua nas Cidades do Interior." Rio de Janeiro,

Revista de administração municipal (10:60), September-October 1963, p. 385-399.

5396 Castelo Branco, Z.
"A 'Realidade Brasileira' em Têrmos de Abastecimento de Agua." Rio de Janeiro, Revista da administração dos municipios (11:64), May-June 1964, p. 195-213.

5397 Cavalcanti, Jeronymo
"Geografia Urbana e sua Influência Sobre o Saneamento das Cidades." Rio de Janeiro, Revista brasileira de geografia, January-March 1941, p. 20-52.

5398 Cervone, A.N. de Abreu
"Reservatórios de Agua." Rio de Janeiro, Revista de administraçao municipal (10:56), January-February 1963, p. 7-16.

5399 Coutinho, A.
"Estrutura Jurídica e Financeira do Serviço de Agua." Rio de Janeiro, Revista de administração municipal (9:51), March-April 1962, p. 133-147.

5400 Garcez, L.N.
"Alguns Aspectos Acerca do Uso de Agua." São Paulo, Arquivos do higiene 26, June 1961, p. 147-155.

5401 "The New Water Service in Bello Horizonte." Rio de Janeiro, Brazilian American March 15, 1930, p. 9-16.

5402 Whitaker, Plinio Penteado
"Abastecimento de Agua da Cidade de São Paulo: sua Solução." São Paulo, Engenharia, October 1946, p. 65-108.

5403 Whitaker, Plinio Penteado
"Abastecimiento de Agua Potavel às Cidades." São Paulo, Engenharia (10:114), February 1952, p. 188-201.

Chile

5404 "Additional Water Supply for Santiago, Chile." Pan American Union bulletin 71, September 1937, p. 732.

5405 Espinosa, Januario
"Santiago's Water Supply. How the Capital's Rapidly Growing Population Has Made Necessary the Development of Modern Water Works High in the Andes." Chile, August 1929, p. 56-59 & 94.

5406 Valle, Ramón del
"Explotación de los Servicios de Agua Potable en Chile." Organo oficial de la Asociación Interamericana de Ingeniería Sanitaria (3:1/4), July 1949-June 1950, p. 28-36.

Colombia

5407 Herrnstadt, Brígida
"El Abastecimiento de Agua en 50 Municipios de Cundinamarca." Bogotá, Revista javeriana (48: 237), August/September 1957, p. 93-97.

5408 "New Waterworks for Cartagena, Colombia." Pan American Union bulletin 73, April 1939, p. 247.

Cuba

5409 Fernández y Simón, Abel
"Evolución Sanitaria de las Aguas de Consumo Público de la Ciudad de la Habana (1592-1930)." Havana, Ingeniería civil (6:3), March 1955, p. 172-195.

5410 Fernández y Simón, Abel
"La Traída de las Aguas del Río de la Chorrera al Puerto y Villa de La Habana. La Zanja Real (1592)." Havana, Ingeniería civil (8:4), April 1957, p. 219-237; (8:6), June 1957, p. 351-375.

5411 Montoulieu, Eduardo I.
"Comentarios Sobre el Aprovechamiento de las Aguas de la Cuenca Sur para el Abasto de Agua de la Ciudad de La Habana." Havana, Revista de la Sociedad Cubana de Ingenieros (53:5), May 1953, p. 147-158.

5412 Núñez Jiménez, Antonio
"Explorando una Cuenca Subterránea que Puede Abastecer de Agua a La Habana." Havana, Carteles (31:36), September 3, 1950, p. 52-53, 97.

5413 Rodríguez Zaldívar, Rodolfo
"Cuba: Isla Sin Agua." Havana, Bohemia (42:26), June 15, 1950, p. 86-90.

5414 Zorrila, Gonzalo
"'Dos Millones de Pesos Bastarán para Dar Agua a La Habana,' Dice en un Informe el Ingeniero Abel Fernández." Havana, Carteles (32:45), November 11, 1951, p. 73-76.

Ecuador

5415 Macias Constante, R.
"Observaciones Sobre Entamoeba Moshkovskii, Amiba Viviendo-Libre en la Ciudad de Guayaquil." Guayaquil, Revista ecuatoriana de higiene 22, May-August 1965, p. 157-161.

Guatemala

5416 Jost, C. F., et al
"Guatemala Acquires . . . Team to Provide Additional Potable Water Supply." American city 65, October 1950, p. 92-94.

5417 Olivero Aycinena, Humberto
"Consideraciones Generales Sobre el Problema de Abastecimiento de Agua en las Poblaciones de Guatemala." Guatemala, Boletín de la Facultad de Ingeniería (5:31), July/August 1955, p. 7-10.

Haiti

5418 "Municipal Waterworks." Pan American Union bulletin 64, May 1930, p. 527-528.

Honduras

5419 "Expanded Water Supply for Puerto Cortés." Pan American Union bulletin 80, February 1946, p. 111.

5420 Seidel, H.
"Empty Water Mains." American city 78, April 1963, p. 33.

Mexico

5421 Blanco M., Gonzalo
"El Abastecimiento de Agua a la Ciudad de México." México, Revista de economía (13:2), February 15, 1950, p. 63-65.

5422 Blanco M., Gonzalo
"El Abastecimiento de Agua a la Ciudad de México." México, Boletín de la Sociedad Mexicana Geográfica y Estadística, March-June 1948, p. 201-222.

5423 Gaido, S., et al
"Evaluo del Tratamiento de Aguas de Albañal en la Planta de Chapultepec." México, Revista del Instituto de Salubridad e Enfermedades Tropicales 23, June 1963, p. 5-34.

5424 Jiménez, Antonio
"Techo Eterno 'Eureka,' S.A. Contribuye a Resolver el Problema de la Escasez de Agua en Guadalajara." México, Todo, June 17, 1948, p. 52-54.

5425 Jiménez López, César
"Política del Agua de México. Puntos de Vista de Ingeniería." México, Ingeniería (27:4), July 1957, p. 1-15.

5426 Jones, Heinz L. & M. Anaya
"Abastecimiento de Agua Potable y Alimentación de Aguas Negras en Mérida, Yucatán." México, Ingeniería hidráulica en México (14:2), April/June 1960, p. 31-49.

5427 "Mexico City Drains Storm Water to Where Farmers Can Use It." Engineering news 173, October 22, 1964, p. 28-29.

5428 Miller, L.A.
"Mexico City Formulates a Plan for Water Supply." American city 59, August 1944, p. 54-55.

5429 Moguel Traconis, Manuel
"¡Agua! ¡Agua! He Allí el Gran Problema." México, Todo, March 27, 1947, p. 51-53.

5430 Rodríguez García, Manuel
"Estudio Sobre Dotaciones de Agua Potable para Poblaciones de la República Mexicana." México, Revista mexicana de ingeniería y arquitectura, July/September 1947, p. 155-163.

5431 Suárez, Luis
"El Drama de un Pueblo. La Laguna que Se Bebió la Ciudad de México." México, Mañana (67:706), March 9, 1957, p. 32-37.

5432 Thornby, Gerald
"Termination of the Lerma Project. Assures Mexico City of Abundant Water Supply." México, Mexican life (28:9), September 1951, p. 15-18.

5433 Villa Acosta, Alfonso
"Seis Siglos de Abastecimiento de Agua en la Ciudad de México." México, Ingeniería, October 1941, p. 298-311.

Nicaragua

5434 "Water Supply for the Capital of Nicaragua." Pan American Union bulletin 63, July 1929, p. 729.

Peru

5435 Denevan, William M.
"Choclococha Diversion Project. A Visit to Choclococha Lagoon: Site of the World's Highest Major Water Diversion Project." Lima, Peruvian times (17:848), March 22, 1957, p. 7-10.

5436 Pérez Santisteban, V.
"Nuevo Régimen de Repartición y Consumo del Agua de Regadío en la Costa Peruana." Lima, Revista de la Facultad de Ciencias Económicas y Comerciales 69, July-December 1964, p. 182-189.

Venezuela

5437 Lasser, T.
"Nuestras Aguas." Caracas, El farol (26:213), April-June 1965, p. 25-31.

5438 Mejías, F.
"El Estado Actual del Abastecimiento de Agua y de

Desagüaderos Albañales y para Aguas Lluvias en Poblaciones Más que 5,000 Habitantes." Caracas, Revista venezolana de sanidad y asistencia social, suplemento 3, September 1961, p. 137-163.

5439 Rojas, A.
"La Derrota de la Sed." Caracas, El farol (22: 190), September-October 1960, p. 8-14.

5440 Saville, Thorndike
"El Abastecimiento de Agua de Caracas, Venezuela, con Notas Relativas a Circunstancias que Influyen Sobre los Abastecimientos de Agua en el País." Caracas, Revista técnica del Ministerio de Obras Públicas, October 1933, p. 7-29.

West Indies and the Caribbean

5441 Moore, E.W.
"British Caribbean Water Supply." Public health reports (74:5), May 1959, p. 428-430.

PUBLIC WELFARE

Books

General

5442 Adrian, Charles R., ed., et al
Social science and community action. East Lansing, 1960, 55p.

5443 Beshers, James M.
Urban social structure. New York, Free Press of Glencoe, 1962, 207p.

5444 Boskoff, Alvin
The sociology of urban regions. New York, Appleton-Century-Crofts, 1962, 370p.

5445 Conference on Service to Families, Chicago, 1964
Neighborhood centers to serve the troubled family; report. New York, National Federation of Settlements & Neighborhood Centers, 1964, 112p.

5446 Delliguardi, F.
Helping the family in urban society. New York, Columbia University Press, 1963, 184p.

5447 Gordon, Margaret S.
The economics of welfare policies. New York, Columbia University Press, 1963, 159p.

5448 Hungate, Joseph I.
A guide for training local public welfare administrators. Washington, Division of Technical Training, Bureau of Family Services, Welfare Administration, U.S. Dept. of Health, Education & Welfare, 1964, 136p.

5449 Mann, P.H.
An approach to urban sociology. London, Routledge & K. Paul, 1965, 232p.

5450 Mendieta y Núñez, Lucio
Urbanismo y sociología. México, Asociación Mexicana de Sociología, 1951? 65p.

5451 National Conference on Social Welfare. Forum. 89th, New York, 1962
Helping the family in urban society. Ed. by Fred Delli Quadri. New York, Columbia University Press, 1963, 184p.

5452 Newson, J., & E. Newson
Patterns of infant care in an urban community. Baltimore, Penguin Books, 1965, 285p.

5453 Owen, Wilfred
Strategy for mobility. Washington, Brookings Institution, 1964, 249p.

5454 Pearl, Arthur, & Frank Riessman
New careers for the poor: the nonprofessional in human service. New York, Free Press, 1965, 287p.

5455 Rosser, C., & C. Harris
The family and social change. London, Routledge & K. Paul, 1965, 337p.

5456 Séminaire International de Recherche sur la Famille et de l'Institut de l'Unesco des Sciences Sociales, Cologne, 1954
Recherches sur la famille. 3v. Tubingen, Mohr, 1956.

5457 Seminar on Social Aspects of Urban Development, Washington, D.C., 1963
Seminar on social aspects of urban development; report. Washington, 1964? 47p.

5458 Sirjamaki, J.
The sociology of cities. New York, Random House, 1964, 328p.

5459 Towle, Charlotte
Common human needs. Rev. ed. New York, National Association of Social Workers, 1965, 174p.

5460 United Nations. Dept. of Economic & Social Affairs
Family, child and youth welfare services; document ST/SOA/59. New York, 1965, 61p.

5461 United Nations. Secretary-General
The relationship between social security and social services; report, document E/CN.5/AC.12/L.2. New York, 1964, 32p.

5462 Weaver, Robert C.
The urban complex; human values in urban life. Garden City, Doubleday, 1964, 297p.

5463 Wickenden, Elizabeth
Social welfare in a changing world; the place of social welfare in the process of development. Washington, Welfare Administration, U.S. Dept. of Health, Education & Welfare, 1965, 41p.

5464 Women's Group on Public Welfare
Loneliness. London, National Council of Social Service, 1964, 72p.

Latin America

5465 Caldera, Rafael
Christian democracy and social reality in Latin America (CICOP working paper C-4-65). Davenport, Latin America Bureau, National Catholic Welfare Conference, 1965, 28p.

5466 Interamerican Children's Institute. Directing Council
Reunión. Montevideo. Annual.

5467 Mardones de Martínez, L.
Estudio de tres escuelas de servicio social en América Latina. Washington, Unión Panamericana, 1959, 73p.

5468 Pan American Union. Division of Labor & Social Affairs
La familia y el servicio social. Washington, 1956, 27 plus 2p.

5469 Pan American Union. Section of Social Work
Supervisión en servicio social; selecciones. Washington, 1958-

5470 Paraíso, V. A.
Social service in Latin America; functions and relationships to development. New York, UN Economic Commission for Latin America, 1965, 62p.

5471 Sajón, Rafael, & J. P. Achard
Situación de la legislación relativa a la minoridad en Latinoamérica. Montevideo, Instituto Interamericano del Niño, 1965, 90p.

5472 Schroeder, Augusta
El servicio social. Montevideo, Ed. Mosca Hnos., 1953, 207p.

5473 Servicio social interamericano. No. 1- , Washington, Consejo Interamericano Económico y Social, Unión Panamericana, 1955-

Bolivia

5474 U. S. Foreign Operations Administration
Report of Santa Cruz, Bolivia, area development group. Washington, 1954, 64p.

Brazil

5475 Cesarino, Ferreira Antônio, & Ingeborg S. Gerson
Direito social brasileiro. 4th ed. enl. 2v. Rio de Janeiro, Livraria Freitas Bastos, 1957.

5476 Congresso Brasileiro de Serviço Social
Teses apresentadas. São Paulo, 1947-

5477 Fischlowitz, Estanislão
Revolução contemporânea na política social. Rio de Janeiro, Ministério do Trabalho, Indústria e Comércio, Serviço de Documentação, 1951, 37p.

5478 São Paulo, Brasil (State) Departamento do Serviço Público
Relatório das atividades. São Paulo, Serviço de Documentação. Annual.

5479 Serviço Social da Indústria. Departamento National
Anuário estatístico. Rio de Janeiro, 1956-

5480 Serviço Social do Comercio
Anais da convenção nacional de técnicos. Rio de Janeiro, 1964-

Chile

5481 Chile. Universidad. Facultad de Ciencias Jurídicas y Sociales
Instituciones de asistencia social de Santiago. Santiago, 1966, 327p.

5482 Servicio social. Santiago, 1958-

5483 Sociedad Chilena de Salubridad
Quintas jornadas, realizadas en Santiago de Chile desde el 15 al 17 de diciembre de 1958. Santiago, 1958, 116p.

Colombia

5484 Calderón Alvarado, Luis
Poder retentivo del "área local urbana" en las relaciones sociales. Investigación en tres áreas de diferente clase social: alta, media y baja, en Bogotá; observaciones desde el punto de vista del movimiento endo-exo-local en las relaciones. Fribourg, Feres, 1963, 216p.

5485 Torres Restrepo, Camilo
La proletarización de Bogotá; ensayo de metodología estadística. Bogotá, Universidad Nacional, Facultad de Sociología, 1961, 42p.

Cuba

5486 El bien como acción social. Havana, Depto. de Propaganda del Ministerio de Obras Públicas, 1953, unpaged.

5487 Cuba. Ministerio de Salubridad y Asistencia Social
Asistencia social en Cuba. Havana, 1960, 38p.

Ecuador

5488 Rubio Orbe, Gonzalo
Servicios e instituciones sociales en el Ecuador; lecturas ilustradas . . . Quito, Tall. Graf. Nacionales, 1948, 66p.

El Salvador

5489 Barrett, M. T.
Social welfare programmes in El Salvador. New York, United Nations, 1954, 18p.

Guatemala

5490 Campos Jiménez, C. M.
Organización y desarrollo de la comunidad para el bienestar social. Guatemala, 1956, 282p.

5491 Comedores y guarderías infantiles de la ciudad de Guatemala y algunas cabeceras departamentales. Guatemala, Ministerio de Educación Pública, 1951, 291p.

5492 Salubridad y asistencia. Guatemala, 1952- .

Haiti

5493 Denis, L., & F. Duvalier
Problèmes des classes à travers l'histoire d'Haiti; sociologie politique. Port-au-Prince, Au Service de la Jeunesse, 1958, 110p.

5494 Kain, Joan
Report on Haiti. Washington, Federal Security Agency, Social Security Administration, Children's Bureau, 1950, variously paged.

Jamaica

5495 Marier, Roger
Social welfare work in Jamaica. Paris, Unesco, 1953, 166p.

Mexico

5496 Alvarez Amézquita, José, et al
Historia de la salubridad y de la asistencia en México. México, Secretaria de Salubridad y Asistencia, 1960-

5497 Bonifaz Ocampo, Blanca
El trabajo social en el Centro de Salud "Dr. Atanasio Garza Ríos." México, 1960, 98p.

5498 Mexico. Social Security Institute
Social security centers for family welfare. México, 1960, 24 plus 52p.

5499 Omaña Suárez, Enidina
Evolución de la ayuda social para llegar al trabajo social en México. México, 1949, 157p.

5500 Trueba Urbina, Alberto
Tratado de legislación social. México, Herrero, 1954, 420p.

5501 Valenzuela Kunckel de Sánchez, María L.
Consideraciones sobre el trabajo social en México. México, 1952, 61p.

Nicaragua

5502 Managua (National District) Junta Local de Asistencia Social
Memoria. Managua. Annual.

Peru

5503 Sociedad de Beneficencia de Lima
Presupuesto. Lima, 1950- .

5504 Sociedad de Beneficencia de Lima
Anuario estadístico. Lima? Annual.

Venezuela

5505 Chiossone, Talio
Temas sociales venezolanos. Caracas, Tip. Americana, 1950, 248p.

5506 Zulia, Venezuela. Secretaría de Asistencia Pública y Social
Memoria y cuenta. Maracaibo, Impr. del Estado Zulia, 1950-

West Indies and the Caribbean

5507 Luke, S.
Development and welfare in the West Indies. London, H.M.S.O., 1955, 129p.

Periodical Articles

General

5508 Anderson, C. L.
"Development of an Objective Measure of Orientation Toward Public Dependence." Social forces 44,

September 1965, p. 107-113.

5509 Reed, E.S.
"Human Values and Organized Welfare." Ottawa, Canadian welfare 41, March-April 1965, p. 74-77.

5510 Schnore, Leo F.
"The City as a Social Organism." Urban affairs quarterly (I:3), March 1966, p. 58-69.

Latin America

5511 Bernal Nicholls, Alberto
"Asistencia Pública." Medellín, Letras y encajes, January 1947, p. 407-412.

5512 Haar, C.M.
"Latin America's Troubled Cities." Foreign affairs (41:3), April 1963, p. 536-549.

5513 Jones, Robert C.
"Bienestar Social en las Américas." México, Revista mexicana de sociología (13:2), May-August 1951, p. 237-243.

5514 Lenroot, K.F.
"Social Welfare in Latin America." Inter-American affairs-1942: annual survey no. 2, 1943, p. 131-145.

5515 Martínez-Marí Odena, J.M.
"Programa de Servicios Sociales Mínimos para un Barrio Satélite de 600 Viviendas." Madrid, Razón y fé 722, March 1958, p. 241-256.

5516 Morales Carrión, Arturo
"As Relações Humanas Entre o Município e os Cidadãos." Rio de Janeiro, Revista brasileira dos municípios (8:29), January-March 1955, p. 1-7.

5517 Paraíso, V.A.
"Social Service in Latin America: Functions and Relationships to Development." Economic bulletin for Latin America (XI:1), April 1966, p. 71-105.

5518 Pereira, L.
"Mulher e Trabalho." Rio de Janeiro, Educação

e ciências sociais (8:15), September 1960, p. 143-158.

5519 Pike, Frederick B.
"Public Work and Social Welfare in Colonial Spanish American Towns." The Americas (13:4), April 1957, p. 361-375.

5520 "Problemas Econômicos e Sociais do Hemisfério." Rio de Janeiro, Revista do comercio, October 1947, p. 38-68.

5521 Smith, Thomas L.
"Problemas Sociales de Actualidad en América Latina." Cuenca, Anales de la Universidad de Cuenca (12:3-4), July-December 1956, p. 145-157.

5522 Souza, Y.H. de
"O Abandono da Criança na América Latina; Aspectos Sociais." Montevideo, Boletín del Instituto Interamericano del Niño (34:2), June 1960, p. 214-232.

5523 Mayone Stycos, J.
"Survey of Research and Population Control in Latin America." Public opinion quarterly (28:3), Autumn 1964, p. 367-372.

5524 Tapia Moore, Astolfo
"Diferentes Condiciones de Vida en la Ciudad y en el Campo." México, Revista mexicana de sociología (20:3), September-December 1958, p. 669-677.

5525 Terra, J.P., et al
"Situación y Perspectivas Demográficas de América Latina." Montevideo, Cuadernos latinoamericanos de economía humana (I:1), 1958, p. 34-59.

5526 Tierno Galván, E.
"Conocimiento y Pobreza." México, Panoramas (2:11), September-October 1964, p. 79-84.

5527 Vekemans, Roger
"Marginalidad y Promoción Popular." Santiago, Mensaje (15:149), June 1966, p. 218-222.

5528 Velásquez, Pedro
"El Problema Social en América y el Catolicismo Social." México, Abside (13:4), October-December 1949, p. 461-495.

Argentina

5529 Argentine Republic. Laws, statutes, etc.
"La 'Fundación Eva Perón' Atenderá los Fines Sociales del Instituto Nacional de las Remuneraciones. Correspondan a los Fijados por el Art. 49 del Decreto 33.302/45. Ley 13.992." Buenos Aires, Boletín oficial, November 10, 1950, p. 1.

5530 Argentine Republic. Laws, statutes, etc.
"Serán Coordinados los Distintos Servicios Sociales de la Administración Nacional. Decreto No. 4.612." Buenos Aires, Boletín oficial, March 31, 1954, p. 1.

5531 Carrillo, Ramón
"Doctrina Peronista del Bienestar Social." Buenos Aires, Yapeyú, June 1947, p. 27-32.

5532 Imaz, José L. de
"Movilidad Social en Argentina." México, Revista mexicana de sociología (20:3), October-December 1958, p. 743-750.

5533 International Labour Office
"Reorganization of Social Welfare Services in Argentina." Geneva, Industry and labour (11:8), April 15, 1954, p. 346-347.

5534 Loiza, Raimundo
"Pinceladas Sobre la Vida Urbana en Buenos Aires." Buenos Aires, Revista geográfica americana, January 1942, p. 1-8.

5535 Lumsden, E.W.H.
"Buenos Aires Childhood." Américas (5:9), September 1953, p. 9-11, 27.

5536 "National Institute of Social Prevision." Buenos Aires, Argentine news, December 1944, p. 21-22.

5537 Teeters, N.K.
"Argentina's College Home for Children." Pan American Union bulletin 80, January 1944, p. 41-44.

Bolivia

5538 Gueiler de Möller, L.
"La Mujer en Bolivia." San José, Combate (3:18), September-October 1961, p. 33-41.

Brazil

5539 Albuquerque, J.B. da Mota e
"A Igreja e a Familia Brasileira." Rio de Janeiro, Síntese política econômica social (2:7), July-September 1960, p. 6-14.

5540 Alcântara, A. Brasileiro
"Bibliografía: Estudos e Pesquisas Sôbre Família no Brasil." Rio de Janeiro, Dados, 2d quarter 1966, p. 176-179.

5541 Brazil. XI Conferencia Internacional de Servicio Social
"Informe Nacional." Montevideo, Boletín del Instituto Interamericano del Niño (37:144), March 1963, p. 33-62.

5542 Cascudo, Luiz da Câmara
"Considerações Sôbre as Relações de Vizinhança." São Paulo, Sociología (17:4), October 1955, p. 348-354.

5543 Carvalho, M. Cavalcanti de
"Pela Reforma do Ministério do Trabalho (T. e Bem-Estar Social) e Criação do Ministério da Economia. Sentido Social e Econômico de um Plano." Rio de Janeiro, Trabalho e seguro social (26:95/96), November/December 1950, p. 185-194.

5544 Dias, A.A.
"Aspectos Atuais da Juventude." Petrópolis, Vozes (54:1), January 1960, p. 26-34.

5545 Dias Velloso, E., & V. Castro Silva
"Alguns Aspectos da Evolução de uma Clínica

Psicológica." Rio de Janeiro, Arquivos brasileiros de psicotécnica (14:1), January-March 1962, p. 5-34.

5546 Fernandes, Florestan
"O Homem e a Cidade-Metrópole." Rio de Janeiro, Educação e ciencias sociais (5:11), August 1959, p. 23-44.

5547 Ferreira, F. de Paula
"O Servico Social em São Paulo; Evolução e Tendências nos Ultimos 25 Anos." Petrópolis, Vozes (56:6), June 1962, p. 439-447.

5548 Freyre, Gilberto
"Região, Pesquisa Social e Educação." Rio de Janeiro, Revista brasileira de estudos pedagógicos (29:69), January-March 1958, p. 31-41.

5549 Gonçalves, O.
"Aspectos Económicos da Previdência Social no Brasil." São Paulo, Revista da Universidade Católica de São Paulo (11:20), December 1956, p. 504-510.

5550 Leite, M.A. da Cruz
"Social Welfare in Brazil." International social work (5:1), 1962, p. 8-13.

5551 Nogueira, Oracy
"A Estratificação Social no Municipio de Itapetininga." São Paulo, Sociología (21:3), August 1959, p. 225-235.

5552 "Orientação Psico-Pedagógica as Instituições que Têm a Seu Cargo Crianças Desprotegidas." Rio de Janeiro, Revista de serviço social, December/March 1946, p. 90-93.

5553 Riley, Nelson J.
"Brazil's Social Welfare Program Aided by American Skill and Funds." Brazil (24:3), March 1950, p. 3-5.

5554 Servicio Social da Industria
"O 'SESI' Tem Novo Regulamento." Rio de Janeiro, Desenvolvimento e conjuntura (6:3), March 1962, p. 90-104.

5555 Smith, J.M.
"The Social Work Institute in Brazil." International social work (5:2), 1962, p. 8-12.

5556 Vergara, F. de Paula
"O Ideal da Coordenação no Campo das Instituições Privadas." Petrópolis, Vozes (57:6), June 1963, p. 414-421.

Central America

5557 Seminario Sobre Bienestar Social para Centroamérica y Panamá, Naciones Unidas, 1964
"Información." Montevideo, Boletín del Instituto Interamericano del Niño (38:150), September 1964, p. 322-330.

Chile

5558 Alexander, Robert J.
"Industrial Social Workers." Social service review (23:3), September 1949, p. 373-376.

5559 Alvarez Andrews, O.
"El Problema de la Familia en Chile." México, Revista mexicana de sociología (20:2), May-August 1958, p. 413-428.

5560 Duarte Gonzalez, A.
"La Protección al Niño de Edad Escolar." Santiago, Nueva era XIV, 1945, p. 171-173.

5561 Chile. Laws, statutes, etc.
"Decreto con Fuerza de Ley No. 120.- Fija Normas por las que se Regirá la Empresa del Estado Denominada Polla Chilena de Beneficiencia." Santiago, Diario oficial (83:24,606), March 29, 1960, p. 618-19.

5562 Galitzi, C.
"Los Problemas del Servicio Social en Chile." Santiago, Servicio social, July-December 1936, p. 115-122.

5563 Institut Français d'Opinion Publique
"Situation et Perspective du Chili en 1957." Paris, Sondages (19:4), 1957, p. 3-88.

5564 Ivovich, Esteban
"Orígenes y Desarrollo de la Beneficiencia Pública en Chile." Santiago, Revista asistencia social, March 1933, p. 95-153.

5565 Salinas, Juan
"Fecundidad y Actitudes Relativas a la Formación de la Familia en Santiago de Chile." Santiago, Boletín de la Universidad de Chile 15, September 1960, p. 44-49.

5566 Sepúlveda, Orlando
"Algunos Problemas de la Salud en el Area Metropolitana del Gran Santiago." Santiago, Boletín de la Universidad de Chile 15, September 1960, p. 41-43.

5567 Tabah, L.
"A Study of Fertility in Santiago, Chile." Marriage & Family living (25:1), February 1963, p. 20-26.

Colombia

5568 Colombia. Departamento Nacional de Trabajo
"La Obra Social del Gobierno." Bogotá, Boletín del Departamento Nacional del Trabajo, April-December 1910, p. 3-20.

5569 Quintana R., E.
"El Servicio Social en la Protección de Menores de Colombia." Bogotá, Revista de la Academia Colombiana de Jurisprudencia (20:158-161), p. 183-215.

5570 Rosenthal, C.S.
"Lower Class Family Organization on the Caribbean Coast of Colombia." Pacific sociological review (3:1), Spring 1960, p. 12-17.

Cuba

5571 Hernández, Amado
"La Lucha por las Leyes Complementarias." Havana, C.T.C, August 20, 1946, p. 24-25, 55.

5572 Portal, H. del
"Las Trabajadoras Sociales en Cuba." Havana, Bohemia (42:13), March 26, 1950, p. 58-60, 112.

Dominican Republic

5573 Alvarez Sánchez, V.
"Protección a la Infancia en la República Dominicana." Ciudad Trujillo, Boletín de salud pública (8:1), January-September 1952, p. 40-51.

5574 Dominican Republic. Laws, statutes, etc.
"Decreto No. 5516, que Crea e Integra la Comisión Nacional de Planificación, Coordinación y Control de Programas de Asistencia Social." Ciudad Trujillo, Gaceta oficial (81:8448), February 16, 1960, p. 13-14.

5575 Dominican Republic. Laws, statutes, etc.
"Reglamento No. 5940, Sobre las Atribuciones y Funcionamiento de la Comisión Nacional de Planificación, Coordinación y Control de Programas de Asistencia Social." Ciudad Trujillo, Gaceta oficial (81:8496), August 3, 1960, p. 18-23.

Ecuador

5576 Díaz, O. A.
"Análisis Espectral de la Sociedad Ecuatoriana." México, Cuadernos americanos 44, September-October 1960, p. 57-60.

5577 Díaz, O. A.
"Cambios Sociales de las Clases Dominantes del Ecuador." México, Revista mexicana de sociología (25:2), May-August 1963, p. 721-736.

5578 Ecuador. Laws, statutes, etc.
"Documento 1329. Expídese Reglamento para la Aplicación de la Ley de Asistencia Pública Codificada." Quito, Registro oficial, November 20, 1950, p. 557-558.

5579 Ecuador. Laws, statutes, etc.
"Reformas a la Ley Vigente de Asistencia Pública." Quito, Registro oficial, December 23, 1948, p. 741-743.

5580 Uzcátegui, Maruja de
"Apuntes para una Historia de la Protección y de los Servicios Sociales en el Ecuador." Quito, Filosofía, letras y ciencias (5:14), April/June 1952, p. 111-140.

Guatemala

5581 Guatemala. Laws, statutes, etc.
"Apruébanse los Estatutos de la 'Asociación Guatemalteca de Rehabilitación de Lisiados'; y Reconócesele su Personalidad Jurídica." Guatemala, El Guatemalteco (151:25), September 9, 1957, p. 393-394.

5582 Nash, Manning
"Multiple Society in Economic Development: Mexico and Guatemala." American anthropologist 59, October 1957, p. 825-833.

Haiti

5583 Nelson, J., ed.
"Contribution du Service Social Polyvalent à l'Amélioration des Conditions de Vie des Familles." Port-au-Prince, Revue du travail 12, May 1963, p. 76-80.

5584 Simpson, G.E.
"Haiti's Social Structure." American sociological review 6, October 1941, p. 640-649.

5585 Troniak, J.
"Services Sociaux en Haiti." Port-au-Prince, Revue du travail 11, May 1962, p. 99-103.

5586 Wingfield, R., & V.J. Parenton
"Class Structure and Class Conflict in Haitian Society." Social forces (43:3), March 1965, p. 338-347.

Honduras

5587 Bernaldo de Quirós, Juan
"Ley del Seguro Social de Honduras." México, Boletín del Instituto de Derecho Comparado de México (11:33), September/December 1958, p. 69-75.

5588 Fernández Bertrán, S.
"El Reto de la Juventud." Tegucigalpa, Honduras rotaria (año XXIII:230), June-July 1966, p. 10-11.

Mexico

5589 Acosta, F., & A. López Bermúdez
"La Ciudad, sus Areas Representativas y un Programa de Bienestar Social Urbano." México, Revista mexicana de sociología (20:1), January-February 1958, p. 241-259.

5590 Arrequín Velez, E.
"Aspectos Sociales del Problema del Servicio Médico al Pueblo Mexicano." México, Revista mexicana de sociología (13:2), May-August 1951, p. 245-255.

5591 Baz, Gustavo
"Fichas Bibliográficas Sobre la Asistencia Pública en México." México, Asistencia, July 1943, p. 1-86.

5592 Beegle, J.A., et al
"Demographic Characteristics of the United States-Mexican Border." Rural sociology (25:1), March 1960, p. 107-162.

5593 Bermúdez Castro, S.
"Algunas Consideraciones en Torno a los Problemas Sociales de México." México, Revista mexicana de sociología (23:3), 1961, p. 841-852.

5594 Borrajo Dacruz, E.
"La Organización Liberal de la Medicina y su Evolución." México, Seguridad social (10:9), May-June 1961, p. 5-25.

5595 Dotson, Floyd
"A Note on Participation in Voluntary Associations in a Mexican City." American sociological review (18:4), August 1953, p. 380-386.

5596 Huerta Maldonado, M.
"El Nivel de Vida en México." México, Revista mexicana de sociología (22:2), May-August 1960, p. 463-526.

5597 Ortega Mata, R.
"La Industrialización y el Nivel de Vida de la Población del País." México, Estudios sociológicos 1955, p. 341-356.

5598 Rorty, J.
"Hay Discriminación en México?" México, América indígena (20:3), July 1960, p. 217-228.

5599 Rubio García, L.
"El Desarrollo Demográfico de México y sus Exigencias Económico-Sociales." Madrid, Revista internacional de sociología (20:77), January-March 1962, p. 53-63.

5600 Sánchez Vargas, G.
"Factores de Desarrollo de la Política de Seguridad Social en México." México, Revista mexicana de sociología (23:3), 1961, p. 897-919.

5601 Yescas Peralta, P.
"Estructura Social de la Ciudad de Oaxaca." México, Revista mexicana de sociología (20:3), October-December 1958, p. 767-781.

Panama

5602 Panama. Laws, statutes, etc.
"Ley No. 92 (de 6 de Diciembre de 1960), por la Cual el Gobierno Nacional Instala Dispensarios de Asistencia Pública Gratuita en los Barrios de Marañón, Calidonia, Pueblo Nuevo, San Miguelito y San Francisco de la Caleta." Panamá, Gaceta oficial (57:14.300), December 30, 1960, p. 1.

5603 Velasco Ceballos, R.
"La Sociedad 'Amigos de los Niños.'" México, Asistencia 8, April 1948, p. 43-59.

Peru

5604 Bustamante Ruiz, C.
"La Rehabilitación en el Perú." Lima, Informaciones sociales (15:2), April-June 1960, p. 3-14.

5605 Cuzco. Archivo Histórico
"Monografías Sobre Problemas Sociales del Perú."

Cuzco, Revista del Archivo Histórico del Cuzco (10:10), 1959, p. 85-93.

Uruguay

5606 Achard, José P.
"La Colacación Familiar para Niños, Temporaria o Definitivamente Abandonados." Montevideo, Boletín del Instituto Interamericano de Protección a la Infancia, April 1942, p. 587-607.

5607 Rama, Carlos M.
"Clases Sociales en el Uruguay: Mito y Realidad." México, Cuadernos americanos (18:2), March-April 1959, p. 102-107.

5608 Uruguay. Laws, statutes, etc.
"Resolución. Se Aprueba la Reglamentación de la Ley 11.925 en lo Referente al Régimen Asistencial que Prestan los Establecimientos del Ministerio de Salud Pública." Montevideo, Diario oficial (217: 15777), October 23, 1959, p. 151A-154A.

Venezuela

5609 Alvarez, P.J.
"La Acción Privada en la Protección de la Infancia en Venezuela." Montevideo, Boletín del Instituto Interamericano del Niño (37:144), March 1963, p. 13-32.

5610 Loreto, Luis, & R. Levervanche Parpacen
"A Resumé of Social Legislation in Venezuela." Venezuela up-to-date (2:3), February 1951, p. 12-13, 20-21.

5611 Lucchesi, A.H. de
"Las Trabajadores Sociales en Venezuela." Caracas, Revista Shell (2:8), September 1953, p. 45-51.

5612 Quintero, Rodolfo
"Las Bases Económicas y Sociales de una Aristocracia Obrera en Venezuela." Caracas, Economía y ciencias sociales (5:2), April-June 1963, p. 90-100.

5613 Villalba Villalba, L.
"El Deber de los Venezolanos ante el Menor Abandonado." Maracaibo, Revista de la Universidad del Zulia (4:14), April-June 1961, p. 23-27.

West Indies and the Caribbean

5614 Ericksen, G.
"The West Indies Population Problem: Dimension for Action." American sociological review (28:4), August 1963, p. 671-673.

5615 Goode, William J.
"Illegitimacy in the Caribbean Social Structure." American sociological review (25:1), February 1960, p. 21-30.

5616 Harewood, J.
"Population Growth in Trinidad and Tobago in the Twentieth Century." Mona, Social & economic studies (12:1), March 1963, p. 1-26.

5617 Ibberson, D.
"Social Development in the British West Indies." Brussels, Civilisations (7:2), 1957, p. 173-186.

5618 Pellier, J.
"La Région des Caraïbes: Problèmes de Population." Paris, Etudes et conjoncture (13:10), October 1958, p. 973-984.

5619 Richardson, J.N.
"Social Security Problems with Special Reference to the British West Indies." Mona, Social & economic studies (5:2), June 1956, p. 139-169.

5620 Roberts, George W.
"The Caribbean Islands." Annals of the American Academy of Political & Social Science 316, March 1958, p. 127-136.

5621 Roberts, George W.
"Some Demographic Considerations of West Indian Federation." Mona, Social & economic studies (6:2), 1957, p. 262-285.

RURAL-URBAN MIGRATION

Books

General

5622 Abrams, Charles
Squatter settlements, the problem and the opportunity. Washington, Division of International Affairs, Dept. of Housing & Urban Development, 1966, 48p.

5623 Duncan, O.D., & Albert J. Reiss
Social characteristics of urban and rural communities, 1950. New York, Wiley, 1956, 421p.

5624 Hauser, Philip M., ed.
The population dilemma. Englewood Cliffs, Prentice-Hall, 1963, 187p.

5625 Levy, Yair
L'apport des organisations du travail au dialogue ville-campagne. Tel Aviv, Institut Afro-Asiatique d'Etudes Syndicales et Coopératives en Israel, 1965, 93p.

5626 Lowry, Ira S.
Migration and metropolitan growth: two analytical models. San Francisco, Chandler, 1966, 241p.

5627 Taylor, Miller L., & Arthur R. Jones
Rural life and urbanized society. New York, Oxford University Press, 1964, 493p.

5628 Southern California Planning Institute
The nature and control of urban dispersal. Ed. by Ernest A. Engelbert. Berkeley, Calif. Chapter of the American Institute of Planners, 1960, 130p.

5629 United Nations. Population Commission
World survey of urban and rural population growth; preliminary report by the Secretary-General;

report E/CN.9/187. New York, 1965, 24p.

5630 United Nations World Population Conference, Belgrade, August 30-September 10, 1965
Information bulletin no. 2; (E/CONF.41/INF.2). New York, United Nations, 1965, 12p.

Latin America

5631 Bendaña, René
Informe; Proyecto II-b-11. La migración a las grandes ciudades de América Latina y soluciones posibles al problema de vivienda creado por migrantes. Bogotá, Centro Interamericano de Vivienda, 1962, 125p.

5632 Boletín CELAP. Santiago, año I, no. 1, 1965-

5633 Frick Davie, Carlos
Cual reforma agraria? Reformas progresistas y regresivas. Montevideo, Barreiro & Ramos, 1964, 175p.

5634 Preston, David A.
Aspects of rural emigration in Latin America. Leeds, Dept. of Geography, University of Leeds, 1966, 51p.

5635 U.S. Bureau of the Census. Census Atlas Project
Census atlas maps of Latin America. Washington, U.S. Bureau of the Census in cooperation with the Foreign Operations Administration, 1955-

5636 Vellard, Jean
Civilisation des Andes; évolution des populations du haut plateau bolivien: géographie humaine. Paris, Gallimard, 1963, 270p.

Argentina

5637 García Martínez, L.
Urbanismo y éxodo rural. Buenos Aires, 1958, 88p.

5638 Germani, Gino
Assimilation of immigrants to urban areas. Buenos

Aires, Centro de Sociología Comparada, Instituto Torcuato di Tella, 1966, 57p.

5639 Miatello, Roberto A.
Migraciones de población de la Provincia de Catamarca . . . Córdoba, Dirección General de Publicidad, Universidad Nacional de Córdoba, 1960, 216p.

5640 Pearson, Ross N.
Recent changes in the distribution of population in Argentina. (In Loomis, R. A., ed. Papers of the Michigan Academy of Science, Arts, and Letters. Ann Arbor, University of Michigan Press, 1964, p. 367-381).

5641 Viale, Jorge O.
Exodos campesinos en la Argentina; principales causas, efectos y medios de contención. Santa Fé, Castellví, 1960, 169p.

Brazil

5642 Almeida, Vicente Unzer de
Migração rural-urbana . . . São Paulo, Directoria de Publicidade Agrícola, Secretaria da Agricultura, Indústria e Comercio do Estado de São Paulo, 1951, 147p.

5643 Barros, Souza
Exodo e fixação; sugestões para uma política de colonização e aldeamento no Nordeste. Rio de Janeiro, Ministério da Agricultura, 1953, 206p.

5644 Camârgo, José F. de
Exodo rural no Brasil; ensaio sôbre formas, causas e consequencias econômicas principais. São Paulo, Faculdade de Ciências Econômicas e Administrativas, Universidade de São Paulo, 1957, 233p.

5645 Harris, Marvin
Town and country in Brazil. New York, Columbia University Press, 1956, 302p.

5646 Leite, Mario
Paulistas e mineiros, plantadores de cidades. São Paulo, Ed. Art, 1961, 292p.

5647 Melo, Mário Lacerda de
As migrações para o Recife; estudo geográfico. 4v. Recife, Insto. Joaquim Nabuco de Pesquisas Sociais, Min. da Educação e Cultura, 1961.

5648 Pereira, J. dos Santos
A previsão do crescimento das populações urbanas. Salvador, Livraria Progresso Ed., 1958, 100p.

Chile

5649 Chile. Universidad. Instituto de Economía
La población del Gran Santiago; fuerza de trabajo, educación, ingresos, migración. Santiago, 1959, 173p.

5650 Chile. Universidad. Instituto de Economía
La migración interna en Chile en el período 1940-1952. Santiago, 1959, 74p.

5651 Chile. Universidad. Valparaíso. Escuela de Economía
Deseo de emigrar de Valparaíso y Viña del Mar. Valparaíso, 1961, 14p.

5652 Herrick, Bruce H.
Urban migration and economic development in Chile. Cambridge, M.I.T. Press, 1966, 126p.

Colombia

5653 Flinn, William L.
Rural to urban migration: a Colombian case. Madison, Land Tenure Center, University of Wisconsin, 1966, 42p.

Costa Rica

5654 Pan American Union. Section of Labor, Migration & Social Security
Migraciones internas en Costa Rica, by W. Jiménez Castro. Washington, 1956, 163p.

Mexico

5655 Stevens, Robert P.
Algunos aspectos de la migración interna y urbanizacion en México, 1950-1960. (In International Geographical Union. Proceedings of the First

Latin American Regional Conference, Mexico City, August 2-8, 1966. v. 1. Mexico, 1966, p. 65-72).

Peru

5656 Arca Parro, Alberto
El medio geográfico y la población del Perú. Lima, 1945, 60p.

5657 Dobyns, Henry F., & Mario C. Vasquez, eds.
Migración e integración en el Perú. Lima, Ed. Estudios Andinos, 1963, 196p.

Venezuela

5658 Montesino Samperio, José V.
Demografía venezolana: la población del área metropolitana de Caracas; factores de crecimiento y tendencia futura. Caracas, Ed. Grafos, 1956, 86p.

5659 Pan American Union. Section of Labor, Migration & Social Security
Causas y efectos del éxodo rural en Venezuela, por Aníbal Buitrón. Washington, Consejo Interamericano Económico y Social, Organización de los Estados Americanos, Unión Panamericana, 1955, 272p.

5660 Tellería, L.
La experiencia migratoria venezolana. Madrid, Journal, 1961, 159p.

5661 Vilá Camposada, Marco A.
De la vida rural a vida urbana en Venezuela. (In International Geographical Union. Proceedings of the First Latin American Regional Conference, Mexico City, August 2-8, 1966. v. 1. Mexico, 1966, p. 666-673).

West Indies and the Caribbean

5662 Augelli, John P.
The country-to-town movement in the West Indies. (In International Geographical Union. Proceedings of the eighth general Assembly and seventeenth international Congress, Washington, D.C., August 8-15, 1952. Washington, 1952, p. 719-723).

Periodical Articles

General

5663 Bachmura, T.
"Man-Land Equalization Through Migration." American economic review 49, December 1959, p. 1004-1017.

5664 Hamilton, C. H.
Population Pressure and Other Factors Affecting Net Rural-Urban Migration." Social forces 30, December 1951, p. 209-215.

5665 Hathaway, D. E.
"Migration from Agriculture: the Historical Record and Its Meaning." American economic review; papers and proceedings 50, May 1960, p. 379-391.

5666 Johnson, D. G.
"Policies to Improve the Labor Transfer Process." American economic review; papers and proceedings 50, May 1960, p. 403-418.

5667 Kempinksi, T.
"Rural Migration." Rural sociology (26:7), March 1961, p. 70-73.

5668 McDonald, S. L.
"Farm Outmigration as an Integrative Adjustment to Economic Growth." Social forces 34, December 1955, p. 119-128.

5669 Maddox, J. G.
"Private and Social Costs of the Movement of People out of Agriculture." American economic review; papers and proceedings 50, May 1960, p. 392-402, 413-418.

5670 Martinson, F. M.
"Personal Adjustment and Rural-Urban Migration." Rural sociology (20:2), June 1955, p. 102-110.

5671 Mendras, Henri
"Rural Exodus and Industrialization." Paris,

Diogenes, Summer 1960, p. 104-119.

5672 Mintz, Sidney W.
"The Folk-Urban Continuum and the Rural Proletarian Community." American journal of sociology 59, September 1953, p. 136-143.

5673 Rose, A., & L. Warshaw
"The Adjustment of Migrants to Cities." Social forces (36:1), October 1957, p. 72-76.

5674 Schwarzweller, H.K.
"Parental Family Ties and Social Integration of Rural to Urban Migrants." Journal of marriage & the family 26, November 1964, p. 410-416.

5675 Simon, W., & J.H. Gagnon
"The Decline and Fall of the Small Town." Trans-Action, April 1967, p. 42-51.

5676 "Urban Problems and Prospects." Law & contemporary problems 30, Winter 1965, p. 9-229.

5677 Wigny, P.
"Migratory Movements in Underdeveloped Countries in Course of Industrialization." International labour review 68, July 1953, p. 1-13.

Latin America

5678 "Aspectos Sociales de la Población en América Latina." Revista interamericana de ciencias sociales (2a. época, 3:3), 1965, p. 29-41.

5679 Baudin, L.
"Exode Rural et Communautés Agraires en Amérique Latine." Paris, Revue politique et parlementaire (144:429), August 10, 1930, p. 269-284.

5680 Borobio Navarro, L.
"Planeamiento de la Población y Exodo Campesino." Bogotá, Arco (2:6), January-February 1960, p. 16-24.

5681 "Education and Social Change in Latin America." Rural sociology (25:1), March 1960, p. 1-173.

5682 Elizaga, J.C.
"Internal Migration in Latin America." Paris, International social science journal (17:2), 1965, p. 213-231.

5683 Margulis, Mario
"Sociología de las Migraciones." Paris, Aportes 3, January 1967, p. 5-23.

5684 Ortiz, Y.
"Algunas Dificultades de Adaptación de las Poblaciones Rurales al Pasar al Medio Urbano en los Países Latinoamericanos, y Especialmente en Colombia." México, Revista mexicana de sociología (19:1), January-April 1957, p. 25-38.

5685 Poblete Toncoso, Moisés
"El Exodo Rural, sus Orígenes, sus Repercusiones." Rio de Janeiro, América latina, January-June 1962, p. 41-50.

5686 Rosario, C.
"La Emigración como Experiencia Vital." Río Piedras, La torre (IV:13), January-March 1956, p. 23-31.

Argentina

5687 "Argentina Checks Rural Migration to Cities." Pan American Union bulletin 72, August 1938, p. 492-493.

5688 Dagnino Pastore, L.
"Dinámica de la Población Argentina." Buenos Aires, Revista de ciencias económicas (49:3), January-March 1961, p. 41-50.

5689 "The Flight to the Cities." Buenos Aires, Review of the River Plate (131:3457), April 30, 1962, p. 141-143.

5690 Margulis, Mario
"Análisis de un Proceso Migratorio Rural-Urbano en Argentina." Paris, Aportes 3, January 1967, p. 73-126.

5691 Margulis, Mario
"Estudio de las Migraciones en su Lugar de Orígen." Rio de Janeiro, América latina (9:4), October-December 1966, p. 41-72.

5692 "Migración de la Joven del Interior a la Capital Federal." Buenos Aires, Inmigración (VIII:11), 1966, p. 969-983.

Bolivia

5693 Crist, Raymond E.
"Bolivians Trek Eastward: Background of and Motivations for the Present Eastward Migration of People in Bolivia." Américas 15, April 1963, p. 33-38.

Brazil

5694 Andrade, J. Lopes de
"Les Migrations dans le Nord-est du Brésil." Paris, Cahiers internationaux de sociologie 16, January-June 1954, p. 146-155.

5695 Barreira, Américo
"Exodo Rural e Reforma Agrária." Rio de Janeiro, Revista do serviço público, ano XVI (3:1), July 1953, p. 37-44.

5696 Beaujeu-Garnier, J.
"Les Migrations vers Salvador." Bordeaux, Cahiers d'outre-mer 59, 1962, p. 291-300.

5697 Camârgo, José F. de
"Alguns Aspectos da Imigração em São Paulo." São Paulo, Digesto econômico 89, 1952, p. 55-61; no. 91, p. 132-136; no. 93, p. 158-164.

5698 "Causas e Efeitos do Exodo Rural." Rio de Janeiro, Revista brasileira dos municípios (9:35-36), July-December 1956, p. 198-208.

5699 Confederação Nacional da Indústria
"Movimento Migratorio para São Paulo." Rio de Janeiro, Desenvolvimento e conjuntura 5, 1960, p. 101-110.

5700 "Exodo Rural na Bahia." Rio de Janeiro, Conjuntura econômica, June 1952, p. 41-47.

5701 Fernandes, R. Queiroz
"O Exodo Rural e o Desenvolvimento das Areas Urbanas no Brasil." Rio de Janeiro, Revista brasileira dos municípios (10:39-40), July-December 1957, p. 129-135.

5702 Ferrari, A. Trujillo
"Atitudes e Comportamento Político do Imigrante Nordestino em São Paulo." São Paulo, Sociologia (XXIV:3), September 1962, p. 159-180.

5703 Filgueiras, D. Melgação
"População Brasileira, uma Analise da Distribuição de seus Grupos Profissionais." Rio de Janeiro, Revista do serviço público (83:3), June 1959, p. 291-320.

5704 Hutchinson, Bertram
"Fertility, Social Mobility and Urban Migration in Brazil." London, Population studies (14:3), March 1961, p. 182-189.

5705 Hutchinson, Bertram
"The Migrant Population of Urban Brasil." Rio de Janeiro, América latina (VI:2), 1963, p. 41-71.

5706 Jordão, A.
"São Paulo e o Problema das Migrações Internas." São Paulo, Sociologia (25:3), September 1963, p. 209-212.

5707 Lúcio, Antônio
"Economia Municipal. Exodo Rural." Rio de Janeiro, Revista do serviço público ano XVI (4:2), November 1953, p. 115-118.

5708 "Migração para São Paulo." Rio de Janeiro, Conjuntura econômica (IX:8), August 1955, p. 73-77.

5709 Mortara, Giorgio
"Nota Sôbre o Cálculo das Migrações Interiores Baseada nos Censos." Rio de Janeiro, Revista

brasileira de estatística (16:61), January-March 1955, p. 9-13.

5710 "Respondem as Migrações Internas a Expansão da Economia Nacional?" Rio de Janeiro, Desenvolvimento e conjuntura (2:7), July 1958, p. 79-92.

5711 Rochefort, Michel
"L'Accroissement de la Population dans Quelques Capitales du Brésil." Toulouse, Caravelle 3, 1964, p. 63-68.

5712 Santos, Milton
"As Migrações para Salvador Através da Análise do Fichário Eleitoral." Bêlo Horizonte, Revista brasileira de estudos políticos 15, January-July 1963, p. 127-150.

5713 Siegel, Bernard J.
"The Role of Perception in Urban-Rural Change: a Brazilian Case Study." Economic development & social change (5:3), April 1957, p. 244-256.

5714 Silva, Alvares da
"A Tragedia dos Deslocados Nacionais: Sertanejos no Asfalto." Rio de Janeiro, O Cruzeiro (23:27), April 21, 1951, p. 14-22.

5715 Souza, R. Pinto
"Deslocamento da População Rural." São Paulo, Digesto econômico (VII:83), October 1951, p. 133-139.

5716 "Uma Arma Contra o Exodo Rural." Rio de Janeiro, Revista do serviço público, April 1953, p. 103-104.

5717 Vasconcelos, L. Leite de
"Migrações Internas no Brasil." Rio de Janeiro, Revista brasileira de economia (10:3), September 1956, p. 83-107.

5718 Zanotti, Isidoro
"Migração dos Campos para as Cidades." Rio de Janeiro, Revista de imigração e colonização, December 1946, p. 628-648.

British Honduras

5719 Ashton, G. T.
"Consecuencias de la Emigración de Zapateros Adolescentes a Belice." México, América indígena (27:2), April 1967, p. 301-316.

Chile

5720 Yañez, I.
"Características de la Migración Hacia el Gran Santiago." Santiago, Economía (18:62), 1st quarter, 1959, p. 79-80.

Colombia

5721 Borobio Navarro, L.
"Planeamiento de la Población y Exodo Campesino." Bogotá, Arco (Revista de las Areas Culturales Bolivarianas) (2:6), January-February 1960, p. 16-24.

Costa Rica

5722 Goldkind, Victor
"Sociocultural Contrasts in Rural and Urban Settlement Types in Costa Rica." Rural sociology (26:4), December 1961, p. 365-380.

Dominican Republic

5723 Ramos, Manuel V.
"La Ciudad y el Campo; Medidas para Contrarrestar la Emigración Rural." Ciudad Trujillo, Renovación (Organo del Instituto Trujilloniano) (7:26), July-September 1960, p. 52-63.

Ecuador

5724 Cisneros Cisneros, César
"Indian Migrations from the Andean Zone of Ecuador to the Lowlands." México, América indígena (19:3), July 1959, p. 225-231.

Guatemala

5725 Arias, J.
"Migración Interna en Guatemala." Estadística 76, 1962, p. 519-527.

Haiti

5726 Fouchard, L. M.
"Migrations et Problèmes de Main-Oeuvre." Port-

au-Prince, Revue du travail (6:6), May 1, 1956, p. 12-16.

Mexico

5727 Butterworth, D.S.
"A Study of the Urbanization Process Among Mixtec Migrants from Tilaltongo in Mexico City." México, América indígena (XXII:3), July 1962, p. 257-274.

5728 Lewis, Oscar
"Nuevas Observaciones Sobre el 'Continuum' con Especial Referencia a México." México, Ciencias políticas y sociales (IX:3), January-March 1963, p. 13-28.

5729 Lewis, Oscar
"Tepoztlán Restudied: A Critique of the Folk-Urban Conceptualization of Social Change." Rural sociology (18:2), June 1953, p. 121-137.

5730 Lewis, Oscar
"Urbanización sin Desorganización; las Familias Tepoztecas en la Ciudad de México." México, América indígena (17:3), July 1957, p. 231-246.

5731 Randall, L.
"La Migración Laboral y el Desarrollo Económico de México." México, Comercio exterior (13:6), June 1963, p. 409-413.

5732 Whetten, Nathan L., & R.G. Burnright
"Internal Migration in Mexico." Rural sociology (21:2), March 1956, p. 140-151.

5733 Winnie, William W.
"Estimates of Interstate Migration in Mexico, 1950-1960: Data and Methods." Caracas, Antropológica 14, June 1966, p. 38-60.

Paraguay

5734 Rivarola, D.M.
"Aspectos de la Migración Paraguaya." Paris, Aportes 3, January 1967, p. 25-73.

Peru

5735 Comité Peruano de Servicio Social
"La Desorganización Familiar y Social por Migración Rural-Urbana." Lima, Informaciones sociales (17:4), October-December 1962, p. 18-39.

5736 Mangin, William P.
"Mental Health and Migration to Cities: a Peruvian Case." Annals of the New York Academy of Sciences 84, December 1960, p. 911-917.

5737 Mangin, William P.
"The Role of Regional Associations in the Adaptations of Rural Population in Peru." Berlin, Sociologus (IX:1), 1959, p. 23-35.

5738 Martínez, H.
"La Migración Puno-Tambopata." Lima, Idea (12:47), April-June 1961, p. 1, 12.

5739 Zuzunaga Flores, Carlos
"Dos Tésis Sobre el Problema de Migración de Provincianos a la Capital." Lima, Servicio social (11:12), December 1953-54, p. 137-138.

Venezuela

5740 Hill, George W.
"The Adjustment of Rural Migrants in an Urban Venezuelan Community." Migration news, March-April 1963, p. 7-14; May-June 1963, p. 15-17.

SOCIAL CHANGE

Books

General

5741 Anderson, Nels, & K. Ishwaran
Urban sociology. New York, Asia Pub. House, 1965, 191p.

5742 Beshers, James M.
Urban social structures. New York, Free Press of Glencoe, 1962, 207p.

5743 Burgess, Ernest W., & Donald J. Bogue, eds.
Contributions to urban sociology. Chicago, University of Chicago Press, 1964, 673p.

5744 Center for the Study of Democratic Institutions
Occasional paper on the city, # 1- . Santa Barbara, 1964- .

5745 Chinitz, Benjamin, ed.
City and suburb; the economics of metropolitan growth. Englewood Cliffs, Prentice-Hall, 1965, 181p.

5746 Clower, R.W.
Growth without development. Evanston, Northwestern University Press, 1966, 266p.

5747 Cohen, Nathan
Should government take a direct hand in promoting social change? Report # MR-51. Los Angeles, Institute of Government & Public Affairs, University of California, 1965, 18p.

5748 Doxiadis, Constantinos A., & Truman B. Douglass
The new world of urban man. Philadelphia, United Church Press, 1965, 127p.

5749 Finkle, J. L., & R. W. Gable
Political development and social change. New York, Wiley, 1966, 599p.

5750 Geddes, Patrick
Cities in evolution . . . New & rev. ed. New York, Oxford University Press, 1950, 241p.

5751 Gutkind, Erwin A.
Revolution of environment. London, K. Paul, Trench, Trabner, 1946, 454p.

5752 Hagen, Everett E.
Cambio social y desarrollo económico. Conferencia pronunciada el 18 de junio de 1962 en el Salón de Actos del Consejo Federal de Inversiones. Buenos Aires, Instituto de Desarrollo Económico y Social, 1963? 23p.

5753 Hirsch, Werner Z., ed.
Urban life and form. New York, Holt, Rinehart & Winston, 1963, 248p.

5754 Interactions of man and his environment; proceedings of a conference held at Northwestern University, January 1965. Ed. by Burgess H. Jennings & John E. Murphy. New York, Plenum Press, 1966, 229p.

5755 International bibliography of sociology. Paris, Unesco, 1957-

5756 Kabir, A. K. M.
Social change and nation building in the developing areas; a selected, annotated bibliography. Dacca, National Institute of Public Administration, 1965, 79p.

5757 Klaasen, L. H.
Area economic and social redevelopment. London, H. M. S. O., 1965, 113p.

5758 Mann, Peter H.
An approach to urban sociology. New York, Humanities Press, 1965, 232p.

5759 Mendes, Richard H. P.
Bibliography on community organization for citizens participation in voluntary democratic associations. Washington, G.P.O., 1965, 98p.

5760 Moore, Wilbert E.
Social change. Englewood Cliffs, Prentice-Hall, 1963, 120p.

5761 Morris, R., et al
Feasible planning for social change. New York, Columbia University Press, 1966, 167p.

5762 Niehoff, A. H.
A casebook of social change. Chicago, Aldine, 1966, 312p.

5763 National Opinion Research Center
NORC social research, 1941-1964; an inventory of studies and publications in social research. Ed. & annotated by John M. Allswang & Patrick Bova. Chicago, 1964, 80p.

5764 Olson, G.
Distance and human interaction: a review and bibliography. Philadelphia, Regional Science Research Institute, 1965, 112p.

5765 Ritter, Paul
Edurecreation: education for creation, growth and change . . . New York, Pergamon Press, 1966, 380p.

5766 Rogers, E.M., & L. Smith
Bibliography on the diffusion of innovations. East Lansing, Dept. of Communication, Michigan State University, 1965, 101p.

5767 Seminar on Social Aspects of Urban Development, Washington, D.C. 1963
Seminar on social aspects of urban development; report. Washington, 1964? 47p.

5768 Sociological abstracts. v. 1, #1, New York, 1952-

5769 Tamiment Institute
The future metropolis. Ed. by Lloyd Rodwin. New York, Braziller, 1961, 253p.

5770 Thompson, Wilbur R.
A preface to urban economics. Baltimore, published for Resources for the Future by Johns Hopkins Press, 1965, 413p.

5771 Tietze, F.T., & J.E. McKeown
The changing metropolis. Boston, Houghton, Mifflin, 1964, 210p.

5772 Toby, Jackson, ed.
Contemporary society: social process and social structure in urban industrial societies. New York, Wiley, 1964, 598p.

5773 United Nations. Bureau of Social Affairs. Population Division, & Sidney Goldstein
Urbanization and economic and social change. (In Inter-Regional Seminar on Development Policies and Planning in Relation to Urbanization, University of Pittsburgh, Pittsburgh, Pa., 24 October-7 November, 1966. Working paper #10, agenda item #2; 66-47166. New York, United Nations, 1966, 50p.)

5774 Unesco
Some characteristics of personality related to upward social mobility in an unstable urban environment; E/CN.12/URB/8; UNESCO/SS/URB/LA/8. New York, 1958, 27p.

5775 United Nations. Secretariat
Social aspects of urban development; report. Document A/AC.35/L.335. New York, 1961, 150p.

5776 Vereker, C., et al
Urban redevelopment and social change. Liverpool, Liverpool University Press, 1961, 150p.

Latin America

5777 Adams, Richard N., et al
Social change in Latin America today; its implica-

tions for United States policy. New York, Harper, 1960, 353p.

5778 American Academy of Political & Social Science
A crowding hemisphere: population change in the Americas, ed. by Kingsley Davis. Philadelphia, 1958, 206p.

5779 Calderón Alvarado, Luis
Poder retentivo del area local urbana en las relaciones sociales. Fribourg, Feres, 1963, 257p.

5780 Camârgo, José F. de
Demografia econômica; variáveis demográficas do desenvolvimento econômico. Bahia, Universidade da Bahia (Publicações IX-6), 1959, 127p.

5781 Caplow, Theodore
The modern Latin American city. (In Tax, Sol, ed. *Acculturation in the Americas.* Chicago, University of Chicago Press, 1952, p. 255-260).

5782 Fals Borda, Orlando
La transformación de la América Latina y sus implicaciones sociales y económicas. Bogotá, Facultad de Sociología, Universidad Nacional de Colombia, 1961, 21p.

5783 Geisert, Harold L.
Population problems in Mexico and Central America. Washington, Population Research Project, George Washington University, 1959, 48p.

5784 Germani, Gino
Política y sociedad en una época de transición; de la sociedad tradicional a la sociedad de masas. Buenos Aires, Ed. Paidos, 1963, 266p.

5785 Heath, Dwight B., & Richard N. Adams, eds.
Contemporary cultures and societies of Latin America; a reader in the social anthropology of Middle and South America and the Caribbean. New York, Random House, 1965, 586p.

5786 Houtart, François
Social structures in Latin America: genesis and evolution (CICOP working paper C-1-65). Davenport, Latin America Bureau, National Catholic Welfare Conference, 1965, 24p.

5787 Inter-American Development Bank
Reformas institucionales y desarrollo social en América Latina. Washington, 1963, 355p.

5788 Johnson, John J., ed.
Continuity and change in Latin America. Stanford, Stanford University Press, 1964, 282p.

5789 Kahl, Joseph A.
Social stratification and values in metropoli and provinces; Brazil and Mexico. Buenos Aires, Centro de Sociología Comparada, Instituto Torcuato di Tella, 1965, 89p.

5790 Kusch, Rodolfo
La ciudad mestiza. Buenos Aires, 1952, 29p.

5791 Latin American Seminar on Population, Rio de Janeiro, Brazil, December 5-16, 1955
Papers. New York, United Nations, 1958, 148p.

5792 Leonard, Olen E., & Charles P. Loomis, eds.
Readings in Latin American social organization and institutions. East Lansing, Michigan State College, 1953, 320p.

5793 Municipalismo. New Orleans, Interamerican Municipal Organization, 1970- (quarterly).

5794 Pan American Union. General Secretariat
Estudio social de América Latina, 1963-1964. Washington, 1964, 265p.

5795 Pan American Union. Division of Labor & Social Affairs
Informe final, seminarios regionales de asuntos sociales: vivienda y urbanismo. Resumen de las discusiones de Mesa Redonda de Vivienda y Urbanismo, Quito, Ecuador, mayo de 1950, San Salvador,

El Salvador, noviembre de 1950; Porto Alegre, Brazil, mayo de 1951. Washington, 1952, 140p.

5796 Revista latinoamericana de sociología. Buenos Aires, (I:1), 1965-

5797 Rosenbluth, G.
La participación de las poblaciones marginales en el crecimiento. Santiago, Division of Social Affairs, UN Economic Commission for Latin America, 1965, 117p.

5798 Rottenberg, Simon
Notes on the economics of urbanization in Latin America. New York, United Nations (Document #E/CN.12/URB6), 1958, 27p.

5799 Schaller, Lyle E.
Community organization: conflict and reconciliation. Nashville, Abingdon Press, 1966, 176p.

5800 Silva Solar, Julio, & Jacques Choncol
El desarrollo de la nueva sociedad en América Latina. Santiago, Ed. Universitaria, 1965, 160p.

5801 Silvert, Kalman H.
The conflict society: reaction and revolution in Latin America. New Orleans, Hauser, 1961, 280p.

5802 Smith, Thomas L.
Current social trends and problems in Latin America. Gainesville, University of Florida Press, 1957, 44p.

5803 Smith, Thomas L.
Latin American population studies. Gainesville, University of Florida Press, 1961, 83p.

5804 United Nations. Economic Commission for Latin America
El desarrollo social de América Latina en la postguerra. Buenos Aires, Solar-Hachette, 1963, 188p.

5805 Vekemans, Roger
Family, political modernization and cultural mutation in Latin America; a preliminary study. Santiago,

DESAL, 1966, 16p.

5806 Vekemans, Roger
The social crisis in Latin America (CICOP working paper C-2-65). Davenport, Latin America Bureau, National Catholic Welfare Conference, 1965, 13p.

5807 Whiteford, Andrew H.
Two cities of Latin America. New York, Doubleday, 1964, 266p.

5808 Willems, Emilio
El cambio cultural dirigido. Bogotá, Impr. Nacional, 1964, 82p.

Argentina

5809 Fillol, Tomás B.
Social factors in economic development: the Argentine case. Cambridge, M.I.T. Press, 1961, 118p.

5810 Germani, Gino
Estructura social de la Argentina. Buenos Aires, Ed. Raigal, 1955, 278p.

5811 Germani, Gino
Inquiry into the social effects of urbanization in a working-class sector of Greater Buenos Aires. (In Hauser, Philip M., ed. Urbanization in Latin America. Paris, Unesco, 1962, p. 206-233).

Bolivia

5812 Leonard, Olen E.
Santa Cruz; estudio económico social de una región. Tr. from English by Douglas Moore. La Paz, Ministerio de Agricultura, Ganadería y Colonización, 1948, 103p.

Brazil

5813 Audrin, José M.
Os sertanejos que en conheci. Rio de Janeiro, Olympio, 1963, 117p.

5814 Bazzanella, Waldemiro
Estratificação e mobilidade social no Brasil, fontes bibliográficas. Rio de Janeiro, Centro Brasileiro de Pesquisas Educacionais, 1956, 116p.

5815 Brazil. Comissão Censitaria Nacional
Censo experimental de Brasília; população, habitação, 17 de maio de 1959. Rio de Janeiro, 1959, 109p.

5816 Fernandes, Gonçalves
Mobilidade, caráter e região . . . Recife, Ministério da Educação e Cultura, Instituto Joaquim Nabuco de Pesquisas Sociais, 1959, 79p.

5817 Freyre, Gilberto
Sobrados e mucambos: decadência do patriarcado rural e desenvolvimento do urbano. 3d ed. 2v. Rio de Janeiro, Livraria Olympio, 1961.

5818 Ianni, Octavio
Industrialização e desenvolvimento social no Brasil. Rio de Janeiro, Ed. Civilização Brasileira, 1963, 270p.

5819 Monbeig, Pierre
La croissance de la ville de São Paulo. Grenoble, Institut et Revue de Géographie Alpine, 1953, 90p.

5820 Morse, Richard M.
From community to metropolis: a biography of São Paulo, Brazil. Gainesville, University of Florida Press, 1958, 341p.

5821 Prado, Caio
Evolução política do Brasil e outros estudos. 2d ed. São Paulo, Ed. Brasilense, 1947, 203p.

Chile

5822 Mattelart, Armand, & Manuel A. Garretón
Integración nacional y marginalidad: ensayo de regionalización social de Chile. Santiago, Ed. del Pacífico, 1965, 199p.

5823 Ruiz, Antonio, et al
Estratificación y movilidad sociales en Chile. Rio de Janeiro, Gráf. Ed. Livro, 1961, 157p.

Colombia

5824 Colombia. Republic
Desarrollo económico y social de Colombia. Washington, Pan American Union, 1962, 146p.

5825 Hagen, Everett E.
El cambio social en Colombia. Bogotá, Eds. Tercer Mundo, 1963, 108p.

5826 Havens, A. E., & Michel Romieux
Barrancabermeja: conflictos sociales en torno a un centro petrolero. Bogotá, Eds. Tercer Mundo, 1966, 186p.

5827 Movimiento Aliado de la Clase Media Económica de Colombia
Manifesto. Bogotá, 1963, 6p.

Costa Rica

5828 Loomis, Charles P., et al
Turrialba; social systems and the introduction of change. Glencoe, Free Press, 1953, 288p.

5829 Nunley, Robert E.
The distribution of population in Costa Rica. Washington, National Research Council, 1960, 71p.

5830 Santoro, Gustavo
Algunos aspectos de la vida urbana en San José, tres problemas apremiantes. San José, Instituto Centroamericano de Investigaciones Sociales y Económicas, 1962, 62p.

Dominican Republic

5831 Mejía Ricart, N. A.
Las clases sociales en Santo Domingo. Ciudad Trujillo, Ed. Librería Dominicana, 1953, 57p.

Ecuador

5832 Beals, Ralph L.
Community in transition: Nayón, Ecuador. Los Angeles, Latin American Center, University of California, 1965, 240p.

5833 Saunders, John V. D.
La población del Ecuador, un análisis del censo de 1950. Quito, Casa de la Cultura Ecuatoriana, 1959, 118p.

Haiti

5834 Bouchereau, M. G.
Haiti et ses femmes; une étude d'evolution culturelle. Port-au-Prince, Impr. Les Presses Libres, 1957, 253p.

Honduras

5835 Honduras. Instituto Nacional de la Vivienda
Belén; estudio socio-económico. Tegucigalpa, 1959, 22p.

5836 Méndez Guillén, N.
La situación de hecho en Honduras. Paris, Unesco, 1962, 15p.

Mexico

5837 Encinas, L.
Progreso y problemas de México. México, 1954, 284p.

5838 Guadalajara, México. Ayuntamiento
Evolución de Guadalajara. Guadalajara, 1955, unpaged.

5839 Sotomayor, Arturo
Los bárbaros sobre la Ciudad de México; ensayo. México, Costa-Amic, 1960, 98p.

5840 Valencia, Enrique
La Merced. Estudio ecológico y social de una zona de la Ciudad de México. México, Instituto Nacional de Antropología e Historia, 1965, 383p.

Panama

5841 Jaén, Ricardo
Problemas socio-económicos de Panamá. Panamá, Librería Avance, 196- , 100p.

5842 Porras, Demetrio A.
Problemas vitales panameños. Panamá, Ministerio de Educación, Depto. de Bellas Artes y Publicaciones, 1960, 127p.

5843 Westerman, George W.
A study of the socio-economic conflicts on the Panama Canal Zone. Panamá, Liga Cívica Nacional, 1948, 26 plus 29p.

Peru
5844 Bourricaud, François
Changements á Puno, étude de sociologie andine. Paris, Institut des Hautes Etudes de l'Amérique Latine, Université de Paris, 1962, 239p.

Uruguay
5845 Grompone, A. M.
Las clases medias en el Uruguay. Montevideo, Eds. del Río de la Plata, 1963, 43p.

5846 Solari, Aldo E.
Estudios sobre la sociedad uruguaya. v.1. Montevideo, Arca, 1964-

Venezuela
5847 Acedo Mendoza, Clemy de
Actitudes ante el cambio social. Caracas, Comisión Nacional del Cuatricentenario de la Fundación de Caracas, 1966, 87p.

5848 Quintero, Rodolfo
Antropología de las ciudades latinoamericanas. Caracas, 1964, 258p.

5849 Watson, Lawrence C.
Guajiro personality and urbanization. Los Angeles, Latin American Center, University of California, 1968, 160p.

West Indies and the Caribbean
5850 Smith, Michael G.
Stratification in Grenada. Berkeley, University of California Press, 1965, 271p.

Periodical Articles

General
5851 Adams, Richard N.
"Sudden Development; Growth Patterns." Américas 17, August 1965, p. 3-6.

5852 Azevedo, F. de
"La Educación Como Agente del Cambio Social." Caracas, Política 24, January-March 1963, p. 22-40.

5853 Camârgo, J.A.J. de
"Cristianismo, Conservação e Mudança Social." Montevideo, Cuadernos latinoamericanos de economía humana (3:8), 1960, p. 118-136.

5854 Davis, Kingsley, & H.H. Golden
"Urbanization and the Development of Pre-Industrial Areas." Economic development & culture change (3:1), October 1954, p. 6-26.

5855 Gross, F.
"Los Valores y el Cambio Social." México, Revista mexicana de sociología (25:1), January-April 1963, p. 289-307.

5856 Guzzardi, W.
"The Crucial Middle Class." Fortune 65, February 1962, p. 98-100.

5857 Hagen, Everett E.
"Como Se Inicia o Desenvolvimento Econômico; uma Teoria Sôbre Mudança Social." São Paulo, Sociologia (26:3), September 1964, p. 321-335.

5858 Hoselitz, Bert F.
"Some Potentialities and Limitations of Research on Social Implications of Technical Change." Brussels, Civilisations (6:2), 1956, p. 157-174.

5859 Houtart, François
"Silent Revolution." Commonweal 62, July 22, 1955, p. 391-394.

5860 Kahl, Joseph A.
"Some Social Concomitants of Industrialization and Urbanization." Human organization (18:2), Summer 1959, p. 53-74.

5861 "Mesa Redonda Sobre Choques de Cultura y Cambio Social, México D. F., 1961. Relatório e Recomendações." Rio de Janeiro, Arquivos brasileiros de psicotécnica (14:2), April-June 1962, p. 57-67.

5862 Miglioli, J.
"Sociología Oficial Versus Desenvolvimento Econômico." Rio de Janeiro, Estudos sociais (3:8), July 1960, p. 419-435.

5863 Mitscherlich, A.
"Gran Ciudad y Neurosis." Bogotá, Arco (9:50), June 1964, p. 199-227.

5864 Moore, Wilbert E.
"El Cambio Social y los Estudios Comparados." Rio de Janeiro, América latina (6:4), October-December 1963, p. 3-12.

5865 Oliveira Tôrres, J.C. da
"Da Falsa e da Verdadeira Reforma Política y Social." Petrôpolis, Vozes (58:4), April 1964, p. 268-278.

5866 Pastore, J.
"As Funcões da Educação numa Sociedade em Mudança." São Paulo, Sociologia (26:1), March 1964, p. 21-31.

5867 Pérez, J. L.
"Movimientos Sociales." Caracs, Sociología (1:1), April 1961, p. 6-26.

5868 Perpiña Rodríguez, A.
"Efectos Sociales del Desarrollo Económico." Madrid, Fomento social (15:57), January-March 1960, p. 9-16.

5869 Silvert, Kalman H.
"El Desarrollo Social y la Idea de Nación en el Mundo Actual." Buenos Aires, Revista de la Universidad de Buenos Aires (7:2), April-June 1962, p. 213-244.

5870 Sjoberg, G.
"Familial Organization in the Preindustrial City." Marriage and family living 18, February 1956, p. 30-36.

5871 Willeke, E.
"Zur Entstehung und Problematik der Grossstadt." Dortmund, Soziale welt (6:1), 1955, p. 1-17.

5872 Yepes del Pozo, J.
"La Patología Social del Desarrollo." Quito, Ensayos 3, March 1963, p. 14-22.

Latin America

5873 Alba, Víctor (pseud.)
"La Nueva Clase Media Latinoamericana." México, Revista mexicana de sociología (22:3), September-December 1960, p. 781-789.

5874 Anderson, H.H., & G.L. Anderson
"Social Values of Teachers in Rio de Janeiro, Mexico City and Los Angeles County, California . . . ." Journal of social psychology (58:2), 1962, p. 207-226.

5875 Benko, F.
"Traditionalisme et Développement: les Villes Latino-Americaines." Le Havre, Psychologie des peuples (20:1), 1st quarter 1965, p. 8-27.

5876 Bonilla, Frank
"Comentarios Sobre la Estructura de Clase en América Latina." Medellín, Ciencias sociales (7:40), December 1956, p. 263-276.

5877 Compton, G.C.
"Prescription for Social Ills: OAS Advisory Committee Looks at Latin America's Problems." Américas 13, February 1961, p. 3-6.

5878 Diez Alvaro, M.
"Los Doctores y la Revolución en la América Latina." México, Revista mexicana de sociología (22:3), September-December 1960, p. 747-779.

5879 Echánove Trujillo, Carlos A.
"Latin American Sociology?" Américas 14, November 1962, p. 16-19.

5880 Galindez, Jesús de
"Revolución Socio-Económica en Iberoamérica." México, Cuadernos americanos (14:2), March-April 1954, p. 7-18.

5881 Germani, Gino
"Social Stratification and Social Mobility in Four Latin American Cities: a Note on the Research Design." Rio de Janeiro, América Latina (6:3), July-September 1963, p. 91-93.

5882 Gibaja, R.
"Aspectos Sociales y Culturales de la Modernización." Buenos Aires, Revista latinoamericana de sociología (I:1), March 1965, p. 111-114.

5883 Giedion, S.
"Fundación de Ciudades y Metamórfosis de la Estructura Urbana en la Crisis del Presente." Santiago, Boletín de la Universidad de Chile 46, April 1964, p. 4-9.

5884 Hawthorn, H.B., & A.E. Hawthorn
"Stratification in a Latin American City." Social forces 27, 1948, p. 23.

5885 Hopenhayn, B.
"La Organización de una Nueva Sociedad como Requísito para un Proceso de Desarrollo con Estabilidad en América Latina." Buenos Aires, Desarrollo económico (3:3), October-December 1963, p. 453-470.

5886 Koner, M.
"Neighbors Who Are Neither Rich nor Poor." Fortune 65, February 1962, p. 88-97.

5887 Kriesberg, Louis
"Entrepreneurs in Latin America and the Role of Cultural and Situational Processes." Paris, International social science journal (XV:4), 1963, p. 581-594.

5888 Kunkel, J.H.
"Fatôres Psicológicos na Análise do Desenvolvimento Econômico." São Paulo, Sociología (26:3),

September 1964, p. 337-356.

5889 Labbens, J.
"Las Universidades Latinoamericanas y la Movilidad Social." Paris, Aportes 2, October 1966, p. 68-79.

5890 "Latin America in Transition." Commonweal 66, September 13, 1957, p. 697-699.

5891 Lodge, George C.
"Revolution in Latin America." Foreign affairs 44, January 1966, p. 173-197.

5892 Marsal, José F.
"Algunas Características de la Literatura Sobre Cambio Social." Buenos Aires, Revista latinoamericana de sociología (II:2), July 1966, p. 237-253.

5893 Mayone Stycos, J.
"Opinions of Latin American Intellectuals on Population Problems and Birth Control." Annals of the American Academy of Political & Social Science 306, July 1965, p. 11-26.

5894 Nash, Manning
"Social Prerequisites to Economic Growth in Latin America and Southeast Asia." Economic development and cultural change (12:3), April 1964, p. 225-242.

5895 Nelson, E.
"A Revolution in Economic Policy: an Hypothesis of Social Dynamics in Latin America." Southwestern social science quarterly (34:3), December 1953, p. 3-16.

5896 Quintero, Rodolfo
"Dinâmica de los Pueblos Latinoamericanos." Havana, Casa de las Américas (2:13-14), July-October 1962, p. 104-107.

5897 Rieser, C.
"Latin America: the Pains of Growth." Fortune 57, February 1958, p. 112-119.

5898 Romero, J. L.
"El Cambio Social en Latinoamérica." México, Revista de la Universidad de México (17:7), March 1963, p. 15-18.

5899 Segundo, J. L.
"Transformación Latinoamericana y Conducta Moral." Montevideo, Cuadernos latinoamericanos de economía humana (3:9), 1961, p. 252-267.

5900 Silvert, Kalman H.
"Les Valeurs Nationales, le Développement, les Leaders et Leurs Troupes . . ." Paris, Revue internationale des sciences sociales (15:4), 1963, p. 594-605.

5901 Stokes, William S.
"What Hope for Latin America?" National review 17, July 13, 1965, p. 591-594.

5902 Touraine, A.
"Mobilité Sociale Rapports de Classe et Nationalisme en Amérique Latine." Paris, Sociologie du travail (7:1), January-March 1965, p. 71-82.

5903 Trujillo Ferrari, A.
"Incidencias Teóricas en el Estudio de las Clases Sociales en Latinoamérica." México, Revista mexicana de sociología (22:2), May-August 1960, p. 543-558.

Argentina

5904 Agulla, Juan C.
"Aspectos Sociales del Proceso de Industrialización en una Comunidad Urbana." México, Revista mexicana de sociología (25:2), May-August 1963, p. 743-772.

5905 "Buenos Aires y el País en Cifras." Buenos Aires, Hacienda, economía y previsión (3:10), January/March 1952, p. 59-66.

5906 Cuevillas, F.
"La Familia Argentina ante el Cambio Social." Rio de Janeiro, América latina (7:3), July-September 1964, p. 73-86.

5907 Cullere, J.
"Desarrollo y Perspectivas de la Clase Media en la Argentina." Córdoba, Revista de la Universidad de Córdoba, May-August 1960, p. 457-484.

5908 Germani, Gino
"La Movilidad Social en la Argentina." Buenos Aires, Revista de derecho y ciencias sociales 3-4, Summer 1956-57, p. 40-51.

5909 Imaz, José L. de
"Movilidad Social en Argentina." México, Revista mexicana de sociología (20:3), September-December 1958, p. 743-750.

5910 Miller, D.C.
"Estudio del Liderazgo de Córdoba. Estudio del Liderazgo de la Comunidad I.K.A." Córdoba, Cuadernos de los Institutos (17:76), 1964, p. 29-49.

5911 Schultz Cazenueva de Mantovani, F.
"La Mujer en los Ultimos 30 años." Buenos Aires, Sur 267, November-December 1960, p. 20-29.

Brazil

5912 Asimow, Morris
"Project Brazil: a Case Study in Micro-Planning." International development review (6:2), June 1964, p. 26-29.

5913 Cardoso, Fernando H.
"Os Brancos e a Ascensão Social dos Negroes em Pôrto Alegre." São Paulo, Anhembi (39:117), August 1960, p. 583-596.

5914 Cardoso, Fernando H.
"Proletariado e Mudança Social em São Paulo." São Paulo, Sociologia (22:1), March 1960, p. 3-11.

5915 Castro, Josué de
"A Revolução Social Brasileira." Rio de Janeiro, Revista brasileira de ciências sociais (2:2), July 1962, p. 197-215.

5916 Costa Pinto, Luiz Aguiar de
"As Clases Sociais no Brasil; Padrão Tradicional

e Mudanças Recentes." Bêlo Horizonte, Revista brasileira de ciências sociais (3:1), March 1963, p. 217-247.

5917 Díaz, G.
"Quelques Problèmes de la Lutte des Classes au Brésil." Paris, Nouvelle revue internationale (7: 1), January 1964, p. 45-54.

5918 Fernandes, Florestan
"Reflexões Sôbre a Mudança Social no Brasil." Bêlo Horizonte, Revista brasileira de estudos políticos 15, January-July 1963, p. 31-71.

5919 Hammond, H. R.
"Social Mobility and Politics in Brazil." Race (4: 2), May 1963, p. 3-13.

5920 Hutchinson, Bertram
"Class Self-Assessment in a Rio de Janeiro Population." Rio de Janeiro, América latina (6:1), January-March 1963, p. 53-62.

5921 Hutchinson, Bertram
"Urban Social Mobility Rates in Brazil Related to Migration and Changing Occupational Structure." Rio de Janeiro, América latina (6:3), July-September 1963, p. 47-61.

5922 Kahl, Joseph A.
"Urbanização e Mudanças Ocupacionais no Brasil." Rio de Janeiro, América latina (5:4), October-December 1962, p. 21-30.

5923 Lenhard, R.
"Hierarquias Sociais Urbanas." São Paulo, Sociología (25:3), September 1963, p. 253-270.

5924 Morse, Richard M.
"São Paulo in the Twentieth Century: Social and Economic Aspects." Inter-American economic affairs (8:1), Summer 1954, p. 3-60.

5925 Mussolini, G.
"Aspectos da Cultura e da Vida Social no Litoral

Brasileiro." São Paulo, Revista da antropologia (1:2), December 1953, p. 81-98.

5926 "Negroes in the Brazilian Social Structure." Rio de Janeiro, Conjuntura econômica internacional (4:4), April 1957, p. 45-49.

5927 Rochefort, Michel
"Como a Prevença de uma Grande Cidade Diversifica as Aglomerações de uma Região." Rio de Janeiro, Revista brasileira dos municípios (14: 53-54), January-June 1961, p. 7-11.

5928 Soares, G.A. Dillon
"Brasil, la Política de un Desarrollo Desigual." México, Ciencias políticas y sociales (9:32), April-June 1963, p. 159-196.

Chile

5929 Hamuy, Eduardo
"Problemas de Educación Elemental y Desarrollo Económico." Santiago, Economía (18:60-61), 3d-4th quarters 1958, p. 31-41.

5930 Herrick, Bruce H.
"Efectos Económicos de los Cambios Demográficos en Chile, 1940-1960." Santiago, Economía (22:83-84), 1964, p. 47-71.

Colombia

5931 Abrisqueta, Francisco de
"El Desarrollo de Bogotá, 1938-1944." Bogotá, Registro municipal, October 31, 1945, p. 527-529.

5932 Albano, M.J.R.
"Siloe Helps Itself: the Story of a Colombian Neighborhood." Américas (10:5), May 1958, p. 20-22.

5933 Blasier, Cole
"Power and Social Change in Colombia: the Cauca Valley." Journal of inter-American studies (8:3), July 1966, p. 386-410.

5934 Dumont, J.J.
"Le Conflit 'Societal' et le Processus de Changement Politique et Economique. Le Cas de 'Violencia' en Colombie." Brussels, Civilisations (XVI:3), 1966, p. 296-306.

5935 Guerra, Blas
"Esta Es Bogotá, D.E., la del Millón de Almas." Bogotá, Cromos (82:2025), February 27, 1956, p. 12-15, 41, 59-60.

5936 Neissa Rosas, Carlos
"Las Clases Medias en Colombia." Bogotá, Revista de la Universidad Libre (4a. época:18), December-January 1964-65, p. 19-32.

5937 Tellez, H.
"La Mobilidad de los Cuadros Sociales en Colombia." Caracas, Política (3:29), December 1963, p. 59-66.

5938 Whiteford, Andrew H.
"Notas Sobre la Clase Media en Popayán, Colombia." Ciencias sociales (4:19), February 1953, p. 2-10.

Costa Rica

5939 Goldkind, Victor
"Socio-Cultural Contrasts in Rural and Urban Settlement Types in Costa Rica." Rural sociology (26:4), December 1961, p. 365-380.

5940 Santoro, Gustavo
"La Estratificación y la Movilidad Social en la Ciudad de San José." San Salvador, Revista salvadoreña de ciencias sociales (1:1), January-March 1965, p. 9-88.

Cuba

5941 Tannenbaum, Frank
"Castro and Social Change." Political science quarterly 77, June 1962, p. 178-204.

Ecuador

5942 Brachfeld, O.
"Significado y Papel de la Clase Media." Quito,

Anales de la Universidad Central del Ecuador (85: 340), 1956, p. 168-172.

5943 Chavez, F.
"Balance Sumario de los Elementos Culturales." Quito, Anales (83:343), 1959, p. 243-267.

5944 Díaz, A.
"Cambios Sociales de las Clases Dominantes del Ecuador." México, Revista mexicana de sociología (25:2), May-August 1963, p. 721-736.

El Salvador

5945 Larde y Larín, J.
"La Población de El Salvador: su Orígen y Distribución Geográfica." San Salvador, Anales del Museo David Guzmán (4:12), March 1953, p. 73-92.

5946 Tricart, Jean
"Un Exemplaire du Désiquilibre Villes-Campagnes dans une Economie en Voie du Développement: Le Salvador." Paris, Développement et civilisations 11, July-September, 1962, p. 80-102.

Guatemala

5947 Arriola, Jorge L.
"En Torno a la Integración Social de Guatemala." Guatemala, Guatemala indígena (1:1), January-March 1961, p. 7-30.

5948 Bogardus, E.S.
"Social Trends in Guatemala." Sociology & social research, June 1954, p. 323-328.

5949 Reina, Rubén E.
"The Urban World View of a Tropical Forest Community in the Absence of a City, Petén, Guatemala." Human organization (XXIII:4), Winter 1964, p. 265-277.

Guyana

5950 Farley, R.
"The Rise of the Peasantry in British Guiana." Mona, Social & economic studies (2:4), March 1954, p. 87-103.

Haiti

5951 Aristide, Achille
"Los Problemas Demográficos de Haiti." México, América indígena (16:1), January 1956, p. 35-39.

Honduras

5952 Mejía Nieto, A.
"Ha Cambiado Tegucigalpa?" Tegucigalpa, Honduras rotaria (año XXIII:230), June-July 1966, p. 11-14.

Jamaica

5953 Kerr, M.
"Some Areas in Transition: Jamaica." Phylon (14:4), 1953, p. 410-412.

Mexico

5954 Borja, A.
"Alvarado, Veracruz, Programa de Desarrollo Urbano." México, Arquitectura México (22:86), June 1964, p. 79-90.

5955 Burnright, R.G., et al
"Differential Rural-Urban Fertility in Mexico." American sociological review (21:1), February 1956, p. 3-8.

5956 Canchola, A.
"Relaciones Sociales y Económicas de la Ciudad y el Campo en México." México, Revista mexicana de sociología (19:1), January-April 1957, p. 15-23.

5957 Caplow, Theodore
"Tendencias en la Organización Corporada." México, Revista mexicana de sociología (25:2), May-August 1963, p. 695-703.

5958 Durán Ochoa, J.
"El Crecimiento de la Población Mexicana." México, Trimestre económico (22:3), July-September 1955, p. 331-349.

5959 Hayner, Norman S.
"Differential Social Change in a Mexican Town."

Social forces 26, 1948, p. 383.

5960 Hayner, Norman S.
"New Patterns in Old Mexico: Differential Changes in the Social Institutions of Village, Town and Metropolis." Research studies of the State College of Washington (16:1), March 1948, p. 44-50.

5961 Lewis, Oscar
"La Cultura de Vecindad en la Ciudad de México." México, Ciencias políticas y sociales (5:17), July-September 1959, p. 349-364.

5962 Logo, G.
"Notas Sobre Población y Desarrollo Económico." México, Investigación económica (23:90), 1963, p. 319-358.

5963 Mendieta y Núñez, Lucio
"La Clase Media en México." México, Revista mexicana de sociología (17:2), May-December 1955, p. 517-553.

5964 Pozas Arciniega, Ricardo
"Los Niveles del Desarrollo y la Dinámica en la Comunidad." México, Ciencias políticas y sociales (9:34), October-December 1963, p. 539-553.

5965 Yescas Peralta, P.
"Estructura Social de la Ciudad de Oaxaca." México, Revista mexicana de sociología (20:3), September-December 1958, p. 767-780.

Nicaragua

5966 Ycaza Tigerino, J.
"Las Clases Sociales en Nicaragua." Ciencias sociales (6:31), February 1955, p. 2-11.

Peru

5967 Arias Larreta, Abraham
"Evolución Social del Peruano." Havana, América (39:3), June 1953, p. 22-28.

5968 Bourricaud, François, & Olivier Dollfus
"La Population Péruvienne en 1961." Bordeaux,

Cahiers d'outre-mer (16:62), April-June 1963, p. 184-200.

5969 "Community and Regional Development: the Joint Cornell-Peru Experiment." Human organization 21, Summer 1962, p. 107-124.

5970 Matos Mar, José
"Consideraciones Sobre la Situación Social del Perú." Rio de Janeiro, América latina (7:1), January-March 1964, p. 57-70.

5971 Palacios, L.M.
"Encuesta Sobre Condiciones de Vida de las Familias de Trabajadores en Arequipa." Lima, Revista de la Facultad de Ciencias Económicas y Comerciales 61, January-December 1960, p. 154-164.

5972 Palacios, L.M.
"Gastos y Consumo de Artículos Alimenticios por Familias Obreras de Lima y Callao." Lima, Revista de la Facultad de Ciencias Económicas y Comerciales 62, January-June 1961, p. 87-92.

Trinidad

5973 Crowley, D.J.
"Plural and Differential Acculturation in Trinidad." American anthropologist 59, October 1957, p. 817-824.

Uruguay

5974 Abdala, C.E.
"El Desarrollo Económico y Social en la República del Uruguay." México, Seguridad social (12:23), September-October 1963, p. 7-20.

5975 Solari, Aldo E..
"Las Clases Sociales y su Gravitación en la Estructura Política y Social del Uruguay." México, Revista mexicana de sociología (18:2), May-August 1956, p. 257-266.

5976 Solari, Aldo E.
"El 'Envejecimiento' de la Población en el Uruguay y sus Consecuencias." Rio de Janeiro, Boletim

do Centro Latino-Americano de Pesquisas em Ciências Sociais (4:1), February 1961, p. 55-64.

Venezuela

5977 Ahumada, Jorge C.
"Hipótesis para el Diagnóstico de una Situación de Cambio Social: el Caso de Venezuela." Rio de Janeiro, América latina (7:2), April-June 1964, p. 3-14.

5978 Elmer, M.C.
"The Growth of a Middle Class in Venezuela." Social science (38:3), June 1963, p. 145-147.

5979 Friedmann, John R.
"El Crecimiento Económico y la Estructura Urbana de Venezuela." Caracas, Revista de económia latinoamericana (2:6), April-June 1962, p. 115-204.

5980 "Informe que la Comisión Encargada de Realizar la 'Encuesta Sobre las Condiciones de Vida en Caracas' Somete al Ciudadano Ministro de Hacienda." Caracas, Revista de hacienda no. extraordinario, July 24, 1946, p. 5-182.

West Indies and the Caribbean

5981 Ibberson, D.
"Social Development in the British West Indies." Brussels, Civilisations (7:2), 1957, p. 173-186.

SOCIAL SECURITY

Books

General

5982 Asch, Sidney H.
Social security and related welfare programs. 3d ed. Dobbs Ferry, Oceana Publications, 1959, 96p.

5983 Bursztyn Dobry, Rosa
Estudio comparativo de las legislaciones de seguridad social de Chile y Perú. Santiago, Ed. Universitaria, 1962, 114p.

5984 Costoya Coderch, Enrique
Estudio comparativo de las legislaciones sociales de Chile y Paraguay. Santiago, 1953, 96p.

5985 Gajardo Céspedes, Rina
Estudio comparativo de las legislaciones de seguridad social de Chile y Uruguay. Santiago, 1948, 79p.

5986 International Social Security Association
Developments and trends in social security, 1961-1963. Geneva, 1965, 625p.

5987 Richardson, J. H.
Economic and financial aspects of social security. Toronto, University of Toronto Press, 1960, 271p.

Latin America

5988 Barroso Leite, Celso, & Luiz Paranhos Velloso
Previdência social. Rio de Janeiro, Zahar Eds., 1963, 265p.

5989 Figueroa Rojas, Manuel
Aportación iberoamericana al progreso de la seguridad social. Madrid? 1956, 115p.

5990 Inter-American Conference on Social Security. 4th, Mexico, 1952
Memoria de labores. México, 1952, 407p.

5991 International Bank for Reconstruction & Development
Aspectos financieros del seguro social en América Latina. México, Centro de Estudios Monetarios Latinoamericanos, 1963, 158p.

5992 Moles, Ricardo R.
Historia de la previsión social en Hispanoamérica. Buenos Aires, Eds. Depalma, 1962, 153p.

5993 Organización Iberoamericana de Seguridad Social
Curso de cooperación técnica sobre racionalización y mecanización de servicios administrativos de la seguridad social. Madrid, Secretaría General, 1956, 549p.

5994 Pan American Union. Dept. of Social Affairs
Síntesis de la seguridad social americana. Washington, 1961-

5995 Permanent Inter-American Committee on Social Security
The Inter-American Committee on Social Security. 2v. Geneva, International Labor Office, 1950-51.

5996 Permanent Inter-American Committee on Social Security
Manual de instituciones de seguridad social en América Latina. México, Secretaría General del Comité Permanente Interamericano de Seguridad Social, 1957, 222p.

5997 Seguridad social. No. 1- , Bogotá, September-November 1948-

5998 Solminihac Andrade, Jorge de
Estudio comparativo de las legislaciones de seguridad social de Chile y Bolivia. Santiago, 1952, 88p.

Argentina

5999 Antokoletz, Daniel
Derecho del trabajo y previsión social; derecho

argentino y comparado, con referencias especiales a las repúblicas americanas. 2d ed. rev. . . . 2v. Buenos Aires, Kraft, 1953.

6000 Argentina. Congreso. Biblioteca
Seguro social. Buenos Aires, 1966, 56p.

6001 Deveali, Mario L.
Curso de derecho sindical y de la previsión social. Buenos Aires, de Zavalia, 1952, 363p.

6002 Fernández Pastorino, A.
Constitucionalismo social; el derecho del trabajo y el derecho de la seguridad social en la reforma constitucional de 1957. Buenos Aires, Ed. Ergon, 1964, 199p.

6003 Goñi Moreno, José M.
Derecho de la previsión social. 2v. Buenos Aires, EDIAR, 1956.

6004 Goñi Moreno, José M.
Previsión social. Buenos Aires, Abeledo-Perrot, 1959, 77p.

6005 Legaz y Lacambra, Luis
Conferencias . . . Eva Perón, Universidad Nacional, Facultad de Ciencias Jurídicas y Sociales, 1952, 102p.

6006 Martínez, Enrique S.
Inflación y previsión social. Buenos Aires, Librería Perlado, 1960, 109p.

6007 Podetti, Humberto A.
Aspectos del recurso judicial en material de previsión social: conferencia. Buenos Aires, Abeledo-Perrot, 1963, 67p.

6008 Posse, Melchor A.
Los desarraigados. Buenos Aires, Ed. Desarrollo, 1964, 141p.

6009 Remorino, Jerónimo
La nueva legislación social argentina. 2d ed.

Buenos Aires, Kraft, 1955, 428p.

6010 Revista de trabajo y previsión. año 1, no. 1- , Buenos Aires, 1953-

Bolivia

6011 Bolivia. Laws, statutes, etc.
Disposiciones legales sobre seguridad social. Comp. por Ramiro Bedregal I. La Paz, Ed. Casegural, 1964, 303p.

6012 Bolivia. Laws, statutes, etc.
Legislación social boliviana, por Gustavo Salas Linares, & Dulfredo Zambrana R. Potosí, 1946, 428p.

6013 Pérez Platón, R.
La seguridad social en Bolivia. (In Estudios dedicados al Profesor García Oviedo, v. 2. Seville, Universidad de Sevilla, 1954, p. 327-357).

6014 Potosí, Bolivia. Universidad Autónoma "Tomás Frías." Facultad de Economía y Finanzas
El seguro social en Bolivia, ponencias . . . Potosí, Impr. Universitaria, 1950, 224p.

Brazil

6015 Athar, J. A.
Curso de previdência social; programa da cátedra de direito do trabalho de Universidade do Brasil. Rio de Janeiro, Dist. Record Editôra, 1961, 177p.

6016 Alvarenga, Tasso de Vasconcelos
O trabalho na previdência social. 1st ed. Rio de Janeiro, Ed. Nacional de Direito, 1957, 286p.

6017 Borges, Durval R. Sarmento
Seguro social no Brasil . . . Rio de Janeiro, Olympio, 1948, 230p.

6018 Brasil. Instituto de Aposentadoria e Pensões dos Industriários
O seguro social, a indústria brasileira, o Instituto dos Industriários; relatório-estudo do engenheiro Alim Pedro. Rio de Janeiro, 1950, 477p.

6019 Fundação Getulio Vargas
A previdência social no Brasil e no estrangeiro. Rio de Janeiro, 1950, 329p.

6020 Instituto de Direito Social
Seguro social. São Paulo, 1948, 126p.

6021 Martins, M. Magalhães
Seguros social para concursos do I.A.P.I. Rio de Janeiro, ESCOL, 1953? 69p.

6022 São Paulo, Brazil (State) Instituto de Previdência
Relatório. São Paulo. Annual.

6023 Soares, Maria Nogueira
Alguns aspectos do Serviço Social de Menores, 1951-1955; relatório-estudo . . . São Paulo, 1955, 83p.

6024 Susskind, A. L.
Previdência social brasileira. Rio de Janeiro, Freitas Bartos, 1955, 399p.

Chile

6025 Gaete Berrios, Alfredo, & Inés Santana Davis
Seguridad social; estudio teórico-práctico de la nueva legislación chilena y comparada. Buenos Aires, Depalma, 1957, 205p.

6026 Klein & Saks. Economic & Financial Mission to Chile
El sistema de previsión chileno; informe de la misión Klein & Saks. Santiago, 1958, 157p.

6027 Poblete Troncoso, Moisés
El derecho de trabajo y la seguridad social en Chile; sus realizaciones panorama americano, 25 años de legislación social. Santiago, Ed. Jurídica, 1949, 206p.

6028 Ruiz Troncoso, Jorge
La seguridad social y su repercusión en la economía nacional. Santiago, Ed. Universitaria, 1959, 120p.

6029 Solar Pero, Luis I. del
Estudio comparativo de las legislaciones de seguridad social de Chile y Costa Rica. Santiago, 1952, 82p.

6030 Walker Linares, Francisco
Esquema del derecho del trabajo y de la seguridad social en Chile. Santiago, Ed. Jurídica de Chile, 1965, 186p.

6031 Walker Linares, Francisco
Panorama del derecho social chileno. Santiago, Ed. Jurídica de Chile, 1950, 188p.

Colombia

6032 Foreign Tax Law Association
Colombian social security tax service. Ed. by Donald O. Wallace. Hempstead, 1952-

6033 Herrnstadt, Ernesto
Tratado del derecho social colombiano. Comentarios. Codigos . . . 4th ed. rev. & enl. Bogotá, Ed. Kelly, 1951, 777p.

6034 Instituto Colombiano de Seguros Sociales
Antecedentes y documentos de los seguros sociales en Colombia. Compiló Jesús María Rengifo. 2v. Bogotá, Antares, 1952.

6035 Salguero Basto, Gonzálo
Legislación social del ramo de guerra. Bogotá, Talleres de Ed. Retina, 1964, 96p.

Costa Rica

6036 Costa Rica. Caja Costarricense de Seguro Social
Memoria. San José. Annual.

6037 Costa Rica. Laws, statutes, etc.
Leyes y reglamentos de seguros. San José, 1946, 109p.

6038 Trejos Escalante, Fernando
Libertad y seguridad; libertad económico y seguridad social. San José, Asociación Nacional de Fomento Económico, 1963, 197p.

Cuba

6039 Cuba. Consejo Nacional de Economía
El problema de los seguros sociales en Cuba . . . 2v. Havana, 1955.

6040 Cuba. Laws, statutes, etc.
Legislación social. Havana, Divulgación Fiscal, 1952-

6041 Grupo Cubano de Investigaciones Económicas
Social security in Cuba. Coral Gables, Cuban Economic Research Project, University of Miami, 1964, 290p.

6042 International Labor Office
Informe al Gobierno de Cuba sobre la Ley de seguridad social de 1963. Geneva, 1963, 51p.

6043 International Labor Office
Informe al Gobierno de Cuba sobre seguridad social. Geneva, 1960, 75p.

Dominican Republic

6044 Cordero, Armando
La filosofía de la seguridad social y su aplicación en la República Dominicana. Ciudad Trujillo, Ed. Montalvo, 1953, 103p.

6045 Dominican Republic. Laws, statutes, etc.
Previsión social en la República Dominicana, por Orestes Herrera Bornia. Ciudad Trujillo, Ed. Arte y Cine, 1952, 595p.

6046 Dominican Republic. Laws, statutes, etc.
Tareas de previsión social en la República Dominicana. Ciudad Trujillo, Impr. Arte y Cine, 1951, 274p.

6047 Dominican Republic. Secretaría de Previsión Social
Memoria. Ciudad Trujillo. Annual.

6048 Sobá, José G.
Algunos programas sociales y construcción de viviendas durante los últimos 30 años en la República Dominicana. Ciudad Trujillo, 1961, 50p.

Ecuador

6049 Campaña Barrera, Aníbal
El seguro social en el Ecuador. Quito, Impr. de la Caja del Seguro, 1954, 192p.

6050 Ecuador. Laws, statutes, etc.
Legislación social ecuatoriana. Quito, Ministerio de Previsión Social y Trabajo, 1948-

6051 Jaramillo, Carlos A.
Regímenes de seguros sociales en España y posibilidades del seguro social ecuatoriano. Madrid, Oficina Iberoamericana de Seguridad Social, 1953, 141p.

6052 Salamanca Jorguera, Raúl
Estudio comparativo de las legislaciones de seguridad social de Chile y Ecuador. La Serena, 1948, 75p.

El Salvador

6053 Frank, Beryl
Proyecto de programa de seguridad social para El Salvador . . . San Salvador, Impr. Nacional, 1951, 51p.

6054 Instituto Salvadoreño del Seguro Social
Estadísticas. San Salvador. Annual.

6055 Salvador. Laws, statutes, etc.
Recopilación de leyes y reglamentos sobre trabajo y seguridad social. San Salvador, Impr. Nacional, 1954, 465p.

Guatemala

6056 Guatemala. Consejo de Bienestar Social
Introducción al estudio de la asistencia gerontológica en Guatemala. Guatemala, Ed. del Ministerio de Educación Pública, 1959, 98p.

6057 Guillen Villalobos, José
Estructuración de una seguridad social guatemalteca. Guatemala, 1952, 38p.

6058 Instituto Guatemalteco de Seguridad Social
Bases de la seguridad social en Guatemala. Guatemala, 1947, 386p.

6059 Instituto Guatemalteco de Seguridad Social
Desarrollo y proyecciones del régimen guatemalteco de seguridad social . . . Guatemala, 1956, 76p.

6060 Suslow, L. A.
Social security in Guatemala; a case study in bureaucracy and social welfare planning. Ann Arbor, University Microfilms, 1955, 359p.

Haiti

6061 Falk, Isidore S.
Rapport sur le régime d'assurance sociale d'Haiti. Port-au-Prince, 1951, 176p.

6062 Haiti (Republic) Commission Chargée de l'Organisation de l'Institut d'Assurances Sociales
Guide pratique pour les assurances sociales . . . Port-au-Prince, Impr. de l'Etat, 1951, 30p.

6063 Haiti (Republic) Institut d'Assurances Sociales
Rapport. Port-au-Prince. Annual.

Honduras

6064 Villeda Morales, Ramón
Discurso, con motivo de la inauguración del seguro social. Tegucigalpa, 1962, 11p.

Mexico

6065 Alvarez, Oscar C.
La cuestión social en México. México, Publicaciones Mundiales, 1950, 479p.

6066 Astudillo Sandoval, Homero
Inconstitucionalidad de los capitales constitutivos en la Ley mexicana del seguro social. México, 1963, 101p.

6067 García Cruz, Miguel
La seguridad social: bases, evolución, importancia económica, social y política. México, 1955, 231p.

6068 Garduño Váldez, Carmen
El trabajo social en el Centro Materno Infantil "General Maximino Avila Camacho." México, 1953, 33p.

6069 González Díaz Lombardo, Francisco X.
Cursillo de seguridad social mexicana. Monterrey, Universidad de Nuevo León, 1959, 205p.

6070 Instituto Mexicano de Seguro Social
Anuario estadístico. México, 1947-

6071 Instituto Mexicano del Seguro Social
Boletín de información. México, 1951-

6072 Mexico. Laws, statutes, etc.
Ley federal del trabajo reformada y adicionada; con bibliografía, comentarios y jurisprudencia. Ley del seguro social reformada . . . 38th ed. México, Ed. Porrúa, 1963, 463p.

6073 Mexico. Laws, statutes, etc.
Ley de seguro social y disposiciones complementarias. 3d ed. México, Ed. Porrúa, 1963, 427p.

6074 Mexico. Laws, statutes, etc.
Ley de trabajo de la República Mexicana; Ley del seguro social; Estatuto de los trabajadores al servicio de los poderes de la Unión . . . México, Impr. Didot, 1957, 397p.

6075 Molina Trujillo, Mario
La creación del Instituto Nacional de Seguridad y Servicios Sociales para los Campesinos y Trabajadores del Campo. México, 1964, 122p.

6076 Porte-Petit Candaudap, Celestino
El Instituto de la Juventud Mexicana. México, Ed. Ruta, 1950, 77p.

6077 Sandozeky Acosta, Graciela G.
El seguro social en México y la necesidad de desarrollar un programa de salud mental como complemento a sus prestaciones. México, 1960, 128p.

6078 Venegas Castañeda, Humberto
La seguridad social en México. México, 1949, 97p.

6079 Tena Morelos, Adolfo
Ideas generales sobre el seguro social. México, 1950, 94p.

Nicaragua

6080 International Labor Office
Informe financiero y actuarial sobre los seguros sociales de Nicaragua. Geneva, 1960, 86p.

6081 Roiz Granera, Noel
El seguro social. León, 1952, 44p.

Panama
6082 Castillo, Rosa
Diversos aspectos del seguro social en España y en Panamá. Madrid, Oficina Iberoamericana de Seguridad Social, 1953, 74p.

6083 Panama (Republic) Ministerio de Trabajo, Previsión Social y Salud Pública
Boletín de previsión social. Año 1, # 1- , Panamá, 1946- .

Paraguay
6084 Paraguay. Instituto de Previsión Social
Instituto de Previsión Social; 19 años, 1943-1962. Asunción, 1962, 20p.

6085 Pecci, Jorge M.
Los seguros sociales de enfermedad y accidentes de trabajo y la seguridad social en el Paraguay. Madrid, Oficina Iberoamericana de Seguridad Social, Instituto de Cultura Hispánica, 1954, 132p.

Peru
6086 Ferrero Rebagliati, Raúl
El derecho de trabajo en el Perú. . . Lima, 1955, 96p.

6087 Ferrero, Rómulo A.
Estudio económico de la legislación social peruana para obreros. Lima, Centro de Estudios Económicos y Sociales, 1960, 110p.

6088 Ferrerro, Rómulo A., & A.J. Altmeyer
Estudio económico de la legislación social peruana y sugerencias para su mejoramiento. Lima, 1957, 176p.

6089 Peru. Laws, statutes, etc.
Codificación de la legislación del trabajo y de previsión social del Perú, por Jorge Ramírez Otarola. Lima, 1955, 760p.

6090 Rozas Navarro, Guillermo
Seguridad social. Lima, 1947, 152p.

Uruguay

6091 Durán Cano, Ricardo
Seguro social integral; contribución a su estudio. Montevideo, 1957, 24p.

6092 International Labor Office
Informe al Gobierno de la República Oriental del Uruguay sobre seguridad social. Geneva, 1964, 71p.

Venezuela

6093 Foreign Tax Law Association
Venezuelan income tax service. Tr. & ed. by David S. Stern & Donald O. Wallace. Hempstead, 1951?-

6094 Gutiérrez Alfaro, Tito
Documentos inéditos para la historia de la introducción de seguro social obligatorio en Venezuela. Caracas, 1960, 33p.

6095 Instituto Venezolano de los Seguros Sociales
Anales. Caracas, 1955, 170p.

6096 Sánchez Piña, G.
Los seguros sociales y su aplicación en Venezuela; estudio jurídico y social. Caracas, Tip. Vargas, 1957, 310p.

6097 Venezuela. Ministerio del Trabajo
Realidades de la seguridad social. 2v. Caracas, 1955.

West Indies and the Caribbean

6098 International Labor Office
Report to the Government of Trinidad and Tobago on a proposed social security scheme. Geneva, 1960, 153p.

Periodical Articles

General

6099 Rohrlich, G. F.
"Social Security in World-Wide Perspective." Social Service review 38, Dec. 1964, p. 443-454.

6100 Rys, V.
"The Sociology of Social Security." International Social Security Association bulletin 17, January-February 1964, p. 3-34.

6101 Schewe, D.
"Old-Age and Survivors' Protection for the Self-Employed: an International Comparison." International labour review 91, January 1965, p. 1-13.

6102 "Social Security Programs of Foreign Countries." Social security bulletin 27, September 1964, p. 16-26.

Latin America

6103 Andrade Ramos, F. de
"Orientações para o Desenvolvimento do Seguro Social nas Américas." Rio de Janeiro, Revista do serviço público (3:1), July 1951, p. 22-24.

6104 Arroba, Gonzalo
"La Seguridad Social en el Marco del Desarrollo Económico y Social del Continente." México, Seguridad social (12:20-21), March-June 1963, p. 72-99.

6105 Brazil. Ministério do Trabalho, Indústria, e Comércio
"Panorama da Seguridade Social Americana em 1951." Rio de Janeiro, Boletim do Ministério do Trabalho, Indústria e Comércio (1:4), October/December 1951, p. 65-74.

6106 Campaña Barrera, Aníbal
"El Niño en el Seguro Social Americano." Ciudad Trujillo, Seguridad social (8:45), September/October 1955, p. 37-51.

6107 Carvallo Hederra, S.
"Aspectos Generales de la Previsión Social en

Latino América." Lima, Informaciones sociales (8:1), January/March 1953, p. 27-34.

6108 Conferencia Interamericana de Seguridad Social. 7th, Asunción, Paraguay, 1964.
"Informe." México, Seguridad social (13:28), July-August 1964, p. 3-100.

6109 "Desarrollos de la Seguridad Social en los Diversos Países." Bogotá, Seguridad social 13/16, January/December 1952, p. 209-219.

6110 Farman, C.H.
"Social Security in Latin America, 1945-47." Social security bulletin, September 1947, p. 18-26, 48.

6111 International Labour Office
"Gradual Extension of Social Insurance Schemes in Latin American Countries." Geneva, International labour review (78:3), September 1958, p. 257-283.

6112 Martí Bufill, Carlos
"Crónica Hispanoamericana de Seguridad Social." Ciudad Trujillo, Seguridad social (3:15), September/October 1950, p. 35-44.

6113 Martí Bufill, Carlos
"Estilo y Profundidad de la Seguridad Social Iberoamericana." Madrid, Cuadernos hispanoamericanos 27, March 1952, p. 374-384.

6114 Mijares Ulloa, L.
"Consideraciones Sobre el Seguro de Enfermedad en América Latina." México, Seguridad social (4:16), September-October 1955, p. 7-24.

6115 Moles, Ricardo R.
"Importancia de las Investigaciones Sociales para la Orientación y el Desarrollo de la Seguridad Social Americana." La Paz, Protección social (15:177/178), November/December 1952, p. 9-18.

6116 Schwarz, E.
"Algunas Notas y Observaciones Sobre la Seguridad Social en América Latina." México, Seguridad so-

cial (5:21), May/June 1956, p. 57-60.

6117 Stafforini, E.R.
"Orientaciones para el Desarrollo de la Seguridad Social en las Américas." Madrid, Revista española de seguridad social (5:4/5), April/May 1951, p. 571-597.

6118 Tixier, A.
"The Development of Social Insurance in Argentina, Brazil, Chile and Uruguay." London, International labour review, November 1935, p. 610-636; December 1935, p. 751-791.

6119 Venezuela. Ministerio del Trabajo
"La Habitación y la Seguridad Social." Caracas, Revista del trabajo (5:18), January/March 1955, p. 19-116.

6120 Viado, M. de
"Panorama General de la Seguridad Social Americana." Madrid, Revista Española de Seguridad Social (5:4/5), April/May 1951, p. 539-569.

6121 Villa, L.E. de la
"Sistemas para la Cobertura del Riesgo de Paro Forzoso." Madrid, Revista iberoamericana de seguros sociales (10:6), November-December 1961, p. 1407-1439.

6122 Zapata-Ballón, E.
"L'Assurance-Maladie en Amérique Latine." Geneva, Bulletin de l'Association Internationale de Sécurité Social 4, April 1956, p. 135-165.

Argentina

6123 Argentine Republic. Laws, statutes, etc.
"New Social Insurance Scheme for Domestic Workers in Argentina." Geneva, Industry and labour (17:1), January 1, 1957, p. 35.

6124 Arnaudo, A.A.
"La Inversión de las Reservas de las Instituciones Jubilatorias en Argentina Durante el Período 1946-52." Córdoba, Revista de economía (8:14), January 1956-December 1957, p. 31-58.

6125 Bernardo, L. H.
"Previsión Social Argentina." Rosario, Estudios (1:3), September/October 1951, p. 130-149.

6126 Botero Restrepo, J.
"El Seguro Social en Chile y la Argentina." Medellín, Universidad de Antioquia (22:88), September/October 1948, p. 663-672.

6127 Campaño, A. R.
"La Seguridad Social y el Servicio del Empleo." Buenos Aires, Revista del Ministerio de Trabajo y Previsión (2:15), July 1958, p. 20-26.

6128 Deveali, H. L.
"El Sistema de Previsión Argentino. Su Evolución y Perspectivas." Buenos Aires, Derecho del trabajo (14:4), April 1954, p. 193-203.

6129 Flores, Anselmo M.
"Las Instituciones de Previsión Social de Buenos Aires." Santiago, Previsión social, January-February 1938, p. 405-429.

6130 Goñi Moreno, José M.
"Antecedentes Históricos de la Previsión Social Argentina." Buenos Aires, Revista de la Facultad de Derecho y Ciencias Sociales (8:36), November/December 1953, p. 1449-1465.

6131 Goñi Moreno, José M.
"El Nuevo Ordenamiento Administrativo de la Previsión Social Argentina." Geneva, Seguridad social, May 1954, p. 7-14.

6132 Goñi Moreno, José M.
"La Reforma del Régimen Jubilatorio en Argentina." México, Seguridad social (1:1), January-February 1958, p. 47-64.

6133 International Social Security Association
"Reorganization of Social Welfare Services. Argentina." Geneva, Bulletin of the International Social Security Association (7:4), April 1954, p. 133-135.

6134 Perón, M.E. Duarte de
"Reflexiones Sobre la III Conferencia Interamericana de Seguridad Social." Buenos Aires, Hechos e ideas (21:84), March 1951, p. 29-42.

6135 Rolandi, R.D.
"El Jubileo Jubilatorio y el Seguro Social." Buenos Aires, Revista de ciencias económicas, March 1946, p. 177-187.

Bolivia

6136 Andrade, V.
"El Problema de los Seguros Sociales en Bolivia." La Paz, Protección social, September-October 1942, p. 7-15.

6137 Bolivia. Consejo Universitario
"La Universidad y el Régimen de Seguridad Social Vigente." La Paz, Revista de derecho (10:31/32), January/June 1958, p. 115-122.

6138 Céspedes, M.A.
"El Seguro Social en Bolivia." Santiago, Previsión social, October/December 1946, p. 395-406.

6139 International Labour Office
"A General Social Insurance Scheme in Bolivia." Geneva, Industrial & Labour Information, November 16, 1936, p. 272.

6140 International Labour Office
"The Social Insurance Movement in Bolivia." Montreal, International labour review, June 1943, p. 788-789.

6141 International Social Security Association
"Extension of Sickness Insurance to Public Employees. Bolivia." Geneva, Bulletin of the International Social Security Association (7:4), April 1954, p. 140.

6142 Iturralde, L. de
"El Seguro Social en Bolivia." La Paz, Kollasayo, October 1939, p. 21-49.

6143 Martí Bufill, Carlos
"La Seguridad Social en Bolivia." Madrid, Revista iberoamericana de seguridad social (1:1), May-June 1952, p. 51-92.

6144 Pérez Platón, R.
"El Seguro Social en Bolivia." Sucre, Revista de estudios jurídicos, políticos y sociales 10, May 1950, p. 119-146.

6145 Quiroga Pereyra, H.
" Centralización o Descentralización para Implantar el Seguro Social General en Bolivia?" Oruro, Revista económica (13:16/17), January/December 1955-January/June 1956, p. 42-64.

6146 Quiroga Pereyra, H.
"Documentos del Seguro Social Boliviano." Oruro, Revista de la Facultad de Económia y Finanzas, July/December 1952, p. 63-120.

6147 "El Seguro Social en Bolivia." La Paz, Protección social (13:147/148), May/June 1950, p. 57-146.

6148 Stein, O.
"Introducción de los Seguros Sociales en Bolivia." La Paz, Protección social, March 1940, p. 5-16; April 1940, p. 2-19.

6149 Venegas Iporre, J.S.
"Bolivia y la Seguridad Social." México, Seguridad social (11:14), March-April 1962, p. 23-35.

Brazil

6150 "A.C.A.P. de Serviços Públicos em São Paulo." Rio de Janeiro, O observador económico e financiero (16:193), February 1952, p. 86-121.

6151 Assis, A. de Oliveira
"A Quota de Previdência e o Município." Rio de Janeiro, Revista de administração municipal (10: 58), May-June 1963, p. 216-226.

6152 Assis, A. de Oliveira
"La Sécurité Sociale au Brésil." Geneva, Bulletin

de l'Association Internationale de la Sécurité Sociale (4:1/2), January/February 1951, p. 3-19; (4:3), March 1951, p. 97-105.

6153 Firmeza, M.
"Previdência Social, Unificada ao Não." São Paulo, Revista brasiliense 19, September/October 1958, p. 176-188.

6154 Fischlowitz, Estanislão
"Previdência Social: Reforma ou Contra-Reforma." Rio de Janeiro, O observador económico e financeiro (23:265), March 1958, p. 32-39.

6155 Fischlowitz, Estanislão
"Proteção à Familia na Legislação Social Brasileira." Rio de Janeiro, Revista do serviço público, ano XVII (3:3), September 1954, p. 10-17.

6156 Fischlowitz, Estanislão
"Os Sistemas de Organização da Providência Social e a Realidade Brasileira." Rio de Janeiro, Revista do serviço público (3:1), July 1951, p. 17-21.

6157 Gonçalves, O.
"Aspectos Econômicos da Previdência Social no Brasil." São Paulo, Revista da Universidade Católica de São Paulo (11:20), December 1956, p. 504-510.

6158 "Instituição Larragoiti." Rio de Janeiro, Sul América (32:123), January/March 1951, p. 9-14.

6159 No entry

6160 International Labour Office
"General Regulations Governing Social Insurance Institutes in Brazil." Geneva, Industry and labour (12:5), September 1, 1954, p. 257-259.

6161 International Labour Office
"New Benefits for Industrial Workers in Brasil." Geneva, Industry and labour, May 15, 1953, p. 334.

6162 International Social Security Association
"New Hospitals; the Situation of the Social Welfare Institutes; New Medical Service Scheme: Brazil." Geneva, Bulletin of the International Social Security Association (7:4), April 1954, p. 141.

6163 Iório, O.
"Situação Econômico-Financeira da Previdência Social no Brasil, em Geral, e a do I.A.P.I., em Particular." Rio de Janeiro, Industriários 65, October 1958, p. 3-11.

6164 Leal, R.
"A Previdência Social no Brasil. Aspectos Gerais da Questão Social." Rio de Janeiro, Revista do serviço público, ano XVI (4:2), November 1953, p. 36-43.

6165 Lima, Heitor Ferreira
"O Aspecto Financeiro da Previdência Social." São Paulo, Revista brasiliense 30, July-August 1960, p. 148-154.

6166 Oliveira, M. Veloso Cardoso de
"Panorama de Previdencia Social Brasileira." Madrid, Revista iberoamericana de seguridad social (4:2), March-April 1955, p. 205-216.

6167 Oliveira, M. Veloso Cardoso de
"La Sécurité Sociale au Brésil." Geneva, Revue internationale du travail (84:5), November 1961, p. 412-430.

6168 Paranhos, R. da Rocha
"Assistência Social aos Servidores do Estado." Rio de Janeiro, Revista do serviço público, ano XIII (2:3), June 1950, p. 1-21.

6169 "Reorganisation des Assurances Sociales du Brésil." Geneva, Bulletin de l'Association Internationale de la Sécurité Sociale (7:6-7), June-July 1954, p. 253-261.

6170 Silva, W. Nogueira da
"Assistência Médica da Previdência Social." São

Paulo, Revista brasiliense 29, May-June 1960, p. 94-102.

6171 "Síntese Social: a Reforma da Previdência Social." Rio de Janeiro, Síntese política econômica social (7:25), January-March 1965, p. 75-80.

6172 "Social Security: Present Situation and Prospects." Rio de Janeiro, Conjuntura econômica internacional, November 1964, p. 39-45.

Central America

6173 International Labour Office
"Social Security in the Central American Countries: I-II." Geneva, International labour review (64:1), January 1952, p. 93-105; (65:2), February 1952, p. 211-231.

Chile

6174 Agüero, O.
"Ensayo Sobre la Previsión Social en Chile." Madrid, Revista española de seguridad social (4:3), March 1950, p. 247-277.

6175 Alexander, Robert J.
"Social Security in Chile." Social forces (28:1), October 1949, p. 53-58.

6176 Biggemann, H.
"La Seguridad Social Chilena." Santiago, Economía y finanzas (18:218), December 1954, p. 22-31.

6177 Davis, Tom E.
"Dualism, Stagnation and Inequality: the Impact of Pension Legislation in the Chilean Labor Market." Industrial & labor relations review 17, April 1964, p. 380-398.

6178 Gaete Berrios, Alfredo
"Panorama de la Seguridad Social en Chile." México, Seguridad social (9:3), May/June 1960, p. 33-45.

6179 International Labour Office
"Social Security in Chile." Geneva, Industry and labour, January 15, 1953, p. 52-60.

6180 Miranda Salas, E.
"La Seguridad Social en Chile." México, Seguridad social (11:16), July-August 1962, p. 7-44.

6181 "Monografía Sobre los Seguros Sociales en Chile." Madrid, Revista iberoamericana de seguros sociales (9:6), November-December 1960, p. 1541-1582.

6182 Garayar P., Gregorio
"Prestaciones Familiares Generales y su Aplicación en Chile." Lima, Informaciones sociales (8:3), July/September 1953, p. 3-11.

6183 Rabí C., Miguel
"La Seguridad Social de los Obreros en Chile." Lima, Informaciones sociales (14:3), July/September 1959, p. 3-24.

6184 Silva Espejo, E.
"Aspectos Prácticos del Seguro Social Chileno Relacionados con Registros, Cotizaciones y Fuentes Estadísticas." México, Seguridad social (12:22), July-August 1963, p. 7-19.

6185 Sinn Montez, Luis
"La Previsión Social en Chile." México, Latinoamérica (3:27), March 1, 1951, p. 107-109.

6186 Valenzuela Lavín, Guillermo
"Situación Actual de Seguridad Social en Chile." Santiago, Previsión social (20:82), 1952-53, p. 170-176.

Colombia

6187 Botero Restrepo, J.
"El Seguro Social en Colombia." Havana, América (39:1), April 1953, p. 14-20.

6188 Caicedo Ayerbe, Aurelio
"Problemas de la Seguridad Social." Bogotá, Económía colombiana (3:7), November 1954, p. 11-16.

6189 Castro, Miguel I.
"Seguro Social Colombiano." Madrid, Cooperación de la Seguridad Social Iberoamericana, February 1953, p. 12-19.

6190 Castro, Rodolfo
"Aspectos do Seguro Social Colombiano." Rio de Janeiro, Industriários 53, October 1956, p. 11-14.

6191 "Monografía Sobre los Seguros Sociales en Colombia." Madrid, Revista iberoamericana de seguros sociales (10:3), May-June 1961, p. 551-585.

6192 "Nueva Organización del Instituto Colombiano de Seguros Sociales." México, Seguridad social (3a. época, 9:6), November-December 1960, p. 65-67.

6193 Rengifo, J.M.
"Incorporación de las Universidades al Estudio de la Seguridad Social." Bogotá, Universitas 26, June 1964, p. 320-329.

Costa Rica

6194 Araus Armando, A., et al
"La Seguridad Social en Costa Rica." San José, Revista de ciencias jurídico-sociales (1:2), December 1957, p. 191-234.

6195 Céspedes Gutierrez, M.
"El Seguro Social en Costa Rica." México, Seguridad social (13:29), September-October 1964, p. 57-95.

6196 "Monografías Nacionales Sobre Seguridad Social: Costa Rica." México, Seguridad social (12:23), September-October 1963, p. 49-59.

Cuba

6197 Molina Parrado, L.
"El Seguro Social de los Ingenieros Civiles." Havana, Ingeniería civil (6:2), February 1955, p. 113-116.

6198 Muñiz Rodríguez, Nicolás
"La Seguridad Social en Cuba." Havana, Cuba económica y financiera (30:350), May 1955, p. 11-12.

6199 Raggi y Ageo, Carlos M.
"El Progreso de la Seguridad Social en Cuba." México, Seguridad social (9:3), May/June 1960, p. 13-31.

Dominican Republic

6200 Cabral Ortega, Héctor A.
"Transcendencia y Alcances del Seguro Social en la República Dominicana." Ciudad Trujillo, Renovación (6:23), October/December 1959, p. 47-60.

6201 Dominican Republic. U.S. Embassy
"Social Security Benefits in the Dominican Republic." Dominican Republic 151, April 15, 1952, p. 1-4.

6202 Lamarche, Juan B.
"La Política Social en la Republica Dominicana." Ciudad Trujillo, Seguridad social (8:54), March/April 1957, p. 51-53.

6203 Sánchez Bethancourt, Frank C.
"Organización de los Servicios Asistenciales del Seguro Social en la República Dominicana. II." Ciudad Trujillo, Seguridad social (5:36), March/April 1954, p. 47-53.

6204 Sobá, José G.
"La Asistencia Social en la Era de Trujillo." Ciudad Trujillo, Boletín de divulgaciones 5, December 1959, p. 20-22.

Ecuador

6205 Barrera B., Jaime
"Administración del Seguro Social Ecuatoriano." Bogotá, Seguridad social 13/16, January/December 1952, p. 163-166.

6206 Campaña Barrera, Aníbal
"20 Años de Vida del Seguro Social Ecuatoriano." Quito, Seguridad social (12:116), September/October 1955, p. 2-3.

6207 Ecuador. Instituto Nacional de Previsión
"Programa de Seguro Social en el Ecuador." Quito, Boletín de informaciones y de estudios sociales y económicos (20:78/79), July/December 1957, p. 38-49.

El Salvador

6208 Frank, Beryl
"Proyecto de Programa de Seguridad Social para

El Salvador." San Salvador, Revista de trabajo (2:4), January/March 1951, p. 57-110.

6209 "Le Nouveau Régime d'Assurance Sociale du Salvador." Geneva, Bulletin de l'Association Internationale de la Sécurité Sociale (3:12), July 1954, p. 31-42.

Guatemala

6210 Barahona Streber, Oscar
"Principios Financieros del Régimen de Seguridad Social de Guatemala." Quito, Boletín de informaciones y de estudios sociales y económicos (13: 48&49), January/June 1950, p. 112-118.

6211 Betancur, J., et al
"Problemas de Seguridad Social Creados por el Progreso Técnico: el Caso de Guatemala." Bogotá, Revista javeriana (61:305), June 1964, p. 424-437.

6212 Girón, M.A.
"La Medicina del Trabajo y la Seguridad Social en Guatemala." México, Revista mexicana del trabajo (10:9-10), September-October 1963, p. 73-81.

6213 International Social Security Association
"Guatemala: Hospital Services of the Social Security Institute." Geneva, Bulletin of the International Social Security Association (5:1), January 1952, p. 33.

Haiti

6214 Alcindor, J.F.
"Vers la Généralisation de la Sécurité Sociale." Port-au-Prince, Revue du travail 11, May 1962, p. 69-79.

6215 Salomon, Y.
"Sécurité Sociale des Serviteurs à Gages." Port-au-Prince, Revue du travail (10:10), May 1961, p. 28-30.

Honduras

6216 "Los Seguros Sociales en Honduras." Madrid, Revista iberoamericana de seguros sociales (12:1), January-February 1963, p. 11-31.

Mexico

6217 Aguilar Vasquez, J.H.
"Algunas Notas Sobre Seguridad Social." México, Revista de economía (28:1), January 1965, p. 18-21.

6218 Bernaldo de Quirós, Juan
"Seguridad Social y Desarrollo Económico."" México, Seguro social (10:10), July-August 1961, p. 9-40.

6219 Bonilla Marín, G.
"Política de Seguros Sociales." México, Revista de la Facultad del Derecho de México (5:19), July-September 1955, p. 9-33.

6220 Díaz Lombardo, F.G.
"El Bienestar Social Integral de los Jubilados y Pensionados." México, Estudios sociológicos 12, 1961, p. 409-419.

6221 Drill, A.
"Social Security in Mexico." México, Mexican-American review (31:7), July 1963, p. 20-24.

6222 Echenique, Ramón
"La Rehabilitación para el Trabajo en el Seguro Social Mexicano." México, Seguridad social (1:2), March/April 1958, p. 85-93.

6223 Frank, Beryl
"Social Security in Latin America." México, Mexican life (38:3), March 1962, p. 56-57.

6224 Gersdorff, R. von
"L'Assurance Sociale au Méxique." Geneva, Bulletin de l'Association Internationale de la Sécurité Sociale (12:3), March 1959, p. 83-91.

6225 Gómez Corral, R.
"Los Seguros Sociales en México." Madrid, Revista iberoamericana de seguros sociales (11:6), November-December 1962, p. 1411-1442.

6226 Gonzalez Arciniegas, N.
"El Trabajador Indígena, el Pescador y la Mujer

Trabajadora como Laborantes Desprotegidos." México, Estudios sociológicos 12, 1961, p. 313-320.

6227 González Díaz Lombardo, Francisco
"Esquema de la Seguridad Social Mexicana." México, Revista mexicana del trabajo (11:7-8), July-August 1964, p. 51-92.

6228 González Díaz Lombardo, Francisco
"La Extensión de la Seguridad Social a los Trabajadores no Asalariados o Dependientes." México, Revista ITAT 8, 1959, p. 9-25.

6229 González Díaz Lombardo, Francisco
"Instituto de Bienestar Social Militar." México, Revista ITAT 10, 1960, p. 35-75.

6230 González Díaz Lombardo, Francisco
"Mutualidad Nacional del Profesionista." México, Revista ITAT 11, 1960, p. 89-149.

6231 González Peña, Pedro
"La Asistencia Social General en México." México, Salubridad y asistencia (8:4), July/August 1948, p. 203-218.

6232 Hernández, Carlos Pascual
"La Previsión Social Dentro del México Nuevo." México, Revista del trabajo (2:140), September 1949, p. 51-54.

6233 Herrera Gutiérrez, Alfonso
"El Régimen del Seguro Social en México." México, Universidad de México (6:57), July 1952, p. 2-3.

6234 López Mateos, Adolfo
"Relaciones Obreropatronales y Seguridad Social." México, Revista mexicana del trabajo (8:9-10), September-October 1961, p. 7-11.

6235 Mena, A.O.
"Le Développement de la Sécurité Sociale au Mexique." Geneva, Bulletin de l'Association Internationale de la Sécurité Sociale (9:1-2), January-February 1956, p. 41-66.

6236 Mexico (Federal District). Centro Patronal
"Aclaraciones al Seguro Social. Deben Tratarse como Tales y no como Inconformidades." México, Revista patronal (6:100), June 1952, p. 19-22.

6237 Morales, H.I.
"Perfiles y Evoluciones de la Seguridad Social en México." México, Revista mexicana del trabajo (11:7-8), July-August 1964, p. 93-103.

6238 Navarrete, A.
"Desempleo y Seguridad Social." México, Ciencias políticas y sociales (5:16), April-June 1959, p. 179-191.

6239 Navarro Zimbrón, E.
"Un Importante Servicio Más, del Seguro Social: La Unidad de Neuropsiquiatría." México, Vida, September 22, 1947, p. 8-11.

6240 Olson, Jerry
"Ten Years of Seguro Social." México, Mexican-American review (22:9), August 1953, p. 10-11, 32-34.

6241 Pérez Jácome, Eduardo
"Los Procedimientos ante el Seguro Social." México, Revista ITAT 10, 1960, p. 83-128.

6242 "Régimen Mexicano de Seguridad Social." Madrid, Revista de trabajo 5, May 1956, p. 407-422.

6243 Rodríguez Sala, M. L.
"Las Víctimas de Accidentes de Trabajo y las Indemnizaciones Pagadas en los Estados Unidos Mexicanos." México, Estudios sociológicos 12, 1961, p. 199-220.

6244 Rosa G., Francisco J. de la
"Historia del Seguro Social en México." México, La justicia (27:309), January 1956, p. 12314-12320.

6245 Sánchez Vargas, G.
"Factores de Desarrollo de la Política de Seguridad Social en México." México, Revista mexicana de

<u>sociología</u> (23:3), September-December 1961, p. 897-919.

6246 Torres H., R.
"Trabajadores Eventuales y Temporales en el Seguro Social." México, <u>Revista ITAT 16</u>, January-April 1962, p. 147-170.

<u>Nicaragua</u>
6247 Bernaldo de Quirós, Juan
"Nicaragua, Ley Orgánica de Seguridad Social." México, <u>Boletín del Instituto de Derecho Comparado de México</u> (9:26), May-August 1956, p. 224-230.

<u>Panama</u>
6248 Castillo, Rosa
"La Seguridad Social Panameña." Madrid, <u>Cooperación de la Seguridad Social Iberoamericana</u>, November 1953, p. 10-15.

6249 "Monografías Nacionales Americanas de Seguridad Social: Panamá." México, <u>Seguridad social</u> (12:19), January-February 1963, p. 119-142.

6250 Vives S., A. A.
"Apuntes para una Historia de la Seguridad Social en Panamá." Panamá, <u>Lotería</u> (7:80), July 1962, p. 29-40.

<u>Paraguay</u>
6251 "Monografías Nacionales de Seguridad Social: Paraguay." México, <u>Seguridad social</u> (12:24), November-December 1963, p. 85-91.

6252 "Los Seguros Sociales en el Paraguay." Madrid, <u>Revista iberoamericana de seguros sociales</u> (10:2), March-April 1961, p. 283-324.

<u>Peru</u>
6253 Escuela de Servicio Social del Peru
"Desarrollo del Programa de Servicio Social en el Perú, de 1945 a 1953." Lima, <u>Servicio social</u> (11/12:11/12), December 1953-1954, p. 3-16.

6254 Fuentes A., Pastor
"El Seguro Social Peruano y el Seminario Regional de Seguridad Social de Lima." La Paz, Protección social (15:167/168), January-February 1952, p. 5-17.

6255 Hernandez, Francisco J.
"Social Insurance in Peru." Pan American Union bulletin 70, December 1936, p. 978-981.

6256 "Monografía Sobre los Seguros Sociales en el Perú." Madrid, Revista iberoamericana de seguros sociales (9:6), November-December 1960, p. 1583-1628.

6257 "Monografías Nacionales Americanas de Seguridad Social: Perú." México, Seguridad social (13:26-27), March-June 1964, p. 39-78.

6258 Montenegro Baca, José
"El Seguro Social Obligatorio en el Perú." Caracas, Revista del trabajo (5:18), January-March 1955, p. 137-155.

6259 "Obligatory Social Insurance in Peru. Results of the First Year's Operation." Lima, West Coast leader, August 24, 1937, p. 5-8.

6260 Silva Viteri, Genaro
"Campo de Aplicación y Riesgos Cubiertos por los Seguros Sociales en el Perú." Lima, Revista de la Facultad de Ciencias Económicas y Comerciales 52, January/June 1955, p. 80-138.

Uruguay

6261 Abdala, C.E.
"El Desarrollo Económico y Social en la República del Uruguay." México, Seguridad social (12:23), September-October 1963, p. 7-20.

6262 Vieitez Novo, H.
"Sistema de Previsión Social del Uruguay." Montevideo, Revista de la Facultad de Ciencias Económicas y de Administración 22, June 1963, p. 133-163.

Venezuela

6263 Arroba, Gonzalo
"Informe Sobre el Desarrollo Financiero del Seguro Social Venezolano de Enfermedad-Maternidad en el Período 1º de Julio 1951 a 30 de Junio 1954." Caracas, Revista del trabajo (5:20), July/September 1955, p. 81-137.

6264 Barrios Mora, J.R.
"Ensayo para Establecer el Seguro Social del Empleado Público en Venezuela." México, Revista mexicana del trabajo (10:3-4), March-April 1963, p. 23-37.

6265 Clarke Pérez, Jesús
"El Régimen de las Prestaciones de los Seguros Sociales." Caracas, Revista del trabajo (6:25), October/December 1956, p. 21-92.

6266 Cornielles, Amado
"Consideraciones Sobre el Seguro Social Venezolano." Madrid, Cooperación, April 1953, p. 12-13.

6267 Instituto Venezolano de los Seguros Sociales
"Los 20 Años." Caracas, Política (3:36), September-December 1964, p. 121-126.

6268 International Social Security Association
"Compulsory Social Insurance in Venezuela." Geneva, Bulletin of the International Social Security Association (7:1/2), January/February 1954, p. 32-39.

6269 Iribarren Borges, J.
"Intervención del Instituto Venezolano de los Seguros Sociales." Caracas, Política 22, June-July 1962, p. 71A-71E.

6270 "La Asistencia Social en Venezuela." Caracas, Infancia y adolescencia (8:16), 1954, p. 86-91.

6271 "La Nouvelle Législation d'Assurances Sociales du Venezuela." Geneva, Bulletin de l'Association Internationale de la Sécurité Sociale (7:1/2), January-February 1954, p. 34-42.

6272 "Los Seguros Sociales en Venezuela." Madrid, Revista iberoamericana de seguros sociales (10:4), July-August 1961, p. 895-914.

6273 Pisani Ricci, R.
"El Seguro Social en Venezuela." México, Seguridad social (2:8/9), July-October 1959, p. 49-62.

6274 Reyes, Italia
"Servicio Social Municipal de Caracas, República de Venezuela." Santiago, Servicio social (27:1), January/April 1953, p. 27-29.

6275 Rhode, A. J.
"La Rehabilitación de Incapacitados en el Instituto Venezolano de los Seguros Sociales." Caracas, Revista del trabajo (9:36-38), July 1959-March 1960, p. 23-31.

6276 Sánchez R., Roberto
"Venezuela y su Panorama Social." Madrid, Acción de la Seguridad Social Iberoamericana 2, July/August 1955, p. 3-7.

6277 Uzcátegui D., R. A.
"Seguro Social Obligatorio." Caracas, Economía y ciencias sociales (6:3), July-September 1964, p. 80-108.

6278 Venezuela. Ministerio del Trabajo
"El Seguro Social en Venezuela." Caracas, Revista del trabajo (2:7), April/June 1952, p. 15-54.

6279 Zúñiga Cisneros, M.
"Un Programa de Seguridad Social." Caracas, Boletín de la Academia de Ciencias Políticas y Sociales 15, December 1959, p. 13-45.

West Indies and the Caribbean

6280 "St. Pierre and Miquelon: Amendment of Social Security Scheme." International labour review 90, September 1964, p. 285.

Part V
URBANIZATION AS A PHENOMENON AND RESEARCH FIELD

URBANIZATION (GENERAL)

Books

General

6281 Abrams, Charles
The city is the frontier. New York, Harper & Row, 1965, 394p.

6282 Anderson, Nels
Urban community: a world perspective. New York, Holt, 1959, 500p.

6283 Arensberg, Conrad M., & Solon T. Kimball
Culture and community. New York, Harcourt, Brace & World, 1965, 349p.

6284 ATI-ACE newsletter. Athens, Athens Center of Ekistics (3:20), February 15, 1967-

6285 Atlanta Economic Review (periodical)
The ideal city. Atlanta, Bureau of Business & Economic Research, School of Business Administration, Georgia State College, 1964, 120p.

6286 Beaujeu-Garnier, J., & G. Chabot
Traité de géographie urbaine. Paris, Colin, 1963, 200p.

6287 Bergel, Egon E.
Urban sociology. New York, McGraw, 1955, 558p.

6288 Bollens, John C., & Henry J. Schmandt
The metropolis: its people, politics, and economic life. New York, Harper & Row, 1966, 643p.

6289 Breese, Gerald
Urbanization in newly developing countries. Englewood Cliffs, Prentice-Hall, 1966, 151p.

6290 Burgess, Ernest W., & Donald J. Bogue, eds. Contributions to urban sociology. Chicago, University of Chicago Press, 1964, 673p.

6291 California. University. International Urban Research The world's metropolitan areas. Berkeley, University of California Press, 1959, 115p.

6292 California. University. University at Los Angeles. Real Estate Research Program Essays in urban land economics, in honor of the sixty-fifth birthday of Leo Grebler. Los Angeles, 1966, 351p.

6293 Carrière, F., & P. Pinchemel Le fait urbain en France. Paris, Colin, 1963, 374p.

6294 Center for the Study of Democratic Institutions Occasional paper on the city. no. 1- Santa Barbara, 1964-

6295 Chamber of Commerce of the United States of America. Construction & Community Development Dept. Urban development guidebook. Washington, 1955, 102p.

6296 Choay, Françoise, ed. L'urbanisme, utopies et realités, une anthologie. Paris, Editions du Seuil, 1965, 448p.

6297 Chombart de Lauwe, Paul H. Des hommes et des villes. Paris, Payot, 1965, 249p.

6298 Christensen, David E. Urban development. New York, Holt, Rinehart & Winston, 1964, 95p.

6299 Cole, William E. Urban society. Boston, Houghton, Mifflin, 1958, 591p.

6300 Commonwealth Conference on Urban Development and Leadership, University Park, Pa., 1964 Urban development and leadership; proceedings ... Ed. by Roy C. Buck & Robert A. Rath. University Park? 1964, 95p.

6301 Cornell University. Latin American Program
Conference on the Role of the City in the Modernization of Latin America, November, 1965. Ithaca, Cornell University Press, 1967, variously paged.

6302 Dickinson, Robert E.
City and region; a geographical interpretation. London, Routledge & K. Paul, 1964, 588p.

6303 Duggar, G. S.
Renovation de nos villes et communes. 2v. The Hague, Nijhoff, 1965.

6304 Ekistics. Athens, Doxiadis Associates (20:116-119), July-October, 1965-

6305 Evans, Luther H., ed.
The impact of urbanization. (In his Background book: the Tenth National Conference of the U.S. National Commission for UNESCO. Washington, Dept. of State, U.S. National Commission for UNESCO, 1965, p. 33-36).

6306 Everett, R.O., & R.H. Leach, eds.
Urban problems and prospects. Dobbs Ferry, Oceana Publications, 1966, 229p.

6307 Field, Arthur J., ed.
Urbanization and work in modernizing societies; a working paper. Detroit, Glengary Press, 1967, 209p.

6308 Folguera Grassi, Francisco
Urbanismo para todos. Barcelona, Colegio Oficial de Arquitectos de Cataluña y Baleares, 1959, 104p.

6309 Gist, Noel P., & Sylvia (Fleis) Fava
Urban society. 5th ed. New York, Crowell, 1964, 623p.

6310 Green, Constance (McLaughlin)
The rise of urban America. New York, Harper, 1967, 224p.

6311 Hatt, Paul K., & Albert J. Reiss, eds.
Cities and society: the revised reader in urban socio-

logy. 2d ed. Glencoe, Free Press, 1957, 852p.

6312 Hauser, Philip M., & Leo F. Schnore, eds.
The study of urbanization. New York, Wiley, 1965, 554p.

6313 Haworth, Lawrence
The good city. Bloomington, Indiana University Press, 1963, 160p.

6314 Hirsch, Werner Z.
Urban resources decisions; report # MR-35. Los Angeles, Institute of Government & Public Affairs, University of California, 1965, 26p.

6315 International Union of Local Authorities
The large town and the small municipality, their strength and their weakness; reports prepared for the Vienna Congress, 15-20 June 1953. The Hague, 1953, 239p.

6316 Kuper, Leo et al
Living in towns; selected papers in urban sociology. London, Cresset Press, 1953, 370p.

6317 Lee, R.H.
The city: urbanism and urbanization in major world regions. Philadelphia, Lippincott, 1955, 568p.

6318 Lowry, Ira S.
Migration and metropolitan growth. San Francisco Chandler, 1966, 120p.

6319 Mayer, Harold M., & Clyde F. Kohn, eds.
Readings in urban geography. Chicago, University of Chicago Press, 1959, 625p.

6320 Park, Robert E., et al
The city. Chicago, University of Chicago Press, 1925, 239p.

6321 Quinn, James A.
Urban sociology. New York, American Book Co., 1955, 534p.

6322 Reissman, Leonard
The urban process; cities in industrial societies. New York, Free Press, 1964, 269p.

6323 Reps, J.W.
The making of urban America. Princeton, Princeton University Press, 1965, 574p.

6324 Reviews in urban economics. St. Louis, Institute for Urban & Regional Studies, Washington University, 1967-

6325 Revista de estudios de la vida local (17:100), Madrid, Instituto de Estudios de Administración Local, July-August, 1958-

6326 Rivkin, Malcolm D.
Urbanization and national development: some approaches to the dilemma. (In Inter-Regional Seminar on Development Policies and Planning in Relation to Urbanization, University of Pittsburgh, Pittsburgh, Pa., 24 October-7 November 1966. Working paper # 2, agenda item # 3: 66-46978. New York, United Nations, 1966, 72 plus 4p.).

6327 Roca Roca, Eduardo
Urbanismo y grandes ciudades, su dimensión jurídico-social. Granada, Escuela Social de Granada, 1960, 26p.

6328 Sanders, Irwin T.
The community: an introduction to a social system. New York, Ronald Press, 1958, 431p.

6329 Santos, Milton
A cidade nos países subdesenvolvidos. Rio de Janeiro, Ed. Civilização Brasileira, 1965, 175p.

6330 Schlivek, Louis B.
Man in metropolis; a book about the people and prospects of a metropolitan region. Garden City, Doubleday, 1965, 432p.

6331 Schnore, Leo F.
The urban scene: human ecology and demography.

New York, Free Press of Glencoe, 1965, 374p.

6332 Scientific American (periodical)
Cities. New York, Knopf, 1965, 211p.

6333 Sheraton, Mimi
City portraits; a guide to 60 of the world's great cities. 1st ed. New York, Harper & Row, 1964, 601p.

6334 Social problems of development and urbanization (Science, technology and development, v. 7). United States papers prepared for the United Nations Conference on the Application of Science and Technology for the Benefit of the Less Developed Areas. Washington, G.P.O., 1962, 89p.

6335 Sorokin, Pitirim A., & Carle C. Zimmerman
Principals of rural-urban sociology. New York, Holt, 1929, 652p.

6336 Stauber, R., ed.
Approaches to the study of urbanization; proceedings. Lawrence, Government Research Center, University of Kansas, 1964, 250p.

6337 Troedsson, Carl B.
Architecture, urbanism, and socio-political developments in our western civilization. Gothenburg, Akademiförlaget, 1964, 313p.

6338 Turner, John F.C.
Uncontrolled urban settlement: problems and policies. (In Inter-Regional Seminar on Development Policies and Planning in Relation to Urbanization, University of Pittsburgh, Pittsburgh, Pa., 24 October- 7 November, 1966; working paper # 11, agenda item # 4: 66-47393). New York, United Nations, 1966, 112p.

6339 United Nations. Dept. of Economic & Social Affairs
The applicability of community development to urban areas: E/CN.5/356. New York, 1961, 53p.

6340 U.S. Dept. of Housing & Urban Development
Science and the city; publication MP-39. Washington, 1967, 43p.

6341 Urban affairs quarterly. v. 1- , Beverly Hills, Sage, 1967-

6342 Urban land. Washington, (24:7), July-August 1965-

6343 Urban research news. Beverly Hills, Sage Publications, (I:1), November 14, 1966-

6344 Latin American Urbanization Research. Beverly Hills, Sage Publications, 1971- . Annual.

6345 EURE: Revista Latinoamericana de Estudios Urbano Regionales. Santiago, Centro Interdisciplinario de Desarrollo Urbano y Regional, Universidad Católica de Chile, 1970- (three times per year).

6346 Urbanisme, revue française. Paris (35:93), March-April, 1966-

6347 Van Nieuwenhuijze, C.A.O.
The nation and the ideal city: three studies in social identity. The Hague, Mouton, 1966, 148p.

6348 Vernon, Raymond
The myth and reality of our urban problems. Cambridge, Harvard University Press, 1966, 209p.

6349 La vie urbaine. Paris, Institut d'Urbanisme de l'Université de Paris, new series, #4, October-December, 1965-

6350 Weber, M.
Die stadt (In Wirtschaft und gesellschaft. 3d ed. 2v. Tübingen, Mohr, 1947, p. 514-601).

6351 World urbanization trends, 1920-1960. (In Inter-Regional Seminar on Development Policies and Planning in Relation to Urbanization, University of Pittsburgh, Pittsburgh, Pa., 24 October-7 November, 1966. Working paper #6, agenda item #2: 66-47007. New York, United Nations, Bureau of Social Affairs, Population Division, 1966, 57p.).

Latin America

6352 Beyer, Glenn H., ed.
The urban explosion in Latin America: a continent in process of modernization. Ithaca, Cornell University Press, 1967, 406p.

6353 Boltshauer, João
Noções de evolução urbana nas Américas. 3v. Belo Horizonte, Escola de Arquitetura, Universidade de Minas Gerais, 1959-61.

6354 Calderón, Luis, et al
Problemas de urbanización en América Latina: los grupos sociales, las barriadas marginales, la acción religiosa. Madrid, Oficina Internacional de Investigaciones Sociales de FERES, 1963, 243p.

6355 Chase Manhattan Bank. Economic Research Division
Urbanization in Latin America. New York, 1967, 17p.

6356 Cole, John P.
Notes on the fifty largest towns of Latin America. Nottingham, Dept. of Geography, University of Nottingham, 1966, 40p.

6357 Conference on Problems of Urbanization in Latin America, El Paso, Texas, June 9-10, 1967
Proceedings. El Paso, University of Texas at El Paso Press, 1967, variously paged.

6358 Currie, Lauchlin
Una política urbana para los países en desarrollo. Bogotá, Ed. Tercer Mundo, 1965, 188p.

6359 Davis, Kingsley
Las causas y efectos del fenómeno de primacía urbana con referencia especial a América Latina; reprint no. 144, general series. Berkeley, Institute of International Studies, University of California, 1962, p. 361-379.

6360 Dorselaer, Jaime
Les facteurs de l'urbanisation et la "crise tertiaire" en Amérique Latine. Paris, Institut des Hautes Etudes de l'Amérique Latine, 1960? 24p.

6361 Dorselaer, Jaime, & Alfonso Gregory
La urbanización en América Latina. 2v. Bogotá, Centro Internacional de Investigaciones Sociales de FERES, 1962.

6362 Hansen, A. T.
The ecology of a Latin American city. (In American Sociological Society. Race and culture contacts. Ed. by E. B. Reuter. New York, McGraw-Hill, 1934, p. 124-142).

6363 Herrera, Felipe
The role of the communities in the development of Latin America. Washington, Inter-American Development Bank, 1964, 6p.

6364 Inter-American Development Bank
Inter-American Development Bank activities, 1961-1966. Washington, 1967, 133p.

6365 International Geographical Union
Proceedings of the First Latin American Regional Conference, Mexico City, August 2-8, 1966. 5v. Mexico, 1966.

6366 Neira Alva, Eduardo
Urbanization policies (Meeting on population policies in relation to development in Latin America); UP/Ser. H/V/REPO/I/8. Washington, Pan American Union, 1967, 19p.

6367 Programa interamericano de planeamiento urbano y regional: proyecto 205 del Programa de Cooperación Técnica de la OEA en el Instituto de Planeamiento de Lima, Universidad Nacional de Ingeniería del Perú. Washington, Pan American Union, 1963, 53p.

6368 Ruoss, Meryl
New factors in the expanding urban situation. New York, Committee on Cooperation in Latin America, United Presbyterian Church in the U.S.A., 1960, 37p.

6369 Quintero, Rodolfo
Antropología de las ciudades latinoamericanas. Caracas, Dirección de Cultura de la Universidad Central de Venezuela, 1964, 258p.

6370 Rycroft, William S., & Myrtle M. Clemmer
A factual study of Latin America. New York,

Commission on Ecumenical Mission & Relations, United Presbyterian Church in the U.S.A., 1963, 246p.

6371 Schurz, William L.
This new world: the civilization of Latin America. London, Allen & Unwin, 1956, 429p.

6372 Seminar on Urbanization Problems in Latin America, Santiago de Chile, 1959
Seminar on urbanization problems in Latin America, jointly sponsored by the United Nations Educational, Scientific and Cultural Organization, the United Nations Bureau of Social Affairs, and the Secretariat of the United Nations Economic Commission for Latin America, in cooperation with the International Labor Office, and the Organization of American States, Santiago, Chile, 6-18 July, 1959. 4v. Santiago, United Nations Economic & Social Council, 1959.

6373 Seminar on Urbanization Problems in Latin America, Santiago de Chile, 1959
Urbanization in Latin America; proceedings. Ed. by Philip M. Hauser. Paris, Unesco, 1961, 331p.

6374 Sireau, Albert
Culture et peuplement: évolution du municipe de Mercedes dans la province de Buenos Aires . . . Louvain, Eds. Nauwelaerts, 1965, 322p.

6375 Smith, Thomas L.
Urbanization in Latin America. (In Anderson, Nels, ed. Urbanism and urbanization. Leiden, Brill, 1964, p. 127-142).

6376 Tamiment Institute
"The Future Metropolis; a Conference, Tamiment-in-Poconos, Spring 1960." Daedalus, Winter 1961-

6377 Unesco
Report of Seminar on Urbanization Problems in Latin America; E/CN.12/URB/26 Rev. 1. New York, 1960, 116p.

6378 Unesco
Urbanization in Latin America; E/CN.12/662. New York, 1963, 36p.

6379 United Nations. Economic Commission for Latin America
Recent changes in urban and rural settlement patterns in Latin America: some implications for social organization and development. (In Inter-Regional Seminar on Development Policies and Planning in Relation to Urbanization, University of Pittsburgh, Pittsburgh, Pa., 24 October-7 November 1966. Working paper # 3; agenda items # 1 & # 3; 66-46977. New York, 1966, 21p.).

6380 United Presbyterian Church in the U.S.A.
A study of urbanization in Latin America. By W. Stanley Rycroft, & Myrtle M. Clemmer. New York, 1963, 130p.

Argentina

6381 Bielsa, Rafael
Buenos Aires. (In Robson, William A., ed. Great cities of the world. 2d ed. London, Allen & Unwin, 1957, p. 167-188).

6382 Canal-Feijoo, Bernardo
Teoría de la ciudad argentina; idealismo y realismo en el proceso constitucional. Buenos Aires, Ed. Sudamericana, 1951, 265p.

6383 Czajka, Willi
Buenos Aires als weltstadt. (In Schultze, J.H., ed. Zur problem der weltstadt. Berlin, 1959, p. 158-202).

6384 Gerchunoff, Alberto
Buenos Aires, la metrópoli de manaña. Buenos Aires (Cuadernos de Buenos Aires XIII), 1960, 141p.

6385 Miatello, Roberto A.
El proceso de urbanización de la provincia de Córdoba. (In International Geographical Union. Proceedings of the First Latin American Regional Conference, Mexico City, August 2-8, 1966. v. 1.

Mexico, 1966, p. 453-477).

6386 Primer Congreso de la Población, organizado por el Museo Social Argentino, 26 a 31 de octubre de 1940. Buenos Aires, Museo Social Argentino, 1941, 470p.

6387 Scobie, James R.
Argentina: a city and a nation. New York, Oxford University Press, 1964, 294p.

6388 Sireau, Albert
Culture et peuplement: évolution du municipe de Mercedes dans la province de Buenos Aires ... Louvain, Eds. Nauwelaerts, 1965, 322p.

6389 Zamorano, Mariano
La red de ciudades de la República Argentina; evolución y problemas. (In International Geographical Union. Proceedings of the First Latin American Regional Conference, Mexico City, August 2-8, 1966. v. 1. Mexico, 1966, p. 493-504).

Brazil

6390 Andrade e Silva, R., & O. Nogueira de Matos
A evolução urbana de São Paulo. São Paulo, Revista de historia, Universidade do São Paulo, 1955, 122p.

6391 Arnau, Frank
Phantasie und wirklichkeit. Munich, Prestel-Verlag, 1960, 120p.

6392 Azevedo, Aroldo de
A cidade de São Paulo, estudos de geografia urbana . . . 4v. São Paulo, Cia. Ed. Nacional, 1958.

6393 Azevedo, Aroldo de
Suburbios orientais de São Paulo. São Paulo, 1945, 184p.

6394 Brazil. Conselho Nacional de Geografia
Aspectos da geografia carioca. Rio de Janeiro, 1962, 284p.

6395 Brazil. Serviço de Estatística da Educação e Cultura
Melhoramentos urbanos. Rio de Janeiro, I.B.G.E. Annual.

6396 Brazilian Government Trade Bureau
Brazilia, Brazil's dream city, a capital for the jet age. New York, 1960, 21p.

6397 Carmin, Robert L.
Anapolis, Brazil, regional capital of an agricultural frontier; research paper no. 35. Chicago, Dept. of Geography, University of Chicago, 1953, 172p.

6398 Castro, Josué de
A cidade do Recife; ensaio de geografia urbana. Rio de Janeiro, Livraria Ed. da Casa do Estudante do Brasil, 1954, 166p.

6399 Centro Latinoamericano de Demografía
Guanabara demographic pilot survey: final report. Santiago, 1962, 91p.

6400 Congresso Nacional dos Municipios
Anais. v. 4- , Rio de Janeiro, 1957-

6401 Diegues, Manoel
Imigração, urbanização, industrialização. Rio de Janeiro, Centro Brasileiro de Pesquisas Educacionais, Instituto Nacional de Estudos Pedagógicos, Ministério da Educação e Cultura, 1964, 385p.

6402 Enciclopédia dos municipios brasileiros. 36v. Rio de Janeiro, Instituto Brasileiro de Geografia e Estatística, 1957-58.

6403 Ferraz, O.
Brasilia. São Paulo, Ed. Fúlgor, 1961, 268p.

6404 Instituto Brasileiro de Geografía e Estatística.
Conselho Nacional de Geografia
O Rio de Janeiro e sua região. Rio de Janeiro, 1964, 476p.

6405 Kubitschek, Juscelino
A marcha do amanhecer. São Paulo, "Bestseller"

Importadora de Livros, 1962, 234p.

6406 Lagenest, H. D. Barruel de
Marabá, cidade do diamante e da castanha: estudo sociológico. São Paulo, Ed. Anhêmbi, 1958, 105p.

6407 Lima, Heitor B. Calmon de Cerqueira
Movimento mutualista nacional, distritos sociais em comunidades mutualistas. Rio de Janeiro, 1961, 4p.

6408 Lins, Rachel Caldas
Cidades-gasolina. Recife, Arquivo Público Estadual, 1960, 48p.

6409 Magalhaes, A., & E. Feldman
Doorway to Brasilia. Philadelphia, Falcon Press, 1959, variously paged.

6410 Monbeig, Pierre
La croissance de la ville de São Paulo. Grenoble, Institut de Géographie Alpine, 1953, 94p.

6411 Orico, O.
Brasil, capital Brasilia. Rio de Janeiro, Serviço Gráfico do IBGE, 1960, 435p.

6412 Pereira, Jorge dos Santos
A previsão de crescimento das populações urbanas . . . Salvador, Progresso, 1958? 100p.

6413 Petrone, Pasquale
A cidade de São Paulo no século XX. São Paulo, Revista de historia, Universidade de São Paulo, 1955, 122p.

6414 Pinto, M. M. Vieira
Brasil, a nova capital do país. Rio de Janeiro, Conselho Nacional da Geografia, 1960, 48p.

6415 Rado, George, comp.
São Paulo: fastest-growing city in the world. São Paulo, Livraria Kosmos, 1954, 128p.

6416 Recife, Brazil. Direitoria de Documentação e Cultura
Boletim da cidade e do porto de Recife. Recife, 1947-

6417 Rio de Janeiro (Federal District) Depto. de Geografia e Estatística
Estudos e análises. no. 1, Rio de Janeiro, 1946-

6418 Ríos, José A.
Rio de Janeiro. (In Robson, William A., ed. Great cities of the world. 2d ed. London, Allen & Unwin, 1957, p. 489-513).

6419 Silva, Alvares da
Cidade de Salvador: aspectos geográficos, históricos, sociais e antropológicos. Salvador, Impr. Oficial da Bahia, 1960, 154p.

6420 Silveira, José Peixoto da
A nova capital; por que, para onde e como mudar a Capital Federal. 2d ed. Rio de Janeiro, Pongetti, 1959, 357p.

6421 United Nations
Enquete démographique expérimentale de Guanabara. New York, 1964, 81p.

Chile

6422 Guerrero, Raúl, & Hilario Hernandez
Los barrios del sector norte de la ciudad de Concepción, Chile . . . (In International Geographical Union. Proceedings of the First Latin American Regional Conference, Mexico City, August 2-8, 1966. v. 1. México, 1966, p. 505-522).

6423 Sánchez Aguilera, Víctor
La ciudad de los confines. Santiago, Impr. Atenea, 1953, 433p.

6424 Sepúlveda L., Candelario
Chillán, capital de provincia: contribución a su crecimiento y progreso. Santiago, Impr. Linares, 1962, 254p.

Colombia

6425 Iragorri, V.J.M.
Evolución demográfica colombiana. Bogotá, Ed. Universidad, 1959, 76p.

6426 Nussa Rosas, Carlos
Algunos aspectos del Barrio Once de Noviembre en Bogotá. (In Primer Congreso de Sociologia, 8-10 Marzo, 1963. Memoria. Bogotá, Asociación Colombiana de Sociología, 1963, p. 55-70).

Dominican Republic

6427 Pieter, Leoncio
Ciudad Trujillo; transformación urbanística, social y política de la capital de la República Dominicana durante la gloriosa era de Trujillo. Ciudad Trujillo, Ed. Arte y Cine, 1958, 113p.

Guatemala

6428 Arias B., Jorge, et al
Problemas de la urbanización en Guatemala. Guatemala, Depto. de Educación "José de Pineda Ibarra," 1965, 290p.

6429 Minkel, Clarence W.
Urban analysis, Quezaltenango. Guatemala, Instituto Geográfico Nacional, 1964, 93p.

Honduras

6430 Randales, Angel
Fundación, desarrollo y porvenir de San Pedro Sula. San Pedro Sula, 1950, 72p.

Mexico

6431 Brigham, Martin E.
Monterrey, Mexico: a study in urban geography; publication #3474. Ann Arbor, University Microfilms, 1952, Microfilm AC-1, #3474.

6432 Hayner, Norman S.
New patterns in old Mexico; a study of town and metropolis. New Haven, College & University Press, 1966, 316p.

6433 Megee, Mary C.
Monterrey, Mexico: internal patterns and external relations; research paper # 59. Chicago, Dept. of Geography, University of Chicago, 1958, 118p.

6434 Snyder, David E.
La urbanización y el crecimiento de la población en

México. (In Internationa Geographical Union. Proceedings of the First Latin American Regional Conference, Mexico City, August 2-8, 1966. v. 1. Mexico, 1966, p. 624-637.

6435 Stanislawski, Dan
The anatony of 11 towns in Michoacán; Latin American Studies # 10. Austin, University of Texas Press, 1950, 51p.

Panama

6436 Rubio y Muñoz-Bocanegra, Angel
La ciudad de Panamá; biografía urbana, funciones, diagnosis de la ciudad, paisaje, callejero. Panamá, 1950, 238p.

Peru

6437 Cavanaugh, Joseph A.
Características socio-demográficas de Lima, Perú. Lima, Servicio Cooperativo Interamericano de Salud Pública, 1955, 44p.

6438 Gade, Daniel W.
Ayacucho, Peru: un caso notable de aislamiento regional en Latinoamérica. (In International Geographical Union. Proceedings of the First Latin American Regional Conference, Mexico City, August 2-8, 1966. v. 1. Mexico, 1966, p. 89-96).

6439 Miró Quesada Laos, Carlos
En defensa de Callao. Lima, Talleres Gráficos de la Ed. Lumen, 1943, 208p.

6440 Perú. Ministerio de Salud Pública y Asistencia Social
Barriadas de Lima metropolitana. Lima, 1960, 45p.

Uruguay

6441 Abella Trías, J.C.
Montevideo, la ciudad en que vivimos; su desarrollo, su evolución y sus planes. Montevideo, Ed. Alfa, 1960, 334p.

Venezuela

6442 Consejo Municipal de Valencia
Plan de crecimiento del Distrito Valencia, estudio base; presentación del trabajo y resúmen de las principales conclusiones. 4v. Caracas, Ed. Arte, 1963.

6443 Fundacion Creole report. Caracas, nos. 15-16, March-April 1966-

6444 Rodwin, Lloyd
Ciudad Guayana: a new city. (In Scientific American, periodical. Cities. New York, Knopf, 1965, p. 88-104).

6445 Vilá Campusano, Marco A.
Area metropolitana de Caracas. Caracas, Comisión Ejecutiva del Cuatricentenario de Caracas, 1961, 161p.

West Indies and the Caribbean

6446 Niddrie, David L.
Land use and population in Tobago. London, Geographic Pub., 1961, 59p.

Periodical Articles

General

6447 Abu-Lughod, J.
"The City is Dead--Long Live the City. Some Thoughts on Urbanity." American behavioral scientist (10:1), September 1966, p. 3-5.

6448 Adams, L.W.
"The Attraction Exercised by Urban Centres in Countries in Process of Industrialization." Paris, International social science bulletin (5:1), 1953, p. 132-134.

6449 Adams, Richard N.
"Origin of Cities." Scientific American 203, September 1960, p. 153-155, 276.

6450 Anderson, Nels
"Urbanism and Urbanization." American journal

of sociology 65, July 1959, p. 68-73.

6451 Anderson, R. T., & G. Anderson
"Voluntary Associations and Urbanization; a Diachronic Analysis." American journal of sociology 65, November 1959, p. 265-273.

6452 Bauer, C.
"Pattern of Urban and Economic Development: Social Implications." Annals of the Academy of Political & Social Science 305, May 1956, p. 60-69.

6453 Beals, Ralph L.
"Urbanism, Urbanization and Acculturation." American anthropologist 53, January 1951, p. 1-10.

6454 Blumenfeld, H.
"On the Growth of Metropolitan Areas." Social forces 28, October 1949, p. 59-64.

6455 Boffi, Luis L.
"Urbanismo y su Relación con el Espíritu Humano." Salvador, Revista de direito municipal (12:33-34), May-August 1951, p. 9-17.

6456 "City in Society." Confluence 7, Spring-Summer 1958, p. 1-69, 107-156.

6457 Crespo, Renato
"Urbanismo: Ensayo Sociológico Sobre la Ciudad y la Vivienda." Cochabamba, Revista jurídica (14:53), September 1950, p. 27-88.

6458 "Crisis in the Cities: LBJ's Plan of Action." U.S. news & world report 60, February 7, 1966, p. 55-57.

6459 Davis, Kingsley
"The Origin and Growth of Urbanization in the World." American journal of sociology 60, March 1955, p. 429-437.

6460 Davis, Kingsley
"Urbanization of the Human Population." Scientific American 213, September 1965, p. 40-53.

6461 Davis, Kingsley, & H. Hertz
"The World Distribution of Urbanization." Rome, Bulletin of the International Statistical Institute (33: IV), 1956, p. 227-242.

6462 Delorenzo Nêto, Antonio
"O Estudo Sociológico da Cidade." São Paulo, Sociologia (21:1), March 1959, p. 3-22.

6463 Delorenzo Nêto, Antonio
"O Proceso de Desenvolvimento Urbano." São Paulo, Sociologia (25:1), March 1963, p. 87-92.

6464 Dennis, N.
"Changes in Function and Leadership Renewal: a Study of the Community Association Movement and Problems of Voluntary Small Groups in the Urban Locality." Sociological review 9, March 1961, p. 55-84.

6465 Duhl, Leonard J.
"The Crisis of World Urbanization." Community development review (8:2), June 1963, p. 3-5.

6466 Filippone, D.
"Urbanismo Como Técnica Social." Caracas, Política 14, February-March 1961, p. 56-63.

6467 Germani, Gino
"El Estudio de las Comunidades." México, Revista mexicana de sociología (12:3), September-December 1950, p. 307-332.

6468 Gibbs, Jack P., & Leo F. Schnore
"Metropolitan Growth: an International Study." American journal of sociology 66, September 1960, p. 160-170.

6469 Gibbs, Jack P., & W. T. Martin
"Urbanization and Natural Resources: a Study in Organizational Ecology." American sociological review 23, June 1958, p. 266-277.

6470 Ginsburg, Norton
"The International Conference on 'the Study of Urbanization.'" Items (19:4), December 1965, p. 49-50.

6471 Gottman, Jean
"The Corrupt and Creative City." Center diary:14, September-October 1966, p. 7-12.

6472 Gottmann, Jean
"L'Urbanisation dans le Monde Contemporain et ses Conséquences Politiques." Paris, Politique étrangére (25:6), 1960, p. 557-571.

6473 Greer, S.
"Urbanism Reconsidered: a Comparative Study of Local Areas in a Metropolis." American sociological review (21:1), February 1956, p. 19-25.

6474 Hauser, Philip M.
"Social Upheaval in the Cities." Yale political 2, April 1963, p. 13.

6475 Henderson, J.J.
"Urbanization and the World Community." Annals of the American Academy of Political & Social Science 314, November 1957, p. 147-155.

6476 Hoselitz, Bert F.
"Cities in Advanced and Underdeveloped Countries." Confluence 4, October 1955, p. 321-334.

6477 Hoselitz, Bert F.
"The City, the Factory and Economic Growth." The American economic review (XLV:2), May 1955, p. 166-184.

6478 Hoselitz, Bert F.
"The Role of Cities in the Economic Growth of Underdeveloped Countries." Journal of political economy (LXI:3), June 1953, p. 195-208.

6479 Joseph, Richard
"Overdue for Discovery." Esquire 55, January 1961, p. 142-145.

6480 Kahl, Joseph A.
"Some Social Concomitants of Industrialization and Urbanization." Human organization 18, Summer 1959, p. 53-74.

6481 Kaufman, H. F.
"Approach to the Study of Urban Stratification." American sociological review 17, August 1952, p. 430-437.

6482 Klove, R. C.
"Definition of Standard Metropolitan Areas." Annals of the Association of American Geographers 41, June 1951, p. 168.

6483 Leach, R. H.
"Metro: Challenge of the Sixties." America 102, January 9, 1960, p. 414-416.

6484 Lewis, Oscar
"Urbanization Without Breakdown." The scientific monthly (LXXV:1), July 1952, p. 31-41.

6485 Linsky, A. S.
"Some Generalizations Concerning Primate Cities." Annals of the Association of American Geographers 55, September 1965, p. 506-513.

6486 Lópes, B., & F. Lópes
"O Fenómeno da Urbanização e Suas Incidências em Portugal." Lisbon, Informação social (1:3), July-September 1966, p. 18-38.

6487 Lubove, R.
"The Urbanization Process: an Approach to Historical Research." Journal of the American Institute of Planners, January 1967, p. 33-39.

6488 Lynch, K.
"The City as Environment." Scientific American 213, September 1965, p. 209-214, 280.

6489 "Making American Cities More Liveable; Symposium . . ." Satuday review 49, January 8, 1966, p. 37-41.

6490 Manheim, E.
"Theoretical Prospects of Urban Sociology in an Urbanized Society." Americal journal of sociology 66, November 1960, p. 226-229.

6491 Mariño, T.R.
"What Makes Cities Grow?" Américas 14, May 1962, p. 26-29.

6492 Martin, Y.
"Phenomène Métropolitain et Organisation Sociale." Rome, International review of community development 7, 1961, p. 34-39.

6493 Mead, Margaret
"Cruise into the Past and a Glimpse of the Future; Concerning the Delos Symposium in Athens, Summer of 1965." Redbook 126, February 1966, p. 30.

6494 Meadows, P.
"The City, Technology and History." Social forces 36, December 1957, p. 141-147.

6495 Melamid, A.
"Economic Development and Urban Geography." Geographical review 51, January 1961, p. 137-139.

6496 Mercier, P.
"Urban Explosion in Developing Nations." Unesco courier 16, July 1963, p. 50-55.

6497 Meyerson, Martin, ed., et al
"Metropolis in Ferment: Symposium." Annals of the American Academy of Political & Social Science 314, November 1957, p. 1-104.

6498 Neuberger, Richard L.
"Country Slicker vs. the City Yokel." New York times magazine, July 31, 1949, p. 17.

6499 Neuberger, Richard L.
"Why People Are Moving to Town." Survey, March 1951, p. 119-122.

6500 O'Shea, D.
"Urban Evolution." America 101, July 25, 1959, p. 552-554.

6501 Pennsylvania. University. Institute for Urban Studies
"Establishment." Architectural record 109, June 1951, p. 258.

6502 Philbrick, A.K.
"Principles of Areal Functional Organization in Regional Human Geography." Economic geography 33, October 1957, p. 299-336.

6503 Popenoe, David
"On the Meaning of 'Urban' in Urban Studies." Urban affairs quarterly (I:1), September 1965, p. 17-34.

6504 Poviña, Alfredo
"Introducción a la Sociología Urbana." Córdoba, Revista de la Universidad Nacional de Córdoba (4: 3-4), July-October 1963, p. 417-432.

6505 "Problems Are Not All Solved; New Tools to Refashion Our Cities." American city 80, November 1965, p. 6.

6506 Schnore, Leo F.
"Urban and Metropolitan Development in the United States and Canada." Annals of the American Academy of Political & Social Science 316, March 1958, p. 60-68.

6507 Schnore, Leo F.
"The Study of Urbanization: Report of a Council Committee." Items (19:4), December 1965, p. 45-48.

6508 Sovani, N.V.
"The Analysis of Over-Urbanization." Economic & cultural change (12:2), January 1964, p. 113-122.

6509 Ulken, H.Z.
"Algunas Consecuencias del Movimiento de Urbanización." México, Revista mexicana de sociología (20:3), October-December 1958, p. 707-711.

6510 "Urban Growth and Development." American economic review; papers & proceedings 46, May 1956, p. 284-304.

6511 Weissman, E.
"Los Problemas del Urbanismo en los Países Subdesarrollados." Río Piedras, Revista de ciencias

sociales (1:2), June 1957, p. 285-300.

6512 Weissmann, E.
"The Urban Crisis in the World." Urban affairs quarterly 1, September 1965, p. 65-82.

6513 Wirth, L.
"Urbanism as a Way of Life." American journal of sociology 44, July 1938, p. 1-24.

6514 Woodbury, C.
"Economic Implications of Urban Growth." Science 129, June 12, 1959, p. 1585-1590.

6515 Woortmann, K.
"Implicações Sociais do Desenvolvimento e da Urbanização." Rio de Janeiro, Educação e ciências sociais (10:20), May-August 1962, p. 110-119.

6516 Zimmer, B.G.
"Farm Background and Urban Participation." American journal of sociology 61, March 1956, p. 470-475.

Latin America

6517 Argoytia Roiz, Miguel
"Algunos Aspectos de la Urbanización en América Latina." México, Comercio exterior (10:1), January 1960, p. 32-35.

6518 Borobio Navarro, L.
"Incógnita de la Ciudad Moderna." Bogotá, Arco 48, September 1964, p. 618-621.

6519 Browning, Harley L.
"Recent Trends in Latin American Urbanization." Annals of the American Academy of Political & Social Science 316, March 1958, p. 111-120.

6520 Carlson, C.E.
"Large United States Delegation Attends Montevideo Inter-American Municipal Congress." American city 68, April 1953, p. 119.

6521 Casis, Ana, & Kingsley Davis
"Concentración y Desarrollo Urbano en América

Latina." México, El trimestre económico, October/ December 1947, p. 406-456.

6522 Cavalcanti, Jeronymo, ed.
"Segundo Congreso Inter-Americano de Municipios, Realizado en Santiago de Chile." Rio de Janeiro, Revista municipal de engenharia, October 1947, p. 185-207.

6523 Chaunu, Pierre
"Urbanisation et Croissance en Amérique Latine." Le Havre, Cahiers de sociologie économique 10, May 1964, p. 209-246.

6524 "Cities of America." Saturday evening post 224, August 4, 1951, p. 32-33; April 12, 1951, p. 32-33; May 24, 1951, p. 26-27.

6525 "City Growth and Bigger Markets." Latin American business highlights 11, 3d quarter 1961, p. 8-11.

6526 Cole, John P.
"The Million Cities of Latin America." Sheffield, Geography 4, 1962, p. 414-415.

6527 Davee, R. L.
"Urbanization in Latin America." The Hague, Local government throughout the world 1, February 1962, p. 3-5.

6528 Davis, Kingsley, & Ana Casis
"Urbanization in Latin America." Milbank Memorial Fund quarterly (24:2, 3), April, July 1946, p. 1-45.

6529 Frank, Andrew G.
"La Inestabilidad Urbana en América Latina." México, Cuadernos americanos (144:1), January-February 1966, p. 55-73.

6530 "Expansión Urbana en la América Latina Durante el Siglo XIX." Seville, Estudios americanos (XIII:67-68), 1957, p. 255-293.

6531 Gallart, Horacio
"Las Segundas Ciudades de América." Buenos Aires,

Revista geográfica americana, May 1943, p. 241-248.

6532 Germani, Gino
"Urbanización, Secularización y Desarrollo Económico." México, Revista mexicana de sociología (25:2), May-August 1963, p. 625-646.

6533 Goldman, Frank P.
"Big Métropole, América do Sul." Journal of inter-American studies 7, October 1965, p. 514-540.

6534 Goldrich, Daniel
"Peasants' Sons in City Schools: an Inquiry into the Politics of Urbanization in Panama and Costa Rica." Human organization 23, Winter 1964, p. 328-333.

6535 Gomez Mayorga, Mauricio
"El Fenómeno Urbano en Latinoamérica." México, Panoramas 5, September-October 1963, p. 7-52.

6536 Guillén Martínez, F.
"What's Happened to Latin America's Small Towns?" Américas 8, April 1956, p. 8-12.

6537 Haar, C.M.
"Latin America's Troubled Cities." Foreign affairs 41, April 1963, p. 536-549.

6538 Hardoy, Jorge E., et al
"Conclusions and Evaluation of the Symposium on 'The Process of Urbanization in America Since its Origins to the Present Time' (Held at Mar del Plata, Argentina, as a Part of the 37th International Congress of Americanists, September 4th Through 10th, 1966)." Latin American research review (II: 2), Spring 1967, p. 76-90.

6539 Hernández Millares, J.
"Ciudades de América." México, Humanismo (3: 14), September 1953, p. 52-55.

6540 Hoyt, H.
"The Residential and Retail Patterns of Leading Latin American Cities." Land economics 39, 1963, p. 449-454.

6541 Lambert, Denis
"L'Urbanisation Accélérée de l'Amérique Latine et la Formation d'un Secteur Tertiaire Refuge." Brussels, Civilisations (XV:3), 1965, p. 309-325.

6542 Lambert, Denis
"Urbanisation et Développement Economique en Amérique Latine." Toulouse, Caravelle 3, 1964, p. 266-274.

6543 Martínez Guerrero, A.
"La Urbanización en América Latina." México, Investigación económica (23:89), 1st quarter 1963, p. 275-281.

6544 Métraux, Alfred
"The Changing Face of Latin America." Unesco courier 14, June 1961, p. 24-31.

6545 Miguens, J.E.
"Ciudad, Masificación y Comunidad." Córdoba, Revista de la Universidad Nacional de Córdoba (4: 3-4), July-October 1963, p. 495-512.

6546 Monbeig, Pierre
"Reflexions sur les Capitales Latino-américaines." Toulouse, Caravelle 3, 1964, p. 24-29.

6547 Morse, Richard M.
"Cidades Latino-Americanas: Aspectos da Função e Estrutura." Rio de Janeiro, América latina (5:3), July-September 1962, p. 35-63.

6548 Pastor, José M. F.
"Streets and Spaces." Americas (19:10), October 1967, p. 5-11.

6549 Phillips, J.R.
"Prospects for the Urban Peace Corps." Peace Corps volunteer, July 1967, p. 2-6.

6550 Powelson, John P., & Anatole A. Solow
"Urban and Rural Development in Latin America; with Questions and Answers." Annals of the American Academy of Political & Social Science 360, July 1965, p. 48-62.

6551 Santos, Milton
"As Grandes Cidades Latinoamericanas." Rio de Janeiro, América latina (6:3), July-September 1963, p. 85-89.

6552 Sebastián, Santiago
"El Urbanismo Hispanoamericano." Bogotá, Eco (6:5), March 1963, p. 530-544.

6553 Smith, Thomas L.
"Urbanization in Latin America." International journal of comparative sociology (4:2), September 1963, p. 227-242.

6554 Solari, Aldo E.
"Impacto Político de las Deferencias de los Países en los Grados e Indices de Modernización y Desarrollo Económico en América Latina." Rio de Janeiro, América latina (VIII:1), January-March 1965, p. 5-21.

6555 Solow, Anatole A.
"Urban Progress in Latin America." American city 65-69, September 1950, p. 124-126- June 1954, p. 99-101.

6556 Solow, Anatole A.
"Urbanization in Latin America." Development digest (IV:4), January 1967, p. 2-8.

6557 Tricart, Jean
"Quelques Caractéristiques Générales des Villes Latino-américaines." Toulouse, Caravelle 3, 1964, p. 36-48.

6558 "Urbanization in Latin America." New York, World business 5, Chase Manhattan Bank, March 1967, p. 5-8.

6559 Wingo, Lowdon
"Recent Patterns of Urbanization Among Latin American Countries." Urban affairs quarterly (II:3), March 1967, p. 81-109.

Argentina

6560 Bagú, Sergio
"Argentina." México, Cuadernos americanos (20: 6), November-December 1961, p. 19-32.

6561 Bonilla, José
"Política de Desarrollo Regional y Urbano Argentino; Bases de Desarrollo." Buenos Aires, Nuestra arquitectura (28:347), October 1958, p. 42-48.

6562 Bonilla, José
"Radiografía de la Estructura Urbana Argentina." Buenos Aires, Nuestra arquitectura (28:345), August 1958, p. 43-48.

6563 "Ciudad-Jardín 'El Libertador.' Una Nueva y Moderna Ciudad Consagrada a la Memoria del General Don José de San Martín" Buenos Aires, Revista de arquitectura (35:356), August 1950, p. 242-248.

6564 Fochier-Hauke, G.
"Tucumán, eine Stadt am Ostrand der Vorpuna." Berlin, Die erde 1, 1950, p. 37-53.

6565 Frías, P.J.
"Algo por Hacer: la Ciudad Argentina." Córdoba, Revista de la Universidad Nacional de Córdoba (IV: nos. 3-4, 2d series), 1963, p. 341-353.

6566 Germani, Gino
"El Proceso de Urbanización en la Argentina." Revista interamericana de ciencias sociales (2a. época, 2-3), 1963, p. 287-345.

6567 Martonne, E. de
"Buenos Aires: Etude de Géographie Urbaine." Paris, Annales de géographie 44, 1935, p. 281-304.

6568 Melo, C.R.
"Formación y Desarrollo de las Ciudades Argentinas." Córdoba, Revista de la Universidad Nacional de Córdoba (IV: nos. 3-4, 2d series), 1963, p. 381-414.

6569 Mignanego, Alberto A.
"Ensayo de Antropogeografía del Pueblo en Forma-

ción Manuel B. Gonnet." Buenos Aires, GAEA (Anales de la Sociedad Argentina de Estudios Geográficos) 5, 1937, p. 395-422.

6570 Padula, E. L.
"Orden y Destino de la Ciudad de Córdoba." Córdoba, Revista de la Universidad Nacional de Córdoba (IV: nos. 3-4, 2d series), 1963, p. 359-377.

6571 Zamorano, M.
"Problêmes Géographiques de Buenos Aires." Toulouse, Caravelle 3, 1964, p. 192-198.

Bolivia

6572 Bolivia. Laws, statutes, etc.
"Se Eleva a Categoría de Ciudad la Población de Yacuiba, Capital de la Provincia Gran Chaco del Departamento de Tarija. Ley de 25 de Febrero de 1957." La Paz, Gaceta oficial, año 1, no. 1, January/June 1957, p. 1.

6573 "Causas y Efectos del Exodo Rural." La Paz, Khana (2:17-18), July 1956, p. 65-84.

6574 Hawthorn, H.B., & A.E. Hawthorn
"The Shape of a City: Some Observations on Sucre, Bolivia." Sociology & social research 33, 1948, p. 87-91.

Brazil

6575 Ab'saber, A. Nacib
"A Cidade de Manaus." São Paulo, Boletim paulista de geografia 15, 1953, p. 18-45.

6576 Almeida, R.
"Cidade e Desenvolvimento." Rio de Janeiro, Revista brasileira dos municipalidades (13:49-52), January-December 1960, p. 75-76.

6577 Argué, P.
"Rio de Janeiro et sa Banlieue." Bordeaux, Cahiers d'outre-mer (17:65), January-March 1964, p. 100-105.

6578 Azevedo, Aroldo de
"Aldeias e Aldeamentos de Indios." São Paulo,

Boletim paulista de geografia 33, October 1959, p. 23-40.

6579 Azevedo, Aroldo de
"Brazilian Cities; a Sketch of Urban Geography." Montreal, Revue canadienne de géographie 5, 1951, p. 25-43.

6580 Azevedo, Aroldo de
"Embriões de Cidades Brasileiras." São Paulo, Boletim paulista de geografia 25, 1957, p. 31-69.

6581 Barros, Souza
"Nordestinos: Pioneirismo e Emigração." Rio de Janeiro, O observador econômico e financeiro (21: 250), December 1956, p. 58-61.

6582 Bastos, Antonio Dias Tavares
"A Legendary City is About to Die--for the Second Time." Paris, The courier 11, March 1957, p. 26-30.

6583 Bazzanella, Waldemiro
"Industrialização e Urbanização no Brasil." Rio de Janeiro, Boletim do Centro Latinoamericano de Pesquisas em Ciências Sociais (6:1), January-March 1963, p. 3-27.

6584 Bernardes, L. M. Cavalcanti
"Elementos para o Estudo Geográfico das Cidades." Rio de Janeiro, Boletim geográfico 154, 1960, p. 41-48.

6585 Bernardes, L. M. Cavalcanti
"Setores de Organização Urbana na Região do Rio de Janeiro." Rio de Janeiro, Revista geográfica do Instituto Panamericano de Geografia e Historia (29:55), July-December 1961, p. 37-50.

6586 Bernardes, L. M. Calcavanti, et al
"Bibliografia de Geografia Urbana do Brasil, I-." Rio de Janeiro, Boletim geográfico (19:161), March-April 1961, p. 309-311; (19:162), May-June 1961, p. 408.

6587 Boudeville, J. R.
"Brasilia." Brussels, Industrie (14:1), January 1960, p. 15-24.

6588 Boynard, A. Peixoto, & M. T. Ribeiro Soares
"Santa Teresa, um Bairro Residencial no Centro do Rio de Janeiro." Rio de Janeiro, Boletim carioca de geografia (XI:2), 1958, p. 77-88.

6589 Brazil. Conselho Nacional de Estatística. Diretoria de Documentação e Divulgação
"Municipios. Divisão Territorial do Brasil. Municipios Instalados--31-XII-1956." Rio de Janeiro, Boletim geográfico (15:140), September/October 1957, p. 660-685.

6590 Brazil. Conselho Nacional de Estatística
"Divisão Territorial do Brasil: Municípios Instalados--31-XII-1956." Rio de Janeiro, Revista brasileira dos municípios (9:35/36), June/December 1956, p. 254-274.

6591 "Brazil Holds Cities Progress Contest." National municipal review 46, May 1957, p. 276.

6592 Camârgo, José F. de
"Características e Tendencias Principais das Migrações Internas no Brasil, nas suas Relações com a Urbanização e a Industrialização." São Paulo, Boletim paulista de geografia 33, October 1959, p. 3-22.

6593 Camârgo, José F. de
"Migrações Internas e Desenvolvimento Econômico no Brasil." São Paulo, Boletim paulista de geografia 30, October 1958, p. 5-12.

6594 Carmin, Robert L.
"Rapid Growth of Itapací, Brazil; a Frontier Town." Annals of the Association of American Geographers 47, June 1957, p. 156.

6595 Carvalho, A.
"Ritmos, Procesos e Intensidade de Urbanização no Estado da Bahia, Brasil." Salvador, Boletim baiano de geografia 4, 1961, p. 17-46.

6596 Corrêa, Virgilio
"Cidades Serranas: Teresópolis, Nova Friburgo, Petrópolis." Rio de Janeiro, Revista brasileira de geografía, January/March 1947, p. 3-56.

6597 Deffontaines, Pierre
"Du Patrimonio au Condominio: Contribution a la Géographie Urbaine du Brésil." Bordeaux, Cahiers d'outre-mer (14:53), March-April 1961, p. 98-101.

6598 Deffontaines, Pierre
"The Origin and Growth of the Brazilian Network of Towns." Geographical review, July 1938, p. 379-399.

6599 Delorenzo Nêto, Antonio
"O Aglomerado Urbano de São Paulo." Bêlo Horizonte, Revista brasileira de estudos politicos (3:6), July 1959, p. 111-143.

6600 Delorenzo Nêto, Antonio
"A Desigualdade Entre os Municípios." Rio de Janeiro, Revista brasileira dos municípios (12: 47-48), July-December 1959, p. 122-126.

6601 Delorenzo Nêto, Antonio
"A Realidade e Configuração Social do Município." São Paulo, Sociologia (19:4), October 1947, p. 235-252.

6602 "Dream City Coming True in Brazil." Pan American Union bulletin 81, January 1947, p. 50-51.

6603 Eiselen, E.
"Impressions of Belém, Manaus and Iquitos, Amazonia's Largest Cities." Journal of geography (56: 2), 1957, p. 51-56.

6604 "Encontro dos Municípios Paulistas 1º, São Paulo, 1962; Resoluções." Rio de Janeiro, Revista brasileira dos municípios (15:59-60), July-December 1962, p. 192-194.

6605 "For the Good of Brazil, Improve Your Municipality." American city 71, January 1956, p. 22.

6606 Geiger, Pedro Pinchas
"Ensaio para a Estrutura Urbana do Rio de Janeiro." Rio de Janeiro, Revista brasileira da geografia 1, 1960, p. 3-45.

6607 Geiger, Pedro Pinchas
"Exemplos de Hierarchia de Cidades no Brasil." Rio de Janeiro, Boletim carioca de geografia (X: 3-4), 1957, p. 5-15.

6608 Geiger, Pedro Pinchas, & F. Davidovich
"Aspectos do Fato Urbano no Brasil." Rio de Janeiro, Revista brasileira de geografia 2, 1961, p. 263-362.

6609 Grande, J. C. P.
"Cidades Novas no Brasil." Rio de Janeiro, Revista brasileira dos municípios (8:30), April/June 1955, p. 91-100.

6610 Grande, J. C. P.
"Vilas Maiores que Cidades, Segundo os Censos de 1940 e 1950. (Pará ao Ceará)." Rio de Janeiro, Revista brasileira dos municípios (6:21), January/March 1953, p. 57-58.

6611 Guimarães, A. da Cruz
"Para um Análisis Sociológico de los Centros Semi-Rurales y Semi-Urbanos de Brasil." México, Revista mexicana de sociología (20:3), September-December 1958, p. 751-760.

6612 Guimarães, J. Nunes
"Contrastes Brasileiros. Minas--Rio de Janeiro--São Paulo--Distrito Federal." Rio de Janeiro, Boletim geográfico (16:147), November/December 1958, p. 718-722.

6613 Heller, F.
"Historia Natural de uma Rua Suburbana." São Paulo, Sociologia (5:3), 1943, p. 199-216.

6614 Holford, William
"Brasilia, a New Capital City for Brasil." London, The architectural review (22:731), December 1957, p. 395-402.

6615 James, Preston E.
"Rio de Janeiro and São Paulo." Geographical review 23, 1933, p. 271-298.

6616 James, Preston E., & S. Faissol
"Problem of Brazil's Capital City." Geographical review 46, July 1956, p. 301-317; October 1958, p. 571-572.

6617 Lavedan, Pierre
"Geografia das Cidades. Evolução das Cidades: Cidades Espontáneas." Rio de Janeiro, Boletim geográfico, March 1946, p. 1535-1543.

6618 Leite, Edgard Teixeira
"Problemas Econômicos e Sociais dos Municípios Fluminenses." Rio de Janeiro, Revista brasileira dos municípios (1:3/4), July/December 1948, p. 316-332.

6619 Leloup, Y.
"Tipos de Aglomerações y Hierarchia das Cidades de Minas Gerais." Belo Horizonte, Boletim mineiro de geografia 4-5, July 1962, p. 15-28.

6620 Lenhard, R.
"Hierarquias Sociais Urbanas." São Paulo, Sociologia (25:3), September 1963, p. 253-270.

6621 Lessa de Curtis, Maria L.
"Cidades do Brasil." Rio de Janeiro, Boletim geográfico (15:138), May/June 1957, p. 307-308.

6622 Luz, Christiano Carneiro Ribeiro da
"A Transferência da Capital do País." São Paulo, Engenharía municipal (2:5), March 1957, p. 19-21.

6623 Macedo, E. de F.
"Municípios do Estado da Guanabara." Rio de Janeiro, O observador econômico e financeiro (27: 314), August-September 1962, p. 44-48.

6624 Maia, F. Prestes
"Os Grandes Problemas Urbanísticos de São Paulo." São Paulo, Digesto econômico (9:98, 100), January 1953, p. 46-52; March 1953, p. 34-42.

6625 Medeiros, Ocelio de
"Introdução a Sociologia Jurídica do Município Brasileiro." Rio de Janeiro, Revista do serviço público, November/December 1947, p. 46-56.

6626 Monbeig, Pierre
"Aspectos Geográficos do Crescimento da Cidade de São Paulo." São Paulo, Boletim paulista de geografia 16, March 1954, p. 3-29.

6627 Monbeig, Pierre
"Brésil, Quelques Etudes Récentes de Géographie Urbaine." Paris, Revue de géographie humaine et d'ethnologie (I:4), 1948-49, p. 118-120.

6628 Monbeig, Pierre
"O Estudo Geográfico das Cidades." São Paulo, Revista do Arquivo Municipal, January 1941, p. 5-38.

6629 Monbeig, Pierre
"Une Géographie de la Ville de São Paulo." Bordeaux, Cahiers d'outre-mer 49, 1960, p. 104-109.

6630 Monbeig, Pierre
"Salvador de Bahia: les Paradoxes d'une Ancienne." Paris, Industrie (14:1), January 1960, p. 25-34.

6631 Nogueira, Oracy
"Os Estudos de Comunidades no Brasil." São Paulo, Revista de antropologia (3:2), December 1955, p. 95-103.

6632 Nogueira, Oracy
"Indices do Desenvolvimento de São Paulo." Belo Horizonte, Revista brasileira de ciências sociais (2:2), July 1962, p. 143-196.

6633 Nuñez, Osorio
"O Município na América." Rio de Janeiro, O observador econômico e financeiro (17:200), September 1952, p. 83-87.

6634 Penna, J.O. Meira
"Brasilia." Lima, El arquitecto peruano 270/272,

January/March 1960, p. 18-21.

6635 Penteado, A. Rocha
"Belem: Métropole da Amazônia." São Paulo, Boletim paulista de geografia 9, October 1951, p. 65-74.

6636 "Pesquisa Urbana em São Paulo." Rio de Janeiro, Revista do serviço público (80:1), July 1958, p. 116-120.

6637 Geiger, Pedro Pinchas, & F. Davidovich
"Aspetos do Fato Urbano no Brasil." Rio de Janeiro, Revista brasileira de geografia (23:2), April-June 1961, p. 262-263.

6638 Platt, Robert S.
"Brazilian Capitals and Frontiers." The journal of geography (53:9), December 1954, p. 369-375.

6639 "População Urbana Seguindo o Tamanho das Cidades." Rio de Janeiro, Desenvolvimento e conjuntura 10, 1958, p. 87-92.

6640 "A Preview of Brasilia." Rio de Janeiro, Brazilian business (37:4), April 1957, p. 18-21.

6641 Roche, J.
"Pôrto Alegre, Métropole do Brasil Meridional." São Paulo, Boletim paulista de geografia 19, 1955, p. 30-51.

6642 Rochefort, Michel
"L'Organisation Urbaine de l'Amazonie Moyenne." Paris, Bulletin de l'Association de Géographes Français 282-283, 1959, p. 28-40.

6643 Rochefort, Michel
"Le Rôle Régional de Rio de Janeiro." Brussels, Civilisations (XVI:3), 1966, p. 365-375.

6644 Rondón, F.
"O Município e seus Problemas: Genêse, Estrutura e Destino." Rio de Janeiro, Revista brasileira dos municípios (14:55-56), July-December 1961, p. 113-114.

6645 Rose, William
"Brasilia: Custom-Built Capital in the Brazilian Hinterland." Lima, Peruvian times (18:917), July 11, 1958, p. 11-14.

6646 Santos, Milton
"Alguns Problemas do Crescimento da Cidade do Salvador." Bahia, Boletim Baiano de geografía 5-6, 1961, p. 21-36.

6647 Santos, Milton
"Contribução ao Estudo dos Centros de Cidades, o Exemplo de Cidade do Salvador." São Paulo, Boletim paulista de geografia 32, 1959, p. 17-30.

6648 Santos, Milton
"O Papel Metropolitano da Cidade do Salvador." Rio de Janeiro, Revista brasileira dos municípios (9:35-36), July-December 1956, p. 185-190.

6649 "Seminario Municipalista Baiano 2o, Caetite, Brasil, 1961; Reportagem." Rio de Janeiro, Revista brasileira dos municípios (14:53-54), January-June 1961, p. 59-62.

6650 Silva, F.N.
"'Urbanização de Rio de Janeiro' Após sua Passagem de Cidade a Estado." Rio de Janeiro, Revista de engenharia do Estado da Guanabara (30:1-2), January-June 1963, p. 14-25.

6651 Silva, L.
"Cachoeira do Campo, a Vila das Rivalidades." Rio de Janeiro, Revista brasileira de estudos políticos (1:2), July 1957, p. 132-147.

6652 Silva, Moacir M. F.
"Tentativa de Classificação das Cidades Brasileiras." Rio de Janeiro, Revista brasileira de geografia, July/September 1946, p. 283-316.

6653 Snyder, David E.
"Alternate Perspectives on Brasilia." Economic geography (40:1), January 1964, p. 34-45.

6654 Soares, M. T. de Segadas
"Nova Iguaçu: Absorção de uma Célula Urbana pelo

Grande Rio de Janeiro." Rio de Janeiro, Revista brasileira de geografia (24:2), April-June 1962, p. 155-256.

6655 "Symposium sur Brasilia." Toulouse, Caravelle 3, 1964, p. 363-390.

6656 Tavares de Sá, Hernane
"Metropolis Made to Order: Brasilia." The National Geographic magazine (117:5), May 1960, p. 704-724.

6657 "Urbanization of the New City in Rio de Janeiro." Rio de Janeiro, Conjuntura econômica internacional (XIII:3), March 1967, p. 61-65.

6658 "Verbetes para um Dicionário dos Municípios." Rio de Janeiro, Revista brasileira dos municípios (9: 34), April/June 1956, p. 140-145.

6659 Violich, Francis
"Crecimiento Urbano y Planeamiento en Brasil." Havana, Revista nacional de la propiedad urbana (26:308), October 1959, p. 25-28.

6660 Wagner, Philip L.
"Political Implications of Rapid Urbanization in Caribbean Countries." Annals of the Association of American Geographers 52, September 1962, p. 367.

Central America

6661 "Capitales Centroamericanas." San José, Repertorio centro-americano 5, April, 1966, p. 6-13.

6662 Enjalbert, Henri
"Les Capitales de l'Amérique Centrale, Sites Anciens et Essor Récent." Toulouse, Caravelle 3, 1964, p. 303-312.

Chile

6663 Borde, J.
"L'Essor d'une Capitale: Santiago de Chile." Bordeaux, Cahiers d'outre-mer 7, 1954, p. 5-24.

6664 Chilean Municipalities Congress. 1st, Viña del Mar, 1942
"Agenda y Reglamento del Primer Congreso Nacional de Municipalidades Chilenas. Agenda. Reglamento." Havana, Boletín de la Comisión Panamericana de Cooperación Intermunicipal, January-April 1942, p. 46-47.

6665 De Laubenfels, D.J.
"Urban Centers of South Central Chile." Annals of the Association of American Geographers 47, June 1957, p. 158.

6666 Friedmann, John R., & T. Lackington
"Hyperurbanization and National Development in Chile: Some Hypotheses." Urban affairs quarterly (II:4), June 1967, p. 3-29.

6667 Rottenberg, Simon
"Economic Urbana." Santiago de Chile, Finis terrae (5:17), 1st quarter 1958, p. 11-18.

6668 Silva, Herminio de Andrade e
"O Urbanismo--e o Regulamento de Construções e Urbanização da República do Chile." Rio de Janeiro, Revista municipal de engenharia, May 1942, p. 161-168.

Colombia

6669 Acevedo Latorre, E.
"Panorama Geo-Económico del Departamento del Valle." Bogotá, Economía y estadística (10:80), February 20, 1955, p. 5-48.

6670 Colombian Municipalities Congress. 1st, Bogotá, 1941
"Primer Congreso de Municipalidades Colombianas." Bogotá, Registro municipal, September 15, 1941, p. 431-465.

6671 Crist, Raymond E.
"The Personality of Popayán." Rural sociology 15, 1950, p. 130-140.

6672 Eder, G.J.
"Urban Concentration, Agriculture, and Agrarian Reform." Annals of the American Academy of Poli-

tical & Social Science 360, July 1965, p. 27-47.

6673 Fletcher, Frank
"Ciudades de Colombia." Buenos Aires, Revista geográfica americana, April 1945, p. 221-225.

6674 Forero, Manuel J.
"Ciudades de Colombia." Bogotá, Vida 40, October/November 1950, p. 41-43; 41, December 1950, p. 46-49; 42, January/February 1951, p. 17-19.

6675 Pérez Ramírez, Gustavo
"La Urbanización y el Cambio Social en Colombia." Río Piedras, Revista de ciencias sociales (IX:2), June 1965, p. 203-220.

6676 Rivas Putnam, Ignacio
"Chocontá." Bogotá, Boletin de historia y antigüedades (35:407/408), September/October 1948, p. 585-591.

6677 Vidales, Luis
"La Realidad Colombiana a Través del Censo. La Demografía del Municipio en Colombia. Por Luis Vidales, Director Nacional de Estadística." Bogotá, Anales de economía y estadística, November 5, 1942, p. 33-38.

6678 Walker, Guild
"Cali, Colombia. I-VI." Lima, Peruvian times (14:693), May 7, 1954, p. 7-9; (14:699), May 14, 1954, p. 6, 8; (14:700), May 21, 1954, p. 4, 6; (14:701), May 28, 1954, p. 4-6; (14:705), June 25, 1954, p. 4, 6, 21.

Cuba

6679 Garnett, B.
"Comités de los Mil Undertake Improvements in Cuban Cities." American city 65, April 1950, p. 82-83.

Dominican Republic

6680 "League of Municipalities in the Dominican Republic." Pan American Union bulletin 73, April 1939, p. 243.

Ecuador

6681 Albornoz, Miguel
"Una Aldea Andina. Se Adormece en el Regazo del Macizo Cordillerano." Visión (1:23), September 18, 1951, p. 37-39.

6682 Ecuadorean Municipalities Congress. 1st, Quito, 1931
"El Primer Congreso de Municipalidades Agenda. Temario General. Estatutos de la Asociación de Municipios." Havana, Boletín de la Comisión Panamericana de Cooperación Inter-municipal, January-April 1942, p. 3-6.

6683 Forero, Manuel J.
"Ciudades del Ecuador." Bogotá, Vida 51, May/June 1952, p. 43-45.

Guatemala

6684 Caplow, Theodore
"The Social Ecology of Guatemala City." Social forces 28, December 1949, p. 113-133.

6685 Reina, Rubén E.
"Urban World View of a Tropical Forest Community in the Absence of a City; Petén, Guatemala." Human organization 23, Winter 1964, p. 265-277.

Haiti

6686 Devauges, Roland
"Une Capitale Antillaise: Port-au-Prince (Haiti)." Bordeaux, Cahiers d'outre-mer (7:26), April-June 1954, p. 105-136.

Mexico

6687 Bataillon, Claude
"La Geografía Urbana de la Ciudad de México." Rio de Janeiro, América latina (7:4), October-December 1964, p. 71-87.

6688 Bataillon, Marcel
"México, Capital Mestiza." México, Ciencias políticas y sociales (10:35), January-March 1964, p. 161-184.

6689 Borja, A.
"Alvarado, Veracruz, Programa de Desarrollo Urbano." México, Arquitectura México (22:86), June 1964, p. 79-90.

6690 Cacho, R.
"La Ciudad de México." México, Revista de economía (24:4), April 1961, p. 123-133.

6691 Dotson, Floyd
"Notes on Participation in Voluntary Associations in a Mexican City." American sociological review 18, August 1953, p. 380-386.

6692 Dotson, Floyd, & L.O. Dotson
"Ecological Trends in the City of Guadalajara, Mexico." Social forces 32, May 1954, p. 367-374.

6693 Dotson, Floyd, & L.O. Dotson
"La Estructura Sociológica de las Ciudades Mexicanas." México, Revista mexicana de sociología (19:1), January-April 1957, p. 39-66.

6694 Flores, Edmundo
"El Crecimiento de la Ciudad de México." México, Investigaciones económicas, 2d quarter (XIX:74), 1959, p. 247-281.

6695 Form, William H., & William V. D'Antonio
"Integration and Cleavage Among Community Influentials in Two Border Cities." American sociological review 24, December 1959, p. 804-814.

6696 Gerstenhauer, A.
"Acapulco, die Riviera Mexikos." Berlin, Die erde 3-4, 1956, p. 270-281.

6697 González Aparicio, Luis
"El Problema Urbano Como Factor en la Formulación de un Problema." México, Revista de economía (26:3), March 1963, p. 90-95.

6698 Hayner, Norman S.
"Mexico City: its Growth and Configuration." American journal of sociology 50, January 1945, p. 295-304.

6699 Hayner, Norman S.
"Oaxaca, City of Old Mexico." Sociology & social research 29, 1944, p. 87-95.

6700 Luna, Guillermo. "Megalopolis Trends in Mexico." Athens, Ekistics (24:140), July 1967, p. 15-20.

6701 Peña, Moisés T. de la
"Problemas Demográficos y Agrarios." México, Problemas agrícolas e industriales de México (2:3-4), July-December 1950, p. 9-324.

6702 Rivera Marín, G., & R. Montes de Avila
"El Crecimiento de la Ciudad de México y sus Efectos en los Ejidos del D.F." México, Revista de economía (30:6), June 1967, p. 178-186.

6703 Ross, M.
"Mexico's Border Towns." Travel 120, November 1963, p. 32-34.

6704 Zenteno, Benítez
"La Población Rural y Urbana en México." México, Revista mexicana de sociología (24:3), September-December 1962, p. 689-703.

Peru

6705 Dollfus, Olivier
"Lima: Quelques Aspects de la Capitale du Pérou en 1958." Bordeaux, Cahiers d'outre-mer (XI:43), 1958, p. 258-271.

6706 Dollfus, Olivier
"Remarques sur Quelques Aspects de l'Urbanisation Péruvienne." Brussels, Civilisations (XVI:3), 1966, p. 338-353.

6707 Hammel, E.A.
"Some Characteristics of Rural Village and Urban Slum Populations on the Coast of Peru." Southwestern journal of anthropology (20:4), Winter 1964, p. 346-358.

Uruguay

6708 Garmendia, D.J.
"Montevideo, Elementos para una Sociología Urbana."

Montevideo, Cuadernos latinoamericanos de economía humana 2, 1959, p. 267-306.

6709 Rama, Carlos M.
"De la Singularidad de la Urbanización en el Uruguay." Río Piedras, Revista de ciencias sociales (VI:2), June 1962, p. 177-186.

6710 Snyder, David E.
"Urban Places in Uruguay and the Concept of a Hierarchy." Northwestern University studies in geography 6, 1962, p. 29-46.

Venezuela

6711 Snyder, David E.
"Ciudad Guayana, a Planned Metropolis on the Orinoco." Journal of inter-American studies 5, July 1963, p. 405-412.

6712 Sosa Rodriguez, Eduardo
"Radicación de la Población Urbana Inestable." Caracas, Cruz del sur (4:46), July 1959, p. 25-29.

West Indies and the Caribbean

6713 Lowenthal, David
"The West Indies Chooses a Capital." Geographical review XLVIII, 1958, p. 336-364.

6714 Meier, G.
"El Embalse: the Creation of a Community Organization and Urban Renewal." Community development review (5:2), June 1960, p. 18-47.

6715 "Metropolitan Influences in the Caribbean." Annals of the New York Academy of Science (83:5), January 1960, p. 763-815.

6716 Mulville, D.
"Curacão." London, Geographical magazine (34:11), 1962, p. 658-670.

URBANIZATION BIBLIOGRAPHY

Books

General

6717 American Society of Planning Officials
Guides for community planning, a bibliography. Chicago, 1956, 47p.

6718 Barnum, H.G., et al
Supplement through 1964 to central place studies; bibliography series #1. Philadelphia, Regional Science Research Institute, 1965, 50p.

6719 Berry, Brian J. L., & Allen Pred
Central place studies; a bibliography of theory and applications. Philadelphia, Regional Science Research Institute, 1961, 153p.

6720 Bestor, George C., & Holway R. Jones
City planning; a basic bibliography of sources and trends. Sacramento, California Council of Civil Engineers & Land Surveyors, 1962, 195p.

6721 Davis, Elizabeth (Gould), et al
Urbanization and changing land uses; a bibliography of selected references, 1950-58. (Miscellaneous publication # 825). Washington, U.S. Dept. of Agriculture, 1960, 212p.

6722 London. University. Centre for Urban Studies
Land use planning and the social sciences, a selected bibliography. Literature on town and country planning and related social studies in Great Britain, 1930-1963. London, 1964, 44p.

6723 Lorenz, Robert, et al, eds.
A world of cities; across-cultural urban bibliography. Syracuse, Center for Overseas Operations & Research, Maxwell Graduate School of Citizenship & Public Affairs, Syracuse University, 1964, 150p.

6724 Shillaber, Caroline, comp.
References on city and regional planning. Cambridge, M.I.T. Press, 1959, 41p.

6725 Spielvogel, Samuel
A selected bibliography on city and regional planning. Washington, Scarecrow Press, 1951, 276p.

6726 Viet, Jean
Les villes nouvelles, éléments d'une bibliographie annotée . . . New towns, a selected annotated bibliography. Paris, Unesco, 1960, 82p.

Latin America

6727 Bazzanella, Waldemiro
Problemas de urbanização na América Latina; fontes bibliográficas. Rio de Janeiro, Centro Latino-Americano de Pesquisas em Ciências Sociais, 1960, 123p.

6728 Bicker, William, et al
Comparative urban development: an annotated bibliography. Washington, American Society for Public Administration, 1965, 151p.

6729 Centro Latinoamericano de Pesquisas em Ciências Sociais
Bibliografia sôbre estudios de comunidades en América Latina. Rio de Janeiro, 1964, 24p.

6730 Guzmán, Louis E.
An annotated bibliography of publications on urban Latin America. Chicago, Dept. of Geography, University of Chicago, 1952, 53p.

6731 Rubio y Muñoz Bocanegra, Angel
Bibliografía de geografía urbana de América. Rio de Janeiro, Instituto Pan-Americano de Geografía e Historia, 1961, 229p.

Brazil

6732 Council of Planning Librarians
Bibliography on urban planning in Brazil. Eugene, 1964, 7p.

6733 Violich, Francis, & Ismael J. Cantínho Gouveia
Bibliography on urban planning in Brazil. Eugene,

Council of Planning Librarians, 1964, 25p.

Colombia

6734 Violich, Francis, & Alberto Fulleda
Bibliography on urban planning in Colombia. Eugene, Council of Planning Librarians, 1962, 11p.

Periodical Articles

General

6735 "The Literature of Urban Studies: Important Books of the Last Decade." American behavioral scientist 6, February 1963, p. 6-10.

6736 Ornati, O.
"On Metropolitan Growth: a Review of Recent Literature." Social research 28, Fall 1961, p. 359-369.

6737 "Recent Publications on Metropolitan Area Problems." Metropolitan area problems 5, September-October 1962, p. 6.

6738 Sullenger, T.E.
"Source Material in Urban Sociology." Sociology & social research 34, November 1949, p. 112-115.

6739 United Nations. Statistical Office
Demographic yearbook. 1st- , New York, 1948-

Brazil

6740 Costa Pinto, Luiz Aguiar de
"Nota Bibliográfica Sôbre Alguns Aspectos da Formação das Cidades Brasileiras." São Paulo, Boletim bibliográfico, October-December 1945, p. 19-25.

URBANIZATION RESEARCH

General

6741 Bogue, Donald J., & Dorothy L. Harris
Comparative population and urban research via multiple regression and covariance analysis; a methodological experiment with an illustrative application to the study of factors in the growth and suburbanization of metropolitan population. Oxford, Scripps Foundation for Research in Population Problems, Miami University, 1954, 75p.

6742 Bogue, Donald J., ed.
Needed urban and metropolitan research. Contributions by Harvey S. Perloff, et al. Oxford, Scripps Foundation for Research in Population Problems, Miami University, 1953, 88p.

6743 Burgess, Ernest W.
The ecology and social psychology of the city. (In Bogue, Donald J., ed. Needed urban and metropolitan research. Oxford, Scripps Foundation for Research in Population Problems, Miami University, and Population Research Training Center, University of Chicago, 1953, p. 80-81).

6744 Burgess, Ernest W.
The growth of the city: an introduction to a research project. (In Park, Robert E., et al. The city. Chicago, University of Chicago Press, 1925, p. 47-62).

6745 Burgess, Ernest W.
Urban areas. (In Smith, T.V., & L.D. White, eds. An experiment in social science research. Chicago, University of Chicago Press, 1929, p. 114-123).

6746 Chapin, F.S.
Experimental designs in sociological research. Rev. ed. New York, Harper, 1955, 297p.

6747 Chombart de Lauwe, Paul H., et al
Méthodes de recherches pour l'étude d'une grande cité. 2v. Paris, Presses Universitaires de France, 1952.

6748 Colwell, Robert C.
Economic factors in urban planning studies. Washington, G.P.O., 1966, 40p.

6749 Conference on Urban Systems Research in Underdeveloped & Advanced Economies, University of Oregon, 1959
Urban systems and economic development: papers and proceedings. Ed. by Forrest R. Pitts. Eugene, School of Business Administration, University of Oregon, 1962, 126p.

6750 Duke, R.D.
Bibliography for gaming in urban research. East Lansing, Institute for Community Development & Services, Michigan State University, 1963, 4p.

6751 Duke, R.D.
Gaming-simulation in urban research. East Lansing, Institute for Community Development, 1964, 72p.

6752 Duverger, M.
Méthodes des sciences sociales. Paris, Presses Universitaires de France, 1961, 501p.

6753 Festinger, L., & D. Katz
Research methods in the behavioral sciences. New York, Dryden Press, 1953, 660p.

6754 Gibbs, Jack P., ed.
Urban research methods. Princeton, Van Nostrand, 1961, 625p.

6755 Granai, G.
Techniques de l'enquête sociologique. (In Gurvitch, G., ed. Traité de sociologie, v. 1. Paris, Presses Universitaires de France, 1958, p. 135-151).

6756 Gryztell, Karl G.
The demarcation of comparable city areas by

means of population density. Lund, Gleerup, 1963, 111p.

6757 Gutman, Robert, & David Popenoe, eds.
Urban studies: present trends and future prospects in an emerging academic field. Princeton, American behavioral scientist (6:6), February 1963, 62p. (separately printed)

6758 Hansen, Morris H.
Improved federal statistics to serve tomorrow's urban and regional problems; report # MR-72. Los Angeles, Institute of Government & Public Affairs, University of California, 1966, 28p.

6759 Hauser, Philip M., ed.
Handbook for social research in urban areas. Paris, Unesco, 1965, 214p.

6760 Institut International de Statistique
International statistical yearbook of large towns. The Hague, 1954-

6761 Inter-University Seminar on Urbanization in the Missouri River Basin
Approaches to the study of urbanization; proceedings. Ed. by Richard L. Stauber. Lawrence, Governmental Research Center, University of Kansas, 1964, 250p.

6762 Lebret, Louis J., et al
L'enquête urbaine; l'analyse du quartier et de la ville. Paris, Presses Universitaires de France, 1955, 187p.

6763 Mayer, H.M., & C.F. Kohn, eds.
Readings in urban geography. Chicago, University of Chicago Press, 1959, 625p.

6764 Mitchell, J.C., & F.R.H. Shaul
An approach to the measurement of commitment to urban residence. (In Central African Scientific and Medical Congress, Lusaka, Zambia, 1963. Science and medicine in Central Africa. Oxford, Pergamon Press, 1964, p. 625-633).

6765 North Carolina. University. Institute for Research in Social Sciences. Urban Studies Program
Annual report of research in progress. Chapel Hill, Annual.

6766 Oklahoma. University. College of Continuing Education
Terminal report: programs in urban sciences by Joe E. Brown, Director. Norman, 1964, 194p.

6767 Perloff, Harvey S., & Henry Cohen, eds.
Urban research and education in the New York metropolitan region (Volume 2, The university in regional affairs, a report). New York, Regional Plan Association, 1965, variously paged.

6768 Pfeil, E.
Grosstadtforschung. Bremen, Horn, 1950, 272p.

6769 Pfouts, Ralph W., ed.
The techniques of urban economic analysis. West Trenton, Chandler-Davis Pub., 1960, 410p.

6770 Pickard, Jerome P., & Gene C. Tweraser
Urban real estate research, 1963. Washington, Urban Land Institute, 1964-

6771 Plog, Stanley C.
An inventory of urban studies conducted by selected faculty members of the University of California, Los Angeles: report # MR-60. Los Angeles, Institute of Government & Public Affairs, University of California, 1966, 20p.

6772 Polansky, N.A., ed.
Social work research. Chicago, University of Chicago Press, 1960, 306p.

6773 The relationship between population growth, capital formation and employment opportunities in underdeveloped countries. (In Proceedings of the World Population Conference, Rome, August 31-September 10, 1954. v. 5. Paris, United Nations, 1955, p. 695-711).

6774 Resources for the Future
A national program of research in housing and urban

development; the major requirements and a suggested approach . . . by Harvey S. Perloff. Washington, 1961, 32p.

6775 Resources for the Future. Committee on Urban Economics
Urban and regional studies at U.S. universities; a report based on a 1963 survey of urban and regional research. Comp. & ed. by Scott Keyes under the sponsorship of the Bureau of Community Planning. Urbana, University of Illinois, 1964, 127p.

6776 Schnore, Leo F., & Henry Fagin, eds.
Urban research and policy planning. Beverly Hills, Sage Publications, 1967, 640p.

6777 Sussman, Marvin B., ed.
Community structure and analysis. New York, Crowell, 1959, 454p.

6778 Sweeney, Stephen B., & George S. Blair, eds.
Metropolitan analysis: important elements of study and action. Philadelphia, University of Pennsylvania Press, 1958, 189p.

6779 Territorial Planning-Housing-Information. International Group for Cooperation & Research on Documentation
Report of the first session of the group, Paris, December 1966 (Doc. Ref. AG-1-CR). Paris, 1967? 35p.

6780 Texas. University. Institute of Public Affairs
A quarter century of municipal research. Austin, 1947, 22p.

6781 Town Planning Institute
Planning research. London, 1965, 226p.

6782 U.S. Bureau of the Budget
Urban research under federal auspices: a survey prepared for the Subcommittee on Intergovernmental Operations, United States Senate. Washington, G.P.O., 1964, 77p.

6783 Urban research and policy planning (Urban affairs annual reviews, v. 1). Beverly Hills, Sage Publications, 1967- Annual.

6784 Urban research news. Beverly Hills, Sage Publications, 1966-

6785 Vidich, A.J., et al
Reflections on community studies. New York, Wiley, 1964, 359p.

6786 Wallace, Rosemary H.
International bibliography and reference guide on urban affairs. Ramsey, Ramsey-Wallace Corp., 1966, 92p.

6787 Warren, R.L.
Studying your community. New York, Sage Foundation, 1955, 385p.

6788 Webber, M.M., et al
Explorations into urban structure. Philadelphia, University of Pennsylvania Press, 1964, 246p.

6789 Woodbury, Coleman
Urban studies: some questions of outlook and selection. Pittsburgh, Institute of Local Government, University of Pittsburgh, 1960, 20p.

6790 Young, P.V.
Scientific social surveys and research. 3d ed. Englewood Cliffs, Prentice-Hall, 1956, 540p.

Latin America

6791 Bacigalupo, J.L., et al
El proceso de urbanización en América Latina. Buenos Aires, Centro de Estudios Urbanos y Regionales, Instituto Torcuato Di Tella, 1968, 307p.

6792 Latin American Conference on Regional Science. 1st, Caracas, 1962
Papers. Caracas, 1963, 222p.

6793 Miró, Carmen A.
Experience and problems in the population of demographic training and research in developing countries;

the case of Latin America (Meeting on population policies in relation to development in Latin America); UP/Ser. H/V/REPO/I/13. Washington, Pan American Union, 1967, 18p.

6794 Pan American Union. Dept. of Statistics. Inter-American Statistical Institute
América en cifras. Washington, 1961-

6795 Seminar on Urbanization Problems in Latin America, Santiago de Chile, 1959
Urbanization in Latin America; proceedings. Ed. by Philip M. Hauser. New York, International Documents Service, 1961, 331p.

Argentina

6796 Córdoba, Argentine Republic (Province) Dirección General de Estadística, Censos e Investigaciones
Revista. Córdoba, 1950-

6797 Fundación de Investigaciones Económicas Latinoamericanas
Indicadores de coyuntura. Buenos Aires, # 9, November 1966-

6798 Germani, Gino
Estructura social de la Argentina: análisis estadístico. Buenos Aires, Ed. Raigal, 1955, 279p.

6799 Santa Fé, Argentine Republic (Province) Dirección General de Investigaciones, Estadística y Censos
Anuario estadístico. Santa Fé, 1948-

Brazil

6800 Anuario estadístico do Brasil, 1965. Rio de Janeiro, Conselho Nacional da Estatística, 1965- Annual.

6801 Brazil. Comissão Censitaria Nacional
Censo experimental de Brasilia; população, habitação, 17 de maio de 1959. Rio de Janeiro, 1959, 109p.

6802 Brazil. Conselho Nacional de Estatística
Sinopse estatística dos municípios . . . de Estado de São Paulo. Rio de Janeiro, Serviço Gráfico do Instituto Brasileiro de Geografia e Estatística, 1948-

6803 A cidade industrial em números. Bêlo Horizonte, Centro das Indústrias da Cidade Industrial, 1964, 20p.

6804 São Paulo, Brazil (City) Depto. de Cultura. Div. de Estatística e Documentação Social
Boletim. São Paulo, 1949-

6805 São Paulo, Brazil (State) Depto. de Estatística
Resumo anual. São Paulo. Annual.

Chile

6806 Chile. Dirección de Estadística y Censos
Algunos resultados provinciales del XIII censo de población obtenido por muestreo. Santiago, 1963, 284p.

6807 Chile. Universidad. Depto. de Extensión Cultural
Boletín informativo: número especial dedicado a la primera etapa del Seminario del Gran Santiago, April-May 1957. Santiago, 1957, 118p.

6808 Mattelart, Armand
Enfoque metodológico del estudio demográfico en un proyecto de desarrollo regional (Proyecto Maule Norte). Santiago, 1964, 120 plus 5p.

Colombia

6809 Anuario general de estadística. Bogotá, 1955-

6810 Colombia en cifras: síntesis de la actividad económica, social y cultural de la nación. Bogotá, Librería Colombiana Camacho Roldán, 1963, 793p.

Costa Rica

6811 Costa Rica. Dirección General de Estadística y Censos
Censo de vivienda, 1963. San José, 1966, 458p.

6812 Costa Rica. Dirección General de Estadística y Censos
1864 censo de población. San José, 1964, 103 plus 71p.

Ecuador

6813 Ecuador. Dirección General de Estadística y Censos
Censo experimental de la ciudad de Quito, año 1957.

Quito, 1959, 69p.

6814 Guayaquil. Universidad. Instituto de Investigaciones Económicas y Políticas
Guayaquil en cifras. 2d ed. Guayaquil, 1962, 201p.

El Salvador

6815 Salvador. Dirección General de Estadística y Censos
Censo industrial, 3er, 1961. San Salvador, 1966, 314p.

Haiti

6816 Haiti. Récensement de la République
Premier dénombrement de la population. Port-au-Prince, Cité Dumarsais Estime, 1950, 47p.

Mexico

6817 Mexico. Dirección General de Estadística
Memoria de los censos nacionales, 1960-1961. México, 1965, 297p.

Nicaragua

6818 Nicaragua. Dirección General de Estadística. División Demográfica y Administrativa
Población por departamentos y municipios, según sexo, urbana y rural. Managua? Irregular.

Peru

6819 Boletín de estadística peruana. Lima, Ministerio de Finanza y Comercio, 1958-

6820 Lima (Province) Depto. de Estadística y Demografía
Decenio demográfico, 1938-1947. Lima, 1948, 36p.

Uruguay

6821 Montevideo. Intendencia Municipal
Boletín; censo y estadística. Montevideo, Irregular.

6822 Uruguay. Dirección General de Estadística y Censos
Características demográficas del Uruguay. Montevideo? Ministerio de Hacienda, 1962, 39p.

Venezuela

6823 Organization of American States. Inter-American Statistical Institute

Venezuela. 2d ed. Washington, Pan American Union, 1966, 78p.

6824 Universidad de los Andes. Facultad de Economía. Instituto de Investigaciones Económicas Anuario estadístico de los Andes: Venezuela, 1966. Mérida, 1966-

West Indies and the Caribbean

6825 Annuaire statistique de la Guadeloupe, 1959-1962. Paris, I.N.S.E., 1962, 80p.

6826 Trinidad & Tobago. Central Statistical Office Trinidad & Tobago today. #1- , Port-of-Spain, 1966-

Periodical Articles

General

6827 Adrian, Charles R. "Metropology: Folklore and Field Research." Public administration review 21, Summer 1961, p. 148-157.

6828 Agnew, J.W. "Out of Chaos: Some Answers." American city 67, May 1952, p. 117.

6829 Alexander, J.W. "The Case for Applied Community Studies." Economic geography 28, October 1952, p. 375-376.

6830 Arensberg, Conrad M. "The Community as Object and Sample." American anthropologist (63:2), Part 1, April 1961, p. 241-264.

6831 Arensberg, Conrad M. "The Community-Study Method." American journal of sociology (60:2), September 1954, p. 109-124.

6832 Bebout, J.E. "Urban Extension: University Services to the Urban Community." American behavioral scientist (VI:6), February 1963, p. 21-39.

6833 Belknap, G.M., & M.J. Schussheim
"Urban Research from a Federal Standpoint." Urban affairs quarterly (I:1), September 1965, p. 3-16.

6834 Blizzard, S.W.
"Research on the Rural-Urban Fringe: a Case Study." Sociology & sociological research 38, January 1954, p. 143-149.

6835 Blumer, Herbert
"The Study of Urbanization and Industrialization Methodological Deficiencies." Rio de Janeiro, Boletim del Centro Latino-Americano de Pesquisas em Ciências Sociais (2:2), May 1959, p. 17-34.

6836 Broude, H.W.
"Significance of Regional Studies for the Elaboration of National Economic History." Journal of economic history 20, December 1960, p. 588-596.

6837 Chombart de Lauwe, Paul H., & L. Couvreur
"La Sociologie Urbaine en France; Tendances Actuelles de la Recherche et Bibliographie." Paris, Current sociology (4:1), 1955, p. 1-52.

6838 "The City of the Future." Athens, Ekistics 20, July 1965, p. 4-52.

6839 "City 600 Miles Long is Subject of Yale University Planning Study." American city 70, May 1955, p. 108.

6840 Clinard, Marshall B.
"Evaluation and Research in Urban Development." Bucharest, Centro social (10:53-54), 1963, p. 187-198.

6841 Collison, P.
"Social Research and Community Centre Leadership in Urban Areas." International review of community development 3, 1959, p. 159-167.

6842 "Community: the Relation of the Concept 'Community' to Urban Research." Urban affairs quarterly (I:1), September 1965, p. 27-33.

6843 Dever, J.E.
"Developing a Municipal Research Program." Public management 45, April 1963, p. 79-83.

6844 Devereux, E.C., & J. Harding
"Community Participation as a Research Problem." Journal of social issues (16:4), 1960, p. 1-7.

6845 DeVesty, R.E.
"Official and Unofficial Research Bureaus Serve the City of Syracuse." American city 68, May 1953, p. 136-137.

6846 Engelbert, W.
"Mapas de Cidades." Rio de Janeiro, Boletim geográfico (20:167), March-April 1962, p. 198-199.

6847 Ferguson, C.E.
"Statistical Study of Urbanization." Social forces 37, October 1958, p. 19-26.

6848 Gans, Herbert J.
"Sociology of New Towns: Opportunities for Research." Sociology & social research 40, March 1956, p. 231-239.

6849 Garmendia, D.J.
"Problemática de su Comprobación y Aplicaciones de la Teoría Propuesta." Córdoba, Revista de la Universidad Nacional de Córdoba (4:3-4), July-October 1963, p. 469-493.

6850 Gaus, J.M.
"Education for the Emerging Field of Regional Planning and Development." Social forces 29, March 1951, p. 229-237.

6851 George, P.
Présent et Avenir des 'Grands Ensembles.'" Paris, Cahiers internationaux de sociologie (10:35), July-December 1963, p. 25-42.

6852 Gibbs, Jack P., & Kingsley Davis
"Características de los Datos Utilizables en un Estudio Internacional Sobre la Urbanización." México, Revista mexicana de sociología (20:3), September-December 1958, p. 649-667.

6853 Gibbs, Jack P., & Kingsley Davis
"Conventional Versus Metropolitan Data in the International Study of Urbanization." American sociological review 23, October 1958, p. 504-514.

6854 "Greatest Year of My Life." American city 74, November 1959, p. 7.

6855 Gutman, Robert
"Urban Studies as a Field of Research." American behavioral scientist (VI:6), February 1963, p. 9-14.

6856 Gutman, Robert & David Popenoe
"The Literature of Urban Studies: Important Books of the Last Decade." American behavioral scientist (VI:6), February 1963, p. 5-9.

6857 Gutman, Robert, & Francine F. Rabinovitz
"The Relevance of Domestic Urban Studies to International Urban Research." Urban affairs quarterly (I:4), June 1966, p. 45-64.

6858 Harris, B.
"The Uses of Theory in the Simulation of Urban Phenomena." Journal of American Institute of Planners, September 1966, p. 258-272.

6859 Hoffman, H. U.
"Amerikanische Community-Forschung." Dortmund, Soziale welt (5:2), 1954, p. 122-132.

6860 Holtzmann, Wayne H.
"Community Action Research--An Approach to Social Problems in Texas Cities." Public affairs comment 6, September 1960, p. 1-4.

6861 "ICMA Adopts Policy on Urban Research." National civic review 53, May 1964, p. 278-279.

6862 Isard, W.
"Notes on the Use of Regional Science Methods in economic History." Journal of economic history 20, December 1960, p. 597-600.

6863 Johnson, D. G.
"Mobility as a Field of Economic Research." Southern economic journal 15, October 1948, p. 152-161.

6864 Kercher, L.C., et al
"Public Opinion Survey in Kalamazoo, Michigan." American city 68, May 1953, p. 127.

6865 Kuper, Leo
"Social Science Research and the Planning of Urban Neighborhoods." Social forces 29, March 1951, p. 237-243.

6866 Lane, T.
"The Urban Base Multiplier: an Evaluation of the State of the Art." Land economics (XLII:3), August 1966, p. 339-347.

6867 Mabry, J.H.
"Census Tract Variation in Urban Research." American sociological review (23:2), April 1958, p. 193-196.

6868 Mars, D.
"Work for the Future." National civic review 52, May 1963, p. 251-254.

6869 Nash, P.H.
"Interdisciplinary Approaches to the Study of Emerging Polynuclear Metropolitan Regions." Annals of the Association of American Geographers 49, June 1959, p. 204.

6870 "New Urban Research Group is Formed." American city 72, June 1957, p. 201.

6871 Peters, W.S.
"A Method of Deriving Geographic Patterns of Associated Demographic Characteristics Within Urban Areas." Social forces (35:1), October 1956, p. 62-67.

6872 "Pittsburgh's Mayor Acclaims Research and Citizen Aid." American city 64, October 1949, p. 5.

6873 Popenoe, David, & Robert Gutman
"Centers for Urban Studies: a Review." American behavioral scientist (VI:6), February 1963, p. 48-54.

6874 Reiss, Albert J.
"Research Problems in Metropolitan Population Re-

distribution." American sociological review 21, October 1956, p. 571-577.

6875 Rottier, G.
"Remarques sur les Méthodes d'Etude Urbaine." Paris, Revue française de recherche opérationnelle (7:29), 1963, p. 335-338.

6876 Shibata, T.
"Points of Attack in International Urban Studies." American behavioral scientist (VI:6), February 1963, p. 44-48.

6877 Sjoberg, G.
"Urban Community Theory and Research: a Partial Evaluation." American journal of economics & sociology (14:2), January 1955, p. 199-206.

6878 Stover, C. F.
"Technology for Cities." National civic review 53, June 1964, p. 297-300.

6879 Szabo, D.
"L'Etude de la Société Urbaine: Synthèse de Recherches." Louvain, Bulletin de l'Institut de Recherches Economiques et Sociales de Louvain 7, November 1953, p. 599-669.

6880 "Urban Problems and Prospects." Law and contemporary problems 30, Winter 1965, p. 9-229.

6881 Van Arsdol, M.D., et al
"The Generality of Urban Social Area Indexes." American sociological review (23:3), June 1958, p. 277-284.

6882 Weaver, Robert C.
"Urban Growth Problems and Research." Construction review 8, June 1962, p. 4-9.

6883 Wilson, Ray W.
"Organization for Administrative Research in the City Hall." Public management 40, September 1958, p. 206-211.

6884 "World Society for the Study of Human Settlements." Architectural record 137, April 1965, p. 358.

Latin America

6885 Chombart de Lauwe, Paul H.
"Esbozo de un Plan de Investigaciones Acerca de la Vida Social en el Medio Urbano." México, Revista mexicana de sociología (20:3), September-December 1958, p. 637-648.

6886 Costa Pinto, Luiz Aguiar de
"Investigaciones Sobre Estratificación y Movilidad Social en América Latina." Caracas, Sociología (1:2), December 1962, p. 5-27.

6887 Delorenzo Nêto Antônio
"O Estudo Sociolôgico da Cidade." São Paulo, Sociologia (21:1), March 1959, p. 3-22.

6888 Gaete Darbo, A.
"Evaluación de las Estadísticas Vitales en América Latina." Rio de Janeiro, América latina (7:2), April-June 1964, p. 59-73.

6889 Herrera, Felipe
"La Universidad y los Problemas del Crecimiento Urbano." Santiago, Revista Consejo de Rectores Universidades Chilenas (II:2), June 1967, p. 9-10.

6890 Keyfitz, Nathan
"Assessment of Teaching and Training Programs in the Universities of Latin America." Milbank Memorial Fund quarterly (42:2), 1964, p. 236-255.

6891 Luna Clara, C.
"El Método de Observaciones Participantes Aplicado al Estudio de Zonas Urbanas." San Salvador, Revista salvadoreña de ciencias sociales 1, January-March 1965, p. 158-168.

6892 Mortara, Giorgio
"Appraisal of Census Data for Latin America." Milbank Memorial Fund quarterly (62:2), 1964, p. 57-86.

6893 Pozas Arciniega, Ricardo
"Los Límites del Método para el Estudio de la Comunidad." Rio de Janeiro, América latina (7:3), July-September 1964, p. 89-102.

6894 Rochefort, Michel
"Métodos de Estudo das Rêdes Urbanas." Rio de Janeiro, Boletim geográfico (19:160), January-February 1961, p. 3-18.

6895 Somoza, J.
Demographic Research of the Centro Latinoamericano de Demografía (CELADE) and the Economic Commission for Latin America." Milbank Memorial Fund quarterly (62:2), 1964, p. 121-147.

Brazil

6896 "Dados Demográficos do Distrito Federal." Rio de Janeiro, Conjuntura econômica (V:9), 1951, p. 44-45.

6897 "Fatos Demográficos do Distrito Federal e São Paulo, de 1904 a 1950." Rio de Janeiro, Conjuntura econômica (V:1), 1951, p. 54-61.

6898 Ianni, Octavio
"O Método em Uma Comunidad Amazônica." São Paulo, Sociología (20:4), October 1958, p. 574-580.

Central America

6899 Romero G., M.
"The Teaching of Statistics and Demography in Central America." Milbank Memorial Fund quarterly (62:2), 1964, p. 256-275.

Chile

6900 Rojas, O.
"Chile y su Población a Través de los Censos." Santiago, Revista geográfica de Chile "Terra Australis" 2, December 1949, p. 37-49.

West Indies and the Caribbean

6901 Broom, Leonard
"Urban Research in the British Caribbean: a Prospectus." Mona, Social & economic studies (I:1), February 1953, p. 113-119.

6902 Debien, G.
"Estudios Sobre los Problemas de las Antillas Francesas." Seville, Estudios americanos (XIV:75), 1957, p. 255-260.

6903 Roberts, George W.
"The Census Research Program for the West Indies." Milbank Memorial Fund quarterly (62:2), 1964, p. 175-197.

DIRECTORY SECTION

DIRECTORY = 1: RESEARCH CENTERS, INSTITUTES AND RESEARCH ORGANIZATIONS CONCERNED WITH URBANIZATION AND ALLIED FIELDS

DIRECTORY = 2: "WORKING" ORGANIZATIONS (Departments of city, state, and federal governments, and business and professional associations, foundations, and international organizations concerned with urbanization).

DIRECTORY = 3: SPECIALISTS IN URBANIZATION AND CONCOMITANT AREAS OF ACTIVITY

In Directories = 1 and = 2 there are three sections covering the United States, Latin America, and other world areas, respectively. Within each section arrangement is as follows: (1) alphabetical by nation or state (for the United States); and (2) alphabetical by name of institution or organization. In Directory = 3, names and addresses of specialists are arranged (1) under professional fields of activity; (2) geographically according to nation and/or region of Latin America; and (3) alphabetically. In instances where individuals have competence in specialties additional to those under which they have been listed, such professional subject-fields and geographic areas of specialization are indicated following the respective names and addresses. In all instances the abbreviation "L.A." stands for Latin America.

Disclaimer Statement

This Directory Section is furnished as a matter of service only. While efforts have been made to include correct, current information, no guarantee is given nor should any be inferred, with regard to accuracy and/or timeliness of any and all data contained herein.

The author, the publisher and the officers, agents, and employees thereof, make no warranties, express or implied, representations or promises whatsoever concerning the individuals, firms, agencies, organizations or other entities referred to or named in this Directory Section. Users of this Directory Section communicate and negotiate with individuals, firms, or organizations listed herein solely at their own risk. The author, the publisher and the officers, agents, and employees thereof, shall not be liable for any damages whatsoever arising from any errors or omissions made in the compiling or printing of this Directory Section.

DIRECTORY # 1:

RESEARCH CENTERS, INSTITUTES AND RESEARCH ORGANIZATIONS CONCERNED WITH URBANIZATION AND ALLIED FIELDS LOCATED

(A) IN THE UNITED STATES OF AMERICA

(B) IN LATIN AMERICA

(C) ELSEWHERE

1A. RESEARCH CENTERS, INSTITUTES AND RESEARCH ORGANIZATIONS CONCERNED WITH URBANIZATION AND ALLIED FIELDS, LOCATED IN THE UNITED STATES OF AMERICA

(Note: An explanation is given in certain instances where the title of the individual unit listed does not specify its field of activity)

Alabama

1 Latin American Area Program
University of Alabama
University, Ala. 35486

Arizona

2 Bureau of Government Research
Arizona State University
Tempe, Ariz. 85281

3 Center for Latin American Studies
Arizona State University
Tempe, Ariz. 85281
(communications, municipal government)

4 Institute of Public Administration
Arizona State University
Tempe, Ariz. 85281

5 Latin American Area Center
University of Arizona
Tucson, Ariz. 85721

6 Latin American Res. Program & Data Center
Dept. of Latin American Area Studies
American Institute for Foreign Trade
Phoenix, Ariz. 85001

California

7 Center for Latin American Studies
California State College at Los Angeles
Los Angeles, Calif. 90032

8 Center for Latin American Studies
University of California
Berkeley, Calif. 94720

9 Center for Planning & Development Res.
College of Environmental Design
University of California
Berkeley, Calif. 94720

10 Center for Res. on Economic Development
Dept. of Economics
San Diego State College
San Diego, Calif. 92115

11 Center for the Study of Democratic Institutions
2056 Eucalyptus Hill Rd.
Santa Barbara, Calif. 93103

12 Church Growth Institute for Latin America
Fuller Seminary
135 North Oakland Avenue
Pasadena, Calif. 91101

13 Committee on Latin American Studies
Bolivar House
Stanford University
Stanford, Calif. 94305

14 Dept. of Architecture
University of California
Berkeley, Calif. 97420

15 Dept. of City & Regional Planning
University of California
Berkeley, Calif. 94720

16 Institute for Communications Research
Stanford University
Stanford, Calif. 94305

17 Institute of Urban & Regional Development
University of California
Berkeley, Calif. 94720

18 Inter-America Institute of Calif. State Colleges
California State College at Fullerton
800 North State College Blvd.
Fullerton, Calif. 92631

19 Inter-American Studies Program
Elbert-Covell College
University of the Pacific
Stockton, Calif. 95204

20 International Development Center
Stanford University
Stanford, Calif. 94305

21 International Institute of Housing Technology
Fresno State College
Fresno, Calif. 93726

22 International Population & Urban Research
University of California
Berkeley, Calif. 94720

23 Latin American Studies Program
San Diego State College
San Diego, Calif. 92115

24 Latin American Center
University of California
Los Angeles, Calif. 90024

25 Latin American Res. Program
University of California
Riverside, Calif. 92502

26 Latin American Studies Center
California State College at Long Beach
Long Beach, Calif.

27 Missions Advanced Res. & Communication
919 West Huntington Drive
Monrovia, Calif. 91016
(religion, communications)

28 Population Res. Laboratory
University of Southern California
Los Angeles, Calif. 90007

29 Consortium of Mexican Border Universities
c/o Center for Latin American Studies
San Diego State College
San Diego, Calif. 92115

30 Rand Corporation
1700 Main Street
Santa Monica, Calif. 91406
(demography, migration)

31 School of Architecture & Urban Planning
University of California
Los Angeles, Calif. 90024

32 School of Public Health
University of California
Los Angeles, Calif. 90024

33 Survey Research Center
University of California
Berkeley, Calif. 94720
(demography, religion, education)

Colorado

34 Aspen Institute for Humanistic Studies
P.O. Box 219
Aspen, Colo. 81611
(demography)

35 Bureau of Government Res. & Service
University of Colorado
Boulder, Colo. 80302

36 Center for Latin American Studies
Colorado State University
Ft. Collins, Colo. 80521

37 Center for Latin American Studies
University of Denver
Denver, Colo. 80210

38 Committee on Latin American Studies
University of Colorado
Boulder, Colo. 80302

39 Institute of Behavioral Science
University of Colorado
Boulder, Colo. 80302

40 International Economic Studies Center
University of Colorado
Boulder, Colo. 80302

41 National Center of Communication Arts & Sciences
P.O. Box 207
Denver, Colo. 80201

Connecticut

42 Council on Latin American Studies
Yale University
New Haven, Conn. 06520

43 Dept. of History
Yale University
New Haven, Conn. 06520

44 Economic Growth Center
Yale University
New Haven, Conn. 06520
(industrialization)

45 Human Relations Area Files
Yale University
New Haven, Conn. 06520
(res. materials on demography)

46 Latin American Studies Program
University of Connecticut
Storrs, Conn. 06268

47 Program of Urban & Regional Planning
Yale University
New Haven, Conn. 06520

District of Columbia

48 Brookings Institution
1775 Massachusetts Avenue, N.W.
Washington, D.C. 20036
(industrialization, demography, transportation)

49 Bureau of Labor Statistics
U.S. Dept. of Labor
Washington, D.C. 20210

50 Center for Population Res.
Georgetown University
Washington, D.C. 20007

51 Center for Res. in Social Systems
American University
Washington, D.C. 20016

52 Committee on Sanitary Engineering & Environment
National Academy of Sciences-National Research Council
Washington, D.C. 20037

53 Community Water Supply Branch, AID
U.S. Dept. of State
Washington, D.C. 20523

54 Dept. of Geography & Regional Science
George Washington University
Washington, D.C. 20007

55 Division of Research & Statistics
Social Security Administration
U.S. Dept. of Health, Education & Welfare
Washington, D.C. 20201

56 Economic Development Institute
International Bank for Reconstruction & Development
1818 H Street, N.W.
Washington, D.C. 20005

57 Highway Research Board
National Academy of Sciences-National Research Council
Washington, D.C. 20037

58 Institute of Ibero-American Studies
Catholic University of America
Washington, D.C. 20017

59 Inter-American Center
School of Advanced International Studies
Johns Hopkins University
Washington, D.C. 20036

60 Inter-American Development Bank
1818 H Street, N.W.
Washington, D.C. 20005

61 Inter-American Program for Advanced Studies in Social Sciences for the Caribbean Region (PICSES)
Pan American Union
Washington, D.C. 20006

62 International Business Res. Laboratory
American University
Washington, D.C. 20016

63 International Study Center
1755 Massachusetts Avenue, N.W.
Washington, D.C. 20036

64 Latin American Development Administration Committee
American Society for Public Administration

1225 Connecticut Avenue, N.W.
Washington, D.C. 20036

65 Latin American Information Center on Mental Health
Pan American Health Organization
525 - 23rd Street, N.W.
Washington, D.C. 20036

66 Latin American Language & Area Program
American University
Washington, D.C. 20016

67 Latin American Science Board
National Academy of Sciences-National Research Council
Washington, D.C. 20037

68 Latin American Studies Program
Georgetown University
Washington, D.C. 20007

69 National Planning Association
1525 - 18th Street, N.W.
Washington, D.C. 20036

70 Pan American Health Organization
525 - 23rd Street, N.W.
Washington, D.C. 20036

71 Planning Foundation of America
c/o American Institute of Planners
917 - 15th Street, N.W.
Washington, D.C. 20005

72 Policy on Arterial Highways in Urban Areas
c/o Inter-American Highway Commission
Pan American Union
Washington, D.C. 20006

73 Population Council, Inc.
1735 "I" Street, N.W.
Washington, D.C. 20001

74 Population Crisis Committee
1730 K Street, N.W.
Washington, D.C. 20006

75 Population Reference Bureau
1755 Massachusetts Avenue, N.W.
Washington, D.C. 20036

76 Program of Study on Latin America
School of Education
Catholic University of America
Washington, D.C. 20017

77 Program on Western Hemisphere Studies
Catholic University of America
Washington, D.C. 20017

78 Regional Economic Development Institute
1725 DeSales Street, N.W.
Washington, D.C. 20036

79 Resources for the Future, Inc.
1755 Massachusetts Avenue N.W.
Washington, D.C. 20036

80 Select Commission on Western Hemisphere Immigration
U.S. Senate
Washington, D.C.

81 Social Science & Community Programs Branch, Life Sciences Division
Science Information Exchange
Smithsonian Institution
1730 M Street, N.W.
Washington, D.C. 20036

82 Special Operations Research Office
(Human Relations Research Organization)
American University
Washington, D.C. 20016

83 Subcommittee on Urban Affairs
Joint Economic Committee
U.S. Congress
House Office Bldg.
Washington, D.C.

84 Urban Land Institute
1200 - 18th Street, N.W.
Washington, D.C. 20036

Florida

85 Andean Institute
University of West Florida
Pensacola, Fla. 32504

86 Center for Advanced International Studies

University of Miami
Coral Gables, Fla. 33124

87 Center for Inter-American Studies
Florida State University
Tallahassee, Fla. 33206

88 Center for Latin American Studies
University of Florida
Gainesville, Fla. 32601

89 Res. Institute for Cuba & the Caribbean
University of Miami
Coral Gables, Fla. 33124

Georgia

90 Dept. of Sociology
University of Georgia
Athens, Ga. 30601

Illinois

91 The Adlai Stevenson Institute of International Affairs
Robie House
5757 South Woodlawn Avenue
Chicago, Ill. 60637
(urbanization)

92 Center for International Comparative Studies
University of Illinois
Urbana, Ill. 61801

93 Center for Latin American Economic Studies
University of Chicago
Chicago, Ill. 60637

94 Center for Latin American Studies
University of Illinois
Urbana, Ill. 61801

95 Center for Urban Studies
University of Chicago
Chicago, Ill. 60601

96 Comparative Education Center
University of Chicago
Chicago, Ill. 60601

97 Cooperative League of the U.S.A.
59 E. Van Buren Street
Chicago, Ill. 60605

98 Council of Planning Librarians
P.O. Box 229
Monticello, Ill. 61856

99 Dept. of City & Regional Planning
Illinois Institute of Technology
Chicago, Ill. 60616

100 Latin American Studies Program
Bradley University
Peoria, Ill. 61606

101 Dept. of Communications
University of Illinois
Urbana, Ill. 61801

102 Dept. of Economics
University of Chicago
Chicago, Ill. 60601

103 Division of Latin American Studies
Eastern Illinois University
Charleston, Ill. 61920

104 Institute for Training in Municipal Administration
1313 E. 60th Street
Chicago, Ill. 60636

105 Institute of Latin American Studies
Southern Illinois University
Carbondale, Ill. 62901

106 International Information Service
Library of International Relations
000 North Wabash Avenue
Chicago, Ill. 60611

107 Latin American Center
University of Illinois
Chicago Circle
Chicago, Ill. 60680

108 Population Res. & Training Center
University of Chicago
Chicago, Ill. 60601

109 Transportation Center Library
Northwestern University
1810 Hinman Avenue
Evanston, Ill. 62201

110 Urban Journalism Center
Medill School of Journalism
Evanston, Ill. 62201

Indiana

111 Center for the Study of Man
University of Notre Dame
Notre Dame, Ind. 46556
(demography, religion, social change)

112 Dept. of Mass Communications
Indiana University
Bloomington, Ind. 47401

113 Dept. of Sociology
Goshen College
Goshen, Ind.
(demography, religion)

114 International Development Res. Center
Indiana University
Bloomington, Ind. 47403
(industrialization)

115 Language & Area Center for Latin America
Indiana University
Bloomington, Ind. 47401

116 Latin American Studies Institute
Indiana University
Bloomington, Ind. 47405

Iowa

117 Dept. of Mass Communications
University of Iowa
Iowa City, Iowa 52240

Kansas

118 Center of Latin American Studies
University of Kansas
Lawrence, Kansas 66044

119 International Theater Studies Center
University of Kansas
Lawrence, Kansas 66044

Kentucky

120 Spindletop Research, Inc.
Lexington, Kentucky 40505
(industrialization)

Louisiana

121 Center for Latin American Studies
Tulane University
New Orleans, La. 70118

122 Dept. of Social Work
Tulane University
New Orleans, La. 70112

123 Institute of Latin American Studies
Louisiana State University
Baton Rouge, La. 70803

124 Institute of Population Research
Louisiana State University
Baton Rouge, La. 70803

125 Inter-American Center for Medical Res. & Training
Tulane University
New Orleans, La. 70112

126 Middle American Research Institute
Tulane University
New Orleans, La. 70118

127 Urban Life Research Institute
Tulane University
New Orleans, La. 70112

Maryland

128 Dept. of Population & Family Health
School of Public Health
Johns Hopkins University
Baltimore, Md. 21205

129 Latin American Studies Committee
University of Maryland
College Park, Md. 20742

130 National Clearinghouse for Mental Health Information
National Institutes of Mental Health
Bethesda, Md.

Massachusetts

131 Center for Development Economics
Williams College
Williamstown, Mass. 01267
(industrialization)

132 Center for Population Studies
Harvard University
Cambridge, Mass. 02138

133 Center for Studies in Education and Development
Harvard University
Cambridge, Mass. 02138

134 Center for Urban Studies
Graduate School of Design
Harvard University
Cambridge, Mass. 02138

135 Dept. of Architecture, Landscape Architecture, and City and Regional Planning
Harvard University
Cambridge, Mass. 02138

136 Dept. of City & Regional Planning
Massachusetts Institute of Technology
Cambridge, Mass. 02138

137 Dept. of Demography & Human Ecology
School of Public Health
Harvard University
Boston, Mass. 02115

138 Four-College Cooperative Program in Latin American Studies
c/o Dr. Howard J. Wiarda
Dept. of Government
University of Massachusetts
Amherst, Mass. 01002

139 Harvard-M.I.T. Joint Center for Urban Studies
Massachusetts Institute of Technology
66 Church Street
Cambridge, Mass. 02138

140 Inter-American Civil Engineering Program
Dept. of Civil Engineering
Massachusetts Institute of Technology
Cambridge, Mass. 02138

141 Labor Relations & Res. Center
University of Massachusetts
Amherst, Mass. 01002

142 Latin American Program
Smith College
Northampton, Mass. 01060

143 Latin American Studies Program
Brandeis University
Waltham, Mass. 02154

144 Latin American Studies Program
Harvard University
Cambridge, Mass. 02138

145 Latin American Studies Program
Mount Holyoke College
South Hadley, Mass. 01075

146 Roper Public Opinion Res. Center
Williams College
Williamstown, Mass. 01267

147 Urban Studies in Developing Areas Program
Dept. of City & Regional Planning
Massachusetts Institute of Technology
Cambridge, Mass. 02138

Michigan

148 Bureau of Social & Political Research
Michigan State University
East Lansing, Mich. 48823

149 Center for Population Planning
School of Public Health
University of Michigan
Ann Arbor, Mich. 48104

150 Dept. of Anthropology
University of Michigan
Ann Arbor, Mich. 48104
(urbanization in pre-Conquest Mexico)

151 Dept. of Communications
Michigan State University
East Lansing, Mich. 48823

152 Dept. of Communications
University of Michigan
Ann Arbor, Mich. 48104

153 Dept. of Microbiology & Public Health
Michigan State University
East Lansing, Mich. 48823

154 Economic Development Research Center
University of Michigan
Ann Arbor, Mich. 48104

155 Institute for International Studies in Education
Michigan State University
East Lansing, Mich. 48823

156 Latin American Studies Center
Michigan State University
East Lansing, Mich. 48823

157 Latin American Studies Program
Western Michigan University
Kalamazoo, Mich. 49001

Minnesota

158 Center for International Relations & Area Studies
University of Minnesota
Minneapolis, Minn. 55455

159 Committee on Latin American Studies
University of Minnesota
Minneapolis, Minn. 55455

160 Dept. of Sociology
University of Minnesota
Minneapolis, Minn. 55455

161 Latin American Area Division
International Studies Program
Macalester College
St. Paul, Minn. 55101

Mississippi

162 Latin American Studies Center
University of Southern Mississippi
Southern Station
Hattiesburg, Miss. 39401

Missouri

163 Graduate Program in Latin American Studies
Washington University
St. Louis, Mo. 63130

164 Institute of Urban & Regional Studies
Washington University
St. Louis, Mo. 63130

165 Inter-American Group for Comparative Sociology
c/o Latin American Area Committee
Dept. of Sociology
Washington University
St. Louis, Mo. 63130

166 Latin American Studies Program
St. Louis University
St. Louis, Mo. 63130

167 School of Music
Washington University
St. Louis, Mo. 63130
(work on music of Mexico)

168 Social Science Institute
Washington University
St. Louis, Mo. 63130

Nebraska

169 Institute for Latin American & International Studies
University of Nebraska
Lincoln, Nebraska 68508

New Jersey

170 Bureau of Urban Research
Princeton University
Princeton, N.J. 08540

171 Office of Fopulation Research
Princeton University
Princeton, N.J. 08540

172 Industrial Relations Section
Princeton University
Princeton, N.J. 08540
(labor)

173 Latin American Institute
Rutgers, the State University
New Brunswick, N.J. 08903

174 Program in Latin American Studies
Princeton University
Princeton, N.J. 08540

175 Urban Studies Center
Rutgers, the State University
New Brunswick, N.J. 08903

New Mexico

176 Center for Community Action Services
University of New Mexico
Albuquerque, N.M. 87106

177 Division of Inter-American Affairs
University of New Mexico
Albuquerque, N.M. 87106

New York

178 American Public Health Association
1790 Broadway
New York, N.Y.

179 Bureau of Applied Social Research
Columbia University
New York, N.Y. 10027

180 Bureau of Social Affairs
United Nations
New York, N.Y. 10017

181 Center for Aerial Photographic Studies
Cornell University
Ithaca, N.Y. 14850

182 Center for Development Education
School of Education
Syracuse University
New York, N.Y. 13210

183 Center for Housing, Planning & Building
United Nations
New York, N.Y. 10017

184 Center for Latin American Studies
City University of New York
New York, N.Y. 10031

185 Center for Latin American Studies
Queens College
Flushing, Long Island, N.Y. 11367

186 Center for Overseas Operations & Res.
Maxwell Graduate School of Citizenship & Public Affairs
Syracuse University
Syracuse, N.Y. 13210

187 Center for Res. on International Development
State University of New York
Buffalo, N.Y. 14214
(industrialization)

188 Committee on Andean Studies
c/o Dr. Albert Solá
Linguistics Dept.
Cornell University
Ithaca, N.Y. 14850
(includes Pennsylvania State University, Cornell, Syracuse University, and State University of New York at Buffalo)

189 Committee on International Social Welfare
National Social Welfare Assembly
345 E. 46th Street
New York, N.Y. 10017

190 Committee on Urbanization
Social Science Research Council
230 Park Avenue
New York, N.Y. 10017

191 Community Development Foundation
345 E. 46th Street
New York, N.Y. 10017

192 Community Research Associates, Inc.
124 E. 40th Street
New York, N.Y. 10016

193 Comparative Criminal Law Program
New York University
New York, N.Y. 10003
(criminology)

194 Comparative Education Society
525 W. 120th Street
New York, N.Y.

195 Council on Higher Education in the American Republics (CHEAR)
799 United Nations Plaza
New York, N.Y. 10017

196 Dept. of Architecture & Urban Planning
Columbia University
New York, N.Y. 10027

197 Dept. of City & Regional Planning
Cornell University
Ithaca, N.Y. 14850

198 Dept. of Communications
Syracuse University
Syracuse, N.Y. 13210

199 Dept. of History
State University of New York at Stony Brook
Stony Brook, Long Island, N.Y.

200 Dept. of Housing
Cornell University
Ithaca, N.Y. 14850

201 Dept. of Sociology
Columbia University
New York, N.Y. 10027

202 Division of Urban Studies
Center for Housing & Environmental Studies
Cornell University
Ithaca, N.Y. 14850

203 Foreign Area Fellowship Program
110 E. 59th Street
New York, N.Y. 10022
(awards for research training and internships in Latin America)

204 Institute of International Studies
Columbia University
New York, N.Y. 10027
(education)

205 Institute of Latin American Studies
Columbia University
New York, N.Y. 10027

206 Institute of Planning & Housing
New York University
New York, N.Y. 10003

207 Institute of Public Administration
55 W. 44th Street
New York, N.Y. 10036

208 Institute of Urban Environment
Division of Urban Planning
Columbia University
New York, N.Y. 10027

209 International Economic Integration Program
Columbia University
New York, N.Y. 10027
(industrialization)

210 International Legal Res. Program
Columbia University
New York, N.Y. 10027

211 International Population Program
McGraw Hall
Cornell University
Ithaca, N.Y. 14850

212 Latin American Studies Program
Long Island University
385 Flatbush Avenue
Brooklyn, N.Y. 11201

213 Latin American Urban Housing Policy Project
Latin American Program
Cornell University
Ithaca, N.Y. 14850

214 Milbank Memorial Fund
40 Wall Street
New York, N.Y. 10005

215 Missionary Research Library
3041 Broadway
New York, N.Y. 10027

216 Planned Parenthood-World Population
515 Madison Avenue
New York, N.Y. 10010

217 Population Council
245 Park Avenue
New York, N.Y. 10017

218 Population Program
Ford Foundation
477 Madison Avenue
New York, N.Y. 10010

219 Research Center in Comparative Politics & Administration
Brooklyn College
Brooklyn, N.Y. 11210

220 Research Institute for the Study of Man
162 E. 78th Street
New York, N.Y. 10021
(demography and public health, mainly in Caribbean area)

221 Research Project in International Economics

Columbia University
New York, N.Y. 10027
(industrialization)

222 St. John's University
Latin American Area Program
Jamaica, Long Island, N.Y.
11432

223 Social Work Research Group
345 E. 46th Street
New York, N.Y. 10017

224 Sociological Research Laboratory
Fordham University
New York, N.Y. 10007

225 State University of New York at Buffalo
Dept. of Anthropology
Buffalo, N.Y. 14214

226 UN Center for Housing, Building & Planning
United Nations Plaza
New York, N.Y. 10017

227 UN Institute for Training & Research (UNITAR)
801 United Nations Plaza
New York, N.Y. 10017

228 "Urbanization in Latin America" course
Columbia University
New York, N.Y. 10027

229 World Council of Churches
Room 439
475 Riverside Drive
New York, N.Y. 10027

North Carolina

230 Center for Urban & Regional Studies
University of North Carolina
Chapel Hill, North Carolina
27514

231 Dept. of City & Regional Planning
University of North Carolina
Chapel Hill, North Carolina
27514

232 International Program in Sanitary Engineering Design
Dept. of Environmental Sciences & Engineering, School of Public Health
University of North Carolina
Chapel Hill, North Carolina
27514

233 Latin American Social Science Faculty (FLACSO)
Institute of Latin American Studies
University of North Carolina
Chapel Hill, North Carolina
27514

234 Program in Mass Communications Res.
School of Journalism
University of North Carolina
Chapel Hill, North Carolina
27514

Ohio

235 Center for Human Resources Research
Ohio State University
Columbus, Ohio 43210
(labor)

236 Dept. of Economics
Ohio State University
Columbus, Ohio 43210

237 International Education Institute
Ohio University
Athens, Ohio 45701

238 Latin American Program
Great Lakes College Association
Antioch College
Yellow Springs, Ohio 45387

239 Scripps Foundation for Res. in Population
Miami University
Oxford, Ohio 45056

Oregon

240 Latin American Language & Area Studies Center
Portland State College
P.O. Box 751
Portland, Oregon 97207

241 Latin American Studies Committee
University of Oregon
Eugene, Oregon 97403

Pennsylvania

242 Dept. of Regional Science
University of Pennsylvania
Philadelphia, Pa. 19104

243 Economic & Social Development Program
University of Pittsburgh
Pittsburgh, Pa. 15213

244 Inter-American Studies Center
Temple University
Philadelphia, Pa. 19122

245 International Education Program
School of Education
University of Pittsburgh
Pittsburgh, Pa. 15213

246 Latin American Education Program
Pennsylvania State University
University Park, Pa. 16802

247 Latin American Studies Committee
University of Pennsylvania
Philadelphia, Pa. 19104

248 Latin American Studies Program
Pennsylvania State University
University Park, Pa. 16802

249 Population Studies Center
University of Pennsylvania
Philadelphia, Pa. 19104

250 Regional Science Research Institute
3831 Walnut Street
Philadelphia, Pa. 19104

Rhode Island

251 Dept. of Anthropology
Brown University
Providence, R.I.
(community development)

252 Dept. of Economics
Vanderbilt University
Nashville, Tenn.
(industrialization)

Texas

253 Center for Intercultural Studies in Folklore & Oral History
University of Texas
Austin, Texas 78712
(oral history & literature)

254 Center for Economic Development
University of Texas
Austin, Texas 78712
(industrialization)

255 Center for Communication Research
School of Communication
University of Texas
Austin, Texas 78712

256 Latin American Area Studies
Texas Technological College
Lubbock, Texas 79509

257 Latin American Studies Program
University of Texas at El Paso
El Paso, Texas 79902

258 Language & Area Center for Latin America
Southern Methodist University
Dallas, Texas 75222

259 Law Institute of the Americas
Southern Methodist University
Dallas, Texas 75222

260 Population Research Center
Dept. of Sociology
University of Texas
Austin, Texas 79112

261 Program of Inter-American Education
Texas A & M University
Academic Bldg. 106
College Station, Texas 77840

262 School of Education
University of Texas
Austin, Texas 78712

Virginia

263 Center for Latin American Studies
University of Virginia
Charlottesville, Va. 22903

264 Center for the Study of Science, Technology & Public Policy
University of Virginia
Charlottesville, Va. 22903
(demography, urban problems)

Washington

265 International Communications Studies Center

University of Washington
Seattle, Washington 98105

Wisconsin

266 Center for International Communication Studies
Dept. of Mass Communications
University of Wisconsin
Madison, Wisconsin 53706

267 Dept. of Rural Sociology
University of Wisconsin
Madison, Wisconsin 53706
(community development)

268 Ibero-American Studies Program
University of Wisconsin
Madison, Wisconsin 53706

269 Laboratory of International Research in Education
University of Wisconsin
Madison, Wisconsin 53706

270 Land Tenure Center
University of Wisconsin
Madison, Wisconsin 53706

271 Language & Area Center for Latin America
University of Wisconsin-Milwaukee
Milwaukee, Wisconsin 53201

272 Latin American Program
Ripon College
Ripon, Wisconsin 54971

273 Latin American Studies Program
Wisconsin State University
Ear Claire, Wisconsin 54701

274 Latin American Studies Program
Wisconsin State University
Stevens Point, Wisconsin 54481

275 Midwest Universities Consortium for International Activities
Office of International Studies & Programs
University of Wisconsin
Madison, Wisconsin 53706
(the Universities of Illinois, Indiana, and Wisconsin, and the Michigan State University have joined to cooperate in international activities).

Puerto Rico

276 Caribbean Studies Institute
University of Puerto Rico
Rio Piedras, Puerto Rico 00931

277 Center for the Study of Contemporary Latin America
Inter-American University
San Germán, Puerto Rico 00753

278 Institute of Labor Relations
University of Puerto Rico
Rio Piedras, Puerto Rico 00931

Virgin Islands

279 Caribbean Research Institute
College of the Virgin Islands
St. Thomas, Virgin Islands

1B. RESEARCH CENTERS AND INSTITUTES CONCERNED WITH URBANIZATION AND ALLIED FIELDS LOCATED IN LATIN AMERICA

(Note: a note is given in instances where the title of the individual institute or center does not specify its field of activity. Designations of fields of research activity apply to the nation in which the given research center or institute is located, unless specified otherwise).

Argentina

280 Academia Argentina de Bellas Artes
(Argentine Academy of Fine Arts)
Cuba 1823
Buenos Aires, Argentina

281 Academia Argentina de Letras
(Argentine Academy of Letters)
Sánchez de Bustamante 2663
Buenos Aires, Argentina

282 Centro Argentino de Técnicos en Estudios del Trabajo
(Argentine Center for Labor Studies Experts)
Buenos Aires, Argentina

283 Centro de Documentación e Información para Asuntos Municipales
(Documentation and Information Center for Municipal Affairs)
Santa Fé, Argentina

284 Centro de Documentación Sociológica
(Center of Sociological Documentation)
c/o Instituto Latinoamericano de Relaciones Internacionales
Montevideo 666
Buenos Aires, Argentina (L. A.)

285 Centro de Investigación y Acción Social
(Center of Research and Social Action)
Palpa 2440
Buenos Aires, Argentina (L. A.)

286 Centro de Estudios Urbanos y Regionales
(Center for Urban and Regional Research)
Instituto Torcuato di Tella
Virrey del Pino 3230
Buenos Aires, Argentina (L. A.)

287 Centro de Investigaciones en Ciencias del Hombre
(Center for Research in the Sciences of Man)
c/o Centro del Instituto Latinoamericano de Relaciones Internacionales
Montevideo 666
Buenos Aires, Argentina (L. A.)

288 Centro de Sociológia Comparada
(Center for Comparative Sociology)
Instituto Torcuato di Tella
Virrey del Pino 3230
Buenos Aires, Argentina (L. A.)

289 Centro Interamericano de Administración de Programas de Bienestar Social de la O. E. A.
(Inter-American Center for Administration of O. A. S. Social Welfare Programs)
Buenos Aires, Argentina (L. A.)

290 Centro para Estudios Urbanos y Regionales
(Center for Regional and Urban Studies)
Consejo Nacional de Investigaciones Científicas y Técnicas
Rivadavia 1917
Buenos Aires, Argentina (L. A.)

291 Equipo de Planeamiento Regional y Urbano
(Regional and Urban Planning Team)
Centro de Investigación Aplicada
Universidad de Buenos Aires
Buenos Aires, Argentina

292 Faculty of Architecture and City Planning

Universidad Católica de Córdoba
Córdoba, Argentina

293 Faculty of Architecture and City Planning
Universidad de Buenos Aires
Buenos Aires, Argentina

294 Faculty of Architecture and City Planning
Universidad Nacional de Córdoba
Córdoba, Argentina

295 Dept. of Urban and Rural Improvements
Faculty of Architecture and City Planning
Universidad Nacional de La Plata
La Plata, Argentina

296 Fundación de Investigaciones Economicas Latinoamericanas
(Latin American Economic Research Foundation)
Esmeralda 320, 4°. piso
Buenos Aires, Argentina (L.A.)

297 Institute of Regional and City Planning
Universidad Nacional del Litoral
Bulevar Pellegrini 2750
Santa Fé, Argentina

298 Institute of Social and Economic Development
Universidad de Buenos Aires
Viamonte 430
Buenos Aires, Argentina (L.A.)

299 Instituto Argentino de Estudios Municipales
(Argentine Institute of Municipal Studies)
Buenos Aires, Argentina

300 Instituto Argentino de la Vivienda, A.C.
(Argentine Housing Institute)
Paseo Colón 823
Buenos Aires, Argentina

301 Instituto Argentino de Urbanismo
(Argentine City Planning Institute)
Viamonte 1359
Buenos Aires, Argentina

302 Instituto de Arquitectura y Urbanismo
(Institute of Architecture and City Planning)
Universidad Nacional de Tucumán
Tucumán, Argentina

303 Instituto de Ciencia Política
(Institute of Political Science)
Universidad del Salvador
Buenos Aires, Argentina

304 Instituto de Desarrollo Económico y Social
(Institute of Economic and Social Development)
Sarmiento 1179
Buenos Aires, Argentina

305 Instituto de Economía de los Transportes
(Institute of Transportation Economy)
Universidad de Buenos Aires
Buenos Aires, Argentina

306 Instituto de Investigaciones Estéticas
(Institute of Aesthetic Research)
Universidad Nacional de Cuyo
Mendoza, Argentina (L.A.)

307 Instituto de Investigaciones y Docencia Criminológicas
(Institute of Criminological Research and Training)
Ministerio de Gobierno
Provincia de Buenos Aires
Pueyrredón 572
San Martín
Buenos Aires, Argentina

308 Instituto de Literatura Argentina
(Institute of Argentine Literature)
Universidad de Buenos Aires
Buenos Aires, Argentina

309 Instituto de Planeamiento Regional y Urbano
(Institute of Regional and Urban Planning)
Universidad de Buenos Aires
Buenos Aires, Argentina

310 Instituto de Sociografía y Planeación

(Institute for the Study of Sociology and Planning)
Facultad de Derecho y Ciencias Sociales
Universidad Nacional de Tucumán
Tucumán, Argentina

311 Instituto de Sociología
(Institute of Sociology)
Universidad de Buenos Aires
Buenos Aires, Argentina (L. A.)

312 Instituto de Sociología Aplicada
(Institute of Applied Sociology)
Casilla de Correo 5703, Correo Central
Buenos Aires, Argentina (L. A.)

313 Instituto de Vivienda y Planeamiento
(Housing and Planning Institute)
Universidad Nacional del Nordeste
Resistencia, Argentina

314 Instituto Histórico de la Ciudad de Buenos Aires
(Historical Institute of Buenos Aires)
Paraguay 1033
Buenos Aires, Argentina (Buenos Aires)

315 Instituto Nacional de Salud Mental
(National Mental Health Institute)
Vieytes 489
Buenos Aires, Argentina

316 Instituto Torcuato di Tella
Centro de Sociología Comparada
(Center of Comparative Sociology)
Virrey del Pino 3230
Buenos Aires, Argentina (L. A.)

317 International Institute of Sociology
Universidad Nacional de Córdoba
Córdoba, Argentina (L. A.)

318 Seminar on Studies of the Urban World
Universidad de Buenos Aires
Viamonte 444
Buenos Aires, Argentina (L. A.)

319 University Program of Community Action
Urban and Regional Planning Institute
Universidad Nacional del Litoral
Santa Fé, Argentina

Bolivia

320 Institute of Bolivian Sociology
Faculty of Law, Political and Social Sciences
Universidad Mayor de San Francisco Xavier de Chuquisaca
Aptdo. 212
Sucre, Bolivia

321 Instituto de Estudios Sociales y Económicos
(Institute of Social and Economic Studies)
Facultad de Ciencias Económicas
Universidad Mayor de San Simón
Casilla 1392
Cochabamba, Bolivia (L. A.)

322 Programa Interamericano para el Desarrollo de la Comunidad de la O. E. A.
(O. A. S. Inter-American Program for Community Development)
La Paz, Bolivia (L. A.)
(Branches in Quito, Ecuador, and Las Casas, Mexico)

Brazil

323 Associação Brasileira Contra a Fome
(Brazilian Association Against Hunger)
124 Ministro Viveiros Castro
Rio de Janeiro, GB, Brazil

324 Center for Architectural & City Planning Studies
Universidade do Brasilia
Brasilia, D. F., Brazil

325 Centro Acadêmico de Criminologia
(Academic Criminology Center)
Escola de Policia do Estado de São Paulo
602 São Joaquim
São Paulo, S. P., Brazil

326 Centro de Estudos e Acção Social
(Center for Studies and Social Action)

413 Sabará
São Paulo, S.P., Brazil

327 Centro Latino-Americano de Pesquisas em Ciências Sociais
Av. Pasteur 431, Praia Vermelha
Rio de Janeiro, GB, Brazil

328 Committee on Urban Geography
Pan-American Institute of Geography and History
Rio de Janeiro, GB, Brazil
(L.A.)

329 Departamento de Urbanismo
(City Planning Dept.)
Universidad de São Paulo
São Paulo, S.P., Brazil

330 Dept. of Urban Studies
Universidade do Brasil
Rio de Janeiro, GB, Brazil

331 Faculty of Architecture and City Planning
Universidade do São Paulo
São Paulo, S.P., Brazil

332 Fundação Getulio Vargas
Escola Brasileira de Administração Pública
184 Pr. Botafôgo
Rio de Janeiro, GB, Brazil

333 Inspetoria Regional da Estatística Municipal
(Regional Office of Municipal Statistics)
Instituto Brasileiro de Geografia e Estatística
166 Av. F. Roosevelt
Rio de Janeiro, GB, Brazil

334 Institute of Municipal Studies
Escola de Sociologia e Política da Bahia
Joana Angêlica 89
Salvador, Bahia, Brazil

335 Institute of Municipal Studies
School of Sociology & Politics
Universidade de São Paulo
São Paulo, S.P., Brazil

336 Instituto Brasileiro de Administração Municipal
(Brazilian Institute of Municipal Administration)
Miguel Pereira 34, Humaita
Rio de Janeiro, GB, Brazil

337 Instituto Brasileiro de Economia
(Brazilian Institute of Economics)
Fundação Getulio Vargas
Caixa Postal 4081-ZC-05
Rio de Janeiro, GB, Brazil

338 Instituto Central do Pôvo
(Central Population Institute)
188 Rivadavia Corrêia
Rio de Janeiro, GB, Brazil

339 Instituto de Criminologia
(Criminology Institute)
Universidade do Distrito Federal
243 Catete
Rio de Janeiro, GB, Brazil
(L.A.)

340 Instituto de Estudos e Pesquisas Econômicas
(Institute of Economic Research and Studies)
Universidade Federal de Rio Grande do Sul
Pôrto Alegre, Brazil (L.A.)

341 Instituto de Estudos Municipais
(Municipal Studies Institute)
Fundação Escola de Sociología e Política de São Paulo
São Paulo, S.P., Brazil

342 Instituto de Pesquisas e Estudos Sociais
(Institute of Social Studies and Research)
Av. Rio Branco 156
Rio de Janeiro, GB, Brazil
(L.A.)

343 Instituto de Relações Sociais e Industriais
(Institute of Social and Industrial Relations)
97, 2º cj 2B7 Abril
São Paulo, S.P., Brazil

344 Instituto Histórico e Geográphico de São Paulo
(São Paulo Institute of Geography and History)

158 Benjamin Constant
São Paulo, S.P., Brazil
(São Paulo)

345 Instituto Histórico Geográphico Brasileiro
(Brazilian Institute of History and Geography)
8 Av. Augusto Severo
Rio de Janeiro, GB, Brazil

346 Instituto Latinoamericano de Criminología
(Latin American Institute of Criminology)
Rua Rêgo Freitas 454, 6º andar
São Paulo, S.P., Brazil (L.A.)

347 Instituto Municipal de Administração e Ciências Contábeis
(Municipal Institute for Administration and Accounting)
Parque Municipal
Bêlo Horizonte, Minas Gerais
Brazil

348 Instituto Piratininga de Saúde Mental
(Piratininga Institute of Mental Health)
204 Veiga Filho
São Paulo, S.P., Brazil

349 Laboratôrio de Geomorfologia e Estudos Regionais
(Laboratory of Geomorphology and Regional Studies)
Universidade da Bahia
Salvador, Bahia, Brazil

350 Latin American Research Center in the Social Sciences
Av. Pasteur 431
Rio de Janeiro, GB, Brazil
(L.A.)

Chile

351 Center for Urban Development Studies
Universidad Católica Pontificia
Santiago, Chile

352 Center of Sociological Research
Faculty of Economic and Social Sciences
Universidad Católica de Chile
Santiago, Chile (L.A.)

353 Centro de Estudios Demográficos
(Demographic Studies Center)
Universidad de Chile
Toledo 1965
Santiago, Chile (L.A.)

354 Centro de Historia Colonial
(Colonial History Center)
Universidad de Chile
Paulino Alfonso 16
Santiago, Chile

355 Centro de Investigaciones de Historia Americana
(Center for American History Research)
Universidad de Chile
Castro 158-B
Santiago, Chile (L.A.)

356 Centro de Investigaciones Económicas
(Economic Research Center)
Universidad Católica Pontificia
Av. Alameda 340
Santiago, Chile

357 Centro de Planeamiento
(Planning Center)
Facultad de Ciencias Físicas y Matemáticas
Universidad de Chile
Compañía 1270
Santiago, Chile

358 Centro de Vivienda y Construcción
(Construction and Housing Center)
Facultad de Ciencias Físicas y Matemáticas
Universidad de Chile
Av. Beauchef 850
Santiago, Chile

359 Centro Latinoamericano de Demografía
(Latin American Center of Demography)
Exeq. Fernández 703
Santiago, Chile (L.A.)

360 Centro Latinoamericano de Formación de Especialistas en Educación
(Latin American Center for Training of Education Specialists)
Universidad de Chile
Merced 152, piso 5
Santiago, Chile (L.A.)

361 Comité Interdisciplinario de Desarrollo Urbano (CIDU)
(Interdisciplinary Committee for Urban Development)
Universidad Católica de Chile
Mardoqueo Fernández 15, Oficina 74
Santiago, Chile

362 Escuela Latinoamericana de Sociología
(Latin American School of Sociology)
Facultad Latinoamericana de Ciencias Sociales
Casilla 3213
Santiago, Chile (L.A.)

363 Institute of Housing, Urbanization and Planning
Facultad de Arquitectura
Universidad de Chile
Santiago, Chile

364 Institute of Occupational Health and Air Pollution
Escuela de Salud Pública
Universidad de Chile
Santiago, Chile

365 Instituto Americano para el Desarrollo del Sindicalismo Libre
(American Institute for the Development of Free Trade Unions)
Compañía 1516
Santiago, Chile

366 Instituto de Capacitación Sindical
(Trade Union Training Institute)
Cienfuegos 28
Santiago, Chile

367 Instituto de Ciencias Penales
(Penal Sciences Institute)
Huérfanos 1147, Oficina 546
Santiago, Chile

368 Instituto de Estudios Sindicales
(Institute of Trade Union Studies)
Riquelme 15
Santiago, Chile

369 Instituto de Comunicaciones Sociales
(Institute of Social Communication)
Alameda B. O'Higgins 1801
Casilla 1045
Santiago, Chile

370 Instituto de Vivienda, Urbanismo y Planeación
(Institute of Housing & City Planning)
Facultad de Arquitectura
Universidad de Chile
Av. P. Aguirre Cerdá 6655
Santiago, Chile

371 Instituto del Teatro
(Institute of the Theater)
Facultad de Ciencias y Artes Musicales
Universidad de Chile
Santiago, Chile

372 Instituto Latinoamericano de Planeamiento Económico y Social
(Latin American Institute of Economic and Social Planning)
José Miguel Infante 9
Santiago, Chile (L.A.)

373 Instituto Nacional de Acción Poblacional e Investigación
(National Institute of Population Action and Research)
Príncipe de Gales 87
Santiago, Chile

374 Latin American School of Sociology
Latin American Faculty of Social Sciences (FLACSO)
J.P. Alessandri 832
Santiago, Chile (L.A.)

375 Research Committee on Urban Sociology
World Congress on Sociology
J. Medina Echavarría
UN Economic Commission for Latin America
Casilla 179-D
Santiago, Chile (L.A.)

376 Urban & Regional Development Advisory Program
Ford Foundation
Santo Domingo 504, Oficina 81
Santiago, Chile

Colombia

377 Asociación Colombiana para el Estudio Científico de la Población
(Colombian Association for the Scientific Study of Population)
c/o Depto. de Sociología
Universidad Nacional de Colombia, Cuidad Universitaria
Bogotá, Colombia

378 Centro de Estudios Colombianos
(Colombian Studies Center)
Calle 13, 5-93, piso # 2
Bogotá, Colombia

379 Centro de Investigación y Acción Social
(Center of Social Research and Action)
Carrera 23, 39-69
Bogotá, Colombia

380 Centro de Investigaciones Sociales
(Social Research Center)
Aptdo. Aéreo 11996
Bogotá, Colombia (L. A.)

381 Dept. of Urban Planning
Faculty of Architecture
Universidad del Valle
Cali, Colombia

382 División de Estudios de la Población
(Population Studies Division)
Asociación Colombiana de Facultades de Medicina
Av. 1, 10-01, Oficina 815
Bogotá, Colombia

383 Harvard University Development Advisory Service
Bogotá, Colombia

384 Institute of Labor Legislation
Universidad Nacional de Colombia
Bogotá, Colombia

385 Institute of Municipal Studies
Universidad INCCA de Colombia
Carrera 7, 23-49
Bogotá, Colombia

386 Instituto Caro y Cuervo
Calle 24, 5-60, piso 2
Bogotá, Colombia
(linguistic studies) in cities

387 Instituto Colombiano de Desarrollo Social
(Colombian Institute of Social Development)
Apartado Aéreo 11966
Bogotá, Colombia

388 Instituto de Ciencia Política
(Institute of Political Science)
Facultad de Derecho
Universidad de Antioquia
Aptdo. 229
Medellín, Colombia (L. A.)

389 Inter-American Housing & Planning Center
Ciudad Universitaria
Calle 45, Carrera 30
Bogotá, Colombia (L. A.)

390 Oficina Coordinadora del Programa Internacional de Población en América Latina
(Coordinating Office of the International Program of Population in Latin America)
Bogotá, Colombia (L. A.)
(A branch of the Population Reference Bureau,
1755 Massachusetts Avenue, N. W.
Washington, D. C.)

391 City Planning Center
Universidad de los Andes
Aptdo. Aéreo 4976
Bogotá, Colombia

Costa Rica

392 Central American University Institute of Social and Economic Research
Universidad de Costa Rica
Ciudad Universitaria "Rodrigo Facio"
San José, Costa Rica (L. A.)

393 Programa Interamericano de Información Popular
(Inter-American Program for Popular Information)
San José, Costa Rica

Cuba

394 Casa de las Américas
G y Tercera, Vedado
Havana, Cuba

395 Centro Regional de la Unesco en el Hemisferio Occidental
(Unesco Regional Center in the Western Hemisphere)
Calle 5, no. 306, Vedado
Aptdo. 1358
Havana, Cuba (L.A.)

396 Negociado de Censo y Estadística
(Office of Census and Statistics)
Ministerio de Educación
4, no. 502, Vedado
Havana, Cuba

397 Oficina del Historiador de la Ciudad
(Office of the City Historian)
Havana, Cuba

Dominican Republic

398 Dominican Institute of Social Research
Universidad Autónoma de Santo Domingo
Cuidad Universitaria
Santo Domingo,
Dominican Republic

Ecuador

399 Centro de Desarrollo
(Development Center)
Casilla 2321
Quito, Ecuador

400 Centro Internacional de Estudios Superiores de Periodismo para América Latina
(International Center for Higher Journalism Studies for Latin America)
Ciudad Universitaria
Casilla 584
Quito, Ecuador (L.A.)

401 Faculty of Architecture and City Planning
Universidad de Cuenca
Aptdo. 168
Cuenca, Ecuador

402 Instituto de Criminología
(Institute of Criminology)
Universidad Central
Ciudad Universitaria
Quito, Ecuador

403 Instituto de Investigaciones Económicas y Políticas
(Economic and Political Research Institute)
Universidad de Guayaquil
Guayaquil, Ecuador

404 Seminar of Ecuadoran Social Matters
Faculty of Jurisprudence, Political and Social Sciences
Universidad Central del Ecuador
Casilla 166
Quito, Ecuador

El Salvador

405 Asociación Salvadoreña de Sociologia y de la Escuela de Ciencias Sociales
(Salvadoran Association of Sociology and of the School of Social Sciences)
Facultad de Humanidades
Universidad de El Salvador
San Salvador, El Salvador

Guatemala

406 Escuela de Salud Pública
(School of Public Health)
5a. Calle, 4-53
Guatemala, Guatemala

407 Institute of Economic-Social Research
Facultad de Ciencias Económicas
Universidad de San Carlos Nacional y Autónoma
Guatemala, Guatemala

408 Instituto de Antropología e Historia
(Institute of Anthropology and History)
La Aurora
Guatemala, Guatemala

409 Instituto de Criminología
(Institute of Criminology)
Palacio de Justicia
Guatemala, Guatemala

410 Instituto de Nutrición de Centro América y Panamá (INCAP)

(Nutrition Institute of Central America and Panama)
Carretera Roosevelt
Guatemala, Guatemala (L. A.)

Haiti

411 Haitian Center for Research in the Social Sciences
B. P. 1294
Port-au-Prince, Haiti

Honduras

412 Institute of Socio-Economic Research
Universidad Nacional Autónoma de Honduras
Ave. Centenario
Tegucigalpa, Honduras

Jamaica

413 Institute of Social and Economic Research
University of the West Indies
Mona, Jamaica

Mexico

414 Centro de Estudios Económicos y Demográficos
(Center of Economic and Demographic Studies)
Colegio de México
Guanajuato 125
México, D. F., México (L. A.)

415 Centro de Estudios Monetarios Latinoamericanos
(Center of Latin American Monetary Studies)
Durango 54
México, D. F., México (L. A.)

416 Centro de Investigación Histórica
(Center of Historical Research)
Fray Martín de Valencia Escuela
Av. Hidalgo 5, no. 406
México, D. F., México

417 Centro de Investigaciones Económicas
(Economic Research Center)
Universidad de Nuevo León
Monterrey, N. L., México

418 Centro de Investigaciones Sociológicas
(Sociological Research Center)
Universidad de Michoacán
Morelia, Michoacán, México

419 Committee on Urban Redevelopment
Commission on Cartography
Panamerican Institute of Geography and History
Exarzobispado 29
Tacubaya
México, D. F., México (L. A.)

420 Escuela de Salud Pública
(School of Public Health)
Prolongación de Carpio 470
México, D. F., México

421 Fundación para Estudios de la Población
(Foundation for Population Studies)
c/o Instituto de Investigaciones Sociológicas
Universidad Nacional Autónoma de México
México, D. F., México

422 Institute of Social Research
Universidad Nacional Autónoma de México
Ciudad Universitaria
México, D. F., México (L. A.)

423 Instituto de Estudios Sociales
(Social Studies Institute)
Universidad de Nuevo León
Monterrey, N. L., México

424 Instituto de Investigaciones Estéticas
(Institute of Aesthetic Research)
Universidad Nacional Autónoma de México
Ciudad Universitaria
México, D. F., México

425 Instituto de Investigaciones Sociales
(Social Research Institute)
Universidad Nacional Autónoma de México
Lic. Verdad 3
México, D. F., México (L. A.)

426 Instituto Mexicano de Estudios Sociales, A. C.
(Mexican Institute of Social Studies)

Londres 40, piso no. 5
México, D. F., México

427 Organización de las Cooperativas de América
Av. Juarez 76, no. 704-705-706
México, D. F., México

428 Social Work Institute
Universidad de Nuevo León
Colegio Civil y Washington
Monterrey, N. L., México

429 Socio-Religious Research Center
Aptdo. Aéreo 1647
México, D. F., México (L. A.)

Paraguay

430 Centro de Estudios Sociológicos
(Sociological Studies Center)
c/o Instituto Latinoamericano de Relaciones Internacionales
Eligio Ayala 971
Asunción, Paraguay (L. A.)

431 Centro Paraguayo de Estudios Sociológicos
(Paraguayan Sociological Studies Center)
Eligio Ayala 973
Asunción, Paraguay

432 Centro Paraguayo para Desarrollo Económico y Social
(Paraguayan Center for Economic and Social Development)
Casilla 1189
Asunción, Paraguay

433 Escuela Superior de Ciencias Sociales
(Higher School of Social Sciences)
Asunción, Paraguay

Peru

434 Center of Studies of Population and Development
c/o Ford Foundation
Edificio "El Pacifico-Washington"
Plaza Washington 125
Lima, Perú

435 Centro Artesanal de Cerámica
(Artisan Ceramics Center)
Lima, Perú

436 Centro de Estudios sobre Población y Desarrollo
(Center for Population and Development Studies)
Ministerio de Salud Pública
Lima, Perú

437 Institute of Human Relations and Productivity
Facultad de Ciencias Económicas y Comerciales
Universidad Nacional Mayor de San Marcos
Lima, Perú

438 Instituto de Investigaciones Económicas
(Institute of Economic Research)
Facultad de Ciencias Económicas y Comerciales
Universidad Nacional Mayor de San Marcos
Lima, Perú

439 Inter-American Program for Urban & Regional Planning (PIAPUR)
Instituto de Planeamiento de Lima
UniversidadNacional de Ingeniería
Aptdo. 1301
Lima, Perú (L. A.)

440 Professional Institute for Development of Villages, Towns and Communities
Universidad Comunal del Centro del Perú
Real 160
Huancayo, Perú

441 Program in Communications (for M. S. degree)
Depto. de Sociología
Facultad de la Universidad Agraria La Molina
Aptdo. 456
Lima, Perú

442 Urban Institute
Universidad Nacional de Ingeniería
Aptdo. 1301
Lima, Perú

Puerto Rico

443 Curso Piloto de Adiestramiento para Mujeres Dirigentes de la O.E.A.
(O.A.S. Pilot Training Course for Women Leaders)
San Juan, Puerto Rico

444 Social Science Research Center
University of Puerto Rico
Río Piedras, Puerto Rico (L.A.)

Trinidad

445 Dept. of Social Work
University College of the West Indies
St. Augustine, Trinidad

Uruguay

446 Academia Uruguaya de Letras
(Uruguayan Academy of Letters)
Montevideo, Uruguay

447 Centro de Estadísticas Nacionales y Comercio Internacional
(Center of National Statistics and International Commerce)
Misiones 1361
Montevideo, Uruguay

448 Centro de Estudiantes de Arquitectura
(Center of Architecture Students)
Universidad de la República
Montevideo, Uruguay

449 Centro Latino-Americano de Economía Humana
(Latin American Center of Human Economy)
Minas 1250
Montevideo, Uruguay (L.A.)

450 Centro Uruguayo de Promoción Cultural
(Uruguayan Center of Cultural Promotion)
Montevideo, Uruguay

451 Depto. de Estadística de la División de Higiene
(Statistics Department of the Hygiene Division)
Ministerio de Salud Pública
Mesa Central
Av. 18 de Julio 1892
Montevideo, Uruguay

452 Facultad de Derecho y Ciencias Sociales
(Faculty of Law and Social Sciences)
Universidad de la República
Av. 18 de Julio 1824
Montevideo, Uruguay

453 Institute of Theory of Architecture and City Planning
Facultad de Arquitectura
Universidad de la República Oriental del Uruguay
18 de Julio 1824
Montevideo, Uruguay

454 Instituto de Investigaciones Históricas
(Historical Research Institute)
Universidad de la República Oriental del Uruguay
Montevideo, Uruguay

455 Instituto Histórico y Geográfico del Uruguay
(Historical and Geographical Institute of Uruguay)
18 de Julio 1195
Montevideo, Uruguay

456 Instituto Interamericano del Niño
(Inter-American Children's Institute)
8 de Octubre 2882
Montevideo, Uruguay (L.A.)

457 Instituto Nacional de Viviendas Económicas
(National Institute of Low-Cost Housing)
Avenida Agraciada 1409
Montevideo, Uruguay

Venezuela

458 Centro de Investigaciones Administrativas y Sociales
(Administrative and Social Research Center)
Escuela de Administración Pública
Edificio Banco Industrial
Esq. de Traposos
Caracas, Venezuela

459 Depto. de Estudios Latinoamericanos
(Latin American Studies Department)

Universidad del Oriente
Cumaná, Oriente, Venezuela
(L. A.)

460 Escuela de Historia
(School of History)
Universidad Central de Venezuela
Caracas, Venezuela

461 Escuela de Periodismo
(School of Journalism)
Universidad Central de Venezuela
Caracas, Venezuela

462 URVEN (Research group on urban and regional development)
CENDES (Center of Development Studies)
Universidad Central de Venezuela
Caracas, Venezuela

463 Institute of Regional and Urban Planning
Facultad de Arquitectura y Urbanismo
Universidad Central de Venezuela
Ciudad Universitaria
Caracas, Venezuela

464 Instituto de Ciencias Penales y Criminológicas
(Institute of Penal and Criminological Sciences)
Universidad Central de Venezuela
Ciudad Universitaria
Caracas, Venezuela

465 Instituto de Derecho Penal
(Institute of Penal Law)
Universidad Central de Venezuela
Caracas, Venezuela

466 Instituto para Recreación y Capacitación de los Trabajadores
(Institute for Recreation and Training of Workers)
Ministerio del Trabajo
Torre Sur, Av. Bolívar
Caracas, Venezuela

467 Oficina del Estudio de Caracas
(Office for the Study of Caracas)
Edificio Biblioteca Nacional, piso 11
Oficina 1124
Caracas, Venezuela

468 Instituto Venezolano de Análisis Económico y Social
(Venezuelan Institute of Economic and Social Analysis)
Caracas, Venezuela

469 Urban Research Program
Universidad Católica Andrés Bello
Caracas, Venezuela

1C. RESEARCH CENTERS AND INSTITUTES CONCERNED WITH URBANIZATION AND ALLIED FIELDS LOCATED ELSEWHERE

(Note: a note is given in instances where the title of the individual institute or center does not specify its field of activity).

Austria

470 Institüt für Zukunftsfragen
(Institute for Problems of the Future)
Vienna, Austria

471 Oesterreichisches Institüt für Raumplanung
(Austrian Institute for Regional Planning)
1, Reichsratsstrasse
Vienna, Austria

Belgium

472 Catholic International Union for Social Service
111, rue Poste
Brussels, Belgium

473 Institute of City Planning
Université Libre de Bruxelles
50 Ave. F.D. Roosevelt
Brussels, Belgium

474 Inter-Faculty Institute of City & Country Planning
Catholic University of Louvain
Vieux Marché
Louvain, Belgium

475 Studiecentrum voor Regionale Ontwikkeling
(Studies Center for Regional Development)
Ghent, Belgium

Canada

476 Bureau of Municipal Research
12 Richmond, East
Toronto, Ontario, Canada

477 Canadian Council on Urban & Regional Research
225 Metcalfe, Suite 308
Ottawa, Ontario, Canada

478 The Canadian Research Center for Anthropology
223 Main St.
Ottawa, Ontario, Canada

479 Institute of Research in Industrial Hygiene and Air Pollution
University of Montreal
Montreal, P.Q., Canada

480 Research Unit for Urban Studies
McMaster University
Hamilton, Ontario, Canada

England

481 Centre for Environmental Studies
c/o Prof. Henry Chilver
Dept. of Civil Engineering
University of London
London, England

482 Centre for Urban Studies
Flaxman House
Flaxman Terrace
London W.C. 1, England

483 Communications Research Centre
University of London
London, England

484 Community Development and Clearing House
University of London
London, England

485 Council for Technical Education & Training for Overseas Countries
Eland House
Palace St.
London S.W. 1, England

486 Dept. of Community Development Studies
University of London
London, England

487 Institute of Local Government Studies
University of Birmingham
Birmingham, England

488 Population Investigation Committee
Houghton St.
Aldwych
London W.C. 2, England

489 School of Planning
University of Birmingham
Birmingham, England

490 City Planning Institute
26 Portland Place
London W. 1, England

France

491 Association Internationale de Droit Penal
(International Association of Penal Law)
c/o Faculté de Droit et des Sciences Economiques
12 Place Panthéon
Paris, France

492 Center of Urbanization Research
4, Ave. du Recteur-Poincaré
Paris, France

493 Centre d'Etudes des Groupes Sociaux
(Center for Studies of Social Groups)
Montrouge, France

494 Centre d'Information et d'Etude du Crédit
(Information Center for the Study of Credit)
Paris, France

495 Centre International de Recherches et d'Echanges Culturels
(International Center of Research and Cultural Exchange)
18 rue Tanneries
Paris, France

496 Centre International du Formation et de Recherche en vue du Développement Harmonisé
(International Center for Training and Research for Coordinated Development)
Place du Marché St.-Honoré 29
Paris, France

497 Comité International des Sciences Historiques
(International Committee of Historical Sciences)
International Council of Philosophic and Humanistic Sciences
Place de Fontenoy
Paris, France

498 Ecole Pratique des Hautes Etudes
(Practical School of Higher Studies)
Section 6 (Sciences Economiques et Sociales)
54 rue de Varenne
Paris 7, France

499 Groupe d'Ethnologie Sociale
(Social Ethnology Group)
Ecole Pratique des Hautes Etudes
Centre Nationale de la Recherche Scientifique
Paris, France

500 Institut des Hautes Etudes de'Outre Mer
(Institute of Higher Overseas Studies)
2 Av. Observatoire
Paris, France

501 Institut des Sciences Humaines Appliquées
(Institute of Applied Human Sciences)
17 rue Richer
Paris, France

502 Institut d'Etude du Développement Economique et Social
(Institute for the Study of Economic and Social Development)
96, Bd. Raspail
Paris, France

503 Institut d'Urbanisme
(Institute of City Planning)
Université de Paris
3 rue Michelet
Paris, France

504 Institut National d'Etudes Démographiques
(National Institute of Demographic Studies)
23 Ave. Franklin Roosevelt
Paris, France

505 Institut Supérieur et International d'Urbanisme Appliqué
(Higher International Institute of Applied City Planning)
Paris, France

506 Institute of Spanish, Latin American and Luso-Brazilian Studies
Université de Toulouse
Toulouse, France

507 International Committee for Documentation in Social Sciences
International Social Science Council
Unesco House
Place de Fontenoy
Paris, France

508 International Institute for Educational Planning
UNESCO
7, rue Eugène-Delacroix
Paris 16, France

509 Union Internationale des Organismes Familiaux
(International Union of Family Organizations)
28 Place St. Georges
Paris, France

Germany

510 Bundesanstalt für Vegetationskunde, Naturschutz und Landschaftspflege
(Alliance for Information on Care of Plants)
Heerstrasse 10, Bad Godesberg
Mainz, Federal Republic of Germany

511 Dept. of Sociology & Development
Institut für Soziologie
Free University of Berlin
Babelsbergerstrasse 14-16
Berlin, Federal Republic of Germany

512 Institute of Comparative International Research in Social Sciences
University of Cologne
Cologne, Federal Republic of Germany

513 Institut für Raumforschung
(Institute for Space Research)
Michaelshof
Bad Godesberg, Mainz
Federal Republic of Germany

514 Social Research Center
Universität Münster
Münster
Dortmund, Federal Republic of Germany

Greece

515 Centre of Ekistics
24 Strat. Syndesmou Street
Athens, Greece

516 Faculty of Architecture and City Planning
National Technical University of Athens
Odos Octovriou 42
Athens, Greece

Israel

517 Eliezer Kaplan School of Social Sciences and Economics
Hebrew University
Jerusalem, Israel

518 Mount Carmel International Training Center for Community Services
12 David Pinsky Street
Haifa, Israel

Italy

519 Istituto di Urbanística
(Institute of City Planning)
University of Rome
Rome, Italy

520 Istituto per gli Studi di Servizio Sociale
(Institute for the Study of Social Service)
42, via Mario de Fiori
Rome, Italy

521 Istituto Lombardo per gli Studi Economici e Sociali
(Lombardy Institute for Social & Economic Studies)
19, via Mascheroni
Milan, Italy

522 Italian Committee for the Study of Population Problems
Via delle Terme di Diocleziano, 10
Rome, Italy

Japan

523 Community Research Institute

Aichi University
Machihata-cho, Toyohashi
Aichi Prefecture, Japan

Netherlands

524 Dept. of Architecture and City Planning, Technological University of Delft
134 Julianalaan
Delft, Netherlands

525 Dept. of Geographic Demography and Planning
University of Amsterdam
Amsterdam, Netherlands

526 Institute for the Socio-Economic Study of Developing Regions
Linaeusstraat 2a.
Amsterdam, Netherlands

527 Institute of Social Studies
27 Molenstraat
The Hague, Netherlands

528 International Federation for Housing and Planning
L.C. Cattenb. 123
The Hague, Netherlands

529 International Federation of Municipal Engineers
c/o Dr. C. Wegener
St. Afnietenstraat 4-I
Amsterdam, Netherlands

530 International Information Center for Local Credit
International Federation for Housing and Town Planning
L.C. Cattenb. 123
The Hague, Netherlands

531 International Union of Local Authorities
Paleisstr. 5
The Hague, Netherlands

Norway

532 The Chr. Michelsen Institute for Science and Intellectual Freedom
Dept. of Humanities and Social Sciences
Kalvadalsvei 12
Bergen, Norway

Philippines

533 Center of Community Development and Public Administration
Mindanao State University
Marawi City, Philippines

Poland

534 Planning Institute
Faculty of Economics
University of Warsaw
Warsaw, Poland

Portugal

535 Centro de Estudos Históricos Ultramarinos
(Center of Overseas Historical Studies)
Calçada da Boa Hora, 30
Lisbon, Portugal

536 Instituto Superior de Estudos Ultramarinos
(Higher Institute of Foreign Studies)
20 Praça Príncipe Real
Lisbon, Portugal

Spain

537 Centro de Estudios Jurídicos Hispanoamericanos
(Center of Juridical Hispanic American Studies)
Av. de los Reyes Católicos
Madrid, Spain

538 Centro de Información y Sociología
(Center of Information and Sociology)
Obras de Cooperación Sacerdotal Hispanoamericana (OCSHA)
Ciudad Universitaria
Madrid, Spain

539 Congreso de Historia Municipal de la Comunidad Hispánica
Calle de Atocha, 91
Madrid, Spain

540 Seminario de Estudios Americanistas
(Americanist Studies Seminar)
Facultad de Filosofía y Letras
Universidad de Madrid
Ciudad Universitaria
Madrid, Spain

541 Seminario de Urbanismo
(City Planning Seminar)
Instituto de Estudios de Administración Local
Joaquín García Morato 7
Madrid, Spain

Switzerland

542 Association Internationale des Etudes et Recherches sur l'Information
(International Association for Studies and Research on Information)
c/o M. Jacques Bourquin
Petit-chêne 18-B
Lausanne, Switzerland

543 Institute of Sociology
University of Geneva
Geneva, Switzerland

544 International Board of Education
Palais Wilson
52 rue des Pâquis
Geneva, Switzerland

545 International Catholic Institute for Social Research
1 rue Cornavin
Geneva, Switzerland

546 International Federation of Catholic Institutions of Social and Socio-Religious Research
1 Route du Jura
Fribourg, Switzerland

547 International Labor Office
Geneva, Switzerland

548 International Road Federation
8 Route de Meyrin
Geneva, Switzerland

549 Research Institute for Social Development
United Nations
Geneva, Switzerland

550 School of Architecture and City Planning
University of Geneva
3 rue de Candolle
Geneva, Switzerland

551 World Health Organization
Palais des Nations
8-14 Av. de la Paix
Geneva, Switzerland

U.S.S.R.

552 Institut Mezdunarodnogo Rabochego Dvizenija
(International Workers Movement Institute)
Kolpachnyi dom 9-a
Moscow, U.S.S.R.

553 Siberian Section
Academy of Sciences
Novosibirsk, U.S.S.R.

DIRECTORY #2:

"WORKING" ORGANIZATIONS (Departments of city, state, and federal governments, and business and professional associations, foundations and international organizations concerned with urbanization) located

(A) IN THE UNITED STATES OF AMERICA

(B) IN LATIN AMERICA

(C) ELSEWHERE

2A. "WORKING" ORGANIZATIONS (Departments of city, state, and federal governments, and business and professional associations, foundations, and international organizations concerned with urbanization) LOCATED IN THE UNITED STATES OF AMERICA

(Note: a note is given in instances where the title of the individual department, association, foundation, or organization does not specify its field of activity).

California

554 Coordinating Council on Urban Policy
State of California
Sacramento, Calif. 95814

555 League of California Cities
Los Angeles County Division
900 Wilshire Blvd.
Los Angeles, Calif. 90017

District of Columbia

556 Action Council for Better Cities
1220-16th St., N.W.
Washington, D.C. 20036

557 American Association of Road Builders
c/o Pan American Union
Washington, D.C. 20006

558 American Institute of Architects
1735 New York Ave., N.W.
Washington, D.C. 20006

559 American Institute of Planners
917-15th St., N.W.
Washington, D.C. 20005

560 American Municipal Association
1612 K St., N.W.
Washington, D.C. 20006

561 American Planning & Civic Association
901 Union Trust Bldg.
Washington, D.C. 20005

562 American Political Science Association
1527 New Hampshire Ave., N.W.
Washington, D.C. 20036

563 American Sociological Association
1755 Massachusetts Ave., N.W.
Washington, D.C. 20036

564 American Technical Assistance Co.
1725 "I" St., N.W.
Suite 310
Washington, D.C. 20006

565 Area Development Division
U.S. Dept. of Commerce
Washington, D.C. 20235

566 Association for Childhood Education International
3615 Wisconsin Ave., N.W.
Washington, D.C. 20016

567 Bureau of International Labor Affairs
U.S. Dept. of Labor
Washington, D.C. 20210

568 Community Development Information Center
Dept. of Housing & Urban Development
1626 K St., N.W.
Washington, D.C. 20006

569 Construction & Community Development Dept.
Chamber of Commerce of the United States of America
1615 H St., N.W.
Washington, D.C. 20006

570 Dept. of Urban & Regional Development
Robert R. Nathan Associates, Inc.
1218-16th St., N.W.
Washington, D.C. 20036

571 Division of Air Pollution
U.S. Public Health Service
Washington, D.C. 20201

572 Division of Housing & Urban Development

Bureau for Latin America
Agency for International Development
Dept. of State
Washington, D.C. 20523

573 Foundation for Cooperative Housing
1001-15th St., N.W.
Washington, D.C. 20005

574 Human Nutrition Research Branch
Agricultural Research Service
U.S. Dept. of Agriculture
Washington, D.C. 20250

575 Inter-American Cooperative Public Health Service
c/o Pan American Health Organization
525-23rd St., N.W.
Washington, D.C. 20037

576 Inter-American Development Bank
808-17th St., N.W.
Washington, D.C. 20006

577 Inter-American Telecommunications Union
Pan American Union
Washington, D.C. 20006

578 Inter-American Volunteers for Development Purposes
c/o Pan American Union
Washington, D.C. 20006

579 International Coop. Housing Development Association
c/o Mr. Wallace J. Campbell, President
Foundation for Cooperative Housing
1001-15th St., N.W.
Washington, D.C. 20005

580 Inter-Departmental Committee on Nutrition for National Defense
U.S. Dept. of Defense
Washington, D.C. 20301

581 International Secretariat for Volunteer Services (ISVS)
1000-16th St., N.W.
Washington, D.C. 20036

582 International Service
U.S. Social Security Administration
Washington, D.C.

583 International Voluntary Services
1555 Connecticut Ave., N.W.
Washington, D.C. 20036

584 Joint Committee on Careers
Association of American Geographers
1146-16th St., N.W.
Washington, D.C. 20036

585 Kosh-Glassman Associates, Inc.
1145 19th St., N.W.
Washington, D.C. 20036
(private firm researching on public utilities)

586 Latin American Association of Schools of Public Health
c/o Pan American Union
Washington, D.C. 20006

587 Latin American Division
Office of International Housing
Housing & Home Finance Agency
Dept. of Housing & Urban Development
Washington, D.C. 20410

588 Model Cities Administration
Dept. of Housing & Urban Development
Washington, D.C. 20410

589 National Association of Housing & Redevelopment Officials
1413 K St., N.W.
Washington, D.C. 20005

590 National Clearinghouse for Information on Urban Problems
Dept. of Housing & Urban Development
Washington, D.C. 20410

591 National Housing Center
National Association of Home Builders
1625 L St., N.W.
Washington, D.C. 20036

592 National Institutes of Health

U.S. Dept. of Health, Education & Welfare
Washington, D.C. 20201

593 National Institute of Municipal Law Officers
839 17th St., N.W.
Washington, D.C. 20006

594 Office of Metropolitan Development
Dept. of Housing & Urban Development
Washington, D.C. 20410

595 Pan American Development Foundation
19th St. & Constitution Ave., N.W.
Washington, D.C. 20036

596 Pan American Federation of Architects
American Institute of Architects
1735 New York Ave., N.W.
Washington, D.C. 20006

597 People-to-People Health Foundation
1016 20th St., N.W.
Washington, D.C. 20009

598 Population Association of America
c/o Population Division
U.S. Bureau of the Census
Washington, D.C. 20233

599 Public Welfare Foundation, Inc.
3242 Woodland Dr., N.W.
Washington, D.C. 20008

600 Public Welfare Training Center of the District of Columbia
Washington, D.C. 20203

601 Rural and Community Development Service
Office of Technical Cooperation & Research
Agency for International Development
U.S. Dept. of State
Washington, D.C. 20520

602 Trade Union Technical Advisory Committee (COSATE)
Pan American Union
Washington, D.C. 20006

603 U.S. Area Redevelopment Administration
Washington, D.C. 20230

604 U.S. Conference of City Health Officers
1707 H St., N.W.
Washington, D.C. 20006

605 U.S. Conference of Mayors
1707 H St., N.W.
Washington, D.C. 20006

606 U.S. Peace Corps
State Dept.
Washington, D.C. 20521

607 Urban Passenger Transportation Association
1707 H St., N.W.
Washington, D.C. 20006

608 U.S. Urban Renewal Administration
811 Vermont Ave., N.W.
Washington, D.C. 20005

609 Urban Transportation Administration
Dept. of Housing & Urban Development
Washington, D.C. 20410

610 Water Pollution Control Federation
3900 Wisconsin Ave., N.W.
Washington, D.C. 20016

611 Welfare Administration
U.S. Dept. of Health, Education & Welfare
Washington, D.C. 20201

Illinois

612 American Institute of Real Estate Appraisers
36 South Wabash Ave.
Chicago, Ill. 60603

613 American Public Welfare Association
1313 E. 60th St.
Chicago, Ill. 60637

614 American Public Works Association
1313 E. 60th St.
Chicago, Ill. 60637

615 American Society of Planning Officials
1313 E. 60th St.
Chicago, Ill. 60637

616 Carl A. Bays & Associates, Inc.
P.O. Box 36
Urbana, Ill. 61801

617 Committee for International Municipal Cooperation-U.S.A.
1313 E. 60th St.
Chicago, Ill. 60637

618 Community Renewal Foundation, Inc.
19 South LaSalle St.
Chicago, Ill. 60603

619 Dept. of Recreation & Municipal Park Administration
University of Illinois
Urbana, Ill. 61801

620 Federation of Tax Administrators
1313 E. 60th St.
Chicago, Ill. 60637

621 International Association of Assessing Officers
1313 E. 60th St.
Chicago, Ill. 60637

622 International City Managers' Association
1313 E. 60th St.
Chicago, Ill. 60637

623 International Institute of Municipal Clerks
1313 E. 60th St.
Chicago, Ill. 60637

624 Municipal Finance Officers Association of U.S. and Canada
1313 E. 60th St.
Chicago, Ill. 60637

625 Office of Urban Affairs of the Catholic Bishop of Chicago
200 E. Ontario
Chicago, Ill. 60611

626 Public Personnel Association
1313 E. 60th St.
Chicago, Ill. 60637

Kansas

627 Pan American Highway Association
c/o John C. Dart, Chairman
Belleville, Kansas 66935

Louisiana

628 Inter-American Organization for Municipal Cooperation
541 International Trade Mart
New Orleans, La. 70130

Michigan

629 Latin American Division
Kellogg Foundation
Battle Creek, Mich. 49017

New Mexico

630 Conference of Municipal Public Health Engineers
c/o Larry J. Gordon
Box 1293
Albuquerque, N.M. 87103

New York

631 Acción International
145 E. 52nd St.
New York, N.Y. 10022
(urban education, public welfare, community development)

632 Action, Inc.
2 W. 46th St.
New York, N.Y. 10036
(housing)

633 Ad Hoc Group of Experts on Housing & Urban Development
United Nations
New York, N.Y. 10017

634 American Civic Association
8 Pine St.
Binghamton, N.Y. 13901

635 American Public Health Association
1790 Broadway
New York, N.Y. 10019

636 American Society of Civil Engineers
United Engineering Center
345 E. 47th St.
New York, N.Y. 10017

637 Business Council for International Understanding
420 Lexington Ave.
New York, N.Y. 10017

638 CARE, Inc.
660 First Ave.
New York, N.Y. 10016
(public health, public welfare, housing)

639 Child Welfare League of America
44 E. 23rd St.
New York, N.Y. 10010

640 Committee on Latin America
American Council of Voluntary Associations for Foreign Service, Inc.
44 E. 23rd St.
New York, N.Y. 10010

641 Community Development Foundation
345 E. 46th St.
New York, N.Y. 10017

642 Council for Latin America
120 E. 56th St.
New York, N.Y. 10022

643 Council on Social Work Education
345 E. 46th St.
New York, N.Y. 10017

644 Family Service Association of America
44 E. 23rd St.
New York, N.Y. 10010

645 Ford Foundation
477 Madison Ave.
New York, N.Y. 10022

646 Foundation for Internation Child Health, Inc.
1290 Ave. of the Americas
New York, N.Y. 10019

647 Graduate Area Studies Association
Area Studies Program
Graduate School of Arts & Sciences
New York University
New York, N.Y. 10003

648 Health for the World's Needy
104 E. 40th St.
New York, N.Y. 10016

649 Inter-American Education Association
1150-6th Ave.
New York, N.Y. 10009

650 Inter-American Press Association
667 Madison Ave.
New York, N.Y. 10021

651 Inter-American Safety Council, Inc.
140 Cedar St.
New York, N.Y. 10006

652 International Conference on Social Work
345 E. 46th St.
New York, N.Y. 10017

653 International Municipal Signal Association
130 W. 42nd St.
New York, N.Y. 10017

654 International Recreation Association
345 E. 46th St.
New York, N.Y. 10017

655 National Association of Social Workers
2 Park Avenue
New York, N.Y. 10016

656 National Council of Local Administrators of Vocational Education & Practical Arts
c/o Trade & Technical Education
Board of Education, City of New York
110 Livingston St.
Brooklyn, N.Y. 11201

657 National Federation of Settlements and Neighborhood Centers
232 Madison Avenue
New York, N.Y. 10016

658 National Municipal League
47 E. 68th St.
New York, N.Y. 10021

659 National Recreation Association
8 W. 8th St.
New York, N.Y. 10014

660 National Social Welfare Assembly
Committee on International Social Welfare
345 E. 46th St.
New York, N.Y. 10017

661 National Urban League
14 E. 48th St.
New York, N.Y. 10017

662 New York State Federation of Official Planning Organizations
State of New York
Albany, N.Y.

663 Population Branch
Bureau of Social Affairs
United Nations
New York, N.Y. 10017

664 Project Hope
Room 1454
Time-Life Bldg.
1271 Ave. of the Americas
New York, N.Y. 10020

665 Regional Plan Association
230 W. 41st St.
New York, N.Y. 10036

666 Rockefeller Foundation
111 W. 50th St.
New York, N.Y. 10020

667 Salvation Army
120 W. 14th St.
New York, N.Y. 10011

668 UNICEF
c/o United Nations
New York, N.Y. 10017

669 United Community Funds & Councils of America, Inc.
345 E. 46th St.
New York, N.Y. 10017

670 United Nations Development Program
United Nations
New York, N.Y. 10017

671 Urban Training Center for Christian Mission
c/o National Council of Churches of Christ
475 Riverside Dr.
New York, N.Y. 10027

672 World Medical Association
10 Columbus Circle
New York, N.Y. 10019

673 Young Men's Christian Association
422-9th Avenue
New York, N.Y. 10034

Ohio

674 Association of Urban Universities
c/o Norman P. Auburn
University of Akron
Akron, Ohio 44304

675 Inter-American Association of Sanitary Engineering
c/o Ohio River Valley Water Sanitation Commission
F.W. Montanari, Secretary-General
414 Walnut St.
Cincinnati, Ohio 45216

Pennsylvania

676 Air Pollution Control Association
4400 Fifth Ave.
Pittsburgh, Pa. 15213

677 Regional Science Association
Wharton School
University of Pennsylvania
Philadelphia, Pa. 19104

678 Cyrus W. Rice & Co.
15 Noble Ave.
Pittsburgh, Pa. 15205
(private firm working on waste disposal)

Washington

679 National Association of Civic Secretaries
c/o Municipal League of Seattle
431 Lyon Bldg.
Seattle, Washington 98104

Wisconsin

680 Urban Information Systems Association
c/o Kenneth Dueker
Dept. of Civil Engineering
University of Wisconsin
Madison, Wisc. 53706

2B. "WORKING" ORGANIZATIONS (Departments of city, state, and federal governments, and business and professional associations, foundations, and international organizations concerned with urbanization) LOCATED IN LATIN AMERICA

(Note: a note is given in instances where the title of the individual department, association, foundation, or organization does not specify its field of activity. Designations of fields of activity apply to the nation in which the given entity is located, unless otherwise specified).

Argentina

681 Academia de Artes y Ciencias Cinematográficas de la República Argentina
(Academy of Cinema Arts and Sciences of the Argentine Republic)
Buenos Aires, Argentina

682 Acción Sindical Argentina
(Argentine Trade Union Action)
Alsina 1133
Buenos Aires, Argentina

683 Asociación Latinoamericana de Sociología
(Latin American Association of Sociology)
Colón 627
Buenos Aires, Argentina

684 Cámara Argentina de la Construcción
(Argentine Building Trades Council)
Paseo Colón 823
Buenos Aires, Argentina

685 Comisión Municipal de la Vivienda
(Municipal Commission of Housing)
Buenos Aires, Argentina

686 Comisión Municipal de Precios
(Municipal Price Commission)
Abastecimiento Policía Municipal
Av. de Mayo 525
Buenos Aires, Argentina

687 Depto. de Publicaciones
(Publications Department)
Municipalidad de La Plata
La Plata, Argentina

688 Depto. Electrónica
(Electronic Department)
Municipalidad de la Ciudad de Buenos Aires)
Av. de Mayo 525
Buenos Aires, Argentina

689 Dirección de Paseos Públicos
(Department of Public Thoroughfares)
Municipalidad de la Ciudad de Buenos Aires
Av. de Mayo 525
Buenos Aires, Argentina

690 Dirección de Servicios Públicos
(Department of Public Services)
Municipalidad de la Ciudad de Buenos Aires
Carlos Calvo 1052
Buenos Aires, Argentina

691 Dirección General de Obras Públicas y Urbanismo
(General Department of Public Works and City Planning)
Buenos Aires, Argentina

692 Dirección General de Vías de Communicación
(General Department of Highways)
Buenos Aires, Argentina

693 Dirección Municipal de Deporte
(Municipal Department of Recreation)
Arenales 2548
Buenos Aires, Argentina

694 Escuela de Servicio Social
(School of Social Service)
Ciudad de Santa Fé
Santa Fé, Argentina

695 Instituto de Obra Social del Ejército
(Social Work Institute of the Army)
Secretaría de Estado de Guerra
Paso 547
Buenos Aires, Argentina

696 Instituto Municipal de Previsión Social
(Municipal Institute of Social Security)
Cerrito 750
Buenos Aires, Argentina

697 Instituto Nacional de la Salud
(National Health Institute)
Av. G. Mosconi y Perdriel
Buenos Aires, Argentina

698 Instituto Nacional de Previsión Social
(National Institute of Social Security)
Rivadavia 1739
Buenos Aires, Argentina

699 Instituto Promotor de la Vivienda
(Institute for the Advancement of Housing)
Av. de Mayo 666
Buenos Aires, Argentina

700 Secretaría de Cultura y Acción Social
(Ministry of Culture and Social Action)
Municipalidad de la Ciudad de Buenos Aires
Av. de Mayo 525
Buenos Aires, Argentina

701 Secretaría de Salud Pública
(Public Health Ministry)
Municipalidad de la Ciudad de Buenos Aires
Av. de Mayo 525
Buenos Aires, Argentina

Barbados

702 Barbados Association for Mental Health
P.O. Box 6590
Bridgetown, Barbados

703 Development and Welfare Organization
Bridgetown, Barbados

Bolivia

704 Asociación de Vivienda Popular (VIPO)
(Popular Housing Association)
La Paz, Bolivia

705 Comisión Boliviana de Acción Social Evangélica (COMBASE)
La Paz, Bolivia
(Protestant social-service organization)

Brazil

706 Associação Brasileira de Luta Contra a Fome
(Brazilian Association for the Fight Against Hunger)
Largo Misericordia 24
Rio de Janeiro, GB, Brazil

707 Associação Brasileira de Municípios
(Brazilian Association of Counties)
2 Av. Almirante Barroso
Rio de Janeiro, GB, Brazil

708 Banco Nacional da Habitação
(National Housing Bank)
Rio de Janeiro, GB, Brazil

709 Brasil-Estados Unidos Movimento para Desenvolvimento e Organização da Comunidade
(Brazil United States Movement for Community Development and Organization)
Government of the State of Guanabara
Rio de Janeiro, Brazil

710 Centro de Assistência Social Brasil-Moóca
(Brazil-Moóca Social Service Center)
574 Catumbi
São Paulo, S.P., Brazil

711 Centro Nacional de Productividad Industrial
(National Center of Industrial Productivity)

Ministério da Indústria e Comercio
375 Av. Pres. A. Carlos
Rio de Janeiro, GB, Brazil

712 COHAB
(Guanabara State Housing Agency)
Rio de Janeiro, GB, Brazil

713 Comissão de Abastecimentos e Preços
(Supplies and Prices Commission)
Ministério da Indústria e Comércio
375 Av. Pres. A. Carlos
Rio de Janeiro, GB, Brazil

714 Comissão de Desenvolvimento Econômico de Pernambuco
(Economic Development Commission of Pernambuco)
Recife, Pernambuco, Brazil

715 Companhia do Alojamento Popular
(Popular Housing Company)
Rio de Janeiro, GB, Brazil

716 Conselho de Política Urbana (COPURB)
(Urban Politics Council)
Presidência de la República
Brasilia, Brazil

717 Cruzada São Sebastião
Rua da Gloria 446
Rio de Janeiro, GB, Brazil
(Catholic aid to the needy)

718 Depto. Administrativo do Serviço Público
(Administrative Department of Public Service)
Esplanada dos Ministérios, Bl. 7
Brasilia, Brazil

719 Depto. de Aguas e Energia Eléctria
(Department of Water and Electrical Energy)
30 ramais 115, piso 4
Riachuelo
São Paulo, S.P., Brazil

720 Depto. de Aguas e Esgôtos
(Dept. of Water & Sewage)
194 Antônia Queirós
São Paulo, S.P., Brazil

721 Depto. de Esgôtos Sanitários
(Dept. of Sanitation & Sewage)
Superintendência, Urbanização, Saneamento Govêrno do Estado Guanabara
118 Av. Erasmo Braga
Rio de Janeiro, GB, Brazil

722 Depto. de Habitação Popular
(Department of Popular Housing)
Secretaria Geral da Viação das Obras
Govêrno do Estado Guanabara
350 Av. Marechal Câmara
Rio de Janeiro, GB, Brazil

723 Depto. de Limpeza Urbano
(Department of Urban Sanitation)
Secretaria Geral da Viação das Obras
Govêrno do Estado Guanabara
10 Joaquim Palhares
Rio de Janeiro, GB, Brazil

724 Depto. de Urbanismo
(Department of City Planning)
Curitiba, Paraná, Brazil

725 Departamento de Urbanismo
(Department of City Planning)
São Paulo, S.P., Brazil

726 Depto. de Urbanização
(Urbanization Department)
Superintendência Urbanização Saneamento--SURSAN
(Superintendency of Urbanization & Sanitation)
Govêrno do Estado Guanabara
186 Av. Marechal Câmara
Rio de Janeiro, GB, Brazil

727 Depto. dos Institutos Penais
(Department of Penal Institutions)
Estado de São Paulo
30 ramais
88 Barão Itapetininga
São Paulo, S.P., Brazil

728 Diretoria Serviço do Trânsito
(Office of Transit Service)
Depto. Estadual da Segurança Pública

Govêrno do Estado Guanabara
67 Praça Tiradentes
Rio de Janeiro, GB, Brazil

729 Federação de Orgãos para Assistência Social e Educacional)
(Federation of Organizations for Social & Educational Aid)
Rua Mena Barreto 161, no. 3
Botafôgo, Rio de Janeiro, Brazil

730 Fundação Serviço Especial Saúde Pública
(Foundation for Special Public Health Service)
251 Av. Rio Branco
Rio de Janeiro, GB, Brazil

731 Grupo Facultativo de Assistência a Media e Pequena Emprêsa
(Facultative Group for Aid to Medium and Small Business)
Ministério da Indústria e Comércio
375 Av. Pres. A. Carlos
Rio de Janeiro, GB, Brazil

732 Instituto Brasileiro de Administração Municipal
(Brazilian Institute of Municipal Administration)
34 Miguel Pereira
Rio de Janeiro, GB, Brazil

733 Instituto Brasileiro de Habitação
(Brazilian Housing Institute)
c/o Ministério da Viação e Obras Públicas
Praça 15 de Novembro
Rio de Janeiro, GB, Brazil

734 Instituto Cultural do Trabalho
(Cultural Institute of Labor)
São Paulo, S. P., Brazil

735 Instituto de Criminalística
(Criminology Institute)
Depto. Estadual de Segurança Pública
Govêrno do Estado Guanabara
Praça Maúa
Rio de Janeiro, GB, Brazil

736 Instituto de Organização Racional do Trabalho
30, 10º Praça D. José Gaspar
São Paulo, S. P., Brazil

737 Instituto de Previdência do Estado de São Paulo
(Social Security Institute of the State of São Paulo)
139, 1º s. 102 Bráulio Gomes
São Paulo, S. P., Brazil

738 Programa de Financiamento à Pequena e Média Emprêsa
(Program for Financing Small and Medium Businesses)
Banco Nacional do Desenvolvimento Econômico
Av. Rio Branco 53
Rio de Janeiro, GB, Brazil

739 Rio Light, S. A.
168 Av. Marechal Floriano
Rio de Janeiro, GB, Brazil
(public utilities)

740 Secretaria dos Serviços e Obras Públicas
(Office of Public Services and Works)
15 ramais, 115 Riachuelo
São Paulo, S. P., Brazil

741 Secretaria dos Transportes
(Transportation Ministry)
80 ramais, Av. Santos Dumont
São Paulo, S. P., Brazil

742 Secretaria Geral das Finanças
(General Finance Office)
Govêrno do Estado Guanabara
42 Alfândega
Rio de Janeiro, GB, Brazil

743 Serviço de Centros de Saúde da Capital
(Health Centers Service of the Capital)
Av. São Luis 99, 6º
São Paulo, S. P., Brazil

744 Serviço Nacional Aprendizagem Comercial (SENAC)

(National Commercial Apprenticeship Service)
307 Av. Geral Justo
Rio de Janeiro, GB, Brazil

745 Serviço Social da Indústria
(Industrial Social Service)
3 México
Rio de Janeiro, GB, Brazil

746 Teatro Rio de Janeiro
(Rio de Janeiro Theater)
Govêrno do Estado Guanabara
Av. Rio Branco
Rio de Janeiro, GB, Brazil

Chile

747 Asociación Chilena de Asistencia Social
(Chilean Social Assistance Association)
Santiago, Chile

748 Asociación Chilena de Protección a la Familia
(Chilean Family Protection Association)
Valentín Letelier 1373
Santiago, Chile

749 Asociación Football de Santiago
(Santiago Football Association)
Santo Domingo 1334
Santiago, Chile

750 Centro de Acción Comunitaria
(Community Action Center)
El Tijeral 1770
Santiago, Chile

751 Centro de Vivienda y Construcción
(Housing and Construction Center)
Facultad de Ciencias Físicas y Matematicas
Universidad de Chile
Av. Beauchef 850
Santiago, Chile

752 Centro Interamericano de Enseñanza de Estadística
(Inter-American Center for Teaching of Statistics)
Casilla 10015
Santiago, Chile (L.A.)

753 Comité de Programación Económica y Reconstrucción (COPERE)
(Economic Planning and Reconstruction Committee)
Ministerio de Economía, Fomento y Reconstrucción
Santiago, Chile

754 Consejo de Defensa del Niño
(Council for Child Protection)
Hnos. Amunátegui 109
Santiago, Chile

755 Consejo Nacional de Deportes
(National Sports Council)
Compañía 1630
Santiago, Chile

756 Corporación de Servicios Habitacionales de Chile
(Housing Services Corporation of Chile)
Santiago, Chile

757 Depto. de Inspección General y Control Sanitario
(Dept. of General Inspection and Sanitary Control)
Municipalidad de Santiago
Plaza de Armas--21 de Mayo
Santiago, Chile

758 Depto. de Urbanismo y Vivienda
(City Planning and Housing Dept.)
Sección Plan Intercomunal de Santiago
Ministerio de Obras Públicas
Morandé 45, 59-71
Santiago, Chile

759 Dirección del Tránsito
(Traffic Department)
Municipalidad de Santiago
Plaza de Armas--21 de Mayo
Santiago, Chile

760 Empresa Nacional de Electricidad, S.A.
(National Electric Company, Inc.)
Moneda 812
Santiago, Chile

761 Empresa Nacional de Telecomunicaciones (ENTEL)
(National Telecommunications Company)

Universidad de Chile
Santiago, Chile

762 Fundación de Viviendas y Asistencia Social
(Housing and Social Assistance Foundation)
Bandera 24, Oficina 713
Santiago, Chile

763 Fundación Viviendas de Emergencia
(Foundation for Emergency Housing)
Santiago, Chile

764 Hogar de Cristo
Santiago, Chile
(Self-help housing development project)

765 Instituto de Rehabilitación Infantil
(Institute for Rehabilitation of Children)
Huérfanos 2681
Santiago, Chile

766 Instituto de Rehabilitación y Educación Especial
(Institute for Rehabilitation and Special Education)
Av. Los Leones 1701
Santiago, Chile

767 Instituto de Salubridad y Educación Comunitaria
(Institute for Health and Community Education)
Fernández Albano 3075
Santiago, Chile

768 Instituto de Viviendas Populares Caritas
(Institute for General Welfare Housing)
Santiago, Chile

769 Ministerio de la Vivienda y Urbanismo
(Department of Housing and City Planning)
Serrano 45, piso 4
Santiago, Chile

770 Organización de Universidades Católicas de América Latina
(Organization of Catholic Universities of Latin America)
Universidad Católica de Chile
O'Higgins 340, piso 2
Santiago, Chile

771 Plan Intercomunal para Santiago
(Inter-Community Plan for Santiago)
Ministerio de Obras Públicas
Santiago, Chile

772 Tesorería Municipal
(Municipal Treasury)
Municipalidad de Santiago
Plaza de Armas--21 de Mayo
Santiago, Chile

Colombia

773 Asociación Colombiana Popular de Industriales
(Colombian Manufacturers' Association)
Carrera 6, no. 11-87, Oficina 807
Bogotá, Colombia

774 Asociación Nacional de Industriales (ANDI)
(National Association of Industrialists)
Carrera 10, 14-33, piso 16
Bogotá, Colombia

775 Casa de la Cultura
(House of Culture)
Girardot, Colombia

776 Corporación Financiera de Caldas
(Financial Corporation of Caldas)
Manizales, Colombia

777 Depto. Administrativo de Planificación
(Administrative Planning Dept.)
Distrito Especial de Bogotá
Carrera 8, no. 10-65, piso 4
Bogotá, Colombia

778 Inspecciones de Tránsito y Transportes
(Traffic and Transportation Inspector's Office)
Distrito Especial de Bogotá
1a. Carrera 19, 11-17
Bogotá, Colombia

779 Instituto Colombiano de Seguros Sociales
(Colombian Social Security Institute)
Tr. 17, 25-39
Bogotá, Colombia

780 Instituto de Aprovechamiento de Aguas y Fomento Eléctrico
(Institute for Water Improvement and Electrical Development)
Carrera 13, no. 27-00, piso 3
Bogotá, Colombia

781 Instituto de Fomento Industrial
(Institute for Industrial Development)
Av. Jiménez de Quesada 8-49, piso 9
Bogotá, Colombia

782 Instituto Nacional de Fomento Municipal
(National Municipal Development Institute)
Autopista, Aeropuerto Eldorado
Bogotá, Colombia

783 Instituto Popular de Cultura
(Popular Institute of Culture)
Ministerio de Educación Nacional
Carrera 8, no. 6-40
Bogotá, Colombia

784 Seccion de Parques y Avenidas
(Parks and Streets Department)
Depto. de Conservación
Distrito Especial de Bogotá
Carrera 8, no. 10-65
Bogotá, Colombia

785 Secretaría de Salud Pública
(Public Health Department)
Distrito Especial de Bogotá
Calle 11, no. 8-49
Bogotá, Colombia

Costa Rica

786 Agencia Judicial Municipal
(Municipal Judicial Agency)
Calle 14 a 4
San José, Costa Rica

787 Compañía Nacional de Fuerza y Luz
(National Power and Light Company)
Av. 1-5
San José, Costa Rica

788 Instituto Costarricense de Electricidad
(Costa Rican Institute of Electricity)
Central Local
San José, Costa Rica

789 Instituto Nacional de Vivienda y Urbanismo
(National Institute for Housing and City Planning)
Calle 9a., 2
San José, Costa Rica

790 Sección de Urbanismo
(City Planning Section)
Depto. de Ingeniería
Municipalidad de San José
Calle 14 a 4
San José, Costa Rica

791 Sección de Vías Públicas
(Public Roads Section)
Depto. de Ingeniería
Municipalidad de San José
Calle 14 a 4
San José, Costa Rica

Cuba

792 Casa de las Américas
(House of the Americas)
Havana, Cuba

793 Central de Trabajadores de Cuba Revolucionaria
(Workers' Center of Revolutionary Cuba)
San Carlos y Peñalver
Centro Privado
Havana, Cuba

794 Comisión de Economía
(Economic Commission)
36, no. 2702, Marianao
Havana, Cuba

795 Consejo Nacional de Cultura
(National Culture Council)
Av. 49, no. 12008, Marianao
Centro Privado
Havana, Cuba

796 Consejo Superior de la Reforma Urbana

(Higher Council on Urban Reform)
O. no. 216, Vedado
Havana, Cuba

797 Empresa de Correos y Telégrafos
(Mail and Telegraph Enterprises)
Ministerio de Comunicaciones
Plaza de la Revolución José Martí
Havana, Cuba

798 Empresas Metropolitanas
(Metropolitan Enterprises)
Ministerio del Comercio Interior
Edificio MINCIN
Obispo 61--Centro Privado
Havana, Cuba

799 Escuela Nacional Sindical "Carlos Rodríguez Carreaga"
(Carlos Rodríguez Carreaga National Trade Union School)
23 no. 21425, Marianao
Havana, Cuba

800 Institución de Servicios de Divulgación
(Information Services Institution)
Mier y 23 Vedado
Hotel Havana Libre
Havana, Cuba

801 Instituto Cubano de Radiodifusión
(Cuban Broadcasting Institute)
Edificio Radio Centro
Havana, Cuba

802 Instituto Nacional de Ahorro y Viviendas
(National Savings & Housing Institute)
Ayestarán y 20 de Mayo
Havana, Cuba

803 Instituto Nacional de Deportes, Educación Física y Recreación
(National Institute of Sports, Physical Education and Recreation)
Av. Porvenir y Santa Catalina
Havana, Cuba

804 Ministerio de la Construcción
(Ministry of Construction)
Plaza de la Revolución José Martí
Havana, Cuba

805 Ministerio de Salud Pública
(Ministry of Public Health)
Padre Varela y E. Barnet
Havana, Cuba

806 Omnibus de la Habana
(Havana Bus Co.)
Ministerio de Transportes
P. Varela 362
Havana, Cuba

807 Vice-Ministerio de Viviendas
(Vice-Ministry of Housing)
Amargura 53
Havana, Cuba

Dominican Republic

808 Centro Sanitario de Santo Domingo
(Santo Domingo Sanitary Center)
Santiago 4
Santo Domingo, Dominican Republic

809 Central Sindical de Trabajadores Dominicanos
(Dominican Workers' Trade Union Center)
Arzobispo Meriño 117
Santo Domingo, Dominican Republic

810 Dirección de Limpieza y Ornato
(Sanitation and Beautification Department)
Vertedero de Basura
Autopista Santo Domingo-Haina
Santo Domingo, Dominican Republic

811 Dirección de Transporte Urbano
(Urban Transportation Department)
Ayuntamiento del Distrito Nacional
Palacio del Ayuntamiento Feria
Santo Domingo, Dominican Republic

812 Dirección General de Obras Públicas
(General Office of Public Works)
Ayuntamiento de Distrito Nacional
Palacio del Ayuntamiento Feria
Santo Domingo, Dominican Republic

813 Fundación Dominicana de Desarrollo
(Dominican Development Foundation)
c/o Dr. José Armenteros, President
Ghandi 23
Santo Domingo, Dominican Republic

814 Instituto de Auxilios y Viviendas
(Institute of Assistance and Housing)
B. Monción 11
Santo Domingo, Dominican Republic

815 Instituto Nacional de Aguas Potables y Alcantarillados
(National Institute of Potable Water and Sewage Systems)
Santo Domingo, Dominican Republic

816 Oficina de Sanidad Aérea
(Air Pollution Control Office)
Secretaría de Salud y Previsión Social
Aeropuerto Internacional de Pta. Caucedo
Santo Domingo, Dominican Republic

817 Oficina para el Desarrollo de la Comunidad
(Office for Community Development)
Santo Domingo, Dominican Republic

818 Secretaría de Educación, Bellas Artes y Cultos
(Secretariat of Education, Fine Arts and Religion)
Santo Domingo, Dominican Republic

Ecuador

819 Bombas de El Sena
(El Sena Pumping Division)
Empresa Municipal de Agua Potable
Angel P. Chavez 360
Quito, Ecuador

820 Centro Médico
(Medical Center)
Junta de Asistencia Social
Cotocollao
Quito, Ecuador

821 Confederación Ecuatoriana de Organizaciones Sindicales Libres
(Ecuadorean Confederation of Free Trade Union Organizations)
García Moreno 1244
Quito, Ecuador

822 Depto. de Obras Públicas Municipales
(Dept. of Municipal Public Works)
Comisaría de Construcciones
Pasaje Amador 350, piso 4
Quito, Ecuador

823 Depto. Financiero
(Financial Dept.)
Municipalidad de Quito
Olmedo 497
Quito, Ecuador

824 Instituto de Ingeniería Sanitaria
(Sanitary Engineering Institute)
Rocafuerte 1545
Quito, Ecuador

825 Instituto Ecuatoriano de Electrificación
(Ecuadorean Electrification Institute)
Auditoría
Bogotá 123
Quito, Ecuador

826 Instituto Municipal de Cultura
(Municipal Institute of Culture)
Quito, Ecuador

827 Instituto Nacional de Nutrición
(National Nutrition Institute)
Av. Colombia
Quito, Ecuador

828 Instituto Nacional de Previsión
(National Social Security Institute)
Estrada y Av. Tarqui
Quito, Ecuador

829 Junta Central de Asistencia Social
(Central Social Welfare Board)
Montúfar 352
Guayaquil, Ecuador

830 Radiodifusora Municipal
(Municipal Radio Station)
Depto. Municipal de Cultura
García Moreno 887
Quito, Ecuador

831 Zonas Sanitarias Sur y Norte
(North and South Sanitary Zones)
Dirección de Higiene
Av. Colombia 362
Quito, Ecuador

El Salvador

832 Administración Nacional de Acueductos y Alcantarillados
(National Administration of Aqueducts and Sewage Systems)
5a. Av. no. 512
San Salvador, El Salvador

833 Compañía de Alumbrado Eléctrico de San Salvador
(San Salvador Electric Lighting Company)
Apartado Postal 186
San Salvador, El Salvador

834 Instituto de Vivienda Urbana
(Urban Housing Institute)
Calle Urb. Libertad
San Salvador, El Salvador

Guatemala

835 Asociación de Bienestar Social Infantil
(Association for Social Welfare of Children)
Av. Bolívar no. 25-00
Guatemala, Guatemala

836 Asociación de Trabajadores Sociales
(Social Workers Association)
6a. Av. no. 15-40
Guatemala, Guatemala

837 Asociación Nacional de Municipalidades de la República de Guatemala
(National Association of Municipalities of the Republic of Guatemala)
Guatemala, Guatemala

838 Centro de Bienestar Social Guatemalteco
(Guatemalan Social Welfare Center)
6a. Av. 3-74
Guatemala, Guatemala

839 Depto. de Bomberos Municipales
(Municipal Fire Department)
1a. Calle 2-13
Guatemala, Guatemala

840 Depto. de Ingeniería Municipal
(Dept. of Municipal Engineering)
22 Calle "A" y 6a. Avenida
Guatemala, Guatemala

841 Depto. de Ingeniería Sanitaria
(Sanitary Engineering Department)
Av. La Reforma
Guatemala, Guatemala

842 Depto. General de Aguas Municipales
(General City Water Department)
39a. Calle y 8a. Avenida
Guatemala, Guatemala

843 Instituto de Fomento Municipal
(Municipal Development Institute)
6a. Av. 1-73
Guatemala, Guatemala

844 Inter-American Cooperative Housing Institute
Ruta 2, 0-52
Guatemala, Guatemala

845 Sindicato de Trabajadores Municipales
(Municipal Workers' Union)
19 Calle 2-58
Guatemala, Guatemala

Guyana

846 Central Housing and Planning Authority
Georgetown, Guyana

Haiti

847 Office d'Administration des Cités Ouvrières
(Administrative Office of Workers' Cities)
Port-au-Prince, Haiti

Honduras

848 Asociación Hondureña de Planeamiento Familiar

(Honduran Family Planning Association)
c/o Hospital San Felipe
Tegucigalpa, Honduras

849 Departamento Socio-Económico
(Socio-Economic Department)
Instituto de la Vivienda
6a. Calle, 1551
Tegucigalpa, Honduras

850 Dirección de Municipalidades
(Municipalities Bureau)
Tegucigalpa, Honduras

851 Dirección General de Caminos
(General Bureau of Roads)
Bo. La Bolsa
Tegucigalpa, Honduras

852 Dirección General de Comunicaciones Eléctricas
(Bureau of Electrical Communications)
5a. Calle, 4a. y 5a. Avenida
Tegucigalpa, Honduras

853 Dirección General de Salud Pública
(General Bureau of Public Health)
3a. Calle y 4a. Avenida
Tegucigalpa, Honduras

854 Dirección General de Seguridad Social
(General Bureau of Social Security)
5a. Av. 707
Tegucigalpa, Honduras

855 Dirección General del Trabajo
(General Bureau of Labor)
3a. Calle
Tegucigalpa, Honduras

856 Federación Sindical de Trabajadores Nacionales (FESINTRAH)
(Trade Union Federation of Honduran Workers)
Tegucigalpa, Honduras

Jamaica

857 Foundation for Cooperative Housing
Kingston, Jamaica

Martinique

858 Caribbean Federation for Mental Health
c/o Mme. Charles St.-Cyr
Ravine Vilaine
Fort-de-France, Martinique

Mexico

859 Banco Nacional Hipotecario Urbano y de Obras Públicas, S.A.
Plaza de la República 16
México, D. F., México

860 Centro Familiar Obrero
(Workers' Family Center)
Prolongación Av. Central 400
México, D. F., México

861 Centro Urbanístico
(City Planning Center)
Secretaría de Comunicaciones
Ministerio de Comunicaciones y Obras Públicas
México, D. F., México

862 Ciudad Deportiva
(Sports City)
Depto. del Distrito Federal
16 de Septiembre, no. 66
México, D. F., México

863 Comisión de Estudios Técnicos de Transportes en el Distrito Federal
(Comission on Technical Studies of Transportation in the Federal District)
Depto. del Distrito Federal
16 de Septiembre, no. 66
México, D. F., México

864 Comisión de Tarifas de Electricidad y Gas
(Electricity and Gas Rates Commission)
A. Herrera 15, 1º - 2º - 3º pisos
México, D. F., México

865 Comisión Nacional de Salarios Mínimos
(National Minimum Wage Commission)
Av. Paseo de la Reforma 72--piso 4
México, D. F., México

866 Comisión Nacional Organizadora de los Municipios en México
(National Organizing Commission of Municipalities in Mexico)
México, D. F., México

867 Delegaciones del Ministerio Público Urbanas
(Urban Delegations of the Public Ministry)
Depto. del Distrito Federal
Av. Revolución 127
Tacubaya
México, D. F., México

868 Departamento de Planeación
(Planning Department)
Secretaría de Comunicaciones y Transportes
México, D. F., México

869 Dirección de Salubridad en el Distrito Federal
(Federal District Board of Health)
Secretaría de Salubridad y Asistencia
Donceles 39
México, D. F., México

870 Dirección General de Aguas y Saneamiento
(General Department of Water and Health)
Depto. del Distrito Federal
Edificio de la Tesorería
México, D. F., México

871 Dirección General de Tránsito
(General Traffic Department)
Depto. del Distrito Federal
F.S.T. de Mier y Plaza de Tlaxcoaque
México, D. F., México

872 Instituto de Seguridad y Servicios Sociales de los Trabajadores del Estado
(Institute of Social Security and Services for State Workers)
Plaza de la República 6
México, D. F., México

873 Instituto Mexicano de Rehabilitación
(Mexican Rehabilitation Institute)
San Fernando 15
Tlalpam, D. F., Mexico

874 Instituto Mexicano del Seguro Social
(Mexican Social Security Institute)
Reforma 476
México, D. F., México

875 Instituto Nacional de Bellas Artes
(National Institute of Fine Arts)
Palacio de Bellas Artes
México, D. F., México

876 Instituto Nacional de la Juventud Mexicana
(National Institute of Mexican Youth)
México, D. F., México

877 Instituto Nacional de Vivienda
(National Housing Institute)
Niños Héroes 139
México, D. F., México

878 Inter-American Confederation of Catholic Social Action
Roma 1
México, D. F., México

879 Oficina de Parques y Jardines
(Office of Parks and Gardens)
Depto. del Distrito Federal
Bosque de Chapultepec
México, D. F., México

880 Organización Regional Interamericano de Trabajadores (ORIT)
(Regional Inter-American Organization of Workers)
Plaza de la República 30
México, D. F., México

881 Permanent Interamerican Committee on Social Security,
c/o O.E.A.
Guanajuato 277, piso 7
Mexico, D. F., Mexico

882 Servicio de Aguas Potables
(Potable Water Service)
Depto. de Distrito Federal
Pino Suárez 42
México, D. F., México

883 Sociedad de Auxilios Voluntarios Económicos
(Society for Voluntary Economic Aid)
México, D. F., México

Netherlands West Indies

884 Promotion for the Foundation of Responsible Parenthood
Curaçāo, Netherlands West Indies

Nicaragua

885 Instituto Nicaragüense de la Vivienda
(Nicaraguan Housing Institute)
Central Sur, 402
Managua, Nicaragua

886 Junta Local de Asistencia Social
(Local Social Assistance Board)
Managua, Nicaragua

887 Oficina Nacional de Urbanismo
(National City Planning Office)
Ministerio de Fomento
Managua, Nicaragua

Panama

888 Alcaldía Municipal
Av. 7 Central, 20
Panamá, Panamá

889 Banco de Urbanización y Rehabilitación
(Bank of Urbanization and Rehabilitation)
Panamá, Panamá

890 Depto. de Ingeniería Municipal
(Dept. of Civil Engineering)
Calle 11, Nuevo Cristóbal
Panamá, Panamá

891 Depto. de Obras y Construcciones Municipales
(Dept. of Municipal Works and Construction)
Transversal 1, 65
Panamá, Panamá

892 Depto. De Urbanización y Rehabilitación
(Urbanization and Rehabilitation Department)
Instituto de Fomento Económico
Av. 4, 24-120, y Calle 21
Panamá, Panamá

893 Dirección de Transportes y Talleres
(Department of Transportation & Shops)
Calle 28 Final
Panamá, Panamá

894 IFHA
(Institute for the Development of Insured Mortgages)
Panamá, Panamá

895 Instituto de Acueductos y Alcantarillados Nacionales
(Institute of National Aqueducts and Sewage Systems)
Depto. de Ingeniería Municipal
Panamá, Panamá

896 Instituto de la Vivienda y Urbanismo
(Housing and City Planning Institute)
Av. 3 y Calle 24
Panamá, Panamá

897 Inter-American Association of Sanitary Engineering
Aptdo. 8246
Panamá, Panamá

898 Oficina de Salubridad
(Office of Health)
Ministerio de Trabajo, Previsión Social y Salud Pública
Av. 5
Panamá, Panamá

899 Sección de Asistencia Familiar
(Family Assistance Center)
Ministerio de Trabajo, Previsión Social y Salud Pública
Av. 5
Panamá, Panamá

900 Tesorería Municipal
(Municipal Treasury)
Av. Herrera, 5060
Panamá, Panamá

Paraguay

901 Depto. de Salubridad
(Health Department)
Municipalidad de la Capital
Palma 371
Asunción, Paraguay

902 Depto. de Transporte
(Transportation Department)
Municipalidad de la Capital
Palma 371
Asunción, Paraguay

903 Direcciones de Catástro y Saneamiento
(Taxation and Health Departments)
Municipalidad de la Capital
Palma 371
Asunción, Paraguay

904 Direccion de Obras Públicas
(Public Works Department)
Ministerio de Obras Públicas y Comunicaciones
General Díaz y Alberdi
Asunción, Paraguay

905 Dirección General de Institutos Penales de la República
(General Office of Penal Institutions of the Republic)
Tacumbú
Asunción, Paraguay

906 Instituto de Previsión Social
(Social Security Institute)
Constitución y Luis A. Herrera
Asunción, Paraguay

907 Ministerio de Salud Pública y Bienestar Social
(Ministry of Public Health and Social Welfare)
Av. Pettirossi y Brasil
Asunción, Paraguay

908 Teatro Municipal
(Municipal Theater)
Municipalidad de la Capital
Palma 371
Asunción, Paraguay

Peru

909 ASINCOOP
(Peruvian Workers' Housing Bank)
Lima, Perú

910 Asociación Nacional de Escritores y Artistas
(National Writers' and Artists' Association)
112 Moquegua
Lima, Perú

911 Asociación de Propietarios de Omnibus Urbanos e Interurbanos
(Association of Urban and Interurban Bus Line Owners)
295 P. Bermúdez
Lima, Perú

912 Centro Nacional de Acción para el Incremento de la Productividad
(National Action Center for Productivity Increase)
Lima, Perú

913 Cooperación Popular y Desarrollo Comunal
(Popular Cooperation & Community Development)
Lima, Perú

914 Corporación Nacional de Vivienda
(National Housing Corporation)
Lima, Perú

915 Depto. de Asistencia Pública
(Dept. of Public Assistance)
Ministerio de Salud Pública y Asistencia Social
Av. Salaverry
Lima, Perú

916 Depto. de Control Urbano y de Terrenos del Estado
(Dept. of Urban Control and State Lands)
Ministerio de Fomento y Obras Públicas
Av. 28 de Julio
Lima, Perú

917 Depto. Municipal de Sanidad
(Municipal Department of Health)
Plaza de Armas
Lima, Perú

918 Dirección General de Establecimientos Penales y de Tutela
(General Department of Penal and Protection Institutions)
Ministerio de Justicia y Culto
Palacio de Gobierno
Lima, Perú

919 Inspección de Alumbrado y Tranvías
(Office of Lighting and Streetcars)
Municipalidad de Lima
Plaza de Armas
Lima, Perú

920 Instituto Nacional de Planificación
(National Planning Institute)
Lampa 277
Lima, Perú

921 Oficina Nacional de Planeamiento y Urbanismo
(National Planning and City Planning Office)
115 P. Thouars
Lima, Perú

922 Parlamento Latinoamericano
(Latin American Parliament)
Casilla Postal 6041
Lima, Perú (L.A.)

923 Servicio de Empleo y Recursos Humanos
(Employment and Human Resources Service)
Ministerio de Trabajo y Asuntos Indígenas
Av. Salaverry
Lima, Perú

924 Superintendencia de Agua Potable de Lima
(Supervisory Office for Potable Water of Lima)
Av. Venezuela
Lima, Perú

Puerto Rico

925 Inter-American Municipal Organization
P.O. Box 4355
San Juan, Puerto Rico

926 Inter-American Planning Society
P.O. Box 1779
San Juan, Puerto Rico

Uruguay

927 Administración General de las Usinas Eléctricas y los Teléfonos del Estado
(Federal Administration of Power Plants and Telephones)
Palacio de la Luz
Montevideo, Uruguay

928 Comisión de Inversiones y Desarrollo Económico
(Investment and Economic Development Commission)
Convención 1523
Montevideo, Uruguay

929 Comisión de Teatros Municipales
(Municipal Theaters Commission)
Bartolomé Mitre 1270
Montevideo, Uruguay

930 Comisión Municipal de Fiestas
(Municipal Fiestas Commission)
Av. Centenario
Montevideo, Uruguay

931 Comisión Nacional de Municipalidades
(National Commission of Municipalities)
Montevideo, Uruguay

932 Comisión para la Integración Eléctrica Regional
(Commission for Regional Electrical Integration)
Montevideo, Uruguay

933 Dirección de Vialidad Nacional
(National Bureau of Roads)
Ministerio de Obras Públicas
Mesa Central
18 de Julio 1112, piso 2
Montevideo, Uruguay

934 Instituto de Previsión Social y Asistencia Médica "Patria"
("Patria" Institute of Social Security and Medical Assistance)
Sierra 2133
Montevideo, Uruguay

935 Instituto Nacional de Viviendas Económicas
(National Institute of Low-Income Housing)
Av. Agraciada 1409
Montevideo, Uruguay

936 Inter-American Children's Institute
Av. 8 de Octubre 2882
Montevideo, Uruguay

937 Ministerio de Industrias y Trabajo
(Ministry of Industries and Labor)
Rincón 737
Montevideo, Uruguay

938 Ministerio de Instrucción Pública y Previsión Social
(Ministry of Public Education and Social Security)
25 de Mayo 376
Montevideo, Uruguay

Venezuela

939 Acción de Venezuela
Edificio Distromédica
Av. Urdaneta
Caracas, Venezuela
(Community development, urban education, public welfare)

940 Banco Obrero
(Workers' Bank)
Instituto de la Vivienda del Estado Venezolano
Edificio Centro Comercial Altagracia
Caracas, Venezuela

941 Compañía Anónima de Administración y Fomento Eléctrico
(Electrical Development Administration)
Caracas, Venezuela

942 Corporación Venezolana de Fomento
(Venezuelan Development Corporation)
Edificio Norte
Centro Simón Bolívar
Caracas, Venezuela

943 Depto. de Higiene Mental
(Mental Hygiene Department)
Ministerio de Salubridad y Asistencia Social
Centro Simón Bolívar
Edificio Sur, piso 4, Oficina 429
Caracas, Venezuela

944 Dirección de Aseo Urbano
(Department of Urban Sanitation)
Av. L. Samanes
La Flórida
Caracas, Venezuela

945 Dirección de Asistencia Social del Ministerio de Sanidad
(Department of Social Assistance of the Ministry of Health)
Edificio Sur, Centro Simón Bolívar, piso 4, oficina 335
Caracas, Venezuela

946 Dirección de Planeamiento
(Planning Department)
Ministerio de Obras Públicas
Caracas, Venezuela

947 Dirección General de Obras Municipales
(General Department of Municipal Works)
Gobernación del Distrito Federal
Esq. de Principal
Caracas, Venezuela

948 Dirección Municipal de Educación
(Municipal Department of Education)
Gobernación del Distrito Federal
Av. San Martín
Caracas, Venezuela

949 Dividendo Voluntario para la Comunidad
(Businessmen's Community Development Organization)
Caracas, Venezuela

950 División de Voluntarios para la Comunidad, Edificio Gran Avenida, piso 6
Calle Real de Sabana Grande
Caracas, Venezuela
(Community development service organization)

951 Federación de Instituciones Privades de Atención al Niño (FIPAN)
(Federation of Private Institutions for the Care of Children)
Edificio VAM, Penthouse
Av. Andrés Bello
Caracas, Venezuela

952 Fundación Instituto Venezolano de Productividad
(Venezuelan Foundation Institute for Productivity)
Edificio Sur, piso 9, Centro Simón Bolívar
Caracas, Venezuela

953 Fundación para el Desarrollo de la Comunidad y Fomento Municipal
(Foundation for Community Development and Municipal Promotion)
Residencias Santiago de León, piso 4
Av. Casanova
Bello Monte
Caracas, Venezuela

954 Inspección General de Teatros y Espectáculos Públicos
(General Office of Theaters and Public Presentations)
Gobernación del Distrito Federal
Esq. de Principal
Caracas, Venezuela

955 Instituto Municipal Transporte Colectivo D. F.
(Municipal Institute of Mass Transportation, Federal District)
3a. Calle Transversal
Av. San Martín, Los Molinos
Caracas, Venezuela

956 Instituto Nacional de Cooperación Educativa (INCE)
(National Institute for Educational Cooperation)
Edificio Torre del Cují, piso 9, Esq. del Cují
Caracas, Venezuela

957 Instituto Nacional de Nutrición
(National Nutrition Institute)
Esq. El Carmen
Caracas, Venezuela

958 Instituto Nacional de Obras Sanitarias
(National Institute of Sanitary Works)
Edificio Las Mercedes
Esq. de Tienda Honda
Caracas, Venezuela

959 Instituto para Capacitación y Recreación de los Trabajadores (INCRET)
(Institute for Training and Recreation of Workers)
Centro Simón Bolívar
Caracas, Venezuela

960 Instituto para el Desarrollo Económico y Social
(Institute for Economic and Social Development)
Aptdo. 5105
Caracas, Venezuela

961 Instituto Venezolano de Acción Comunitaria
(Venezuelan Institute for Community Action)
Edificio La Línea, 3er. piso 34
Av. Libertador
Caracas, Venezuela

962 Instituto Venezolano de los Seguros Sociales
(Venezuelan Social Security Institute), Edificio Sur, 403
Av. Bolívar
Caracas, Venezuela

963 Oficina Central de Coordinación y Planificatión (CORDIPLAN)
(Central Coordination and Planning Office)
c/o Ministerio de Fomento
Caracas, Venezuela

964 Sociedad Venezolana de Planificación
(Venezuelan Planning Society)
Aptdo. 622
Caracas, Venezuela

2C. "WORKING" ORGANIZATIONS (Departments of city, state, and federal governments, and business and professional associations, foundations, and international organizations concerned with urbanization) LOCATED ELSEWHERE

(Note: a note is given in instances where the title of the individual department, association, foundation, or organization does not specify its field of activity).

Belgium

965 Fédération Belge de l'Urbanisme, de l'Habitation et de l'Aménagement du Territoire
(Belgian Federation of City Planning, Housing, and Land Management)
61, rue Montoyer
Brussels, Belgium

966 International Confederation of Free Trade Unions
37-47 rue Montagne aux Herbes Potagères
Brussels, Belgium

967 International Union of Public Transport
18 Ave. de la Toison d'Or
Brussels, Belgium

Canada

968 Boy Scouts World Bureau
77 Metcalf
Ottawa, Ontario, Canada

969 Canadian Federation of Mayors and Municipalities
Mt. Royal Hotel
Montreal, P. Q., Canada

970 Community Planning Association of Canada
32 Isabella
Toronto, Ontario, Canada

England

971 Centre for Educational Television Overseas
Nuffield Idg.
Regents Park
London N.W. 1, England

972 Community Service Volunteers
15 Trinity Sq.
London, E.C. 3, England

973 International Road Federation, Ltd.
Abbey House
Victoria St.
London, S.W. 1, England

974 International Water Supply Aso-sociation
34 Park St.
London W. 1, England

975 Ministry of Housing and Local Government
Whitehall
London S.W. 1, England

976 National Council of Social Service, Inc.
26 Bedford Square
London W.C. 1, England

977 Public Services International
54 Bartholomew
London E.C. 1, England

978 Town and Country Planning Association
28 King St.
London W.C. 2, England

979 Voluntary Service Overseas
3 Hanover St.
London W. 1, England

980 World Bureau
World Association of Girl Guides & Girl Scouts
132 Ebury St.
London S.W. 1, England

981 World Federation of Mental Health
19 Manchester St.
London W. 1, England

France

982 Centre de Formation des Experts de la Coopération Technique Internationale
(Center for Training of Experts in International Technical Cooperation)
Foundation Nationale des Sciences Politiques
27 rue St. Guillaume
Paris, France

983 Centre International de l'Enfance
(International Children's Center)
26 Blvd. Brune
Paris, France

984 Centre International du Logement
(International Housing Center)
12 Av. Grande Armée
Paris, France

985 Centre Mondial Familial
(World Family Center)
43 rue Lafitte
Paris, France

986 Conseil International des Musées
(International Museums Council)
International Council of Philosophic & Humanistic Sciences
Place de Fontenoy
Paris, France

987 General Association of Municipal Health & Technical Experts
9 Rue de Phalsbourg
Paris, France

988 International Society of City & Regional Planners
c/o A.I.U.
52 Rue Mathurin Régnier
Paris, France

989 Société d'Etudes pour l'Urbanisme, l'Equipement et les Canalisations
91 Ave. Kleber
Paris, France
(water supply)

Germany

990 Kommunale Gemeinschaftsstelle für Verwaltungsvereinfachung
(Community Office for Operational Efficiency)
Cologne, Federal Republic of Germany

India

991 Dept. of Community Development Panchayati Raj, Government of India
Delhi, India

992 National Institute for Community Development
Rajendranagar, India

Israel

993 Mt. Carmel International Training Center for Community Services
Haifa, Israel

994 National Housing Cooperation for Immigrants, Ltd.
Amidar, Israel

Italy

995 European Federation for Prefabrication & Other Industrialized Building Methods
(EUROPREFAB)
Milan, Italy

996 International Federation of Settlements and Neighborhood Centers
Rome, Italy

Netherlands

997 International Union of Local Authorities
Paleisstraat 5
The Hague, Netherlands

Scotland

998 World Society for Ekistics
(World Society for the Study of Human Settlements)
c/o Professor Sir Robert Matthew
Dept. of Architecture
University of Edinburgh
Edinburgh, Scotland

Spain

999 Asociación de Sociólogos de Lengua Española y Portugués
(Association of Sociologists of the Spanish and Portuguese Languages)
Instituto de Cultura Hispánica
Av. de los Reyes Católicos
Ciudad Universitaria
Madrid, Spain

1000 Comisión Informativa de Urbanismo
(City Planning Information Commission)
Ayuntamiento de Sevilla
Seville, Spain

1001 Dirección General de Urbanismo
(General City Planning Department)
Ministerio de la Vivienda
Agustín Betancourt 2
Madrid, Spain

1002 Oficina Iberoamericana de Seguridad Social
Madrid, Spain

Switzerland

1003 Bureau Européen
(European Office)
Organization of American States
44, rue de Lausanne
Geneva, Switzerland

1004 Expert Committee on Atmospheric Pollutants
World Health Organization
Palais des Nations
Geneva, Switzerland

1005 International Catholic Migration Commission
11 rue Cornavin
Geneva, Switzerland

1006 International Social Service
14 Rue Hollande
Geneva, Switzerland

DIRECTORY # 3:

SPECIALISTS IN URBANIZATION AND CONCOMITANT AREAS OF ACTIVITY:

3A. AESTHETICS AND HUMANITIES

- Planning
- Religion
- Travel
- Urban History
- Urban Matrix for Literature & the Arts
- Urban Speech

3B. ECONOMICS-INDUSTRY COMMERCE

- Cost and Standard of Living
- Employment
- Industrialization
- Poverty
- Transportation

3C. GOVERNMENT-LAW

- Municipal Finance
- Municipal Government and Legal Matters
- Public Utilities

3D. SOCIOLOGY

- Urban Sociology
- Communications
- Community Development
- Crime and Juvenile Delinquency
- Demography
- Education
- Housing
- Public Health
- Public Welfare
- Rural-Urban Migration
- Social Change
- Social Security
- Urban Geography

3E. URBANIZATION

- Urbanization, General
- Urbanization Bibliography

(Note: Under each professional field of activity, names and addresses of specialists are arranged (1) geographically according to nation and/or region of Latin America; and (2) alphabetically. In instances where individuals have competence in specialties additional to those under which they have been listed, such professional subject-fields and geographic areas of specialization are indicated following the respective names and addresses).

3A. AESTHETICS AND HUMANITIES

Planning

Latin America

1007 Astica Mascaró, Juan B.
Chief, Housing Dept.
Planning Bureau
Ministry of Public Works
Santiago, Chile
(housing)

1008 Bullrich, Francisco J.
Visiting Lecturer in History of Art
Yale University
New Haven, Conn. 06520
(architecture, urbanism)

1009 Hardoy, Jorge E., Director
Institute of Urban & Regional Planning
National University of Litoral
Santa Fé 2008
Rosario, Argentina

1010 Mardones-Restat, Héctor
Málaga 316
Santiago, Chile

1011 Morcillo, Pedro P.
Aptdo. Aéreo 1738
Cali, Colombia

1012 Parker, John A.
Chairman, City & Regional Planning
University of North Carolina
Chapel Hill, N.C. 27514
(education, Chile, Central America)

1013 Quereizaeta Enríquez, A.
Dirección General de Urbanismo
Ministerio de Vivienda
Plaza San Juan de la Cruz 1
Madrid, Spain

1014 Sañudo, Celestino
Organization of American States
Washington, D.C. 20006

1015 Stein, Stuart W.
College of Architecture
Cornell University
Ithaca, New York 14850

1016 Ventre, Francis T.
Associate Professor
Dept. of Architecture & Urban Planning
University of California
Los Angeles, Calif. 90024

1017 Violich, Francis
Dept. of City & Regional Planning
College of Environmental Design
University of California
Berkeley, Calif. 94720

1018 Wilhelmy, Herbert
16 Seestrasse
Stuttgart, Federal Republic of Germany

Argentina

1019 Buschiazzo, Mario J.
Facultad de Arquitectura y Planeación Municipal
Universidad de Buenos Aires
Buenos Aires, Argentina

1020 Calcaprina, Ciro
Instituto de Arquitectura y Urbanismo
Universidad Nacional de Tucumán
Tucumán, Argentina

1021 Casares, Alfredo C.
Facultad de Arquitectura y Planeación Municipal
Universidad de Buenos Aires
Buenos Aires, Argentina

1022 Ferraz, Enrique
Profesor de Planeación Municipal
Depto. de Ingeniería
Universidad Nacional del Sur
Bahia Blanca, Argentina

1023 Figueroa Román, Miguel
Instituto de Sociografía y Planeación
Universidad Nacional de Tucumán
Tucumán, Argentina

1024 Kleinert, Alfredo J.

Facultad de Arquitectura y Planeación Municipal
Universidad Nacional de La Plata
La Plata, Argentina

1025 Masllorens, Juan
Escuela de Arquitectura
Universidad de Buenos Aires
Buenos Aires, Argentina

1026 Morea, Luis M.
25 Av. de Mayo 267
Buenos Aires, Argentina

1027 Mouchet, Carlos
Avenida de Mayo 749
Buenos Aires, Argentina

1028 Nícoli, Víctor F.
Museo Etnográfico
Santa Fé, S. F., Argentina

1029 Pastor, José M. F.
México 625
Buenos Aires, Argentina

1030 Pinzani, Julio E.
Facultad de Arquitectura y Planeación Municipal
Universidad Católica de Córdoba
Córdoba, Argentina

1031 Rebora, Luis A.
Facultad de Arquitectura y Planeación Municipal
Universidad Nacional de Córdoba
Córdoba, Argentina

Bolivia

1032 Ovando, Guillermo
Profesor de Arquitectura y Urbanismo
Facultad de Ingeniería
Universidad Mayor y Autónoma Tomás Frías
Potosí, Bolivia

1033 Rivera Escobar, Hugo
Profesor de Planeación Regional y Urbana, Facultad de Arquitectura
Universidad Mayor de San Andrés
La Paz, Bolivia

Brazil

1034 Bastos Birkholz, Lauro
Faculdade da Arquitetura e Planeação Municipal
Universidade de São Paulo
São Paulo, S. P., Brazil

1035 Braga Guimarães, Admar
Prof. da Organização Social Urbana, Faculdade da Arquitetura
Universidade da Bahia
Salvador, Bahia, Brazil

1036 Brandão Lopes, Juarez R.
Faculdade da Arquitetura e Planeação Municipal
Universidade do São Paulo
São Paulo, S. P., Brazil

1037 Evenson, Norma
Dept. of City Planning
University of California
Berkeley, Calif. 94720

1038 Lübke, Max W.
Faculdade da Arquitetura
Universidade do Rio Grande do Sul
Pôrto Alegre, R. G. S., Brazil

1039 Mello, F. de Sá
Centro de Estudios de Urbanismo e Habitação "Eng. Duarte Pacheco" M. O. P.
Av. Antônio Augusto de Aguiar 17. 4º
Lisbon, Portugal

1040 Niemeyer, Oscar
Escola da Arquitetura
Universidade de Brasilia
Brasilia, Brazil

1041 Nogueira Batista, Paulo
Institute of Brazilian Architects
Av. Rio Branco 277
Rio de Janeiro, GB, Brazil

1042 Pereira Paiva, E.
Faculdade da Arquitetura
Universidade do Rio Grande do Sul
Pôrto Alegre, R. G. S., Brazil

1043 Rodrigues de Carvalho, Adalberto
Faculdade da Arquitetura

Universidade do Rio Grande do Sul
Pôrto Alegre, R.G.S., Brazil

1044 Szilard, Adalberto
155 Av. Nilo Peçanha
Rio de Janeiro, GB, Brazil

Central America

1045 Guernsey, James L.
Professor of Geography
Indiana State University
Terre Haute, Indiana 47809

1046 Solow, Anatole A.
Associate Professor of Urban & Regional Planning
University of Pittsburgh
Pittsburgh, Pa. 15213
(housing)

Chile

1047 Aguirre del Canto, Santiago
Facultad de Arquitectura
Universidad de Chile
Santiago, Chile

1048 Aliaga, Carlos
Depto. de Obras Públicas
Municipalidad de Santiago
Santiago, Chile

1049 Allen, Ivan J.
Associate Professor of Urban Planning
Michigan State University
East Lansing, Mich. 48823

1050 Baez, Jorge R.
Faculty of Architecture and Engineering
Universidad de Santo Domingo
Santo Domingo, Dominican Republic

1051 Bedrack, Moisés
Profesor de Urbanismo
Facultad de Arquitectura
Universidad de Chile
Santiago, Chile

1052 Böhm Rosas, Hernán
Facultad de Arquitectura
Universidad de Chile
Santiago, Chile

1053 Brieba, Amador
División de Programación Reguladora
Depto. de Planeación
Ministerio de Obras Públicas
Morandé 45
Santiago, Chile

1054 Calvo, Hernán
Depto. de Obras Públicas
Municipalidad de Santiago
Santiago, Chile

1055 Cañas, Carlos
Depto. de Obras Públicas
Municipalidad de Santiago
Santiago, Chile

1056 Honold Duener, Juan
Ministerio de Obras Públicas
Santiago, Chile

1057 Mann, Lawrence D.
Program Specialist
Ford Foundation
I. Valdés Vergara 340, Depto. 11
Santiago, Chile

1058 Ramírez, Aída
Depto. de Obras Públicas
Municipalidad de Santiago
Santiago, Chile

1059 Reyes Vicuña, Tomás
Cámara de Diputados
Santiago, Chile

Colombia

1060 Bernal Villa, Segundo
Chief, Research Dept.
Oficina de Planeación del Distrito Especial
Bogotá, Colombia

1061 Bright, Alex
Professor of Architecture
Universidad de los Andes
Bogotá, Colombia

1062 Harris, Walter De S.
Associate Professor of City Planning
Yale University
New Haven, Conn. 06520
(housing)

1063 Piñeros Torres, Ignacio
Facultad de Arquitectura
Universidad Nacional de Colombia
Bogotá, Colombia

1064 Velasco, Armando
Depto. de Urbanismo
Facultad de Arquitectura
Universidad del Valle
Cali, Colombia

Cuba

1065 Sisto Guerra, Luis
Municipalidad de La Habana
Havana, Cuba

Dominican Republic

1066 Haza del Castillo, Luis
Facultad de Ingeniería y Arquitectura
Universidad de Santo Domingo
Santo Domingo, Dominican Republic

Ecuador

1067 Costales, Alfredo
Welfare Section
Technical Division
Ecuadoran National Planning & Economic Coordination Board
Quito, Ecuator

1068 Rubio Orbe, Gonzálo
Chief, Welfare Section
Technical Division
Ecuadoran National Planning & Economic Coordination Board
Quito, Ecuador

1069 Torres Caicedo, Reinaldo
General Studies Section
Technical Division
Ecuadoran National Planning & Economic Coordination Board
Quito, Ecuador

Honduras

1070 Rivera, M.
Consejo Superior de Planificación Económica
Edificio Banco Central
Tegucigalpa, Honduras

Jamaica

1071 Clarke, Colin G.
Professor of Urban Planning
University of Liverpool
Liverpool, England (Kingston)

Mexico

1072 García Ramos, Domingo
Escuela Nacional de Arquitectura
Universidad Nacional Autónoma de México
México, D. F., México

1073 Gómez Mayorga, Mauricio
Explanada 1345
México, D. F., México

1074 Pani, Mario
Paseo de la Reforma 369, Mezzanine
México, D. F., México

1075 Perez-Duarte, Javier
Universidad Iberoamericana
Av. Cerro Las Torres 395
México, D. F., México

1076 Reich, Larry
Asst. Commissioner, City Planning
City of Chicago
Room 800, 211 W. Wacker Dr.
Chicago, Ill. 60606
(housing)

Panama

1077 Moreno, Ramón A.
Assistant Director
Depto. de Planeamiento Regional
Instituto de Vivienda y Urbanismo
Panamá, Panamá

1078 Quirós, Felix
Depto. de Planificación
Dirección General de Planificación y Administración
Presidencia de la República
Panamá, Panamá

1079 Riba, Jorge
Profesor de Planeación Municipal
Facultad de Arquitectura
Universidad de Panamá
Panamá, Panamá

1080 Vergara, Emmanuel
Sub-Director

Instituto de Vivienda y Urbanismo
Panamá, Panamá

Paraguay

1081 Williams, Carlos
Assistant Town-Planner
United Nations Technical Assistance Administration
New York, N.Y. 10017

Peru

1082 Gakenheimer, Ralph A.
Associate Professor of City & Regional Planning
University of North Carolina
Chapel Hill, North Carolina 27514

1083 Harth Terró, Emilio
Facultad de Arquitectura
Escuela de Bellas Artes
Universidad Católica del Perú
Lima, Perú

1084 Jaworski, Cárdenas, Helan
Instituto de Planeamiento
Universidad Nacional de Ingeniería
Lima, Perú

1085 Pérez del Pozo, Roberto
Profesor de Planeación Municipal
Facultad de Ingeniería
Pontificia Universidad Católica del Perú
Lima, Perú

Puerto Rico

1086 Arconi, María E.
Depto. de Edificios Públicos
San Juan, Puerto Rico

1087 Collazo, José L.
Hernández 720
Santurce, Puerto Rico 00907

1088 Corrada Guerrero, Rafael
Escuela Graduada de Planificación
Universidad de Puerto Rico
Río Piedras, Puerto Rico 00931

1089 Cruz, Santos I. de la
Italia 306
Ext. E. Comandante
Río Piedras, Puerto Rico 00924

1090 Dilipkumar Ratanchand, Jhaveri
Box 3586
San Juan, Puerto Rico 00928

1091 Drives, Daniel
Depto. de Obras Públicas
San Juan, Puerto Rico

1092 Hernández-Alvarez, José G.
Instructor
Centro de Investigaciones Sociales
Universidad de Puerto Rico
Río Piedras, Puerto Rico 00931

1093 Montoulieu García, Eduardo
Escuela Graduada de Planificación
Universidad de Puerto Rico
Río Piedras, Puerto Rico 00931

1094 Rathburn, James
International Basic Economy Corp.
San Juan, Puerto Rico

1095 Rodríguez Calzada, Héctor
Junta de Planes
San Juan, Puerto Rico

1096 Rodríguez Lebrón, Luis M.
Calle [illegible]
La Riviera
Río Piedras, Puerto Rico 00924

1097 Vargas, Iván
Junta de Planes
San Juan, Puerto Rico

Uruguay

1098 Abella Trías, Julio C.
Buxareo 1220
Montevideo, Uruguay

1099 Campos Thèvenin, Guillermo
Chief, Technical Planning Group
Planning Commission
Departmental Council of Montevideo
Montevideo, Uruguay

Venezuela

1100 Lander, Luis
Director, CENDES
Universidad Central de Venezuela
Ciudad Universitaria
Caracas, Venezuela

1101 Peattie, Lisa
Dept. of City Planning
Massachusetts Institute of Technology
Cambridge, Mass. 02139

1102 Puig, José
Facultad de Arquitectura y Planeación Municipal
Universidad Central de Venezuela
Caracas, Venezuela

1103 Rivas, Luis
Depto. de Urbanismo
Ministerio de Obras Públicas
Caracas, Venezuela

1104 Vidal, Elio
Depto. de Urbanismo
Ministerio de Obras Públicas
Caracas, Venezuela

1105 Villanueva, Carlos R.
Quinta Gaoma, Av. Jllos. L. Flórida
Caracas, Venezuela

Religion

Latin America

1106 Barbieri, Sante U.
L. Ceibos 56
Ciudad Jardín Lomas del Palomar
Buenos Aires, Argentina
(Protestant religion)

1107 Borremans, Valentine
Executive Director
Centro Intercultural de Documentación, Aptdo. 479
Cuernavaca, Mexico
(Catholic religion)

1108 Coggins, Wade T.
Evangelical Foreign Missions Association
1405 G St., N.W.
Washington, D.C. 20005
(Protestant religion)

1109 Colonnese, Louis M., S.J.
Administrative Director
Latin America Bureau
National Catholic Welfare Conference
1312 Massachusetts Ave., N.W.
Washington, D.C. 20005
(Catholic religion)

1110 Damboriena, Prudencio
Centro de Investigaciones Sociales de FERES
Aptdo. Aéreo 11996
Bogotá, Colombia
(Catholic and Protestant religions)

1111 Derby, Marian
Executive Secretary
Board of Missions of the Methodist Church
475 Riverside Dr.
New York, N.Y. 10027
(Protestant religion)

1112 Dussel, Enrique
Centro de Investigaciones Sociales de FERES
Aptdo. Aéreo 11996
Bogotá, Colombia
(Protestant and Catholic religions)

1113 Ellis, James E.
Board of Missions of the Methodist Church
475 Riverside Dr.
New York, N.Y. 10027
(Protestant religion)

1114 Estrada, Adriana
Centro Intercultural de Documentación
Aptdo. 479
Cuernavaca, Mexico
(Catholic religion)

1115 Green, Dana S.
Latin American Dept.
Division of Overseas Ministries
National Council of Churches of Christ in the U. S. A.
475 Riverside Dr.
New York, N.Y. 10027
(Protestant religion)

1116 Hernández, Pedro, S.J.
Centro de Investigación y Acción Social
Universidad Iberoamericana
Av. Cerro Las Torres 395
Mexico, D. F., Mexico
(Catholic religion)

1117 Kadt, Emmanuel J. de
Assistant Professor of Sociology
London School of Economics
London, England

1118 Pin, Emile, S.J.
Piazza della Pilotta
Rome, Italy
(Catholic religion)

1119 Read, William
Fuller Theological Seminary
135 North Oakland Avenue
Pasadena, Calif. 91101
(Protestant religion)

1120 Roberts, W. Dayton
Latin American Mission
Aptdo. 1307
San José, Costa Rica
(Protestant religion)

1121 Rycroft, W. Stanley
Office for Research
Commission on Ecumenical Mission & Relations
United Presbyterian Church in the U.S.A.
475 Riverside Dr.
New York, N.Y. 10027
(urbanization)

1122 Taylor, Clyde W.
Evangelical Foreign Missions Association
1405 G St., N.W.
Washington, D.C. 20005
(Protestant religion)

1123 Wipfler, William L.
Latin American Dept.
National Council of Churches
475 Riverside Dr.
New York, N.Y. 10027

Argentina

1124 Bonino, José M.
President
Union Theological Seminary
Buenos Aires, Argentina

1125 Cyperstein, Avigdor, Rabbi
Av. Córdoba 1507
Buenos Aires, Argentina
(Jewish religion)

1126 Quarracino, Antonio, Archbishop
c/o Catedral Metropolitana
Rivadavia 437
Buenos Aires, Argentina
(Catholic religion)

Brazil

1127 Britto, Rosa M. de
c/o Centro de Estadísticas Religiosas e Investigações Sociais (CERIS)
Rio de Janeiro, GB, Brazil
(Catholic religion)

1128 Dayton, Edward R.
Missions Advanced Research & Communication Center
919 W. Huntington Drive
Monrovia, Calif. 91016
(Protestant religion)

Chile

1129 Grunwald, D., Rabbi
San Francisco 1028
Santiago, Chile
(Jewish religion)

Colombia

1130 Beckman, Jan D.
Sozialforschungsstelle an der Universität Münster (COSAL)

Dortmund
Federal Republic of Germany

Mexico

1131 Avidor, Jacob, Rabbi
Culiacán 37-102
México, D. F., México
(Jewish religion)

1132 Rivera R., Pedro, S.J.
Universidad Iberoamericana
Av. Cerro Las Torres 395
México, D. F., México
(Protestant and Catholic religions)

Panama

1133 Levy, Sion R., Rabbi
Congregation Sheveth Ahim
Aptdo. 6222
Panamá, Panamá
(Jewish religion)

Puerto Rico

1134 Clear, Val B.
Chairman, Sociology & Social Work
Anderson College
Anderson, Indiana
(social service)

Travel

Latin America

1135 Chiles, Dwight
Braniff International Airways
Love Field
Dallas, Texas 75235

1136 Havelka, George
Pan American World Airways
80 E. 42nd St.
New York, N.Y. 10017

1137 Jacobs, Babette R.
Travel Digests
1100 Glendon Ave., Suite 1517
Los Angeles, Calif. 90024

1138 Jacobs, Charles R.
Travel Digests
1100 Glendon Ave., Suite 1517
Los Angeles, Calif. 90024

1139 Meyer, Edward
Grace Line, Inc.
3 Hanover Sq.
New York, N.Y. 10004

1140 Pellerano, Carlos V.
Executive Director
South American Travel Organization
100 Biscayne Blvd., Suite 501
Miami, Fla. 33132

Argentina

1141 Quiroga, Oscar
Suipac 472
Buenos Aires, Argentina

Brazil

1142 Silveira, Joaquim X. de
President
Emprêsa Brasileira de Turismo
Brasilia, Brazil

1143 Trigueiros, Jr., Osvaldo
VARIG Airlines
365 Av. Almirante S. Noronha
Rio de Janeiro, GB, Brazil

Chile

1144 Steinsapir, J.
Pacific Tour
Agustinas 1028
Santiago, Chile

Colombia

1145 Chaves C., Jorge
Agencia Central de Viajes
Aptdo. Aéreo 72-84
Bogotá, Colombia

Costa Rica

1146 Quirós C., Rodolfo
Panamericana de Viajes
Calle A. Volio a 1
San José, Costa Rica

Dominican Republic
1147 Winter, Luis E.
El Conde 5
Santo Domingo,
Dominican Republic

Ecuador
1148 Proaño, Eduardo
Metropolitan Touring
Benalcázar 699
Quito, Ecuador

El Salvador
1149 Carillo, Alfredo
Truinter
la. Calle Oriente, 424
San Salvador, El Salvador

Mexico
1150 Sacal, Salomón
Romfel Travel Service, S.A.
Av. Horacio No. 124
Colonia Polanco
Correo Mayor 92-B
México, D.F., Mexico

Panama
1151 Díaz, Pedro
Turismo de Panamá
Panamá, Panamá

1152 Smith, Shirley
Persons Travel Bureau
Av. 7 España, no. 117
Panamá, Panamá

Paraguay
1153 Fretes, Raúl A.
14 de mayo, 57, Planta Baja
Asunción, Paraguay

Peru
1154 Lemor, José
Dasatour, S.A.
671 Carabaya
Lima, Perú

1155 Villegas, Julio C.
Compañía Peruana de Turismo, S.A.
Lima, Perú

Venezuela
1156 Barrera Melendez, Antonio
Depto. de Turismo
Caracas, Venezuela

Urban History

Latin America
1157 Fowler, Melvin L.
Dept. of Anthropology
University of Wisconsin
Milwaukee, Wisc. 53211

1158 Garzón Macedo, Ceferino
Instituto de Estudios Americanistas
Universidad Nacional de Córdoba
Córdoba, Argentina

1159 Gibson, Charles
Dept. of History
University of Michigan
Ann Arbor, Mich. 48104

1160 Longacre, William A.
Dept. of Anthropology
University of Arizona
Tucson, Arizona 85721

1161 Romero, José L.
Director
Seminar on Studies of the Urban World
Universidad de Buenos Aires
Viamonte 444
Buenos Aires, Argentina

1162 Sentou, Jean
28, rue St.-Luc
Toulouse, France

1163 Wolff, Philippe
Dept. of History
Faculté des Lettres
Université de Toulouse
Toulouse, France

1164 Yacono, Xavier
Dept. of History
Faculté des Lettres
Université de Toulouse
Toulouse, France

1165 Zuidema, R. T.
Universidad Nacional de San Cristóbal de Huamanga
Ayacucho, Peru

Argentina

1166 Gandía, Enrique de
Elflein 3567
La Lucila
Buenos Aires, Argentina

1167 Madrazo, Guillermo B.
Museo Etnográfico Municipal "Dámaso Arce"
Olavarría
Buenos Aires, Argentina

1168 Ottonello de García Reynoso, Marta
Museo Etnográfico Municipal "Dámaso Arce"
Olavarría
Buenos Aires, Argentina

1169 Randle, Patricio
Consejo Nacional de Investigaciones Científicas y Técnicas
Rivadavia 1917
Buenos Aires, Argentina
(Buenos Aires)

1170 Scobie, James R.
Dept. of History
University of Indiana
Bloomington, Indiana 46556
(Buenos Aires)

1171 Zapata Gollán, Agustín
Museo Etnográfico
Santa Fé, S. F., Argentina
(Santa Fé)

Brazil

1172 Escragnolle Taunay, Affonso de
Rua Lupércio Camârgo, 74
São Paulo, Brazil

1173 Monbeig, Pierre
Institut des Hautes Études de l'Amérique Latine
28, rue St. Guillaume
Paris, France

1174 Morse, Richard M.
Professor of History
Yale University
New Haven, Conn. 06520

Chile

1175 Guarda, Gabriel
Universidad Católica de Chile
O'Higgins 340
Santiago, Chile

Ecuador

1176 Szasdi, Dora León Borja de
Dept. of History
Inter-American University of Puerto Rico
Hato Rey, Puerto Rico

El Salvador

1177 Barón Castro, Rodolfo
M. Lafuente, 88
Madrid, Spain

Guatemala

1178 Lanning, John T.
Dept. of History
Duke University
Durham, North Carolina 27706

Mexico

1179 Hartung, Horst
Universidad de Guadalajara
Guadalajara, Jalisco, Mexico

1180 Mayer-Oakes, William J.
Dept. of Anthropology
University of Manitoba
Winnipeg, Manitoba, Canada

1181 Millon, René
Dept. of Anthropology
University of Rochester
Rochester, N.Y. 14627

1182 Palm, Erwin
History Dept.
University of Heidelberg
Heidelberg, Federal Republic of Germany

1183 Sanders, William T.
Dept. of Anthropology
Pennsylvania State University
University Park, Pa. 16802

Panama

1184 Castillero Reyes, Ernesto de J.
Calle 31, no. 34
Aptdo. 1563
Panamá, Panamá

Peru

1185 Bonavía, Duccio
Museo Nacional de Antropología y Arqueología
1515 Av. Bolívar
Lima, Peru

1186 Mariátegui Oliva, Ricardo
326 B. Flores
Lima, Peru

1187 Miró Quesada Sosa, Aurelio
339 Eucaliptus
Lima, Peru

1188 Moore, John P.
Dept. of History
Louisiana State University
Baton Rouge, Louisiana 70803

1189 Thompson, Donald E.
Dept. of Anthropology
University of Wisconsin
Madison, Wisconsin 53706

Venezuela

1190 Acosta Saignes, Miguel
Escuela de Historia
Universidad Central de Venezuela
Caracas, Venezuela

1191 Carrera Damas, Germán
Escuela de Historia
Universidad Central de Venezuela
Ciudad Universitaria
Caracas, Venezuela

1192 Gabaldón Márquez, Joaquín
Quinta Bahia, Av. Guaicaipuro
El Rosal
Caracas, Venezuela

1193 Nava, Julian
Dept. of History
San Fernando Valley State Colleg
Northridge, Calif. 91324

1194 Quintero, Rodolfo
Oficina de Estudios de Caracas
Edificio Biblioteca Central, piso 11
Oficina 1124
Caracas, Venezuela

1195 Uslar Pietri, Arturo
Av. L. Pinos 49
L. Florida
Caracas, Venezuela

West Indies and the Caribbean

1196 Hoetink, Harry, Director
Studie- en Documentatiecentrum voor Latijns Amerika
(Study and Documentation Center for Latin America)
University of Amsterdam
Mauritskade 63
Amsterdam, Netherlands

1197 Parry, John
Dept. of History
Harvard University
Cambridge, Mass. 02138

Urban Matrix for Literature and the Arts

Latin America

1198 Franco, Jean
Asst. Professor of Spanish American Literature
King's College
University of London
London, England

1199 Sánchez, Luis A.
Rector
Universidad Nacional Mayor de San Marcos
Lima, Perú

1200 Vera, Oscar L.
Assistant Director
Unesco Regional Centre for the Western Hemisphere
Aptdo. 1358
Havana, Cuba

Argentina

1201 De Krize, Jeannette
Rodríguez Peña 1882
Buenos Aires, Argentina

1202 Murena, Héctor A.
Centro del Instituto Latinoamericano de Relaciones Internacionales
Montevideo 666
Buenos Aires, Argentina

1203 Rottin, Luciano
Solís 674
Buenos Aires, Argentina

1204 Squirrú, Rafael
Dept. of Visual Arts
Pan American Union
Washington, D.C.

Bolivia

1205 MacLean, Eduardo
Centro del Instituto Latinoamericano de Relaciones Internacionales
Juan de la Riva 1411
La Paz, Bolivia

Brazil

1206 Amoroso Lima, Alceu
Paissandú 200, Apto. 701
Rio de Janeiro, GB, Brazil

1207 Arroyo, Leonardo
243, 2º Dr. Lima Barreto
São Paulo, S.P., Brazil

1208 Cavalcanti, Valdemar
66 J. Carlos
Rio de Janeiro, GB, Brazil

1209 Leepa, Allen
Dept. of Art
Michigan State University
E. Lansing, Mich. 48823

1210 Valladares, Clarivel
Centro del Instituto Latinoamericano de Relaciones Internacionales
Rua Prudente de Morais 129
Ipanema
Rio de Janeiro, GB, Brazil

Chile

1211 Carvacho, Víctor
Centro del Instituto Latinoamericano de Relaciones Internacionales
MacIver 142
Santiago, Chile

1212 Pereira Salas, Eugenio
Av. I. Goyenechea 2888
Santiago, Chile

Peru

1213 Recavarrén, Jorge L.
Centro del Instituto Latinoamericano de Relaciones Internacionales
Hernán Velarde 240
Lima, Peru

Uruguay

1214 Millá, Benito
Centro del Instituto Latinoamericano de Relaciones Internacionales
Bacacay 1334-1
Edificio Ciudadela
Montevideo, Uruguay

Venezuela

1215 Calcaño, José A.
Quinta Anacoa, C. Madrid
Mercedes
Caracas, Venezuela

1216 Díaz Seijas, Pedro
Vice President
Instituto Nacional de Cultura y Bellas Artes
Caracas, Venezuela

1217 Samerano Urdaneta, Oscar
Editor-in-Chief
Revista Nacional de Cultura
Instituto Nacional de Cultura y Bellas Artes
Caracas, Venezuela

Urban Speech

Latin America

1218 Alvar, Manuel
Universidad de Granada
Granada, Spain

1219 Boggs, Ralph S.
536 Altara Ave.
Coral Gables, Fla. 33306

1220 Bolinger, Dwight L.
Dept. of Spanish
University of Colorado
Boulder, Colorado 80302

1221 Criado, Manuel
Oficina Internacional de
Información y Observación del
Español
Madrid, Spain

1222 Lado, Robert
Institute of Languages &
Linguistics
Georgetown University
Washington, D.C. 20007

1223 Lapesa, Rafael
Academia Española de la
Lengua
Felipe IV, 4
Madrid, Spain

1224 Pottier, Bernard
Instituto de Estudios Hispá-
nicos
31 rue Guy Lussac
Paris, France

1225 Praag, J.A. van
Professor of Spanish Language
and Literature
University of Amsterdam
Amsterdam, Netherlands

Argentina

1226 Barrenechea, Ana M.
Director
Institute of Spanish Philology
Universidad de Buenos Aires
Buenos Aires, Argentina

1227 Lagmanovich, David
Universidad Nacional de
Tucumán
Tucumán, Argentina

Bolivia

1228 Loma Pardo, Ernestina
Instituto de Lenguas
Calama 3101
Cochabamba, Bolivia

Brazil

1229 Campos Cônego, Apio
Professor of Philology
Universidade de Pará
Belem, Pará, Brazil

1230 Feldman, David
Dept. of Foreign Languages
California State College at
Fullerton
800 No. State College Blvd.
Fullerton, Calif. 92631

1231 Gudschinsky, Sarah C.
Professor of Linguistics
Universidade de Brasilia
Brasilia, Brazil

1232 Mattoso Câmara, Jr., J.
Professor of Linguistics
Universidade de Brasil
Rio de Janeiro, GB, Brazil

1233 Rossi, Nelson
Director, Phonetics Laboratory
Universidade de Bahia
Bahia, Salvador, Brazil

Chile

1234 Contreras Figueroa de
Rabanales, Lidia
Professor of Linguistics
Universidad de Chile
Casilla 147
Santiago, Chile

1235 Rabanales Ortiz, Ambrosio
Instituto de Filología
Universidad de Chile

Casilla 147
Santiago, Chile

1236 Wigdorsky, Leopoldo
Professor of Applied Linguistics
Universidad Católica
Santiago, Chile

Colombia

1237 Flórez, Luis
Instituto Caro y Cuervo
Apartado Aéreo 20002
Bogotá, Colombia

1238 Martin, John W.
Instituto Colombo-Americano
Apartado Aéreo 13407
Bogotá, Colombia

1239 Montes Giraldo, José J.
Instituto Caro y Cuervo
Aptdo. Aéreo 20002
Bogotá, Colombia

Costa Rica

1240 Agüero Chavez, Arturo
Dept. of Philology, Linguistics & Literature
Facultad de Filosofía y Letras
Universidad de Costa Rica
Ciudad Universitaria
San José, Costa Rica

Haiti

1241 Pressoir, Charles F.
13 rue Villate
Pétionville, Haiti

1242 Valdman, Albert
Dept. of Linguistics
Indiana University
Bloomington, Indiana 47401

Mexico

1243 Lastra, Yolanda
Latin American Center
University of California
Los Angeles, Calif. 90024

1244 Lope Blanch, Juan M.
Presidente, Comisión de Lingüística y Dialectología Iberoamericanas
Programa Interamericano de Lingüística y Enseñanza de Idiomas
Colegio de México
Guanajuato 125
México, D. F., Mexico

1245 Romero Castillo, Moisés
Professor of Linguistics
Escuela Nacional de Antropología e Historia de México
Córdoba 45
México, D. F., Mexico

Nicaragua

1246 Coloma González, Fidel
Depto. de Letras
Universidad Nacional de Nicaragua
Managua, Nicaragua

Panama

1247 Robe, Stanley L.
Dept. of Spanish & Portuguese
University of California
Los Angeles, Calif. 90024

Peru

1248 Benvenutto Murrieta, Pedro
Universidad Nacional Mayor de San Marcos
Lima, Perú

1249 López Morales, H.
Depto. de Lingüística
Facultad de Filosofía y Letras
Universidad Nacional Mayor de San Marcos
Lima, Perú

Puerto Rico

1250 Mergal, Angel M.
Universidad de Puerto Rico
Aptdo. 1562
Río Piedras, Puerto Rico

Uruguay

1251 Rona, José P.
Depto. de Lingüística
Universidad de la República Oriental del Uruguay
Montevideo, Uruguay

Venezuela

1252 Rosenblat, Angel
Professor of Spanish Linguistics
Universidad Central de Venezuela
Ciudad Universitaria
Caracas, Venezuela

Cost and Standard of Living

Brazil

1253 Câmara, Lourival
555 Conde Irajá
Rio de Janeiro, GB, Brazil

1254 Paiva, Glycon de
156 Av. Rio Branco
Rio de Janeiro, GB, Brazil

Colombia

1255 Lannoy, Juan L. de
Centro de Investigaciones Sociales de FERES
Aptdo. Aéreo 11996
Bogotá, Colombia

1256 Mallol de Recasens, María R., & José de Recasens Tuset
Transversal 5, 47-25, Aptdo. 201
Bogotá, Colombia

1257 Prieto Durán, Rafael
Carrera 20, 40-A-05S
Bogotá, Colombia

1258 Torres León, Fernán
Universidad de Bogotá "Jorge Tadeo Lozano"
Carrera 7a., 23-08
Bogotá, Colombia

Costa Rica

1259 Esquivel Fernandez, Ricardo
Calle Alfredo Volio/1a1
San José, Costa Rica

Mexico

1260 Gómez Robledo, José
Instituto de Investigaciones Sociales
Universidad Nacional Autónoma de México
México, D. F., Mexico

1261 Suárez, Eduardo L.
Centro de Investigaciones Económicas
Universidad de Nuevo León
Monterrey, N. L., Mexico

Uruguay

1262 Gianola, Angel M.
Libertad 2669
Montevideo, Uruguay

1263 Iglesias, Enrique
Director, Instituto de Investigaciones Económicas
Universidad de la República Oriental del Uruguay
Montevideo, Uruguay

West Indies and the Caribbean

1264 Taylor, Leroy
Institute of Social & Economic Research
University of the West Indies
Mona, Jamaica

Employment

Latin America

1265 Alba, Víctor
(pseudonym of Pedro Pagès)
American Institute for Free Labor Development
1925 K Street, N.W.
Washington, D.C. 20006

1266 Catharino, José Martins
Instituto de Ciencias Sociais
Universidade da Bahia
Salvador, Bahia, Brazil

1267 Ericson, A.S.
Bureau of Labor Statistics
U.S. Dept. of Labor
Washington, D.C. 20210
(Bolivia, Venezuela)

1268 Goldenberg, Boris
Forschungsinstitut der Friedrich Ebert Siftung e. V.
Bad Godesberg, Federal Republic of Germany

1269 Illanes Edwards, Jaime
International Labor Office
Geneva, Switzerland

1270 Romualdi, Serafino
Inter-American Representative
AFL-CIO
815-16th St., N.W.
Washington, D.C. 20006

1271 Venegas Carrasco, Ramón
Latin American Federation of Christian Trade Unions
Alfonso Ovalle 1475
Santiago, Chile

Argentina

1272 March, Armando
Hamburgo 2951
Buenos Aires, Argentina

1273 Pinilla de Las Heras, Esteban
c/o Centro de Investigaciones Sociales
Instituto Torcuato di Tella
Virrey del Pino 3230
Buenos Aires, Argentina

Brazil

1274 Kahl, Joseph A.
Professor of Sociology & Anthropology
Washington University
St. Louis, Missouri 63130

Central America

1275 Ducoff, Louis J.
U.S. Dept. of Agriculture
Washington, D.C. 20250
(demography, rural urban migration)

1276 Friedman, J.A.
Bureau of Labor Statistics
U.S. Dept. of Labor
Washington, D.C. 20210

Colombia

1277 Braun, Kurt H.
Bureau of Labor Statistics
U.S. Dept. of Labor
Washington, D.C. 20210

1278 Posada, Esteban
Centro de Investigaciones Económicas
Universidad de Antioquia
Medellín, Colombia (Medellín)

Cuba

1279 Sust Méndez, José
Facultad de Ingeniería
Universidad de La Habana
Havana, Cuba

Guyana

1280 Davis, Horace B.
University of Guyana
Georgetown, Guyana

Honduras

1281 Gonzáles A., Carlos H.
2a. Av., 516-C
Tegucigalpa, Honduras

Jamaica

1282 Graham, Sara
Institute of Social & Economic Research
University of the West Indies
Mona, Jamaica

Mexico

1283 Jáuregui Hurtado, Arturo
O.R.I.T.
Plaza de la República, 30
México, D.F., México

1284 Neef, Arthur F.
Bureau of Labor Statistics
U.S. Dept. of Labor
Washington, D.C. 20210

Panama

1285 Sinclair, W.
Public Service International
Aptdo. 4982
Panamá, Panamá

Peru

1286 Romero, Fernando
430 Grau
Lima, Perú

1287 Samamé, Benjamín
Assistant Director
Servicio de Empleo y Recursos Humanos

(Employment & Human Resources Service)
Ministerio de Trabajo y Comunidades
Lima, Perú

Trinidad

1288 Alexis, A. C.
Minister of Labor
Port-of-Spain, Trinidad

Venezuela

1289 Croce Orozco, Francisco
Director
Dirección de Empleo
Caracas, Venezuela

1290 Malavé Villalba, A.
Tajamar a la Cruz 46
Caracas, Venezuela

Industrialization

Latin America

1291 Robock, Stefan H.
Director, International Business Programs
Indiana University
Bloomington, Indiana 46556

1292 Rottenberg, Simon
Dept. of Industrial Relations
University of Buffalo
Buffalo, N.Y. 14222

1293 Stokes, Charles J.
Dept. of Economics
University of Bridgeport
Bridgeport, Conn. 06602

1294 Strassman, W. P.
Dept. of Economics
Michigan State University
E. Lansing, Mich. 48823
(employment)

1295 Vellas, Pierre
Director
Institut des Relations Internationales et Pays en Voie du Dévellopement
Villa St. Louis
Auzeville par Castanet, Haute-Gironde
France

1296 Vera, José
Advisor
Economic & Social Development Division
Inter-American Development Bank
808-17th St., N.W.
Washington, D.C. 20006

1297 Wood, James R.
Dept. of Sociology
Vanderbilt University
Nashville, Tenn. 37203

Argentina

1298 Frondizi, Silvio
c/o Latin American Studies Program
University of Texas
Austin, Texas 78719

1299 Knox, John B.
Professor of Sociology
University of Tennessee
Knoxville, Tenn. 37916
(industrial sociology)

1300 Laura, Lauro C.
Cabezón 2639
Buenos Aires, Argentina

1301 Ríos, Raúl A.
Facultad de Ciencias Económicas
Universidad Nacional de Córdoba
Córdoba, Argentina

Bolivia

1302 Anaya, Ricardo
Decano, Facultad de Economía
Universidad de Cochabamba
Cochabamba, Bolivia

1303 Canelas O., Amado
c/o El Diario
La Paz, Bolivia

1304 Prado Balcazar, Juan
Depto. de Economía
Universidad Tomás Frías
Potosí, Bolivia

1305 Vasquez, César A.
Dirección de Programación Global
Secretaría Nacional de Planificación
La Paz, Bolivia

Brazil

1306 Aguiar Costa Pinto, Luiz
Dept. of Economics
Universidade da Bahia
Salvador, Bahia, Brazil

1307 Bazzanella, Waldemiro
49 E. Ramos
Rio de Janeiro, GB, Brazil

1308 Cardoso, Fernando H.
School of Sociology & Politics
Universidade de São Paulo
São Paulo, S.P., Brazil

1309 Goodman, David
Dept. of Economics
University of California
Berkeley, Calif. 94720

1310 Nicholls, William H.
Dept. of Sociology
Vanderbilt University
Nashville, Tenn. 37203
(São Paulo, Brazil)

1311 Silveira, Cid
Facultad Nacional de Economia
Universidade do Brasil
Rio de Janeiro, GB, Brazil

1312 Velloso, Péricles S.
Commíssão do Planeamento Econômico de Bahia
Salvador, Bahia, Brazil
(Salvador)

Chile

1313 Lluch Soler, Salvador
Director Gerente
Instituto Chileno de Acero (ICHA)
Moneda 1160
Santiago, Chile

1314 Sierra Castro, Enrique
Escuela de Economía y Administración
Universidad de Concepción
Concepción, Chile

Colombia

1315 Colorado, Iván
Facultad de Ciencias Económicas
Universidad de América
Calle 10, no. 6-44
Bogotá, Colombia

1316 Consuegra Higgins, José
Facultad de Economía
Universidad de Cartagena
Cartagena, Colombia

1317 Delgadillo Parra, Alfonso
Facultad de Ciencias Económicas
Universidad de América
Calle 10, no. 6-44
Bogotá, Colombia

1318 González Santos, Jaime
Facultad de Economía
Universidad Nacional
Bogotá, Colombia

Dominican Republic

1319 Mejía Constanzo, Héctor B.
Facultad de Ciencias Económicas
Universidad Autónoma de Santo Domingo
Santo Domingo, Dominican Republic

1320 Mejía Ricart, Marco
Facultad de Ciencias Económicas
Universidad Autónoma de Santo Domingo
Santo Domingo, Dominican Republic

El Salvador

1321 Marroquín, Alejandro D.
Decano de la Facultad de Humanidades
Universidad de El Salvador
San Salvador, El Salvador

Guatemala

1322 Sierra Franco, Raúl
Director, Facultad de Ciencias Económicas
Universidad de San Carlos
Guatemala, Guatemala

Haiti

1323 Pierre-Charles, Gérard
University of Haiti
Port-au-Prince, Haiti

Honduras

1324 Carías, Marco V.
Facultad de Ciencias Económicas
Universidad Nacional Autónoma de Honduras
Tegucigalpa, Honduras

1325 Euceda G., Jorge A.
Facultad de Ciencias Económicas
Universidad Nacional Autónoma de Honduras
Tegucigalpa, Honduras

Mexico

1326 Aaron, Henry J.
Dept. of Economics
Harvard University
Cambridge, Mass. 02138
(Mexico City)

1327 Bassols Batalla, Angel
Profesor de Geografía
Facultad de Filosofía y Letras
Universidad Nacional Autónoma de México
Ciudad Universitaria
México, D. F., México

1328 Brom O., Juan
Escuela Nacional de Economía
Universidad Nacional Autónoma de México
Ciudad Universitaria
México, D. F., México

1329 Browning, Clyde E.
Dept. of Geography
University of North Carolina
Chapel Hill, North Carolina 27514 (Mexico City)

1330 Burns, Leland S.
Graduate School of Business Administration
University of California
Los Angeles, Calif. 90024
(Mexico City, Monterrey)

1331 Meceña, José L.
Director, Instituto de Investigaciones Económicas
Universidad Nacional Autónoma de México
Ciudad Universitaria
México, D. F., México

1332 Frank, André Gunder
Escuela Nacional de Economía
Universidad Nacional Autónoma de México
Ciudad Universitaria
México, D. F., México

1333 López Esparza, Manuel
Asst. Director, Centro de Investigaciones Económicas
Escuela Superior de Economía
Instituto Politécnico Nacional
Ciudad Universitaria
México, D. F., México

1334 Mauro, Frédéric
Professor of Economic History
Faculté des Lettres et Sciences Humaines
Université de Toulouse
Toulouse, France

1335 Puigrós, Rodolfo
Escuela Nacional de Economía
Universidad Nacional Autónoma de México
Ciudad Universitaria
México, D. F., México

1336 Tata, Robert
Dept. of Geography
Florida Atlantic University
Boca Raton, Florida 33432

1337 Villanueva de la Rosa, Sebastián
Escuela de Economía
Universidad Autónoma de Puebla
Puebla, Puebla, México

Nicaragua

1338 Castellón D., Raúl
Facultad de Ciencias Económicas
Universidad Nacional Autónoma de Nicaragua
Managua, Nicaragua

1339 Conrado Gómez, Eduardo
Facultad de Ciencias Económicas
Universidad Nacional Autónoma de Nicaragua
Managua, Nicaragua

1340 Marcenaro, Fernando R.
Facultad de Ciencias Económicas
Universidad Nacional Autónoma de Nicaragua
Managua, Nicaragua

Paraguay

1341 Jadua Saba, Roberto
Corporación de Fomento
Asunción, Paraguay

Puerto Rico

1342 González, Antonio J.
Depto. de Economía
Facultad de Ciencias Sociales
Universidad de Puerto Rico
Río Piedras, Puerto Rico

1343 Herrero, José A.
Depto. de Economía
Facultad de Ciencias Sociales
Universidad de Puerto Rico
Río Piedras, Puerto Rico

1344 Picó, Rafael
Banco Popular
San Juan, Puerto Rico

Uruguay

1345 Lichtensztejn, Samuel
Facultad de Ciencias Económicas y de Administración
Universidad de la República Oriental del Uruguay
Montevideo, Uruguay

1346 Quijano, Carlos
Ex-Director de los Cursos de Investigaciones
Facultad de Ciencias Económicas
Universidad de la República Oriental del Uruguay
Montevideo, Uruguay

Venezuela

1347 Malavé Mata, Héctor
Facultad de Economía
Universidad Central de Venezuela
Ciudad Universitaria
Caracas, Venezuela

1348 Margheritti, Rubén C.
Jefe, Depto. de Investigaciones Económicas
Facultad de Ciencias Económicas y Sociales
Universidad de Zulia
Maracaibo, Venezuela

1349 Marrero, J.S.
Profesor de Economía Urbana
Facultad de Ingeniería
Universidad de Los Andes
Mérida, Mérida, Venezuela

1350 Maza Zavala, Domingo F.
Quinta Alicia, 7a. Transversal
Maripérez
Caracas, Venezuela

1351 Morales Valorino, Jesús
Fundación Instituto Venezolano de Productividad
Edificio Sur, piso 9, Centro Simon Bolívar
Caracas, Venezuela

1352 Rodríguez Mena, Manuel
Facultad de Ciencias Económicas y Sociales
Universidad de Zulia
Maracaibo, Venezuela

1353 Valéry, Maurice
Director-General
Oficina Central de Coordinación y Planificación (CORDIPLAN)
Presidencia de la República
Caracas, Venezuela

1354 Valladares, Ligia
Instituto de Investigaciones Económicas
Edificio Banco Industrial, piso 5
Esquina de Sociedad
Caracas, Venezuela

West Indies and the Caribbean

1355 Best, Lloyd
Research Fellow
Institute of Social & Economic Research
University of the West Indies
Mona, Jamaica

Poverty

Latin America

1356 d'Escoto, Miguel
University of Santa Clara
Santa Clara, Calif. 95050
(Chile, Peru)

1357 Mamalakis, Markos A.
Dept. of Economics
University of Wisconsin
Milwaukee, Wis. 53201

Bolivia

1358 Patch, Richard
Anthropology Dept.
State Univ. of N.Y.
Buffalo, N.Y.

Brazil

1359 Bonilla, Frank
Center for International Studies
Massachusetts Institute of Technology
Cambridge, Mass. 02139

1360 Goulart, José A.
664 Av. Copacabana
Rio de Janeiro, GB, Brazil

1361 Modesto, Helio
91 Av. Almirante Barroso
Rio de Janeiro, GB, Brazil
(housing)

Chile

1362 Braun Lyon, Juan
Instituto de Economía
Universidad de Chile
Santiago, Chile
(employment)

1363 Rosenbluth L., Guillermo
Marcel Duhaut 2818
Santiago, Chile (Santiago)

Colombia

1364 Antequera Stand, Miguel A.
Centro de Desarrollo Económico
Universidad de Los Andes
Bogotá, Colombia
(employment, Bogotá)

Guatemala

1365 Lopez T., José
Dirección de Obras Públicas
Guatemala, Guatemala
(Guatemala City)

Panama

1366 Gutíerrez, Samuel
Instituto de Vivienda y Urbanismo
Av. 3 y Calle 34
Panamá, Panamá
(Panama City)

Peru

1367 Hammel, Eugene A.
Dept. of Anthropology
University of California
Berkeley, Calif. 94720

Uruguay

1368 Bon Espasandín, Mario C.
Coe 3903 bis
Montevideo, Uruguay

West Indies and the Caribbean

1369 Rottenberg, Simon
Dept. of Industrial Relations
University of Buffalo
Buffalo, N.Y. 14222

Transportation

Latin America

1370 Murcia-Camacho, Efraim
Inter-American Statistical Institute
Pan American Union
Washington, D.C. 20006

Argentina

1371 Lopez Airaghi, Antonio C.
c/o Instituto de Vías de Comunicación
Universidad Nacional de Tucumán
Tucumán, Argentina

Brazil

1372 Bastos, Humberto
194 Gústavo Sampaio
Rio de Janeiro, GB, Brazil

1373 Cavalcanti, Lysia M. de Bernardes
Faculdade do Brasil
Rio de Janeiro, GB, Brazil

1374 Snyder, David E.
Dept. of Geography
Yale University
New Haven, Conn. 06520
(Uruguay)

1375 Goulart, José Alipio
664 Av. Copacabana
Rio de Janeiro, GB, Brazil

1376 Grossman, William L.
Dept. of Economics
New York University
New York, N.Y. 10011

1377 Lopes, José Codeceira
1246 Av. Copacabana
Rio de Janeiro, GB, Brazil

1378 Wanderly, Alberto
32 Carangola
Bêlo Horizonte, R.G.S., Brazil

Chile

1379 Hurtado Ruiz-Tagle, Fernando
Av. Bulnes 060
Santiago, Chile

1380 Paolinelli Monti, Italo
c/o Dr. Livio Paolinelli Monti
G. Edwards 2844
Santiago, Chile

Colombia

1381 Restrepo Castro, Jorge
Calle 37, 13A-28
Bogotá, Colombia

Mexico

1382 Mondragón Moreno, Pablo J.
Av. Universidad 199-12
México, D. F., México

Paraguay

1383 Bejarano, Ramón C.
18 y 3a., Sajonia
Asunción, Paraguay

Puerto Rico

1384 Ast, K. J.
Transportation & Planning Division
De Leuw, Cather & Company
165 West Wacker Drive
Chicago, Ill. 60601

1385 Vivoni, William
Depto. de Obras Públicas
San Juan, Puerto Rico

Uruguay

1386 Arredondo, Horacio
Búlevar Artigas 1203
Montevideo, Uruguay

Venezuela

1387 Bingham, Sidney H.
109 E. 35th St.
New York, N.Y. 10016
(Caracas)

Municipal Finance

Latin America

1388 Munizaga, Gustavo
Comité Interdisciplinario de Desarollo Urbano
Universidad Católica de Chile
Av. Alameda 340
Santiago, Chile

Brazil

1389 Barbosa de Campos, Paulo
2073 Bela Cintra
São Paulo, S.P., Brazil

Central America

1390 Adler, John H.
International Bank for Reconstruction and Development
1818 H St., N.W.
Washington, D.C. 20006

Chile

1391 Berwart, Luisa
Comité Interdisciplinario de Desarrollo Urbano
Universidad Católica de Chile
Av. Alameda 340
Santiago, Chile

Colombia

1392 Alvarez Cardona, Javier E.
Diagonal 31, 37-92, piso 1
Bogotá, Colombia

Costa Rica

1393 Portocarrero Argüello, Alfonso Lourdes
San José, Costa Rica

Mexico

1394 Bird, Richard M.
Dept. of Economics
Harvard University
Cambridge, Mass. 02138
(Mexico City)

1395 Moore, O.E.
Centro de Estudios Monetarios Latinoamericanos
Durango 54
México, D.F., México

1396 Orantes Durazo, Teodoro
California 85
México, D.F., Mexico

Venezuela

1397 Shoup, Carl S.
Dept. of Economics
Colombia University
New York, N.Y. 10027

Municipal Government and Legal Matters

Latin America

1398 Ascher, Charles S.
Dept. of Political Science
Brooklyn College
Brooklyn, N.Y. 11210
(urbanization)

1399 Bollens, John C.
Dept. of Political Science
University of California
Los Angeles, Calif. 90024

1400 Bourricaud, François
Dept. of History
Université de Bordeaux
Bordeaux, France

1401 Garay, Mario
Professor of Political Science
University of Chile
Santiago, Chile

1402 Hamon, Léo
Faculty of Law
Université de Dijon
Dijon, France

1403 Isaac, Guy
Faculty of Law
Université de Toulouse
Toulouse, France

1404 Lambert, Jacques
Faculty of Law & Economic Sciences
Université de Lyon
Lyon, France

1405 Sweeney, Stephen B.
Dept. of Political Science
University of Pennsylvania
Philadelphia, Pa. 19104

Argentina

1406 Klein, Alberto
Oblig. 2166
Buenos Aires, Argentina

1407 Linares Quintana, Segundo V.
Profesor de Leyes Públicas y Municipales
Universidad Nacional de La Plata
La Plata, Argentina

1408 Mazzocco, Angel R.
Valle 1157
Buenos Aires, Argentina

1409 Miller, Delbert C.
Dept. of Sociology
Indiana University
Bloomington, Indiana 46556

Brazil

1410 Anglade, Christian
Professor of Political Science
Université de Toulouse
Toulouse, France

1411 Brandão, Maria
Professor, Escola da Administração
Universidade da Bahia
Salvador, Bahia
Brazil

1412 Bueno, Antonio S. Cunha
Conselho Nacional de Estatística
Rio de Janeiro, GB, Brazil

1413 Carneiro, Levi
244 Gústavo Sampaio
Rio de Janeiro, GB, Brazil

1414 Costa, Margarida
Escola de Administração
Universidade da Bahia
Salvador, Bahia
Brazil

1415 Delorenzo Nêto, Antonio
Instituto de Estudos Municipais
Fundação Escola de Sociologia e Política de São Paulo
São Paulo, S.P., Brazil

1416 Gomes, Francelino de Araujo
c/o Seção Brasileira
Instituto Internacional de Ciências Administrativas
Rio de Janeiro, GB, Brazil

1417 Lordello de Mello, Diogo
Assistant Director
Instituto Brasileiro de Administração Municipal
Rio de Janeiro, G.B, Brazil

1418 Machado Pauperio, Artur
Av. Rio Branco 128, s/506
Rio de Janeiro, GB, Brazil

1419 Matta, João Eurico
Escola de Administração
Universidade da Bahia
Salvador, Bahia
Brazil

1420 Medeiros, Ocelio de
Depto. Administrativo do Serviço Público
Rio de Janeiro, GB, Brazil

1421 Paulson, Belden E.
Dept. of Political Science
University of Wisconsin-Milwaukee
Milwaukee, Wisconsin 53201

1422 Reis, José Osório
Escola de Administração
Universidade da Bahia
Salvador, Bahia
Brazil

1423 Ribeiro, Manoel
Universidade da Bahia
Salvador, Bahia, Brazil

1424 Richardson, Ivan
Dept. of Political Science
California State College at Fullerton

Fullerton, Calif. 92631
(Rio de Janeiro)

1425 Sherwood, Frank
Dept. of Economics
University of Massachusetts
Amherst, Mass. 01002

1426 Sobrinho, Jorge Haje
Escola de Administração
Universidade da Bahia
Salvador, Bahia
Brazil

1427 Xavier, Rafael
26 Paula Freitas
Rio de Janeiro, GB, Brazil

Chile

1428 Flisfisch E., Mauricio
Jefe, Depto. Jurídico
Municipalidad de Santiago
Santiago, Chile

1429 Gil, Federíco G.
Institute of Latin American Studies
University of North Carolina
Chapel Hill, North Carolina 27514

1430 Muñoz Maluschka, Luis
Regulatory Programming Bureau
Viña del Mar, Chile

Colombia

1431 Camargo Angulo, Fernando
Calle 45, no. 28-48
Bogotá, Colombia

1432 Galvis Gaitán, Fernando
Av. Jiménez 7-25
Oficina 723
Bogotá, Colombia

1433 Guzmán Botero, Carlos A.
Carrera 9, no. 14-36, Oficina 608
Bogotá, Colombia

Ecuador

1434 Aguirre Ruiz, Tomás
Profesor de Leyes Municipales
Facultad de Leyes
Universidad Nacional de Lója
Loja, Ecuador

1435 Cordero León, Gerardo
Profesor de Leyes Municipales
Facultad de Jurisprudencia y Ciencias Sociales
Universidad de Cuenca
Cuenca, Ecuador

1436 Ríofrío Villagómez, Eduardo
Benalcázar 1066
Quito, Ecuador

Guatemala

1437 Orellana Cardona, Manuel
14a. Calle, no. 7-26
Guatemala, Guatemala

Mexico

1438 Blough, William J.
Dept. of Political Science
University of North Carolina
Chapel Hill, North Carolina 27514

1439 Cardenas, Leonard
Dept. of Political Science
Louisiana State University
Baton Rouge, La.

1440 D'Antonio, William V.
Dept. of Sociology
University of Notre Dame
Notre Dame, Indiana 46556

1441 Form, William H.
Dept. of Sociology
Michigan State University
E. Lansing, Mich. 48823
(industrialization)

1442 Puente Arteaga, Martín
Palma Norte 413-304
México, D. F., Mexico

1443 Rabinovitz, Francine
Dept. of Political Science
University of California
Los Angeles, Calif. 90024

Peru

1444 Agulla, Juan C., c/o Dr. Delbert C. Miller
Dept. of Sociology
Indiana University
Bloomington, Indiana 47401

Puerto Rico

1445 Rincón de Gautier, Felisa
Alcaldía
San Juan, Puerto Rico

Venezuela

1446 Gabaldón Márquez, Joaquín
Edificio La Bolsa
Caracas, Venezuela

1447 Karst, Kenneth L.
School of Law
University of California
Los Angeles, Calif. 90024
(Caracas)

1448 Ríos, Erasmo
Centro de Investigaciones Administrativas y Sociales
Escuela de Administración Pública
Edificio Banco Industrial
Esq. de Traposos
Caracas, Venezuela

1449 Schwartz, Murray L.
Associate Dean, School of Law
University of California
Los Angeles, Calif. 90024
(Caracas)

1450 Silva Michelena, José
Escuela de Ciencias Políticas
Universidad Central de Venezuela
Caracas, Venezuela
(Caracas)

Public Utilities

Brazil

1451 Barbosa de Oliveira, Américo L.
6 Av. Almirante Barroso
Rio de Janeiro, GB, Brazil

1452 Bhering, Mário
President, ELETROBRAS
Brasilia, Brazil

1453 Maranhão, Jarbas C. A.
Depto. Administrativo do Serviço Público e Instituto Brasileiro de Ciências Administrativas
Rio de Janeiro, GB, Brazil

Cuba

1454 Alvarez del Río, Daniel
Ministerio de Obras Públicas
Havana, Cuba

1455 Catellbi, Enrique
Ministerio de Obras Públicas
Havana, Cuba

1456 Gutierrez García, Manuel
Ministerio de Obras Públicas
Havana, Cuba

1457 Jongh, Enrique de
Ministerio de Obras Públicas
Havana, Cuba

1458 Morales Hernández, José
Ministerio de Obras Públicas
Havana, Cuba

Paraguay

1459 Peña Villamil, Manuel
Sarmiento 312
Asunción, Paraguay

Trinidad

1460 Mahabit, Errol
Minister of Public Utilities
Port-of-Spain, Trinidad

Uruguay

1461 Ganón, Isaac
Treinta y Tres 1420, E-13
Montevideo, Uruguay

3D. SOCIOLOGY

Urban Sociology

Latin America

1462 Abramo, Perseu
Instituto de Ciências Sociais
Universidade da Bahia
Salvador, Bahia, Brazil

1463 Andrews, Wade H.
Social Science Analyst
Farm Population Branch
U.S. Dept. of Agriculture
Washington, D.C. 20250

1464 Birou, Alain
262, rue St. Honoré
Paris, France

1465 Bogue, Donald J.
Dept. of Sociology
University of Chicago
Chicago, Ill. 60637

1466 Caplow, Theodore
Dept. of Sociology
Columbia University
New York, N.Y. 10027
(industrialization and social change)

1467 Erickson, Ephraim G.
Chairman, Dept. of Sociology
University of Tennessee
Knoxville, Tenn. 37916
(British West Indies, Costa Rica)

1468 Gibbs, Jack P.
Dept. of Sociology
University of Texas
Austin, Texas 78712

1469 Goldstein, Sidney
Chairman, Dept. of Anthropology & Sociology
Brown University
Providence, Rhode Island 02912
(urbanization)

1470 Gutman, Robert
Dept. of Sociology
Rutgers, the State University
New Brunswick, N.J. 08903
(demography)

1471 Horowitz, Irving L.
Dept. of Sociology
Rutgers, the State University
New Brunswick, N. J.
(Jewish communities, Argentina)

1472 Houtart, Francis H.
Director
Centre de Recherches Socio-Religieuses
5, rue de Guimard
Brussels, Belgium

1473 Jansson, Kurt
Bureau of Social Affairs
United Nations
New York, N.Y. 10017

1474 Leeds, Anthony
Dept. of Anthropology
University of Texas
Austin, Texas 78712

1475 Mattelart, Armand
DESAL
Casilla 10,445
Santiago, Chile

1476 Medina Echevarria, José
UN Economic Commission for Latin America
Casilla 179-D
Santiago, Chile

1477 Orleans, Peter
Dept. of Sociology
University of California
Los Angeles, Calif. 90024
(housing, population)

1478 Perloff, Harvey S.
Resources for the Future
1775 Massachusetts Ave., N.W.
Washington, D.C. 20036

1479 Petersen, William
Dept. of Sociology
University of California
Berkeley, Calif. 94720
(urbanization)

1480 Ratinoff, Luis
Director

Instituto Latinoamericano de Sociología
Bogotá, Colombia

1481 Rennie, Douglas L. C.
Dept. of Sociology
Southern Illinois University
Carbondale, Ill. 62901

1482 Roig, Julio C.
Mar Mediterráneo 5510
Montevideo, Uruguay

1483 Rosenberg, Bernard
Associate Professor of Sociology
City University of New York
New York, N.Y. 10010
(urbanization, juvenile delinquency; Chile, Argentina, Uruguay)

1484 Simmons, Ozzie G.
Professor of Sociology
University of Colorado
Boulder, Colorado 80302
(urbanization, Peru, Chile)

1485 Sjoberg, Gideon
Dept. of Sociology
University of Texas
Austin, Texas 78712

1486 Volpi, Alberto E.
Assistant Director
Centro Latinoamericano de Población y Familia (CELAP)
Miguel Claro 136
Santiago, Chile

1487 Yagupsky, Máximo
American Jewish Committee
165 E. 56th St.
New York, N.Y. 10022
(Jewish communities)

Argentina

1488 Poviña, Alfredo
Dept. of Sociology
Universidad Nacional de Córdoba
Córdoba, Argentina

Brazil

1489 Azzi, Rodolpho
Associação Brasileira de Psicólogos
Caixa Postal 8105
São Paulo, S.P., Brazil

1490 Bastide, Roger
Professor of Ethnology, Sociology, & Religion
Faculté des Lettres
Université de Paris
Paris, France

1491 Klebe, John A.
Dept. of Sociology
University of Oregon
Eugene, Oregon 97403

1492 Saito, Hiroshi
Escola de Sociologia e Política
Rua General Jardim, 522
C. Postal 30619
São Paulo, S.P., Brazil

Chile

1493 Ezquerra, Mercedes
Chilean Committee on Social Work
International Conference of Social Work
345 E. 46th St.
New York, N.Y. 10017

1494 Maturana de Mallafe, Lucía
International Conference on Social Work
345 E. 46th St.
New York, N.Y. 10017

Cuba

1495 Rodríguez, J.
Depto. de Sociología
Universidad de la Habana
Havana, Cuba

Mexico

1496 Demerath, Nicholas J.
Professor of Sociology
Washington University
St. Louis, Missouri 63130
(community development, public health, housing)

1497 Dotson, Floyd W.
Professor of Sociology
University of Connecticut
Storrs, Conn. 06268

1498 Hayner, Norman S.
Professor of Sociology

University of Washington
Seatle, Washington 98102
(criminology)

1499 Takayama, Tomohiro
Ibero-American Institute
Sophia University
Chiyoda-ku, Kioicho 7
Tokyo, Japan

1500 Zárate, Alvan O.
Population Research Center
Dept. of Sociology
University of Texas
Austin, Texas 78712

Nicaragua

1501 Alvarez Montalvan, Emilio
Instituto Social Nicaraguense
Managua, Nicaragua

Peru

1502 Durand, José
Asst. Professor
Faculté des Lettres
Université de Toulouse
Toulouse, France

Uruguay

1503 Carbounel de Groupons, María A.
c/o Sociedad Uruguaya de Psicología
Mariscal Estigarribia 858, Aptdo. 2
Montevideo, Uruguay

Venezuela

1504 Salazar Jiménez, José M.
c/o Associación Venezolana de Psicología
Aptdo. 10650 Este
Caracas, Venezuela

West Indies and the Caribbean

1505 Braithwaite, Lloyd W.S.
Dept. of Sociology, Faculty of Social Sciences
University of the West Indies
Mona, Jamaica

1506 Field, Arthur J.
Dept. of Sociology & Anthropology
Wayne State University
Detroit, Mich. 48202

1507 Hill, George W.
Dept. of Sociology
Universidad Central de Venezuela
Ciudad Universitaria
Caracas, Venezuela

Communications

Latin America

1508 Anderson, H. Calvert
Regional Director
Programa Interamericano de Información Popular
American International Association
Casilla 5060, Sucursal 1
Montevideo, Uruguay

1509 Carty, James
Dept. of Journalism
Bethany College
Bethany, West Virginia 26032

1510 Delman, Neil M.
American Broadcasting Companies, Inc.
1330 Avenue of the Americas
New York, N.Y. 10019

1511 McAnany, Emile G., S.J.
Institute for Communication Research
Stanford University
Stanford, Calif. 94305

1512 Merrill, John
Dept. of Journalism
University of Missouri
Columbia, Missouri 65201

1513 Meyer, Joaquín
Director, Information Division
Interamerican Development Bank

808-17th St., N.W.
Washington, D.C. 20006

1514 Pierce, Roy E.
Dept. of Journalism & Mass Communications
University of Minnesota
Minneapolis, Minnesota 55455

1515 Suescun, Alfredo
San Juan 1132
Buenos Aires, Argentina

1516 Terán, Edison
Professor
School of Information Sciences
Universidad Central del Ecuador
Quito, Ecuador

Argentina

1517 Badell, Carlos E.
Director of Public Relations
Instituto Nacional de Tecnología Agropecuaria
Buenos Aires, Argentina

1518 Bringuer Ayala, Julio
Rodríguez Peña 641
Buenos Aires, Argentina

1519 Domingo Morras, Casimiro
Jefe de Noticias
Radio Rivadavia
Arenales 2467
Buenos Aires, Argentina

1520 Gainza Paz, Alberto
Diario "La Prensa"
Av. de Mayo 575
Buenos Aires, Argentina

1521 Ingrey, Norman
"Buenos Aires Herald"
Rivadavia 767
Buenos Aires, Argentina

1522 Vanzolini, Angel
"La Nueva Provincia"
Sarmiento 64
Bahia Blanca, Buenos Aires Province
Argentina

Bolivia

1523 Carrasco, Mario
President
Radiodifusoras Altiplana
c/o "El Diario"
La Paz, Bolivia

Brazil

1524 Alves, Marilia Antunes
381, 1º Lavradio
São Paulo, S.P., Brazil

1525 Bandeira, Marina
Movimento da Educação da Base
Botafôgo
Rio de Janeiro, GB, Brazil

1526 Barbosa Lima, Fernando
Director
Agencia "Esquire"
15, A Alcindo Guanabara
Rio de Janeiro, GB, Brazil

1527 Brown, Joseph F.
"Brazil Herald"
México 3
Rio de Janeiro, GB, Brazil

1528 Galvão, Augusto de Sousa Gomes
President, Emprêsa Brasileira de Telecomunicacões
EMBRATEL
Brasilia, Brazil

1529 Marinho, Roberto
"O Globo"
35 Irineu Marinho
Rio de Janeiro, GB, Brazil

Central America

1530 Rivas, Jr., Leo
Director
United Nations Information Center for Central America
San Salvador, El Salvador

Chile

1531 Aliaga Lopez, Darío
Extension Dept.
Canal 13--Televisión
Universidad Católica de Chile
O'Higgins 340
Santiago, Chile

1532 Deformes, Renato
Radio "Cruz del Sur" CB 138
Nataniel 47, piso no. 8
Santiago, Chile

1533 Maluenda, Rafael
Diario "El Mercurio"
Estado 337, piso 6
Santiago, Chile

Colombia

1534 Castaño C., Alvaro
Director
Radio Station H.J.C.K. "El Mundo"
Carrera 7, no. 7-14, piso 3
Bogotá, Colombia

1535 Castro, José F.
c/o Colegio Superior de Telecomunicaciones
Calle 24, no. 7-59
Bogotá, Colombia

1536 Santos, Eduardo
Diario "El Tiempo"
Av. Jimenez de Quesada 6-77
Bogotá, Colombia

Costa Rica

1537 Vargas Gené, Joaquín
Director, "Diario"
Calle Alfredo Volio a F. Guell
San José, Costa Rica

Dominican Republic

1538 Herrera, Rafael A.
"El Caribe"
El Conde, no. 1
Santo Domingo, Dominican Republic

Ecuador

1539 Araujo Sánchez, Diego
Oficina de Medios de Comunicación (OMECO)
Quito, Ecuador

1540 Cevallos H., Miguel A.
Director, Dept. of Sociology
Universidad Central del Ecuador
Quito, Ecuador

1541 Clark, Robert B.
Director, Channel 4--TV
Quito, Ecuador

1542 Guerrero V., Rafael
President
Asociación Ecuatoriana de Radiodifusoras (AER)
Station C.R.E.
Guayaquil, Ecuador

1543 Herrera Crespo, Patricio
Head, Dept. of Public Relations
Universidad Central del Ecuador
Ciudad Universitaria
Quito, Ecuador

1544 Maldonado Q., Gonzalo
Director
Radio "Atahualpa"
Venezuela 537
Quito, Ecuador

1545 Mantilla Mata, Manuel
Asociación Ecuatoriana de Radiodifusoras (AER)
c/o Asociación Radio Ecuatoriana
Espejo 924
Quito, Ecuador

1546 Mantilla Ortega, Carlos
Director
Diario "El Comercio"
Chile 1347
Quito, Ecuador

1547 Naranjo, Eduardo F.
Professor of Public Relations
Instituto Nacional de Policía
Quito, Ecuador

El Salvador

1548 Samayoa Martínez, Carlos
Director
"Diario Latino"
23 Av. Sur, 225
San Salvador, El Salvador

Guatemala

1549 Ramírez Maldonado, Angel
Diario "El Imparcial"
7a. Calle, no. 10-54
Guatemala, Guatemala

Guyana

1550 Blackman, Carl
Editor
"Sunday Graphic"
Georgetown, Guyana

1551 Willock, G.E.
"The Daily Chronicle"

23 Main St.
Georgetown, Guyana

Haiti

1552 Gaillard, Roger
Director
"Le Matin"
Port-au-Prince, Haiti

Honduras

1553 Acosta, Oscar
Jefe, Oficina de Información y Prensa Presidencia
Tegucigalpa, Honduras

1554 Ramos Alvarado, Vestura
Director
Diario "El Cronista"
6a. Av., 511, T.
Tegucigalpa, Honduras

Jamaica

1555 Sealy, T.E.
"The Daily Gleaner"
148 Harbor St.
Kingston, Jamaica

Mexico

1556 Bravo Santos, Oscar
López 143-4
México, D.F., México

1557 Ibarra López, Francisco
President
Cámara Nacional de la Industria de la Radiodifusión
Paseo de la Reforma 400-302
México, D.F., Mexico

1558 Llana, Rodrigo de
"Excelsior"
Paseo de la Reforma 18
México, D.F., Mexico

Nicaragua

1559 Cisneros, César
Director
Radiodifusora Nacional
Managua, Nicaragua

1560 Cuadra Chamberlain, Vicente
Publicidad Cuadra Chamberlain
Managua, Nicaragua

1561 Luna, Sergio
Director
"Radio Periódico"
Managua, Nicaragua

1562 Saenz, Dagoberto
Director
Diario "El Universal"
Managua, Nicaragua

1563 Vivas, César
Asociación de Reporteros de Managua
Managua, Nicaragua

Panama

1564 Picard Ami, Miguel
Diario "La Hora"
Av. 13, no. 13-37
Panamá, Panamá

1565 Rodríguez, Indalecio
Professor of Journalism
Universidad de Panamá
Panamá, Panamá

Paraguay

1566 Bejarano, Ramón C.
18 y 3a. Av.
Sajonia
Asunción, Paraguay

Peru

1567 Michenfelder, Joseph
Centro de Información Católica
Lima, Perú

1568 Ortiz de Zevallos, B.
"Ultima Hora"
745 Unión
Lima, Perú

1569 Tello Cadenas, Pedro
President
Organización de Radiodifusoras Bolivarianas (ORBO)
Lima, Perú

Puerto Rico

1570 Vargas Badillo, Pablo
"El Mundo"
383 F.D. Roosevelt
San Juan, Puerto Rico

Uruguay

1571 Quinteros Islas, Héctor
"La Mañana y El Diario"
Bartolomé Mitre 1275
Montevideo, Uruguay

Venezuela

1572 Alcalá, Gilberto
Editor

"El Nacional"
Caracas, Venezuela

1573 Gómez, Luis A.
Escuela de Periodismo
Universidad Central de Venezuela
Ciudad Universitaria
Caracas, Venezuela

1574 Otero Silva, Miguel
"El Nacional"
Puerto Escondido a Puente Nuevo
Caracas, Venezuela

Community Development

Latin America

1575 Biesanz, John B.
Professor of Sociology & Anthropology
Wayne State University
Detroit, Mich. 48202
(community development; Central America, Caribbean areas)

1576 Blumer, Herbert G.
Dept. of Sociology
University of California
Berkeley, Calif. 94720
(industrialization)

1577 Jordán Pando, Roberto
Consultant
Inter-American Development Bank
808-17th St., N.W.
Washington, D.C. 20006

1578 Moore, Lawrence B.
Regional Advisor in Community Development
UN Economic Commission for Latin America
Santiago, Chile

1579 Rivkin, Malcolm D.
Director of Urban & Regional Development
Robert R. Nathan Associates, Inc.
1218-16th St., N.W.
Washington, D.C. 20036

Brazil

1580 Bombart, J.B.
Centro Latino-Americano de Pesquisas em Ciências Sociais
Av. Pasteur 431, Praia Vermelha
Rio de Janeiro, GB, Brazil

1581 Machado de Silva, Luis A.
Centro Latino-Americano de Pesquisas em Ciências Sociais
Av. Pasteur 431, Praia Vermelha
Rio de Janeiro, GB, Brazil

Colombia

1582 Fals-Borda, Orlando
Ministerio de Agricultura
Dirección General
Bogotá, Colombia

1583 Fonseca Mejía, Carlos
Director del Plan Multiplicador
Oficina para el Desarrollo de la Comunidad
Universidad de Antioquia
Medellín, Colombia

Central America

1584 Putnam, Emilia B.
Community Development Adviser
Regional Office
U.S.A.I.D.
c/o U.S. Embassy
San José, Costa Rica

Guatemala

1585 Lucas, Max E.
Programa de Desarrollo de la Comunidad
Guatemala, Guatemala

1586 Reina, Rubén E.
Dept. of Anthropology
University of Pennsylvania

Philadelphia, Pa. 19104

Haiti

1587 Schaedel, Richard P., Editor
Latin American Research Review
Box L, University Station
Austin, Texas 78712

Mexico

1588 Aguirre Beltrán, Gonzalo
Assistant Director
Instituto Nacional Indigenista
México, D. F., Mexico

1589 Edmunson, Munro S.
Dept. of Anthropology
Tulane University
New Orleans, Louisiana 70118

1590 Hancock, Richard H.
Director of International Programs
Center for Continuing Education
University of Oklahoma
Norman, Oklahoma 73069

1591 Young, Frank W.
Professor of Rural Sociology
Cornell University
Ithaca, N.Y. 14850

Peru

1592 Dobyns, Henry F.
Dept. of Anthropology
Cornell University
Ithaca, N.Y. 14850

1593 d'Ugard, Carlos
Regional Director
Acción Andina
Lima, Perú

Venezuela

1594 Acedo Mendoza, Carlos
Instituto Venezolano de Acción Comunitaria
Edificio La Línea, 3er piso 34
Av. Libertador
Caracas, Venezuela

1595 Groscoors, Rolando
Fundación para el Desarrollo de la Comunidad y Fomento Municipal
Residencias Santiago de León, 4o. piso
Av. Casanova
Bello Monte
Caracas, Venezuela

1596 Mayorca, Juan M.
División de Voluntarios para la Comunidad
Edificio Gran Avenida, piso 6
Calle Real de Sábana Grande
Caracas, Venezuela

1597 Pardo, Arturo
Acción de Venezuela
Edificio Distromédica
Av. Urdaneta
Caracas, Venezuela

1598 Ravell, Carola
CORDIPLAN, Desarrollo de la Comunidad
Palacio Blanco, piso 3
Caracas, Venezuela

West Indies and the Caribbean

1599 Hackshaw, James O. F.
School of Social Work
Columbia University
New York, N.Y. 10027

Crime and Juvenile Delinquency

Latin America

1600 Alfaro González, Anastasio
Calle 5, no. 1234
San José, Costa Rica

1601 Quiróz Cuarón, Alfonso
Instituto de Investigaciones Sociales
Universidad Nacional Autónoma de México
México, D. F., México

Argentina

1602 Aftalión, Enrique R.
Charcas 2253
Buenos Aires, Argentina

1603 Defleur, Lois B.
Sociology Dept.
Washington State University
Pullman, Wash. 99163

1604 Pagano, José L.
Olleros 1800
Buenos Aires, Argentina

Chile

1605 Jackson, Christopher
Instituto de Sociología
Universidad de Chile
Santiago, Chile

1606 Munizaga, Carlos
Instituto de Sociología
Universidad de Chile
Santiago, Chile

1607 Zamorano, Manuel
Instituto de Sociología
Universidad de Chile
Santiago, Chile

Colombia

1608 Barbosa Herrera, Clodoveo
Carrera 29A, no. 70A-07
Bogotá, Colombia

1609 Canal Ramírez, Gonzalo
Carrera 4, no. 25B-50
Bogotá, Colombia

1610 Gutierrez Anzola, Jorge E.
Calle 39, no. 19-46
Bogotá, Colombia

1611 Sevillano Quiñones, Lino A.
Carrera 9, no. 13-12, Oficina 405
Bogotá, Colombia

Haiti

1612 Noel, Ulrick J.
Professor of Applied Criminology
Faculty of Ethnology
Université d'Etat d'Haiti
Port-au-Prince, Haiti

Mexico

1613 Bernaldo de Quirós y Pérez, Constancio
Zamora 80-14
México, D. F., Mexico

Peru

1614 Solano, Susana
271 P. Thouars
Lima, Perú

Uruguay

1615 Morató Rodríguez, Octavio
Itacurubí 1362
Montevideo, Uruguay

Venezuela

1616 Canestri, Francisco
Instituto de Ciencias Penales y Criminológicas
Universidad Central de Venezuela
Ciudad Universitaria
Caracas, Venezuela

1617 Chiosone, Tulio
Instituto de Derecho Penal
Universidad Central de Venezuela
Caracas, Venezuela

1618 Gomez Grillo, Elio
Facultad de Derecho
Universidad Central de Venezuela
Ciudad Universitaria
Caracas, Venezuela

1619 Villalba Villalba, Luis
Villa Clara
Puente Hierro
Caracas, Venezuela
(juvenile delinquency)

West Indies and the Caribbean

1620 Cartey, Desmond
Institute of Social & Economic Research
University of the West Indies
Mona, Jamaica

Demography

Latin America

1621 Anderson, Theodore R.
Dept. of Sociology
Iowa State University
Iowa City, Iowa 52240
(urbanization)

1622 Benítez Zenteno, Raúl
Centro de Estudios Económicos y Demográficos
El Colegio de México
Guanajuato 125
México, D. F., México

1623 Breese, Gerald
Bureau of Urban Research
Princeton University
Princeton, N.J. 08540

1624 Browning, Harley L.
Director, Population Research Center
University of Texas
Austin, Texas 78712
(Urbanization)

1625 Cabrera, Gustavo
Centro de Estudios Económicos y Demográficos
El Colegio de México
Guanajuato 125
México, D. F., México

1626 Campañó, Arnaldo R.
Chief, Population Program
Dept. of Social Affairs
Pan American Union
Washington, D.C. 20006

1627 Claxton, Philander P.
Special Assistant for Population Matters
Dept. of State
Washington, D.C. 20520

1628 Collver, O.A.
Research Sociologist
International Population & Urban Research
University of California
Berkeley, Calif. 94720

1629 Davis, Kingsley
Chairman, International Population & Urban Research
University of California
Berkeley, Calif. 94720

1630 Diegues Junior, Manoel
Director
Latin American Center for Research in Social Sciences
431 Av. Pasteur
Rio de Janeiro, GB, Brazil

1631 Draper, William H.
National Chairman
Population Crisis Committee
1730 K St., N.W.
Washington, D.C. 20006

1632 Duncan, Beverly
Population Training Center
University of Chicago
Chicago, Ill. 60637

1633 Durand, John D.
Population Studies Center
University of Pennsylvania
Philadelphia, Pa. 19104

1634 Elizaga, Juan C.
Centro Latinoamericano de Demografía
Exeq. Fernández 703
Santiago, Chile

1635 Friedmann, John R.P.
Dept. of Architecture & Urban Planning
University of California
Los Angeles, Calif. 90024
(Brazil, Venezuela)

1636 Fuentes, Guillermo
Inter-American Statistical Institute
Pan American Union
Washington, D.C. 20006

1637 García-Frías, Roque
Inter-American Statistical Institute

Pan American Union
Washington, D.C. 20006
(education)

1638 García-Peña, Alvaro
Director
Latin American Program
Population Reference Bureau
1755 Massachusetts Ave., N.W.
Washington, D.C. 20005

1639 Harkavy, Oscar
Director, Population Program
Ford Foundation
441 Madison Avenue
New York, N.Y. 10017

1640 Harris, Marvin
Dept. of Anthropology
Columbia University
New York, N.Y. 10027

1641 Hauser, Philip M.
Director, Population Research & Training Center
University of Chicago
Chicago, Ill. 60637
(urbanization)

1642 Jones, Gavin
Demographic Division
The Population Council, Inc.
230 Park Ave.
New York, N.Y. 10017

1643 Kirk, Dudley
Director, Demographic Division
The Population Council, Inc.
230 Park Avenue
New York, N.Y. 10017

1644 Lerner, Susana
Centro de Estudios Económicos y Demográficos
El Colegio de México
Guanajuato 125
México, D.F., Mexico

1645 Macisco, John J.
Center of Population Research
Georgetown University
Washington, D.C. 20007

1646 Macura, Milos
Chief, Population Division
United Nations
New York, N.Y. 10017

1647 Miró, Carmen
Director
Latin American Institute for Economic & Social Planning (ILPES)
Santiago, Chile

1648 Maris van Blaaderen, Andreas N.
Dept. of Sociology
University of Oregon
Eugene, Oregon 97430

1649 Notestein, Frank
President
The Population Council, Inc.
230 Park Ave.
New York, N.Y. 10017

1650 Ramírez, Mariano
Specialist, Human Resources Program
Dept. of Scientific Affairs
Pan American Union
Washington, D.C. 20006

1651 Pease, Clifford A.
Assistant Director
Technical Assistance Division
The Population Council, Inc.
230 Park Ave.
New York, N.Y. 10017

1652 Pfau, Luisa
President
Asociación Chilena para la Protección de la Familia
Santiago, Chile

1653 Sobrero, Aquilés J.
Director
Margaret Sanger Research Bureau
17 W. 16th St.
New York, N.Y. 10011

1654 Taeuber, Irene B.
Senior Research Demographer
Office of Population Research
Princeton University
Princeton, N.J. 08540

1655 Vallier, Ivan R.
Assistant Director
Institute of International Research
University of California
Berkeley, Calif. 94720

1656 Veliz, Claudio
Director
Instituto de Asuntos Internacionales
Universidad de Chile
Santiago, Chile

1657 Yampey, Mohamed
Estados Unidos 505 y San Carlos
Asunción, Paraguay

Argentina

1658 Ortiguera, Roberto
Instituto de Sociología Aplicada
Casilla de Correo 5703, Correo Central
Buenos Aires, Argentina
(urban sociology)

Barbados

1659 Gollop, Clyde
Barbados Family Planning Association
Bridgetown, Barbados

Bolivia

1660 Taborga, Huáscar
Coordinating Secretary
Centro de Estudio de Población y Familia
Casilla 469
La Paz, Bolivia
(public health)

Brazil

1661 Azevedo, Thales de
Faculdade da Filosofia
Universidade da Bahia
Salvador, Bahia, Brazil

1662 Banton, M.
Dept. of Sociology
University of Bristol
Britsol, England

1663 Fernandes, Florestan
Rua Maria Antônia, 294
São Paulo, S.P., Brazil

1664 Freyre, Gilberto
Apipucos
Recife, Brazil

1665 Henriques, Fernando
Research Unit for the Study of Multi-Racial Societies
University of Sussex
Brighton, Sussex, England

1666 Ianni, Ottávio
Universidade de São Paulo
São Paulo, S.P., Brazil

1667 Kubat, Daniel
Dept. of Sociology
University of Florida
Gainesville, Fla. 32601

1668 Mourao Filho, Fernando
Dept. of Sociology
Universidade de São Paulo
São Paulo, S.P., Brazil

1669 Smith, Thomas L.
Dept. of Sociology
University of Florida
Gainesville, Fla. 32601

Colombia

1670 Mendoza Hoyos, Hernán
Chief, Division of Population Studies
Asociación Colombiana de Facultades de Medicina
Bogotá, Colombia
(public health)

1671 Page, Thomas L.
Dept. of Political Science
University of Florida
Gainesville, Fla. 32601

Costa Rica

1672 Jiménez, Ricardo
Universidad de Costa Rica
San José, Costa Rica

1673 Ramírez Arias, Mariano
Profesor de Estadística
Facultad de Ciencias Económicas y Sociales
Universidad de Costa Rica
San José, Costa Rica

Cuba

1674 Pérez de la Riva, Juan
Professor of Geography & Demography
Universidad de La Habana
Havana, Cuba

Dominican Republic

1675 Hoetink, Harry

Studie-en Documentatiecentrum voor Latijns Amerika
University of Amsterdam
Mauritskade 63
Amsterdam, Netherlands
(communications)

Guyana

1676 Trembley, William
University of Guyana
Georgetown, Guyana

Jamaica

1677 Knox, Graham
Howard University
Dept. of Sociology
Washington, D.C. 20001

Mexico

1678 Benítez-Zenteno, Raúl
Professor of Sociology & Demography
Facultad de Filosofía y Letras
Universidad Nacional Autónoma de México
México, D. F., Mexico

1679 Burnright, Robert G.
Dept. of Anthropology & Sociology
Brown University
Providence, R.I. 02912

1680 Cabrera, Gustavo
Centro de Estudios Económicos y Demográficos
El Colegio de México
Guanajuato 125
México, D. F., México

1681 Gyves Falcón, Zaida de
Professor of Geography
Facultad de Filosofía y Letras
Universidad Nacional Autónoma de México
México, D. F., México

1682 MacGregor, Maria T. Gutiérrez de
Professor of Geography
Facultad de Filosofía y Letras
Universidad Nacional Autónoma de México
Ciudad Universitaria
México, D. F., México

1683 Urquidi, Victor L.
Centro de Estudios Económicos y Demográficos
Colegio de México
Guanajuato 125
México, D. F., México
(industrialization)

Venezuela

1684 Alamo Blanco, Roberto
Corporación Venezolana de Guyana
Edificio Shell
Urbanización Chuao
Caracas, Venezuela

West Indies and the Caribbean

1685 Brass, M.W.
Lecturer in Medical Demography
London School of Hygiene & Tropical Medicine
London, England

1686 Roberts, G.W.
Professor of Demography
Dept. of Sociology
University of the West Indies
Mona, Jamaica

1687 Stycos, J.M.
Dept. of Anthropology & Sociology
Cornell University
Ithaca, N.Y. 14850

1688 Teychnié, Henri
Lycée d'Etat de Reims
Rheims, France

Education

Latin America

1689 Ponce de León, Jaime
Carrera 8, 83-74
Bogotá, Colombia

1690 Desmaras, Raúl C.
Universidad Católica Argentina
Río Bamba 1227
Buenos Aires, Argentina

1691 García-Frías, Roque
Inter-American Statistical Institute
Pan American Union
Washington, D.C. 20006
(population)

1692 Havighurst, Robert J.
School of Education
University of Chicago
Chicago, Ill. 60637

1693 Lesch, Leo A.
Specialist for Educational TV Programs
United Nations
7 rue Eugène Delacroix
Paris, France

1694 Orrego, Teresa
Higher Education Section
Project Analysis Division
Inter-American Development Bank
808-17th St., N.W.
Washington, D.C. 20006

1695 Reissig, Luis
Callao 545
Buenos Aires, Argentina

1696 Ruíz, Alberto
Dept. of Educational Affairs
Pan American Union
Washington, D.C. 20006

1697 Sánchez, George I.
Dept. of Education
University of Texas
Austin, Texas 78712

1698 Steger, Hans-Albert
Center for Social Research
University of Munich
Munich, Federal Republic of Germany

Bolivia

1699 Donoso Torres, Vicente
Casilla 1483
La Paz, Bolivia

Brazil

1700 Díaz Sánchez, Demetrio
Oficina Internacional de Investigaciones Sociales de FERES
Fribourg, Switzerland

1701 Faust, Augustus F.
Dept. of Educational Administration
University of Utah
Salt Lake City, Utah 84112

1702 Goldman, Frank P.
Professor of Educational Sociology
Faculdade de Filosofía, Ciências e Letras de Rio Claro
Rio Claro, S.P., Brazil

1703 Hutchinson, Bertram
Centro Brasileiro de Pesquisas Educacionais
107 Voluntarios da Patria
Rio de Janeiro, GB, Brazil

1704 Moreira, João R.
90 Constante Ramos
Rio de Janeiro, GB, Brazil

Central America

1705 Thompson, N.W.
U.S. Office of Education
Dept. of Health, Education & Welfare
Washington, D.C. 20202

Chile

1706 Gill, Clark C.
American Republics Branch
U.S. Office of Education
Dept. of Health, Education & Welfare
Washington, D.C.

1707 Samper, Armando
Dept. of Educational Affairs
Pan American Union
Washington, D.C. 20006

Ecuador

1708 Carrasco, Santiago
Bellarmine School of Theology
Loyola University
230 So. Lincoln Way
North Aurora, Ill. 60542

Haiti

1709 Dale, George A.
U.S. Office of Education
Dept. of Health, Education & Welfare
Washington, D.C. 20202

Mexico

1710 Johnston, Marjorie C.
U.S. Office of Education
Dept. of Health, Education & Welfare
Washington, D.C. 20202

1711 Kneller, George F.
School of Education
University of California
Los Angeles, Calif. 90024

1712 Ruscoe, Gordon C.
School of Education
Syracuse University
Syracuse, N.Y. 13210

Peru

1713 Freeburger, Adela R.
U.S. Office of Education
Dept. of Health, Education & Welfare
Washington, D.C. 20202

Trinidad

1714 Pierre, Donald
Minister for Education & Culture
Port-of-Spain, Trinidad

Venezuela

1715 Chacón, Hernán
Instituto Nacional de Cooperación Educativa (INCE)
Edificio Torre del Cují, piso no. 9, Esquina del Cují
Caracas, Venezuela

1716 Cortesía, José R.
Depto. de Investigaciones Educacionales (EDUPLAN)
Edificio Esmeralda
Av. Los Próceres
San Bernardino
Caracas, Venezuela

1717 Hall, George
Deputy Executive Director
Fundación Creole
Apartado 889
Caracas, Venezuela

1718 McGinn, Noel
Center for Studies in Education & Development
Graduate School of Education
Harvard University
Cambridge, Mass. 02138

1719 Perls, Katherine
Research Assistant
Center for Studies in Education & Development
Graduate School of Education
Harvard University
Cambridge, Mass. 02138
(rural-urban migration)

West Indies and the Caribbean

1720 Wilgus, A.C.
Room 160
University Library
University of Florida
Gainesville, Fla. 32601

Housing

Latin America

1721 Abrams, Charles
Chairman, Division of Urban Planning
Columbia University
New York, N.Y. 10027
(urban planning)

1722 Beyer, Glenn H.
Dept. of Housing & Design
Cornell University
Ithaca, N.Y. 14850

1723 Burrows, Malcolm
National Association of Home Builders

1625 L St., N.W.
Washington, D.C.

1724 Casís, Ana
Inter-American Statistical Institute
Pan American Union
Washington, D.C. 20006

1725 Dietz, Albert G.H.
Center for International Studies
Massachusetts Institute of Technology
90 Massachusetts Ave.
Cambridge, Mass. 02139

1726 Koth, Marcia N.
Center for International Studies
Massachusetts Institute of Technology
90 Massachusetts Ave.
Cambridge, Mass. 02139

1727 Pineda Giraldo, Roberto
Centro Interamericano de Vivienda y Planeamiento
Apartado Aéreo 6209
Bogotá, Colombia

1728 Silva Michelena, Julio A.
Center for International Studies
Massachusetts Institute of Technology
90 Massachusetts Ave.
Cambridge, Mass. 02139

1729 Schafers, B.
Center for Social Research
University of Munich
Munich, Federal Republic of Germany
(poverty)

1730 Weissman, Ernest
Assistant Director in Charge of Housing, Building, & Planning Branch
Bureau of Social Affairs
United Nations Secretariat
New York, N.Y. 10017

Argentina

1731 Alvarez Alonso, Salvador
Lavalle 1425
Buenos Aires, Argentina

1732 Babini, Nicolás
Córdoba 2540
Buenos Aires, Argentina

1733 Bereterbide, Fermín H.
Segurola 3525
Buenos Aires, Argentina

1734 Coghlan, Eduardo A.
Guido 1852
Buenos Aires, Argentina

Bolivia

1735 Lavayen J., José
President
Instituto Nacional de Vivienda
La Paz, Bolivia

1736 Murillo S., Wálter
Director
Instituto Nacional de Vivienda
La Paz, Bolivia

Brazil

1737 Lodi, Carlos
Brazilian Federation for Housing and Planning
Rua Salvador Mendoça 100
São Paulo, S.P., Brazil

1738 Wagner, Bernard
Urban Housing Development Administration
U.S. Agency for International Development
Manila, Philippines
(Rio de Janeiro)

Chile

1739 Videla, Jorge A.
United Nations Economic Comission for Latin America
Casilla 179-D
Santiago, Chile

1740 Weeks, Harvey C.
IBEC Chilena, S.A.
Teatinos 449, piso no. 7
Santiago, Chile

Colombia

1741 Mora Rubio, Rafael
CINVA
Ciudad Universitaria
Calle 45, Carrera 30
Bogotá, Colombia

1742 Turner, Charles B.
Inter-American Housing & Planning Center
Ciudad Universitaria
Calle 45, Carrera 30
Bogotá, Colombia (Bogotá)

Mexico

1743 Aaron, Henry
Council of Economic Advisors
Executive Office of the President
Washington, D.C. (Mexico City)

1744 Coquet, Benito
Instituto Mexicano del Seguro Social
Secretaría del Trabajo y Previsión Social
México, D.F., México

1745 Zamora, Fernando
Instituto Nacional de la Vivienda
Ninos Héroes 139
México, D.F., México

Panama

1746 Alegre, Cecilia
Instituto de Vivienda
Av. 3 y Calle 24
Panamá, Panamá

Peru

1747 Land, P.D.
Banco de la Vivienda
P.O. Box 5425
Lima, Perú

1748 Vega Christie, David
Asociación Nacional de Vivienda
Lima, Perú

1749 Wenzel, E.H.
Hogares Peruanos
Lima, Perú

Puerto Rico

1750 Carrero, Telésforo
Atlantic View IV
San Juan, Puerto Rico

1751 Safa, Helen
Youth Development Center
926 South Crouse Avenue
Syracuse, N.Y. 13210

Trinidad

1752 Teshea, Isabel
Minister of Housing
Port-of-Spain, Trinidad

Venezuela

1753 Espino Padrón, Gustavo
Fundación de la Vivienda Popular
Edificio Las Fundaciones
Local 6--Av. Andrés Bello
Caracas, Venezuela

Public Health

Latin America

1754 Allen, Raymond B.
Chief, Office of Health & Population Dynamics
Pan American Health Organization
525-23rd St., N.W.
Washington, D.C. 20037

1755 Coleman, George
Chief, Health, Population & Nutrition Division
AID, Dept. of State
Washington, D.C. 20520

1756 Kaprio, L.
Division of Public Health Services
World Health Organization
Geneva, Switzerland

1757 Kisch, Arnold I.
School of Public Health, UCLA
Los Angeles, Calif. 90024

1758 McKenzie-Pollack, James
Chief, Office of National Health Planning
Pan American Health Organization
Washington, D.C. 20037

1759 MacKinnon, C. F.
Regional Domestic Economy Officer
UN Food & Agriculture Organization
Rome, Italy
(nutrition)

1760 Paz Soldán, Carlos E.
876 Unión
Lima, Peru

1761 Puffer, Ruth R.
Chief, Health Statistics Branch
Pan American Health Organization
Washington, D.C. 20037

1762 Ramírez, Marco A.
Instituto de Nutrición de Centroamérica y Panama (INCAP)
Calle Roosevelt
Guatemala, Guatemala
(nutrition)

1763 Roche, Jean C.
Station Berthelot
Bellevue, Seine-et-Oise
Paris, France

1764 Roemer, Milton I.
Professor of Public Health
School of Public Health
University of California
Los Angeles, Calif. 90024

1765 Rueda Williamson, Robert
Director, National Institute of Nutrition
Bogotá, Colombia
(nutrition)

1766 Ruiz, Próspero
World Health Organization
Geneva, Switzerland
(sanitary engineering)

1767 Santa Cruz, Hernán
Regional Representative
United Nations Food & Agriculture Organization
Rome, Italy
(nutrition)

1768 Saxton, Nadine
Health, Population & Nutrition Division
Latin American Bureau
U.S. Agency for International Development
Dept. of State
Washington, D.C. 20521

1769 Suchman, Edward A.
School of Public Health
Columbia University
New York, N.Y. 10027

1770 Van Burkalow, Anastasia
Dept. of Geography
Hunter College
Bedford Park Blvd., West
New York, N.Y. 10021
(nutrition)

1771 Wegman, Myron
Pan American Health Organization
525-23rd St., N.W.
Washington, D.C. 20037

1772 Wishik, Samuel M.
School of Public Health
University of Pittsburgh
Pittsburgh, Pa. 15213

Argentina

1773 Grau, Carlos A.
Calle 13, no. 635
La Plata, Argentina

Barbados

1774 Cummins, G. T. M.
Barbados Family Planning Association
Bridgetown, Barbados

Brazil

1775 Barbosa Albuquerque, Manuel H.
Universidade do Ceará
Fortaleza, Ceará, Brazil
(water supply)

1776 Castro, Josué de
124 Ministro Viveiros Castro
Rio de Janeiro, GB, Brazil
(nutrition)

1777 Figueiredo Lima, Antonio
State Sanitation Dept.
Recife, Pernambuco, Brazil
(sanitary engineering, Recife)

1778 Pacheco e Silva, A. C.
388, 4º Av. Brigadeiro Luis Antônio
São Paulo, S. P., Brazil
(mental hygiene)

1779 Pinotti, Mario
67 Desembargador Alfredo Russell
Rio de Janeiro, GB, Brazil

1780 Santos, Waldir
FSESP
Regional Sanitation Engineering
Recife, Pernambuco, Brazil
(sanitary engineering, Recife)

1781 Sena, Ottavio L. S. de
Universidade Federal da Bahia
Rua Augusto Viana, Palacio da Reitoria
Salvador, Bahia, Brazil
(sanitary engineering)

1782 Silva Mello, Antônio da
90 Av. Almirante Barroso
Rio de Janeiro, GB, Brazil

1783 Torres Pires, José
Director
Polytechnic School of Pernumbuco
Recife, Pernambuco, Brazil
(sanitary engineering)

Chile

1784 Ahumada Pacheco, Hermes
Teatinos 371
Santiago, Chile

1785 Faundes-Latham, Aníbal
Servicio de Obstetricía y Ginecología
Hospital Barros Luco-Trudeau
Gran Avenida 3204
Santiago, Chile
(demography)

1786 Mardones-Restat, Francisco
Director-General
Servicio Nacional de Salud Pública
Santiago, Chile

1787 Romero, Hernán
Facultad de Medicina
Universidad de Chile
Santiago, Chile

1788 Viel, Benjamín
Facultad de Medicina
Universidad de Chile
Santiago, Chile

Colombia

1789 Bejarano, Jorge
Calle 39-A, no. 20-55
Bogotá, Colombia

1790 Golden, Archie
Project Hope
Aptdo. Aéreo 2879
Cartagena, Colombia

Costa Rica

1791 Quirós Sasso, Mario
Profesor de Ingeniería Sanitaria
Facultad de Ingeniería
Universidad de Costa Rica
San José, Costa Rica

El Salvador

1792 Santana, Manuel
Profesor de Ingeniería Sanitaria
Facultad de Ingeniería
Universidad Nacional de El Salvador
San Salvador, El Salvador

Guatemala

1793 Valladares Ortiz, Oscar
1a. Calle, no. 0-90
Guatemala, Guatemala

Mexico

1794 Alvarez Amézquita, José
Paseo de la Reforma 400-202
México, D. F., México

1795 Aragonés, Ruipérez R. de
Profesor de Geografía
Facultad de Filosofía y Letras
Universidad Nacional Autónoma
Ciudad Universitaria
México, D. F., México

1796 Kirby, Anne V. T.
Centre of Latin American Studies
Cambridge University

Cambridge, England
(water supply, Oaxaca)

1797 Millán, Alfonso
Juarez 48
México, D. F., México
(mental hygiene)

1798 Ramírez Fonseca, Hugo
Profesor de Ingeniería Sanitaria
Facultad de Ingeniería
Universidad Autónoma de Guadalajara
Guadalajara, Jalisco, México
(sanitary engineering)

Panama

1799 Falk, Isidore S.
R.D. 1
Stonington, Conn. 06378

Peru

1800 Caravedo, Baltazar
National Advisor for Mental Health
Ministerio de Salud Pública
Lima, Perú

1801 Collazos Chiriboga, Carlos
140 Olavida
Lima, Perú

1802 Fried, Jacob
Dept. of Anthropology
McGill University
Montreal, P.Q., Canada
(mental health)

1803 Mantilla Fernandini, Luis
Profesor de Ingeniería Sanitaria Municipal y Legislación
Facultad de Ingeniería Sanitaria
Universidad Nacional de Ingeniería
Lima, Perú

1804 Rotondo, Humberto
4343 Av. Arequipa
Lima, Perú
(mental health)

Puerto Rico

1805 Rogler, Lloyd H.
Associate Professor of Sociology
Yale University
New Haven, Conn. 06520
(mental health)

Trinidad

1806 Awon, Maxwell P.
Minister of Health
Port-of-Spain, Trinidad

Venezuela

1807 Arboleda, Jorge
c/o Instituto Nacional de Obras Sanitarias
Edificio Las Mercedes
Esquina de Tierra Honda
Caracas, Venezuela
(sanitary engineering, Caracas)

1808 Archila, Ricardo
Quinta Solemar
Av. Barquisimeto
Palmas
Caracas, Venezuela

1809 Berti, Arturo L.
Jefe, División de Malariología
Ministerio de Salud Pública
Caracas, Venezuela

1810 Dominguez, Luis
Depto. de Higiene Mental
Ministerio de Salubridad y Asistencia Social
Centro Simón Solívar
Edificio Sur, piso 4, Oficina 429
Caracas, Venezuela
(mental hygiene)

1811 Mateo Alonzo, A.
Av. Avila 31, Altamira
Caracas, Venezuela
(mental hygiene)

1812 Mijares, Gustavo R.
c/o Instituto Nacional de Obras Sanitarias
Edificio Las Mercedes
Esquina de Tierra Honda
Caracas, Venezuela
(sanitary engineering, Caracas)

1813 Olivares, Pedro
División de Malariología
Ministerio de Salud Pública
Caracas, Venezuela

1814 Santos Mendoza, Espíritu
Asesoría del Ministerio de Sanidad y Asistencia Social
Edificio Sur, piso 3, Oficina 340, Centro Simón Bolívar
Caracas, Venezuela

1815 Vêlez Boza, Fermín
Instituto Nacional de Nutrición
Plaza España
Caracas, Venezuela

West Indies and the Caribbean

1816 Eldemire, Herbert W.
Minister of Health
Government of Jamaica
Kingston, Jamaica
(population)

1817 Jacobs, Lenworth
President, Jamaica Family Planning Association
Kingston, Jamaica

Public Welfare

Latin America

1818 Izquierdo Phillips, Adriana
Catholic International Union for Social Service
111 rue de la Poste
Brussels, Belgium

1819 Sullivan, Dorothea F.
Director of Social Services
Cuban Children's Program
Catholic Welfare Bureau
1325 W. Flagler St.
Miami, Fla. 33135

1820 Vergara, Laura
Regional Social Welfare Officer
Bureau of Social Affairs
United Nations
New York, N.Y. 10017

Brazil

1821 Fischlowitz, Estanislao
2440 Av. Atlântica
Rio de Janeiro, GB, Brazil

Colombia

1822 Calderón Alvarado, Luis
Centro de Investigaciones Sociales de FERES
Aptdo. Aéreo 11996
Bogotá, Colombia

1823 Pulecio de Betancur, Yolanda
Director
Asistencia Social
Bogotá, Colombia

Costa Rica

1824 Trejos Escalante, Fernando
Los Yoses
San José, Costa Rica

Dominican Republic

1825 Sobá, José G.
Av. Pasteur 56
Santo Domingo, Dominican Republic

Ecuador

1826 Tobar, Blanca R.
Jefa, Depto. de Servicio Social
Sociedad para la Protección de la Infancia
Guayaquil, Ecuador

Mexico

1827 Mendieta y Núnez, Lúcio
Av. Madero 60-4
México, D.F., Mexico

Venezuela

1828 Quijada, Hernán
Dirección de Asistencia Social de Ministerio de Sanidad
Edificio Sur, Centro Simón Bolívar, 4º piso, Oficina 335
Caracas, Venezuela

1829 Ruesta, María E.
Federacion de Instituciones Privadas de Atención al Niño (FIPAN)
Edificio VAM, Pent House
Av. Andrés Bello
Caracas, Venezuela

West Indies and the Caribbean

1830 Smith, Michael G.
Dept. of Anthropology
University of California
Los Angeles, Calif. 90024

Rural- Urban Migration

Latin America

1831 Davies, D.I.
Assistant Professor of Sociology
University of Essex
Colchester, England

1832 Hanson, Robert C.
Institute of Behavioral Science
University of Colorado
Boulder, Colorado 80302

1833 McGreevey, William P.
Center for Latin American Studies
University of California
Berkeley, Calif. 94720

1834 Wanderer, Jules J.
Institute of Behavioral Science
University of Colorado
Boulder, Colorado 80302

Argentina

2835 Germani, Gino
Monroe Gutman Professor of Latin American Affairs
Harvard University
Cambridge, Mass. 02138

1836 Margulis, Mario
Research Associate
Centro de Investigaciones de las Ciencias del Hombre
Buenos Aires, Argentina

Brazil

1837 Camârgo, José F. de
Universidade do São Paulo
São Paulo, S.P., Brazil

1838 Unzer de Almeida, Vicente
473 Campinas
São Paulo, S.P., Brazil

1839 Wilkening, Eugene A.
Land Tenure Center
University of Wisconsin
Madison, Wisconsin 53706

Central America

1840 Goldkind, Victor
Dept. of Anthropology
San Diego State College
San Diego, Calif. 92115

Chile

1841 Herrick, Bruce H.
Dept. of Economics
University of California
Los Angeles, Calif. 90024

Colombia

1842 Flinn, William L.
Land Tenure Center
University of Wisconsin
Madison, Wisc. 53706

Guatemala

1843 Arias B., Jorge
10a. Avenida, no. 4-40
Guatemala, Guatemela

Mexico

1844 Ball, John M.
Department of Geography
University of Georgia
Athens, Ga. 30601

Peru

1845 Mangin, William

Dept. of Anthropology
Syracuse University
Syracuse, N.Y. 13210
(mental health)

1846 Matos Mar, José
Instituto Etnográfico
Universidad de San Marcos
Lima, Perú

Venezuela

1847 Hill, George W.
Facultades de Humanidades y Educación
Universidad Central de Venezuela
Ciudad Universitaria
Caracas, Venezuela

1848 Vilá Camposada, Marco A.
Professor of Geography
Universidad Central de Venezuela
Ciudad Universitaria
Caracas, Venezuela

Social Change

Latin America

1849 Alcântara, Pythagoras Cavalcanti
Instituto de Ciencias Sociais
Universidade da Bahia
Salvador, Bahia, Brazil

1850 Barreto, Leonor de
Specialist
Dept. of Social Affairs
Pan American Union
Washington, D.C. 20006

1851 Crevenna, Theo R.
Acting Director
Dept. of Social Affairs
Pan American Union
Washington, D.C. 20006

1852 Di Tella, Torcuato
Instituto Torcuato Di Tella
Virrey del Pino 3230
Buenos Aires, Argentina

1853 Goldrich, Daniel
Dept. of Political Science
University of Oregon
Eugene, Oregon 97403

1854 Hagen, Everett E.
Center for International Studies
Massachusetts Institute of Technology
90 Massachusetts Ave.
Cambridge, Mass. 02139

1855 Heintz, Peter
Facultad Latinoamericana de Ciencias Sociales
Universidad de Chile
Santiago, Chile

1856 Johnson, John J.
Dept. of Political Science
Stanford University
Stanford, Calif. 94305

1857 Ladin, David
Chief, Studies on Social Development
Dept. of Social Affairs
Pan American Union
Washington, D.C. 20006

1858 Loeb, Thomas A.
Center for Social Research
University of Munich
Munich, Federal Republic of Germany

1859 Olivos, Luis
Assistant Deputy Director for Social Development
Dept. of Social Affairs
Pan American Union
Washington, D.C. 20006

1860 Schaedel, Richard P.
Center of Latin American Studies
University of Texas
Austin, Texas 78712

1861 Solari, Aldo
Instituto de Ciencias Sociales
25 de Mayo 477, piso no. 2
Montevideo, Uruguay

1862 Whiteford, Andrew H.
Dept. of Anthropology
Beloit College
Beloit, Wisconsin 53511

Argentina

1863 Rodriguez Bustamante, Norberto
Maipú 81
Banfield
Buenos Aires, Argentina

Brazil

1864 Baird, Rebecca
Dept. of History
Stanford University
Stanford, Calif. 94305

1865 Tutaka, Sugiyama
Research Associate
Institute of Latin American Studies
University of Texas
Austin, Texas 78712

Central America

1866 Geisert, H.L.
Dept. of Anthropology & Sociology
George Washington University
Washington, D.C. 20006
(population)

Chile

1867 Debuyst, Frédéric
DESAL
Casilla 10,445
Santiago, Chile

Colombia

1868 Dumont, Jacques J.
Research Associate
Catholic University of Louvain
Louvain, Belgium

Costa Rica

1869 Loomis, Charles P.
Dept. of Anthropology & Sociology
Michigan State University
E. Lansing, Mich. 48823

Dominican Republic

1870 Corten, André
Asst. Professor of Sociology
Catholic University of Louvain
Louvain, Belgium
(Santo Domingo)

Puerto Rico

1871 Feldman, Arnold S.
Professor of Sociology
Northwestern University
Evanston, Ill. 60201

Social Security

Latin America

1872 Farman, Carl H.
Social Science Analyst
U.S. Dept. of Health, Education & Welfare
Washington, D.C. 20201
(Chile, Mexico)

1873 Martí Bufill, Carlos
Paseo Ptor. Rosales, 40
Madrid, Spain

Argentina

1874 Remorino, Jerónimo
Don Bosco, S.K.
Buenos Aires, Argentina

Brazil

1875 Fischlowitz, Estanislau
Professor
Pontificia Universidade Católica
Rio de Janeiro, GB, Brazil

Chile

1876 Gaete Berrios, Alfredo
Rafael Cañas, 84
Santiago, Chile

Colombia

1877 Martínez Muñoz, Enrique
433 Carrera 6A, # 14-42
Bogotá, Colombia

1878 Restrepo Hoyos, Jorge
818 Carrera 7, # 14-78
Bogotá, Colombia

Ecuador

1879 Campaña Barrera, Anibal
2a. Transversal a la Av. 6 de Diciembre
Quito, Ecuador

Guatemala

1880 Barahona Streber, Oscar
14 Calle, # 7-54
Guatemala, Guatemala

Haiti

1881 Falk, Isidore S.
Road District
Stonington, Conn. 06378

Mexico

1882 Martínez Manautou, Jorge
Director de Investigaciones
Instituto de Seguro Social
México, D. F., México

Peru

1883 Altmeyer, Arthur J.
4201 Cathedral Ave., N.W.
Washington, D.C.

1884 Ferrero, Rómulo A.
376 A.M. Quesada
Lima, Perú

Urban Geography

Latin America

1885 Cole, J.P.
Dept. of Geography
University of Nottingham
Nottingham, England

1886 Crist, Raymond E.
Dept. of Geography
University of Florida
Gainesville, Fla. 32601
(Colombia, Venezuela)

1887 Gauthier, Howard L.
Professor of Geography
Ohio State University
Columbus, Ohio 43210
(urban planning, transportation)

1888 Gormsen, Erdmann
Dept. of Geography
University of Heidelberg
Marktplatz 4
Heidelberg, Federal Republic of Germany

1889 James, Preston E.
Dept. of Geography
Syracuse University
Syracuse, N.Y. 13210

1890 Kayser, Bernard
Professor of Geography
Faculté des Lettres
Université de Toulouse
Toulouse, France

1891 León, Raquel de
Depto. de Geografía
Universidad de Panamá
Panamá, Panamá

1892 Oya, Jesús
Depto. de Geografía
Universidad de Madrid
Madrid, Spain

1893 Snyder, David E.
Assistant Professor of Geography
Yale University
New Haven, Conn. 06520
(transportation, Venezuela, Brazil, Uruguay)

1894 Stanislawski, Dan
Chairman, Dept. of Geography
University of Arizona
Tucson, Arizona 85721
(Mexico, Brazil)

1895 Wagner, Philip L.
Dept. of Geography
University of California
Davis, Calif. 95616
(Costa Rica, Mexico)

Argentina

1896 Chiozza, Elena
Dept. of Geography
Facultad de Filosofía y Letras
Universidad de Buenos Aires
Buenos Aires, Argentina

1897 Miatello, Roberto A.
Professor of Geography
Universidad Nacional de Córdoba
Córdoba, Argentina

1898 Zamorano, Mariano
Professor of Geography
Universidad Nacional de Cuyo
Mendoza, Argentina

Brazil

1899 Azevedo, Aroldo de
93 Ferdinando Laboriau
São Paulo, S.P., Brazil

1900 Carmin, Robert L.
Dept. of Geography
Ball State University
Muncie, Indiana 47306
(community development)

1901 Deffontaines, Pierre
224 Av. Balmes
Barcelona, Spain

1902 Soares, Maria T. de Segadas
Professor of Geography
Faculdade de Letras
Universidade do Brasil
Rio de Janeiro, GB, Brazil

1903 Vergolino Días, Catharina
Conselho Nacional de Geografia
I.B.G.E.
Rio de Janeiro, GB, Brazil

Central America

1904 Enjalbert, Henri
Professor of Geography
Faculté des Lettres
Université de Bordeaux
Bordeaux, France
(history)

1905 Thompson, John
Professor of Geography
University of Illinois
Urbana, Ill. 61801
(urban food supply, Chile, Central America)

Chile

1906 Flores Silva, Eusebio
Profesor de Geografía
Facultad de Filosofía y Educación
Universidad de Chile
Santiago, Chile

1907 Guerrero, Raúl
Professor of Geography
Facultad de Letras
Universidad de Concepción
Concepción, Chile

1908 Hernández, Hilario
Professor of Geography
Universidad de Concepción
Concepción, Chile

Ecuador

1909 Dambaugh, Luella N.
Dept. of Geography
University of Miami
Coral Gables, Fla. 33146

1910 Sheck, Ronald C.
Dept. of Geography
Ohio State University
Columbus, Ohio 43210

Mexico

1911 Pyle, Jane
Dept. of Geography
University of Oregon
Eugene, Oregon 97403
(Mexico City)

1912 Tichy, Franz
Professor of Geography
University of Erlangen
Erlangen, Federal Republic of Germany

Panama

1913 Rubio y Muñoz-Bocanegra, Angel
Av. E. Lefevre 40
Panamá, Panamá

Peru

1914 Gade, Daniel W.
Dept. of Geography
University of Oregon
Eugene, Oregon 97403

Urbanization, General

Latin America

1915 Brunet, Roger
Dept. of Geography
Faculté des Lettres
Université de Toulouse
Toulouse, France

1916 Canaux, Jean
Director, Centre de Recherches d'Urbanisme
4, Av. du Recteur-Poincaré
Paris, France

1917 Chapoulie, Jean P.
Faculté des Lettres et Sciences Humaines
Université de Toulouse
Toulouse, France

1918 Chaunu, Pierre
Professor
Faculté des Lettres
Université de Caen
Caen, France

1919 Coppolani, Jean
Urbaniste d'Etat
59, Av. J. -Rieux
Toulouse, France

1920 Donald, Carr L.
Programs Officer, Pan American Union
Washington, D.C. 20006

1921 Dorselaer, J.
Institut des Hautes Etudes de d'Amérique Latine
28 rue St. Guillaume
Paris, France
(rural-urban migration)

1922 Durán, Gustavo
Research & Development Branch
Bureau of Social Affairs
United Nations
New York, N.Y. 10017

1923 Gans, Herbert J.
Dept. of City Planning
University of Pennsylvania
Philadelphia, Pa. 19104

1924 Geisse G., Guillermo
Director
Comité Interdisciplinario de Desarrollo Urbano
Universidad Católica de Chile
Mardoqueo Fernández 15, Oficina 74
Santiago, Chile

1925 Herrera, Felipe
Director-General
Inter-American Development Bank
1818 H St., N.W.
Washington, D.C. 20006
(industrialization)

1926 Johnson, Kenneth F.
Dept. of Political Science
University of Southern California
Los Angeles, Calif. 90007

1927 Kitchen, James D.
Public Administration Center
San Diego State College
San Diego, Calif. 92115

1928 Mauro, Frédéric
Institute of Spanish, Latin American & Luso-Brazilian Studies
Université de Toulouse
Toulouse, France

1929 Moore, Wilbert E.
Dept. of Sociology & Anthropology
Princeton University
Princeton, N.J. 08540
(industrialization)

1930 Neira Alves, Eduardo
Consultant on Urban Development
Office of the Program Advisor
Inter-American Development Bank
808-17th St., N.W.
Washington, D.C. 20006

1931 Pérez Ramírez, Gustavo

Centro de Investigaciones Sociales DESAL
Aptdo. Aéreo 11966
Bogotá, Colombia
(social change)

1932 Pfeiffer, Gottfried
Dept. of Geography
University of Heidelberg
Heidelberg, Federal Republic of Germany

1933 Roberts, B.R.
Dept. of Sociology
University of Manchester
Manchester, England
(Central America)

1934 Seda-Bonilla, Eduardo
Dept. of Sociology
New York University
New York, N.Y. 10003

1935 Tavares de Sá, Hernane
Pan American Union
Washington, D.C. 20006

1936 Tricart, Jean
Institute of Geography
Faculté des Lettres
Université de Strasbourg
Strasbourg, France

1937 Turner, John F.C.
Research Associate
Joint Center for Urban Studies, M.I.T.-
Harvard University
66 Church St.
Cambridge, Mass. 02138

1938 Wingo, Lowdon
Resources for the Future, Inc.
1755 Massachusetts Ave., N.W.
Washington, D.C. 20036

Argentina

1939 Canal-Feijoo, Bernardo
Juncal 1775
Buenos Aires, Argentina

1940 Denis, Paul-Yves
Dept. of Geography
University of Montreal
Montreal, P.Q., Canada

1941 Coutinho Lobo, Durval
Depto. dos Estudos Urbanos
Universidade do Brasil
Rio de Janeiro, GB, Brazil

1942 Oliveiro Reis, José de
Depto. dos Estudos Urbanos
Universidade do Brasil
Rio de Janeiro, GB, Brazil

1943 Orico, Osvaldo
213 Santa Clara
Rio de Janeiro, GB, Brazil

1944 Rochefort, Michel
Institute of Geography
Université de Paris
Paris, France

1945 Santos, Milton
56, Calle 13 e 19 Fevreiro
Rio de Janeiro, GB, Brazil

1946 Xavier Andrade Pedrosa, Homero
Depto. dos Estudos Urbanos
Universidade do Brasil
Rio de Janeiro, GB, Brazil

Brazil

1947 Adelman, Jeffry
Dept. of History
Indiana University
Bloomington, Indiana 47401
(Bêlo Horizonte)

1948 Banton, M.
Dept. of Sociology
University of Bristol
Bristol, England
(demography)

1949 Morse, Richard M.
Dept. of History
Yale University
New Haven, Conn. 06520
(São Paulo)

Chile

1950 Lackington, Tomás
Faculty of Economic & Social Sciences
Universidad Católica de Chile
Santiago, Chile

1951 Medina Echavarría, José
Director
Escuela Latinoamericana de Sociología
Universidad de Chile
Santiago, Chile
(social change)

Colombia

1952 Bernal Aranza, Hernando
Av. 28, 39B-25, piso # 4
Bogotá, Colombia
(Buenaventura)

1953 Currie, Lauchlin
Carrera 5, 25A-38
Aptdo. 400
Bogotá, Colombia
(industrialization)

1954 Dorselaer, Jaime
Centro de Investigaciones Sociales de FERES
Aptdo. Aéreo 11996
Bogotá, Colombia

1955 Gregory, Alfonso
Centro de Investigaciones Sociales de FERES
Aptdo. Aéreo 11996
Bogotá, Colombia

1956 Samper, Armando
Director-General
Inter-American Institute of Agricultural Sciences
Executive Headquarters
San José, Costa Rica
(communications)

1957 Torres León, Fernán
Facultad de Ciencias Económicas
Fundación Jorge Tadeo Lozano
Universidad de Bogotá
Apartado Aereo 9912
Bogotá, Colombia (Bogotá)

1958 Torres Restrepo, Camilo
Facultad de Sociología
Universidad Nacional de Colombia
Bogotá, Colombia

Dominican Republic

1959 Pieter, Leoncio
Av. J. Perdomo 30
Santo Domingo,
Dominican Republic

Mexico

1960 Bataillon, Claude
Professor, Institut Français
Calle Laplace 33
México, D. F., México

1961 Gutiérrez-Zamora, Renato
Escuela Náutica de Tampico
Tampico, Tamaulipas, México

1962 Luna, Guillermo
Athens Center of Ekistics
24 Strat. Syndesmou
Athens, Greece

1963 Megee, Mary C.
1570 E. Swan Circle
St. Louis, Missouri 63144

1964 Pozas Arciniega, Ricardo
c/o Instituto Nacional Indigenista
México, D. F., México

1965 Sánchez Baylon, Félix
Escuela Nacional de Arquitectura
Universidad Nacional de México
México, D. F., México
(housing)

1966 Unikel Miller, Luis
Sierra Ventana 564
México, D. F., México

Peru

1967 Dollfus, Olivier
Institute of Geography
Université de Strasbourg
Strasbourg, France

1968 Rodríguez Suy Suy, Antonio
Universidad Nacional de Trujillo
Aptdo. 315
Trujillo, Perú

Venezuela

1970 Jones, Emrys
Professor of Geography

London School of Economics
University of London
London, England

1971 Rodwin, Lloyd
Chairman, Faculty Committee
Joint Center for Urban Studies, M.I.T.-Harvard University
66 Church St.
Cambridge, Mass. 02138

West Indies and the Caribbean

1972 Millette, James
Dept. of History
University of the West Indies
Mona, Jamaica

1973 Rubel, Arthur J.
Dept. of Anthropology
University of Notre Dame
Notre Dame, Indiana 46556

1974 Stanton, Howard R.
Graduate School of Planning
University of Puerto Rico
Río Piedras, Puerto Rico

Urbanization Bibliography

Latin America

1975 Bazzanella, Waldemiro
49 E. Ramos
Rio de Janeiro, GB, Brazil

1976 Guzmán, Louis F.
Dept. of Geography
San Fernando Valley State College
Northridge, Calif. 91324

1977 Rubio y Muñoz Bocanegra, Angel
Av. E Lefevre 40
Panamá, Panamá

1978 Sable, Martin H.
Associate Professor
School of Library and Information Science
University of Wisconsin-Milwaukee
Milwaukee, Wis. 53201

AUTHOR INDEX TO BIBLIOGRAPHY SECTION

SUBJECT INDEX TO BIBLIOGRAPHY SECTION

INDEX TO DIRECTORY SECTION

Author Index to Bibliography Section

Note: Numbers immediately following names of personal and corporate authors, as well as titles entered as authors, refer to individual, numbered bibliographic items, and not to pages. In cases where a given author has also been editor (or compiler, translator, etc.) of additional works, his name is re-entered in the index, followed by the appropriate designation. The names of joint authors (not exceeding a total of two individuals) have also been included. It should be noted that periodicals have been identified as such.

A

B

C

D

E

F

G

H

J

K

L

M

N

S

T

U

V

W

X - Y

Z

Subject Index to Bibliographies Section

Note: Numbers immediately following topics, sub-topics, places and individuals treated as subjects refer not to pages, but rather to individual, numbered bibliographic items. It should be noted that geographic designations follow topics so as to render the index as nearly geographic in character as is possible, thereby leading the user speedily to his field (and geographic area) of interest. In instances where geographic descriptions do not antecede given topics, it should be assumed that the item is general in nature, and universal in scope; hence the term "General" is appended. For further details please consult the corresponding explanatory material in the Preface and in the Introduction to the Table of Contents. "Literature" as used in this Subject Index refers to the essay, a combination of two or more of the genres or all genres (drama, novel, poetry, short story), correspondence and reminiscences, as well as sketches and descriptions of life in Latin American cities.

A

B

D

F

G

H

I

J - K

L

M

N

O

Q

R

T

Y

Z

Index to Directory Section

Note: The fields of activity listed in this index refer to research institutes and centers, as well as "working" organizations, which are to be found in directories numbers 1 and 2, respectively. Immediately following the listing of research institutes and "working" organizations in each field, there is a listing of the specialists in that particular area of knowledge. All numbers refer to individual organizations or individuals, and not to pages.

R

S

T

U

W